Programming C# 12
Build Cloud, Web, and Desktop Applications

Ian Griffiths

Beijing · Boston · Farnham · Sebastopol · Tokyo

Programming C# 12

by Ian Griffiths

Copyright © 2024 Ian Griffiths. All rights reserved.

Published by O'Reilly Media, Inc., 1005 Gravenstein Highway North, Sebastopol, CA 95472.

O'Reilly books may be purchased for educational, business, or sales promotional use. Online editions are also available for most titles (*http://oreilly.com*). For more information, contact our corporate/institutional sales department: 800-998-9938 or *corporate@oreilly.com*.

Acquisitions Editor: Brian Guerin
Development Editor: Corbin Collins
Production Editor: Elizabeth Faerm
Copyeditor: Kim Cofer
Proofreader: Piper Editorial Consulting, LLC

Indexer: Sue Klefstad
Interior Designer: David Futato
Cover Designer: Karen Montgomery
Illustrator: Kate Dullea

June 2024:   First Edition

Revision History for the First Edition
2024-06-07:   First Release

See *http://oreilly.com/catalog/errata.csp?isbn=9781098158361* for release details.

978-1-098-15836-1

[LSI]

I dedicate this book to my excellent wife, Deborah, and to my wonderful daughters, Hazel, Victoria, and Lyra. Thank you for enriching my life.

Table of Contents

Preface

C# has now existed for around two decades. It has grown steadily in both power and size, but Microsoft has always kept the essential characteristics intact. Each new capability is designed to integrate cleanly with the rest, enhancing the language without turning it into an incoherent bag of miscellaneous features.

Even though C# continues to be a fairly straightforward language at its heart, there is a great deal more to say about it now than in its first incarnation. Because there is so much ground to cover, this book expects a certain level of technical ability from its readers.

Who This Book Is For

I have written this book for experienced developers—I've been programming for years, and I set out to make this the book I would want to read if that experience had been in other languages, and I were learning C# today. Whereas earlier editions explained some basic concepts such as classes, polymorphism, and collections, I am assuming that readers will already know what these are. The early chapters still describe how C# presents these common ideas, but the focus is on the details specific to C#, rather than the broad concepts.

Conventions Used in This Book

The following typographical conventions are used in this book:

Italic
> Indicates new terms, URLs, email addresses, filenames, and file extensions.

`Constant width`
> Used for program listings, as well as within paragraphs to refer to program elements such as variable or function names, databases, data types, environment variables, statements, and keywords.

Constant width bold
> Shows commands or other text that should be typed literally by the user. In examples, highlights code of particular interest.

Constant width italic
> Shows text that should be replaced with user-supplied values or by values determined by context.

 This element signifies a tip or suggestion.

 This element signifies a general note.

 This element indicates a warning or caution.

Using Code Examples

Supplemental material (code examples, exercises, etc.) is available for download at *https://oreil.ly/prog-cs-12-repo*.

If you have a technical question or a problem using the code examples, please send email to *bookquestions@oreilly.com*.

This book is here to help you get your job done. In general, if example code is offered with this book, you may use it in your programs and documentation. You do not need to contact us for permission unless you're reproducing a significant portion of the code. For example, writing a program that uses several chunks of code from this book does not require permission. Selling or distributing examples from O'Reilly books does require permission. Answering a question by citing this book and quoting example code does not require permission. Incorporating a significant amount of example code from this book into your product's documentation does require permission.

We appreciate, but generally do not require, attribution. An attribution usually includes the title, author, publisher, and ISBN. For example: "*Programming C# 12* by Ian Griffiths (O'Reilly). Copyright 2024 by Ian Griffiths, 978-1-098-15836-1."

If you feel your use of code examples falls outside fair use or the permission given above, feel free to contact us at *permissions@oreilly.com*.

O'Reilly Online Learning

 For more than 40 years, *O'Reilly Media* has provided technology and business training, knowledge, and insight to help companies succeed.

Our unique network of experts and innovators share their knowledge and expertise through books, articles, and our online learning platform. O'Reilly's online learning platform gives you on-demand access to live training courses, in-depth learning paths, interactive coding environments, and a vast collection of text and video from O'Reilly and 200+ other publishers. For more information, visit *https://oreilly.com*.

How to Contact Us

Please address comments and questions concerning this book to the publisher:

O'Reilly Media, Inc.
1005 Gravenstein Highway North
Sebastopol, CA 95472
800-889-8969 (in the United States or Canada)
707-827-7019 (international or local)
707-829-0104 (fax)
support@oreilly.com
https://www.oreilly.com/about/contact.html

We have a web page for this book, where we list errata, examples, and any additional information. You can access this page at *https://oreil.ly/prgrmg-c-12*.

For news and information about our books and courses, visit *https://oreilly.com*.

Find us on LinkedIn: *https://linkedin.com/company/oreilly-media*.

Watch us on YouTube: *https://youtube.com/oreillymedia*.

Acknowledgments

Many thanks to the book's technical reviewers: Stephen Toub, Doug Holland, Howard van Rooijen, and Glyn Griffiths. I'd also like to give a big thank you to those who reviewed individual chapters or otherwise offered help or information that improved this book: Brian Rasmussen, Eric Lippert, Andrew Kennedy, Daniel Sinclair, Brian Randell, Mike Woodring, Mike Taulty, Bart De Smet, Matthew Adams, Jess Panni, Jonathan George, Mike Larah, Carmel Eve, Ed Freeman, Elisenda Gascon, Jessica Hill, Liam Mooney, Nehemiah Campbell, and Shahryar Saljoughi. Thanks in particular to endjin, both for allowing me to take time out from work to write this book and for creating such a great place to work.

Thank you to everyone at O'Reilly whose work brought this book into existence. In particular, thanks to Corbin Collins for his support in making this book happen, and to Brian Guerin for his support in getting this project started. Elizabeth Faerm is the best production editor an author could wish for. Thanks also to Cassandra Furtado, Ron Bilodeau, Nick Adams, Kate Dullea, Karen Montgomery, and Kristen Brown, for their help in bringing the work to completion. Further thanks to Sue Klefstad for her work on the index. Thanks also to Kim Cofer for her thorough and thoughtful copy editing and to Piper Editorial Consulting, LLC, for their diligent proofreading. Finally, thank you to Amanda Quinn for getting me involved as an author for this title several editions ago, and to John Osborn, for taking me on as an O'Reilly author back when I wrote my first book.

CHAPTER 1

Introducing C#

The C# programming language (pronounced "see sharp") is used for many kinds of applications, including websites, cloud-based systems, artificial intelligence, IoT devices, desktop applications, embedded controllers, mobile apps, games, and command-line utilities. C#, along with the supporting runtime, libraries, and tools known collectively as .NET, has been center stage for Windows developers for over 20 years. Today, .NET is cross-platform and open source, enabling applications and services written in C# to run on operating systems including Android, iOS, macOS, and Linux, as well as on Windows.

Every new version of C# has enhanced developer productivity. For example, the most recent versions include new pattern-matching features to make our code more expressive and succinct. Primary constructors and collection expressions help to reduce verbosity in some common scenarios. Various type-system enhancements allow our code to express its requirements and characteristics in more detail, enabling us to write more flexible libraries, and to enjoy better compile-time diagnostics.

C# 11.0 and 12.0 have gained performance-oriented features including generic math, and improved control over memory handling for performance-sensitive low-level code. Every new .NET release has improved execution speed, but there have also been significant reductions in startup times, memory footprint, and binary size. This, along with improved support for containerization, enhances .NET's fit for modern cloud development. There have also been significant improvements for cross-platform client-side development, thanks to Blazor and .NET MAUI (Multi-platform App UI). .NET has supported ARM and WebAssembly (WASM) for many years, but continuous recent improvements for those targets are important for cloud, mobile, and web development.

C# and .NET are open source projects, although it didn't start out that way. In C#'s early history, Microsoft guarded all of its source code closely; however, in 2014, the .NET Foundation (*https://oreil.ly/vYiMY*) was created to foster the development of open source projects in the .NET world. Many of Microsoft's most important C# and .NET projects are now under the foundation's governance (in addition to many non-Microsoft projects). This includes the C# language standard (*https://github.com/dotnet/csharpstandard*), Microsoft's C# compiler (*https://github.com/dotnet/roslyn*), and also the .NET runtime and libraries (*https://github.com/dotnet/runtime*). Today, pretty much everything surrounding C# is developed in the open, with code contributions from outside of Microsoft being welcome. New language feature proposals are managed on GitHub, enabling community involvement from the earliest stages.

Why C#?

Although there are many ways you can use C#, other languages are always an option. Why might you choose C# over those? It will depend on what you need to do and what you like and dislike in a programming language. I find that C# provides considerable power, flexibility, and performance and works at a high enough level of abstraction that I don't expend vast amounts of effort on little details not directly related to the problems my programs are trying to solve.

Much of C#'s power comes from the range of programming techniques it supports. For example, it offers object-oriented features, generics, and functional programming. It supports both dynamic and static typing. It provides powerful list- and set-oriented features, thanks to Language Integrated Query (LINQ). It has intrinsic support for asynchronous programming. Moreover, the various development environments that support C# all offer a wide range of productivity-enhancing features.

C# provides options for balancing ease of development against performance. The runtime has always provided a garbage collector (GC) that frees developers from much of the work associated with recovering memory that the program is no longer using. A GC is a common feature in modern programming languages, and while it is a boon for most programs, there are some specialized scenarios where its performance implications are problematic. That's why C# also enables more explicit memory management, giving you the option to trade ease of development for runtime performance but without the loss of type safety. This makes C# suitable for certain performance-critical applications that for years were the preserve of less safe languages such as C and C++.

Languages do not exist in a vacuum—high-quality libraries with a broad range of features are essential. Some elegant and academically beautiful languages are glorious right up until you want to do something prosaic, such as talking to a database or determining where to store user settings. No matter how powerful a set of programming idioms a language offers, it also needs to provide full and convenient access to the underlying platform's services. C# is on very strong ground here, thanks to its runtime, built-in class libraries, and extensive third-party library support.

.NET encompasses both the runtime and the main class libraries that C# programs use. The runtime part is called the *Common Language Runtime* (usually abbreviated to CLR) because it supports not just C# but any .NET language. Microsoft also offers Visual Basic, F#, and .NET extensions for C++, for example. The CLR has a *Common Type System* (CTS) that enables code from multiple languages to interoperate freely, which means that .NET libraries can normally be used from any .NET language—F# can consume libraries written in C#, C# can use Visual Basic libraries, and so on.

There is an extensive set of class libraries built into .NET. These have gone by a few names over the years, including Base Class Library (BCL), Framework Class Library, and framework libraries, but Microsoft now seems to have settled on *runtime libraries* as the name for this part of .NET. These libraries provide wrappers for many features of the underlying operating system (OS), but they also provide a considerable amount of functionality of their own, such as collection classes and JSON processing.

The .NET runtime class libraries are not the whole story—many other systems provide their own .NET libraries. For example, there are libraries that enable C# programs to use popular cloud services. As you'd expect, Microsoft provides comprehensive .NET libraries for working with services in its Azure cloud platform. Likewise, Amazon provides a fully featured development kit for using Amazon Web Services (AWS) from C# and other .NET languages. And libraries do not have to be associated with particular services. There's a large ecosystem of .NET libraries, some commercial and some free, including mathematical utilities, parsing libraries, and user interface (UI) components, to name just a few. Even if you get unlucky and need to use an OS feature that doesn't have any .NET library wrappers, C# offers various mechanisms for working with other kinds of APIs, such as the C-style APIs available in Win32, macOS, and Linux, or APIs based on the Component Object Model (COM) in Windows.

In addition to libraries, there are also numerous application frameworks. .NET has built-in frameworks for creating web apps and web APIs, desktop applications, and mobile applications. There are also open source frameworks for various styles of distributed systems development, such as high-volume event processing with Reaqtor (*https://reaqtive.net*) or high-availability globally distributed systems with Orleans (*https://oreil.ly/kxaEg*).

Finally, with .NET having been around for over two decades, many organizations have invested extensively in technology built on this platform. So C# is often the natural choice for reaping the rewards of these investments.

In summary, C# gives us a strong set of abstractions built into the language, a powerful runtime, and easy access to an enormous amount of library and platform functionality.

Managed Code and the CLR

C# was the first language designed to be a native in the world of the CLR. This gives C# a distinctive feel. It also means that if you want to understand C#, you need to understand the CLR and the way in which it runs code.

For years, the most common way for a compiler to work was to process source code and to produce output in a form that could be executed directly by the computer's CPU. Compilers would produce *machine code*—a series of instructions in whatever binary format was required by the kind of CPU the computer had. This is sometimes referred to as *native* code, because it's the language the CPU inherently understands. Many compilers still work this way, but although we can compile C# into machine code, we often don't. This is optional because C# uses a model called *managed code*.

With managed code, the compiler does not generate the machine code that the CPU executes. Instead, the compiler produces a form of binary code called the *intermediate language* (IL). The executable binary is produced later, usually, although not always, at runtime. The use of IL enables features that are hard or even impossible to provide under the more traditional model.

Perhaps the most visible benefit of the managed model is that the compiler's output is not tied to a single CPU architecture. For example, the Intel and AMD CPUs used in many modern computers support both 32-bit and 64-bit instruction sets (known, respectively, for historical reasons as *x86* and *x64*). With the old model of compiling source code into machine language, you'd need to choose which of these to support, building multiple versions of your component if you need to target more than one. But with .NET, you can build a single component that can run without modification in either 32-bit or 64-bit processes. The same component could even run on completely different architectures such as ARM (a processor architecture widely used in mobile phones, Macs with *Apple Silicon*, and also in tiny devices such as the Raspberry Pi). With a language that compiles directly to machine code, you'd need to build different binaries for each of these, or in some cases you might build a single file that contains multiple copies of the code, one for each supported architecture. With .NET, you can compile a single component that contains just one version of the code, and it can run on any of them. It would even be able to run on platforms that weren't supported at the time you compiled the code if a suitable runtime became available in the future. (For example, .NET components written years before Apple released its first ARM-based Macs can run without relying on the *Rosetta* (*https://oreil.ly/MO6W1*) translation technology that normally enables older code to work on the newer processors.)

More generally, any kind of improvement to the CLR's code generation—whether that's support for new CPU architectures or just performance improvements for existing ones—instantly benefits all .NET languages. For example, older versions of the CLR did not take advantage of the vector processing extensions available on modern processors, but the current versions will now often exploit these when generating code for loops. All code running on current versions of .NET benefits from this, including components that were compiled years before this enhancement was added.

The exact moment at which the CLR generates executable machine code can vary. By default, it uses an approach called *just-in-time* (JIT) compilation, in which each individual function's machine code is generated the first time it runs. However, it doesn't have to work this way. One of the runtime implementations, called Mono, is able to interpret IL directly without ever converting it to runnable machine language, which is useful on platforms such as iOS where legal constraints may prevent JIT compilation. The .NET Software Development Kit (SDK) also provides ways to build precompiled code alongside the IL. This *ahead-of-time* (AOT) compilation can improve an application's startup time.

 Generation of executable code can still happen at runtime. The CLR's *tiered compilation* feature may choose to recompile a method dynamically to optimize it better for the ways it is being used at runtime, and it can do this even when you use AOT compilation because the IL is still available at runtime.

The .NET SDK offers a more extreme option called *Native AOT*. Instead of combining IL and native code, applications built with Native AOT contain only native code.[1] Runtime features including the garbage collector and any runtime library components the application requires are included in the output, making Native AOT applications completely self-contained. (The bundled runtime features do not include the JIT compiler. It's unnecessary, because all IL is compiled to machine language at build time.) Unlike with other .NET compilation models, Native AOT applications do not need a copy of the .NET runtime to be either preinstalled or shipped alongside the application code. Not all applications can use Native AOT, because some .NET libraries exploit the CLR's ability to JIT compile code by generating new code at runtime, so these don't work (or have limited functionality) on Native AOT. But in cases where it is applicable, it can dramatically lower startup times for applications that are able to use it.

Managed code has ubiquitous type information. The .NET runtime requires this to be present to enable certain features. For example, .NET offers various automatic serialization services, in which objects can be converted into binary or textual representations of their state, and those representations can later be turned back into objects, perhaps on a different machine. This sort of service relies on a complete and accurate

---

1 Native AOT therefore can't offer tiered compilation.

description of an object's structure, something that's guaranteed to be available in managed code. Type information can be used in other ways. For example, unit test frameworks can use it to inspect code in a test project and discover all of the unit tests you have written. These kinds of features typically rely on the CLR's *reflection* services, which are the topic of Chapter 13. However, Native AOT imposes some restrictions—full type information is available at the point where Native AOT starts to generate native code, but unless it can deduce that your code will rely on that type information at runtime, it will often trim some of this out. This makes the compiled output significantly smaller, which can improve startup times, but it also means that by default, the final output might have an incomplete picture, which is another reason not all libraries work with Native AOT. However, the .NET team intends to make Native AOT viable for as many applications as possible, which is why the last few versions of the .NET SDK have added compile-time code generation features that can reduce the reliance on runtime reflection. For example, it can generate code enabling the JSON libraries described in Chapter 15 to perform serialization without using reflection. This still relies on full type information being available for all .NET code during the build process; it just enables it to be dropped from the final build output.

Although C#'s close connection with the runtime is one of its main defining features, it's not the only one. There's a certain philosophy underpinning C#'s design.

C# Prefers Generality to Specialization

C# favors general-purpose language features over specialized ones. C# is now on its 12th major version, and with every release, the language's designers had specific scenarios in mind when designing new features. However, they have always tried hard to ensure that each element they add is useful beyond these primary scenarios.

For example, several years ago, the C# language designers decided to add features to C# to make database access feel well integrated with the language. The resulting technology, Language Integrated Query (LINQ, described in Chapter 10), certainly supports that goal, but they achieved this without adding any direct support for data access to the language. Instead, the design team introduced a series of quite diverse-seeming capabilities. These included better support for functional programming idioms, the ability to add new methods to existing types without resorting to inheritance, support for anonymous types, the ability to obtain an object model representing the structure of an expression, and the introduction of query syntax. The last of these has an obvious connection to data access, but the rest are harder to relate to the task at hand. Nonetheless, these can be used collectively in a way that makes certain data access tasks significantly simpler. But the features are all useful in their own right, so as well as supporting data access, they enable a much wider range of scenarios. For example, these additions made it much easier to process lists, sets, and other groups of objects, because the new features work for collections of things from any origin, not just databases.

One illustration of this philosophy of generality was a language feature that was prototyped for C# but which its designers ultimately chose not to go ahead with. The feature would have enabled you to write XML directly in your source code, embedding expressions to calculate values for certain bits of content at runtime. The prototype compiled this into code that generated the completed XML at runtime. Microsoft Research demonstrated this publicly, but this feature didn't ultimately make it into C#, although it did later ship in another .NET language, Visual Basic, which also got some specialized query features for extracting information from XML documents. Embedded XML expressions are a relatively narrow facility, only useful when you're creating XML documents. As for querying XML documents, C# supports this functionality through its general-purpose LINQ features, without needing any XML-specific language features. XML's star has waned since this language concept was mooted, having been usurped in many cases by JSON (which may well be eclipsed by something else in years to come). Had embedded XML made it into C#, it would by now feel like an anachronistic curiosity.

The new features added in subsequent versions of C# continue in the same vein. For example, the relatively new *range* syntax (described in Chapter 5) was motivated partly by some machine learning and AI scenarios, but the feature is not limited to any particular application area. Likewise, generic math is one of the more significant new capabilities in C# 11.0, but it is enabled by some general-purpose enhancements of the type system.

C# Standards and Implementations

Before we can get going with some actual code, we need to know which implementation of C# and the runtime we are targeting. The standards body Ecma has written specifications that define language and runtime behavior (ECMA-334 and ECMA-335, respectively) for C# implementations. This has made it possible for multiple implementations of C# and the runtime to emerge. At the time of writing, there are four in widespread use: .NET, Mono, .NET Native (a forerunner of .NET Native AOT still used by applications targeting the Universal Windows Platform), and .NET Framework. Somewhat confusingly, Microsoft is behind all of these, although it didn't start out that way.

Many .NETs

The Mono project was launched in 2001 and did not originate from Microsoft. (This is why it doesn't have .NET in its name—it can use the name C# because that's what the standards call the language, but back in the pre-.NET Foundation days, the .NET brand was exclusively used by Microsoft.) Mono started out with the goal of enabling Linux desktop application development in C#, but it went on to add support for iOS and Android. That crucial move helped Mono find its niche, because it is now mainly used to create cross-platform mobile device applications in C#. Mono also introduced support for targeting WebAssembly (also known as WASM) and includes an implementation of the CLR that can run in any standards-compliant web browser, enabling C# code to run on the client side in web applications. This is often used in conjunction with a .NET application framework called Blazor, which enables you to build HTML-based user interfaces while using C# to implement behavior. The Blazor-with-WASM combination also makes C# a viable language for working with platforms such as Electron, which use web client technologies to create cross-platform desktop applications. (Blazor doesn't require WASM—it can also work with C# code compiled normally and running on the .NET runtime; .NET's Multi-platform App UI [MAUI] exploits this to make it possible to write a single application that can run on Android, iOS, macOS, and Windows.)

Mono was open source from the start and has been supported by a variety of companies over its existence. In 2016, Microsoft acquired the company that had stewardship of Mono: Xamarin. For now, Microsoft retains Xamarin as a distinct brand, positioning it as the way to write cross-platform C# applications that can run on mobile devices. Mono's core technology has been merged into Microsoft's .NET runtime codebase. This was the endpoint of several years of convergence in which Mono gradually shared more and more in common with .NET. Initially, Mono provided its own implementations of everything: C# compiler, libraries, and the CLR. But when Microsoft released an open source version of its own compiler, the Mono tools moved over to that. Mono used to have its own complete implementation of the .NET runtime libraries, but ever since Microsoft released the first open source version of .NET, Mono has been depending increasingly on that. Today, Mono is no longer a separate .NET, being effectively one of two CLR implementations in the main .NET runtime repository, enabling support for mobile and WebAssembly runtime environments.

What about the other three implementations, all of which seem to be called .NET? There is .NET Native, a predecessor of Native AOT. It is used in Universal Windows Platform (UWP) apps, but developers are discouraged from building new applications this way, since there are no plans for either UWP or the old .NET Native to be updated except for bug or security fixes. So in practice we have just two current, non-doomed versions: .NET Framework (Windows only, closed-source) and .NET (cross-platform, open source). However, as mentioned earlier, Microsoft is not planning to add any new features to the Windows-only .NET Framework, so this leaves .NET 8.0 as effectively the only current version.

Nonetheless, .NET Framework continues to be used because there are a handful of things it can do that .NET 8.0 cannot. .NET Framework only runs on Windows, whereas .NET 8.0 supports Windows, macOS, iOS, and Linux, and although this makes .NET Framework less widely usable, it means it can support some Windows-specific features. For example, there is a section of the .NET Framework Class Library dedicated to working with COM+ Component Services, a Windows feature for hosting components that integrate with Microsoft Transaction Server. This isn't possible on the newer, cross-platform versions of .NET because code might be running on Linux, where equivalent features either don't exist or are too different to be presented through the same .NET API.

The number of .NET-Framework-only features has dropped dramatically over the last few releases, because Microsoft has been working to enable even Windows-only applications to use the latest version of .NET. Even many Windows-specific features can be used from .NET. For example, the System.Speech .NET library used to be available only on .NET Framework because it provides access to Windows-specific speech recognition and synthesis functionality, but there is now a .NET version of this library. That library only works on Windows, but its availability means that application developers relying on it are now free to move from .NET Framework to .NET. The remaining .NET Framework features that have not been brought forward are those that are not used extensively enough to justify the engineering effort. COM+ support was not just a library—it had implications for how the CLR executed code, so supporting it in modern .NET would have had costs that were not justifiable for what is now a rarely used feature.

The cross-platform .NET is where most of the new development of .NET has occurred for the last few years. .NET Framework is still supported, and will be for many years to come, but Microsoft has stated that it will not get any new features, and it has been falling behind for some time. For example, Microsoft's web application framework, ASP.NET Core, dropped support for .NET Framework back in 2019. So .NET Framework's retirement, and .NET's status as the one true .NET, is the inevitable conclusion of a process that has been underway for a few years. Since many legacy projects continue to run on .NET Framework, .NET library developers often want to support both runtimes, so I will call out places where there are significant differences, but new C# applications should use .NET, not .NET Framework.

Release Cycles and Long Term Support

Microsoft currently releases new versions of C# and .NET every year, normally around November or December, but not all versions are created equal. Alternate releases get *Long Term Support* (LTS), meaning that Microsoft commits to supporting the release for at least three years. Throughout that period, the tools, libraries, and runtime will be updated regularly with security patches. .NET 8.0, released in November 2023, is an LTS release, so it will be supported until December 2026. The preceding LTS release was .NET 6.0, which was released in December 2021 and therefore remains in support until December 2024; the LTS release before that was .NET Core 3.1,[2] which went out of support in December 2022.

What about non-LTS releases? These are supported from release but only for 18 months. For example, .NET 5.0 was supported when it was released in December 2020, but support ended in May 2022, six months after .NET 6.0 shipped (and six months *before* support for its predecessor .NET Core 3.1 ended).

It often takes a few months for the ecosystem to catch up with a new release. You might not be able to use a new version of .NET on the day of its release in practice, because your cloud platform provider might not support it yet, or there may be incompatibilities with libraries that you need to use. This significantly shortens the effective useful lifetime of non-LTS releases, and it can leave you with an uncomfortably narrow window in which to upgrade when the next version appears. If it takes a few months for the tools, platforms, and libraries you depend on to align with the new release, you will have very little time to move on before it falls out of support. In extreme situations, this window of opportunity might not even exist: .NET Core 2.2 reached the end of its supported life before Azure Functions offered full support for either .NET Core 3.0 or 3.1, so developers who had used the non-LTS .NET Core 2.2 on Azure Functions found themselves in a situation where the latest supported version actually went backward: they had to choose between either downgrading back to .NET Core 2.1 or using an unsupported runtime in production for a few months. For this reason, some developers look at the non-LTS versions as previews—you can experimentally target new features in anticipation of using them in production once they arrive in an LTS release.

Targeting Multiple .NET Runtimes

For many years, the multiplicity of .NET runtimes, each with its own different version of the runtime libraries, presented a challenge for anyone wanting to make their C# code available to other developers. This has been improving in recent years because Microsoft made convergence a major goal with recent releases, so these days if a component targets the oldest version of .NET in support (.NET 6.0 as I write this) it will be able to run on the majority of .NET runtimes. However, it is common to want to continue to support systems that run on the old .NET Framework. This means that it will be useful to produce components that target multiple .NET runtimes for the foreseeable future.

---

2 Older versions of the runtime we now call .NET were called .NET Core, and when this was rebranded as plain .NET, it skipped from 3.1 to 5.0 to emphasize the move away from .NET Framework, the latest version of which is 4.8.1.

There's a package repository for .NET components called NuGet (*https://nuget.org*), which is where Microsoft publishes all of the .NET libraries it produces that are not built into .NET itself, and it is also where most .NET developers publish libraries they'd like to share. But which version should you build for? This is a two-dimensional question: there is the runtime implementation (.NET, .NET Framework, UWP) and also the version (for example, .NET 6.0 or .NET 8.0; .NET Framework 4.7.2 or 4.8). Many authors of popular open source packages distributed through NuGet support a plethora of versions, old and new.

Component authors often used to support multiple runtimes by building multiple variants of their libraries. When you distribute .NET libraries via NuGet, you can embed several sets of binaries in the package, each targeting different flavors of .NET. However, one major problem with this is that as new forms of .NET have appeared over the years, existing libraries wouldn't run on all newer runtimes. A component written for .NET Framework 4.0 would work on all subsequent versions of .NET Framework but not necessarily on, say, .NET 6.0. Even if the component's source code was entirely compatible with the newer runtime, you would need to compile a separate version to target that platform. And if the author of a library that you use had only provided .NET Framework binaries, it might not work on .NET. (You can tell .NET to try to use .NET Framework binaries, and it goes to some lengths to accommodate them. You might find that it does just work, but there are no guarantees.) This was bad for everyone. Various versions of .NET have come and gone over the years (such as Silverlight and several Windows Phone variants; UWP's .NET Native is still hanging in there), meaning that component authors found themselves on a treadmill of having to churn out new variants of their component. Since that relies on those authors having the inclination and time to do this work, component consumers might find that not all of the components they want to use are available on their chosen platform.

To avoid this, Microsoft introduced .NET Standard, which defines common subsets of the .NET runtime libraries' API surface area. Many of the older runtimes have gone away, but the split between .NET and .NET Framework remains, so today, .NET Standard 2.0 is likely to be the best choice for component authors wishing to support a wide range of platforms, because all recently released versions of .NET support it, and it provides access to a very broad set of features. If you don't need to support .NET Framework, it would make more sense to target .NET 6.0 or .NET 8.0 instead. Chapter 12 describes some of the considerations around .NET Standard in more detail.

When a version of .NET goes out of support, this does not deprecate components that target it. .NET supports using components built for older versions, so if you find a component on NuGet that targets .NET 5.0, you can use it on .NET 8.0. It would be wise to check whether such a component is still under active development, but old targets don't necessarily imply that a component is out of date. Sometimes component authors choose to help out people who are running systems on unsupported runtimes.

Microsoft provides more than just a language and the various runtimes with its associated class libraries. There are also development environments that can help you write, test, debug, and maintain your code.

Visual Studio, Visual Studio Code, and JetBrains Rider

Microsoft offers two desktop development environments: Visual Studio Code and Visual Studio. Both provide the basic features—such as a text editor, build tools, and a debugger—but Visual Studio provides the most extensive support for developing C# applications, whether those applications will run on Windows or other platforms. It has been around the longest—for as long as C#—so it comes from the pre–open source days and continues to be a closed-source product. The various editions available range from free to eye-wateringly expensive. Microsoft is not the only option: the developer productivity company JetBrains sells a fully fledged .NET IDE called Rider, which runs on Windows, Linux, and macOS.

Visual Studio is an Integrated Development Environment (IDE), so it takes an "everything included" approach. In addition to a fully featured text editor, it offers visual editing tools for UIs. There is deep integration with source control systems such as Git and with online systems such as GitHub and Microsoft's Azure DevOps system that provide source repositories, issue tracking, and other Application Lifecycle Management (ALM) features. Visual Studio offers built-in performance monitoring and diagnostic tools. It has various features for working with applications developed for and deployed to Microsoft's Azure cloud platform. It has the most extensive set of refactoring features out of the three Microsoft environments described here. Note that this version of Visual Studio runs only on Windows.

The JetBrains Rider IDE is a single product that runs on Windows, macOS, and Linux. It is more focused than Visual Studio, in that it was designed purely to support .NET application development. (Visual Studio also supports C++.) It has a similar "everything included" approach, and it offers a particularly powerful range of refactoring tools.

Visual Studio Code (often shortened to VS Code) was first released in 2015. It is open source and cross platform, supporting Linux as well as Windows and Mac. It is based on the Electron platform and is written predominantly in TypeScript. (This means that VS Code really is the same program on all operating systems.) VS Code is a more lightweight product than Visual Studio: a basic installation of VS Code has little more than text editing support. However, as you open up files, it will discover downloadable extensions that, if you choose to install them, can add support for C#, F#, TypeScript, PowerShell, Python, and a wide range of other languages. (The extension mechanism is open, so anyone who wants to can publish an extension.) So although in its initial form it is less of an IDE and more like a simple text editor, its extensibility model makes it pretty powerful. The wide range of extensions has led to VS Code becoming remarkably popular outside of the world of Microsoft languages, and this in turn has encouraged a virtuous cycle of even greater growth in the range of extensions.

Visual Studio and JetBrains Rider offer the most straightforward path to getting started in C#—you don't need to install any extensions or modify any configuration to get up and running. However, Visual Studio Code is available to a wider audience, so I'll be using that in the quick introduction to working with C# that follows. The same basic concepts apply to all environments, though, so if you will be using Visual Studio or Rider, most of what I describe here still applies.

 You can download Visual Studio Code for free (*https://oreil.ly/ m0vaY*). You will also need to install the .NET SDK (*https://oreil.ly/ 8Ok2Z*). If you are using Windows and would prefer to use Visual Studio, you can download the free version of Visual Studio, called Visual Studio Community (*https://oreil.ly/3RUGS*). This will install the .NET SDK for you, as long as you select at least one .NET *workload* during installation.

Any nontrivial C# application will have multiple source code files, and these will belong to a *project*. Each project builds a single output, or *target*. The build target might be as simple as a single file—a C# project could produce an executable file or a library, for example—but some projects produce more complicated outputs. For instance, some project types build websites. A website will normally contain multiple files, but collectively, these files represent a single entity: one website. Each project's output will be deployed as a unit, even if it consists of multiple files.

Executables typically have a *.exe* file extension in Windows, while libraries use *.dll* (historically short for *dynamic link library*). With .NET, however, all code goes into *.dll* files, even on macOS and Linux. The SDK can also generate a *host* executable (with a *.exe* extension on Windows), but this just starts the runtime and then loads the *.dll* containing the main compiled output. (It's slightly different if you target .NET Framework: that compiles the application directly into a self-bootstrapping *.exe* with no separate *.dll*.) In any case, the only difference between the main compiled output of an application and a library is that the former specifies an application entry point.

Both file types can export features to be consumed by other components. These are both examples of *assemblies*, the subject of Chapter 12. (If you use Native AOT you will end up with a *.exe* on Windows and a similarly executable binary on other platforms, but Native AOT essentially works as an extra final step: it takes the various *.dll* files produced by the normal .NET build process and compiles these into a single native executable.)

C# project files have a *.csproj* extension, and if you examine these files with a text editor, you'll find that they contain XML. A *.csproj* file describes the contents of the project and configures how it should be built. The Visual Studio and Rider IDEs know how to process these, and so do the .NET extensions for VS Code. They are also understood by various command-line build utilities such as the `dotnet` command-line tool installed by the .NET SDK, and also Microsoft's older MSBuild tool. (MSBuild supports numerous languages and targets, not just .NET. In fact, when you build a C# project with the .NET SDK's `dotnet build` command, it is effectively a wrapper around MSBuild.)

You will often want to work with groups of projects. For example, it is good practice to write tests for your code, but most test code does not need to be deployed as part of the application, so you would typically put automated tests into separate projects. And you may want to split up your code for other reasons. Perhaps the system you're building has a desktop application and a website, and you have common code you'd like to use in both applications. In this case, you'd need one project that builds a library containing the common code, another producing the desktop application executable, another to build the website, and three more projects containing the tests for each of the main projects.

The build tools and IDEs that understand .NET help you work with multiple related projects through what they call a *solution*. A solution is a file with a *.sln* extension, defining a collection of projects. While the projects in a solution are usually related, they don't have to be.

If you're using Visual Studio, be aware that it requires projects to belong to a solution, even if you have only one project. Visual Studio Code is happy to open a single project if you want, but its .NET extensions also recognize solutions.

A project can belong to more than one solution. In a large codebase, it's common to have multiple *.sln* files with different combinations of projects. You would typically have a main solution that contains every single project, but not all developers will want to work with all the code all of the time. Someone working on the desktop application in our hypothetical example will also want the shared library but probably has no interest in loading the web project.

I'll show how to create a new project, open it in Visual Studio Code, and run it. I'll then walk through the various features of a new C# project as an introduction to the language. I'll also show how to add a unit test project and how to create a solution containing both projects.

Anatomy of a Simple Program

Once you've installed the .NET 8.0 SDK either directly or by installing an IDE, you can create a new .NET program. Start by creating a new directory called *HelloWorld* on your computer to hold the code. Open up a command prompt and ensure that its current directory is set to that, and then run this command:

```
dotnet new console
```

This makes a new C# console application by creating two files. It creates a project file with a name based on the parent directory: *HelloWorld.csproj* in this case. And there will be a *Program.cs* file containing the code. If you open that file up in a text editor, you'll see it's pretty simple, as Example 1-1 shows.

Example 1-1. Our first program

```
// See https://aka.ms/new-console-template for more information
Console.WriteLine("Hello, World!");
```

You can compile and run this program with the following command:

```
dotnet run
```

As you've probably already guessed, this will display the text Hello, World!, the traditional behavior for the opening example in any programming book.

Over half of this example is just a comment. The second line here is all you need, with the first just showing a link explaining the "new" style this project uses. It's not all that new anymore—it came in with the .NET 6.0 SDK—but there was a significant change in the language, and the .NET SDK authors felt it necessary to provide an explanation. The last few versions of C# have added various features intended to reduce the amount of *boilerplate*. Boilerplate is the name used to describe code that needs to be present to satisfy certain rules or conventions but that looks more or less the same in any project. For example, C# requires code to be defined inside a *method*, and a method must always be defined inside a *type*. You can see evidence of these rules in Example 1-1. To produce output, it relies on the .NET runtime's ability to display text, which is embodied in a method called WriteLine. But we don't just say WriteLine because C# methods always belong to types, which is why the code qualifies this as Console.WriteLine.

Any C# code that we write is subject to the rules, so our code that invokes the Console.WriteLine method must itself live inside a method inside a type. And in the majority of C# code, this would be explicit: in most cases, you'll see something a bit more like Example 1-2.

Example 1-2. "Hello, World!" with visible boilerplate

```
using System;

namespace HelloWorld;

internal class Program
{
    private static void Main(string[] args)
    {
        Console.WriteLine("Hello, World!");
    }
}
```

There's still only one line here that defines the behavior of the application, and it's the same as in Example 1-1. The obvious advantage of the first example is that it lets us focus on what our program actually does, although the downside is that quite a lot of what's going on becomes invisible. With the explicit style in Example 1-2, nothing is hidden. Example 1-1 uses the *top-level statement* style, but the compiler still puts the code in a method defined inside a type called Program; it's just that you can't see that from the code. With Example 1-2, the method and type are clearly visible.

The C# boilerplate reduction feature that enables us to dive straight in with the code is just for the program entry point. When you're writing the code you want to execute whenever your program starts, you don't need to define a containing class or method. But a program has only one entry point, and for everything else, you still need to spell it out. So in practice, most C# code looks more like Example 1-2 than Example 1-1, and with older codebases even the program entry point will use this explicit style.

Since real projects involve multiple files, and usually multiple projects, let's move on to a slightly more realistic example. I'm going to create a program that calculates the average (the arithmetic mean, to be precise) of some numbers. I will also create a second project that will automatically test our first one. Since I've got two projects, this time I'll need a solution. I'll create a new directory called *Averages*. If you're following along, it doesn't matter where it goes, although it's a good idea *not* to put it inside the *HelloWorld* project's directory. I'll open a command prompt in the *Averages* directory and run this command:

```
dotnet new sln
```

This will create a new solution file named *Averages.sln*. (By default, dotnet new usually names new projects and solutions after their containing directories, although you can specify other names.) Now I willll add the two projects I need with these two commands:

```
dotnet new console -o Averages
dotnet new mstest -o Averages.Tests
```

The -o option here (short for output) indicates that I want the tool to create a new subdirectory for each of these new projects—when you have multiple projects, each needs its own directory.

I now need to add these to the solution:

```
dotnet sln add ./Averages/Averages.csproj
dotnet sln add ./Averages.Tests/Averages.Tests.csproj
```

I'm going to use that second project to define some tests that will check the code in the first project (which is why I specified a project type of mstest—this project will use Microsoft's unit test framework). This means that the second project will need access to the code in the first project. To enable that, I run this command:

```
dotnet add ./Averages.Tests/Averages.Tests.csproj reference
./Averages/Averages.csproj
```

(I've split this over two lines to make it fit, but it needs to be run as a single command.) Finally, to edit the project, I can launch VS Code in the current directory with this command:

```
code .
```

If you're following along, and if this is the first time you've run VS Code, it will ask you to make some decisions, such as choosing a color scheme. It might also ask you whether you trust the folder location, in which case you should tell it that you do. You might be tempted to ignore its questions, but one of the things it might offer to do at this point is install extensions for language support. People use VS Code with all sorts of languages, and the installer makes no assumptions about which you will be using, so you have to install an extension to get C# support. If you follow VS Code's instructions to browse for language extensions, it will offer Microsoft's C# Dev Kit extension. Don't panic if VS Code does not offer to do this. The automatic extension suggestion behavior has changed from time to time, and it might have changed again after I wrote this. You might need to open one of the .cs files before it shows a prompt similar to the one in Figure 1-1.

Figure 1-1. Visual Studio Code's extension suggestion prompt

If you don't see this, perhaps you already had the C# Dev Kit extension installed. To find out, click the Extensions icon on the bar on the lefthand side. It's the one shown at the bottom left of Figure 1-2, with four squares. If you've opened VS code in a directory with a *.csproj* file in it, the C# Dev Kit extension should appear in the INSTALLED section if you've already installed it, and in the RECOMMENDED section if you don't have it yet.

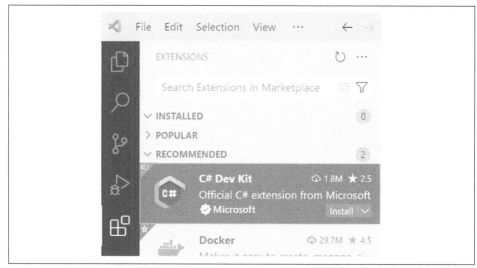

Figure 1-2. Visual Studio Code's C# Dev Kit extension

If you still don't see it, type **C#** into the search text box at the top. A few results will appear, so if you're following along, make sure you get the right one. If you click the search result, it will show more detailed information, which should show its full name as "C# Dev Kit" with a subtitle of "Official C# extension from Microsoft" and it will show "Microsoft" as the publisher. Click the Install button to install the extension.

It might take a few minutes to download and install the C# Dev Kit extension, but once that's done, at the bottom left of the window the status bar should look similar to Figure 1-3, showing it has found the two projects we created.

Figure 1-3. Visual Studio Code's status bar

The C# Dev Kit extension will inspect all of the source code in all of the projects in the solution. Obviously there's not much in these yet, but it will continue to analyze code as I type, enabling it to identify problems and make helpful suggestions.

I can take a look at the code by switching to the Explorer view, using the button at the top of the toolbar on the left. As Figure 1-4 shows, it displays the directories and files. I've expanded the *Averages.Tests* directory and have selected its *UnitTest1.cs* file.

Figure 1-4. Visual Studio Code's Explorer

If you single-click a file in the Explorer panel, VS Code shows it in a *preview tab*, meaning that it won't stay open for long: as soon as you click some other file, that displaces the one you had open before. This is designed to avoid ending up with hundreds of open tabs, but if you're working back and forth across two files, this can be annoying. You can avoid this by double-clicking the file when you open it—that opens a nonpreview tab, which will remain open until you deliberately close it. If you already have a file open in a preview tab, you can double-click the filename to turn it into an ordinary tab. VS Code shows the filename in italics in preview tabs, and you'll see it change to nonitalic when you double-click.

You might be wondering why I expanded the *Averages.Tests* directory. The purpose of this test project will be to ensure that the main project does what it's supposed to. With this example, I'll be following the engineering practice of defining tests that embody my requirements before writing the code being tested (sometimes known as *test driven development* or TDD). That means starting with the test project.

Writing a Unit Test

When I ran the command to create this project earlier, I specified a project type of mstest. This project template has provided me with a test class to get me started, in a file called *UnitTest1.cs*. I want to pick a more informative name. There are various schools of thought as to how you should structure your unit tests. Some developers advocate one test class for each class you wish to test, but I like the style where you write a class for each *scenario* in which you want to test a particular class, with one method for each of the things that should be true about your code in that scenario. This program will only have one behavior: it will calculate the arithmetic mean of its inputs. So I'll rename the *UnitTest1.cs* source file to *WhenCalculatingAverages.cs*. (You can rename a file by right-clicking it in VS Code's Explorer panel and selecting the Rename entry.) This test should verify that we get the expected results for a few representative inputs. Example 1-3 shows a complete source file that does this; there are two tests here, shown in bold.

Example 1-3. A unit test class for our first program

```csharp
using Microsoft.VisualStudio.TestTools.UnitTesting;

namespace Averages.Tests;

[TestClass]
public class WhenCalculatingAverages
{
    [TestMethod]
    public void SingleInputShouldProduceSameValueAsResult()
    {
        string[] inputs = { "1" };
        double result = AverageCalculator.ArithmeticMean(inputs);
        Assert.AreEqual(1.0, result, 1E-14);
    }

    [TestMethod]
    public void MultipleInputsShouldProduceAverageAsResult()
    {
        string[] inputs = { "1", "2", "3" };
        double result = AverageCalculator.ArithmeticMean(inputs);
        Assert.AreEqual(2.0, result, 1E-14);
    }
}
```

I will explain each of the features in this file once I've shown the program itself. For now, the most interesting parts of this example are the two methods. First, we have the SingleInputShouldProduceSameValueAsResult method, which checks that our program correctly handles the case where there is a single input. The first line inside this method describes the input—a single number. (Slightly surprisingly, this test represents the numbers as strings. This is because our inputs will ultimately come as command-line arguments, so our test needs to reflect that.) The second line executes the code under test (which I've not actually written yet). And the third line states that the calculated average should be equal to the one and only input. If it's not, this test will report a failure. The second method, `MultipleInputsShouldProduceAverageAs Result`, checks a slightly more complex case, in which there are three inputs, but has the same basic shape as the first.

This code uses C#'s `double` type, a double-precision floating-point number, to be able to represent results that are not whole numbers. I'll be describing C#'s built-in data types in more detail in the next chapter, but be aware that as with most programming languages, floating-point arithmetic in C# has limited precision. The `Assert.AreEqual` method I'm using to check the results here takes this into account and lets me specify maximum tolerance for imprecision. The final argument of `1E-14` in each case denotes the number 1 divided by 10 raised to the power of 14, so these tests are stating that they require the answer to be correct to 14 decimal places.

Let's focus on one particular line from these tests: the one that runs the code I want to test. Example 1-4 shows the relevant line from Example 1-3. This is how you invoke a method that returns a result in C#. This line starts by declaring a variable to hold the result. (The text `double` indicates the data type, and `result` is the variable's name.) All methods in C# need to be defined inside a type, so just as we saw earlier with the `Console.WriteLine` example, we have the same form here: a type name, then a period, then a method name. And then, in parentheses, the input to the method.

Example 1-4. Calling a method

```
double result = AverageCalculator.ArithmeticMean(inputs);
```

If you are following along by typing the code in as you read, then if you look at the two places this line of code appears (once in each test method), you might notice that VS Code has drawn a squiggly line underneath `AverageCalculator`. Hovering the mouse over this kind of squiggly shows an error message, as Figure 1-5 shows.

```
[TestMethod]
0 references
public void SingleIn        The name 'AverageCalculator' does not exist in the current
{                           context (CS0103)

    string[] inputs   View Problem (Alt+F8)   Quick Fix... (Ctrl+.)
    double result = AverageCalculator.ArithmeticMean(inputs);
    Assert.AreEqual(1.0, result, 1E-14);
}
```

Figure 1-5. An unrecognized type

This is telling us something we already knew: I haven't yet written the code that this test aims to test. Let's fix that. I need to add a new file, which I can do in VS Code's Explorer view by clicking the *Averages* directory and then, with that selected, clicking the leftmost button on the toolbar near the top of the Explorer. Figure 1-6 shows that when you hover the mouse over this button, it shows a tool tip confirming its purpose. After clicking it, I can type in *AverageCalculator.cs* as the name for the new file.

Figure 1-6. Adding a new file

VS Code will create a new, empty file. I'll add the smallest amount of code I can to fix the error reported in Figure 1-5. Example 1-5 will satisfy the C# compiler. It's not complete yet—it doesn't perform the necessary calculations, but we'll come to that.

Example 1-5. A simple class

```
namespace Averages;

public static class AverageCalculator
{
    public static double ArithmeticMean(string[] args)
    {
        return 1.0;
    }
}
```

You can now build the code. If you look at the bottom of VS Code's Explorer, you should see a Solution Explorer section. If you expand this, it will show the solution and its two projects. You can right-click the solution and select Build, as Figure 1-7 shows. Alternatively, you can just type `dotnet build` at the command line. Or you can use the Ctrl-Shift-B shortcut. The first time you use that shortcut, it may ask you to confirm that you want to use the `dotnet build` command to perform the build.

Figure 1-7. Building the solution

Once the build is complete, you should see a flask icon on the button bar on the left of the VS Code window, as Figure 1-8 shows. If you click this, it will show the Testing panel, enabling you to run tests and see the results.

Figure 1-8. The Testing button

The Testing panel shows the tests hierarchically, first grouped by project and then by namespace. (Since your test project is called `Averages.Tests`, and all its tests are in a namespace called `Averages.Tests`, you'll see that appear twice, as Figure 1-9 shows.) At the top of the Testing panel is a row of buttons. One shows a couple of triangles, one on top of the other. If you click this it will run all of the tests.

Figure 1-9. Test results

Since we've not finished writing the library yet, one of these tests will fail. As Figure 1-9 shows, this is indicated by showing a cross next to the test. If you click the failing test, VS Code will show you the point in the code at which the test failed, along with details including the failure message and a stack trace, as Figure 1-10 shows.

```
16          [TestMethod]
            0 references
17          public void MultipleInputsShouldProduceAverageAsResult()
18          {
19              string[] inputs = { "1", "2", "3" };
20              double result = AverageCalculator.ArithmeticMean(inputs);
21              Assert.AreEqual(2.0, result, 1E-14);    Assert.AreEqual failed
```

Assert.AreEqual failed. Expected a difference no greater... MultipleInputsShou... ↑ ↓ ↺ | ≡ₓ ⬒ ×

```
    Assert.AreEqual failed. Expected a difference no greater than <1E-14>
    between expected value <2> and actual value <1>.
      at Averages.Tests.WhenCalculatingAverages.
      MultipleInputsShouldProduceAverageAsResult() in
      C:\dev\temp\Averages\Averages.Tests\UnitTest1.cs:line 21
      at System.RuntimeMethodHandle.InvokeMethod(Object target, Void**
      arguments, Signature sig, Boolean isConstructor)
      at System.Reflection.MethodBaseInvoker.InvokeWithNoArgs(Object
      obj, BindingFlags invokeAttr)
```

Figure 1-10. A failing test

You can alternatively run tests with the command dotnet test. It shows the same information as Visual Studio Code did, but just as normal console output:

```
Failed MultipleInputsShouldProduceAverageAsResult [291 ms]
Error Message:
 Assert.AreEqual failed. Expected a difference no greater than <1E-14>
between expected value <2> and actual value <1>.
 Stack Trace:
   at Averages.Tests.WhenCalculatingAverages.
MultipleInputsShouldProduceAverageAsResult() in
C:\book\Averages\Averages.Tests\WhenCalculatingAverages.cs:line 21
   at System.RuntimeMethodHandle.InvokeMethod(Object target, Void** arguments,
Signature sig, Boolean isConstructor)
   at System.Reflection.MethodBaseInvoker.InvokeWithNoArgs(Object obj,
BindingFlags invokeAttr)

Failed!  - Failed:     1, Passed:     1, Skipped:     0, Total:     2,
Duration: 364 ms - Averages.Tests.dll (net6.0)
```

As expected, we get failures because I've not written a proper implementation yet. But first, I want to explain each element of Example 1-5 in turn, as it provides a useful introduction to some important elements of C# syntax and structure. The very first thing in this file is a *namespace declaration*.

Namespaces

Namespaces bring order and structure to what would otherwise be a horrible mess. The .NET runtime libraries contain thousands of types, and there are many more out there in NuGet packages both from Microsoft and third parties, not to mention the classes you will write yourself. There are two problems that can occur when dealing with this many named entities. First, it becomes hard to guarantee uniqueness. Second, it can become challenging to discover the API you need; unless you know or can guess the right name, it's difficult to find what you need from an unstructured list of tens of thousands of things. Namespaces solve both of these problems.

Most .NET types are defined in a namespace. There are certain conventions for namespaces that you'll see a lot. For example, types in .NET's runtime libraries are in namespaces that start with System. Additionally, Microsoft has made a wide range of useful libraries available that are not a core part of .NET, and these usually begin with Microsoft, or, if they are for use only with some particular technology, they might be named for that. (For example, there are libraries for using Microsoft's Azure cloud platform that define types in namespaces that start with Azure.) Libraries from other vendors tend to start with the company name or a product name, while open source libraries often use their project name. You are not forced to put your own types into namespaces, but it's recommended that you do. C# does not treat System as a special namespace, so nothing's stopping you from using that for your own types, but unless you're writing a contribution to the .NET runtime libraries that you will be submitting as a pull request to the .NET runtime source repository (*https://github.com/dotnet/runtime*), then it's a bad idea because it will tend to confuse other developers. You should pick something more distinctive for your own code, such as your company or project name. As you can see from the first line of Example 1-5, I've chosen to define our `AverageCalculator` class inside a namespace called `Averages`, matching our project name.

The style of namespace declaration in Example 1-5 is relatively new, so you are likely to come across the older, slightly more verbose style shown in Example 1-6. The difference is that the namespace declaration is followed by braces (`{}`), and its effect applies only to the contents of those braces. This makes it possible for a single file to contain multiple namespace declarations. But in practice, the overwhelming majority of C# files contain exactly one namespace declaration. With the old syntax, this means that the majority of the contents of each file has to sit inside a pair of braces, indented by one tab stop. The newer style shown in Example 1-5 applies to all types declared in the file without needing to wrap them explicitly, reducing unproductive clutter in our source files.

Example 1-6. Explicitly scoped namespace declaration

```
namespace Averages
{
    public static class AverageCalculator
    {
        ...as before...
    }
}
```

The namespace usually gives a clue as to the purpose of a type. For example, all the runtime library types that relate to file handling can be found in the `System.IO` namespace, while those concerned with networking are under `System.Net`. Namespaces can form a hierarchy. The runtime libraries' `System` namespace contains types and also other namespaces, such as `System.Net`, and these often contain yet more namespaces, such as `System.Net.Sockets` and `System.Net.Mail`. These examples show that namespaces act as a sort of description, which can help you navigate the library. If you were looking for regular expression handling, for example, you might look through the available namespaces and notice the `System.Text` namespace. Looking in there, you'd find a `System.Text.RegularExpressions` namespace, at which point you'd be pretty confident that you were looking in the right place.

Namespaces also provide a way to ensure uniqueness. The namespace in which a type is defined is part of that type's full name. This lets libraries use short, simple names for things. For example, the regular expression API includes a `Capture` class that represents the results from a regular expression capture. If you are working on software that deals with images, the term *capture* is commonly used to mean the acquisition of some image data, and you might feel that `Capture` is the most descriptive name for a class in your own code. It would be annoying to have to pick a different name just because the best one is already taken, particularly if your image acquisition code has no use for regular expressions, meaning that you weren't even planning to use the existing `Capture` type.

But in fact, it's fine. Both types can be called `Capture`, and they will still have different names. The full name of the regular expression `Capture` class is effectively `System.Text.RegularExpressions.Capture`, and likewise, your class's full name would include its containing namespace (for example, `SpiffingSoftworks.Imaging.Capture`).

If you really want to, you can write the fully qualified name of a type every time you use it, but most developers don't want to do anything quite so tedious, which is where the `using` directives you can see at the start of Examples 1-2 and 1-3 come in. It's common to see a list of directives at the top of each source file, stating the namespaces of the types that file intends to use. You will normally edit this list to match your file's requirements. In this example, the `dotnet` command-line tool added `using Microsoft.VisualStudio.TestTools.UnitTesting;` when it created the test project. You'll see different sets in different contexts. If you add a class representing a UI element, for example, Visual Studio would include various UI-related namespaces in the list.

If a project makes heavy use of a particular namespace, we can avoid having to put the same `using` directive in every single source file by writing a *global using directive*. If we put the `global` keyword in front of the directive, as Example 1-7 does, the directive applies to all files in a project. The .NET SDK takes this a step further, by generating a hidden file in your project with a set of these `global using` directives to ensure that commonly used namespaces such as `System` and `System.Collections.Generic` are available. (The exact set of namespaces added as implicit global imports varies by project type—web projects get a few extra, for example. If you're wondering why unit test projects don't already do what Example 1-7 does, it's because the .NET SDK doesn't have a specific project type for test projects—the `mstest` template we told `dotnet new` to use just creates an ordinary class library project with a reference to the unit test library packages.)

Example 1-7. A global using directive

```
global using Microsoft.VisualStudio.TestTools.UnitTesting;
```

With `using` declarations like these (either per-file or global) in place, you can just use the short, unqualified name for a class. The line of code that enables Example 1-1 to do its job uses the `System.Console` class, but because the SDK adds an implicit `global using` directive for the `System` namespace, it can refer to it as just `Console`.

Namespaces and component names

Earlier, I used the `dotnet` CLI to add a reference from our `Averages.Tests` project to our `Averages` project. You might think that references are redundant—can't the compiler work out which external libraries we are using from the namespaces? It could if there was a direct correspondence between namespaces and either libraries or packages, but there isn't.

Library names sometimes align with namespaces—the popular `Newtonsoft.Json` NuGet package contains a *Newtonsoft.Json.dll* file that contains classes in the `Newton soft.Json` namespace, for example. But this is an optional convention, and often there's no such connection—the .NET runtime libraries include a *System.Private. CoreLib.dll* file, but there is no `System.Private.CoreLib` namespace. So it is necessary to tell the compiler which libraries your project depends on, and also which namespaces it uses. We will look at the nature and structure of library files in more detail in Chapter 12.

Resolving ambiguity

Even with namespaces, there's potential for ambiguity. A single source file might use two namespaces that both happen to define a class of the same name. If you want to use that class, then you will need to be explicit, referring to it by its full name. If you need to use such classes a lot in the file, you can still save yourself some typing: you only need to use the full name once because you can define a *using alias*. Example 1-8 defines two aliases to resolve a clash that I've run into a few times: .NET's desktop UI framework, the Windows Presentation Foundation (WPF), defines a `Path` class for working with Bézier curves, polygons, and other shapes, but there's also a `Path` class for working with filesystem paths, and you might want to use both types together to produce a graphical representation of the contents of a file. Just adding `using` directives for both namespaces would make the simple name `Path` ambiguous if unqualified. But as Example 1-8 shows, you can define distinctive aliases for each.

Example 1-8. Resolving ambiguity with aliases

```
using System.IO;
using System.Windows.Shapes;
using IoPath = System.IO.Path;
using WpfPath = System.Windows.Shapes.Path;
```

With these aliases in place, you can use `IoPath` as a synonym for the file-related `Path` class, and `WpfPath` for the graphical one.

By the way, you can refer to types in your own namespace without qualification, without needing a `using` directive. That's why the test code in Example 1-3 doesn't have a `using Averages;` directive. However, you might be wondering how this works, since the test code declares a different namespace, `Averages.Tests`. To understand this, we need to look at namespace nesting.

Nested namespaces

As you've already seen, the .NET runtime libraries nest their namespaces, sometimes quite extensively, and you will often want to do the same. There are two ways you can do this. You can nest namespace declarations, as Example 1-9 shows.

Example 1-9. Nesting namespace declarations

```
namespace MyApp
{
    namespace Storage
    {
        ...
    }
}
```

Alternatively, you can just specify the full namespace in a single declaration, as Example 1-10 shows. This is the more commonly used style. This single-declaration style works with either the newer kind of declaration shown in Example 1-10 or with the older style using braces.

Example 1-10. Nested namespace with a single declaration

```
namespace MyApp.Storage;
```

Any code you write in a nested namespace will be able to use types not just from that namespace but also from its containing namespaces without qualification. Code in Examples 1-9 or 1-10 would not need explicit qualification or `using` directives to use types either in the `MyApp.Storage` namespace or the `MyApp` namespace. This is why in Example 1-3 I didn't need to add a `using Averages;` directive to be able to access the `AverageCalculator` in the `Averages` namespace: the test was declared in the `Averages.Tests` namespace, and since that is nested in the `Averages` namespace, the code automatically has access to that outer namespace.

When you define nested namespaces, the convention is to create a matching directory hierarchy. Some tools expect this. Although VS Code doesn't currently have any particular expectations here, Visual Studio does follow this convention. If your project is called MyApp, it will put new classes in the MyApp namespace when you add them to the project. But if you create a new directory in the project called, say, *Storage*, Visual Studio will put any new classes you create in that directory into the MyApp.Storage namespace. Again, you're not required to keep this—Visual Studio just adds a namespace declaration when creating the file, and you're free to change it. The compiler does not need the namespace to match your directory hierarchy. But since the convention is supported by various tools, including Visual Studio, life will be easier if you follow it.

Classes

After the namespace declaration, our *AverageCalculator.cs* file defines a *class*. Example 1-11 shows this part of the file. This starts with the public keyword, which enables this class to be accessed by other components. Next is the static keyword, which indicates that this class is not meant to be instantiated—it offers only class-level operations and no per-instance features. Then comes the class keyword followed by the name, and of course the full name of the type is effectively Averages.AverageCalculator, because of the namespace declaration. As you can see, C# uses braces ({}) to delimit all sorts of things—we already saw this in the older (but still widely used) namespace declaration syntax, and here you can see the same thing with the class, as well as the method it contains.

Example 1-11. A class with a method

```
public static class AverageCalculator
{
    public static double ArithmeticMean(string[] args)
    {
        return 1.0;
    }
}
```

Classes are C#'s mechanism for defining entities that combine state and behavior, a common object-oriented idiom. But this class contains nothing more than a single method. C# does not support global methods—all code has to be written as a member of some type. So this particular class isn't very interesting—its only job is to act as the container for the method that will do the actual work. We'll see some more interesting uses for classes in Chapter 3.

As with the class, I've marked the method as public to enable access from other components. I've also declared this to be a *static method*, meaning that it is not necessary to create an instance of the containing type (AverageCalculator, in this case) in order to invoke the method. The double keyword that follows indicates that the type of data this method returns is a double-precision floating-point number.

The method declaration is followed by the method body, which in this example contains code that returns a placeholder value, so all that remains is to modify the code inside the braces delimiting the method body. Example 1-12 shows code that calculates the average instead of just returning 1.0.

Example 1-12. Calculating the average

```
return args.Select(numText => double.Parse(numText)).Average();
```

This relies on library functions for working with collections that are part of the set of features collectively known as LINQ, which is the subject of Chapter 10. But just to describe quickly what's going on here, the `Select` method lets us apply an operation to every single item in a collection, and in this case, the operation I'm applying is the `double.Parse` method, a .NET runtime library function that converts a textual string containing a number into the native double-precision floating-point type. And then we push these transformed results through LINQ's `Average` method, which does the calculation for us.

With this in place, if I run my tests again, they will all pass. So apparently the code is working. However, I see a problem if I try to verify that informally by running the program, which I can do with this command:

```
./Averages/bin/Debug/net8.0/Averages 1 2 3 4 5
```

This just writes out `Hello, World!` to the screen. I've written and tested the code that performs the required calculation, but I've not yet connected that up to the program's entry point. The code that runs when the program starts lives in *Program.cs*, although there's nothing special about that filename. The program entry point can live in any file. In older versions of C#, you denoted the entry point by defining a `static` method called `Main`, as Example 1-2 showed, and you can still do that with C# 12.0, but we normally use the newer, more succinct approach: we write a file that contains executable statements without putting them explicitly inside a method in a type, and the C# compiler will treat that as the entry point. (You're only allowed to have one file in your project written that way, because your program can have only one entry point.) If I replace the entire contents of *Program.cs* with the code shown in Example 1-13, it will have the desired effect.

Example 1-13. Program entry point with arguments

```
using Averages;

Console.WriteLine(AverageCalculator.ArithmeticMean(args));
```

Notice that I've had to add a `using` directive—when you use this stripped-down program entry point syntax, the code in that file is not in any namespace by default, so I need to state that I want to use the class I defined in the Averages namespace. After that, this code invokes the method I wrote earlier, passing args as an argument, and then calls Console.WriteLine to display the result. When you use this style of program entry point, args is a special name—it's effectively an implicitly defined local variable that provides access to the command-line arguments. This will be an array of strings, with one entry for each argument. If you want to run the program again with the same arguments as before, run the dotnet build command first to rebuild it.

 Some C-family languages include the filename of the program itself as the first argument, on the grounds that it's part of what the user typed at the command prompt. C# does not follow this convention. If the program is launched without arguments, the array's length will be 0. You might have noticed that the code does not cope well with that. Feel free to add a new test scenario that defines the relevant behavior, and to modify the program to match.

Unit Tests

Now that the program is working, I want to return to the tests, because they illustrate a C# feature that the main program does not. If you go back to Example 1-3, it starts in a pretty ordinary way: we have a using directive and then a namespace declaration, for Averages.Tests this time, matching the test project name. But the class looks different. Example 1-14 shows the relevant part of Example 1-3.

Example 1-14. Test class with attribute

```
[TestClass]
public class WhenCalculatingAverages
{
```

Immediately before the class declaration is the text [TestClass]. This is an *attribute*. Attributes are annotations you can apply to classes, methods, and other features of the code. Most of them do nothing on their own—the compiler records the fact that the attribute is present in the compiled output, but that is all. Attributes are useful only when something goes looking for them, so they tend to be used by frameworks. In this case, I'm using Microsoft's unit testing framework, and it goes looking for classes annotated with this TestClass attribute. It will ignore classes that do not have this annotation. Attributes are typically specific to a particular framework, and you can define your own, as we'll see in Chapter 14.

The two methods in the class are also annotated with attributes. Example 1-15 shows the relevant excerpts from Example 1-3. The test runner will execute any methods marked with the [TestMethod] attribute.

Example 1-15. Annotated methods

```
[TestMethod]
public void SingleInputShouldProduceSameValueAsResult()
...

[TestMethod]
public void MultipleInputsShouldProduceAverageAsResult()
...
```

And with that, we've examined every element of a program and the test project that verifies that it works as intended.

Summary

You've now seen the basic structure of C# programs. I created a solution containing two projects, one for tests and one for the program itself. This was a simple example, so each project had only one or two source files of interest. Where necessary, these files began with `using` directives indicating which types the file uses. The program's entry point used a stripped-down style, but the other two used a more conventional structure, containing a namespace declaration stating the namespace that the file populates, and a class containing one or more methods or other members, such as fields.

We will look at types and their members in much more detail in Chapter 3, but first, Chapter 2 will deal with the code that lives inside methods, where we express what we want our programs to do.

Basic Coding in C#

All programming languages have to provide certain capabilities. It must be possible to express the calculations and operations that our code should perform. Programs need to be able to make decisions based on their input. Sometimes we will need to perform tasks repeatedly. These fundamental features are the very stuff of programming, and this chapter will show how these things work in C#.

Depending on your background, some of this chapter's content may seem very familiar. C# is said to be from the "C family" of languages. C is a hugely influential programming language, and numerous languages have borrowed much of its syntax. There are direct descendants, such as C++ and Objective-C. There are also more distantly related languages, including Java, JavaScript, and C# itself, that have no compatibility with C but that still copy many aspects of its syntax. If you are familiar with any of these languages, you will recognize many of the language features we are about to explore.

We saw the basic elements of a program in Chapter 1. In this chapter, we will be looking just at code inside methods. As you've seen, C# requires a certain amount of structure: code is made up of statements that live inside a method, which belongs to a type, which is typically inside a namespace, all inside a file that is part of a project, typically contained by a solution. In the special case of a program's entry point, the containing method and type might be hidden thanks to C#'s clutter-reducing *top-level statements* feature, but they're visible in most files. For clarity, most of the examples in this chapter will show the code of interest in isolation, as in Example 2-1.

Example 2-1. The code and nothing but the code

```
Console.WriteLine("Hello, World!");
```

And although the compiler will accept that shorter example as the entirety of the program, any program larger than a single file (i.e., almost any useful program) will need to include the other elements explicitly. So unless I say otherwise, this kind of extract is shorthand for showing the code in context inside a suitably structured file. Examples such as Example 2-1 are equivalent to something more like Example 2-2.

Example 2-2. The whole code

```
using System;

public class MyType
{
    public static void SomeMethod()
    {
        Console.WriteLine("Hello, World!");
    }
}
```

Although I'll be introducing fundamental elements of the language in this section, this book is for people who are already familiar with at least one programming language, so I'll be relatively brief with the most ordinary features of the language and will go into more detail on those aspects that are particular to C#.

Local Variables

The inevitable "Hello, World!" example is missing a vital element: it doesn't really deal with information. Useful programs normally fetch, process, and produce data, so the ability to define and identify it is one of the most important features of a language. Like most languages, C# lets you define *local variables*, which are named elements inside a method that each hold a piece of information.

 In the C# specification, the term *variable* can refer to local variables but also to fields in objects and array elements. This section is concerned entirely with local variables, but it gets tiring to keep reading the *local* prefix. So, from now on in this section, *variable* means a local variable.

C# is a *statically typed* language, which is to say that any element of code that represents or produces information, such as a variable or an expression, has a data type determined at compile time. This is different than *dynamically typed* languages, such as JavaScript, in which types are determined at runtime.

The easiest way to see C#'s static typing in action is with simple variable declarations, such as the ones in Example 2-3. Each of these starts with the data type—the first two variables are of type `string`, followed by two `int` variables. These types represent text strings and 32-bit signed integers, respectively.

Example 2-3. Variable declarations

```
string part1 = "the ultimate question";
string part2 = "of something";
int theAnswer = 42;
int andAnotherThing;
```

The data type is followed immediately by the variable's name. The name must begin with either a letter or an underscore, which can be followed by any combination of letters, decimal digits, and underscores. (At least, those are the options if you stick to ASCII. C# supports Unicode, so if you save your file in UTF-8 or UTF-16 format, anything after the first character in an identifier can be any of the characters described in the "Identifier and Pattern Syntax" annex of the Unicode specification. This includes various accents and diacritics, and also numerous punctuation marks, but only those intended for use *within* words—characters that Unicode identifies as being intended for *separating* words cannot be used.) These same rules determine what constitutes a legal identifier for any user-defined entity in C#, such as a class or a method.

Example 2-3 shows that there are a couple of forms of variable declarations. The first three variables include an *initializer*, which provides the variable's initial value, but as the final variable shows, this is optional. That's because you can assign new values into variables at any point. Example 2-4 continues on from Example 2-3 and shows that you can set a variable regardless of whether it had an initial value.

Example 2-4. Assigning values to previously declared variables

```
part2 = " of life, the universe, and everything";
andAnotherThing = 123;
```

Because variables have a static type, the compiler will reject attempts to assign the wrong kind of data. So if we were to follow on from Example 2-3 with the code in Example 2-5, the compiler would complain. It knows that `theAnswer` is a variable of type `int`, which is a numeric type, so it will report an error if we attempt to assign a text string into it.

Example 2-5. An error: the wrong type

```
theAnswer = "The compiler will reject this";
```

You'd be allowed to do this in dynamic languages such as JavaScript, because in those languages, a variable doesn't have its own type—all that matters is the type of the value it contains, and that can change as the code runs. It's possible to do something similar in C# by declaring a variable with type `dynamic` or `object` (which I'll describe later in "Dynamic" on page 90 and "Object" on page 91). However, the most common practice in C# is for variables to have a more specific type.

 The static type doesn't always provide a complete picture, thanks to inheritance. I'll be discussing this in Chapter 6, but for now, it's enough to know that some types are open to extension through inheritance, and if a variable uses such a type, then it's possible for it to refer to some object of a type derived from the variable's static type. Interfaces, described in Chapter 3, provide a similar kind of flexibility. However, the static type always determines what operations you are allowed to perform on the variable. If you want to use additional members specific to some derived type, you won't be able to do so through a variable of the base type.

You don't have to state the variable type explicitly. You can let the compiler work it out for you by using the keyword `var` in place of the data type. Example 2-6 shows the first three variable declarations from Example 2-3 but using `var` instead of explicit data types.

Example 2-6. Implicit variable types with the `var` keyword

```
var part1 = "the ultimate question";
var part2 = "of something";
var theAnswer = 42;
```

This code often misleads people who know some JavaScript, because that also has a `var` keyword that you can use in a similar-looking way. But `var` does not work the same way in C# as in JavaScript: these variables are still all statically typed. All that's changed is that we haven't said what the type is—we're letting the compiler deduce it for us. It looks at the initializers and can see that the first two variables are strings, whereas the third is an integer. (That's why I left out the fourth variable from Example 2-3, `andAnotherThing`. That doesn't have an initializer, so the compiler would have no way of inferring its type. If you try to use the `var` keyword without an initializer, you'll get a compiler error.)

You can demonstrate that variables declared with `var` are statically typed by attempting to assign something of a different type into them. We could repeat the same thing we tried in Example 2-5 but this time with a `var`-style variable. Example 2-7 does this, and it will produce exactly the same compiler error, because it's the same mistake—we're trying to assign a text string into a variable of an incompatible type. That variable, `theAnswer`, has a type of `int` here, even though we didn't say so explicitly.

Example 2-7. An error: the wrong type (again)

```
var theAnswer = 42;
theAnswer = "The compiler will reject this";
```

Opinion is divided on how and when to use the var keyword, as the sidebar "To var, or Not to var?" describes.

To var, or Not to var?

A variable declared with var behaves in exactly the same way as the equivalent explicitly typed declaration, which raises a question: Which should you use? In a sense, it doesn't matter, because they are equivalent. However, if you like your code to be consistent, you'll want to pick one style and stick to it. Not everyone agrees on which is the "best" style.

Some developers see the extra text required for explicit variable types as unproductive "ceremony," preferring the more succinct var keyword. Let the compiler deduce the type for you, instead of doing the work yourself, or so the argument goes. It also reduces visual clutter in the code.

I take a different view, because I spend more time reading code than writing it—debugging, code review, refactoring, and enhancements seem to dominate. Anything that makes those activities easier is worth the frankly minimal time it takes to write the type names explicitly. Code that uses var everywhere slows you down, because you have to work out what the type really is in order to understand the code. Although var saved you some work when you wrote the code, that gain is quickly wiped out by the additional thought required every time you go back and look at the code. So unless you're the sort of developer who only ever writes new code, leaving others to clean up after you, the only benefit the "var everywhere" philosophy really offers is that it can look neater.

You can even use explicit types and still get the compiler to do the work: in Visual Studio, VS Code, or Rider you can write the keystroke-friendly var, then press Ctrl-. to open the Quick Actions menu. This offers to replace it with the explicit type for you. (This feature uses the C# compiler's API to discover the variable's type.)

That said, there are some situations in which I will use var, such as avoiding writing the name of the type twice. This can happen when you use the new operator to create a new instance of some type, as in this example:

```
List<int> numbers1 = new List<int>();
var numbers2 = new List<int>();
List<int> numbers3 = new();
```

All three lines have the same effect. The third line works because you can use new() without specifying the type as long as the C# compiler can infer the type required. var n = new(); wouldn't work because that doesn't indicate a type. The type name is right

---

there in all three cases, so the first one doesn't gain anything by stating the type twice, which is why I don't mind the second option, although the third is the most succinct. There are similar examples involving casts and generic methods. As long as the type name appears explicitly in the variable declaration, there is no downside to using `var` to avoid writing the type twice.

I also use `var` where it is necessary. As we will see in later chapters, C# supports *anonymous types*, and as the name suggests, it's not possible to write the name of such a type. In these situations, you may be compelled to use `var`. (In fact, the `var` keyword was introduced to C# only when anonymous types were added.)

You can declare and optionally initialize multiple variables in a single statement. If you want multiple variables of the same type, this may reduce clutter in your code. Example 2-8 declares three variables of the same type in a single declaration and initializes two of them.

Example 2-8. Multiple variables in a single declaration

```
double a, b = 2.5, c = -3;
```

Regardless of how you declare it, a variable holds some piece of information of a particular type, and the compiler prevents us from putting data of an incompatible type into that variable. Variables are useful only because we can refer back to them later in our code. Example 2-9 starts with the variable declarations we saw in earlier examples, then goes on to use the values of those variables to initialize some more variables, and then displays the results.

Example 2-9. Using variables

```
string part1 = "the ultimate question";
string part2 = "of something";
int theAnswer = 42;

part2 = "of life, the universe, and everything";

string questionText = "What is the answer to " + part1 + ", " + part2 + "?";
string answerText = "The answer to " + part1 + ", " +
                    part2 + ", is: " + theAnswer;

Console.WriteLine(questionText);
Console.WriteLine(answerText);
```

By the way, this code relies on the fact that C# defines a couple of meanings for the + operator when it's used with strings. First, when you "add" two strings together, it concatenates them. Second, when you "add" something other than a string to the end of a string (as the initializer for `answerText` does—it adds `theAnswer`, which is a number), C# generates code that converts the value to a string before appending it. So Example 2-9 produces this output:

```
What is the answer to the ultimate question, of life, the universe, and everythi
ng?
The answer to the ultimate question, of life, the universe, and everything, is:
42
```

 In this book, text longer than 80 characters is wrapped across multiple lines to fit the page. If you try these examples, they will look different if your console windows have a different width.

When you use a variable, its value is whatever you last assigned to it. If you attempt to use a variable before you have assigned a value, as Example 2-10 does, the C# compiler will report an error.

Example 2-10. Error: using an unassigned variable

```
int willNotWork;
Console.WriteLine(willNotWork);
```

Compiling that produces this error for the second line:

```
error CS0165: Use of unassigned local variable 'willNotWork'
```

The compiler uses a slightly pessimistic system (which it calls the *definite assignment* rules) for determining whether a variable has a value yet. It's not possible to create an algorithm that can determine such things for certain in every possible situation.[1] Since the compiler has to err on the side of caution, there are some situations in which the variable will have a value by the time the offending code runs, and yet the compiler still complains. The solution is to write an initializer so that the variable always contains something, perhaps using 0 for numeric values and `false` for Boolean variables. In Chapter 3, I'll introduce reference types, and as the name suggests, a variable of such a type can hold a reference to an instance of the type. If you need to initialize such a variable before you've got something for it to refer to, you can use the keyword `null`, a special value signifying a reference to nothing. Alternatively, you can initialize a variable of any type with the keyword `default`, which denotes a value of zero, `false`, or `null`.

---

1 See Alan Turing's seminal work on computation for details. Charles Petzold's *The Annotated Turing* (John Wiley & Sons) is an excellent guide to the relevant paper.

The definite assignment rules determine the parts of your code in which the compiler considers a variable to contain a valid value and will therefore let you read from it. Writing into a variable is less restricted, but as you might expect, any given variable is accessible only from certain parts of the code. Let's look at the rules that govern this.

Scope

A variable's *scope* is the range of code in which you can refer to that variable by its name. Variables are not the only things with scope. Methods, properties, types, and, in fact, anything with a name all have scope. These require broadening the definition of scope: it's the parts of your code where you can refer to the entity by its name without needing additional qualification. When I write `Console.WriteLine`, I am referring to the method by its name (`WriteLine`), but I need to qualify it with a class name (`Console`), because the method is not in scope. But with a local variable, scope is absolute: either it's accessible without qualification, or it's not accessible at all.

Broadly speaking, a variable's scope starts at its declaration and finishes at the end of its containing *block*. (Some statements, such as loops, complicate this by putting variable declarations ahead of the block in which they are in scope.) A block is a region of code delimited by a pair of braces ({}). A method body is a block, so a variable defined in one method is not visible in a separate method, because it is out of scope. If you attempt to compile Example 2-11, you'll get an error complaining that The name 'thisWillNotWork' does not exist in the current context.

Example 2-11. Error: out of scope

```
static void SomeMethod()
{
    int thisWillNotWork = 42;
}

static void AnUncompilableMethod()
{
    Console.WriteLine(thisWillNotWork);
}
```

Methods often contain nested blocks, particularly when you work with the loop and flow control constructs we'll be looking at later in this chapter. At the point where a nested block starts, everything that is in scope in the outer block continues to be in scope inside that nested block. Example 2-12 declares a variable called `someValue` and then introduces a nested block as part of an `if` statement. The code inside this block is able to access that variable declared in the containing block.

Example 2-12. Variable declared outside block, used within block

```
int someValue = GetValue();
if (someValue > 100)
{
    Console.WriteLine(someValue);
}
```

The converse is not true. If you declare a variable in a nested block, its scope does not extend outside of that block. So Example 2-13 will fail to compile, because the `will NotWork` variable is only in scope within the nested block. The final line of code will produce a compiler error because it tries to use that variable outside of that block.

Example 2-13. Error: trying to use a variable not in scope

```
int someValue = GetValue();
if (someValue > 100)
{
    int willNotWork = someValue - 100;
}
Console.WriteLine(willNotWork);
```

This might seem fairly straightforward, but things get a bit more complex when it comes to potential naming collisions. C# sometimes catches people by surprise here.

Variable Name Ambiguity

Consider the code in Example 2-14. This declares a variable called `anotherValue` inside a nested block. As you know, that variable is only in scope to the end of that nested block. After that block ends, we try to declare another variable with the same name.

Example 2-14. Error: surprising name collision

```
int someValue = GetValue();
if (someValue > 100)
{
    int anotherValue = someValue - 100;  // Compiler error
    Console.WriteLine(anotherValue);
}

int anotherValue = 123;
```

This causes a compiler error on the first of the lines to declare `anotherValue`:

```
error CS0136: A local or parameter named 'anotherValue' cannot be declared in
  this scope because that name is used in an enclosing local scope to define a
  local or parameter
```

This seems odd. At the final line, the supposedly conflicting earlier declaration is not in scope, because we're outside of the nested block in which it was declared. Furthermore, the second declaration is not in scope within that nested block, because the declaration comes after the block. The scopes do not overlap, but despite this, we're having problems with C#'s rules for avoiding name conflicts. To see why this example fails, we first need to look at a less surprising example.

C# tries to prevent ambiguity by disallowing code where one name might refer to more than one thing. Example 2-15 shows the sort of problem it aims to avoid. Here we've got a variable called errorCount, and the code starts to modify this as it progresses,[2] but partway through, it introduces a new variable in a nested block, also called errorCount. It is possible to imagine a language that allowed this—you could have a rule that says that when multiple items of the same name are in scope, you just pick the one whose declaration happened last.

Example 2-15. Error: hiding a variable

```
int errorCount = 0;
if (problem1)
{
    errorCount += 1;

    if (problem2)
    {
        errorCount += 1;
    }

    // Imagine that in a real program there was a big
    // chunk of code here before the following lines.

    int errorCount = GetErrors();  // Compiler error
    if (problem3)
    {
        errorCount += 1;
    }
}
```

C# chooses not to allow this, because code that did this would be easy to misunderstand. This is an artificially short method because it's a contrived example in a book, making it easy to see the duplicate names, but if the code were a bit longer, it would be very easy to miss the nested variable declaration. Then, we might not realize that errorCount refers to something different at the end of the method than it did earlier on. C# simply disallows this to avoid misunderstanding.

---

2 If you're new to C-family languages, the += operator may be unfamiliar. It is a *compound assignment* operator, described later in this chapter. I'm using it here to increase errorCount by one.

But why does Example 2-14 fail? The scopes of the two variables don't overlap. Well, it turns out that the rule that outlaws Example 2-15 is not based on scopes. It is based on a subtly different concept called a *declaration space*. A declaration space is a region of code in which a single name must not refer to two different entities. Each method introduces a declaration space for variables. Nested blocks also introduce declaration spaces, and it is illegal for a nested declaration space to declare a variable with the same name as one in its parent's declaration space. And that's the rule we've contravened here—the outermost declaration space in Example 2-15 contains a variable named `errorCount`, and a nested block's declaration space tries to introduce another variable of the same name.

If that all seems a bit dry or arbitrary, it may be helpful to know *why* there's a whole separate set of rules for name collisions instead of basing it on scopes. The intent of the declaration space rules is that it mostly shouldn't matter where you put the declaration. If you were to move all of the variable declarations in a block to the start of that block—and some organizations have coding standards that mandate this sort of layout—the idea of these rules is that this shouldn't change what the code means. This wouldn't be possible if Example 2-15 were legal. And this explains why Example 2-14 is illegal. Although the scopes don't overlap, they would if you moved all variable declarations to the tops of their containing blocks.

Local Variable Instances

Variables are features of the source code, so each particular variable has a distinct identity: it is declared in exactly one place in the source code and goes out of scope at exactly one well-defined place. However, that doesn't mean that it corresponds to a single storage location in memory. It is possible for multiple invocations of a single method to be in progress simultaneously, through recursion, multithreading, or asynchronous execution.

Each time a method runs, it gets a distinct set of storage locations to hold the local variables' values. This enables multiple threads to execute the same method simultaneously without problems, because each has its own set of local variables. Likewise, in recursive code, each nested call gets its own set of locals that will not interfere with any of its callers. The same goes for multiple concurrent invocations of an asynchronous method. To be strictly accurate, each execution of a particular *scope* gets its own set of variables. This distinction matters when you use anonymous functions, described in Chapter 9. As an optimization, C# reuses storage locations when it can, so it will only allocate new memory for each scope's execution when it really has to. (For example, it won't allocate new memory for variables declared in the body of a loop for each iteration unless you put it into a situation where it has no choice.) But the effect is as though it allocated new space each time.

Be aware that the C# compiler does not make any particular guarantee about where variables live (except for some special cases, as we'll see in Chapter 18). They might well live on the stack, but sometimes they don't. When we look at anonymous functions in later chapters, you'll see that variables sometimes need to outlive the method that declares them, because they remain in scope for nested methods that will run as callbacks after the containing method has returned.

By the way, before we move on, be aware that just as variables are not the only things to have scope, they are also not the only things to which declaration space rules apply. Other language features that we'll be looking at later, including classes, methods, and properties, also have scoping and name uniqueness rules.

Statements and Expressions

Variables give us somewhere to put the information that our code works with, but to do anything with those variables, we will need to write some code. This will mean writing *statements* and *expressions*.

Statements

When we write a C# method, we are writing a sequence of statements. Informally, the statements in a method describe the actions we want the method to perform. Each line in Example 2-16 is a statement. It might be tempting to think of a statement as an instruction to do one thing (such as initializing a variable or invoking a method). Or you might take a more lexical view, where anything ending in a semicolon is a statement. (And it's the semicolons that are significant here, not the line breaks, by the way. I could have written this as one long line of code and it would have exactly the same meaning.) However, both descriptions are simplistic, even though they happen to be true for this particular example.

Example 2-16. Some statements

```
int a = 19;
int b = 23;
int c;
c = a + b;
Console.WriteLine(c);
```

C# recognizes many different kinds of statements. In Example 2-16, the first three lines are *declaration statements*, statements that declare and optionally initialize a variable. The fourth and fifth lines are *expression statements*. But some statements have more structure than the ones in this example.

When you write a loop, that's an *iteration statement*. When you use the if or switch mechanisms described later in this chapter to choose between various possible actions, those are *selection statements.* In fact, the C# specification distinguishes between 13 categories of statements. Most fit broadly into the scheme of describing either what the code should do next or, for features such as loops or conditional statements, describing how it should decide what to do next. Statements of the second kind usually contain one or more embedded statements describing the action to perform in a loop, or the action to perform when an `if` statement's condition is met.

There's one special case, though. A block is a kind of statement. This makes statements such as loops more useful than they would otherwise be, because a loop iterates over just a single embedded statement. That statement can be a block, and since a block itself is a sequence of statements (delimited by braces), this enables loops to contain more than one statement.

This illustrates why the two simplistic points of view stated earlier—"statements are actions" and "statements are things that end in semicolons"—are wrong. Compare Example 2-16 with 2-17. Both do the same thing, because the various actions we've said we want to perform remain exactly the same, and both contain five semicolons. However, Example 2-17 contains one extra statement. The first two statements are the same, but they are followed by a third statement, a block, which contains the final three statements from Example 2-16. The extra statement, the block, doesn't end in a semicolon, nor does it perform any action. In this particular example, it's pointless, but it can sometimes be useful to introduce a nested block like this to avoid name ambiguity errors. So statements can be structural, rather than causing anything to happen at runtime.

Example 2-17. A block

```
int a = 19;
int b = 23;
{
    int c;
    c = a + b;
    Console.WriteLine(c);
}
```

While your code will use a mixture of statement types, it will inevitably end up containing at least a few expression statements. An expression statement is a statement that consists of a suitable expression, followed by a semicolon. What's a suitable expression? What's an expression, for that matter? I'd better answer that second question before coming back to what constitutes a valid expression for a statement.

Expressions

The official definition of a C# *expression* is rather dry: "a sequence of operators and operands." Admittedly, language specifications tend to be like that, but in addition to this sort of formal prose, the C# specification contains some very readable informal explanations of the more formally expressed ideas. (For example, it describes statements as the means by which "the actions of a program are expressed" before going on to pin that down with less approachable but more technically precise language.) The quote at the start of this paragraph is from the formal definition of an expression, so we might hope that the informal explanation in the introduction will be more helpful. No such luck: it says that expressions "are constructed from operands and operators." That's certainly less precise than the other definition, but it's no easier to understand. The problem is that there are several kinds of expressions, and they do different jobs, so there isn't a single, general, informal description.

It's tempting to describe an expression as some code that produces a value. That's not true for all expressions, but the majority of expressions you'll write will fit this description, so I'll focus on this for now, and I'll come to the exceptions later.

The simplest expressions are *literals*, where we just write the value we want, such as "Hello, World!" or 42. You can also use the name of a variable as an expression. Expressions can involve operators, which describe calculations or other computations to be performed. Operators have some fixed number of inputs, called *operands*. Some take a single operand. For example, you can negate a number by putting a minus sign in front of it. Some take two: the + operator lets you form an expression that adds together the results of the two operands on either side of the + symbol.

Some symbols have different roles depending on the context. The minus sign is not just used for negation. It acts as a two-operand subtraction operator if it appears between two expressions.

In general, operands are also expressions. So, when we write 2 + 2, that's an expression that contains two more expressions—the pair of "2" literals on either side of the + symbol. This means that we can write arbitrarily complicated expressions by nesting expressions within expressions within expressions. Example 2-18 exploits this to evaluate the quadratic formula (the standard way to solve quadratic equations).

Example 2-18. Expressions within expressions

```
double a = 1, b = 2.5, c = -3;
double x = (-b + Math.Sqrt(b * b - 4 * a * c)) / (2 * a);
Console.WriteLine(x);
```

Look at the declaration statement on the second line. The overall structure of its initializer expression is a division operation. But that division operator's two operands are also expressions. Its lefthand operand is a *parenthesized expression*, which tells the compiler that I want that whole expression (`-b + Math.Sqrt(b * b - 4 * a * c)`) to be the first operand of the division. This subexpression contains an addition, whose lefthand operand is a negation expression whose single operand is the variable b. The addition's righthand side takes the square root of another, more complex expression. And the division's righthand operand is another parenthesized expression, containing a multiplication. Figure 2-1 illustrates the full structure of the expression.

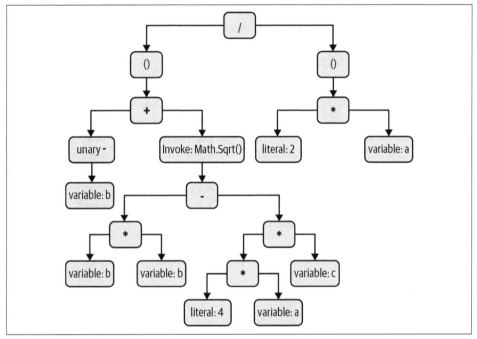

Figure 2-1. The structure of an expression

One important detail of this example is that method invocations are a kind of expression. The `Math.Sqrt` method used in Example 2-18 is a .NET runtime library function that calculates the square root of its input and returns the result. What's perhaps more surprising is that invocations of methods that don't return a value, such as `Console.WriteLine`, are also, technically, expressions. And there are a few other constructs that don't produce values but are still considered to be expressions, including a reference to a type (such as the `Console` in `Console.WriteLine`) or to a namespace. These sorts of constructs take advantage of a set of common rules (such as scoping, how to resolve what a name refers to, etc.) by virtue of being expressions. However, all the non-value-producing expressions can be used only in certain specific circumstances. (You can't use one as an operand in another expression, for example.) So although it's not technically correct to define an expression as a piece of code that produces a value, the ones that do are the ones we use when describing the calculations we want our code to perform.

We can now return to the question: what can we put in an expression statement? Roughly speaking, the expression has to have some effect; it cannot just calculate a value. So although 2 + 2 is a valid expression, you'll get an error if you try to turn it into an expression statement by sticking a semicolon on the end. That expression calculates something but doesn't do anything with the result. To be more precise, you can use the following kinds of expressions as statements: method invocation, assignment, increment, decrement, and new object creation. We'll be looking at increment and decrement later in this chapter, and we'll be looking at objects in later chapters, so that leaves invocation and assignment.

When we write a method invocation as an expression statement, there may be nested expressions of other kinds (such as the method's arguments), but the whole thing must be a method call. Example 2-19 shows some valid examples. Notice that the C# compiler doesn't check whether the method call really has any lasting effect—the Math.Sqrt function is a pure function, in the sense that it does nothing other than returning a value determined entirely by its inputs. So invoking it and then doing nothing with the result doesn't really do anything at all—it's no more of an action than the expression 2 + 2. But as far as the C# compiler is concerned, any method call is allowed as an expression statement.

Example 2-19. Method invocation expressions as statements

```
Console.WriteLine("Hello, World!");
Console.WriteLine(12 + 30);
Console.ReadKey();
Math.Sqrt(4);
```

 If you run this example in VS Code, the call to ReadKey might fail because of how the debugger redirects input and output by default. The documentation explains (*https://oreil.ly/JefbY*) how to avoid this problem when debugging programs that need to read console input.

It seems inconsistent that C# forbids us from using an addition expression as a statement while allowing Math.Sqrt. Both perform a calculation that produces a result, so it makes no sense to use either in this way. Wouldn't it be more consistent if C# allowed only calls to methods that return nothing to be used for expression statements? That would rule out the final line of Example 2-19, which would seem like a good idea because that code does nothing useful. It would also be consistent with the fact that 2 + 2 also cannot form an expression statement. Unfortunately, sometimes you want to ignore the return value. Example 2-19 calls Console.ReadKey(), which waits for a keypress and returns a value indicating which key was pressed. If my program's behavior depends on which particular key the user pressed, I'll need to inspect the method's return value, but if I just want to wait for any key at all, it's OK to ignore the return value. If C# didn't allow methods with return values to be used as expression statements, I wouldn't be able to do this. The compiler has no way to distinguish between methods that make for pointless statements because they have no side effects (such as `Math.Sqrt`) and those that might be good candidates (such as `Console.ReadKey`), so it allows any method.

For an expression to be a valid expression statement, it is not enough merely to contain a method invocation. Example 2-20 shows some expressions that call methods and then go on to use those as part of addition expressions. Although these are valid expressions, they're not valid expression statements, so these will cause compiler errors. What matters is the outermost expression. In both lines here, that's an addition expression, which is why these are not allowed.

Example 2-20. Errors: some expressions that don't work as statements

```
Console.ReadKey().KeyChar + "!";
Math.Sqrt(4) + 1;
```

Earlier I said that one kind of expression we're allowed to use as a statement is an assignment. It's not obvious that assignments should be expressions, but they are, and they do produce a value: the result of an assignment expression is the value being assigned to the variable. This means it's legal to write code like that in Example 2-21. The second line here uses an assignment expression as an argument for a method invocation, which shows the value of that expression. The first two `WriteLine` calls both display 123.

Example 2-21. Assignments are expressions

```
int number;
Console.WriteLine(number = 123);
Console.WriteLine(number);

int x, y;
x = y = 0;
Console.WriteLine(x);
Console.WriteLine(y);
```

The second part of this example assigns one value into two variables in a single step by exploiting the fact that assignments are expressions—it assigns the value of the `y = 0` expression (which evaluates to 0) into `x`.

This shows that evaluating an expression can do more than just produce a value. Some expressions have side effects. We've just seen that an assignment is an expression, and of course it has the effect of changing what's in a variable. Method calls are expressions too, and although you can write pure functions that do nothing besides calculating their result from their input, like `Math.Sqrt`, many methods do something with lasting effects, such as writing data to the screen, updating a database, or triggering the demolition of a building. This means that we might care about the order in which the operands of an expression get evaluated.

An expression's structure imposes some constraints on the order in which operators do their work. For example, I can use parentheses to enforce ordering. The expression `10 + (8 / 2)` has the value 14, while the expression `(10 + 8) / 2` has the value 9, even though both have exactly the same literal operands and arithmetic operators. The parentheses here determine whether the division is performed before or after the addition.[3]

However, while the structure of an expression imposes some ordering constraints, it still leaves some latitude: although both the operands of an addition need to be evaluated before they can be added, the addition operator doesn't care which operand we evaluate first. But if the operands are expressions with side effects, the order could be important. For these simple expressions, it doesn't matter because I've used literals, so we can't really tell when they get evaluated. But what about an expression in which operands call some method? Example 2-22 contains code of this kind.

Example 2-22. Operand evaluation order

```
static int X(string label, int i)
{
    Console.Write(label);
    return i;
}

Console.WriteLine(X("a", 1) + X("b", 1) + X("c", 1) + X("d", 1));
```

This defines a method, X, which takes two arguments. It displays the first and just returns the second. I've then used this a few times in an expression so that we can see exactly when the operands that call X are evaluated. Some languages choose not to define this order, making the behavior of such a program unpredictable, but C# does specify an order here. The rule is that within any expression, the operands are evaluated in the order in which they occur in the source. So, when the `Console.WriteLine`

---

3 In the absence of parentheses, C# has rules of *precedence* that determine the order in which operators are evaluated. For the full (and not very interesting) details, consult the documentation. In this example, because division has higher precedence than addition, without parentheses the expression would evaluate to 14.

in Example 2-22 runs, it makes multiple calls to X, which calls Console.Write each time, so we see this output: abcd4.

However, this glosses over an important subtlety: What do we mean by the order of expressions when nesting occurs? The entire argument to that Console.WriteLine is one big add expression, where the first operand is X("a", 1), and the second is another add expression, which in turn has a first operand of X("b", 1) and a second operand, which is yet another add expression, whose operands are X("c", 1) and X("d", 1). Taking the first of those add expressions, which constitutes the entire argument to Console.WriteLine, does it even make sense to ask whether it comes before or after its first operand? Lexically, the outermost add expression starts at exactly the same point that its first operand starts and ends at the point where its second operand ends (which also happens to be at the exact same point that the final X("d", 1) ends). In this particular case, it doesn't really matter because the only observable effect of the order of evaluation is the output the X method produces when invoked. None of the expressions that invoke X are nested within one another, so we can meaningfully say what order those expressions are in, and the output we see matches that order. However, in some cases, such as Example 2-23, the overlapping of nested expressions can have a visible impact.

Example 2-23. Operand evaluation order with nested expressions

```
Console.WriteLine(
    X("a", 1) +
    X("b", (X("c", 1) + X("d", 1) + X("e", 1))) +
    X("f", 1));
```

Here, Console.WriteLine's argument adds the results of three calls to X; however, the second of those calls to X (first argument "b") takes as its second argument an expression that adds the results of three more calls to X (with arguments of "c", "d", and "e"). With the final call to X (passing "f"), we have a total of six expressions invoking X in that statement. C#'s rule of evaluating expressions in the order in which they appear applies as always, but because there is overlap, the results are initially surprising. Although the letters appear in the source in alphabetical order, the output is "acdebf5". If you're wondering how on earth that can be consistent with expressions being evaluated in order, consider that this code starts the evaluation of each expression in the order in which the expressions start, and finishes the evaluation in the order in which the expressions finish, but that those are two different orderings. In particular, the expression that invokes X with "b" begins its evaluation before those that invoke it with "c", "d", and "e", but it finishes its evaluation *after* them. And it's that *after* ordering that we see in the output. If you find each closing parenthesis that corresponds to a call to X in this example, you'll find that the order of calls exactly matches what's displayed.

Comments and Whitespace

Most programming languages allow source files to contain text that is ignored by the compiler, and C# is no exception. As with most C-family languages, it supports two styles of *comments* for this purpose. There are *single-line comments*, as shown in Example 2-24, in which you write two / characters in a row, and everything from there to the end of the line will be ignored by the compiler.

Example 2-24. Single-line comments

```
Console.WriteLine("Say");        // This text will be ignored, but the code on
Console.WriteLine("Anything");   // the left is still compiled as usual.
```

C# also supports *delimited comments*. You start a comment of this kind with /*, and the compiler will ignore everything that follows until it encounters the first */ character sequence. This can be useful if you don't want the comment to go all the way to the end of the line, as the first line of Example 2-25 illustrates. This example also shows that delimited comments can span multiple lines.

Example 2-25. Delimited comments

```
Console.WriteLine(/* Has side effects */ GetLog());

/* Some developers like to use delimited comments for big blocks of text,
 * where they need to explain something particularly complex or odd in the
 * code. The column of asterisks on the left is for decoration - asterisks
 * are necessary only at the start and end of the comment.
 */
```

There's a minor snag you can run into with delimited comments; it can happen even when the comment is within a single line, but it more often occurs with multiline comments. Example 2-26 shows the problem with a comment that begins in the middle of the first line and ends at the end of the fourth.

Example 2-26. Multiline comments

```
Console.WriteLine("This will run");    /* This comment includes not just the
Console.WriteLine("This won't");        * text on the right but also the text
Console.WriteLine("Nor will this");    /* on the left except the first and last
Console.WriteLine("Nor this");          * lines. */
Console.WriteLine("This will also run");
```

Notice that the /* character sequence appears twice in this example. When this sequence appears in the middle of a comment, it does nothing special—comments don't nest. Even though we've seen two /* sequences, the first */ is enough to end the comment. This is occasionally frustrating, but it's the norm for C-family languages.

It's sometimes useful to take a chunk of code out of action temporarily, in a way that's easy to put back. Turning the code into a comment is a common way to do this, and although a delimited comment might seem like the obvious thing to use, it becomes awkward if the region you commented out happens to include another delimited comment. Since there's no support for nesting, you would need to add a /* after the inner comment's closing */ to ensure that you've commented out the whole range. So it is common to use single-line comments for this purpose. (You can also use the #if directive described in the next section.)

 Visual Studio and VS Code can comment out regions of code for you. If you select several lines of text and type Ctrl-K followed immediately by Ctrl-C, it will add // to the start of every line in the selection. And you can uncomment a region with Ctrl-K, Ctrl-U. (With Visual Studio, if you chose something other than C# as your preferred language when you installed it, these actions may be bound to different key sequences, but they are also available on the Edit→Advanced menu, as well as on the Text Editor toolbar, one of the standard toolbars that Visual Studio shows by default.)

Speaking of ignored text, C# ignores extra whitespace for the most part. Not all whitespace is insignificant, because you need at least some space to separate tokens that consist entirely of alphanumeric symbols. For example, you can't write staticvoid as the start of a method declaration—you'd need at least one space (or tab, newline, or other space-like character) between static and void. But with non-alphanumeric tokens, spaces are optional, and in most cases, a single space is equivalent to any amount of whitespace and new lines. This means that the three statements in Example 2-27 are all equivalent.

Example 2-27. Insignificant whitespace

```
Console.WriteLine("Testing");
Console . WriteLine(   "Testing");
Console.
    WriteLine ("Testing" )
  ;
```

There are a couple of cases where C# is more sensitive to whitespace. Inside a string literal, space is significant, because whatever spaces you write will be present in the string value. Also, while C# mostly doesn't care whether you put each element on its own line, or put all your code in one massive line, or (as seems more likely) something in between, there is an exception: preprocessing directives are required to appear on their own lines.

Preprocessing Directives

If you're familiar with the C language or its direct descendants, you may have been wondering if C# has a preprocessor. It doesn't have a separate preprocessing stage, and it does not offer macros. However, it does have a handful of directives similar to those offered by the C preprocessor, although it is only a very limited selection. Even though C# doesn't have a full preprocessing stage like C, these are known as preprocessing directives nonetheless.

Compilation Symbols

C# offers a `#define` directive that lets you define a *compilation symbol*. These symbols are commonly used in conjunction with the `#if` directive to compile code in different ways for different situations. For example, you might want some code to be present only in Debug builds, or perhaps you need to use different code on different platforms to achieve a particular effect. Often, you won't use the `#define` directive, though—it's more common to define compilation symbols through the compiler build settings. You can open up the *.csproj* file and define the values you want in a `<DefineConstants>` element of any `<PropertyGroup>`. Alternatively, Visual Studio can do this for you: right-click the project's node in Solution Explorer, select Properties, and in the property page that this opens, go to the Build section. This UI lets you configure different symbol values for each build configuration (which it does by adding attributes such as `Condition="'$(Configuration)|$(Platform)'=='Debug|AnyCPU'"` to the `<PropertyGroup>` containing these settings).

 The .NET SDK defines certain symbols by default. It supports two configurations, Debug and Release. It defines a `DEBUG` compilation symbol in the Debug configuration, whereas Release will define `RELEASE` instead. It defines a symbol called `TRACE` in both configurations. Certain project types get additional symbols. A library targeting .NET Standard will have `NETSTANDARD` defined, along with a version-specific symbol such as `NETSTANDARD2_0`, for example. Projects that target .NET 8.0 get a `NET8_0` symbol.

Compilation symbols are typically used in conjunction with the `#if`, `#else`, `#elif`, and `#endif` directives (`#elif` is short for *else if*). Example 2-28 uses some of these directives to ensure that certain lines of code get compiled only in Debug builds. (You can also write `#if false` to prevent sections of code from being compiled at all. This is typically done only as a temporary measure and is an alternative to commenting out that sidesteps some of the lexical pitfalls of attempting to nest comments.)

Example 2-28. Conditional compilation

```
#if DEBUG
    Console.WriteLine("Starting work");
#endif
    DoWork();
#if DEBUG
    Console.WriteLine("Finished work");
#endif
```

C# provides a more subtle mechanism to support this sort of thing, called a *conditional method*. The compiler recognizes an attribute defined by the runtime libraries, called ConditionalAttribute, for which it provides special compile-time behavior. You can annotate any method with this attribute. Example 2-29 uses it to indicate that the annotated method should be used only when the DEBUG compilation symbol is defined.

Example 2-29. Conditional method

```
[System.Diagnostics.Conditional("DEBUG")]
static void ShowDebugInfo(object o)
{
    Console.WriteLine(o);
}
```

If you write code that calls a method that has been annotated in this way, the C# compiler will omit that call in builds that do not define the relevant symbol. So if you write code that calls this ShowDebugInfo method, the compiler strips out all those calls in non-Debug builds. This means you can get the same effect as Example 2-28 but without cluttering up your code with directives.

The runtime libraries' Debug and Trace classes in the System.Diagnostics namespace use this feature. The Debug class offers various methods for generating diagnostic output that are conditional on the DEBUG. compilation symbol, while the Trace class has methods conditional on TRACE. If you leave the default settings for a new C# project in place, any diagnostic output produced through the Trace class will be available in both Debug and Release builds, but any code that calls a method on the Debug class will not get compiled into Release builds.

The Debug class's `Assert` method is conditional on `DEBUG`, which sometimes catches developers out. `Assert` lets you specify a condition that must be true at runtime, and it throws an exception if the condition is false. There are two things developers new to C# sometimes mistakenly put in a `Debug.Assert`: checks that should in fact occur in all builds, and expressions with side effects that the rest of the code depends on. This leads to bugs, because the compiler will strip this code out in non-Debug builds.

#error and #warning

C# lets you choose to generate compiler errors or warnings with the `#error` and `#warning` directives. These are typically used inside conditional regions, as Example 2-30 shows, although an unconditional `#warning` could be useful as a way to remind yourself that you've not written some particularly important bit of the code yet.

Example 2-30. Generating a compiler error

```
#if NETSTANDARD
  #error .NET Standard is not a supported target for this source file
#endif
```

#line

The `#line` directive is useful in generated code. When the compiler produces an error or a warning, it states where the problem occurred, providing the filename, a line number, and an offset within that line. But if the code in question was generated automatically using some other file as input and if that other file contains the root cause of the problem, it may be more useful to report an error in the input file, rather than the generated file. A `#line` directive can instruct the C# compiler to act as though the error occurred at the line number specified and, optionally, as if the error were in an entirely different file. Example 2-31 shows how to use it. The error after the directive will be reported as though it came from line 123 of a file called *Foo.cs*. You can tell the compiler to revert to reporting warnings and errors without fakery by writing `#line default`.

Example 2-31. The #line directive and a deliberate mistake

```
#line 123 "Foo.cs"
    intt x;
```

This directive also affects debugging. When the compiler emits debug information, it takes #line directives into account. This means that when stepping through code in the debugger, you'll see the location that #line refers to.

There's another use for this directive. Instead of a line number (and optional filename), you can write just #line hidden. This affects only the debugger behavior: when single stepping, Visual Studio will run straight through all the code after such a directive without stopping until it encounters a non-hidden #line directive (typically #line default).

#pragma

The #pragma directive provides two features: it can be used to disable selected compiler warnings, and it can also be used to override the checksum values the compiler puts into the *.pdb* file it generates containing debug information. Both of these are designed primarily for code-generation scenarios, although it can occasionally be useful to disable warnings in ordinary code. Example 2-32 shows how to use a #pragma to prevent the compiler from issuing the warning that would normally occur if you declare a variable that you do not then go on to use.

Example 2-32. Disabling a compiler warning

```
#pragma warning disable CS0168
    int a;
```

You should generally avoid disabling warnings. This feature is useful in generated code because code generation can often end up creating items that are not always used, and pragmas may offer the only way to get a clean compilation. But when you're writing code by hand, it should usually be possible to avoid normal compiler warnings in the first place.

Having said that, it can be useful to disable specific warnings if you have opted in to additional diagnostics. Some components on NuGet supply *code analyzers*, components that get connected up to the C# compiler API and that are given the opportunity to inspect the code and generate their own diagnostic messages. (This happens at build time, and in Visual Studio, it also happens during editing, providing live diagnostics as you type. They also work live in Visual Studio Code if you install the C# Dev Kit extension.) The .NET SDK also includes built-in analyzers that can check various aspects of your code such as adherence to naming conventions or the presence of common security mistakes. You can configure these at a project level with the AnalysisMode setting, but as with compiler warnings, you might want to disable analyzer warnings in specific cases. You can use #pragma warning directives to control warnings from code analyzers, not just ones from the C# compiler. Analyzers generally prefix their warning numbers with some letters to enable you to distinguish between them—compiler warnings all start with CS, and warnings from the .NET SDK's analyzers start with CA, for example.

It's possible that future versions of C# may add other features based on #pragma. When the compiler encounters a pragma it does not understand, it generates a warning, not an error, on the grounds that an unrecognized pragma might be valid for some future compiler version or some other vendor's compiler.

#nullable

The #nullable directive allows fine-grained control of the nullable annotation context and the nullable warning context. This is part of the *nullable references* feature. Chapter 3 describes the #nullable directive in more detail.

#region and #endregion

Finally, we have two preprocessing directives that do nothing. If you write #region directives, the only thing the compiler does is ensure that they have corresponding #endregion directives. Mismatches cause compiler errors, but the compiler ignores correctly paired #region and #endregion directives. Regions can be nested.

These directives exist entirely for the benefit of text editors that choose to recognize them. Visual Studio, VS Code, and Rider use them to provide the ability to collapse sections of the code down to a single line on screen. These editors automatically allow certain features to be expanded and collapsed, such as class definitions, methods, and code blocks (a feature they call *outlining*). If you define regions with these two directives, these can also be expanded and collapsed. This allows for outlining at both finer-grained (for example, within a single block) and coarser-grained (for example, multiple related methods) scales than the editor offers automatically.

If you hover the mouse over a collapsed region in Visual Studio, it displays a tool tip showing the region's contents. You can put text after the #region token. When IDEs display a collapsed region, they show this text on the single line that remains. Although you're allowed to omit this, it's usually a good idea to include some descriptive text so that people can have a rough idea of what they'll see if they expand it.

Some people like to put the entire contents of a class into various regions, because by collapsing all regions, you can see a file's structure at a glance. It might even all fit on the screen at once, thanks to the regions being reduced to a single line. On the other hand, some people hate collapsed regions, because they present speed bumps on the way to being able to look at the code and can also encourage people to put too much source code into one file.

Fundamental Data Types

.NET defines thousands of types in its runtime libraries, and you can write your own, so C# can work with an unlimited number of data types. However, a handful of types get special handling from the compiler. You saw earlier in Example 2-9 that if you have a string, and you try to add a number to it, the resulting code converts the number to a string and appends that to the first string. In fact, the behavior is more general than that—it's not limited to numbers. The compiled code works by calling the `String.Concat` method, and if you pass to that any nonstring arguments, it will call their `ToString` methods before performing the append. All types offer a `ToString` method, so this means you can append values of any type to a string.

That's handy, but it only works because the C# compiler knows about strings and provides special services for them. (There's a part of the C# specification that defines the unique string handling for the + operator.) C# provides various special services not just for strings but also for certain numeric data types, Booleans, a family of types called tuples, and two specific types called `dynamic` and `object`. Most of these are special not just to C# but also to the runtime—almost all of the numeric types get direct support in intermediate language (IL), and the `bool`, `string`, and `object` types are also intrinsically understood by the runtime.

Numeric Types

C# supports integer and floating-point arithmetic. The CLR provides intrinsic support for signed and unsigned integer types of various sizes, as Table 2-1 shows. The most commonly used integer type is `int`, not least because it is large enough to represent a usefully wide range of values without being too large to work efficiently on all CPUs that support .NET. (Larger data types might not be handled natively by the CPU and can also have undesirable characteristics in multithreaded code: reads and writes are atomic for 32-bit types[4] but may not be for larger ones.)

Table 2-1. Intrinsic integer types

C# type	CLR name	Signed	Size in bits	Inclusive range
byte	System.Byte	No	8	0 to 255
sbyte	System.SByte	Yes	8	−128 to 127
ushort	System.UInt16	No	16	0 to 65,535
short	System.Int16	Yes	16	−32,768 to 32,767
uint	System.UInt32	No	32	0 to 4,294,967,295

---

4 This is guaranteed only for correctly aligned 32-bit types. However, C# aligns them correctly by default, and you'd normally encounter misaligned data only if your code needs to call out into unmanaged code.

C# type	CLR name	Signed	Size in bits	Inclusive range
int	System.Int32	Yes	32	−2,147,483,648 to 2,147,483,647
ulong	System.UInt64	No	64	0 to 18,446,744,073,709,551,615
long	System.Int64	Yes	64	−9,223,372,036,854,775,808 to 9,223,372,036,854,775,807
nuint	System.UIntPtr	No	Depends	Depends
nint	System.IntPtr	Yes	Depends	Depends

The second column in Table 2-1 shows the name of the type in the CLR. Different languages have different naming conventions, and C# uses names from its C-family roots for numeric types, but those don't fit with the naming conventions that .NET has for its data types. As far as the runtime is concerned, the names in the second column are the real names—there are various APIs that can report information about types at runtime, and they report these CLR names, not the C# ones. The names are synonymous in C# source code, so you're free to use the runtime names if you want to, but the C# names are a better stylistic fit—keywords in C-family languages are all lowercase. Since the compiler handles these types differently than the rest, it's arguably good to have them stand out.

The nint and nuint types are unusual in that their size is not always the same. These are the *native-sized integer* types (hence the n prefix), and they are intended for low-level code that needs to deal directly with the address of data in memory. This is why they don't have a fixed size—they are 32 bits wide in a 32-bit process and 64 bits in a 64-bit process. (These are very specialized types, normally only used when writing wrappers for non-.NET libraries, and I've included them in this table only for completeness.) These types are aliases for System.IntPtr and System.UIntPtr, although this was not true before C# 11.0. The .NET runtime didn't used to support arithmetic with IntPtr and UIntPtr, and the nint and nuint types were originally introduced as a workaround for this. If you declared variables in C# as nint or nuint, their runtime types would be IntPtr or UIntPtr, but you could perform pointer arithmetic on them and the C# compiler would generate the necessary code to make that work. However, .NET 7.0 added arithmetic support for IntPtr and UIntPtr as part of the *generic math* feature (see Chapter 4) meaning C# no longer needed to offer nint and uint as extended versions of these types to enable arithmetic, so these are now merely aliases like everything else in the table.

Not all .NET languages support unsigned numbers, so the .NET runtime libraries tend to avoid them. A runtime that supports multiple languages (such as the CLR) faces a trade-off between offering a type system rich enough to cover most languages' needs and forcing an overcomplicated type system on simple languages. To resolve this, .NET's type system, the CTS, is reasonably comprehensive, but languages don't have to support all of it. .NET also defines the Common Language Specification (CLS), which identifies a relatively small subset of the CTS that all languages should support. Signed integers are in the CLS, but unsigned ones are not. This explains some surprising-looking type choices, such as the Length property of an array being int (rather than uint) despite the fact that it will never return a negative value.

C# also supports floating-point numbers. It has intrinsic support for two types: float and double, which are 32-bit and 64-bit numbers in the standard IEEE 754 formats (*https://oreil.ly/ZMz9o*), and as the CLR names in Table 2-2 suggest, these correspond to what are commonly called *single-precision* and *double-precision numbers*. Floating-point values do not work in the same way as integers, so this table is a little different than the integer types table. Floating-point numbers store a value and an exponent (similar in concept to scientific notation but working in binary instead of decimal). The Precision column shows how many bits are available for the value part, and then the range is expressed as the smallest nonzero value and the largest value that can be represented. (These can be either positive or negative.)

Table 2-2. Intrinsic floating-point types

C# type	CLR name	Size in bits	Precision	Range (magnitude)
float	System.Single	32	23 bits (~7 decimal digits)	1.5×10^{-45} to 3.4×10^{38}
double	System.Double	64	52 bits (~15 decimal digits)	5.0×10^{-324} to 1.8×10^{308}

C# recognizes another noninteger numeric representation called decimal (or System.Decimal in the CLR). This is a 128-bit value, so it can offer greater precision than the other formats, but it is not just a bigger version of double. It is designed for calculations that require predictable handling of decimal fractions, something neither float nor double can offer. If you write code that initializes a variable of type float to 0 and then adds 0.1 to it nine times in a row, you might expect to get a value of 0.9, but in fact you'll get approximately 0.9000001. That's because IEEE 754 stores numbers in binary, which cannot represent all decimal fractions. It can handle some, such as the decimal 0.5; written in base 2, that's 0.1. But the decimal 0.1 turns into a recurring number in binary. (Specifically, it's 0.0 followed by the recurring sequence 0011.) This means float and double can represent only an approximation of the decimal value 0.1, and more generally, only a small subset of decimals can be represented completely accurately. This isn't always instantly obvious, because when floating-point numbers are converted to text, they are rounded to a decimal approximation that can mask the discrepancy. But over multiple calculations, the inaccuracies tend to add up and eventually produce surprising-looking results.

For some kinds of calculations, the lack of exact decimal fidelity doesn't really matter; in simulations or signal processing, for example, some noise and error is expected. But accountants and financial regulators tend to be less forgiving—little discrepancies like this can make it look like money has magically vanished or appeared. We need calculations that involve money to be absolutely accurate, which makes binary floating point a terrible choice for such work. This is why C# offers the `decimal` type, which provides a well-defined level of decimal precision.

 Most of the integer types can be handled natively by the CPU. (All of them can when running in a 64-bit process.) Likewise, many CPUs can work directly with `float` and `double` representations. However, none has intrinsic support for `decimal`, meaning that even simple operations, such as addition, require multiple CPU instructions. This means that arithmetic is significantly slower with `decimal` than with the other numeric types shown so far.

A `decimal` stores numbers as a sign bit (positive or negative) and a pair of integers. There's a 96-bit integer, and the value of the `decimal` is this first integer (negated if the sign bit says so) divided by 10 raised to the power of the second integer, which is a number in the range of 0 to 28.[5] Ninety-six bits is enough to represent any 28-digit decimal integer (and some, but not all, 29-digit ones), so the second integer—the one representing the power of 10 by which the first is divided—effectively says where the decimal point goes. This format makes it possible to represent any decimal with 28 or fewer digits accurately.

When you write a literal numeric value, you can choose the type, or you can let the compiler pick a suitable type for you. If you write a plain integer, such as 123, its type will be `int`, `uint`, `long`, or `ulong`—the compiler picks the first type from that list with a range that contains the value. (So 123 would be an `int`, 3000000000 would be a `uint`, 5000000000 would be a `long`, etc.) If you write a number with a decimal point, such as 1.23, its type is `double`.

If you're dealing with large numbers, it's very easy to get the number of zeros wrong. This is usually bad and possibly very expensive or dangerous, depending on your

---

5 A decimal, therefore, doesn't use all of its 128 bits. Making it smaller would cause alignment difficulties, and using the additional bits for extra precision would have a significant performance impact, because on most CPUs, integers whose length is a multiple of 32 bits are easier to deal with than the alternatives.

application area. C# provides some mitigation by allowing you to add underscores anywhere in numeric literals, to break the numbers up however you please. This is analogous to the common practice in most English-speaking countries of using a comma to separate zeros into groups of three. For example, instead of writing 5000000000, most native English speakers would write 5,000,000,000, instantly making it much easier to see that this is 5 billion and not, say, 50 billion, or 500 million. (What many native English speakers don't know is that several countries around the world use a period for this and would write 5.000.000.000 instead, using the comma where most native English speakers would put a decimal point. Interpreting a value such as €100.000 requires you to know which country's conventions are in use if you don't want to make a disastrous financial miscalculation. But I digress.) In C# we can do something similar by writing the numeric literal as 5_000_000_000.

You can tell the compiler that you want a specific type by adding a suffix. So 123U is a uint, 123L is a long, and 123UL is a ulong. Suffix letters are case- and order-independent, so instead of 123UL, you could write 123Lu, 123uL, or any other permutation. For double, float, and decimal, use the D, F, and M suffixes, respectively.

These last three types all support a decimal exponential literal format for large or small numbers, where you put a decimal, then the letter E followed by an integer. The value is the first number multiplied by 10 raised to the power of the second. For example, the literal value 1.5E-20 is the value 1.5 multiplied by 10^{-20}. (This happens to be of type double, because that's the default for a number with a decimal point, regardless of whether it's in exponential format. You could write 1.5E-20F and 1.5E-20M for float and decimal constants with equivalent values.)

It's often useful to be able to write integer literals in hexadecimal, because the digits map better onto the binary representation used at runtime. This is particularly important when different bit ranges of a number represent different things. For example, you may need to deal with a numeric error code that originated from a Windows system call—these occasionally crop up in exceptions. In some cases, these codes use the topmost bit to indicate success or failure, the next few bits to indicate the origin of the error, and the remaining bits to identify the specific error. For example, the COM error code E_ACCESSDENIED has the value −2,147,024,891. It's hard to see the structure in decimal, but in hexadecimal, it's easier: 80070005. The 8 indicates that this is an error, and the 007 that follows indicates that this was originally a plain Win32 error that has been translated into a COM error. The remaining bits indicate that the Win32 error code was 5 (ERROR_ACCESS_DENIED). C# lets you write integer literals in hexadecimal for scenarios like these, where the hex representation is more readable. You just prefix the number with 0x; therefore, in this case, you would write 0x80070005.

You can also write binary literals by using the 0b prefix. Digit separators can be used in hex and binary just as they can in decimals, although it's more common to group binary digits by fours, like so: 0b_0010_1010. Obviously this makes any binary structure in a number even more evident than hexadecimal does, but 32-bit binary literals are inconveniently long, which is why we often use hexadecimal instead.

Numeric conversions

Each of the built-in numeric types uses a different representation for storing numbers in memory. Converting from one form to another requires some work—even the number 1 looks quite different if you inspect its binary representations as a float, an int, and a decimal. However, C# is able to generate code that converts between formats, and it will often do so automatically. Example 2-33 shows some cases in which this will happen.

Example 2-33. Implicit conversions

```
int i = 42;
double di = i;
Console.WriteLine(i / 5);
Console.WriteLine(di / 5);
Console.WriteLine(i / 5.0);
```

The second line assigns the value of an int variable into a double variable. The C# compiler generates the necessary code to convert the integer value into its equivalent floating-point value. More subtly, the last two lines will perform similar conversions, as we can see from the output of that code:

```
8
8.4
8.4
```

This shows that the first division produced an integer result—dividing the integer variable i by the integer literal 5 caused the compiler to generate code that performs integer division, so the result is 8. But the other two divisions produced a floating-point result. In the second case, we've divided the double variable di by an integer literal 5. C# converts that 5 to floating point before performing the division. (As an optimization, in this particular case the compiler happens to perform that conversion at compile time, so it emits the same code for that expression as it would if we had written di / 5.0.) And in the final line, we're dividing an integer variable by a floating-point literal. This time, it's the variable's value that gets turned from an integer into a floating-point value before the division takes place. (Since i is a variable, not a constant, the compiler emits code that performs that conversion at runtime.)

In general, when you perform arithmetic calculations that involve a mixture of numeric types, C# will pick the type with the largest range and *promote* values of types with a narrower range into that larger one before performing the calculations. (Arithmetic operators generally require all their operands to have the same type, so if you supply operands with different types, one type has to "win" for any particular operator.) For example, double can represent any value that int can, and many that it cannot, so double is the more expressive type.[6]

C# will perform numeric conversions implicitly whenever the conversion is a promotion (i.e., the target type has a wider range than the source), because there is no possibility of the conversion failing. However, it will not implicitly convert in the other direction. The second and third lines of Example 2-34 will fail to compile because they attempt to assign expressions of type double into an int, which is a *narrowing* conversion, meaning that the source might contain values that are out of the target's range.

Example 2-34. Errors: implicit conversions not available

```
int i = 42;
int willFail = 42.0;
int willAlsoFail = i / 1.0;
```

It is possible to convert in this direction, just not implicitly. You can use a *cast*, where you specify the name of the type to which you'd like to convert in parentheses. Example 2-35 shows a modified version of Example 2-34, where we state explicitly that we want a conversion to int, and we either don't mind that this conversion might not work correctly or we have reason to believe that, in this specific case, the value will be in range. Note that on the final line I've put parentheses around the expression after the cast. That makes the cast apply to the whole expression; otherwise, C#'s rules of precedence mean it would apply just to the i variable, and since that's already an int, it would have no effect.

Example 2-35. Explicit conversions with casts

```
int i = 42;
int i2 = (int) 42.0;
int i3 = (int) (i / 1.0);
```

So narrowing conversions require explicit casts, and conversions that cannot lose information occur implicitly. However, with some combinations of types, neither is strictly more expressive than the other. What should happen if you try to add an int to a uint? Or an int to a float? These types are all 32 bits in size, so none of them can possibly offer more than 2^{32} distinct values, but they have different ranges, which

---

6 Promotions are not in fact a feature of C#. There is a more general mechanism: conversion operators. C# defines intrinsic implicit conversion operators for the built-in data types. The promotions discussed here occur as a result of the compiler following its usual rules for conversions.

means that each has values it can represent that the other types cannot. For example, you can represent the value 3,000,000,001 in a uint, but it's too large for an int and can only be approximated in a float. As floating-point numbers get larger, the values that can be represented get farther apart—a float can represent 3,000,000,000 and also 3,000,001,024 but nothing in between. So for the value 3,000,000,001, uint seems better than float. But what about –1? That's a negative number, so uint can't cope with that. Then there are very large numbers that float can represent that are out of range for both int and uint. Each of these types has its strengths and weaknesses, and it makes no sense to say that one of them is generally better than the rest.

Surprisingly, C# allows some implicit conversions even in these potentially lossy scenarios. The rules consider only range, not precision: implicit conversions are allowed if the target type's range completely contains the source type's range. So you can convert from either int or uint to float, because although float is unable to represent some values exactly, there are no int or uint values that it cannot at least approximate. But implicit conversions are not allowed in the other direction, because there are some float values that are simply too big—unlike float, the integer types can't offer approximations for bigger numbers.

You might be wondering what happens if you force a narrowing conversion to int with a cast, as Example 2-35 does, but in situations where the number is out of range. The answer depends on the type from which you are casting. Conversion from one integer type to another works differently than conversion from floating point to integer. In fact, the C# specification does not define how floating-point numbers that are too big should be converted to an integer type—the result could be anything. But when casting between integer types, the outcome is well defined. If the two types are of different sizes, the binary will be either truncated or padded with zeros (or ones, if the source type is signed and the value is negative) to make it the right size for the target type, and then the bits are just treated as if they are of the target type. This is occasionally useful but can more often produce surprising results, so you can choose an alternative behavior for any out-of-range cast by making it a *checked* conversion.

Checked contexts

C# defines the checked keyword, which you can put in front of either a block statement or an expression, making it a *checked context*. This means that certain arithmetic operations, including casts, are checked for range overflow at runtime. If you cast a value to an integer type in a checked context and the value is too high or low to fit, an error will occur—the code will throw a System.OverflowException. (As you'll see in Chapter 4, C# 11.0's *generic math* feature provides some other ways to deal with out-of-range casts, but checked contexts continue to be an important concept when using generic math.)

As well as checking casts, a checked context will detect range overflows in ordinary arithmetic. Addition, subtraction, and other operations can take a value beyond the range of its data type. For integers, this causes the value to "roll over" when unchecked, so adding 1 to the maximum value produces the minimum value, and vice versa for subtraction. Occasionally, this wrapping can be useful. For example, if you want to determine how much time has elapsed between two points in the code, one way to do this is to use the Environment.TickCount property.[7] (This is more reliable than using the current date and time, because that can change as a result of the clock being adjusted or when moving between time zones. The tick count just keeps increasing at a steady rate. That said, in real code you'd probably use the runtime libraries' Stopwatch class.) Example 2-36 shows one way to do this.

Example 2-36. Exploiting unchecked integer overflow

```
int start = Environment.TickCount;
DoSomeWork();
int end = Environment.TickCount;

int totalTicks = end - start;
Console.WriteLine(totalTicks);
```

The tricky thing about Environment.TickCount is that it occasionally "wraps around." It counts the number of milliseconds since the system last rebooted, and since its type is int, it will eventually run out of range. A span of 25 days is 2.16 billion milliseconds—too large a number to fit in an int. (You could avoid this by using the TickCount64 property, which is good for almost 300 million years. But this is unavailable in .NET Framework.) Imagine the tick count is 2,147,483,637, which is 10 short of the maximum value for int. What would you expect it to be 100 ms later? It can't be 100 higher (2,147,483,727), because that's too big a value for an int. We'd expect it to get to the highest possible value after 10 ms, so after 11 ms, it'll roll round to the minimum value; thus, after 100 ms, we'd expect the tick count to be 89 above the minimum value (which would be −2,147,483,559).

 The tick count is not necessarily precise to the nearest millisecond in practice. It often stands still for milliseconds at a time before leaping forward in increments of 10 ms, 15 ms, or even more. However, the value still rolls over—you just might not be able to observe every possible tick value as it does so.

---

[7] A *property* is a member of a type that represents a value that can be read or modified or both. Chapter 3 describes properties in detail.

Interestingly, Example 2-36 handles this perfectly. If the tick count in `start` was obtained just before the count wrapped, and the one in `end` was obtained just after, `end` will contain a much lower value than `start`, which seems upside down, and the difference between them will be large—larger than the range of an `int`. However, when we subtract `start` from `end`, the overflow rolls over in a way that exactly matches the way the tick count rolls over, meaning we end up getting the correct result regardless. For example, if the `start` contains a tick count from 10 ms before rollover, and `end` is from 90 ms afterward, subtracting the relevant tick counts (i.e., subtracting −2,147,483,558 from 2,147,483,627) seems like it should produce a result of 4,294,967,185. But because of the way the subtraction overflows, we actually get a result of 100, which corresponds to the elapsed time of 100 ms.

But in most cases, this sort of integer overflow is undesirable. It means that when dealing with large numbers, you can get results that are completely incorrect. A lot of the time, this is not a big risk, because you will be dealing with fairly small numbers, but if there is any possibility that your calculations might encounter overflow, you might want to use a checked context. Any arithmetic performed in a checked context will throw an exception when overflow occurs. You can request this in an expression with the `checked` operator, as Example 2-37 shows. Everything inside the parentheses will be evaluated in a checked context, so you'll see an `OverflowException` if the addition of a and b overflows. The `checked` keyword does not apply to the whole statement here, so if an overflow happens as a result of adding c, that will not cause an exception.

Example 2-37. Checked expression

```
int result = checked(a + b) + c;
```

You can also turn on checking for an entire block of code with a `checked` statement, which is a block preceded by the `checked` keyword, as Example 2-38 shows. Checked statements always involve a block—you cannot just add the `checked` keyword in front of the `int` keyword in Example 2-37 to turn that into a checked statement. You'd also need to wrap the code in braces.

Example 2-38. Checked statement

```
checked
{
    int r1 = a + b;
    int r2 = r1 - (int) c;
}
```

A checked block only affects the lines of code inside the block. If the code invokes any methods, those will be unaffected by the presence of the checked keyword—there isn't some *checked* bit in the CPU that gets enabled on the current thread inside a checked block. (In other words, this keyword's scope is lexical, not dynamic.)

C# also has an unchecked keyword. You can use this inside a checked block to indicate that a particular expression or nested block should not be a checked context. This makes life easier if you want everything except for one particular expression to be checked—rather than having to label everything except the chosen part as checked, you can put all the code into a checked block and then exclude the one piece that wants to allow overflow without errors.

You can configure the C# compiler to put everything into a checked context by default, so that only explicitly unchecked expressions and statements will be able to overflow silently. In Visual Studio, you can configure this by opening the project properties, going to the Build section's Advanced subsection. Or you can edit the *.csproj* file, adding `<CheckForOverflowUnderflow>true</CheckForOverflowUnderflow>` inside a `<PropertyGroup>`. Be aware that there's a significant cost—checking can make individual integer operations several times slower. The impact on your application as a whole will be smaller, because programs don't spend their whole time performing arithmetic, but the cost may still be nontrivial. Of course, as with any performance matter, you should measure the practical impact. You may find that the performance cost is an acceptable price to pay for the guarantee that you will find out about unexpected overflows.

BigInteger, Int128, UInt128, and Half

The preceding sections discussed the various numeric types that get native support from the runtime, but there are some other numeric types worth being aware of: there is BigInteger (in the System.Numerics namespace), and also Int128, UInt128, and Half (in the System namespace). These are part of the runtime libraries and get no special recognition from the C# compiler, so they don't strictly belong in this section of the book. However, they define arithmetic operators and conversions, meaning that you can use them just like the built-in data types.

They will compile to slightly less compact code—the compiled format for .NET programs can represent the integer and floating-point types described earlier natively, but these other types have to rely on the more general-purpose mechanisms used by ordinary class library types. In theory they are likely to be significantly slower too, although in an awful lot of code, the speed at which you can perform basic arithmetic on small integers is not a limiting factor, so it's quite possible that you won't notice.

And as far as the programming model goes, these types look and feel like normal numeric types in your code.

The Int128 and UInt128 types are similar to the smaller integer types already seen, but since they are stored as 128-bit values, they offer a much wider numeric range. BigInteger, as the name suggests, also represents an integer, but it will grow as large as is necessary to accommodate values. So unlike the built-in numeric types, it has no theoretical limit on its range. Example 2-39 uses it to calculate values in the Fibonacci sequence, showing every 100,000th value. This quickly produces numbers far too large to fit into any of the other integer types. I've shown the full source of this example, including the using directive, to illustrate that this type is defined in the System.Numerics namespace.

Example 2-39. Using BigInteger

```
using System.Numerics;

BigInteger i1 = 1;
BigInteger i2 = 1;
Console.WriteLine(i1);
int count = 0;
while (true)
{
    // The % operator returns the remainder of dividing its 1st operand by its
    // 2nd, so this displays the number only when count is divisible by 100000.
    if (count++ % 100000 == 0)
    {
        Console.WriteLine(i2);
    }
    BigInteger next = i1 + i2;
    i1 = i2;
    i2 = next;
}
```

Although BigInteger imposes no fixed limit, there are practical limits. You might produce a number that's too big to fit in the available memory, for example. Or more likely, the numbers may grow large enough that the amount of CPU time required to perform even basic arithmetic becomes prohibitive. But until you run out of either memory or patience, BigInteger will grow to accommodate numbers as large as you like.

The runtime libraries also offer System.Half, a 16-bit IEEE 754 floating-point format offering 10 bits of precision and a magnitude range from 5.96×10^{-8} to 65,504. This precision is only slightly better than three-decimal digits, so Half is typically useful only in applications where reducing memory consumption is more important than precision. That can be common in artificial intelligence applications, and also in games and some kinds of media processing. Although this type is supported extensively throughout the runtime libraries (for example, JSON serialization supports it, and all the other numeric types offer conversion to and from `Half`) the fact that it is currently just a library feature with no intrinsic runtime support means it can't currently make use of the hardware support for this format that some CPUs offer (although to be fair, very few CPU architectures support this format today). `Half` implements arithmetic by first converting its value to `float`, which is somewhat inefficient. That could conceivably change, but for now, this type's main purpose is to enable natural support for this representation in libraries for systems that can work with it directly. For example, this is a common format when performing calculations on a graphics card. Your C# code might create an array of `Half` values and then send them to the graphics hardware to be processed by the GPU. In this scenario, the relatively weak performance the CLR offers for `Half` doesn't matter, because the GPU is doing the heavy number crunching.

Booleans

C# defines a type called `bool`, or as the runtime calls it, `System.Boolean`. This offers only two values: `true` and `false`. Whereas some C-family languages allow numeric types to stand in for Boolean values, with conventions such as 0 meaning false and anything else meaning true, C# will not accept a number. It demands that values indicating truth or falsehood be represented by a `bool`, and none of the numeric types is convertible to `bool`. For example, in an `if` statement, you cannot write `if (someNumber)` to get some code to run only when `someNumber` is nonzero. If that's what you want, you need to say so explicitly by writing `if (someNumber != 0)`.

Strings and Characters

The `string` type (synonymous with the CLR `System.String` type) represents text. A string is a sequence of values of type `char` (or `System.Char`, as the CLR calls it), and each `char` is a 16-bit value representing a single UTF-16 *code unit*.

A common mistake is to think that each `char` represents a character. (The type's name has to share some of the blame for this.) It's often true, but not always. There are two factors to bear in mind: first, something that we might think of as a single character can be made up from multiple Unicode *code points*. (The code point is Unicode's central concept, and in English at least, each character is represented by a single code point, but some languages are more complex.) Example 2-40 uses Unicode's 0301 "COMBINING ACUTE ACCENT" to add an accent to a letter to form the text cafés.

Example 2-40. Characters versus char

```
char[] chars = ['c', 'a', 'f', 'e', (char) 0x301, 's'];
string text = new string(chars);
```

So this string is a sequence of six char values, but it represents text that seems to contain just five characters. There are other ways to achieve this—I could have used code point 00E9 "LATIN SMALL LETTER E WITH ACUTE" to represent that accented character as a single code point. But either approach is valid, and there are plenty of scenarios in which the only way to create the exact character required is to use this combining character mechanism. This means that certain operations on the char values in a string can have surprising results—if you were to reverse the order of the values, the resulting string would not look like a reversed version of the text—the acute accent would now apply to the s, resulting in śefac! (If I had used 00E9 instead of combining e with 0301, reversing the characters would have produced the less surprising séfac.)

Unicode's combining marks notwithstanding, there is a second factor to consider. The Unicode standard defines more code points than can be represented in a single 16-bit value. (We passed that point back in 2001, when Unicode 3.1 defined 94,205 code points.) UTF-16 represents any code point with a value higher than 65,535 as a pair of UTF-16 code units, referred to as a *surrogate pair*. The Unicode standard defines rules for mapping code points to surrogate pairs in a way that the resulting code units have values in the range 0xD800 to 0xDFFF, a reserved range for which no code points will ever be defined. (For example, code point 10C48, "OLD TURKIC LETTER ORKHON BASH," which looks like ⋈, would become 0xD803, followed by 0xDC48.)

In summary, items that users perceive as single characters might be represented with multiple Unicode code points, and some single code points might be represented as multiple code units. Manipulating the individual char values that make up a string is therefore a job you should approach with caution. Often, a simple approach works well enough—if, for example, you want to search a string for some specific character that you know fits in a single code unit (such as /), a simple char-based search will work perfectly well. However, if you have a more complex scenario that requires you to detect all multi-code-unit sequences correctly, the runtime libraries offer some help here.

The string type offers an EnumerateRunes method that effectively combines surrogate pairs back into the value of the code point they represent. It presents the string as a sequence of values of type Rune, and if a string contained the 0xD803, 0xDC48 sequence just described, this pair of char values would be presented as a single Rune with the value 0x10C48. The Rune type still operates at the level of individual code points, so it won't help you with combining characters, but if you need to go to that next level, the runtime libraries define a StringInfo class in the System. Globalization namespace. This interprets a string as a sequence of "text elements," and in cases such as cafés, it will report the é as a single text element, even when it was formed with two code points using the combining character mechanism.

Immutability of strings

.NET strings are immutable. There are many operations that sound as though they will modify a string, such as concatenation, or the ToUpper and ToLower methods offered by instances of the string type, but each of these generates a new string, leaving the original one unmodified. This means that if you pass strings as arguments, even to code you didn't write, you can be certain that it cannot change your strings.

The downside of immutability is that string processing can be inefficient. If you need to do work that performs a series of modifications to a string, such as building it up character by character, you will end up allocating a lot of memory, because you'll get a separate string for each modification. This creates a lot of extra work for .NET's garbage collector, causing your program to use more CPU time than necessary. In these situations, you can use a type called StringBuilder. (This type gets no special recognition from the C# compiler, unlike string.) This is conceptually similar to a string—it is a sequence of char values and offers various useful string manipulation methods—but it is modifiable. Alternatively, in extremely performance-sensitive scenarios, you might use the techniques shown in Chapter 18.

String manipulation methods

The string type has numerous instance methods for working with strings. I already mentioned ToUpper and ToLower, but there are also methods for finding text within the string, including IndexOf and LastIndexOf. StartsWith and EndsWith return a bool indicating whether the string starts or ends with a particular character or string. Split takes one or more separator characters (e.g., commas or spaces) and returns an array with an entry for each substring between the separators. For example, "One,two,three".Split(',') returns an array containing the three strings "One", "two", and "three". Substring takes a starting position and optional length and returns a new string containing all characters from the start position up to either the end of the string or the specified length; Remove does the opposite: it forms a new string by removing the part of the original string that Substring would have returned. Insert forms a new string by inserting one string into the middle of another. Replace returns a new string formed by replacing all instances of a particular character or string with another. Trim can be used to remove unwanted leading and trailing characters such as whitespace.

Formatting data in strings

C# provides a syntax that makes it easy to produce strings containing a mixture of fixed text and information determined at runtime. (The official name for this feature is *string interpolation*.) For example, if you have local variables called name and age, you could use them in a string, as Example 2-41 shows.

Example 2-41. Expressions in strings

```
string message = $"{name} is {age} years old";
```

When you put a $ symbol in front of a string literal, the C# compiler looks for embedded expressions delimited by braces and produces code that will insert a textual representation of the expression at that point in the string. (So if name and age were Ian and 50, respectively, the string's value would be "Ian is 50 years old".) As Example 2-42 shows, embedded expressions can be more complex than just variable names.

Example 2-42. More complex expressions in strings

```
double width = 3, height = 4;
string info = $"Hypotenuse: {Math.Sqrt(width * width + height * height)}";
```

If a string contains complex expressions, it might become a bit too large to fit on a single line. As Example 2-43 shows, you can split interpolated strings or string literals over multiple lines by breaking them up and using + to join the parts together. (Visual Studio can do this for you: if you put the text cursor where you'd like to split the string and press Enter, it automatically adds the necessary extra " and + symbols.)

Example 2-43. Splitting up an interpolated string

```
string info = $"Hypotenuse:" +
    $" {Math.Sqrt(width * width + height * height)}";
```

The + symbol denotes concatenation, and in general the compiler implements this with the string type's Concat method. However, in this case it will see that we're just using it to split an interpolated string across multiple lines, and it will generate exactly the same code as it would if it were a single interpolated string. This is important because if it generated the two parts separately and then concatenated them, it would create more string objects than necessary, increasing memory usage at runtime.

If an individual expression is complex, you might also want to split that across multiple lines. This wasn't possible before C# 11.0: unless you're writing a *verbatim string* (described in the next section) string literals aren't allowed to contain new lines, and C# used to impose this rule even on the expressions in an interpolated string. C# 11.0 relaxed this restriction, enabling us to split individual expressions in an interpolated string across multiple lines, as Example 2-44 shows. (If you want line breaks in the actual text content, you will still need to use either verbatim strings or raw string literals, which I will describe shortly.)

Example 2-44. Splitting an interpolated expression across lines

```
string info = $"Hypotenuse: {Math.Sqrt(
    width * width +
    height * height)}";
```

If you want to use string interpolation but you also want the resulting string to include opening or closing braces, you double them up. When an interpolated string contains either {{ or }}, the compiler does not interpret them as delimiting embedded expressions and just produces a single { or } in the output. For example, $"Brace: {{, braces: {{}}, width: {width}, braced width: {{{width}}}" evaluates to Brace: {, braces: {}, width: 3, braced width: {3} (assuming width is 3 here).

The runtime libraries offer another mechanism for plugging values into a string called *composite formatting*. The string class's Format method takes a string with numbered placeholders of the form {0} and {1}, followed by a list of arguments supplying the values for these placeholders. Example 2-45 uses this to achieve the same effect as Examples 2-41 and 2-42.

Example 2-45. Using string.Format

```
string message = string.Format("{0} is {1} years old", name, age);
string info = string.Format(
    "Hypotenuse: {0}",
    Math.Sqrt(width * width + height * height));
```

This composite formatting mechanism is older—it has been around since C# 1.0, whereas string interpolation was introduced in C# 6.0—so you will see it cropping up in quite a few places. Console.WriteLine supports it, for example. In most cases, it's not the preferred approach. String interpolation is much less error prone—composite formatting uses position-based placeholders, making it all too easy to put an expression in the wrong place. It's also tedious for anyone reading the code to try and work out how the numbered placeholders relate to the arguments that follow, particularly as the number of expressions increases. Interpolated strings are usually much easier to read. However, composite formatting has one important capability that interpolated strings do not: you can choose the format string at runtime. This is widely used for internationalization: applications can choose which format string to use based on the preferred language the user has configured.

Interpolated strings can sometimes offer performance benefits. If we select a composite format string at runtime, all the processing associated with that string must also be done at runtime, but with string interpolation, the compiler may be able to perform compile-time optimizations. For example, if an expression in an interpolated string is a const string (Chapter 3 describes the const keyword), the compiler will insert its value into the string at compile time. Furthermore, libraries may indicate that they want to be involved in the interpolation process, making it possible to avoid ever creating a string in cases where that string won't be used. When might you write an interpolated string that won't be used? Look at Example 2-46.

Example 2-46. A potentially unused interpolated string

```
Debug.Assert(everythingIsOk, $"Everything is *not* OK: {myApplicationModel}");
```

This uses `Debug.Assert`, a diagnostic method you can add to your code to detect when your application has got into some unexpected state. `Debug.Assert` checks its first argument, and if that's `false`, it will halt the program, displaying the message passed as the second argument. But if the first argument is `true`, it proceeds without ever using the second argument. In this example, if calling `ToString()` on the `myApplicationModel` in the interpolated string were expensive, it would be bad news if that ran even in cases where everything is in fact OK—our program might be doing a great deal of work to create a string that gets thrown away. But Example 2-46 uses an overload of `Debug.Assert` that takes advantage of string interpolation's ability to avoid ever creating that string in cases where it won't be used. This same mechanism could be used by logging frameworks, in which it's common for code to be able to generate a lot of strings to provide detailed descriptions of what's happening but which will be unused in the typical case where verbose logging has not been enabled.

Interpolated strings have another performance benefit: the work of finding all the braces to determine which parts of the string are plain text and which are value placeholders can be done at compile time, so even when a string does get created, interpolation has an advantage over composite formatting. If you really do need to select composite format strings at runtime (e.g., to support internationalization) you can't avoid doing runtime processing. However, .NET 8.0 adds a new type, `Composite Format`, that can avoid *repeating* work in cases where we use the same format string repeatedly. Example 2-47 obtains a format string from a method (`GetPersonFormat`; not shown here, but it could look up the text based on the locale). `CompositeFormat.Parse` will parse this string to find the placeholders. Each time the loop calls `string.Format`, that can use this information instead of having to rescan the format string every time. This is not quite as efficient as string interpolation, which does that work at compile time, but in cases where you use the same composite format string frequently, this avoids repeating work unnecessarily.

Example 2-47. Using `CompositeFormat`

```
CompositeFormat nameAgeFormat = CompositeFormat.Parse(GetPersonFormat());

foreach (Person p in people)
```

```
{
    string message = string.Format(
        CultureInfo.InvariantCulture, nameAgeFormat, p.Name, p.Age);
    Console.WriteLine(message);
}
```

With some data types, there are choices to be made about their textual representation. For example, with floating-point numbers, you might want to limit the number of decimal places, or force the use of exponential notation. (For example, 1e6 instead of 1000000.) In .NET, we control this with a *format specifier*, which is a string describing how to convert some data to a string. Some data types have only one reasonable string representation, so they do not support this, but with types that have multiple string forms, you can pass the format specifier as an argument to the ToString method. For example, System.Math.PI.ToString("f4") formats the PI constant (which is of type double) to four decimal places ("3.1416"). There are nine built-in formats for numbers, and if none of those suits your requirements, there is also a minilanguage for defining custom formats. Moreover, different types use different format strings—dates work quite differently from numbers, for example—so the full range of available formats is too large to list here. Microsoft supplies extensive documentation of the details.

When using composite formatting, you can include a format specifier in the placeholder; for example, {0:f3} indicates that the first expression is to be formatted with three digits after the decimal point. You can include a format specifier in a similar way with string interpolation. Example 2-48 shows the age with one digit after the decimal point.

Example 2-48. Format specifiers

```
string message = $"{name} is {age:f1} years old";
```

There's one wrinkle with this: with many data types, the process of converting to a string is culture-specific. For example, as mentioned earlier, in the US and the UK, decimals are typically written with a period between the whole number part and the fractional part, and you might use commas to group digits for readability, but some European countries invert this: they use periods to group digits, while the comma denotes the start of the fractional part. So what might be written as 1,000.2 in one country could be written as 1.000,2 in another.

As far as numeric literals in source code are concerned, this is a nonissue: C# uses underscores for digit grouping and always uses a period as the decimal point. But what about processing numbers at runtime? By default, you will get conventions determined by the current thread's culture, and unless you've changed that, it will use the regional settings of the computer. Sometimes this is useful—it can mean that numbers, dates, and so on are correctly formatted for whatever locale a program runs in. However, it can be problematic: if your code relies on strings being formatted in a particular way (to serialize data that will be transmitted over a network, for example), you may need to apply a particular set of conventions. For this reason, you can pass the `string.Format` method a *format provider*, an object that controls formatting conventions. Likewise, data types with culture-dependent representations accept an optional format provider argument in their `ToString` methods. But how do you control this when using string interpolation? There's nowhere to put the format provider. You can solve this with the `string` type's `Create` method, as shown in Example 2-49.

Example 2-49. Format specifiers with invariant culture

```
decimal v = 1234567.654m;
string i = string.Create(CultureInfo.InvariantCulture, $"Quantity {v:N}");
string f = string.Create(new CultureInfo("fr"), $"Quantity {v:N}");
string frc = string.Create(new CultureInfo("fr-FR"), $"Quantity {v:C}");
string cac = string.Create(new CultureInfo("fr-CA"), $"Quantity {v:C}");
```

This passes various different format providers to the `string.Create` method, but it uses only a couple of different interpolated strings. Notice that it puts `:N` after the variable name in the first two lines. This asks for normal numeric formatting, including digit separators. The first call passes the *invariant culture*, which guarantees consistent formatting regardless of the locale in which the code runs, with the effect that `i` gets the value `"Quantity 1,234,567.654"`. The third line uses a `CultureInfo` object constructed with the argument `"fr"`. This tells it that we want it to format strings in the ways typically expected in French-speaking cultures, so the `f` variable gets the value `"Quantity 1.234.567,654"`. The final two lines use `:C`, indicating we'd like to show the value as a currency. I've passed cultures representing France and the French-speaking parts of Canada, resulting in euro and dollar symbols, respectively.

It may seem odd that this works: normally, method arguments are evaluated before being passed into the method, so you might expect the interpolated string to be turned into a normal string before the call to `string.Create`, meaning it would be too late to apply the specified format provider. But as I said earlier, methods can indicate that they want to be involved in the string interpolation process. This `string.Create` method does exactly that, enabling it to take control of the process, which is how it is able to apply the format provider.

Verbatim string literals

C# supports an alternative way of expressing a string value: you can prefix a string literal with the @ symbol like so: `@"Hello"`. Strings of this form are called *verbatim string literals*. They are useful for two reasons: they can improve the readability of strings containing backslashes, and they make it possible to write multiline string literals. (The newer *raw string literal* feature described in the next section can also do this, and is more flexible, but verbatim literals can sometimes be simpler. They've also been around for longer so you are likely to come across them in existing codebases.)

In a normal string literal, the compiler treats a backslash as an escape character, enabling various special values to be included. For example, in the literal `"Hello \tWorld!"` the `\t` denotes a single tab character (code point 9). This is a common way to express control characters in C-family languages. You can also use the backslash to include a double quote in a string—the backslash prevents the compiler from interpreting the character as the end of the string. Useful though this is, it makes including a backslash in a string a bit awkward: you have to write two of them. Since Windows uses backslashes in paths, this can get ugly: `"C:\\Windows\\System32\\"`. A verbatim string literal can be useful here, because it treats backslashes literally, enabling you to write just `@"C:\Windows\System32"`. (You can still include double quotes in a verbatim literal: just write two double quotes in a row. For example, `@"Hello ""World"""` produces the string value `Hello "World"`.)

> You can use @ in front of an interpolated string. This combines the benefits of verbatim literals—straightforward use of backslashes and newlines—with support for embedded expressions.

Verbatim string literals also allow values to span multiple lines. With a normal string literal, the compiler will report an error if the closing double quote is not on the same line as the opening one. But with a verbatim string literal, the string can cover as many lines of source as you like.

The resulting string will use whichever line-ending convention your source code uses. Just in case you've not encountered this, one of the unfortunate accidents of computing history is that different systems use different character sequences to denote line endings. The predominant system in internet protocols is to use a pair of control codes for each line end: in either Unicode or ASCII, we use code points 13 and 10, denoting a *carriage return* and a *line feed*, respectively, often abbreviated to CR LF. This is an archaic hangover from the days before computers had screens, and starting a new line meant moving the teletype's print head back to its start position (carriage return) and then moving the paper up by one line (line feed). Anachronistically, the HTTP specification requires this representation, as do the various popular email standards, SMTP, POP3, and IMAP. It is also the standard convention on Windows. Unfortunately, the Unix operating system does things differently, as do most of its derivatives and lookalikes such as macOS and Linux—the convention on these systems is to use just a single line feed character. The C# compiler accepts either and will not complain if a single source file contains a mixture of both conventions. This introduces a potential problem for multiline string literals if you are using a source control system that converts line endings for you. For example, *Git* is a very popular source control system, and thanks to its origins (it was created by Linus Torvalds, who also created Linux), there is a widespread convention of using Unix-style line endings in its repositories. However, on Windows it can be configured to convert working copies of files to a CR LF representation, automatically converting them back to LF when committing changes. This means that files will appear to use different line-ending conventions depending on whether you're looking at them on a Windows system or a Unix one. (And it might even vary from one Windows system to another, because the default line-ending handling is configurable. Individual users can configure the machine-wide default setting and can also set the configuration for their local clone of any repository if the repository does not specify the setting itself.) This in turn means that compiling a file containing a multiline verbatim string literal on a Windows system could produce subtly different behavior than you'd see with the exact same file on a Unix system, if automatic line-ending conversion is enabled (which it is by default on most Windows installations of Git). That might be fine—you typically want CR LF when running on Windows and LF on Unix—but it could cause surprises if you deploy code to a machine running a different OS than the one you built it on. So it's important to provide a *.gitattributes* file in your repositories so that they can specify the required behavior, instead of relying on changeable local settings. If you need to rely on a particular line ending in a string literal, it's best to make your *.gitattributes* disable line-ending conversions.

Raw string literals

Certain text formats can be awkward to produce with string literals. JSON is particularly tricky because it tends to contain lots of braces and double quotes. The safest way to produce JSON is with the `System.Text.Json` API described in Chapter 15, so for most production code I would advise you not to use string literals at all when creating JSON. However, there are some situations (especially test code) where the risks of creating malformed JSON are low, in which case a string literal might be the best choice. However, this can lead to horrors of the kind shown in Example 2-50.

Example 2-50. Messy JSON string interpolation

```
static string MakeRightAngledTriangleJson(double width, double height)
{
    // Wonky indentation is necessary here to get correctly indented output
    return @$"{{
""width"": {width},
""height"": {height},
""calculated"": {{
    ""hypotenuse"": {Math.Sqrt(width * width + height * height)},
    ""area"": {width * height / 2}
}}
}}";
}
```

I've used a verbatim string literal here so that the JSON being produced can run over multiple lines with indentation, but there are several problems here. JSON is a format that uses a lot of double quotes and braces. Since the " character delimits the string, I've had to write "" every time I want my string to contain a double quote. And since I'm using string interpolation, I've had to double up the braces anywhere I want to emit an actual brace.

There's a more subtle problem with indentation. When a statement crosses multiple lines in C#, we would normally indent it so that it's easier to see where each statement ends. But here, the content of my string is mostly aligned with the `return` statement, and the final line of the string is actually to the left of the `return` statement it belongs to, making the final line in the method look like it's the result of a cut and paste mishap. Unfortunately, it has to look like this. If I had indented the string so that it was positioned in the way we normally format C# code, all the extra whitespace would have been included in the string's value, meaning I would no longer be producing the JSON text I want. It's not too bad in this example, but as code becomes more deeply nested inside flow control structures or type definitions, we typically indent it further. This makes verbatim strings look more and more out of place, because they need to remain anchored to the left to avoid adding unwanted whitespace to the string value.

C# 11.0 added a new string literal syntax that addresses all of these problems. It is called the *raw string* syntax, and Example 2-51 shows how to use it in place of the preceding example's verbatim string.

Example 2-51. JSON with an interpolated raw string literal

```
static string MakeRightAngledTriangleJson(double width, double height)
{
    return $$"""
        {
            "width": {{width}},
            "height": {{height}},
            "calculated": {
                "hypotenuse": {{Math.Sqrt(width * width + height * height)}},
                "area": {{width * height / 2}}
            }
        }
        """;
}
```

With this syntax, I can write the double quote and brace characters that show up so often in JSON exactly as they will appear in the output. I've also been able to indent the entire string literal. If I had done that with a verbatim string, that extra indentation would have become part of the string, but not so here. This produces exactly the same output as before. For example, if I call this method with a `width` and `height` of 3 and 5 I get this:

```
{
    "width": 3,
    "height": 4,
    "calculated": {
        "hypotenuse": 5,
        "area": 6
    }
}
```

The opening and closing braces are not indented at all, but I still get all of the necessary indentation within the JSON. That's exactly what I wanted, but how did the compiler know to include some but not all of the whitespace? When you write a multiline raw string literal, you're required to put the start of the string on its own line. (If text follows the """ on the same line, that means you're writing a single-line string, in which case the compiler won't allow embedded new lines.) The closing """ must also appear on its own line, and the compiler looks at its indentation and removes that much indentation from the start of each line of the string. Since my closing """ is aligned with the opening and closing braces in this string, those end up with no indentation at all in the resulting string. (The extra line endings that the syntax requires at the start and end are not included in the resulting string. The very first character of this string is the opening {, not a new line; the final character is the closing } and this is not followed by a new line, despite how it looks in the example. If you want leading and trailing new lines, you would add blank lines at the start and end of the string.)

You might be wondering why I needed two $ symbols. In fact, I could have written just $""", but then I would have needed to double up all the braces that weren't meant to be interpolated expressions. The number of $ symbols tells the compiler how many braces I will be writing if I want to embed an expression instead of just producing an actual { or }. Since Example 2-51 starts with two $ symbols, C# will interpret individual braces as normal characters. Only when braces come in pairs will it treat them as expression delimiters. If for some reason I wanted to produce a string that contained a lot of double braces, I could start the string with $$$, telling the compiler that it should interpret { and {{ literally, and that only if I write {{{ am I embedding an expression. I can also omit the $ signs entirely—if I start a raw string with just """ that means that I don't want string interpolation at all.

Just as we can vary the number of $ signs, we can also use more than three double quotes. If you wanted to produce a string that contains three double quotes in a row, you can use four quotes in the delimiters. The compiler defines no fixed limit on the number of $ or " signs, so no matter how many consecutive double quotes or braces you'd like to put in a string, raw string literals work without any of the messy escaping that normal or verbatim string literals require.

UTF-8 string literals

There's one last way to write a string literal: if you write u8 after the closing ", this tells the compiler that you want the text as a sequence of bytes encoded as UTF-8. This can be useful when working directly with text that is encoded as UTF-8. Most JSON text is in that format, for example, and when you're using the System.Text.Json API described in Chapter 15, it can be more efficient to avoid forcing the API to convert between the UTF-16 representation that .NET uses and the UTF-8 encoding your actual data is using. Example 2-52 uses this API to retrieve some properties from a root element representing a JSON document. (Chapter 15 shows how to obtain such a JsonElement.)

Example 2-52. Specifying JSON property names as UTF-8

```
if (root.TryGetProperty("location"u8, out JsonElement locationElement))
{
    JsonElement latitudeElement = locationElement.GetProperty("latitude"u8);
    JsonElement longitudeElement = locationElement.GetProperty("longitude"u8);
    double latitude = latitudeElement.GetDouble();
    double longitude = longitudeElement.GetDouble();
    Console.WriteLine($"Location: {locationName}: {latitude},{longitude}");
}
```

Notice how each string literal here ends in u8. That means that when we ask Json Element to find a property with a particular name, we've supplied that name using the same text encoding as will be in use in the source JSON itself. You aren't obliged to do this—these methods have overloads that let you specify the property name as an ordinary string, but if you use those, you force JsonElement to compare the UTF-16 data in that string with the UTF-8 in the JSON. Comparing strings that use different encodings will always be more expensive than when they use the same representation, so in cases where you know the name of the property at compile time, a UTF-8 string constant provides an easy performance improvement.

UTF-8 string constants do not produce a string object, because string always uses UTF-16 internally, so you can't do all the things you can do with a normal string— methods such as Split or Replace are not available. In fact, they are not objects at all. UTF-8 literals have the type ReadOnlySpan<byte>, which is a way to refer to a range of bytes in memory. (So you effectively get a managed pointer into the part of the DLL where the compiler put the UTF-8 bytes.) This is a much more lightweight data type than string but it comes with some limitations. Chapter 18 discusses span types in detail. If you need a normal byte[] array instead of a span, you can just call the span's ToArray() method.

Tuples

Tuples let you combine multiple values into a single value. The name tuple (which C# shares with many other programming languages that provide a similar feature) is meant to be a generalized version of words like *double, triple, quadruple,* and so on, but we generally call them tuples even in cases where we don't need the generality. For example, even if we're talking about a tuple with two items in it, we still call it a tuple, not a double. Example 2-53 creates a tuple containing two `int` values and then displays them.

Example 2-53. Creating and using a tuple

```
(int X, int Y) point = (10, 5);
Console.WriteLine($"X: {point.X}, Y: {point.Y}");
```

That first line is a variable declaration with an initializer. It's worth breaking this down, because the syntax for tuples makes for a slightly more complex-looking declaration than we've seen so far. Remember, the general pattern for statements of this form is as follows:

```
type identifier = initial-value;
```

That means that in Example 2-53, the type is `(int X, int Y)`. So we're saying that our variable, `point`, is a tuple containing two values, both of type `int`, and that we want to refer to those as X and Y. The initializer here is `(10, 5)`. So when we run the example, it produces this output:

```
X: 10, Y: 5
```

C# 12.0 has removed a limitation that used to apply to tuple types. For years, the `using` syntax for defining type aliases did not support tuple types, but now, code such as Example 2-54 is permitted. This does not define a new type—it just means that in the source file that defines the alias, we can use an alternative name to refer to the type. I introduced this *using alias* syntax in Chapter 1 as a way to resolve ambiguity between two types in different namespaces with the same simple name, but there is no ambiguity with tuple types—they don't live in a namespace, so `(int X, int Y)` always refers to one particular type. There is a different reason you might want to define an alias for a tuple type: it can make your intent clear. A descriptive name might help someone reading your code to understand more easily what the tuple is meant to represent.

Example 2-54. Defining and using an alias for a tuple type

```
using Point = (int X, int Y);

Point center = (0, 0);
```

If you're a fan of var, you'll be pleased to know that you can specify the names in the initializer using the syntax shown in Example 2-55, enabling you to use var instead of the explicit type. This is equivalent to Example 2-53.

Example 2-55. Naming tuple members in the initializer

```
var point = (X: 10, Y: 5);
Console.WriteLine($"X: {point.X}, Y: {point.Y}");
```

If you initialize a tuple from existing variables and you do not specify names, the compiler will presume that you want to use the names of those variables, as Example 2-56 shows.

Example 2-56. Inferring tuple member names from variables

```
int x = 10, y = 5;
var point = (x, y);
Console.WriteLine($"X: {point.x}, Y: {point.y}");
```

This raises a stylistic question: Should tuple member names start with lowercase or uppercase letters? The members are similar in nature to properties, which we'll be discussing in Chapter 3, and conventionally those start with an uppercase letter. For this reason, many people believe that tuple member names should also be uppercase. To a seasoned .NET developer, that point.x in Example 2-56 just looks weird. However, another .NET convention is that local variables usually start with a lowercase name. If you stick to both of these conventions, tuple name inference doesn't look very useful. Many developers choose to accept lowercase tuple member names for tuples used purely in local variables, because it enables the use of the convenient name inference feature, using the more normal casing style only for tuples that are exposed outside of a method.

Arguably it doesn't matter much, because tuple member names turn out to exist only in the eye of the beholder. First, they're optional. As Example 2-57 shows, it's perfectly legal to omit them. The names just default to Item1, Item2, etc.

Example 2-57. Default tuple member names

```
(int, int) point = (10, 5);
Console.WriteLine($"X: {point.Item1}, Y: {point.Item2}");
```

Second, the names are purely for the convenience of the code using the tuples and are not visible to the runtime. You'll have noticed that I've used the same initializer expression, (10, 5), as I did in Example 2-53. Because it doesn't specify names, the expression's type is (int, int), which matches the type in Example 2-57, but I was also able to assign it straight into an (int X, int Y) in Example 2-53. That's because the names are essentially irrelevant—these are all the same thing under the covers. (As we'll see in Chapter 4, at runtime these are all represented as instances of a type called `ValueTuple<int, int>`.) The C# compiler keeps track of the names we've chosen to use, but as far as the CLR is concerned, all these tuples just have members called `Item1` and `Item2`. An upshot of this is that we can assign any tuple into any variable with the same shape, as Example 2-58 shows.

Example 2-58. Structural equivalence of tuples

```
(int X, int Y) point = (50, 3);
(int Width, int Height) dimensions = point;
(int Age, int NumberOfChildren) person = point;
```

This flexibility is a double-edged sword. The assignments in Example 2-58 seem rather sketchy. It might conceivably be OK to assign something that represents a location into something that represents a size—there are some situations in which that would be valid. But to assign that same value into something apparently representing someone's age and the number of children they have looks likely to be wrong. The compiler won't stop us though, because it considers all tuples comprising a pair of `int` values to have the same type. (It's not really any different from the fact that the compiler won't stop you assigning an `int` variable named `age` into an `int` variable named `height`. They're both of type `int`.)

If you want to enforce a semantic distinction, you would be better off defining custom types as described in Chapter 3. Tuples are really designed as a convenient way to package together a few values in cases where defining a whole new type wouldn't really be justified.

C# does require tuples to have an appropriate shape. You cannot assign an (`int`, `int`) into an (`int`, `string`), nor into an (`int`, `int`, `int`). However, all of the implicit conversions in "Numeric conversions" on page 66 work, so you can assign anything with an (`int`, `int`) shape into an (`int`, `double`) or a (`double`, `long`). So a tuple is really just like having a handful of variables neatly contained inside another variable.

Tuples support comparison, so you can use the `==` and `!=` relational operators described later in this chapter. To be considered equal, two tuples must have the same shape, and each value in the first tuple must be equal to its counterpart in the second tuple.

Tuple Deconstruction

Sometimes you will want to split a tuple back into its component parts. The most straightforward way would be to access each item in turn by its name (or as `Item1`, `Item2`, etc., if you didn't specify names), but C# provides another mechanism, called *deconstruction*. Example 2-59 declares and initializes two tuples and then shows two different ways to deconstruct them.

Example 2-59. Constructing then deconstructing tuples

```
(int X, int Y) point1 = (40, 6);
(int X, int Y) point2 = (12, 34);

(int x, int y) = point1;
Console.WriteLine($"1: {x}, {y}");
(x, y) = point2;
Console.WriteLine($"2: {x}, {y}");
```

Having defined point1 and point2, this deconstructs point1 into two variables, x and y. This particular form of deconstruction also declares the variables into which the tuple is being deconstructed. The alternative form is shown when we deconstruct point2—here, we're deconstructing it into two variables that already exist, so there's no need to declare them.

Until you become accustomed to this syntax, the first deconstruction example can seem confusingly similar to the first couple of lines, in which we declare and initialize new tuples. In those first couple of lines, the (int X, int Y) text signifies a tuple type with two int values named X and Y, but in the deconstruction line when we write (int x, int y), we're actually declaring two variables, each of type int. The only significant difference is that in the lines where we're constructing new tuples, there's a variable name before the = sign. (Also, we're using uppercase names there, but that's just a matter of convention. It would be entirely legal to write (int x, int y) point3 = point1;. That would declare a new tuple with two int values named x and y, stored in a variable named point3, initialized with the same values as are in point1. Equally, we could write (int X, int Y) = point1;. That would deconstruct point into two local variables called X and Y.)

You can mix the two forms of deconstruction: the lefthand side could be (int z, x), which declares a new variable for the first part of the target, and uses an existing variable for the second. If you don't need every element of a tuple, you can use an underscore, as Example 2-60 shows. This is called a *discard*.

Example 2-60. Tuple deconstruction with discard

```
(_, int h) = point1;
```

The underscore character can appear in any number of places in the target, and it tells the compiler that we don't need that part of the tuple to be extracted into a variable.

Dynamic

C# defines a type called dynamic. This doesn't directly correspond to any CLR type—when we use dynamic in C#, the compiler presents it to the runtime as object, which is described in the next section. However, from the perspective of C# code, dynamic is a distinct type, and it enables some special behavior.

With dynamic, the compiler makes no attempt at compile time to check whether operations performed by code are likely to succeed. In other words, it effectively disables the statically typed behavior that we normally get with C#. You are free to attempt almost any operation on a dynamic variable—you can use arithmetic operators, you can attempt to invoke methods on it, you can try to assign it into variables of some other type, and you can try to get or set properties on it. When you do this, the compiler generates code that attempts to make sense of what you've asked it to do at runtime.

If you have come to C# from a language in which this sort of behavior is the norm (such as JavaScript), you might be tempted to use dynamic for everything because it works in a way you are used to. However, you should be aware that there are a couple of issues with it. First, it was designed with a particular scenario in mind: interoperability with certain pre-.NET Windows components. The Component Object Model (COM) in Windows is the basis for automatability of Microsoft 365 (perhaps still better known by its old name, Microsoft Office) and many other applications, and the scripting language built into Office is dynamic in nature. An upshot of this is that a lot of Office's automation APIs used to be hard work to use from C#. One of the big drivers behind adding dynamic to the language was a desire to improve this.

As with all C# features, it was designed with broader applicability in mind and not simply as an Office interop feature. But since that was the most important scenario for this feature, you may find that its ability to support idioms you are familiar with from dynamic languages is disappointing. And the second issue to be aware of is that it is not an area of the language that is getting a lot of new work. When it was introduced, Microsoft went to considerable lengths to ensure that all dynamic behavior was as consistent as possible with the behavior you would have seen if the compiler had known at compile time what types you were going to be using.

This means that the infrastructure supporting dynamic (which is called the Dynamic Language Runtime, or DLR) has to replicate significant portions of C# behavior. However, the DLR has not been updated much since dynamic was added in C# 4.0 back in 2010, even though the language has seen many new features since then. Of course, dynamic still works, but its capabilities reflect how the language looked around a decade ago.

Even when it first appeared, dynamic had some limitations. There are some aspects of C# that depend on the availability of static type information, meaning that dynamic has always had some problems working with delegates and also with LINQ. So even from the start, it was at something of a disadvantage compared to using C# as intended, i.e., as a statically typed language.

Object

The last data type to get special recognition from the C# compiler is `object` (or `System.Object`, as the CLR calls it). This is the base class of almost[8] all C# types. A variable of type `object` is able to refer to a value of any type that derives from `object`. This includes all numeric types, the `bool` and `string` types, and any custom types you can define using the keywords we'll look at in the next chapter, such as `class`, `record`, and `struct`. And it also includes all the types defined by the runtime libraries, with the exception of certain types that can only be stored on the stack and that are described in Chapter 18.

So `object` is the ultimate general-purpose container. You can refer to almost anything with an `object` variable. We will return to this in Chapter 6 when we look at inheritance.

Operators

Earlier you saw that expressions are sequences of operators and operands. I've shown some of the types that can be used as operands, so now it's time to see what operators C# offers. Table 2-3 shows the ones that support common arithmetic operations.

Table 2-3. Basic arithmetic operators

Name	Example
Unary plus (does nothing)	+x
Negation (unary minus)	-x
Postincrement	x++
Postdecrement	x--
Preincrement	++x
Predecrement	--x
Addition	x + y
Subtraction	x - y
Multiplication	x * y
Division	x / y
Remainder	x % y

---

8 There are some specialized exceptions, such as pointer types.

If you've had much experience with any other C-family language, all of these should seem familiar. If not, the most peculiar ones will probably be the increment and decrement operators. These have side effects: they add or subtract one from the variable to which they are applied (meaning they can be applied only to variables). With the postincrement and postdecrement, although the variable gets modified, the containing expression ends up getting the original value. So if x is a variable containing the value 5, the value of x++ is also 5, even though the x variable will have a value of 6 after evaluating the x++ expression. The pre- forms return the modified value, so if x is initially 5, ++x produces the value 6, which is also the value of x after evaluating the expression.

Although the operators in Table 2-3 are used in arithmetic, some are available on certain nonnumeric types. As you saw earlier, the + symbol represents concatenation when working with strings, and as you'll see in Chapter 9, the addition and subtraction operators are also used for combining and removing delegates.

C# also offers some operators that perform certain binary operations on the bits that make up a value, shown in Table 2-4. These are not available on floating-point types. (C# 11.0's generic math feature, described in Chapter 4, does actually provide a way to use all but the shift operators on double, float, and Half values, but you still can't use these operators directly on variables of these types.)

Table 2-4. Binary integer operators

Name	Example
Bitwise negation	~x
Bitwise AND	x & y
Bitwise OR	x | y
Bitwise XOR	x ^ y
Shift left	x << y
Shift right	x >> y
Unsigned shift right	x >>> y

The bitwise negation operator inverts all bits in an integer—any binary digit with a value of 1 becomes 0, and vice versa. The shift operators move all the bits left or right by the number of columns specified by the second operand. A left shift sets the least significant bits to 0. Right shifts of unsigned integers fill the higher order bits with 0. When you right shift a signed integer, you can choose between >>, which fills the most significant bits with whatever value the leftmost bit already had (i.e., negative numbers remain negative because they keep their most significant bit set, while positive numbers keep their upper bit as 0, thus remaining positive), or >>>, which fills these bits with 0. The >>> operator is new in C# 11.0, and can be useful because some libraries use int to represent values that are really unsigned. (This happens sometimes because the CLS disallows the use of unsigned integer types, since not all languages support these.)

The bitwise AND, OR, and XOR (exclusive OR) operators perform Boolean logic operations on each bit of the two operands when applied to integers. These three operators are also available when the operands are of type bool. (In effect, these operators treat a bool as a one-digit binary number.) There are some additional operators available for bool values, shown in Table 2-5. The ! operator does to a bool what the ~ operator does to each bit in an integer.

Table 2-5. Operators for bool

Name	Example
Logical negation (also known as NOT)	!x
Conditional AND	x && y
Conditional OR	x || y

If you have not used other C-family languages, the conditional versions of the AND and OR operators may be new to you. These evaluate their second operand only if necessary. For example, when evaluating (a && b), if the expression a is false, the code generated by the compiler will not even attempt to evaluate b, because the result will be false no matter what value b has. Conversely, the conditional OR operator does not bother to evaluate its second operand if the first is true, because the result will be true regardless of the second operand's value. This is significant if the second operand's expression either contains elements that have side effects (such as method invocation) or might produce an error. For example, you often see code like that shown in Example 2-61.

Example 2-61. The conditional AND operator

```
if (s is not null && s.Length > 10)
...
```

This checks to see if the variable s contains the special value null, meaning that it doesn't currently refer to any value. The use of the && operator here is important, because if s is null, evaluating the expression s.Length would cause a runtime error. If we had used the & operator, the compiler would have generated code that always evaluates both operands, meaning that we would see a NullReferenceException at runtime if s is null. By using the conditional AND operator, we avoid that, because the second operand, s.Length > 10, will be evaluated only if s is not null.

Although code of the kind shown in Example 2-61 was once common, it has gradually become much rarer thanks to a feature introduced back in C# 6.0, *null-conditional operators*. If you write s?.Length instead of just s.Length, the compiler generates code that checks s for null first, avoiding the NullReferenceException. This means the check can become just if (s?.Length > 10). Furthermore, C#'s optional *nullable reference types* (a relatively new feature, discussed in Chapter 3) can help reduce the need for these kinds of tests for null.

Example 2-61 tests to see if a property is greater than 10 by using the > operator. This is one of several *relational operators*, which allow us to compare values. They all take two operands and produce a bool result. Table 2-6 shows these, and they are supported for all numeric types. Some operators are available on some other types too. For example, you can compare string values with the == and != operators. (There is no built-in meaning for the other relational operators with string because different countries have different ideas about the order in which to sort strings. If you want ordered string comparison, .NET offers the StringComparer class, which requires you to select the rules by which you'd like your strings ordered.)

Table 2-6. Relational operators

Name	Example
Less than	x < y
Greater than	x > y
Less than or equal	x <= y
Greater than or equal	x >= y
Equal	x == y
Not equal	x != y

As is usual with C-family languages, the equality operator is a pair of equals signs. This is because a single equals sign means something else: it's an assignment, and assignments are expressions too. This can lead to an unfortunate problem: in some C-family languages, it's all too easy to write if (x = y) when you meant if (x == y). Fortunately, this will usually produce a compiler error in C#, because C# has a special type to represent Boolean values. In languages that allow numbers to stand in for Booleans, both pieces of code are legal even if x and y are numbers. (The first means to assign the value of y into x, and then to execute the body of the if statement if that value is nonzero. That's very different than the second one, which doesn't change the value of anything and executes the body of the if statement only if x and y are equal.)

But in C#, the first example would be meaningful only if x and y were both of type bool.[9]

Another feature that's common to the C family is the conditional operator. (Some people call it the ternary operator, because it's the only operator in the language that takes three operands.) It chooses between two expressions. More precisely, it evaluates its first operand, which must be a Boolean expression, and then returns the value of either the second or third operand, depending on whether the value of the first was true or false, respectively. Example 2-62 uses this to pick the larger of two values. (This is just for illustration. In practice, you'd normally use .NET's Math.Max method, which has the same effect but is rather more readable. Math.Max also has the benefit that if you use expressions with side effects, it will only evaluate each one once, something you can't do with the approach shown in Example 2-62, because you end up writing each expression twice.)

Example 2-62. The conditional operator

```
int max = (x > y) ? x : y;
```

This illustrates why C and its successors have a reputation for terse syntax. If you are familiar with any language from this family, Example 2-62 will be easy to read, but if you're not, its meaning might not be instantly clear. This will evaluate the expression before the ? symbol, which is (x > y) in this case, and that's required to be an expression that produces a bool. (The parentheses are optional. I put them in to make the code easier to read.) If that is true, the expression between the ? and : symbols is used (x, in this case); otherwise, the expression after the : symbol (y here) is used.

The conditional operator is similar to the conditional AND and OR operators in that it will evaluate only the operands it has to. It always evaluates its first operand, but it will never evaluate both the second and third operands. That means you can handle null values by writing something like Example 2-63. This does not risk causing a NullReferenceException, because it will evaluate the third operand only if s is not null.

Example 2-63. Exploiting conditional evaluation

```
int characterCount = s is null ? 0 : s.Length;
```

However, in some cases, there are simpler ways of dealing with null values. Suppose you have a string variable, and if it's null, you'd like to use the empty string instead.

---

9 Language pedants will note that it will also be meaningful in certain situations where custom implicit conversions to bool are available. We'll get to custom conversions in Chapter 3.

You could write (s is null ? "" : s). But you could just use the *null coalescing* operator instead, because it's designed for precisely this job. This operator, shown in Example 2-64 (it's the ?? symbol), evaluates its first operand, and if that's non-null, that's the result of the expression. If the first operand is null, it evaluates its second operand and uses that instead.

Example 2-64. The null coalescing operator

```
string neverNull = s ?? "";
```

We could combine a null-conditional operator with the null coalescing operator to provide a more succinct alternative to Example 2-63, shown in Example 2-65.

Example 2-65. Null-conditional and null coalescing operators

```
int characterCount = s?.Length ?? 0;
```

One of the main benefits offered by the conditional, null-conditional, and null coalescing operators is that they often allow you to write a single expression in cases where you would otherwise have needed to write considerably more code. This can be particularly useful if you're using the expression as an argument to a method, as in Example 2-66.

Example 2-66. Conditional expression as method argument

```
FadeVolume(gateOpen ? MaxVolume : 0.0, FadeDuration, FadeCurve.Linear);
```

Compare this with what you'd need to write if the conditional operator did not exist. You would need an if statement. (I'll get to if statements in the next section, but since this book is not for novices, I'm assuming you're familiar with the rough idea.) And you'd either need to introduce a local variable, as Example 2-67 does, or you'd need to duplicate the method call in the two branches of the if/else, changing just the first argument. So, terse though the conditional and null coalescing operators are, they can remove a lot of clutter from your code.

Example 2-67. Life without the conditional operator

```
double targetVolume;
if (gateOpen)
{
    targetVolume = MaxVolume;
}
else
{
    targetVolume = 0.0;
```

```
}
FadeVolume(targetVolume, FadeDuration, FadeCurve.Linear);
```

There is one last set of operators to look at: the *compound assignment* operators. These combine assignment with some other operation and are available for the +, -, *, /, %, <<, >>, &, ^, |, and ?? operators. They enable you not to have to write the sort of code shown in Example 2-68.

Example 2-68. Assignment and addition

```
x = x + 1;
```

We can write this assignment statement more compactly as the code in Example 2-69. All the compound assignment operators take this form—you just stick an = on the end of the original operator.

Example 2-69. Compound assignment (addition)

```
x += 1;
```

This is a distinctive syntax that makes it very clear that we are modifying the value of a variable in some particular way. So, although those two snippets perform identical work, many developers find the second idiomatically preferable.

That's not quite a comprehensive list of operators. There are a few more specialized ones that I'll get to once we've looked at the areas of the language for which they were defined. (Some relate to classes and other types, some to inheritance, some to collections, and some to delegates. There are chapters coming up on all of these.) By the way, although I've been describing which operators are available on which types, it's possible to write a custom type that defines its own meanings for most of these. That's how .NET's `BigInteger` type can support the same arithmetic operations as the built-in numeric types. I'll show how this can be done in Chapter 3.

Flow Control

Most of the code we have examined so far executes statements in the order they are written and stops when it reaches the end. If that were the only possible way in which execution could flow through our code, C# would not be very useful. So, as you'd expect, it has a variety of constructs for writing loops and for deciding which code to execute based on inputs.

Boolean Decisions with if Statements

An `if` statement decides whether or not to run some particular statement depending on the value of a `bool` expression. For example, the `if` statement in Example 2-70 will execute the block statement that shows a message only if the `age` variable's value is less than 18.

Example 2-70. Simple if statement

```
if (age < 18)
{
    Console.WriteLine("You are too young to buy alcohol in a bar in the UK.");
}
```

You don't have to use a block statement with an `if` statement. You can use any statement type as the body. A block is necessary only if you want the `if` statement to govern the execution of multiple statements. However, some coding style guidelines recommend using a block in all cases. This is partly for consistency but also because it avoids a possible error when modifying the code at a later date: if you have a non-block statement as the body of an `if`, and then you add another statement after that, intending it to be part of the same body, it can be easy to forget to add a block around the two statements, leading to code like that in Example 2-71. The indentation suggests that the developer meant for the final statement to be part of the `if` statement's body, but C# ignores indentation, so that final statement will always run. If you are in the habit of always using a block, you won't make this mistake.

Example 2-71. Probably not what was intended

```
if (authenticationCodesCorrect)
    SendTransferConfirmation();
    TransferFunds();
```

An `if` statement can optionally include an `else` part, which is followed by another statement that runs only if the `if` statement's expression evaluates to `false`. So Example 2-72 will write either the first or the second message, depending on whether the `optimistic` variable is `true` or `false`.

Example 2-72. if and else

```
if (optimistic)
{
    Console.WriteLine("Glass half full");
}
else
{
```

```
    Console.WriteLine("Glass half empty");
}
```

The else keyword can be followed by any statement, and again, this is typically a block. However, there's one scenario in which most developers do not use a block for the body of the else part, and that's when they use another if statement. Example 2-73 shows this—its first if statement has an else part, which has another if statement as its body.

Example 2-73. Picking one of several possibilities

```
if (temperatureInCelsius < 52)
{
    Console.WriteLine("Too cold");
}
else if (temperatureInCelsius > 58)
{
    Console.WriteLine("Too hot");
}
else
{
    Console.WriteLine("Just right");
}
```

This code still looks like it uses a block for that first else, but that block is actually the statement that forms the body of a second if statement. It's that second if statement that is the body of the else. If we were to stick rigidly to the rule of giving each if and else body its own block, we'd rewrite Example 2-73 as Example 2-74. This seems unnecessarily fussy, because the main risk that we're trying to avert by using blocks doesn't really apply in Example 2-73.

Example 2-74. Overdoing the blocks

```
if (temperatureInCelsius < 52)
{
    Console.WriteLine("Too cold");
}
else
{
    if (temperatureInCelsius > 58)
    {
        Console.WriteLine("Too hot");
    }
    else
    {
        Console.WriteLine("Just right");
    }
}
```

Although we can chain if statements together as shown in Example 2-73, C# offers a more specialized statement that can sometimes be easier to read.

Multiple Choice with switch Statements

A switch statement defines multiple groups of statements and either runs one group or does nothing at all, depending on the value of an input expression. As Example 2-75 shows, you put the expression inside parentheses after the switch keyword, and after that, there's a region delimited by braces containing a series of case sections, defining the behavior for each anticipated value for the expression.

Example 2-75. A switch statement with strings

```
switch (workStatus)
{
case "ManagerInRoom":
    WorkDiligently();
    break;

case "HaveNonUrgentDeadline":
case "HaveImminentDeadline":
    CheckSocialMedia();
    CheckEmail();
    CheckSocialMedia();
    ContemplateGettingOnWithSomeWork();
    CheckSocialMedia();
    CheckSocialMedia();
    break;

case "DeadlineOvershot":
    WorkFuriously();
    break;

default:
    CheckSocialMedia();
    CheckEmail();
    break;
}
```

As you can see, a single section can serve multiple possibilities—you can put several different case labels at the start of a section, and the statements in that section will run if any of those cases apply. You can also write a default section, which will run if none of the cases apply. A switch statement does not have to be comprehensive, so if there is no case that matches the expression's value and there is no default section, the switch statement simply does nothing.

Unlike if statements, which take exactly one statement for the body, a case may be followed by multiple statements without needing to wrap them in a block. The sections in Example 2-75 are delimited by break statements, which causes execution to jump to the end of the switch statement. This is not the only way to finish a section—strictly speaking, the rule imposed by the C# compiler is that the end point of the statement list for each case must not be reachable, so anything that causes execution to leave the switch statement is acceptable. You could use a return statement instead, or throw an exception, or you could even use a goto statement.

Some C-family languages (C, for example) allow *fall-through*, meaning that if execution is allowed to reach the end of the statements in a case section, it will continue with the next one. Example 2-76 shows this style, and it is not allowed in C# because of the rule that requires the end of a case statement list not to be reachable.

Example 2-76. C-style fall-through, illegal in C#

```
switch (x)
{
case "One":
    Console.WriteLine("One");
case "Two":   // This line will not compile
    Console.WriteLine("One or two");
    break;
}
```

C# outlaws this, because the vast majority of case sections do not fall through, and when they do in languages that allow it, it's often a mistake caused by the developer forgetting to write a break statement (or some other statement to break out of the switch). Accidental fall-through is likely to produce unwanted behavior, so C# requires more than the mere omission of a break: if you want fall-through, you must ask for it explicitly. As Example 2-77 shows, we use the unloved goto keyword to express that we really do want one case to fall through into the next one.

Example 2-77. Fall-through in C#

```
switch (x)
{
case "One":
    Console.WriteLine("One");
    goto case "Two";
case "Two":
    Console.WriteLine("One or two");
    break;
}
```

This isn't technically a goto statement. It's a goto case statement and can be used only to jump within a switch block. C# also supports more general goto statements—you can add labels to your code and jump around within your methods.

However, `goto` is heavily frowned upon, so the fall-through form offered by `goto`
`case` statements seems to be the only use for this keyword that is considered respectable in modern society.

These examples have all used strings. You can also use `switch` with integer types,
`char`, and any `enum` (a kind of type discussed in the next chapter). But `case` labels
don't necessarily have to be constants: you can also use patterns, which are discussed
later in this chapter.

Loops: while and do

C# supports the usual C-family loop mechanisms. Example 2-78 shows a `while` loop.
This takes a `bool` expression. It evaluates that expression, and if the result is `true`, it
will execute the statement that follows. So far, this is just like an `if` statement, but the
difference is that once the loop's embedded statement is complete, it then evaluates
the expression again, and if it's `true` again, it will execute the embedded statement a
second time. It will keep doing this until the expression evaluates to `false`. As with `if`
statements, the body of the loop does not need to be a block, but it usually is.

Example 2-78. A `while` loop

```
while (!reader.EndOfStream)
{
    Console.WriteLine(reader.ReadLine());
}
```

The body of the loop may decide to finish the loop early with a `break` statement. It
does not matter whether the `while` expression is `true` or `false`—executing a `break`
statement will always terminate the loop.

C# also offers the `continue` statement. Like a `break` statement, this terminates the
current iteration, but unlike `break`, it will then reevaluate the `while` expression, so
iteration may continue. Both `continue` and `break` jump straight to the end of the
loop, but you could think of `continue` as jumping directly to the point just before the
loop's closing }, while `break` jumps to the point just after. By the way, `continue` and
`break` are also available for all of the other loop styles I'm about to show.

Because a `while` statement evaluates its expression before each iteration, it's possible
for a `while` loop not to run its body at all. Sometimes, you may want to write a loop
that runs at least once, only evaluating the `bool` expression after the first iteration.
This is the purpose of a do loop, as shown in Example 2-79.

Example 2-79. A do loop

```
char k;
do
{
    Console.WriteLine("Press x to exit");
    k = Console.ReadKey().KeyChar;
}
while (k != 'x');
```

Notice that Example 2-79 ends in a semicolon, denoting the end of the statement. Compare this with the line containing the while keyword in Example 2-78, which does not, despite otherwise looking very similar. That may look inconsistent, but it's not a typo. Putting a semicolon at the end of the line with the while keyword in Example 2-78 would be legal, but it would change the meaning—it would indicate that we want the body of the while loop to be an empty statement. The block that followed would then be treated as a brand-new statement to execute after the loop completes. The code would get stuck in an infinite loop unless the reader were already at the end of the stream. (The compiler will issue a warning about a "Possible mistaken empty statement" if you do that, by the way.)

C-Style for Loops

Another style of loop that C# inherits from C is the for loop. This is similar to while, but it adds two features to that loop's bool expression: it provides a place to declare and/or initialize one or more variables that will remain in scope for as long as the loop runs, and it provides a place to perform some operation each time around the loop (in addition to the statement that forms the body of the loop). So the structure of a for loop looks like this:

```
for (initializer; condition; iterator) body
```

A very common application of this is to do something to all the elements in an array. Example 2-80 shows a for loop that multiplies every element in an array by 2. The condition part works in exactly the same way as in a while loop—it determines whether the embedded statement forming the loop's body runs, and it will be evaluated before each iteration. Again, the body doesn't strictly have to be a block but usually is.

Example 2-80. Modifying array elements with a for loop

```
for (int i = 0; i < myArray.Length; i++)
{
    myArray[i] *= 2;
}
```

The initializer in this example declares a variable called i and initializes it to 0. The initializer does not need to be a variable declaration—you can use any expression statement—but it's a common choice. The initializer executes just once at the start of the loop, so this variable's lifetime effectively begins just before the loop starts and ends when the loop finishes.

The iterator in Example 2-80 just adds 1 to i. It runs at the end of each loop iteration, after the body runs and before the condition is reevaluated. (So if the condition is initially false, not only does the body not run, the iterator will never be evaluated.) C# does nothing with the result of the iterator expression—it is useful only for its side effects. So it doesn't matter whether you write i++, ++i, i += 1, or even i = i + 1.

A for loop doesn't let you do anything that you couldn't have achieved by writing a while loop and putting the initialization code before the loop and the iterator at the end of the loop body instead.[10] However, there may be readability benefits. A for statement puts the code that defines how we loop in one place, separate from the code that defines what we do each time around the loop, which might help those reading the code to understand what it does. They don't have to scan down to the end of a long loop to find the iterator statement (although a long loop body that trails over pages of code is generally considered to be bad practice, so this last benefit is a little dubious).

Both the initializer and the iterator can contain lists, as Example 2-81 shows, although in this particular case it isn't terribly useful—since all the iterators run every time around, i and j will have the same value as each other throughout.

Example 2-81. Multiple initializers and iterators

```
for (int i = 0, j = 0; i < myArray.Length; i++, j++)
...
```

You can't write a single for loop that performs a multidimensional iteration. If you want that, you would nest one loop inside another, as Example 2-82 illustrates.

Example 2-82. Nested for loops

```
for (int j = 0; j < height; ++j)
{
    for (int i = 0; i < width; ++i)
    {
```

---

10 A continue statement complicates matters, because it provides a way to move to the next iteration without getting all the way to the end of the loop body. Even so, you could still reproduce the effect of the iterator when using continue statements—it would just require more work.

```
        ...
    }
}
```

Although Example 2-80 shows a common enough idiom for iterating through arrays, you will often use a different, more specialized construct.

Collection Iteration with foreach Loops

C# offers a style of loop that is not universal in C-family languages. The foreach loop is designed for iterating through collections. A foreach loop fits this pattern:

```
foreach (item-type iteration-variable in collection) body
```

The *collection* is an expression whose type must match a particular pattern recognized by the compiler. The runtime libraries' IEnumerable<T> interface, which we'll be looking at in Chapter 5, matches this pattern, although the compiler doesn't actually require an implementation of that interface—it just requires the collection to have a GetEnumerator method that resembles the one defined by that interface. Example 2-83 uses foreach to show all the strings in an array. (All arrays provide the method that foreach requires.)

Example 2-83. Iterating over a collection with foreach

```
string[] messages = GetMessagesFromSomewhere();
foreach (string message in messages)
{
    Console.WriteLine(message);
}
```

This loop will run the body once for each item in the array. The *iteration variable* (message, in this example) is different each time around the loop and will refer to the item for the current iteration.

In one way, this is less flexible than the for-based loop shown in Example 2-80: a foreach loop cannot modify the collection it iterates over. That's because not all collections support modification. IEnumerable<T> demands very little of its collections—it does not require modifiability, random access, or even the ability to know up front how many items the collection provides. (In fact, IEnumerable<T> is able to support never-ending collections. For example, it is perfectly legal to write an implementation that will return random numbers for as long as you care to keep fetching values.)

But foreach offers two advantages over for. One advantage is subjective and therefore debatable: it's a bit more readable. But significantly, it's also more general. If you're writing methods that do things to collections, those methods will be more broadly applicable if they use `foreach` rather than `for`, because you'll be able to accept an `IEnumerable<T>`. Example 2-84 can work with any collection that contains strings, rather than being limited to arrays.

Example 2-84. General-purpose collection iteration

```
public static void ShowMessages(IEnumerable<string> messages)
{
    foreach (string message in messages)
    {
        Console.WriteLine(message);
    }
}
```

This code can work with collection types that do not support random access, such as the `LinkedList<T>` class described in Chapter 5. It can also process lazy collections that decide what items to produce on demand, including those produced by iterator functions, also shown in Chapter 5, and by certain LINQ queries, as described in Chapter 10.

Patterns

There's one last essential mechanism to look at in C#: *patterns*. A pattern describes one or more criteria that a value can be tested against. You've already seen some simple patterns in action: each `case` in a `switch` specifies a pattern. But as we'll now see, there are many kinds of patterns, and they aren't just for `switch` statements.

The `switch` examples earlier, such as Example 2-75, used one of the simplest pattern types: they were all *constant patterns*. With these, you specify just a constant value, and an expression matches this pattern if it has that value. Example 2-85 shows a more interesting kind of pattern: it uses *declaration patterns*. An expression matches a declaration pattern if it has the specified type. As you saw earlier in "Object" on page 91, some variables are capable of holding a variety of different types. Variables of type `object` are an extreme case of this, since they can hold more or less anything. Language features such as *interfaces* (discussed in Chapter 3), generics (Chapter 4), and inheritance (Chapter 6) can lead to scenarios where the static type of a variable provides more information than the anything-goes `object` type but still leaves latitude for a range of possible types at runtime. Declaration patterns can be useful in these cases.

Example 2-85. Declaration patterns

```
switch (o)
{
case string s:
```

```
    Console.WriteLine($"A piece of string is {s.Length} long");
    break;

case int i:
    Console.WriteLine($"That's numberwang! {i}");
    break;
}
```

Declaration patterns have an interesting characteristic that constant ones do not: as well as the Boolean match/no-match common to all patterns, a declaration pattern produces an additional output. Each `case` in Example 2-85 introduces a variable, which the code for that `case` then goes on to use. This output is just the input but copied into a variable with the specified static type. So that first `case` will match if o turns out to be a `string`, in which case we can access it through the s variable (which is why that s.Length expression compiles correctly; o.Length would not if o is of type object).

Sometimes, you won't actually need a declaration pattern's output—it might be enough just to know that the input matched a pattern. One way to handle these cases is with a *discard*: if you put an underscore (_) in the place where the output variable name would normally go, that tells the C# compiler that you are only interested in whether the value matches the type. There's a more succinct alternative: *type patterns*. A type pattern looks and works like a declaration pattern without the variable—as Example 2-86 shows, the pattern consists of just the type name.

Example 2-86. Type patterns

```
switch (o)
{
case string:
    Console.WriteLine("This is a piece of string");
    break;

case int:
    Console.WriteLine("That's numberwang!");
    break;
}
```

Some patterns do a little more work to produce their output. For example, Example 2-87 shows a *positional pattern* that matches any tuple containing a pair of int values and extracts those values into two variables, x and y.

Example 2-87. Positional pattern

```
case (int x, int y):
    Console.WriteLine($"I know where it's at: {x}, {y}");
    break;
```

Positional patterns are an example of a *recursive pattern*: they are patterns that contain patterns. In this case, this positional pattern contains a declaration pattern as each of its children. But as Example 2-88 shows, we can use constant values in each position to match tuples with specific values.

Example 2-88. Positional patterns with constant values

```
switch (p)
{
case (0, 0):
    Console.WriteLine("How original");
    break;

case (0, 1):
case (1, 0):
    Console.WriteLine("What an absolute unit");
    break;

case (1, 1):
    Console.WriteLine("Be there and be square");
    break;
}
```

We can mix things up, because positional patterns can contain different pattern types in each position. Example 2-89 shows a positional pattern with a constant pattern in the first position and a declaration pattern in the second.

Example 2-89. Positional pattern with constant and declaration patterns

```
case (0, int y):
    Console.WriteLine($"This is on the X axis at height {y}");
    break;
```

If you are a fan of var, you might be wondering if you can write something like Example 2-90. This will work, and the static types of the x and y variables here will depend on the type of the pattern's input expression. If the compiler can determine how the expression deconstructs (for example, if the switch statement input's static type is an (int, int) tuple), then it will use this information to determine the output variables' static types. In cases where this is unknown, but it's still conceivable that this pattern could match (for example, if the input is object), then x and y here will also have type object.

Example 2-90. Positional pattern with var

```
case (var x, var y):
    Console.WriteLine($"I know where it's at: {x}, {y}");
    break;
```

 The compiler will reject patterns in cases where it can determine that a match is impossible. For example, if it knows the input type is a (string, int, bool) tuple, it cannot possibly match a positional pattern with only two child patterns, so C# won't let you try.

Example 2-90 shows an unusual case where using var instead of an explicit type can introduce a significant change of behavior. These *var patterns* differ in one important respect from the declaration patterns in Example 2-87: a var pattern always matches its input, whereas a declaration pattern inspects its input's type to determine at runtime whether it matches. This check might be optimized away in practice—there are cases where a declaration pattern will always match because its input type is known at compile time. But the only way to express in your code that you definitely don't want the child patterns in a positional pattern to perform a runtime check is to use var. So although a positional pattern containing declaration patterns strongly resembles the deconstruction syntax shown in Example 2-59, the behavior is quite different. Example 2-87 is in effect asking three questions at runtime: Is the value a 2-tuple, is the first value an int, is the second value an int? (So it would work for tuples with a static type of (object, object), as long as each value is an int at runtime.) This shouldn't really be surprising: the point of patterns is to test at runtime whether a value has certain characteristics. However, with some recursive patterns, you may find yourself wanting to express a mixture of runtime matching (for example, is this thing a string?) combined with statically typed deconstruction (for example, if this is a string, I'd like to extract its Length property, which I believe to be of type int, and I want a compiler error if that belief turns out to be wrong). Patterns are not designed to do this, so it's best not to try to use them that way.

What if we don't need to use all of the items in the tuple? You already know one way to handle that. Since we can use any pattern in each position, we could use a declaration pattern that discards its result in, say, the second position: (int x, int _). Or we could use a type pattern: (int x, int). However, Example 2-91 shows a shorter alternative: instead of a type pattern, we can use just a lone underscore. This is a *discard pattern*. You can use it in a recursive pattern anyplace a pattern is required but where you want to indicate that anything will do in that particular position and that you don't need to know what it was.

Example 2-91. Positional pattern with discard pattern

```
case (int x, _):
    Console.WriteLine($"At X: {x}. As for Y, who knows?");
    break;
```

This has subtly different semantics than the discarding declaration pattern or the type pattern: those patterns will check at runtime that the value to be discarded has the specified type, and the pattern will only match if this check succeeds. But a discard pattern always matches, so this would match (10, 20), (10, "Foo"), and (10, (20, 30)), for example.

You might be looking at these tuple patterns and wondering if we can do something similar with lists. C# 11.0 introduced list patterns, enabling us to write the code in Example 2-92.

Example 2-92. List patterns

```
case [int x]:
    Console.WriteLine($"Scalar: {x}");
    break;
case [int x, int y]:
    Console.WriteLine($"2D vector: ({x}, {y})");
    break;
case [int x, int y, int z]:
    Console.WriteLine($"3D vector: ({x}, {y}, {z})");
    break;
```

Each of these patterns starts by asking the question: Is this a list? As you'd expect, arrays qualify, as does the runtime library's List<T>, or indeed anything implementing IList<T>. List patterns don't demand any particular type though. They consider something to be a list if it offers either a Length or Count property, and a numeric indexer. (Indexers are described in "Indexers" on page 205, but in practice, any type that can be used with syntax such as items[42] qualifies.)

 Most patterns perform all their tests at runtime, but list patterns are an exception: the compiler checks that the source type is a list at compile time. This is because it needs to generate different code for different kinds of lists—although List<T> and arrays both support numeric indexing, the compiler emits quite different IL for each.

If the input is a list, the patterns in Example 2-92 will then ask: Is it the right length? (This test *does* happen at runtime.) Suppose the input is an array with two elements. Only the middle pattern will match in that case. Finally, it will test that the two elements match the two patterns supplied—like positional patterns, list patterns are recursive. These examples use declaration patterns, but you can put any pattern you like in each position of a list pattern (including another list pattern, if you are looking for a list of lists).

List patterns don't have to require a fixed size. The .. in Example 2-93 is a *slice pattern*, and it indicates that there can be any number of additional elements at that point. So inputs of ["alpha", "papa", "omega"] or ["alpha", 42, (1.2, true), null, "omega"] would match. Also, ["alpha", "omega"] would match, because a slice will accept zero additional elements. (Slice patterns can appear only inside a list pattern, so these are also new in C# 11.0.)

Example 2-93. A list pattern containing a slice pattern

```
if (list is ["alpha", .., "omega"])
{
    Console.WriteLine("That seems to be in order");
}
```

Example 2-93 is the simplest form of slice pattern: it essentially says we don't care what, if anything, appears at that point in the list. But what if we wanted to do something with that part? The .. can optionally be followed by any other pattern, which will be applied to whichever part of the list the slice represents. Example 2-94 shows a slice pattern that uses a declaration pattern.

Example 2-94. A list pattern containing a slice pattern with a nested pattern

```
if (list is ["alpha", .. string[] theRest, "omega"])
{
    Console.WriteLine(string.Join(", ", theRest));
}
```

This causes an extra compile-time test—the compiler will reject patterns of this kind if it can't determine how to extract the middle section of the list, or if it can, but the resulting type is wrong. (It effectively uses the range syntax, so theRest will be extracted with code equivalent to list[1..^1]. "Addressing Elements with Index and Range Syntax" on page 288 describes this syntax, and not all lists support it.) So Example 2-94 would compile if list was of type string[], but not if it was an IList<T>, because the IList<T> interface doesn't require all implementations to support range indexing. It would also fail if list was a type that did support range indexing but which returned the wrong type. For example, if list were a List<string> (which implements IList<T> but also provides a range indexer—see Chapter 3 for details), then a range indexer would be available, but it returns another List<string>, and since that is incompatible with string[], the compiler would reject Example 2-94. (The declaration pattern for the slice would need to specify

List<string>, or some compatible type such as IEnumerable<string>, instead of string[].)

A slice pattern can use any kind of pattern—it doesn't have to be a declaration pattern. So in addition to checking the list length and all the other nested patterns (checking whether list starts with "alpha" and ends with "omega" in this case) it will also perform whatever runtime tests the slice pattern's nested pattern requires. The whole list pattern only succeeds if all these steps succeed. And in this case, since the nested pattern is a declaration pattern, it will also initialize theRest with an array containing everything except the first and last elements of list.

 A list pattern may contain at most one slice. This is because multiple slices would significantly increase the complexity of pattern matching. To match [1, .., 2] requires a length check (>=2) and to inspect the first and last elements. But to match [1, .., 2, 3, .. 4] would involve searching the entire list to see if the values 2 and 3 occur consecutively at any point. That would be a powerful capability, but it would make it easy to write very expensive or ambiguous patterns by mistake.

Positional and list patterns are not the only recursive ones: you can also write a *property pattern*. We'll look at properties in detail in the next chapter, but for now it's enough to know that they are members of a type that provide some sort of information, such as the string type's Length property, which returns an int telling you how many code units the string contains. Example 2-95 shows a property pattern that inspects this Length property.

Example 2-95. Property pattern

```
case string { Length: 0 }:
    Console.WriteLine("How long is a piece of string? Not very!");
    break;
```

This property pattern starts with a type name, so it effectively incorporates the behavior of a type pattern in addition to its property-based tests. (You can omit this in cases where the type of the pattern's input is sufficiently specific to identify the property. For example, if the input in this case already had a static of type string, we could omit this.) This is then followed by a section in braces listing each of the properties that the pattern wants to inspect and the pattern to apply for that property. (These child patterns are what make this another recursive pattern.) So this example first checks to see if the input is a string. If it is, it then applies a constant pattern to the string's Length, so this pattern matches only if the input is a string with Length of 0.

Property patterns can optionally specify an output. Example 2-95 doesn't do this. Example 2-96 shows the syntax, although in this particular case it's not terribly useful because this pattern will ensure that s only ever refers to an empty string.

Example 2-96. Property pattern with output

```
case string { Length: 0 } s:
    Console.WriteLine($"How long is a piece of string? This long: {s.Length}");
    break;
```

Since each property in a property pattern contains a nested pattern, those too can produce outputs, as Example 2-97 shows.

Example 2-97. Property pattern with nested pattern with output

```
case string { Length: int length }:
    Console.WriteLine($"How long is a piece of string? This long: {length}");
    break;
```

You can nest property patterns within property patterns. Example 2-98 uses this to inspect the operating system version reported by Environment.OSVersion, testing whether the major version is equal to 10.

Example 2-98. Property pattern with nested property pattern

```
switch (Environment.OSVersion)
{
    case { Version: { Major: 10 } }:
        Console.WriteLine("Windows 10, 11, or later");
        break;
}
```

There is a more succinct way to express this. You can replace the case in Example 2-98 with Example 2-99. It has exactly the same effect but is a more compact, and arguably more readable, expression of the intent.

Example 2-99. Extended property pattern

```
case { Version.Major: 10 }:
    Console.WriteLine("Windows 10, 11, or later");
    break;
```

Combining and Negating Patterns

C# offers three logical operations for use in patterns: and, or, and not. The simplest of these is not, and it lets you invert the meaning of a pattern. Example 2-100 uses this to ensure it runs certain code only if a variable is non-null. This applies negation (not) to a constant pattern: the null here is interpreted as a constant pattern. If we had written just null, the pattern would match when the value is null, but with not null the pattern matches when it is not.

Example 2-100. Detecting non-nullness with pattern negation

```
case not null:
    Console.WriteLine($"User's middle name is: {middleName}");
    break;
```

We can use and and or to combine pairs of patterns. (These are officially called *conjunctive* and *disjunctive* patterns; apparently the C# language designers are fans of formal propositional logic.) If we combine two patterns with and, the result is a pattern that matches only if both of the constituent patterns match. For example, if you wanted to write code that had something against my middle name, you could use the approach shown in Example 2-101. This also shows that you can use a mixture of these logical operations: this uses both and and not.

Example 2-101. Using pattern conjunction (and) and negation (not)

```
case not null and not "David":
    Console.WriteLine($"User's middle name is: {middleName}");
    break;
```

We can use or in a similar way, and the effect is a pattern that matches its input if either of its constituent patterns matches. You can build up larger combinations through repeated use of and and/or or.

Relational Patterns

Patterns can use the <, <=, >=, and > operators when the pattern's type supports these kinds of comparison. Example 2-102 shows a switch statement that includes two *relational patterns*, as patterns based on these operators are called.

Example 2-102. Relational patterns

```
switch (value)
{
case > 0: Console.WriteLine("Positive"); break;
case < 0: Console.WriteLine("Negative"); break;
default: Console.WriteLine("Neither strictly positive nor negative"); break;
};
```

You can use relational patterns in any place that any other pattern can be used. So they could appear inside a positional pattern (e.g., if you wanted to match points on the Y axis, above the X axis you could write (0, > 0)). Example 2-103 uses two relational patterns as the constituents of a conjunction to express the requirement that a value falls within a particular range.

Example 2-103. Using relational patterns in a conjunction

```
case >= 168 and <= 189:
    Console.WriteLine("Is within inner 90 percentiles");
    break;
```

Relational patterns support comparisons only with constants. You cannot replace the numbers in the preceding examples with variables.

Getting More Specific with when

Sometimes, the built-in pattern types won't provide the level of precision you need. For example, with positional patterns, we've seen how to write patterns that match, say, any pair of values, or any pair of numbers, or a pair of numbers where one has a particular value. But what if you want to match a pair of numbers where the first is higher than the second? This isn't a big conceptual leap, but there's no built-in support for this—relational patterns can't do this because they can compare only with constants. We could detect the condition with an if statement of course, but it would seem a shame to have to restructure our code from a switch to a series of if and else statements just to make this small step forward. Fortunately we don't have to.

Any pattern in a case label can be qualified by adding a when clause. It allows a Boolean expression to be included. This will be evaluated if the value matches the main part of the pattern, and the value will match the pattern as a whole only if the when clause is true. Example 2-104 shows a positional pattern with a when clause that matches pairs of numbers in which the first number is larger than the second.

Example 2-104. Pattern with when clause

```
case (int w, int h) when w > h:
    Console.WriteLine("Landscape");
    break;
```

Patterns in Expressions

All of the patterns I've shown so far appear in case labels as part of a switch statement. This is not the only way to use patterns. They can also appear inside expressions. To see how this can be useful, look first at the switch statement in Example 2-105. The intent here is to return a single value determined by the input, but it's a little clumsy: I have had to write four separate `return` statements to express that.

Example 2-105. Patterns, but not in expressions

```
switch (shape)
{
    case (int w, int h) when w < h: return "Portrait";
    case (int w, int h) when w > h: return "Landscape";
    case (int _, int _): return "Square";
    default: return "Unknown";
}
```

Example 2-106 shows code that performs the same job but rewritten to use a *switch expression*. As with a `switch` statement, a `switch` expression contains a list of patterns. The difference is that whereas labels in a `switch` statement are followed by a list of statements, in a `switch` expression each pattern is followed by a single expression. The value of a `switch` expression is the result of evaluating the expression associated with the first pattern that matches.

Example 2-106. A switch expression

```
return shape switch
{
    (int w, int h) when w < h => "Portrait",
    (int w, int h) when w > h => "Landscape",
    (int _, int _) => "Square",
    _ => "Unknown"
};
```

`switch` expressions look quite different than `switch` statements, because they don't use the `case` keyword. Instead, they just dive straight in with the pattern, and then use => between the pattern and its corresponding expression. There are a few reasons for this. First, it makes `switch` expressions a bit more compact. Expressions are generally used inside other things—in this case, the `switch` expression is the value of a `return` statement, but you might also use these as a method argument or anywhere else an expression is allowed—so we generally want them to be succinct. Secondly, using `case` here could have led to confusion because the rules for what follows each `case` would be different for `switch` statements and `switch` expressions: in a `switch` statement, each `case` label is followed by one or more statements, but in a `switch` expression, each pattern needs to be followed by a single expression. Finally, although `switch` expressions were added to C# fairly recently, this sort of construct has been around in other languages for many years. C#'s version of it more closely resembles equivalents from other languages than it would have done if the expression form used the `case` keyword.

Notice that the final pattern in Example 2-106 is a discard pattern. This will match anything, and it's there to ensure that the pattern is exhaustive, i.e., that it covers all possible cases. (It has a similar effect to a `default` section in a `switch` statement.) Unlike a `switch` statement, where it's OK for there to be no matches, a `switch` expression has to produce a result, so the compiler will warn you if your patterns don't handle all possible cases for the input type. It would complain in this situation if we were to remove that final case, assuming the `shape` input is of type `object`. (Conversely, if `shape` were of type (`int, int`), we would have to remove that final case, because the first three cases in fact cover all possible values for that type and the compiler will produce an error telling us that the final pattern will never apply.) If you ignore this warning, and then at runtime you evaluate a `switch` expression with an unmatchable value, it will throw a `SwitchExpressionException`. Exceptions are described in Chapter 8.

There's one more way to use a pattern in an expression, and that's with the `is` keyword. It turns any pattern into a Boolean expression. Example 2-107 shows a simple example that determines whether a value is a tuple containing two integers.

Example 2-107. An is expression

```
bool isPoint = value is (int, int);
```

This also provides a way to ensure that a value is non-null before proceeding. Example 2-108 combines a negation with a constant pattern testing for `null`.

Example 2-108. Testing for non-nullness with is

```
if (s is not null)
{
    Console.WriteLine(s.Length);
}
```

You might be wondering why we wouldn't just write `s != null`. In most cases that will work, but it has a potential problem: types are free to customize the behavior of comparison operators such as `!=`. The advantage of the approach in Example 2-108 is that it will invariably perform just a simple comparison with `null` even with types that have customized the behavior of `!=` and `==`. (The positive form, `is null`, has the same advantage.)

As with patterns in `switch` statements or expressions, the pattern in an `is` expression can extract values from its source. Like Example 2-107, the pattern in Example 2-109 tests whether a value is a tuple containing two integers but goes on to use the two values from the tuple.

Example 2-109. Using the values from an `is` expression's pattern

```
if (value is (int x, int y))
{
    Console.WriteLine($"X: {x}, Y: {y}");
}
```

New variables introduced in this way by an `is` expression remain in scope after their containing statement. So in both these examples, x and y would continue to be in scope until the end of the containing block. Since the pattern in Example 2-109 is in the `if` statement's condition expression, that means these variables remain in scope after the body block. However, if you try to use them outside of the body, you'll find that the compiler's definite assignment rules will tell you that they are uninitialized. It allows Example 2-109 because it knows that the body of the `if` statement will run only if the pattern matches, so in that case x and y will have been initialized and are safe to use.

Patterns in `is` expressions cannot include a when clause. It would be redundant: the result is a Boolean expression, so you can just add on any qualification you require using the normal Boolean operators, as Example 2-110 shows.

Example 2-110. No need for when in an `is` expression's pattern

```
if (value is (int w, int h) && w < h)
{
    Console.WriteLine($"(Portrait) Width: {w}, Height: {h}");
}
```

Summary

In this chapter, I showed the nuts and bolts of C# code—variables, statements, expressions, basic data types, operators, flow control, and patterns. Now it's time to take a look at the broader structure of a program. All code in C# programs must belong to a type, and types are the topic of the next chapter.

CHAPTER 3

Types

C# does not limit us to the built-in data types shown in Chapter 2. You can define your own types. In fact, you have no choice: if you want to write code at all, C# requires that code to be inside a type. For the special case of our program's entry point, we might not have to declare the type explicitly, but it's still there. Everything we write, and any functionality we consume from the .NET runtime libraries (or any other .NET library), will belong to a type.

C# recognizes multiple kinds of types. I'll begin with the most important.

Classes

Most of the types you work with in C# will be *classes*. A class can contain both code and data, and it can choose to make some of its features publicly available while keeping others accessible only to code within the class. So classes offer a mechanism for *encapsulation*—they can define a clear public programming interface for other people to use while keeping internal implementation details inaccessible.

If you're familiar with object-oriented languages, this will all seem very ordinary. If you're not, then you might want to read a more introductory-level book first, because this book is not meant to teach programming. I'll just describe the details specific to C# classes.

I've already shown examples of classes in earlier chapters, but let's look at the structure in more detail. Example 3-1 shows a simple class. (For information about names for types and their members, see the sidebar "Naming Conventions" on page 121.)

Example 3-1. A simple class

```
public class Counter
{
    private int _count;

    public int GetNextValue()
    {
        _count += 1;
        return _count;
    }
}
```

Class definitions always contain the `class` keyword followed by the name of the class. C# does not need the name to match the containing file, nor does it limit you to having one class in a file. That said, most C# projects make the class and filenames match by convention. In any case, class names must follow the basic rules described in Chapter 2 for identifiers such as variables; e.g., they cannot start with a number.

The first line of Example 3-1 contains an additional keyword: `public`. Class definitions can optionally specify *accessibility*, which determines what other code is allowed to use the class. Ordinary classes have just two choices here: `public` and `internal`, with the latter being the default. (As I'll show later, you can nest classes inside other types, and nested classes have a slightly wider range of accessibility options.) An internal class is available for use only within the component that defines it. So if you are writing a class library, you are free to define classes that exist purely as part of your library's implementation: by marking them as `internal`, you prevent the rest of the world from using them.

You can choose to make your internal types visible to selected external components. Microsoft sometimes does this with its libraries. The runtime libraries are spread across numerous individual DLLs each of which defines many internal types, and some internal features are used by multiple DLLs. This is made possible by annotating a component with the `[assembly: InternalsVisibleTo ("name")]` attribute, specifying the name of the component with which you wish to share. (Chapter 14 describes this in more detail.) For example, you might want to make every class in your application visible to a test project so that you can write unit tests for code that you don't intend to make publicly available.

Starting with C# 11.0, you can write the `file` keyword instead of specifying the accessibility. This makes the class inaccessible outside of the file in which it was defined. This is intended for code generators—it enables them to define classes without having to worry about whether the chosen name will clash with classes defined elsewhere in the project. This works by changing the name of the type at compile time to ensure that it is unique.

The `Counter` class in Example 3-1 has chosen to be `public`, but that doesn't mean it has to make everything accessible. It defines two members—a field called `_count` that holds an `int` and a method called `GetNextValue` that operates on the information in that field. Fields are a kind of variable, but unlike a local variable, whose scope and lifetime is determined by its containing method, a field is tied to its containing type. `GetNextValue` is able to refer to the `_count` field by its unqualified name because fields are in scope within their defining class.

As is very common with object-oriented programming, this class has chosen to make the data member private, exposing public functionality through a method. Accessibility modifiers are optional for members, just as they are for classes, and again, they default to the most restrictive option available: `private`, in this case. So I could have left off the `private` keyword in Example 3-1 without changing the meaning, but I prefer to be explicit. (If you leave it unspecified, people reading your code may wonder whether the omission was deliberate or accidental.)

Naming Conventions

Microsoft defines a set of conventions for publicly visible identifiers, which it (mostly) conforms to in its class libraries, and I usually follow them in my examples. The .NET SDK incorporates a code analyzer that can help enforce these conventions. It is enabled by default. If you just want to read a description of the rules, they're part of the design guidelines for .NET class libraries (*https://oreil.ly/rlyqm*).

In these conventions, the first letter of a class name is capitalized, and if the name contains multiple words, each new word also starts with a capital letter. (For historical reasons, this convention is called *Pascal casing*, or sometimes *PascalCasing* as a self-referential example.) Although it's legal in C# for identifiers to contain underscores, the conventions don't allow them in class names. Methods also use Pascal casing, as do properties. Fields are rarely public, but when they are, they use the same casing.

Method parameters use a different convention known as *camelCasing*, in which uppercase letters are used at the start of all but the first word. The name refers to the way this convention produces one or more humps in the middle of the word.

The class library design guidelines remain silent regarding implementation details. (The original purpose of these rules was to ensure a consistent feel across the whole public API of the .NET runtime libraries.) So these rules say nothing about how private fields are named. I've used an underscore prefix in Example 3-1 because I like fields to look different from local variables. This makes it easy to see what sort of data my code is working with, and it can also help to avoid situations where method parameter names clash with field names. (Microsoft often uses this same convention for instance fields in the .NET runtime libraries, along with s_ and t_ prefixes for static and thread-local fields.) Some people find this convention ugly and prefer not to distinguish fields visibly but might choose to always access members through the this reference (described later) so that the distinction between variable and field access is still clear.

To use our Counter class, we must create an instance of it. As Example 3-2 shows, we do this using the new keyword followed by the class name. Our Counter class doesn't require any inputs upon creation, so the type name is followed in this case by a pair of parentheses, representing an empty argument list.

Example 3-2. Using a custom class

```
var c1 = new Counter();
Console.WriteLine($"c1: {c1.GetNextValue()}");
Console.WriteLine($"c1: {c1.GetNextValue()}");
Console.WriteLine($"c1: {c1.GetNextValue()}");
```

Running this produces the following output:

```
c1: 1
c1: 2
c1: 3
```

Initialization Inputs

When running that last example, the first call to GetNextValue returned 1. That's because the CLR automatically initializes the _count field to 0 when a Counter is created. What if we wanted a different start value when creating a Counter? A class can specify its initial inputs by defining special members called *constructors*. Example 3-3 shows a variation on the Counter. This CounterWithPrimaryConstructor has a constructor requiring a single argument of type int.

Example 3-3. A class with a primary constructor

```
public class CounterWithPrimaryConstructor(int count)
{
    public int GetNextValue()
```

```
    {
        count += 1;
        return count;
    }
}
```

This syntax, in which the class name is followed by one or more parameters in parentheses, defines a *primary constructor*. This is a new feature of C# 12.0. (This syntax was available only for record types before.) As you'll see in "Constructors" on page 162, constructors are commonly defined inside the body of the class, and look very similar to methods. A primary constructor is much more succinct, because we just write a parameter list. It has no body, so it can't contain any code, and while that certainly enables it to be compact, it also makes primary constructors more limited than the other kinds we'll see later. But if you just want to pass some arguments into a class, their compact style can be appealing.

A primary constructor has two special characteristics. First, the parameters it defines are in scope anywhere in the class. That's why Example 3-3 didn't need a field to hold the count—not only does count define a required constructor argument, it also acts as a variable that we can read or modify anywhere inside the class. (The rules of the language don't dictate exactly how the compiler should make this work, but in practice it generates a hidden field to store the value when we use a primary constructor parameter in this way.) Second, primary constructors must be used when present. As you'll see later, it's possible to define multiple constructors, but if a primary constructor is defined, all other constructors must defer to it. The practical implication of this is that if a class has a primary constructor, you can be confident that any parameters it defines will always be properly initialized.

With a primary constructor defined, I need to pass an argument to new when I construct an instance of this type, as Example 3-4 shows.

Example 3-4. Using multiple instances of a class with a primary constructor

```
var c1 = new CounterWithPrimaryConstructor(0);
var c2 = new CounterWithPrimaryConstructor(10);
Console.WriteLine($"c1: {c1.GetNextValue()}");
Console.WriteLine($"c1: {c1.GetNextValue()}");
Console.WriteLine($"c1: {c1.GetNextValue()}");

Console.WriteLine($"c2: {c2.GetNextValue()}");

Console.WriteLine($"c1: {c1.GetNextValue()}");
```

Since this example uses new twice, I get two Counter objects, each initialized with a different starting count. The program's output shows the effect:

```
c1: 1
c1: 2
c1: 3
c2: 11
c1: 4
```

As you'd expect, the first instance counts up each time we call GetNextValue. When we switch to the second counter, a new sequence starts at 11 (one higher than the value supplied to the constructor). But when we go back to the first counter, it carries on from where it left off. This demonstrates that each instance has its own count. (The same would be true of the _count field in Example 3-1.) But what if we don't want that? Sometimes you will want to keep track of information that doesn't relate to any single object.

Static Members

The static keyword lets us declare that a member is not associated with any particular instance of the class. Example 3-5 shows a modified version of the Counter class from Example 3-1. I've added two new members, both static, for tracking and reporting counts across all instances. (Primary constructor parameters are always per-instance, so if you want this per-class behavior, you have to define a field. I could have continued to use a primary constructor argument instead of the per-instance _count field, but I've chosen to use fields for both here to highlight the difference between static and nonstatic fields.)

Example 3-5. Class with static members

```
public class CounterWithTotal
{
    private int _count;
    private static int _totalCount;

    public int GetNextValue()
    {
        _count += 1;
        _totalCount += 1;
        return _count;
    }

    public static int TotalCount => _totalCount;
}
```

`TotalCount` reports the count, but it doesn't do any work—it just returns a value that the class keeps up to date, and as I'll explain in "Properties" on page 194, this makes it an ideal candidate for being a property rather than a method. The static field `_total Count` keeps track of the total number of calls to `GetNextValue` across all instances of `CounterWithTotal`, unlike the nonstatic `_count`, which just tracks calls to the current instance.

> The => syntax in the `TotalCount` property lets us define the property with a single expression—in this case, whenever code reads the `CounterWithTotal.TotalCount` property, the result will be the value of the `_totalCount` field. As we'll see later, there are ways to write more complex properties, but this is a common approach for simple, read-only properties.

Notice that I'm free to use that static field inside `GetNextValue` in exactly the same way as I use the nonstatic `_count`. The difference is that no matter how many instances of `CounterWithTotal` I create, they each get their own `_count`, but they all share the one and only `_totalCount`. So if I created two instances of `CounterWithTotal`, and called `GetNextValue` twice on the first, and three times on the second, `Counter WithTotal.TotalCount` would return the value 5, the sum of the two counts. To access a static member, I just write *ClassName.MemberName*. In fact, I've been using static member access many times already: the various examples that display output have all used the `Console` class's static `WriteLine` method.

Because I've declared `TotalCount` as a static property, the code it contains has access only to other static members. If it tried to use the nonstatic `_count` field or call the nonstatic `GetNextValue` method from inside the `TotalCount` implementation, the compiler would complain. (Similarly, primary constructor parameters are inaccessible to static members. We supply constructor arguments to new each time we create an instance, so these are inherently associated with a particular instance.) Replacing `_totalCount` with `_count` in the `TotalCount` property results in this error:

```
error CS0120: An object reference is required for the non-static field, method,
  or property Counter._count'
```

Since nonstatic fields are associated with a particular instance of a class, C# needs to know which instance to use. With a nonstatic method or property, that'll be whichever instance the method or property itself was invoked on. So in Example 3-4, I wrote either `c1.GetNextValue()` or `c2.GetNextValue()` to choose which of my two objects to use. C# passed the reference stored in either `c1` or `c2`, respectively, as an implicit hidden first argument. You can get hold of that reference from code inside a class by using the `this` keyword. Example 3-6 shows an alternative way we could have written the first line of `GetNextValue` from Example 3-5, indicating explicitly that we believe _count is a member of the instance on which the GetNextValue method was invoked.

Example 3-6. The this keyword

```
this._count += 1;
```

Explicit member access through this is sometimes necessary due to name collisions. Although all the members of a class are in scope for any code in the same class, the code in a method does not share a *declaration space* with the class. Remember from Chapter 2 that a declaration space is a region of code in which a single name must not refer to two different entities, and since methods do not share theirs with the containing class, you are allowed to declare local variables and method parameters that have the same name as class members. This can easily happen if you don't use a convention such as an underscore prefix for field names. You don't get an error in this case—locals and parameters just hide the class members. But you can still get at the class members by qualifying access with this.

Static methods don't get to use the this keyword, because they are not associated with any particular instance. Also, be aware that because primary constructor arguments are not fields, they cannot be accessed through this. The compiler might choose to generate a field to store them, but from our code's perspective they are just arguments.

Static Classes

Some classes only provide static members. There are several examples in the System.Threading namespace, which contains various classes that offer multithreading utilities. For example, the Interlocked class provides atomic, lock-free, read-modify-write operations; the LazyInitializer class provides helper methods for performing deferred initialization in a way that guarantees to avoid double initialization in multithreaded environments. These classes provide services only through static methods. It makes no sense to create instances of these types, because there's no useful per-instance information they could hold.

You can declare that your class is intended to be used this way by putting the static keyword in front of the class keyword. This compiles the class in a way that prevents instances of it from being constructed. Anyone attempting to construct instances of a class designed to be used this way clearly doesn't understand what it does, so the compiler error will be a useful prod in the direction of the documentation.

You can declare that you want to be able to invoke static methods on certain classes without naming the class every time. This can be useful if you are writing code that makes heavy use of the static methods supplied by a particular type. (This isn't limited to static classes, by the way. You can use this technique with any class that has static members, but it is likely to be most useful with classes whose members are all static.) Example 3-7 uses a static method (Sin) and a static property (PI) of the Math class (in the System namespace). It also uses the Console class's static WriteLine method. (I'm showing the entire source file in this and the next example because the using directives are particularly important. The first example doesn't need a using System; because default implicit global usings make this available everywhere.)

Example 3-7. Using static members normally

```
public static class Normal
{
    public static void UseStatics()
    {
        Console.WriteLine(Math.Sin(Math.PI / 4));
    }
}
```

Example 3-8 is exactly equivalent, but the line that invokes the three static members does not qualify any of them with their defining class's name.

Example 3-8. Using static members without explicit qualification

```
using static System.Console;
using static System.Math;

public static class WithoutQualification
{
    public static void UseStatics()
    {
        WriteLine(Sin(PI / 4));
    }
}
```

To utilize this less verbose alternative, you must declare which classes you want to use in this way with using static directives. Whereas using directives normally specify a namespace, enabling types in that namespace to be used without qualification, using static directives specify a class, enabling its static members to be used without qualification. By the way, as you saw in Chapter 1, you can add the global keyword to using directives. That works for using static directives too, so if you want, say, the Math type's static members to be available without qualification in any file in your project, you can write global using static System.Math; in just one file, and it will apply to all of them.

Records

Although encapsulation is a powerful tool for managing complexity in software development, it can sometimes be useful to have types that just hold information. We might want to represent a message sent over a network, or a row from a table in a database, for example. Types designed for this are sometimes referred to as *POD types*, where POD stands for plain old data. We might try to do this by writing a class containing nothing but public fields, as Example 3-9 shows.

Example 3-9. Plain old data, using public fields

```
public class Person
{
    public string? Name;
    public string? FavoriteColor;
}
```

Some developers will recoil in horror at the lack of encapsulation here. There's nothing to stop anyone from reaching into a `Person` instance and just changing the fields—oh, the humanity! In a type that was doing anything more than just holding some data, that could indeed cause problems. The type's methods might contain code that relies on those fields being used in particular ways, and the problem with making fields public is that anything could change them, making it hard to know what state they will be in. But this type has no code—its only job is to hold some data, so this won't be the end of the world. That said, this example has created a problem: these fields contain strings, but I've had to put a ? after the type name. This signifies the fact that these fields might contain the special value `null`. If I don't add those ? qualifiers, the compiler will issue a warning telling me that I've done nothing to ensure that these fields are suitably initialized, and so I shouldn't go around claiming that they are definitely going to contain strings. If I wanted to require that these fields always have non-null values, I'd need to take control of how the type is initialized, which I can do by writing a constructor. Example 3-10 does this using C# 12.0's new primary constructor syntax to ensure that the fields are initialized, enabling us to remove the ? qualifiers.

Example 3-10. Enforcing initialization of fields with a constructor

```
public class Person(string name, string favoriteColor)
{
    public string Name = name;
    public string FavoriteColor = favoriteColor;
}
```

Earlier, in the `CounterWithPrimaryConstructor`, I mentioned that the compiler generated a hidden field to make the value of the constructor parameter available across the class, so you might be wondering if Example 3-10 is going to end up with two fields for each value. It won't, because the compiler only generates the hidden field if it has to. In this case it will see that the only place we're using the constructor arguments is the field initializers, and since the compiler ends up putting field initializer code into the constructor, it doesn't need to generate additional fields in this case.

This is now looking slightly more verbose than we might like—I've ended up writing each name three times over: once as primary constructor argument, once as a field name, and once where we initialize the field with the constructor argument. Record types offer a simpler way to write a plain old data type, as Example 3-11 shows.

Example 3-11. A record type with a primary constructor

```
public record Person(string Name, string FavoriteColor);
```

Example 3-12 shows how we can use this record type. If we have a variable referring to a `Person`, like the `p` argument in the `ShowPerson` method, we can write `p.Name` and `p.FavoriteColor` to access the data it contains, just as we would if `Person` were defined as in Examples 3-9 or 3-10. (My record type isn't exactly equivalent. Those earlier examples both define public fields, but Example 3-12 is better aligned with normal .NET practice, because it defines `Name` and `FavoriteColor` as properties. I'll be describing properties in more detail later in this chapter.) As you can see, we create instances of record types with the `new` keyword, just as we do with a class. When a record type has a primary constructor as Example 3-11 does, we have to pass in all of the properties to the constructor, and in the right order. A record's primary constructor is also referred to as the *positional syntax* to contrast it with the object initializer syntax I'll be showing later.[1]

Example 3-12. Using a record type

```
void ShowPerson(Person p)
{
    Console.WriteLine($"{p.Name}'s favorite color is {p.FavoriteColor}");
}

var ian = new Person("Ian", "Blue");
var deborah = new Person("Deborah", "Green");
```

---

1 There are two names because `record` introduced this syntax several years before other types, and *positional syntax* was once the only name for it. The name *primary constructor* is new in C# 12.0, and you will sometimes see the older name used when talking about records.

```
ShowPerson(ian);
ShowPerson(deborah);
```

When you use the syntax in Example 3-11, the resulting record type is immutable: if you wrote code that tried to modify either of the properties of an existing `Person`, the compiler would report an error. Immutable data types can make it much easier to analyze code, especially multithreaded code, because you can count on them not to change under your feet. This is one of the reasons strings are immutable in .NET. However, before record types were introduced, immutable custom types were typically inconvenient to work with in C#. For example, if you need to produce some new value that is a modified version of an existing value, you can be in for a lot of tedious work. Whereas the built-in `string` type provides numerous methods for producing new strings built out of existing strings (e.g., substrings, or conversions to lower- or uppercase), you're on your own when you write a class.

For example, suppose you are writing an application in which you've defined a data type representing the state of someone's payment account at a particular moment in time. If you define this as an immutable type, then when processing a new transaction, you will need to make a copy that's identical except for the current balance. Historically, doing this in C# meant you ended up needing to write code to copy over any unchanged data when creating the new instance. The main purpose of record types is to make it much easier to define and use immutable data types, so they offer an easy way to create a copy of an existing instance but with certain properties modified. As Example 3-13 shows, you can write `with` after a record expression, followed by a brace-delimited list of the properties you'd like to change.

Example 3-13. Making a modified copy of an immutable record

```
var startingRecord = new Person("Ian", "Blue");
var modifiedCopy = startingRecord with
{
    FavoriteColor = "Green"
};
```

In this particular case, our type has only two properties, so this isn't dramatically better than just writing `new Person(startingRecord.Name, "Green")`. However, for records with larger numbers of properties, this syntax is much more convenient than rebuilding the whole thing every time.

While records make it much easier to create and use immutable data types, they don't have to be immutable. Example 3-14 shows a `Person` record in which the properties can be modified after construction. (The `{ get; set; }` syntax indicates that these are auto-implemented properties. I'll be describing them in more detail later, but they are essentially just simple read/write properties.)

Example 3-14. A record type with modifiable properties

```
public record Person(string Name, string FavoriteColor)
{
    public string Name { get; set; } = Name;
    public string FavoriteColor { get; set; } = FavoriteColor;
}
```

At this point, we're very nearly back to what we had in Example 3-10, with the only obvious difference being that `Name` and `FavoriteColor` are now properties instead of fields. (Also, the primary constructor parameter names are Pascal-cased here. That matters because a `record` will always ensure that there is a property for each primary constructor parameter. If the first constructor parameter were called `name`, we'd end up with a property called `name` as well as the property called `Name`. That didn't happen in Example 3-10 because only record types require each primary constructor parameter to have a corresponding property.) We could just replace the `record` keyword in this example with `class` and it would still compile. So what exactly changes when we make this a `record`?

Although the primary purpose of records is to make it easy to build immutable data types, the `record` keyword also adds a couple of useful features. In addition to the `with` syntax for building modified copies, records get built-in support for equality testing. This enables you to use the `==` operator to compare two records, and as long as all their properties have the same values, they are considered to be equal. The same functionality is available through the `Equals` method. All types provide an `Equals` method (which I'll describe in more detail later), and records arrange for this method to provide value-based comparison. You might wonder why record types are special in this regard—wouldn't `Equals` work the same way for all types? Not so. Look at Example 3-15.

Example 3-15. Comparing two instances of a type

```
var p1 = new Person("Ian", "Blue");
var p2 = new Person("Ian", "Blue");
if (p1 == p2)
{
    Console.WriteLine("Equal");
}
```

If you run this against any of the `Person` types defined in earlier examples as a `record` type, it will display the text `Equal`. However, if you were to use the definition of `Person` in Example 3-10 (which defines it as a `class`), this will not display that message. Even though all the fields have the same value, `Equals` will report that they are not equal in that case. That's because the default comparison behavior for classes is identity based: two variables are equal only if they refer to the very same object. When variables refer to two different objects, then even if those objects are of exactly the same type and have all the same property and field values, they are still distinct, and Equals reflects that. You can change this behavior when you write a class, but you have to write your own Equals method. With record, the compiler generates that for you.

The other behavior record gives you is a specialized ToString implementation. All types in .NET offer a ToString method, and you can call this either directly or through some mechanism that invokes it implicitly, such as string interpolation. In types that don't provide their own ToString, the default implementation just returns the type name, so if you call ToString on the class defined in Example 3-10, it will always return "Person", no matter what value the members have. Types are free to supply their own ToString, and the compiler does this for you for any record type. So if you call ToString on either of the Person instances created in Example 3-15, it will return "Person { Name = Ian, FavoriteColor = Blue }".

You can define records with properties whose types are also record types. Example 3-16 defines a Person record type, and also a Relation record type to indicate some way in which two people are related.

Example 3-16. Nested record types

```
public record Person(string Name, string FavoriteColor);
public record Relation(Person Subject, Person Other, string RelationshipType);
```

When you have this sort of composite structure—records within records—both Equals and ToString traverse into nested records. Example 3-17 demonstrates this.

Example 3-17. Using nested record types

```
var ian = new Person("Ian", "Blue");
var gina = new Person("Gina", "Green");
var ian2 = new Person("Ian", "Blue");
var gina2 = new Person("Gina", "Green");
var r1 = new Relation(ian, gina, "Sister");
var r2 = new Relation(gina, ian, "Brother");
var r3 = new Relation(ian2, gina2, "Sister");

Console.WriteLine(r1);
Console.WriteLine(r2);
Console.WriteLine(r3);
Console.WriteLine(r1 == r2);
Console.WriteLine(r1 == r3);
Console.WriteLine(r2 == r3);
```

Running this produces the following output (with lines split up to fit on the page):

```
Relation { Subject = Person { Name = Ian, FavoriteColor = Blue },
  Other = Person { Name = Gina, FavoriteColor = Green },
  RelationshipType = Sister }
Relation { Subject = Person { Name = Gina, FavoriteColor = Green },
  Other = Person { Name = Ian, FavoriteColor = Blue },
  RelationshipType = Brother }
Relation { Subject = Person { Name = Ian, FavoriteColor = Blue },
  Other = Person { Name = Gina, FavoriteColor = Green },
  RelationshipType = Sister }
False
True
False
```

As you can see, the Relation type's ToString has shown all of the properties of each of its nested Person records (and also the RelationshipType property, which is just a plain string). Likewise, the comparison logic works for nested records. Nothing special is happening here—a record type compares each property in turn by calling Equals on its value for that property, passing in the corresponding property from the record with which it is being compared. So when it happens to reach a record-type property, it calls its Equals method just as it would any other property, at which point that record type's own Equals implementation will execute, comparing each nested property in turn.

None of the record keyword features I've described do anything you couldn't have done by hand. It would be tedious but uncomplicated to write equivalent implementations of ToString and Equals by hand. (The compiler also provides implementations of the == and != operators and methods called GetHashCode and Deconstruct that I'll be describing later. But you could write all of those by hand too.) And as far as the .NET runtime is concerned, there's nothing special about record types—it just sees them as ordinary classes.

Record types are a language-level feature. The C# compiler generates these types in such a way that it can recognize when types in external libraries were declared as records,[2] but they are essentially just classes for which the compiler generates a few extra members. In fact, you can be explicit about this by declaring the type as record class instead of just record—these two syntaxes are equivalent.

---

2 Specifically, it generates a method with a special name, <Clone>$. That name is an illegal identifier in C#, so this method is in effect hidden from your code, but you will be using it indirectly if you use the with syntax to build a modified copy of a record.

References and Nulls

Any type defined with the class keyword will be a *reference type* (as will any type declared as record, or the equivalent record class). A variable of any reference type will not contain the data that makes up an instance of the type; instead, it can contain a *reference* to an instance of the type. Consequently, assignments don't copy the object; they just copy the reference. Example 3-18 contains similar code to Example 3-4, except instead of using the new keyword to initialize the c2 variable, it initializes it with a copy of c1.

Example 3-18. Copying references

```
Counter c1 = new Counter();
var c2 = c1;
Console.WriteLine($"c1: {c1.GetNextValue()}");
Console.WriteLine($"c1: {c1.GetNextValue()}");
Console.WriteLine($"c1: {c1.GetNextValue()}");

Console.WriteLine($"c2: {c2.GetNextValue()}");

Console.WriteLine($"c1: {c1.GetNextValue()}");
```

Because this example uses new just once, there is only one Counter instance, and the two variables both refer to this same instance. So we get different output:

```
c1: 1
c1: 2
c1: 3
c2: 4
c1: 5
```

It's not just locals that do this—if you use a reference type for any other kind of variable, such as a field or property, assignment works the same way, copying the reference and not the whole object. This is the defining characteristic of a reference type, and it is different from the behavior we saw with the built-in numeric types in Chapter 2. With those, each variable contains a value, not a reference to a value, so assignment necessarily involves copying the value. (This value-copying behavior is not available for most reference types—see the sidebar, "Copying Instances.")

Copying Instances

Some C-family languages define a standard way to make a copy of an object. For example, in C++ you can write a copy constructor, and you can overload the assignment operator; the language has rules for how these are applied when duplicating an object. In C#, some types can be copied, such as the built-in numeric types. Later in this chapter you'll see how to define a *struct*, which is a custom value type, and these can always be copied. There is no way to customize this process for value types: assignment just copies all the fields, and if any fields are of reference type, this just copies the reference. This is sometimes called a *shallow* copy, because it does not make copies of any of the things the struct refers to. Records can always be copied through the `with` syntax. The compiler enables this by generating a constructor that performs a shallow copy in any `record` or `record class`, although when I come to describe *constructors* I'll show how you can customize this.

Although certain types get special copying behavior, there is no general mechanism for making a copy of a class instance. The runtime libraries define `ICloneable`, an interface for duplicating objects, but this is not widely supported. It's a problematic API, because it doesn't specify how to handle objects with references to other objects. Should a clone also duplicate the objects to which it refers (a deep copy) or just copy the references (a shallow copy)? In practice, classes that wish to allow themselves to be copied often just provide an ad hoc method for the job, rather than conforming to any pattern.

We can write code that detects whether two references refer to the same thing. To enable us to look closely at what's happening, I'm going to add the property in Example 3-19 to `Counter`. This returns an instant's current count without changing it. (We'll be getting into properties in detail later in the chapter.)

Example 3-19. A `Count` property for the `Counter` class

```
public int Count => _count;
```

Example 3-20 arranges for three variables to refer to two counters with the same count, and then compares their identities. By default, the == operator does exactly this sort of object identity comparison when its operands are reference types. However, types are allowed to redefine the == operator. The `string` type changes == to perform value comparisons, so if you pass two distinct string objects as the operands of ==, the result will be true if they contain identical text. If you want to force comparison of object identity, you can use the static `object.ReferenceEquals` method.

Example 3-20. Comparing references

```
var c1 = new Counter();
c1.GetNextValue();
Counter c2 = c1;
var c3 = new Counter();
c3.GetNextValue();

Console.WriteLine(c1.Count);
Console.WriteLine(c2.Count);
Console.WriteLine(c3.Count);
Console.WriteLine(c1 == c2);
Console.WriteLine(c1 == c3);
Console.WriteLine(c2 == c3);
Console.WriteLine(object.ReferenceEquals(c1, c2));
Console.WriteLine(object.ReferenceEquals(c1, c3));
Console.WriteLine(object.ReferenceEquals(c2, c3));
```

The first three lines of output use the property in Example 3-19 to confirm that all three variables refer to counters with the same count:

```
1
1
1
True
False
False
True
False
False
```

It also illustrates that while they all have the same count, only c1 and c2 are considered to be the same thing. That's because we assigned c1 into c2, meaning that c1 and c2 will both refer to the same object, which is why the first comparison succeeds. But c3 refers to a different object entirely (even though it happens to have the same value), which is why the second comparison fails. (I've used both the == and object.ReferenceEquals comparisons here to illustrate that they do the same thing in this case, because Counter has not defined a custom meaning for ==.)

We could try the same thing with int instead of a Counter, as Example 3-21 shows. (This initializes the variables in a slightly idiosyncratic way in order to resemble Example 3-20 as closely as possible.)

Example 3-21. Comparing values

```
int c1 = new int();
c1++;
int c2 = c1;
int c3 = new int();
c3++;
```

```
Console.WriteLine(c1);
Console.WriteLine(c2);
Console.WriteLine(c3);
Console.WriteLine(c1 == c2);
Console.WriteLine(c1 == c3);
Console.WriteLine(c2 == c3);
Console.WriteLine(object.ReferenceEquals(c1, c2));
Console.WriteLine(object.ReferenceEquals(c1, c3));
Console.WriteLine(object.ReferenceEquals(c2, c3));
Console.WriteLine(object.ReferenceEquals(c1, c1));
```

As before, we can see that all three variables have the same value:

```
1
1
1
True
True
True
False
False
False
False
```

This also illustrates that the int type defines a special meaning for ==. With int, this operator compares the values, so those three comparisons succeed. But object. ReferenceEquals never succeeds for value types—in fact, I've added an extra, fourth comparison here, where I compare c1 with itself, and even that fails! That surprising result occurs because it's not meaningful to perform a reference comparison with int—it's not a reference type. The compiler has to perform implicit conversions from int to object for the last four lines of Example 3-21: it has wrapped each argument to object.ReferenceEquals in something called a *box*, which we'll be looking at in Chapter 7. Each argument gets a distinct box, which is why even the final comparison fails.

There's another difference between reference types and types like int. By default, any reference type variable can contain a special value, null, meaning that the variable does not refer to any object at all. You cannot assign this value into any of the built-in numeric types (although see the sidebar, "Nullable<T>").

Nullable<T>

.NET defines a wrapper type called Nullable<T>, which adds nullability to value types. Although an int variable cannot hold null, a Nullable<int> can. The angle brackets after the type name indicate that this is a generic type—you can plug various different types into that T placeholder—and I'll talk about those more in Chapter 4.

The compiler provides special handling for Nullable<T>. It lets you use a more compact syntax, so you can write int? instead. When nullable numerics appear inside arithmetic expressions, the compiler treats them differently than normal values. For example, if you write a + b, where a and b are both int?, the result is an int? that will be null if either operand was null, and will otherwise contain the sum of the values. This also works if only one of the operands is an int? and the other is an ordinary int.

While you can set an int? to null, it's not a reference type. It's more like a combination of an int and a bool. (Although, as I'll describe in Chapter 7, the CLR performs some tricks with Nullable<T> that sometimes makes it look more like a reference type than a value type.)

If you use the null-conditional operator described in Chapter 2 (?.) or its indexer equivalent (?[index]) to access members with a value type, the resulting expression will be of the nullable version of that type. For example, if str is a variable of type string?, the expression str?.Length has type Nullable<int> (or if you prefer, int?) because Length is of type int, but the use of a null-conditional operator means the expression could evaluate to null.

Banishing Null with Non-Nullable References

The widespread availability of null references in programming languages dates back to 1965, when computer scientist Tony Hoare added them to the highly influential ALGOL language. He has since apologized for this invention, which he described as his "billion-dollar mistake." The possibility that a reference type variable might contain null makes it hard to know whether it's safe to attempt to perform an action with that variable. (C# programs will throw a NullReferenceException if you attempt this, which will typically crash your program. Chapter 8 discusses exceptions.) Some modern programming languages avoid the practice of allowing references to be nullable by default, offering instead some system for optional values through an explicit opt-in mechanism in the type system. In fact, as you've seen with Nullable<T>, this is the case for C#'s built-in numeric types (and also, as we'll see, any custom value types that you define), but until recently, nullability has not been optional for reference type variables.

The C# team made the ambitious decision to introduce optional nullability for reference types long after the language was already well established. This book is a guide to using C#, not a history book, so I normally only mention specific language versions for recently added features. But in this case, because the change was so significant, and its repercussions are still working their way through the .NET ecosystem, it's helpful to understand the history. Even the latest release, .NET 8.0, includes some changes to the runtime libraries to improve nullability support some four years after the feature first appeared. There are many popular libraries that were designed before this change, and it is useful to know the dates so that you can be aware of when you might be dealing with code that was written before optional nullability was introduced. C# 8.0, which was released in 2019, extended the type system to make a distinction between references that may be null and ones that must not be. This was such a big change that this feature was initially disabled by default, but since C# 10.0 shipped in 2021, newly created projects enable it.

The feature's name is *nullable references*, which seems odd, because references have been able to contain null since C# 1.0. However, this name refers to the fact that with this feature enabled, nullability becomes an opt-in feature: a reference will never contain null unless it is explicitly defined as a nullable reference. At least, that's the theory.

Enabling the type system to distinguish between nullable and non-nullable references was always going to be a tricky thing to retrofit to a language almost two decades into its life. So the reality is that C# cannot always guarantee that a non-nullable reference will never contain a null. However, it can make the guarantee if certain constraints hold, and more generally it will significantly reduce the chances of encountering a NullReferenceException even in cases where it cannot absolutely rule this out.

Enabling non-nullability is a radical change, so the feature is switched off until you enable it explicitly. (Newly created *.csproj* files include the setting that turns this feature on, but without that setting, the feature continues to be off by default. Projects created before then will not suddenly find this feature enabled just because they upgraded to the latest version of C#.) Switching it on can have a dramatic impact on existing code, so it is possible to control the feature at a fine-grained level to enable a gradual transition between the old world and the new nullable-references-aware world.

C# provides two dimensions of control, which it calls the *nullable annotation context* and the *nullable warning context*. Each line of code in a C# program is associated with one of each kind of context. The default is that all your code is in a *disabled* nullable annotation context and a *disabled* nullable warning context. You can change these defaults at a project level (and a newly created project will do that). You can also use the #nullable directive to change either of the nullable annotation contexts at a more fine-grained level—a different one every line if you want. So how do these two contexts work?

The nullable annotation context determines whether we get to declare the nullability of a particular variable that uses a reference type. (I'm using C#'s broader definition of *variable* here, which includes not just local variables but also fields, parameters, and properties.) In a disabled annotation context (the default), we cannot express this, and all references are implicitly nullable. The official categorization describes these as *oblivious* to nullability, distinguishing them from references you have deliberately annotated as being nullable. However, in an enabled annotation context, we get to choose. Example 3-22 shows how.

Example 3-22. Specifying nullability

```
string cannotBeNull = "Text";
string? mayBeNull = null;
```

This mirrors the syntax for nullability of built-in numeric types and custom value types. If you just write the type name, that denotes something non-nullable. If you want it to be nullable, you append a ?.

The most important point to notice here is that in an enabled nullable annotation context, the old syntax gets the new behavior, and if you want the old behavior, you need to use the new syntax. This means that if you take existing code originally written without any awareness of nullability, and you put it into an enabled annotation context, *all* reference type variables are now effectively annotated as being non-nullable, the opposite of how the compiler treated the exact same code before. This may seem surprising, but since nulls are typically not expected most of the time, this works well in practice.

The most direct way to put code into an enabled nullable annotation context is with a #nullable enable annotations directive. You can put this at the top of a source file to enable it for the whole file, or you can use it more locally, followed by a #nullable restore annotations to put back the project-wide default. On its own this will produce no visible change. The compiler won't act on these annotations if the nullable warning context is disabled, and it is disabled by default. You can enable it locally with #nullable enable warnings (and #nullable restore warnings reverts to the project-wide default). You can control the project-wide defaults in the *.csproj* file by adding a <Nullable> property. Example 3-23 sets the defaults to an enabled nullable warning context and an enabled nullable annotation context. You will find a setting like this in any newly created C# project (whether created from Visual Studio or using the dotnet new at the command line).

Example 3-23. Specifying enabled nullable warning and annotation contexts as the project-wide default

```
<PropertyGroup>
  <Nullable>enable</Nullable>
</PropertyGroup>
```

This means that all code will be in an enabled nullable warning context and also in an enabled nullable annotation context unless it explicitly opts out. Other project-wide settings are `disable` (which has the same effect as not setting `<Nullable>` at all), `warnings` (enables warnings but not annotations), and `annotations` (enables annotations but not warnings).

If you've specified an enabled annotation context at the project level, you can use `#nullable disable annotations` to opt out in individual files. Likewise, if you've specified an enabled warning context at the project level, you can opt out with `#null able disable warnings`.

We have all this fine-grained control to make it easier to enable non-nullability for existing code. If you have a large existing codebase that doesn't use nullability annotations, and you fully enable the feature for an entire project in one step, you're likely to encounter a lot of warnings. In practice, it may make more sense to put all code in the project in an enabled warning context but not to enable annotations anywhere to begin with. Since all of your references will be deemed *oblivious* to nullability checking, the only warnings you'll see will relate to use of libraries. And any warnings at this stage are quite likely to be indicative of potential problems, e.g., missing tests for null. Once you've addressed these, you can start to move your own code into an enabled annotation context one file at a time (or in even smaller chunks if you prefer), making any necessary changes.

Over time, the goal would be to get all the code to the point where you can fully enable non-nullable support at the project level. And for newly created projects, it is usually best to have nullable references enabled from the start so that you can prevent problematic null handling ever getting into your code—that's why new projects have this feature enabled.

What does the compiler do for us in code where we've fully enabled non-nullability support? We get two main things. First, the compiler uses rules similar to the definite assignment rules to ensure that we don't attempt to dereference a variable without first checking to see whether it's null. Example 3-24 shows some cases the compiler will accept and some that would cause warnings in an enabled nullable warning context, assuming that `mayBeNull` was declared in an enabled nullable annotation context as being nullable.

Example 3-24. Dereferencing a nullable reference

```
if (mayBeNull is not null)
{
    // Allowed because we can only get here if mayBeNull is not null
    Console.WriteLine(mayBeNull.Length);
}

// Allowed because it checks for null and handles it
Console.WriteLine(mayBeNull?.Length ?? 0);

// The compiler will warn about this in an enabled nullable warning context
Console.WriteLine(mayBeNull.Length);
```

Second, in addition to checking whether dereferencing (use of . to access a member) is safe, the compiler will also warn you when you've attempted to assign a reference that might be null into something that requires a non-nullable reference, or if you pass one as an argument to a method when the corresponding parameter is declared as non-nullable.

Sometimes, you'll run into a roadblock on the path to moving all your code into fully enabled nullability contexts. Perhaps you depend on some component that is unlikely to be upgraded with nullability annotations in the foreseeable future, or perhaps there's a scenario in which C#'s conservative safety rules incorrectly decide that some code is not safe. What can you do in these cases? You wouldn't want to disable warnings for the entire project, and it would be irritating to have to leave the code peppered with #nullable directives. And while you can prevent warnings by adding explicit checks for null, this is undesirable in cases where you are confident that they are unnecessary. There is an alternative: you can tell the C# compiler that you know something it doesn't. If you have a reference that the compiler presumes could be null but that you have good reason to believe will never be null, you can tell the compiler this by using the *null forgiving operator*. This takes the form of an exclamation mark (!) and you can see it near the end of the second line of Example 3-25.

Example 3-25. The null forgiving operator

```
string? referenceFromLegacyComponent = legacy.GetReferenceWeKnowWontBeNull();
string nonNullableReferenceFromLegacyComponent = referenceFromLegacyComponent!;
```

You can use the null forgiving operator in any enabled nullable annotation context. It has the effect of converting a nullable reference to a non-nullable reference. You can then go on to dereference that non-nullable reference, or otherwise use it in places where a nullable reference would not be allowed, without causing any compiler warnings.

The null forgiving operator does not check its input. If you apply it in a scenario where the value turns out to be null at runtime, it will not detect this. Instead, you will get a runtime error at the point where you try to use the reference.

While the null forgiving operator can be useful at the boundary between nullable-aware code and old code that you don't control, there's another way to let the compiler know when an apparently nullable expression will not in fact be null: nullable attributes. .NET defines several attributes that you can use to annotate code to describe when it will or won't return null values. Consider the code in Example 3-26. If you do not enable the nullable reference type features, this works fine, but if you turn them on, you will get a warning. (This uses a dictionary, a collection type that is described in detail in Chapter 5.)

Example 3-26. Nullability and the Try pattern—before nullable reference types

```
public static string Get(IDictionary<int, string> d)
{
    if (d.TryGetValue(42, out string s))
    {
        return s;
    }

    return "Not found";
}
```

With nullability fully enabled, the compiler will complain at the out string s. It will tell you, correctly, that TryGetValue might pass a null through that out argument. (This kind of argument is discussed later; it provides a way to return additional values besides the function's main return value.) This function checks whether the dictionary contains an entry with the specified key. If it does, it will return true and put the relevant value into the out argument, but if not, it returns false and sets that out argument to null. We can modify our code to reflect this fact by putting a ? after the out string. Example 3-27 shows this modification.

Example 3-27. Nullable-aware use of the Try pattern

```
public static string Get(IDictionary<int, string> d)
{
    if (d.TryGetValue(42, out string? s))
    {
        return s;
    }

    return "Not found";
}
```

You might expect this to cause a new problem. Our `Get` method returns a `string`, not a `string?`, so how can that `return s` be correct? We just modified our code to indicate that `s` might be null, so won't the compiler complain when we try to return this possibly null value from a method that declares that it won't return `null`? But in fact this compiles. The compiler accepts this because it knows that `TryGetValue` will only set that out argument to `null` if it returns `false`. That means that the compiler knows that although the `s` variable's type is `string?`, it will not be `null` inside the body of the `if` statement. It knows this thanks to a nullability attribute applied to the `TryGet Value` method's definition. (Attributes are described in Chapter 14.) Example 3-28 shows the attribute in the method's declaration. (This method is part of a generic type, which is why we see `TKey` and `TValue` here and not the `int` and `string` types I used in my examples. Chapter 4 discusses this kind of method in detail. In the examples at hand, `TKey` and `TValue` are, in effect, `int` and `string`.)

Example 3-28. A nullability attribute

```
public bool TryGetValue(TKey key, [MaybeNullWhen(false)] out TValue value)
```

This annotation is how C# knows that the value might be `null` if `TryGetValue` returns `false` but won't be if it returns `true`. Without this attribute, Example 3-26 would have compiled successfully even with nullable warnings enabled, because by writing `IDictionary<int, string>` (and not `IDictionary<int, string?>`) I am indicating that my dictionary does not permit null values. So normally, C# will assume that when a method returns a value from the dictionary, it will also produce a `string`. But `TryGetValue` sometimes has no value to return, which is why it needs this annotation. Table 3-1 describes the various attributes you can apply to give the C# compiler more information about what may or may not be `null`.

Table 3-1. Nullability attributes

Type	Usage
AllowNull	Code is allowed to supply `null` even when the type is non-nullable.
DisallowNull	Code must not supply `null` even when the type is nullable.
DoesNotReturn	Indicates that the method never returns. Typically used for methods that throw exceptions. Although not directly concerned with nullability, this can prevent spurious nullability warnings in the code after a call to such a method.
DoesNotReturnIf	Similar to `DoesNotReturn`, but for methods that take a `bool` argument that will determine whether the method never returns.
MaybeNull	Code should be prepared for this to return the `null` value even when the type is non-nullable.
MaybeNullWhen	Used only with `out` or `ref` parameters; the output may be `null` if the method returns the specified `bool` value.
MemberNotNull	Lists the fields that the method sets with non-`null` values. Typically applied to methods invoked during construction, especially when multiple constructors share common initialization code.

Type	Usage
MemberNotNull When	Similar to MemberNotNull but for use on methods that return bool, and which may return false if they did not set all of the listed fields.
NotNull	Used with parameters. If the method returns without error, the argument was not null. (With out or ref parameters, this typically means the method makes sure to set them; with an inbound-only parameter, this implies the method checks the value and only returns without error if it was not null.)
NotNullWhen	Used only with out or ref parameters; the output may not be null if the method returns the specified bool value.
NotNullIfNotNull	If you pass a non-null value as the argument for the parameter that this attribute names, the value returned by this attribute's target will not be null.

These attributes have been applied where appropriate throughout the .NET runtime libraries to reduce the friction involved in adopting nullable references.

Moving code into enabled nullable warning and annotation contexts can provide a significant boost to code quality. Many developers who migrate existing codebases often uncover some latent bugs in the process, thanks to the additional checks the compiler performs. However, it is not perfect. There are two holes worth being aware of, caused by the fact that nullability was not baked into the type system from the start. The first is that legacy code introduces blind spots—even if all your code is in an enabled nullable annotation context, if it uses APIs that are not, references it obtains from those will be oblivious to nullability. If you need to use the null forgiving operator to keep the compiler happy, there's always the possibility that you are mistaken, at which point you'll end up with a null in what is supposed to be a non-nullable variable. The second is more vexing in that you can hit it in brand-new code, even if you fully enabled this feature from the start: certain storage locations in .NET have their memory filled with zero values when they are initialized. If these locations are of a reference type, they will end up starting out with a null value, and there's currently no way that the C# compiler can enforce their non-nullability. Arrays have this issue. Look at Example 3-29.

Example 3-29. Arrays and nullability

```
var nullableStrings = new string?[10];
var nonNullableStrings = new string[10];
```

This code declares two arrays of strings. The first uses string?, so it allows nullable references. The second does not. However, in .NET you have to create arrays before you can put anything in them, and a newly created array's memory is always zero-initialized. This means that our nonNullableStrings array will start life full of nulls. There is no way to avoid this because of how arrays work in .NET. One way to mitigate this problem is to avoid using arrays directly. If you use List<string> instead (see Chapter 5), it will contain only items that you have added—unlike an array, a

List<T> does not provide a way to initialize it with empty slots. But you can't always substitute a List<T> for an array. Sometimes you will simply need to take care that you initialize all the elements in an array.

A similar problem exists with fields in value types, which are described in the following section. If they have reference type fields, there are situations in which you cannot prevent them from being initialized to null. So the nullable references feature is not perfect. It is nonetheless very useful. Teams that have made the necessary changes to existing projects to use it have reported that this process tends to uncover many previously undiscovered bugs. It is an important tool for improving the quality of your code.

Although non-nullable references diminish one of the distinctions between reference types and built-in numeric types, important differences remain. A variable of type int is not a reference to an int. It contains the value of the int—there is no indirection. In some languages, this choice between reference-like and value-like behavior is determined by the way in which you use a type, but in C#, it is a fixed feature of the type. Any particular type is either a reference type or a *value type*. The built-in numeric types are all value types, as is bool, whereas a class is always a reference type. But this is not a distinction between built-in and custom types. You can write custom value types.

Structs

Sometimes it will be appropriate for a custom type to get the same value-like behavior as the built-in value types. The most obvious example would be a custom numeric type. Although the CLR offers various intrinsic numeric types, some kinds of calculations require a bit more structure than these provide. For example, many scientific and engineering calculations work with complex numbers. The runtime does not define an intrinsic representation for these, but the runtime libraries support them with the Complex type. It would be unhelpful if a numeric type such as this behaved significantly differently from the built-in types. Fortunately, it doesn't, because it is a value type. The way to write a custom value type is to use the struct keyword instead of class.

A struct can have most of the same features as a class; it can contain methods, fields, properties, constructors, and any of the other member types supported by classes (described in "Members" on page 159). We can use the same accessibility keywords, such as public and internal. There are a few restrictions, but with the simple Counter type I wrote earlier, I *could* just replace the class keyword with struct. However, this would not be a useful transformation. Remember, one of the main distinctions between reference types (classes) and value types is that the former have identity: it might be useful for me to create multiple Counter objects so that I can count different kinds of things. But with value types (either the built-in ones or custom structs), the assumption is that they can be copied freely. If I have an instance of the `int` type (e.g., 4) and I store that in several fields, there's no expectation that this value has a life of its own: one instance of the number 4 is indistinguishable from another. The variables that hold values have their own identities and lifetimes, but the values that they hold do not. This is different from how reference types work: not only do the variables that refer to them have identities and lifetimes, the objects they refer to have their own identities and lifetimes independent of any particular variable.

If I add one to the `int` value 4, the result is a completely different `int` value. If I call `GetNextValue()` on a `Counter`, its count goes up by one, but it remains the same `Counter` instance. So although replacing `class` with `struct` in Example 3-5 would compile, we really don't want our `Counter` type to become a struct. Example 3-30 shows a better candidate.

Example 3-30. A simple struct

```
public readonly struct Point(double x, double y)
{
    public double X => x;
    public double Y => y;

    public double DistanceFromOrigin() => Math.Sqrt(X * X + Y * Y);
}
```

This represents a point in two-dimensional space. And while it's certainly possible to imagine wanting the ability to represent particular points with their own identity (in which case we'd want a `class`), it's perfectly reasonable to want to have a value-like type representing a point's location.

This shows that a struct can use the same primary constructor syntax (new in C# 12.0) as a class, but be aware that there is a subtle difference: when a class has a primary constructor, it's not possible to create an instance of that class without invoking its primary constructor. But because structs are often implicitly initialized by setting their fields to zero (or zero-like values such as `false` and `null`), primary constructors might not run. Since the primary constructor defines parameters that are in scope throughout the type, this seems like it shouldn't be possible, because it is equivalent to invoking a method without passing any of the arguments. In practice, the behavior is as though the primary constructor was invoked with default values for all of its arguments.

Although Example 3-30 is OK as far as it goes, it's common for values to support comparison. As mentioned earlier, C# defines a default meaning for the == operator for reference types: it is equivalent to `object.ReferenceEquals`, which compares identities. That's not meaningful for value types, so C# does not automatically support

== for a `struct`. You are not strictly required to provide a definition, but the built-in value types all do, so if we're trying to make a type with similar characteristics to those, we should do this. If you add an == operator on its own, the compiler will inform you that you are required to define a matching != operator. You might think C# would define != as the inverse of ==, since they appear to mean the opposite. However, some types will return `false` for both operators for certain pairs of operands, so C# requires us to define both independently. As Example 3-31 shows, to define a custom meaning for an operator, we use the `operator` keyword followed by the operator we'd like to customize. This example defines the behavior for == and !=, which are very straightforward for our simple type. (Since all of the new methods in this example do nothing more than returning the value of a single expression, I've implemented them using the => syntax, just as I've done with various properties in preceding examples.)

Example 3-31. Support custom comparison

```
public readonly struct Point(double x, double y) : IEquatable<Point>
{
    public double X => x;
    public double Y => y;

    public double DistanceFromOrigin() => Math.Sqrt(X * X + Y * Y);

    public override bool Equals(object? o) => o is Point p && this.Equals(p);
    public bool Equals(Point o) => this.X == o.X && this.Y == o.Y;
    public override int GetHashCode() => HashCode.Combine(X, Y);

    public static bool operator ==(Point a, Point b) => a.Equals(b);
    public static bool operator !=(Point a, Point b) => !(a == b);
}
```

If you just add the == and != operators, you'll find that the compiler generates warnings recommending that you define two methods called `Equals` and `GetHashCode`. `Equals` is a standard method available on all .NET types, and if you have defined a custom meaning for ==, you should ensure that `Equals` does the same thing. In fact Example 3-31 implements two versions of `Equals`: the standard method that accepts any `object` and a more specialized one that allows comparison only with other `Point` values. This allows for more efficient comparisons by avoiding boxing (which is described in Chapter 7), and as is common practice when offering this second form of `Equals`, I've declared support for the `IEquatable<Point>` interface; I'll be describing interfaces in "Interfaces" on page 212. The more specialized `Equals` does the real work. The `Equals` method that permits comparison with any type defers to the other `Equals`, but it first has to check to see if our `Point` is being compared with another `Point`. I've used a declaration pattern to perform this check and also to get the incoming `obj` argument into a variable of type `Point` in the case where the pattern matches. Example 3-31 also implements `GetHashCode`, which we're required to do if we implement `Equals`. See the sidebar, "GetHashCode," for details.

GetHashCode

All .NET types have a `GetHashCode` method. It returns an `int` that in some sense represents the value of your object. Some data structures and algorithms are designed to work with this sort of simplified, reduced version of an object's value. A hash table, for example, can find a particular entry in a very large table very efficiently, as long as the type of value you're searching for offers a good hash code implementation. Some of the collection classes described in Chapter 5 rely on this. The details of this sort of algorithm are beyond the scope of this book, but if you search the web for "hash table" you'll find plenty of information.

A correct implementation of `GetHashCode` must meet two requirements. The first is that whatever number an instance returns as its hash code, that instance must continue to return the same code as long as its own value does not change. The second requirement is that two instances that have equal values according to their `Equals` methods must return the same hash code. Any type that fails to meet either of these requirements might cause code that uses its `GetHashCode` method to malfunction. The default implementation of `GetHashCode` for reference types meets the first requirement but makes no attempt to meet the second—pick any two objects that use the default implementation, and most of the time they'll have different hash codes. That's fine because the default reference type `Equals` implementation only ever returns true if you compare an object with itself, but this is why you need to override `GetHashCode` if you override `Equals`. Value types get default implementations of `GetHashCode` and `Equals` that meet both requirements. However, these can sometimes be slow, so you should normally write your own (unless it's a `record struct`— the compiler generates very efficient `GetHashCode` implementations for all record types).

Ideally, objects that have different values should have different hash codes, but that's not always possible—`GetHashCode` returns an `int`, which has a finite number of possible values (4,294,967,296, to be precise). If your data type offers more distinct values, then it's clearly not possible for every conceivable value to produce a different hash code. For example, the 64-bit integer type, `long`, obviously supports more distinct values than `int`. If you call `GetHashCode` on a `long` with a value of 0, on .NET 8.0 it returns 0, and you'll get the same hash code for a `long` with a value of 4,294,967,297. Duplicates like these are called *hash collisions*, and they are an unavoidable fact of life. Code that depends on hash codes just has to be able to deal with these.

The rules do not require the mapping from values to hash codes to be fixed forever— they only need to be consistent for the lifetime of the process. In fact, there are good reasons to be inconsistent. Criminals who attack online computer systems sometimes try to cause hash collisions. Collisions decrease the efficiency of hash-based algorithms, so an attack that attempts to overwhelm a server's CPU will be more effective if it can induce collisions for values that it knows the server will use in hash-based lookups. Some types in the runtime libraries deliberately change the way they produce hashes each time you restart a program to avoid this problem.

Because hash collisions are unavoidable, the rules cannot forbid them, which means you could return the same value (e.g., 0) from GetHashCode every time, regardless of the instance's actual value. Although not technically against the rules, it tends to produce lousy performance from hash tables and the like. Ideally, you will want to minimize hash collisions. That said, if you don't expect anything to depend on your type's hash code, there's not much point in spending time carefully devising a hash function that produces well-distributed values. Sometimes a lazy approach, such as deferring to a single field, is OK. Or you could use the HashCode.Combine method like Example 3-31 does.

With the version of Point in Example 3-31, we can run a few tests. Example 3-32 works similarly to Examples 3-20 and 3-21.

Example 3-32. Comparing struct instances

```
var p1 = new Point(40, 2);
Point p2 = p1;
var p3 = new Point(40, 2);

Console.WriteLine($"{p1.X}, {p1.Y}");
Console.WriteLine($"{p2.X}, {p2.Y}");
Console.WriteLine($"{p3.X}, {p3.Y}");
Console.WriteLine(p1 == p2);
Console.WriteLine(p1 == p3);
Console.WriteLine(p2 == p3);
Console.WriteLine(object.ReferenceEquals(p1, p2));
Console.WriteLine(object.ReferenceEquals(p1, p3));
Console.WriteLine(object.ReferenceEquals(p2, p3));
Console.WriteLine(object.ReferenceEquals(p1, p1));
```

Running that code produces this output:

```
40, 2
40, 2
40, 2
True
True
True
False
False
False
False
```

All three instances have the same value. With p2 that's because I initialized it by assigning p1 into it, and with p3 I constructed it from scratch but with the same arguments. Then we have the first three comparisons, which, remember, use ==. Since Example 3-31 defines a custom implementation that compares values, all the comparisons succeed. And all the `object.ReferenceEquals` values fail, because this is a value type, just like `int`. In fact, this is the same behavior we saw with Example 3-21, which used `int` instead of `Counter`. So we have achieved our goal of defining a type with similar behavior to built-in value types such as `int`.

When to Write a Value Type

I've shown some of the differences in observable behavior between a reference type (`class` or `record`) and a `struct`, but although I argued why `Counter` was a poor candidate for being a `struct`, I've not fully explained what makes a good one. The short answer is that there are only two circumstances in which you should write a value type. First, if you need to represent something value-like, such as a number, a struct is likely to be ideal. Second, if you have determined that a struct has usefully better performance characteristics for the scenario in which you will use the type, a struct may not be ideal but might still be a good choice. But it's worth understanding the pros and cons in more detail. And I will also address a surprisingly persistent myth about value types.

With reference types, an object is distinct from a variable that refers to it. This can be very useful, because we often use objects as models for real things with identities of their own. But this has some performance implications. An object's lifetime is not necessarily directly related to the lifetime of a variable that refers to it. You can create a new object, store a reference to it in a local variable, and then later copy that reference to a static field. The method that originally created the object might then return, so the local variable that first referred to the object no longer exists, but the object needs to stay alive because it's still possible to reach it by other means.

The CLR goes to considerable lengths to ensure that the memory an object occupies is not reclaimed prematurely but is eventually freed once the object is no longer in use. This is a fairly complex process (described in detail in Chapter 7), and .NET applications can end up causing the CLR to consume a considerable amount of CPU time just tracking objects in order to work out when they fall out of use. Creating lots of objects increases this overhead. Adding complexity in certain ways can also increase the costs of object tracking—if a particular object remains alive only because it is reachable through some very convoluted path, the CLR may need to follow that path each time it tries to work out what memory is still in use. Each level of indirection you add generates extra work. A reference is by definition indirect, so every reference type variable creates work for the CLR.

Value types can often be handled in a much simpler way. For example, consider arrays. If you declare an array of some reference type, you end up with an array of references. This is very flexible—elements can be null if you want, and you're also free to have multiple different elements all referring to the same item. But if what you actually need is a simple sequential collection of items, that flexibility is just overhead. A collection of 1,000 reference type instances requires 1,001 blocks of memory: one block to hold an array of references, and then 1,000 objects for those references to refer to. But with value types, a single block can hold all the values. This simplifies things for memory management purposes—either the array is still in use or it's not, and there's no need for the CLR to check the 1,000 individual elements separately.

It's not just arrays that can benefit from this sort of efficiency. There's also an advantage for fields. Consider a class that contains 10 fields, all of type int. The 40 bytes required to hold those fields' values can live directly inside the memory allocated for an instance of the containing class. Compare that with 10 fields of some reference type. Although those references can be stored inside the object instance's memory, the objects they refer to will be separate entities, so if the fields are all non-null and all refer to different objects, you'll now have 11 blocks of memory—one for the instance that contains all the fields, and then one for each object those fields refer to. Figure 3-1 illustrates these differences between references and values for both arrays and objects (with smaller examples, because the same principle applies even with a handful of instances).

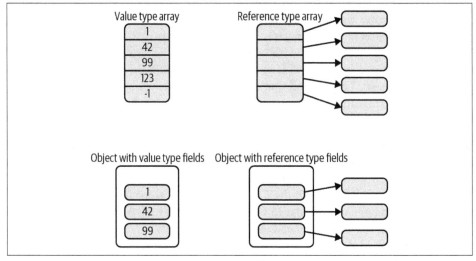

Figure 3-1. References versus values

Value types can also sometimes simplify lifetime handling. Often, the memory allocated for local variables can be freed as soon as a method returns (although, as we'll see in Chapter 9, anonymous functions mean that it's not always that simple). This means the memory for local variables can often live on the stack, which typically has much lower overheads than the heap. For reference types, the memory for a variable is only part of the story—the object it refers to cannot be handled so easily, because that object may continue to be reachable by other paths after the method exits.

In fact, the memory for a value may be reclaimed even before a method returns. New value instances often overwrite older instances. For example, C# can normally just use a single piece of memory to represent a variable, no matter how many different values you put in there. Creating a new instance of a value type doesn't necessarily mean allocating more memory, whereas with reference types, a new instance means a new heap block. This is why it's OK for each operation we perform with a value type —every integer addition or subtraction, for example—to produce a new instance.

One of the most persistent myths about value types says that values are allocated on the stack, unlike objects. It's true that objects always live on the heap, but value types don't always live on the stack,[3] and even in the situations where they do, that's an implementation detail, not a fundamental feature of C#. Figure 3-1 shows two counterexamples. An int value inside an array of type int[] does not live on the stack; it lives inside the array's heap block. Likewise, if a class declares a nonstatic int field, the value of that int lives inside the heap block for its containing object instance. And even local variables of value types don't necessarily end up on the stack. For example, optimizations may make it possible for the value of a local variable to live entirely inside the CPU's registers, rather than needing to go on the stack. And as you'll see in Chapters 9 and 17, locals can sometimes live on the heap.

You might be tempted to summarize the preceding few paragraphs as "there are some complex details, but in essence, value types are more efficient." But that would be a mistake. There are some situations in which value types are significantly more expensive. Remember that a defining feature of a value type is that values get copied on assignment. If the value type is big, that will be relatively expensive. For example, the runtime libraries define the Guid type to represent the 16-byte *globally unique identifiers* that crop up in lots of bits of Windows. This is a struct, so any assignment statement involving a Guid is asking to make a copy of a 16-byte data structure. This is likely to be more expensive than making a copy of a reference, because the CLR uses a pointer-based implementation for references; a pointer typically takes 4 or 8 bytes, but more importantly, it'll be something that fits naturally into a single CPU register.

---

3 There are certain exceptions, described in Chapter 18.

It's not just assignment that causes values to be copied. Passing a value type argument to a method may require a copy. As it happens, with method invocation, it is actually possible to pass a reference to a value, although as we'll see later, it's a slightly limited kind of reference, and the restrictions it imposes are sometimes undesirable, so you may end up deciding that the cost of the copy is preferable.

This is why Microsoft's design guidelines suggest that you should not make a type a struct unless it "has an instance size under 16 bytes" (a guideline that the Guid type technically violates, being exactly 16 bytes in size). But this is not a hard-and-fast rule—it really depends on how you will be using it, and since more recent versions of C# provide more flexibility for using value types indirectly, it is increasingly common for performance-sensitive code to ignore this restriction and instead to take care to minimize copying.

Value types are not automatically going to be more efficient than reference types, so in most cases, your choice should be driven by the behavior you require. The most important question is this: Does the identity of an instance matter to you? In other words, is the distinction between one object and another object important? For our Counter example, the answer is yes: if we want something to keep count for us, it's simplest if that counter is a distinct thing with its own identity. (Otherwise, our Counter type adds nothing beyond what int gives us.) But for our Point type, the answer is no, so it's a reasonable candidate for being a value type.

An important and related question is: Does an instance of your type contain state that changes over time? Modifiable value types tend to be problematic, because it's all too easy to end up working with some copy of a value and not the instance you meant to. (I'll show an important example of this problem later, in "Properties and mutable value types" on page 202, and another when I describe List<T> in Chapter 5.) So it's usually a good idea for value types to be immutable.

This doesn't mean that variables of these types cannot be modified; it just means that to modify the variable, you must replace its contents entirely with a different value. For something simple like an int, this will seem like splitting hairs, but the distinction is important with structs that contain multiple fields, such as .NET's Complex type, which represents numbers that combine a real and an imaginary component. You cannot change the Real or Imaginary property of an existing Complex instance, because the type is immutable. And the Point type shown earlier works the same way. If the value you've got isn't the value you want, immutability just means you need to create a new value, because you can't tweak the existing instance.

Immutability does not necessarily mean you should write a struct—the built-in `string` type is immutable, and that's a class.[4] However, because C# often does not need to allocate new memory to hold new instances of a value type, value types are able to support immutability more efficiently than classes in scenarios where you're creating lots of new values (e.g., in a loop). Immutability is not an absolute requirement for structs—there are some unfortunate exceptions in .NET's runtime libraries. But value types should normally be immutable, so a requirement for mutability is usually a good sign that you want a class rather than a struct.

A type should only be a struct if it represents something that is very clearly similar in nature to other things that are value types. (In most cases it should also be fairly small, because passing large types by value is expensive.) For example, in the runtime libraries, `Complex` is a struct, which is unsurprising because it's a numeric type, and all of the built-in numeric types are value types. `TimeSpan` is also a value type, which makes sense because it's effectively just a number that happens to represent a length of time. In the UI framework WPF, types used for simple geometric data such as `Point` and `Rect` are structs. But if in doubt, write a class.

Guaranteeing Immutability

The two versions of the `Point` struct I've shown so far do not provide any way to modify the value, so they are effectively read-only. In fact, you may well have noticed that I explicitly declared my intention to make these structs read-only by adding the `readonly` keyword in front of `struct`.

Applying the `readonly` keyword to a `struct` has two effects. First, the C# compiler will keep you honest, preventing modification either from outside or from within. If you declare any fields, the compiler will generate an error unless these are also marked `readonly`. Similarly, if you try to define a settable auto-property (one with a `set;` as well as a `get;`), the compiler will produce an error. It also disallows code that tries to modify a primary constructor parameter.

Second, read-only structs enjoy certain optimizations. If in some other type you declare a `readonly` field (either directly, or indirectly with a read-only auto-property) whose type is a `readonly struct`, the compiler may be able to avoid making a copy of the data when something uses that field. Consider the class in Example 3-33.

---

4 You wouldn't want it to be a value type, because strings can be large, so passing them by value would be expensive. In any case, it cannot be a struct, because strings vary in length. However, that's not a factor you need to consider, because you can't write your own variable-length data types in C#. Only strings and array types have variable size.

Example 3-33. A read-only struct in a read-only property

```
public class LocationData(string label, Point location)
{
    public string Label { get; } = label;
    public Point Location { get; } = location;
}
```

Suppose you had a variable r containing a reference to a LocationData. What would happen if you wrote the expression r.Location.DistanceFromOrigin()? Logically, we're asking the LocationData instance referred to by r to retrieve the Location property's value so that we can invoke its DistanceFromOrigin method. The Location property's type is Point, and since that is a value type, retrieving it would entail making a copy of the value. Normally, C# will generate code that really does make a copy because it cannot in general know whether invoking some member of a struct will modify it. These are known as *defensive copies,* and they ensure that expressions like this can't cause a nasty surprise such as changing the value of a property or field that appears to be read-only. However, since Point is a readonly struct, the compiler can know that it does not need to create a defensive copy here. In this case, it would be safe for either the C# compiler or the JIT compiler (or AOT code generator) to optimize this code by invoking DistanceFromOrigin directly on the value stored inside the LocationData without first making a copy.

You are allowed to use a readonly struct in writable fields and properties if you want to—LocationData.Location could have a set accessor despite Point being a read-only struct, for example. The readonly keyword guarantees only that any particular value of this type will not change. If you want to overwrite an existing value with a completely different value, that's up to you.

Record Structs

When you saw Example 3-31, you might have thought to yourself that this seems a lot like the kind of work that the compiler can do for us in a record type. We can get it to do the same work with a value type by declaring a record struct type. This adds the same comparison behavior that we get with a class-based record—the compiler writes GetHashCode and both forms of the Equals methods for you, along with the == and != operators.

Besides the usual differences between classes and value types already described, there are some other more subtle differences between record and record struct types. For example, struct types have a way to declare explicitly that they are immutable (the readonly qualifier). When you use the positional syntax with a record struct, the compiler assumes that if you want a read-only type, you'll say so by declaring it as `readonly record struct`. So although properties defined with the positional syntax are immutable on a `readonly record struct` (just as they are on a `record`), they are modifiable on a `record struct`. So whereas you cannot modify the X and Y properties of a `PointRecord` type in Example 3-34 after construction, you could change the properties of a `PointStructRecord`. But `PointReadonlyStructRecord` gets immutable properties, just like `PointRecord`.

Example 3-34. A read-only record, *a mutable* record struct, *and a* readonly record struct

```
public record PointRecord(int X, int Y);
public record struct PointStructRecord(int X, int Y);
public readonly record struct PointReadonlyStructRecord(int X, int Y);
```

`record structs` also have some subtle differences around constructors, which I'll describe in "Constructors" on page 162.

Class, Structs, Records, or Tuples?

As you've now seen, C# offers many ways to define types. How should we choose between them? Suppose your code needs to work with a pair of coordinates representing a position in two-dimensional space. How should you represent this in C#?

The simplest possible answer would be to declare two variables of type `double`, one for each dimension. This certainly works, but your code will fail to capture something important: the two values are not two separate things. If your chosen type doesn't represent the fact that these two numbers are a single entity, that will cause problems. It is inconvenient when you want to write methods that take a position as an argument —you end up needing two arguments. If you accidentally pass the X value from one coordinate pair and the Y value from a different one, the compiler will have no way of knowing this is wrong. Using two separate values is especially troublesome if you want a function to return a position, because C# methods can return only a single value directly.

Tuples, which were described in Chapter 2, can solve the problems I just described because a single value can contain a pair of numbers: `(1.0, 2.0)`. While this is certainly an improvement, the problem with tuples is that they are unable to distinguish between different kinds of data that happen to have the same structure. This isn't unique to tuples: built-in types have the same issue. A `double` representing a distance in feet has the same C# type as one representing a distance in meters, even though there is a significant difference in meaning. (NASA lost a space probe in 1999 due to confusion over values with identical types but different units.) But these problems go beyond mismatched units. Suppose you have a tuple `(X: 10.0, Y: 10.0)` representing the position of a rectangle in meters, and another `(Width: 2.0, Height: 1.0)` representing its size, also in meters. The units are the same here, but position and size are quite different concepts, and yet these two tuples have exactly the same type. This can seem particularly surprising when the members of the tuples have different names—the first has X and Y, but the second has Width and Height. However, as you saw in the preceding chapter, these tuple member names are a fiction the C# compiler provides for our convenience. The real names are Item1 and Item2.

Given the limitations of tuples, it may be more appropriate to ask: When would you ever want to use a tuple instead of a specialized type such as a record? I have found tuples very useful in private implementation details in places where there is little chance of the structural equivalence of conceptually unrelated tuple types causing a problem. For example, when using the Dictionary<TKey, TValue> container type described in Chapter 5, it is sometimes useful for the dictionary key to be made up of more than one value. Tuples are ideal for this sort of compound key. They can also be useful when a method needs to return multiple related pieces of data in cases where defining a whole new type seems like overkill. For example, if the method is a private one called in only one or two places, is it really worth defining a whole type just to act as the return type of that one method?

Record types would work better than tuples for our structurally similar but conceptually different position and dimension examples: if we define public record Position(double X, double Y) and public record Dimensions(double Width, double Height), we now have two distinct types to represent these two separate kinds of data. If we accidentally try to use positions when dimensions are required, the compiler will point out the mistake. Moreover, unlike the locally defined names we can give tuple members, the names of a record's properties are real, so code using Dimensions will always to refer to its members as Width and Height. Record types automatically implement equality comparisons and hash codes, so they work just as well as tuples as compound keys in dictionaries. There are really only two reasons you might choose a tuple over a record. One is when you actually want the structural equivalence—there are some occasions where deliberately being a bit vague about types can provide extra flexibility that might justify the possible reduction in safety. And the second is in cases where defining a type seems like overkill (e.g., when using a compound key for a dictionary that is used only inside one method).

Since record types are full .NET types, they can contain more than just properties—they can contain any of the other member types described in the following section. Our Dimensions record type could include a method that calculates the area, for example. And we are free to choose between defining a reference type or a value type by using either record or record struct.

When would we use a class (or struct) instead of a record? One reason might be that you don't want the equality logic. If your application has entities with their own identities—perhaps certain objects correspond to people or to particular devices—the value-based comparison logic generated for record types will be inappropriate, because two items can be distinct even if they happen to share the same characteristics. (Imagine objects representing shapes in a drawing program. If you clone a shape, you will have two identical objects, but it's important that they are still considered different because the cloned item may then go on to be moved or otherwise modified.) So you might want to ask: Does your type represent a thing, or does it just hold some information? If it contains some information, a record type is likely to be a good choice, but a class may well be a better bet for representing some real entity, especially if instances of the type have behavior of their own. For example, when building a user interface, an interactive element such as a button would be better modeled as a `class` than a `record`. It's not that a record type couldn't be made to work—they can be made to do more or less anything ordinary classes and structs can do; it's just that they are likely to be a less good fit.

Members

Whether you're writing a class, a struct, or a record, there are several different kinds of members you can put in a custom type. We've seen examples of some already, but let's take a closer and more comprehensive look.

Accessibility

You can specify the accessibility for most class and struct members. Just as a type can be `public` or `internal`, so can each member. Members may also be declared as `private`, making them accessible only to code inside the type, and this is the default accessibility. As we'll see in Chapter 6, inheritance adds three more accessibility levels for members: `protected`, `protected internal`, and `protected private`.

Fields

You've already seen that fields are named storage locations that hold either values or references depending on their type. By default, each instance of a type gets its own set of fields, but if you want a field to be singular, rather than having one per instance, you can use the `static` keyword. You can also apply the `readonly` keyword to a field, which states that it can be set only during initialization and cannot change thereafter.

The readonly keyword does not make any absolute guarantees. There are mechanisms by which it is possible to contrive a change in the value of a readonly field. The reflection mechanisms discussed in Chapter 13 provide one way, and unsafe code, which lets you work directly with raw pointers, provides another. The compiler will prevent you from modifying a field accidentally, but with sufficient determination, you can bypass this protection. And even without such subterfuge, a readonly field is free to change during construction.

C# offers a keyword that seems, superficially, to be similar: you can define a const field. However, this is designed for a somewhat different purpose. A readonly field is initialized and then never changed, whereas a const field defines a value that is invariably the same. A readonly field is much more flexible: it can be of any type, and its value can be calculated at runtime, which means you can define either per-instance or static fields as readonly. A const field's value is determined at compile time, which means it is defined at the class level (because there's no way for individual instances to have different values). This also limits the available types. For most reference types, the only supported const value is null, so in practice, it's normally only useful to use const with types intrinsically supported by the compiler. (Specifically, if you want to use values other than null, a const's type must be one of the built-in numeric types, bool, string, or an enumeration type, as described later in this chapter.)

This makes a const field rather more limited than a readonly one, so you could reasonably ask: What's the point? Well, although a const field is inflexible, it makes a strong statement about the unchanging nature of the value. For example, .NET's Math class defines a const field of type double called PI that contains as close an approximation to the mathematical constant π as a double can represent. That's a value that's fixed forever—thus it is a constant in a very strong sense.

When it comes to less inherently constant values, you need to be a bit careful about const fields; the C# specification allows the compiler to assume that the value really will never change. Code that reads the value of a readonly field will fetch the value from the memory containing the field at runtime. But when you use a const field, the compiler can read the value at compile time and copy it into the IL as though it were a literal. So if you write a library component that declares a const field and you later change its value, this change will not necessarily be picked up by code using your library unless that code gets recompiled.

One of the benefits of a const field is that it is eligible for use in certain contexts in which a readonly field is not. For example, if you want to use a constant pattern (Chapter 2 introduced patterns), perhaps in the label for a case in a switch statement, the value you specify has to be fixed at compile time. So a constant pattern cannot refer to a `readonly` field, but you can use a suitably typed `const` field.

A `const` field declaration is required to contain an expression defining its value, such as the one shown in Example 3-35. This defining expression can refer to other `const` fields, as long as you don't introduce any circular references.

Example 3-35. A `const` *field*

```
const double kilometersPerMile = 1.609344;
```

While mandatory for a `const`, this initializer expression is optional for a class's ordinary and `readonly`[5] fields. If you omit the initializing expression, the field will automatically be initialized to a default value. (That's 0 for numeric values and the equivalents for other types—`false`, `null`, etc.)

Instance field initializers run as part of construction, i.e., when you use the `new` keyword (or some equivalent mechanism such as constructing an instance through reflection, as described in Chapter 13). This means you should be wary of using field initializers in value types. A `struct` can be initialized implicitly, in which case its instance fields are set to 0 (or `false`, etc.). You can write instance field initializers in a `struct`, but these will only run if that `struct` is *explicitly* initialized. If you create an array whose elements are some value type with field initializers, all the fields of all the elements in the array will start out with values of 0; if you want the field initializers to run, you'll need to write a loop that uses `new` to initialize each element in the array. Likewise when you use a `struct` type as a field, it will be zero-initialized, and its field initializers will run only if you explicitly initialize the field with the `new` keyword. (Instance field initializers in a `class` also run only when that `class` is constructed, but the big difference is that it's not possible to get hold of an instance of a `class` without running one of its constructors.[6] There are common situations in which you will be able to use a `struct` instance that was implicitly zero-initialized.) Initializers for noninstance fields (i.e., `const` and `static` fields) will always be executed for structs, though.

If you do supply an initializer expression for a non-`const` field, it does not need to be evaluable at compile time, so it can do runtime work such as calling methods or

---

5 If you omit the initializer for a `readonly` field, you should set it in the constructor or a property's `init` accessor instead; otherwise it's not very useful.

6 There are two exceptions. If a class supports an obsolete CLR feature called *binary serialization*, objects of that type can be deserialized directly from a data stream, bypassing constructors. But even here, you can dictate what data is required. And there's the `MemberwiseClone` method described in Chapter 6.

reading properties. Of course, this sort of code can have side effects, so it's important to be aware of the order in which initializers run.

Nonstatic field initializers run for each instance you create, and they execute in the order in which they appear in the file, immediately before the constructor runs. Static field initializers execute no more than once, no matter how many instances of the type you create. They also execute in the order in which they are declared, but it's harder to pin down exactly when they will run. If your class has no static constructor, C# guarantees to run field initializers before the first time a field in the class is accessed, but it doesn't necessarily wait until the last minute—it retains the right to run field initializers as early as it likes. (The exact moment at which this happens has varied across releases of .NET.) But if a static constructor does exist, then things are slightly clearer: static field initializers run immediately before the static constructor runs. However, that merely raises the questions: What's a static constructor, and when does it run? So we had better take a look at constructors.

Constructors

A newly created object may require some information to do its job. For example, the Uri class in the System namespace represents a *Uniform Resource Identifier* (URI) such as a URL. Since its entire purpose is to contain and provide information about a URI, there wouldn't be much point in having a Uri object that didn't know what its URI was. So it's not actually possible to create one without providing a URI. If you try the code in Example 3-36, you'll get a compiler error.

Example 3-36. Error: failing to provide a Uri with its URI

```
Uri oops = new Uri();  // Will not compile
```

The Uri class defines several *constructors*, members that contain code that initializes a new instance of a type. If a particular class requires certain information to work, you can enforce this requirement through constructors. Creating an instance of a class almost always involves using a constructor at some point, so if the constructors you define all demand certain information, developers will have to provide that information if they want to use your class. So all of the Uri class's constructors need to be given the URI in one form or another.

 If you write a class containing reference-typed instance fields that are non-nullable (e.g., private string name;) the compiler will issue warnings if you do not initialize these fields either with field initializers, or with code in the constructor. The constructor's job is to put an instance in a valid state, and that includes ensuring that all non-nullable fields are not null.

You've seen one kind of constructor already: a primary constructor. These were not available for `class` or `struct` types before C# 12.0, so there is another way. The more general constructor syntax appears inside the body of the type. It first specifies the accessibility (`public`, `private`, `internal`, etc.) and then the name of the containing type. This is followed by a list of parameters in parentheses (which can be empty). Example 3-37 shows a class that defines a single constructor that requires two arguments: one of type `decimal` and one of type `string`. The argument list is followed by a block containing code. So constructors look a lot like methods but with the containing type name in place of the usual return type and method name.

Example 3-37. A class with one constructor

```
public class Item
{
    public Item(decimal price, string name)
    {
        _price = price;
        _name = name;
    }
    private readonly decimal _price;
    private readonly string _name;
}
```

This constructor is pretty simple: it just copies its arguments to fields. A lot of constructors do no more than that, and these cases are a good fit for the *primary constructor* syntax introduced in C# 12.0, used in some earlier examples. We can rewrite Example 3-37 as Example 3-38. Since primary constructor parameters are in scope inside the class, we don't need to define fields.

Example 3-38. A class with a primary constructor and no other constructors

```
public class Item(decimal price, string name)
{
    public override string ToString() => $"{name}: {price:C}";
}
```

If you do want to define fields explicitly when using a primary constructor, you can. Example 3-10 showed how to do this—you just use the primary constructor parameters in the field initializer. And as Example 3-14 showed, you can do the same thing with property initializers. If a primary constructor parameter is used only in expressions evaluated during construction (e.g., field initializers or property initializers) the C# compiler does not generate any code to hold on to its value. It's only if you *capture* the parameter by referring to it in some context that is not part of construction (e.g., inside a method) that the compiler is obliged to ensure that the parameter remains available after construction is complete. (The current compiler implementation does this by generating a field, although the language specification allows it to use any implementation strategy it likes.) If you do put the parameter into a field or property, you should be careful not to capture it as well. Example 3-39 makes this mistake.

Example 3-39. Double storage of a primary constructor argument

```
public class StoresNameTwice(string name)
{
    private readonly string _name = name;

    public override string ToString() => name; // Captures name
}
```

This uses the primary constructor argument to initialize a field. This has enabled it to define the field as `readonly` and also to use the underscore prefix naming convention. (Nothing stops you from putting an underscore prefix on a constructor parameter name, but since those names are publicly visible, it would look odd. It would also defeat the point of using such naming conventions: primary constructor parameters are not fields, so your code should not imply that they are.) Field initialization happens during construction, so this does not cause the argument to be captured. However, the `ToString` method refers to `name`, not `_name`. `ToString` could be called at any time, obliging the compiler to make sure that `name` remains available for the lifetime of the object. The upshot is that `StoresNameTwice` will maintain two copies. Given how the compiler implements this feature, that will mean two instance fields: the explicitly declared `_name`, and a hidden field to hold the captured `name` argument. This is a waste because in this case, these two fields will always have the same value. And if this were not a `readonly` field, having two fields when you intended to have just one could be a source of bugs. The compiler generates a warning if you do this, so it's easy enough to avoid.

In most C# projects, the more verbose syntax shown in Example 3-37 is more widely used than primary constructors. That's partly because prior to C# 12.0 it was the only option. However, even in new projects, the older syntax still offers an advantage: the syntax includes a body, so you can write code. You're free to put as much code in there as you like, but by convention, developers usually expect the constructor to do very little—its main job is to ensure that the object is in a valid initial state. That might involve checking the arguments and throwing an exception if there's a problem, but not much else. You are likely to surprise developers who use your class if you write a constructor that does something nontrivial, such as adding data to a database or sending a message over the network.

Example 3-40 shows how to use the constructor defined by Example 3-37. We just use the `new` operator, passing in suitably typed values as arguments.

Example 3-40. Using a constructor

```
var item1 = new Item(9.99M, "Hammer");
```

If you like your variables' types to be self-evident, and therefore do not use `var` if you can avoid it, you might find Example 3-40 slightly unsatisfactory, because although it does expicitly state the type, it's on the righthand side of the =, and we'd be repeating ourselves if it was on the left too. But as you may recall from "To var, or Not to var?" on page 39, you can write the code in Example 3-41 if you prefer. If the compiler can infer what type of object is required (which it can determine from the variable type here) you can omit the type from the `new` expression.

Example 3-41. Using the target-typed new syntax

```
Item item2 = new(9.99M, "Hammer");
```

A type can define multiple constructors, but it must be possible to distinguish between them: you cannot define two constructors that both take the same number of arguments of the same types, because there would be no way for the `new` keyword to know which one you meant.

Default constructors and zero-argument constructors

If a class does not define any constructors at all, C# will provide a *default constructor* that is equivalent to an empty constructor that takes no arguments.

 Although the C# specification unambiguously defines a default constructor as one generated for you by the compiler, be aware that you will often see the term *default constructor* used to mean any public, parameterless constructor, regardless of whether it was generated by the compiler. There's some logic to this—when using a class, it's not possible to tell the difference between a compiler-generated constructor and an explicit zero-argument constructor, so if the term *default constructor* is to mean anything useful from that perspective, it can mean only a public constructor that takes no arguments. However, that's not how the C# specification defines the term.

The compiler-generated default constructor does nothing beyond the zero initialization of fields, which is the starting point for all new objects. However, there are some situations in which it is necessary to write your own parameterless constructor. You might need the constructor to execute some code. Example 3-42 sets an `_id` field based on a static field that it increments for each new object to give each instance a distinct ID. This doesn't require any arguments to be passed in, but it does involve running some code.

Example 3-42. A nonempty zero-argument constructor

```
public class ItemWithId
{
    private static int _lastId;
    private int _id;

    public ItemWithId()
    {
        _id = ++_lastId;
    }
}
```

There is another way to achieve the same effect as Example 3-42. I could have written a static method called GetNextId, and then used that in the _id field initializer. Then I wouldn't have needed to write this constructor. However, there is one advantage to putting code in the constructor: field initializers are not allowed to invoke the object's own nonstatic methods but constructors are. That's because the object is in an incomplete state during field initialization, so it may be dangerous to call its nonstatic methods—they may rely on fields having valid values. But an object is allowed to call its own nonstatic methods inside a constructor, because although the object's still not fully built yet, it's closer to completion, and so the dangers are reduced.

There are other reasons for writing your own zero-argument constructor. If you define at least one constructor for a class, this will disable the default constructor generation. If you need your class to provide parameterized construction, but you still want to offer a no-arguments constructor, you'll need to write one, even if it's empty. Alternatively, if you want to write a class whose only constructor is an empty, zero-argument one, but with a protection level other than the default of public—you might want to make it internal so that only your code can create instances, for example—you would need to write the constructor explicitly even if it is empty so that you have somewhere to specify the protection level.

 Some frameworks can use only classes that provide a public, zero-argument constructor. For example, if you build a UI with Windows Presentation Foundation (WPF), classes that can act as custom UI elements usually need such a constructor.

It is possible to write your own zero-argument constructor for a struct, but you should exercise caution because there are many scenarios in which that constructor will not run. The CLR's zero initialization is used instead in many cases. Fields and array elements get zero initialized, not constructed, and you can also explicitly ask for a zero-initialized value with default(MyStruct). Only if you invoke the zero-argument constructor explicitly with new MyStruct() will the constructor run. This may sound familiar—earlier we looked at how field initializers often won't run thanks to automatic zero initialization. That's because the compiler turns field initializers into code that runs inside the constructor, so if the constructor doesn't run, neither will the field initializers. (If you attempt to add a field initializer to a struct that has no constructors, you will get a compiler error, because there is nowhere for the field initialization code to go.)

Before C# 11.0, there was another constructor-related quirk of value types: all constructors for structs were obliged to assign values into all fields. This always seemed a little strange, given that in implicit initialization, where no constructor runs at all, all fields are zero-initialized. This rule has been removed, and any fields you do not explicitly initialize in a struct constructor are now implicitly set to their default values.

There's one more important compiler-generated constructor type to be aware of: when you write a record or record class, the compiler generates a constructor that gets used to create a duplicate whenever you use the with syntax shown back in Example 3-13. (This is known as a *copy constructor*, although if you're familiar with C++, don't be misled: this is used only within record types and is not a general-purpose copy mechanism. C# has no support for using a copy constructor in an ordinary class.) It performs a shallow copy by default, much as you get when copying a struct, but if you want to, you can write your own implementation, as Example 3-43 shows.

Example 3-43. Record type with customized copy constructor

```
public record ValueWithId(int Value, int Id)
{
    public ValueWithId(ValueWithId source)
    {
        Value = source.Value;
        Id = source.Id + 1;
    }
}
```

This prevents the compiler from generating the usual copy constructor. Yours will be used whenever the with syntax causes a copy of your type to be created.

The compiler does not generate a copy constructor for a record struct. There's no need, because all struct types are inherently copyable. And although nothing stops you from writing a constructor similar to the one in Example 3-43 for a record struct, the compiler will not use it.

Chaining constructors

If you write a type that offers several constructors, you may find that they have a certain amount in common—there are often initialization tasks that all constructors have to perform. The class in Example 3-42 calculates a numeric identifier for each object in its constructor, and if it were to provide multiple constructors, they might all need to do that same work. Moving the work into a field initializer would be one way to solve that, but what if only some constructors wanted to do it? You might have work that was common to most constructors, but you might want to make an exception by having one constructor that allows the ID to be specified rather than calculated. The field initializer approach would no longer be appropriate, because you'd want individual constructors to be able to opt in or out. Example 3-44 shows a modified version of the code from Example 3-42, defining two extra constructors.

Example 3-44. Optional chaining of constructors

```
public class ItemWithId
{
    private static int _lastId;
    private int _id;
    private string? _name;

    public ItemWithId()
    {
        _id = ++_lastId;
    }

    public ItemWithId(string name)
        : this()
    {
        _name = name;
    }

    public ItemWithId(string name, int id)
    {
        _name = name;
        _id = id;
    }
}
```

If you look at the second constructor in Example 3-44, its parameter list is followed by a colon and then `this()`, which invokes the first constructor. A constructor can invoke any other constructor that way. Example 3-45 shows a different way to structure all three constructors, illustrating how to pass arguments.

Example 3-45. Chained constructor arguments

```
public ItemWithId()
    : this(null)
{
}

public ItemWithId(string? name)
    : this(name, ++_lastId)
{
}

private ItemWithId(string? name, int id)
{
    _name = name;
    _id = id;
}
```

The two-argument constructor here is now the only one that actually sets any fields. The other constructors just pick suitable arguments for that main constructor. This is arguably a cleaner solution than the previous examples, because the work of initializing the fields is done in just one place, rather than having different constructors each performing their own smattering of field initialization.

Notice that I've made the two-argument constructor in Example 3-45 `private`. At first glance, it can look a bit odd to define a way of building an instance of a class and then to make it inaccessible, but it makes perfect sense when chaining constructors. And there are other scenarios in which a private constructor might be useful—we might want to write a method that makes a clone of an existing `ItemWithId`, in which case that constructor would be useful, but by keeping it private, we retain control of exactly how new objects get created. It can sometimes even be useful to make all of a type's constructors `private`, forcing users of the type to go through what's sometimes called a *factory method* (a `static` method that creates an object) to get hold of an instance. There are two common reasons for doing this. One is if full initialization of the object requires additional work of a kind that is inadvisable in a constructor (e.g., if you need to do slow work that uses the asynchronous language features described in Chapter 17, you cannot put that code inside a constructor). Another is if you want to use inheritance (see Chapter 6) to provide multiple variations on a type, but you want to be able to decide at runtime which particular type is returned.

If you write a type with a primary constructor, and you also wish to define some other constructors, those others are all required to call the primary constructor. This uses exactly the same chaining syntax as when calling any other constructors, but the call is mandatory. In a type with a primary constructor, every nonprimary constructor *must* chain to the primary constructor, either directly, or via some other constructor. If Example 3-45 hadn't wanted to make the two-argument constructor `private` it would have made sense to use the primary constructor syntax to emphasize the fact that it always runs. However, primary constructors are always public, so this wasn't an option here.

Static constructors

The constructors we've looked at so far run when a new instance of an object is created. Classes and structs can also define a static constructor. This runs at most once in the lifetime of the application. You do not invoke it explicitly—C# ensures that it runs automatically at some point before you first use the class. So, unlike an instance constructor, there's no opportunity to pass arguments. Since static constructors cannot take arguments, there can be only one per class. Also, because these are never accessed explicitly, you do not declare any kind of accessibility for a static constructor. Example 3-46 shows a class with a static constructor.

Example 3-46. Class with static constructor

```
public class Bar
{
    private readonly static DateTime _firstUsed;
    static Bar()
    {
        Console.WriteLine("Bar's static constructor");
        _firstUsed = DateTime.Now;
    }
}
```

Just as an instance constructor puts the instance into a useful initial state, the static constructor provides an opportunity to initialize any static fields. Since static constructors take no arguments, and the normal reason for writing them is that you can't or don't want to put the relevant initialization code into the corresponding field initializers, there's no such thing as a primary static constructor. (Primary constructors have parameters, and don't contain code because they have no body.)

By the way, you're not obliged to ensure that a constructor (static or instance) initializes every field. When a new instance of a class is created, the instance fields are initially all set to 0 (or the equivalent, such as `false` or `null`). Likewise, a type's static fields are all zeroed out before the class is first used. Unlike with local variables, you only need to initialize fields if you want to set them to something other than the default zero-like value.

Even then, you may not need a constructor. A field initializer may be sufficient. However, it's useful to know exactly when constructors and field initializers run. I mentioned earlier that the behavior varies according to whether constructors are present, so now that we've looked at constructors in a bit more detail, I can finally show a more complete picture of initialization. (There will still be more to come—as Chapter 6 describes, inheritance adds another dimension.)

At runtime, a type's static fields will first be set to 0 (or equivalent values). Next, the field initializers run in the order in which they are written in the source file. This ordering matters if one field's initializer refers to another. In Example 3-47, fields a and c both have the same initializer expression, but they end up with different values (1 and 42, respectively) due to the order in which initializers run.

Example 3-47. Significant ordering of static fields

```
private static int a = b + 1;
private static int b = 41;
private static int c = b + 1;
```

The exact moment at which static field initializers run depends on whether there's a static constructor. As mentioned earlier, if there isn't, then the timing is not precisely defined—C# guarantees to run them no later than the first access to one of the type's fields, but it reserves the right to run them arbitrarily early. The presence of a static constructor changes matters: in that case, the static field initializers run immediately before the constructor. So when does the constructor run? It will be triggered by one of two events, whichever occurs first: creating an instance or accessing any static member of the class.

For nonstatic fields, the story is similar: the fields are first all initialized to 0 (or equivalent values), and then field initializers run in the order in which they appear in the source file, and this happens before the constructor runs. The difference is that instance constructors are invoked explicitly, so it's clear when this initialization occurs.

I've written a class called `InitializationTestClass` designed to illustrate this construction behavior, shown in Example 3-48. The class has both static and nonstatic fields, all of which call a method, `GetValue`, in their initializers. That method always returns the same value, 1, but it prints out a message so we can see when it is called. The class also defines a no-arguments instance constructor and a static constructor, both of which print out messages.

Example 3-48. Initialization order

```
public class InitializationTestClass
{
    public InitializationTestClass()
    {
        Console.WriteLine("Constructor");
    }
```

```
    static InitializationTestClass()
    {
        Console.WriteLine("Static constructor");
    }

    public static int s1 = GetValue("Static field 1");
    public int ns1 = GetValue("Non-static field 1");
    public static int s2 = GetValue("Static field 2");
    public int ns2 = GetValue("Non-static field 2");

    private static int GetValue(string message)
    {
        Console.WriteLine(message);
        return 1;
    }

    public static void Foo()
    {
        Console.WriteLine("Static method");
    }
}

class Program
{
    static void Main()
    {
        Console.WriteLine("Main");
        InitializationTestClass.Foo();
        Console.WriteLine("Constructing 1");
        var i = new InitializationTestClass();
        Console.WriteLine("Constructing 2");
        i = new InitializationTestClass();
    }
}
```

The Main method prints out a message, calls a static method defined by Initial izationTestClass, and then constructs a couple of instances. Running the program, I see the following output:

```
Main
Static field 1
Static field 2
Static constructor
Static method
Constructing 1
Non-static field 1
Non-static field 2
Constructor
Constructing 2
Non-static field 1
Non-static field 2
Constructor
```

Notice that both static field initializers and the static constructor run before the call to the static method (Foo) begins. The field initializers run before the static constructor, and as expected, they run in the order in which they appear in the source file. Because this class includes a static constructor, we know when static initialization will begin—it is triggered by the first use of that type, which in this example is when our Main method calls InitializationTestClass.Foo. You can see that it happens immediately before that point and no earlier, because our Main method manages to print out its first message before the static initialization occurs. If this example did not have a static constructor, and had only static field initializers, there would be no guarantee that static initialization would happen at the exact same point; the C# specification allows the initialization to happen earlier.

You need to be careful about what you do in code that runs during static initialization: it may run earlier than you expect. For example, suppose your program uses some sort of diagnostic logging mechanism, and you need to configure this when the program starts in order to enable logging of messages to the proper location. There's always a possibility that code that runs during static initialization could execute before you've managed to do this, meaning that diagnostic logging will not yet be working correctly. That might make problems in this code hard to debug. Even when you narrow down C#'s options by supplying a static constructor, it's relatively easy to run that earlier than you intended. Use of any static member of a class will trigger its initialization, and you can find yourself in a situation where your static constructor is kicked off by static field initializers in some other class that doesn't have a static constructor—this could happen before your Main method even starts.

You could try to fix this by initializing the logging code in its own static initialization. Because C# guarantees to run initialization before the first use of a type, you might think that this would ensure that the logging initialization would complete before the static initialization of any code that uses the logging system. However, there's a potential problem: C# guarantees only when it will *start* static initialization for any particular class. It doesn't guarantee to wait for it to finish. It cannot make such a guarantee, because if it did, code such as the peculiarly British Example 3-49 would put it in an impossible situation.

Example 3-49. Circular static dependencies

```
public class AfterYou
{
    static AfterYou()
    {
        Console.WriteLine("AfterYou static constructor starting");
        Console.WriteLine($"AfterYou: NoAfterYou.Value = {NoAfterYou.Value}");
        Value = 123;
        Console.WriteLine("AfterYou static constructor ending");
    }
}
```

```
    public static int Value = 42;
}

public class NoAfterYou
{
    static NoAfterYou()
    {
        Console.WriteLine("NoAfterYou static constructor starting");
        Console.WriteLine($"NoAfterYou: AfterYou.Value: = {AfterYou.Value}");
        Value = 456;
        Console.WriteLine("NoAfterYou static constructor ending");
    }

    public static int Value = 42;
}
```

There is a circular relationship between the two types in this example: both have static constructors that attempt to use a static field defined by the other class. The behavior will depend on which of these two classes the program tries to use first. In a program that uses AfterYou first, I see the following output:

```
AfterYou static constructor starting
NoAfterYou static constructor starting
NoAfterYou: AfterYou.Value: = 42
NoAfterYou static constructor ending
AfterYou: NoAfterYou.Value = 456
AfterYou static constructor ending
```

As you'd expect, the static constructor for AfterYou runs first, because that's the class my program is trying to use. It prints out its first message, but then it tries to use the NoAfterYou.Value field. That means the static initialization for NoAfterYou now has to start, so we see the first message from its static constructor. That then goes on to retrieve the AfterYou.Value field, even though the AfterYou static constructor hasn't finished yet. (It retrieved the value set by the field initializer, 42, and not the value set by the static constructor, 123.) That's allowed because the ordering rules say only when static initialization is triggered, and they do not guarantee when it will finish. If they tried to guarantee complete initialization, this code would be unable to proceed—the NoAfterYou static constructor could not move forward because the AfterYou static construction is not yet complete, but that couldn't move forward because it would be waiting for the NoAfterYou static initialization to finish.

The moral of this story is that you should not get too ambitious about what you try to achieve during static initialization. It can be hard to predict the exact order in which things will happen.

The Microsoft.Extensions.Hosting NuGet package provides a much better way to handle initialization problems with its Host Builder class. (Some application frameworks, including the ASP.NET Core web framework, build on this.) It is beyond the scope of this chapter, but it is well worth finding and exploring.

Deconstructors

In Chapter 2, we saw how to deconstruct a tuple into its component parts, but deconstruction is not just for tuples. You can enable deconstruction for any type you write by adding a suitable Deconstruct member, as shown in Example 3-50.

Example 3-50. Enabling deconstruction

```
public readonly struct Size(double w, double h)
{
    public void Deconstruct(out double w, out double h)
    {
        w = W;
        h = H;
    }

    public double W { get; } = w;
    public double H { get; } = h;
}
```

C# recognizes this convention of a method named Deconstruct with a list of out arguments (the next section will describe out in more detail) and enables you to use the same deconstruction syntax as you can with tuples. Example 3-51 uses this to extract the component values of a Size to enable it to express succinctly the calculation it performs.

Example 3-51. Using a custom deconstructor

```
static double DiagonalLength(Size s)
{
    (double w, double h) = s;
    return Math.Sqrt(w * w + h * h);
}
```

Types with a deconstructor automatically support positional pattern matching. Chapter 2 showed how you can use a syntax very similar to deconstruction in a pattern to match tuples. Any type with a custom deconstructor can use this same syntax. Example 3-52 uses the Size type's custom deconstructor to define various patterns for a Size in a switch expression.

Example 3-52. Positional pattern using a custom deconstructor

```
static string DescribeSize(Size s) => s switch
{
    (0, 0) => "Empty",
    (0, _) => "Extremely narrow",
    (double w, 0) => $"Extremely short, and this wide: {w}",
    _ => "Normal"
};
```

Recall from Chapter 2 that positional patterns are recursive: each position within the pattern contains a nested pattern. Since `Size` deconstructs into two elements, each positional pattern has two positions in which to put child patterns. Example 3-52 variously uses constant patterns, a discard, and a declaration pattern.

To use a deconstructor in a pattern, C# needs to know the type to be deconstructed at compile time. This works in Example 3-52 because the input to the `switch` expression is of type `Size`. If a positional pattern's input is of type `object`, the compiler will presume that you're trying to match a tuple instead, unless you explicitly name the type, as Example 3-53 does.

Example 3-53. Positional pattern with explicit type

```
static string Describe(object o) => o switch
{
    Size (0, 0) => "Empty",
    Size (0, _) => "Extremely narrow",
    Size (double w, 0) => $"Extremely short, and this wide: {w}",
    Size _ => "Normal shape",
    _ => "Not a shape"
};
```

If you write a `record` type (either class-based or a `record struct`) with a primary constructor, as Example 3-54 does, the compiler generates a `Deconstruct` method for you. So just as with a tuple, any `record` defined in this way is automatically deconstructable. The deconstructor arguments will be defined in exactly the same order as they appear in the primary constructor.

Example 3-54. `record struct` using positional syntax

```
public readonly record struct Size(double W, double H);
```

Although the compiler provides special handling for the `Deconstruct` member that these examples rely on, from the runtime's perspective, this is just an ordinary method. So this would be a good time to look in more detail at methods.

Methods

Methods are named bits of code that can optionally return a result and that may take arguments. C# makes the fairly common distinction between *parameters* and *arguments*: a method defines a list of the inputs it expects—the parameters—and the code inside the method refers to these parameters by name. The values seen by the code could be different each time the method is invoked, and the term *argument* refers to the specific value supplied for a parameter in a particular invocation.

As you've already seen, when an accessibility specifier, such as `public` or `private`, is present, it appears at the start of the method declaration. The optional `static` keyword comes next, where present. After that, the method declaration states the return type. As with many C-family languages, you can write methods that return nothing, and you indicate this by putting the `void` keyword in place of the return type. Inside the method, you use the `return` keyword followed by an expression to specify the value for the method to return. In the case of a `void` method, you can use the `return` keyword without an expression to terminate the method, although this is optional, because when execution reaches the end of a `void` method, it terminates automatically. You normally only use `return` in a `void` method if your code decides to exit early.

Passing arguments by reference

Methods can return only one item directly in C#. If you want to return multiple values, you can of course make that item a tuple. Alternatively, you can designate parameters as being for output rather than input. Example 3-55 returns two values, both produced by integer division. The main return value is the quotient, but it also returns the remainder through its final parameter, which has been annotated with the `out` keyword.

Example 3-55. Returning multiple values with `out`

```
public static int Divide(int x, int y, out int remainder)
{
    remainder = x % y;
    return x / y;
}
```

Returning a tuple would have been more straightforward. (In fact .NET 7.0's new generic math feature adds an `int.DivRem` method that computes the quotient and remainder in a single operation, and it returns both results as a tuple.) However, tuples were only introduced in C# 7, whereas `out` parameters have been around since the start, so `out` crops up a lot in class libraries in scenarios where tuples might have been simpler. For example, you'll see lots of methods following a similar pattern to `int.TryParse`, in which the return type is a `bool` indicating success or failure, with the actual result being passed through an out parameter.

Example 3-56 shows one way to call a method with an out parameter. Instead of supplying an expression as we do with arguments for normal parameters, we've written the out keyword followed by a variable declaration. This introduces a new variable, which becomes the argument for this out parameter. So in this case, we end up with a new variable r initialized to 1 (the remainder of the division operation).

Example 3-56. Putting an out parameter's result into a new variable

```
int q = Divide(10, 3, out int r);
```

A variable declared in an out argument follows the usual scoping rules, so in Example 3-56, r will remain in scope for as long as q. Less obviously, r is available in the rest of the expression. Example 3-57 uses this to attempt to parse some text as an integer, returning the parsed result if that succeeds and a fallback value of –1 if parsing fails.

Example 3-57. Using an out parameter's result in the same expression

```
int value = int.TryParse(text, out int x) ? x : -1;
```

When you pass an out argument, this works by passing a reference to the local variable. When Example 3-56 calls `Divide`, and when that method assigns a value into `remainder`, it's really assigning it into the caller's r variable. This is an `int`, which is a value type, so it would not normally be passed by reference, and this kind of reference is limited compared to what you can do with a reference type.[7] For example, you can't declare a field in a class that can hold this kind of reference, because the local r variable will cease to exist when it goes out of scope, whereas an instance of a class can live indefinitely in a heap block. C# has to ensure that you cannot put a reference to a local variable in something that might outlive the variable it refers to.

---

7 The CLR calls this kind of reference a *managed pointer*, to distinguish it from a reference to an object on the heap. Unfortunately, C#'s terminology is less clear: it calls both of these things *references*.

Methods annotated with the `async` keyword (described in Chapter 17) cannot have any `out` arguments. This is because asynchronous methods may implicitly return to their caller before they complete, continuing their execution some time later. This in turn means that the caller may also have returned before the `async` method runs again, in which case the variables passed by reference might no longer exist by the time the asynchronous code is ready to set them. The same restriction applies to anonymous functions (described in Chapter 9). Both kinds of methods are allowed to pass `out` arguments into methods that they call, though.

You won't always want to declare a new variable for each `out` argument. As Example 3-58 shows, you can just write `out` followed by the name of an existing variable.

Example 3-58. Putting an out parameter's result into an existing variable

```
int r, q;
q = Divide(10, 3, out r);
Console.WriteLine($"3: {q}, {r}");
q = Divide(10, 4, out r);
Console.WriteLine($"4: {q}, {r}");
```

When invoking a method with an `out` parameter, we are required to indicate explicitly that we are aware of how the method uses the argument. Regardless of whether we use an existing variable or declare a new one, we must use the `out` keyword at call sites as well as in the declaration.

Sometimes you will want to invoke a method that has an `out` argument that you have no use for—maybe you only need the main return value. As Example 3-59 shows, you can just put an underscore after the `out` keyword. This tells C# to discard the result.

Example 3-59. Discarding an out parameter's result

```
int q = Divide(10, 3, out _);
```

You should avoid using _ (a single underscore) as the name of something in C#, because it can prevent the compiler from interpreting it as a discard. If a local variable of this name is in scope, writing `out _` has, since C# 1.0, indicated that you want to assign an `out` result into that variable, so for backward compatibility, current versions of C# have to retain that behavior. You can only use this form of discard if there is no symbol named _ in scope.

An out reference requires information to flow from the method back to the caller, so if you try to write a method that returns without assigning something into all of its out arguments, you'll get a compiler error. C# uses the *definite assignment* rules mentioned in Chapter 2 to check this. (This requirement does not apply if the method throws an exception instead of returning.) There's a related keyword, ref, that has similar reference semantics but allows information to flow bidirectionally. With a ref argument, it's as though the method has direct access to the variable the caller passed in—we can read its current value, as well as modify it. (The caller is obliged to ensure that variables passed with ref contain a value before making the call, so in this case, the method is not required to set it before returning.) If you call a method with a parameter annotated with ref instead of out, you have to make clear at the call site that you meant to pass a reference to a variable as the argument, as Example 3-60 shows.

Example 3-60. Calling a method with a ref argument

```
long x = 41;
Interlocked.Increment(ref x);
```

There's a third way to add a level of indirection to an argument: you can apply the in keyword. Whereas out only enables information to flow out of the method, in only allows it to flow in. It's like a ref argument but where the called method is not allowed to modify the variable the argument refers to. This may seem redundant: If there's no way to pass information back through the argument, why pass it by reference? An in int argument doesn't sound usefully different than an ordinary int argument. In fact, you wouldn't use in with int. You only use it with relatively large types. As you know, value types are normally passed by value, meaning a copy has to be made when passing a value as an argument. The in keyword enables us to avoid this copy by passing a reference instead—we get the same in-only semantics as when passing values the normal way but with the potential efficiency gains of not having to pass the whole value.

You should only use in for types that are larger than a pointer. This is why in int is not useful. An int is 32 bits long, so passing a reference to an int doesn't save us anything. In a 32-bit process, that reference will be a 32-bit pointer, so we have saved nothing, and we end up with the slight extra inefficiency involved in using a value indirectly through a reference. In a 64-bit process, the reference will be a 64-bit pointer, so we've ended up having to pass more data into the method than we would have done if we had just passed the int directly! (Sometimes the CLR can inline the method and avoid the costs of creating the pointer, but this means that at best in int would cost the same as an int. And since in is purely about performance, that's why in is not useful for small types such as int.)

Example 3-61 defines a fairly large value type. It contains four `double` values, each of which is 8 bytes in size, so each instance of this type occupies 32 bytes. The .NET design guidelines have always recommended avoiding making value types this large, and the main reason for this is that passing them as arguments is inefficient. Older versions of C# did not support this use of the `in` keyword, making this guideline more important, but now that `in` can reduce those costs, it might sometimes make sense to define a `struct` this large.

Example 3-61. A large value type

```
public readonly record struct Rect(double X, double Y, double Width, double Height);
```

Example 3-62 shows a method that calculates the area of a rectangle represented by the `Rect` type defined in Example 3-61. We really wouldn't want to have to copy all 32 bytes to call this very simple method, especially since it only uses half of the data in the `Rect`. This method annotates its parameter with `in`, so no such copying will occur: the argument will be passed by reference, which in practice means that only a pointer needs to be passed—either 4 or 8 bytes, depending on whether the code is running in a 32-bit or a 64-bit process.

Example 3-62. A method with an `in` parameter

```
public static double GetArea(in Rect r) => r.Width * r.Height;
```

You might expect that calling a method with `in` parameters would require the call site to indicate that it knows that the argument will be passed by reference by putting `in` in front of the argument, just like we need to write `out` or `ref` at the call site for the other two by-reference styles. And as Example 3-63 shows, you can do this, but it is optional. If you want to be explicit about the by-reference invocation, you can be, but unlike with `ref` and `out`, the compiler just passes the argument by reference anyway if you don't add `in`.

Example 3-63. Calling a method with an `in` parameter

```
var r = new Rect(10, 20, 100, 100);
double area = GetArea(in r);
double area2 = GetArea(r);
```

The `in` keyword is optional at the call site because defining such a parameter as `in` is only a performance optimization that does not change the behavior, unlike `out` and `ref`. Microsoft wanted to make it possible for developers to introduce a source-level-compatible change in which an existing method is modified by adding `in` to a parameter. This is a breaking change at the binary level, but in scenarios where you can be sure people will in any case need to recompile (e.g., when all the code is under your control), it might be useful to introduce such a change for performance reasons. Of course, as with all such enhancements you should measure performance before and after the change to see if it has the intended effect.

What if you want in-like behavior but you don't want it to happen implicitly? C# 11.0 and 12.0 have both added features that enable you to do more with ref, including the ability to store this kind of reference in a field, as Chapter 18 will describe. These features are intended for advanced performance-sensitive scenarios, and it can be preferable for the reference handling to be explicit. So you can now declare a parameter as ref readonly. This enables values to be passed by reference in such a way that the method won't be allowed to modify the value. It is similar to in, but with two significant differences. First, the caller must indicate that they are aware that a reference is being passed by writing ref at the call site. Second, in allows nonvariables to be passed by reference (e.g., SomeMethod(10)), meaning that the method might receive a reference to some temporary storage location that contains the evaluated value of some expression but which is not a variable. Some APIs that work with references only make sense when applied to variables. For example, Interlocked.Read provides a thread-safe way to read a 64-bit value (even in a 32-bit process, where such reads are not normally inherently safe), and attempting to use it on something that's not a variable would be a mistake. Such APIs can use ref readonly to enforce proper usage.

Although the examples just shown work as intended, in sets a trap for the unwary. It works only because I marked the struct in Example 3-61 as readonly. If instead of defining my own Rect I had used the very similar-looking struct with the same name from the System.Windows namespace (part of the WPF UI framework), Example 3-63 would not avoid the copy. It would have compiled and produced the correct results at runtime, but it would not offer any performance benefit. That's because System.Windows.Rect is not read-only. Earlier, I discussed the defensive copies that C# makes when you use a readonly field containing a mutable value type. The same principle applies here, because an in argument is in effect read-only: code that passes arguments expects them not to be modified unless they are explicitly marked as out or ref. So the compiler must ensure that in arguments are not modified even though the method being called has a reference to the caller's variable. When the type in question is already read-only, the compiler doesn't have to do any extra work. But if it is a mutable value type, then if the method to which this argument was passed in turn invokes a method on that value, the compiler generates code that makes a copy and invokes the method on that, because it can't know whether the method might modify the value. You might think that the compiler could enforce this by preventing the method with the in parameter from doing anything that might modify the value, but in practice that would mean stopping it from invoking any methods on the value—the compiler cannot in general determine whether any particular method call might modify the value. (And even if it doesn't today, maybe it will in a future version of the library that defines the type.) Since properties are methods in disguise, this makes in arguments more or less useless when used with mutable types.

 You should use in only with readonly value types, because mutable value types can undo the performance benefits. (Mutable value types are typically a bad idea in any case.)

C# offers a feature that can loosen this constraint a little. It allows the readonly keyword to be applied to methods and properties so that they can declare that they will not modify the value of which they are a member. This makes it possible to avoid these defensive copies on mutable values.

You can use the out and ref keywords with reference types too. That may sound redundant, but it can be useful. It provides double indirection—the method receives a reference to a variable that holds a reference. When you pass a reference type argument to a method, that method gets access to whatever object you choose to pass it. While the method can use members of that object, it can't normally replace it with a different object. But if you mark a reference type argument with ref, the method has access to your variable, so it could replace it with a reference to a completely different object.

It's technically possible for constructors to have out and ref parameters too, although it's unusual. Also, just to be clear, the out or ref qualifiers are part of the method or constructor signature. A caller can pass an out (or ref) argument if and only if the parameter was declared as out (or ref). Callers can't decide unilaterally to pass an argument by reference to a method that does not expect it.

Reference variables and return values

Now that you've seen various ways in which you can pass a method a reference to a value (or a reference to a reference), you might be wondering whether you can get hold of these references in other ways. You can, as Example 3-64 shows, but there are some constraints.

Example 3-64. A local ref variable

```
string? rose = null;
ref string? rosaIndica = ref rose;
rosaIndica = "smell as sweet";
Console.WriteLine($"A rose by any other name would {rose}");
```

This example declares a variable called `rose`. It then declares a new variable of type `ref string?`. The `ref` here has exactly the same effect as it does on a method parameter: it indicates that this variable is a reference to some other variable. Since the code initializes it with `ref rose`, the variable `rosaIndica` is a reference to that `rose` variable. So when the code assigns a value into `rosaIndica`, that value goes into the `rose` variable that `rosaIndica` refers to. When the final line reads the value of the `rose` variable, it will see the value that was written into `rosaIndica` by the preceding line.

So what are the constraints? C# has to ensure that you cannot put a reference to a local variable in something that might outlive the variable it refers to. So you cannot use this keyword on a field except in very specialized cases. Static fields live for as long as their defining type is loaded (typically until the process exits), and member fields of classes live on the heap enabling them to outlive any particular method call. (Most struct types can also live on the heap in some circumstances. But that's not true of `ref struct` types, which are described in Chapter 18, and those are the only types that can use the `ref` keyword on a field.) And even in cases where you might think lifetime isn't a problem (because the target of the reference is itself a field in an object, for example), it turns out that the runtime simply doesn't support storing this kind of reference in a field for most types, or as an element type in an array. More subtly, this also means you can't use a `ref` local variable in a context where C# would store the variable in a class. That rules out their use in `async` methods and iterators and also prevents them being captured by anonymous functions (which are described in Chapters 17, 5, and 9, respectively).

Although most types cannot define fields with `ref`, they can define methods that return a `ref`-style reference (and since properties are methods in disguise, a property getter may also return a reference). As always, the C# compiler has to ensure that a reference cannot outlive the thing it refers to, so it will prevent use of this feature in cases where it cannot be certain that it can enforce this rule. Example 3-65 shows various uses of `ref` return types, some of which the compiler accepts, and some it does not.

Example 3-65. Valid and invalid uses of ref returns

```
public class Referable
{
    private int i;
    private int[] items = new int[10];

    public ref int FieldRef => ref i;

    public ref int GetArrayElementRef(int index) => ref items[index];

    public ref int GetBackSameRef(ref int arg) => ref arg;
```

```
    public ref int WillNotCompile()
    {
        int v = 42;
        return ref v;
    }

    public ref int WillAlsoNotCompile()
    {
        int i = 42;
        return ref GetBackSameRef(ref i);
    }

    public ref int WillCompile(ref int i)
    {
        return ref GetBackSameRef(ref i);
    }
}
```

The methods that return a reference to either a field or an element in an array are allowed, because ref-style references can always refer *to* items inside objects on the heap. (They just can't live *in* them.) Heap objects can exist for as long as they are needed. (The garbage collector, discussed in Chapter 7, is aware of these kinds of references and will ensure that heap objects with references pointing to their interiors are kept alive.) A method can return any of its ref arguments, because the caller was already required to ensure that they remain valid for the duration of the call. However, a method cannot return a reference to one of its local variables, because in cases where those variables end up living on the stack, the stack frame will cease to exist when the method returns. It would be a problem if a method could return a reference to a variable in a now-defunct stack frame.

The rules get a little more subtle when it comes to returning a reference that was obtained from some other method. The final two methods in Example 3-65 both attempt to return the reference returned by GetBackSameRef. One works, and the other does not. The outcome makes sense. WillAlsoNotCompile needs to be rejected for the same reason WillNotCompile was: both attempt to return a reference to a local variable, and WillAlsoNotCompile is just trying to disguise this by going through another method, GetBackSameRef. In cases like these, the C# compiler makes the conservative assumption that any method that returns a ref and that also takes one or more ref arguments might choose to return a reference to one of those arguments. So the compiler prevents us from returning the ref returned by GetBackSameRef in WillAlsoNotCompile on the grounds that it might be a reference to the same local variable that was passed in by reference. (And it happens to be right in this case. But it would reject any call of this form even if the method in question returned a reference to something else entirely.) But it allows WillCompile to return the ref returned by GetBackSameRef because in that case, the reference we pass in is one we would be allowed to return directly.

As with `in` arguments, the main reason for using `ref` returns is that they can enable greater runtime efficiency by avoiding copies. Instead of returning the entire value, methods of this kind can just return a pointer to the existing value. It also has the effect of enabling callers to modify whatever is referred to. For example, in Example 3-65, I can assign a value into the `FieldRef` property, even though the property appears to be read-only. The absence of a setter doesn't matter in this case because its type is `ref int`, which is valid as the target of an assignment. So by writing `r.FieldRef = 42;` (where `r` is of type `Referable`), I get to modify the `i` field. Likewise, the reference returned by `GetArrayElementRef` can be used to modify the relevant element in the array. If this is not your intention, you can make the return type `ref readonly` instead of just `ref`. In this case, the compiler will not allow the resulting reference to be used as the target of an assignment.

 You should only use `ref readonly` returns with a `readonly` `struct`, beause otherwise you will run into the same defensive copy issues we saw earlier.

Optional arguments

You can make non-`out`, non-`ref` arguments optional by defining default values. The method in Example 3-66 specifies the values that the arguments should have if the caller doesn't supply them.

Example 3-66. A method with optional arguments

```
public static void Blame(string perpetrator = "the youth of today",
    string problem = "the downfall of society")
{
    Console.WriteLine($"I blame {perpetrator} for {problem}.");
}
```

This method can then be invoked with no arguments, one argument, or both arguments. Example 3-67 just supplies the first, taking the default for the `problem` argument.

Example 3-67. Omitting one argument

```
Blame("mischievous gnomes");
```

Normally, when invoking a method, you specify the arguments in order. However, what if you want to call the method in Example 3-66, but you want to provide a value only for the second argument, using the default value for the first? You can't just leave the first argument empty—if you tried to write `Blame( , "everything")`, you'd get a compiler error. Instead, you can specify the name of the argument you'd like to supply, using the syntax shown in Example 3-68. C# will fill in the arguments you omit with the specified default values.

Example 3-68. Specifying an argument name

```
Blame(problem: "everything");
```

Obviously, you can omit arguments like this only when you're invoking methods that define default argument values. However, you are free to specify argument names when invoking any method—sometimes it can be useful to do this even when you're not omitting any arguments, because it can make it easier to see what the arguments are for when reading the code. This is particularly helpful if you're faced with an API that takes arguments of type bool and it's not immediately clear what they mean. Example 3-69 constructs a StreamReader and a StreamWriter (described in Chapter 15), each using constructors taking many arguments. It's arguably clear enough what the stream, filepath, and the Encoding.UTF8 arguments represent, but the others are likely to be something of a mystery to anyone reading the code, unless they happen to have committed all 13 StreamReader and 10 StreamWriter constructor overloads to memory. (In Chapter 7 the *using declaration* syntax shown here is described.)

Example 3-69. Unclear arguments

```
using var r = new StreamReader(stream, Encoding.UTF8, true, 8192, false);
using var w = new StreamWriter(filepath, true, Encoding.UTF8);
```

Although argument names are not required here, we can make it much easier to understand what the code does by including some anyway. As Example 3-70 shows, we're free just to name the more cryptic ones, as long as we're supplying arguments for all of the parameters.

Example 3-70. Improving clarity by naming arguments

```
using var r = new StreamReader(stream, Encoding.UTF8,
  detectEncodingFromByteOrderMarks: true, bufferSize: 8192, leaveOpen: false);
using var w = new StreamWriter(filepath, append: true, Encoding.UTF8);
```

It's important to understand how C# implements default argument values because it has an impact on evolving library design. When you invoke a method without providing all the arguments, as Example 3-68 does, the compiler generates code that passes a full set of arguments as normal. It effectively rewrites your code, adding back in the arguments you left out. The significance of this is that if you write a library that defines default argument values like this, you will run into problems if you ever change the defaults. Code that was compiled against the old version of the library will have copied the old defaults into the call sites and won't pick up the new values unless it is recompiled.

Overloading

You will sometimes see an alternative mechanism used for allowing arguments to be omitted, which avoids baking default values into call sites: *overloading*. This is a slightly histrionic term for the rather mundane idea that a single name or symbol can be given multiple meanings. In fact, we already saw this technique with constructors —in Example 3-45, I defined one main constructor that did the real work, and then two other constructors that called into that one. We can use the same trick with methods, as Example 3-71 shows.

Example 3-71. Overloaded method

```
public static void Blame(string perpetrator, string problem)
{
    Console.WriteLine($"I blame {perpetrator} for {problem}.");
}

public static void Blame(string perpetrator)
{
    Blame(perpetrator, "the downfall of society");
}

public static void Blame()
{
    Blame("the youth of today", "the downfall of society");
}
```

In one sense, this is slightly less flexible than default argument values, because code calling the `Blame` method no longer has any way to specify a value for the `problem` argument while picking up the default `perpetrator` (although it would be easy enough to solve that by adding a method with a different name). On the other hand, method overloading offers two potential advantages: it allows you to decide on the default values at runtime if necessary, and it also provides a way to make `out` and `ref` arguments optional. Those require references to variables, so there's no way to define a default value, but you can always provide overloads with and without those arguments if you need to. And you can use a mixture of the two techniques—you might rely mainly on optional arguments, using overloads only to enable `out` or `ref` arguments to be omitted.

Variable argument count with the params keyword

Some methods need to be able to accept different amounts of data in different situations. Take the mechanism that I've used a few times in this book to display information. In most cases, I've passed a simple string to `Console.WriteLine`, and when I've wanted to format and display other pieces of information, I've used string interpolation to embed expressions in strings. However, as you may recall, Chapter 2 showed an alternative, the older composite formatting approach, shown in Example 3-72.

Example 3-72. String formatting

```
var r = new Random();
Console.WriteLine(
    "{0}, {1}, {2}, {3}",
    r.Next(10), r.Next(10), r.Next(10), r.Next(10));
```

If you look at the documentation for `Console.WriteLine`, you'll see that it offers several overloads taking various numbers of arguments. The number of overloads has to be finite, but if you try it, you'll find that this is nonetheless an open-ended arrangement. You can pass as many arguments as you like after the string, and the numbers in the placeholders can go as high as necessary to refer to these arguments. (This is also true for other types that support composite formatting, such as `string.Format`.) The final line of Example 3-72 passes four arguments after the string, and even though the `Console` class does not define an overload accepting that many arguments, it works.

One particular overload of the `Console.WriteLine` method takes over once you pass more than a certain number of arguments after the string (more than three, as it happens). This overload just takes two arguments: a `string` and an `object[]` array. The code that the compiler creates to invoke the method builds an array to hold all the arguments after the string and passes that. So the final statement of Example 3-72 is effectively equivalent to the code in Example 3-73. (Chapter 5 describes arrays.)

Example 3-73. Explicitly passing multiple arguments as an array

```
Console.WriteLine(
    "{0}, {1}, {2}, {3}",
    new object[] { r.Next(10), r.Next(10), r.Next(10), r.Next(10) });
```

The compiler will do this only with parameters that are annotated with the `params` keyword. Example 3-74 shows how the relevant `Console.WriteLine` method's declaration looks.

Example 3-74. The params keyword

```
public static void WriteLine(
    [StringSyntax("CompositeFormat")] string format,
    params object?[]? arg);
```

The params keyword can appear only on a method's final parameter, and that parameter type must be an array. In this case, it's an object?[], meaning that we can pass objects of any type (or nulls), but if you use params in your own methods you can be more specific to limit what can be passed in.

 When a method is overloaded, the C# compiler looks for the method whose parameters best match the arguments supplied. It will consider using a method with a params argument only if a more specific match is not available.

You may be wondering why the Console class bothers to offer overloads that accept one, two, or three object arguments. The presence of this params version seems to make those redundant—it lets you pass any number of arguments after the string, so what's the point of the overloads that take a specific number of arguments? Those overloads exist to make it possible to avoid allocating an array. That's not to say that arrays are particularly expensive; they cost no more than any other object of the same size. However, allocating memory is not free. Every object you allocate will eventually have to be freed by the garbage collector (except for objects that hang around for the whole life of the program), so reducing the number of allocations is usually good for performance. Because of this, most APIs in the runtime libraries that accept a variable number of arguments through params also offer overloads that allow a small number of arguments to be passed without needing to allocate an array to hold them.

Local functions

You can define methods inside other methods. These are called *local functions*, and Example 3-75 defines two of them. (You can also put them inside other method-like features, such as constructors or property accessors.)

Example 3-75. Local functions

```
static double GetAverageDistanceFrom(
    (double X, double Y) referencePoint,
    (double X, double Y)[] points)
{
    double total = 0;
    for (int i = 0; i < points.Length; ++i)
    {
        total += GetDistanceFromReference(points[i]);
```

```
    }
    return total / points.Length;

    double GetDistanceFromReference((double X, double Y) p)
    {
        return GetDistance(p, referencePoint);
    }

    static double GetDistance((double X, double Y) p1, (double X, double Y) p2)
    {
        double dx = p1.X - p2.X;
        double dy = p1.Y - p2.Y;
        return Math.Sqrt(dx * dx + dy * dy);
    }
}
```

One reason for using local functions is that they can make the code easier to read by moving steps into named methods—it's easier to see what's happening when there's a method call to GetDistance than it is if we just have the calculations inline. Be aware that there can be overheads, although in this particular example, when I run the Release build of this code on .NET 8.0, the JIT compiler is smart enough to inline both of the local calls here, so the two local functions vanish, and GetAverage DistanceFrom ends up being just one method.[8] So we've paid no penalty here, but with more complex nested functions, the JIT compiler may decide not to inline. And when that happens, it's useful to know how the C# compiler enables this code to work.

The GetDistanceFromReference method here takes a single tuple argument, but it uses the referencePoint variable defined by its containing method. For this to work, the C# compiler moves that variable into a generated struct, which it passes by reference to the GetDistanceFromReference method as a hidden argument. This is how a single local variable can be accessible to both methods. Since this generated struct is passed by reference, the referencePoint variable can still remain on the stack in this example. However, if you obtain a delegate referring to a local method, any variables shared in this way have to move into a class that lives on the garbage-collected heap, which will have higher overheads. (See Chapters 7 and 9 for more details.) If you want to avoid any such overheads, you can always just not share any variables between the inner and outer methods. You can tell the compiler that this is your intention by applying the static keyword to the local function, as Example 3-75 does with GetDistance. This will cause the compiler to report an error if the method attempts to use a variable from its containing method.

---

8 As Chapter 1 described, the JIT compiler uses *tiered compilation* to improve startup times without sacrificing throughput: it doesn't optimize aggressively at first. The CLR detects when methods are heavily used and recompiles them with full optimization. Only this second pass inlined both local functions.

Besides providing a way to split methods up for readability, local functions are sometimes used to work around some limitations with iterators (see Chapter 5) and async methods (Chapter 17). These are methods that might return partway through execution and then continue later, which means the compiler needs to arrange to store all of their local variables in an object living on the heap so that those variables can survive for as long as is required. This prevents these kinds of methods from declaring variables of certain types, such as reference variables, or Span<T> (described in Chapter 18). In cases where you need to use both async and Span<T>, it is common to move code using the latter into a local, non-async function that lives inside the async function. This enables the local function to use local variable references with these constrained types.

Expression-bodied methods

If you write a method simple enough to consist of nothing more than a single return statement, you can use a more concise syntax. Example 3-76 shows an alternative way to write the GetDistanceFromReference method from Example 3-75. (If you're reading this book in order, you've probably noticed that I've already used this style in a few other examples.) By the way, I can't do this for GetDistance because that contains multiple statements.

Example 3-76. An expression-bodied method

```
double GetDistanceFromReference((double X, double Y) p)
    => GetDistance(p, referencePoint);
```

Instead of a method body, you write => followed by the expression that would otherwise have followed the return keyword. This => syntax intentionally resembles the lambda syntax you can use for writing inline functions and building expression trees. These are discussed in Chapter 9. But when using => to write an expression-bodied member, it's just a convenient shorthand. The code works exactly as if you had written a full method containing just a return statement. You can also use this syntax with void methods. Since those don't return a value, this syntax is equivalent to writing a full method containing a single expression.

Extension methods

C# lets you write methods that appear to be new members of existing types. *Extension methods*, as they are called, look like normal static methods but with the this keyword added before the first parameter. You are allowed to define extension methods only in a static class. Example 3-77 adds a not especially useful extension method to the string type, called Show.

Example 3-77. An extension method

```
namespace MyApplication;

public static class StringExtensions
{
    public static void Show(this string s) => Console.WriteLine(s);
}
```

I've shown the namespace declaration in this example because namespaces are significant: extension methods are available only if you've written a using directive for the namespace in which the extension is defined, or if the code you're writing is defined in the same namespace. In code that does neither of these things, the string class will look normal and will not acquire the Show method defined by Example 3-77. However, code such as Example 3-78, which is defined in the same namespace as the extension method, will find that the method is available.

Example 3-78. Extension method available due to namespace declaration

```
namespace MyApplication;

internal class Showy
{
    public static void Greet() => "Hello".Show();
}
```

The code in Example 3-79 is in a different namespace, but it also has access to the extension method, thanks to a using directive.

Example 3-79. Extension method available due to using directive

```
using MyApplication;

namespace Other;

internal class Vocal
{
    public static void Hail() => "Hello".Show();
}
```

Extension methods are not really members of the class for which they are defined—the string class does not truly gain an extra method in these examples. It's just an illusion maintained by the C# compiler, one that it keeps up even in situations where method invocation happens implicitly. This is particularly useful with C# features that require certain methods to be available. In Chapter 2, you saw that foreach loops depend on a GetEnumerator method. Many of the LINQ features we'll look at in Chapter 10 also depend on certain methods being present, as do the asynchronous language features described in Chapter 17. In all cases, you can enable these language features for types that do not support them directly by writing suitable extension methods.

Properties

Classes and structs can define *properties*, which are really just methods in disguise. To access a property, you use a syntax that looks like field access but ends up invoking a method. Properties can be useful for signaling intent. When something is exposed as a property, the implication is that it represents information about the object, rather than an operation the object performs, so reading a property is usually inexpensive and should have no significant side effects. Methods, on the other hand, are more likely to cause an object to do something.

Of course, since properties are just a kind of method, nothing enforces this. You are free to write a property that takes hours to run and makes significant changes to your application's state whenever its value is read, but that would be a pretty unhelpful way to design code.

Properties typically provide a pair of methods: one to get the value and one to set it. Example 3-80 shows a very common pattern: a property with get and set methods that provide access to a field. Why not just make the field public? That's often frowned upon, because it makes it possible for external code to change an object's state without the object knowing about it. It might be that in future revisions of the code, the object needs to do something—perhaps update the UI—every time the value changes. In any case, because properties contain code, they offer more flexibility than public fields. For example, you might want to store the data in a different format than is returned by the property, or you may even be able to implement a property that calculates its value from other properties. Another reason for using properties is simply that some systems require it—for example, some UI databinding systems are only prepared to consume properties. Also, some types do not support instance fields; later in this chapter, I'll show how to define an abstract type using an *interface*, and interfaces can contain properties but not instance fields.

Example 3-80. Class with simple property

```
public class HasProperty
{
    private int _x;
    public int X
    {
        get
        {
            return _x;
        }
        set
```

```
    {
        _x = value;
    }
  }
}
```

 Inside a set accessor, value has a special meaning. It's a *contextual keyword*—text that the language treats as a keyword in certain contexts. Outside of a property, you can use value as an identifier, but within a property, it represents the value that the caller wants to assign to the property.

In cases where the entire body of the get is just a return statement, or where the set is a single expression statement, you can use the *expression-bodied member* syntax shown in Example 3-81. (This is very similar to the method syntax shown in Example 3-76.)

Example 3-81. Expression-bodied get and set

```
public class HasProperty
{
    private int _x;
    public int X
    {
        get => _x;
        set => _x = value;
    }
}
```

The pattern in Examples 3-80 and 3-81 is so common that C# can write most of it for you. Example 3-82 is more or less equivalent—the compiler generates a field for us and produces get and set methods that retrieve and modify the value just like those in Example 3-80. The only difference is that code elsewhere in the same class can't get directly at the field in Example 3-82, because the compiler hides it. The official name in the language specification for this is an *automatically implemented property*, but these are typically referred to as just *auto-properties*.

Example 3-82. An auto-property

```
public class HasProperty
{
    public int X { get; set; }
}
```

Whether you use explicit or automatic properties, this is just a fancy syntax for a pair of methods. The get method returns a value of the property's declared type—an int, in this case—while the setter takes a single argument of that type through the implicit value parameter. Example 3-80 makes use of that argument to update the field. You're not obliged to store the value in a field, of course. In fact, nothing even forces you to make the get and set methods related in any way—you could write a getter that returns random values and a setter that completely ignores the value you supply. However, just because you *can* doesn't mean you *should*. In practice, anyone using your class will expect properties to remember the values they've been given, not least because in use, properties look just like fields, as Example 3-83 shows.

Example 3-83. Using a property

```
var o = new HasProperty();
o.X = 123;
o.X += 432;
Console.WriteLine(o.X);
```

If you're using the full syntax shown in Example 3-80 to implement a property, or the expression-bodied form shown in Example 3-81, you can leave out either the set or the get to make a read-only or write-only property. Read-only properties can be useful for aspects of an object that are fixed for its lifetime, such as an identifier, or that are calculated from other properties. Write-only properties are less useful, although they can crop up in dependency injection systems. You can't make a write-only property with the auto-property syntax shown in Example 3-82, because you wouldn't be able to do anything useful with the value being set.

There are two variations on read-only properties. Sometimes it is useful to have a property that is publicly read-only but that your class is free to change. You can define a property where the getter is public but the setter is not (or vice versa for a publicly write-only property). You can do this with either the full or the automatic syntax. Example 3-84 shows how this looks with the latter.

Example 3-84. Auto-property with private setter

```
public int X { get; private set; }
```

If you want your property to be read-only in the sense that its value never changes after construction, you can leave out the setter entirely when using the auto-property syntax, as Example 3-85 shows.

Example 3-85. Auto-property with no setter

```
public int X { get; }
```

With no setter and no directly accessible field, you may be wondering how you can set the value of such a property. The answer is that inside your object's constructor, the property appears to be settable. (There isn't really a setter if you omit the set—the compiler generates code that just sets the backing field directly when you "set" the property in the constructor.) A get-only auto-property is effectively equivalent to a readonly field wrapped with an ordinary get-only property. As with fields, you can also write an initializer to provide an initial value. Example 3-86 uses both styles; if you use the constructor that takes no arguments, the property's value will be 42, and if you use the other constructor, it will have whatever value you supply.

Example 3-86. Initializing an auto-property with no setter

```
public class WithAutos
{
    public int X { get; } = 42;

    public WithAutos()
    {
    }

    public WithAutos(int val)
    {
        X = val;
    }
}
```

This initializer syntax works for read-write properties, by the way. You can also use it if you want to create a record type that uses the positional syntax but that wants the properties to be writable, as Example 3-87 shows. This is slightly unusual, since the features offered by record types are mainly intended to make it easier to define immutable data types. But mutability is supported, and it can be useful to require certain properties to be initialized even when they are writable, to avoid the nullable reference type system complaining that your non-nullable property might initially have a null value.

Example 3-87. Record requiring initial values but allowing later modification

```
public record EnforcedInitButMutable(string Name, string FavoriteColor)
{
    public string Name { get; set; } = Name;
    public string FavoriteColor { get; set; } = FavoriteColor;
}
```

Since the positional syntax defines a primary constructor, you might be tempted in cases like Example 3-87 to use more conventionally cased names for the constructor arguments, e.g., name and favoriteColor. If this type were an ordinary class or struct, that would be a reasonable thing to do—when those have primary constructor parameters used only in initializer expressions, the compiler doesn't create any hidden fields to hold on to those parameters after the constructor completes. But with record types, the compiler *always* generates a property for each constructor parameter. So the effect of using normal constructor argument naming conventions would be to create a record with four properties: name, Name, favoriteColor, and Favorite Color. It might look like Example 3-87 has defined the same properties twice, but in fact the duplicate names are how C# knows that we are just saying we want to replace the normal generated properties here.

Initializer syntax

You will often want to set certain properties when you create an object, because it might not be possible to supply all relevant information through constructor arguments. This is particularly common with objects that represent settings for controlling some operation. For example, the ProcessStartInfo type enables you to configure many different aspects of a newly created OS process. It has 16 properties, but you would typically only need to set a few of these in any particular scenario. Even if you assume that the name of the file to run should always be present, there are still 32,768 possible combinations of properties. You wouldn't want to have a constructor for every one of those.

In practice, a class might offer constructors for a handful of particularly common combinations, but for everything else, you just set the properties after construction. C# offers a succinct way to create an object and set some of its properties in a single expression. Example 3-88 uses this *object initializer* syntax. This also works with fields, although it's relatively unusual to have writable public fields.

Example 3-88. Using an object initializer

```
Process.Start(new ProcessStartInfo
{
    FileName = "cmd.exe",
    UseShellExecute = true,
    WindowStyle = ProcessWindowStyle.Maximized,
});
```

You can supply constructor arguments too. Example 3-89 has the same effect as Example 3-88 but chooses to supply the filename as a constructor argument. (This is one of the few properties ProcessStartInfo lets you supply that way.)

Example 3-89. Using a constructor and an object initializer

```
Process.Start(new ProcessStartInfo("cmd.exe")
{
```

```
    UseShellExecute = true,
    WindowStyle = ProcessWindowStyle.Maximized,
});
```

The object initializer syntax can remove the need for a separate variable to refer to the object while you set the properties you need. As Examples 3-88 and 3-89 show, you can pass an object initialized in this way directly as an argument to a method. More generally, this style of initialization can be contained entirely within a single expression. This is important in scenarios that use expression trees, which we'll be looking at in Chapter 9. Another important benefit of initializers is that they can use an `init` accessor.

Init-only properties

Example 3-90 shows a variation on the theme of read-only properties. In place of the `set`, we have the `init` keyword. (By the way, when a `record` type generates a property for one of its primary constructor parameters, that will also have `get` and `init` accessors.)

Example 3-90. Class with auto-property with init-only setter

```
public class WithInit
{
    public int X { get; init; }
}
```

This is almost identical to a read-only property: it indicates that the property is not to be modified after the object is initialized. However, there's one significant difference: the compiler generates a public setter when you use this syntax. It refuses to compile code that attempts to modify the property after the object has been initialized, so for most scenarios it behaves just like a read-only property, but this enables one critical scenario: it lets you set the property in an object initializer as Example 3-91 shows.

Example 3-91. Setting an init-only property

```
var x = new WithInit
{
    X = 42
};
```

You can also set init-only properties in any place where it would be permissible to set a read-only property. The only distinction between an init-only property and a read-only one is the ability to set the property in an object initializer.

The restrictions on init-only properties are enforced only by the compiler. From the CLR's perspective, they are read-write properties, so if you were to use this sort of property from some language that did not recognize this init-only feature, or using indirect means such as reflection (see Chapter 13), you could set the property at any time, not just during initialization.

Init-only properties provide a way to enable immutable `struct` types to use the same `with` syntax that is available to record types. Example 3-92 shows another variation on the `Point` type used in various earlier examples, this time featuring init-only properties.

Example 3-92. A `readonly struct` with init-only properties

```
public readonly struct Point(double x, double y)
{
    public double X { get; init; } = x;
    public double Y { get; init; } = y;
}
```

This defines setters for the properties, which would normally not be allowed with a `readonly struct`, but because they can be set only during initialization, they don't cause a problem here. And they enable code such as Example 3-93.

Example 3-93. Using the `with` syntax on a nonrecord `readonly struct`

```
Point p1 = new(0, 10);
Point p2 = p1 with { X = 20 };
```

Since you can use the `with` syntax with a nonrecord `struct`, you might be wondering whether it also works for a nonrecord `class`. It doesn't. The `with` keyword depends on the ability to create a copy of an existing instance. This is not a problem with `struct` types—their defining feature is that they can be copied. But there is no reliable general-purpose way to clone an instance of a `class`, so with reference types, `with` only works on records, because record types *are* reliably cloneable.

Required properties

What should we do if we want to define a property and require anyone creating an instance of our type to supply a value for that property? You already know one answer to that question: define one or more constructors, and make sure that all of the constructors require an argument that will become that property's value. And while that certainly works, there are some situations in which this might not be ideal.

For example, if you use inheritance (the subject of Chapter 6), and you choose to inherit from a type that enforces property initialization through mandatory constructor arguments, your type will need to define a constructor that accepts all of these same arguments and passes them on to the base class. In effect, each derived class ends up having to duplicate bits of its base class, which is disappointing if you were looking to inheritance as a reuse mechanism. Also, as previously mentioned, some frameworks initialize objects using reflection, and require them to provide a default constructor.

C# 11.0 introduced a different way to make properties mandatory. If you apply the `required` keyword to a property declaration, this indicates that your type requires the property to be supplied with a value during initialization. This relies on the compiler to enforce this rule by the way—unlike with constructors, the CLR does nothing to check that all necessary values have been supplied. So it would be possible to create an instance of such a type with the reflection API (discussed in Chapter 13) without setting `required` properties. However, there are plenty of scenarios for which compile-time checking is good enough. Example 3-94 shows how to use it.

Example 3-94. Required properties

```
public class Person
{
    public required int YearOfBirth { get; init; }
    public required string FavoriteColor { get; set; }
}
```

The `required` keyword comes after the accessibility modifier (if there is one) and before the property's type. Notice that in addition to both of these properties being required, `YearOfBirth` has an `init` accessor, indicating that this property can't be changed after initialization. The `FavoriteColor`, on the other hand, just has a normal `set`, so although it must be set during initialization (because of the `required` keyword), it can be modified later.

Calculated properties

Sometimes it is useful to write a read-only property with a value calculated entirely in terms of other properties. For example, if you have written a type representing a vector with properties called `X` and `Y`, you could add a property that returns the magnitude of the vector, calculated from those other two properties, as shown in Example 3-95.

Example 3-95. A calculated property

```
public double Magnitude
{
```

```
    get
    {
        return Math.Sqrt(X * X + Y * Y);
    }
}
```

There is a more compact way of writing this. We could use the expression-bodied syntax shown in Example 3-81, but for a read-only property, we can go one step further: you can put the => and expression directly after the property name. (This enables us to leave out the braces and the get keyword.) Example 3-96 is exactly equivalent to Example 3-95.

Example 3-96. An expression-bodied read-only property

```
public double Magnitude => Math.Sqrt(X * X + Y * Y);
```

Speaking of read-only properties, there's an important issue to be aware of involving properties, value types, and immutability.

Properties and mutable value types

As I mentioned earlier, value types tend to be more straightforward if they're immutable, but it's not a requirement. One reason to avoid modifiable value types is that you can end up accidentally modifying a copy of the value rather than the one you meant, and this issue becomes apparent if you define a property that uses a mutable value type. The Point struct in the System.Windows namespace is modifiable, so we can use it to illustrate the problem. Example 3-97 defines a Location property of this type.

Example 3-97. A property using a mutable value type

```
using System.Windows;

public class Item
{
    public Point Location { get; set; }
}
```

The Point type defines read/write properties called X and Y, so given a variable of type Point, you can set these properties. However, if you try to set either of these properties via another property, the code will not compile. Example 3-98 tries this—it attempts to modify the X property of a Point retrieved from an Item object's Location property.

Example 3-98. Error: cannot modify a property of a value type property

```
var item = new Item();
item.Location.X = 123;  // Will not compile
```

This example produces the following error:

```
error CS1612: Cannot modify the return value of 'Item.Location' because it is
not a variable
```

C# considers fields to be variables as well as local variables and method arguments, so if we were to modify Example 3-97 so that `Location` was a public field rather than a property, Example 3-98 would then compile and would work as expected. But why doesn't it work with a property? Remember that properties are just methods, so Example 3-97 is more or less equivalent to Example 3-99.

Example 3-99. Replacing a property with methods

```
using System.Windows;

public class Item
{
    private Point _location;
    public Point get_Location()
    {
        return _location;
    }
    public void set_Location(Point value)
    {
        _location = value;
    }
}
```

Since `Point` is a value type, `get_Location` returns a copy. You might be wondering if we could use the `ref` return feature described earlier. We certainly could with plain methods, but there are a couple of constraints to doing this with properties. First, you cannot define an auto-property with a `ref` type. Second, you cannot define a writable property with a `ref` type. However, you can define a read-only `ref` property, as Example 3-100 shows.

Example 3-100. A property returning a reference

```
using System.Windows;

public class Item
{
    private Point _location;
```

```
    public ref Point Location => ref _location;
}
```

With this implementation of Item, the code in Example 3-98 now works fine. (Ironically, to make the property modifiable, we had to turn it into a read-only property.)

Before ref returns were added in C# 7.0, there was no way to make this work. All possible implementations of the property would end up returning a copy of the property value, so if the compiler were to allow Example 3-98 to compile, we would be setting the X property on the copy returned by the property, and not the actual value in the Item object that the property represents. Example 3-101 makes this explicit, and it will in fact compile—the compiler will let us shoot ourselves in the foot if we make it sufficiently clear that we really want to. And with this version of the code, it's quite obvious that this will not modify the value in the Item object.

Example 3-101. Making the copy explicit

```
var item = new Item();
Point location = item.Location;
location.X = 123;
```

However, with the property implementation in Example 3-100, the code in Example 3-98 does compile and ends up behaving like the code shown in Example 3-102. Here we can see that we've retrieved a reference to a Point, so when we set its X property, we're acting on whatever that refers to (the _location field in the Item in this case), rather than a local copy.

Example 3-102. Making the reference explicit

```
var item = new Item();
ref Point location = ref item.Location;
location.X = 123;
```

So it's technically possible to make subproperties of a value-typed property settable, but there is arguably a loss of encapsulation here: the behavior is now more or less equivalent to defining a public field. It's also easy to get it wrong. Fortunately, most value types are immutable, and this problem arises only with mutable value types.

 Immutability doesn't exactly solve the problem—you still can't write the code you might want to, such as item.Location.X = 123. But at least immutable structs don't mislead you by making it look like you should be able to do that.

Since all properties are really just methods (typically defined in pairs), in theory they could accept more arguments in addition to the implicit `value` argument used by `set` methods. The CLR allows this, but C# does not support it except for one special kind of property: an indexer.

Indexers

An *indexer* is a property that takes one or more arguments and is accessed with the same syntax as is used for arrays. This is useful when you're writing a class that contains a collection of objects. Example 3-103 uses one of the collection classes provided by the runtime libraries, `List<T>`. It is essentially a variable-length array, and it feels like a native array thanks to its indexer, used on the second and third lines. (I'll describe arrays and collection types in detail in Chapter 5. And I'll describe generic types, of which `List<T>` is an example, in Chapter 4.)

Example 3-103. Using an indexer

```
List<int> numbers = [1, 2, 1, 4];
numbers[2] += numbers[1];
Console.WriteLine(numbers[0]);
```

From the CLR's point of view, an indexer is a property much like any other, except that it has been designated as the *default property*. This concept is a holdover from the old COM-based versions of Visual Basic that got carried over into .NET, and that C# mostly ignores. Indexers are the only C# feature that treats default properties as being special. If a type designates a property as being the default one, and if the property accepts at least one argument, C# will let you use that property through the indexer syntax.

The syntax for declaring indexers is somewhat idiosyncratic. Example 3-104 shows a read-only indexer. You could add a `set` accessor to make it read/write, just like with any other property.[9]

Example 3-104. Class with indexer

```
public class Indexed
{
    public string this[int index]
    {
        get => index < 5 ? "Foo" : "bar";
```

---

9 Incidentally, the default property has a name, because all properties are required to. C# calls the indexer property `Item` and automatically adds the annotation indicating that it's the default property. You won't normally refer to an indexer by name, but the name is visible in some tools. The .NET documentation lists indexers under `Item`, even though it's rare to use that name in code.

```
        }
}
```

C# supports multidimensional indexers. These are indexers with more than one parameter—since properties are really just methods, you can define indexers with any number of parameters. You are free to use any mixture of types for the parameters. Indexers also support overloading, so you can define any number of indexers, as long as each takes a distinct set of parameter types.

As you may recall from Chapter 2, C# offers *null-conditional* operators. In that chapter, we saw this being used to access properties and fields—e.g., myString?.Length will be of type int?—and its value will be null if myString is null, and the value of the Length property otherwise. There is one other form of null-conditional operator, which can be used with an indexer, shown in Example 3-105.

Example 3-105. Null-conditional index access

```
string? s = objectWithIndexer?[2];
```

As with the null-conditional field or property access, this generates code that checks whether the lefthand part (objectWithIndexer in this case) is null. If it is, the whole expression evaluates to null; it only invokes the indexer if the lefthand part of the expression is not null. It is effectively equivalent to the code shown in Example 3-106.

Example 3-106. Code equivalent to null-conditional index access

```
string? s = objectWithIndexer == null ? null : objectWithIndexer[2];
```

This null-conditional index syntax also works with arrays.

There's a variation on the object initializer syntax that enables you to supply values to an indexer in an object initializer. Example 3-107 uses this to initialize a dictionary. (Chapter 5 describes dictionaries and other collection types in detail.)

Example 3-107. Using an indexer in an object initializer

```
var d = new Dictionary<string, int>
{
    ["One"] = 1,
    ["Two"] = 2,
    ["Three"] = 3
};
```

Operators

Classes and structs can define customized meanings for operators. I showed some custom operators earlier: Example 3-31 supplied definitions for == and !=. A class or struct can support almost all of the arithmetic, logical, and relational operators introduced in Chapter 2. Of the operators shown in Tables 2-3, 2-4, 2-5, and 2-6, you can define custom meanings for all except the conditional AND (&&) and conditional OR (||) operators. Those operators are evaluated in terms of other operators, however, so by defining logical AND (&), logical OR (|), and also the logical true and false operators (described shortly), you can control the way that && and || work for your type, even though you cannot implement them directly.

All custom operator implementations follow a certain pattern. They look like static methods, but in the place where you'd normally expect the method name, you instead have the operator keyword followed by the operator for which you want to define a custom meaning. After that comes a parameter list, where the number of parameters is determined by the number of operands the operator requires. Example 3-108 shows how the binary + operator would look for the Counter class defined earlier in this chapter.

Example 3-108. Implementing the + operator

```
public static Counter operator +(Counter x, Counter y)
{
    return new Counter { _count = x._count + y._count };
}
```

Although the argument count must match the number of operands the operator requires, only one of the arguments has to be the same as the defining type. Example 3-109 exploits this to allow the Counter class to be added to an int.

Example 3-109. Supporting other operand types

```
public static Counter operator +(Counter x, int y)
{
    return new Counter { _count = x._count + y };
}

public static Counter operator +(int x, Counter y)
{
    return new Counter { _count = x + y._count };
}
```

We can define different versions of these operators to be use in a *checked context*. As Chapter 2 described, arithmetic performed inside an expression or block labeled as checked performs runtime checks to detect when the results of a calculation fall outside the range of the target type. Before C# 11.0, this applied only to the built-in numeric types, but it is now possible to define checked custom operator overloads. As Example 3-110 shows, you just put the checked keyword after the operator keyword. In scenarios where you want to supply a checked custom operator, you must also supply an unchecked implementation, so this example would not replace Example 3-108, it would be in addition to it.

Example 3-110. Checked + operator

```
public static Counter operator checked +(Counter x, Counter y)
{
    return new Counter { _count = checked(x._count + y._count) };
}
```

C# requires certain operators to be defined in pairs. We already saw this with the == and != operators—it is illegal to define one and not the other. Likewise, if you define the > operator for your type, you must also define the < operator, and vice versa. The same is true for >= and <=. (There's one more pair, the true and false operators, but they're slightly different; I'll get to those shortly.)

When you overload an operator for which a compound assignment operator exists, you are in effect defining behavior for both. For example, if you define custom behavior for the + operator, the += operator will automatically work too.

The operator keyword can also define custom conversions—methods that convert your type to or from some other type. For example, if we wanted to be able to convert Counter objects to and from int, we could add the two methods in Example 3-111 to the class.

Example 3-111. Conversion operators

```
public static explicit operator int(Counter value)
{
    return value._count;
}

public static explicit operator Counter(int value)
{
    return new Counter { _count = value };
}
```

I've used the explicit keyword here, which means that these conversions are accessed with the cast syntax, as Example 3-112 shows.

Example 3-112. Using explicit conversion operators

```
var c = (Counter) 123;
var v = (int) c;
```

If you use the implicit keyword instead of explicit, your conversion will be able to happen without needing a cast. In Chapter 2 we saw that some conversions happen implicitly: in certain situations, C# will automatically promote numeric types. For example, you can use an int where a long is expected, perhaps as an argument for a method or in an assignment. Conversion from int to long will always succeed and can never lose information, so the compiler will automatically generate code to perform the conversion without requiring an explicit cast. If you write implicit conversion operators, the C# compiler will silently use them in exactly the same way, enabling your custom type to be used in places where some other type was expected. (In fact, the C# specification defines numeric promotions such as conversion from int to long as built-in implicit conversions.)

Implicit conversion operators are something you shouldn't need to write very often. You should normally do so only when you can meet the same standards as built-in promotions: the conversion must always be possible and should never throw an exception. Moreover, the conversion should be unsurprising—implicit conversions are a little sneaky in that they allow you to cause methods to be invoked in code that doesn't look like it's calling a method. So unless you're intending to confuse other developers, you should write implicit conversions only where they seem to make unequivocal sense.

C# recognizes two more operators: true and false. If you define either of these, you are required to define both. These are a bit of an oddball pair, because although the C# specification defines them as unary operator overloads, they don't correspond directly to any operator you can write in an expression. They come into play in two scenarios.

If you have not defined an implicit conversion to bool, but you have defined the true and false operators, C# will use the true operator if you use your type as the expression for an if statement or a do or while loop, or as the condition expression in a for loop. However, the compiler prefers the implicit bool operator, so this is not the main reason the true and false operators exist.

The main scenario for the true and false operators is to enable your custom type to be used as an operand of a conditional Boolean operator (either && or ||). Remember that these operators will evaluate their second operand only if the first outcome does not fully determine the result. If you want to customize the behavior of these operators, you cannot implement them directly. Instead, you must define the nonconditional versions of the operators (& and |), and you must also define the true and false operators. When evaluating &&, C# will use your false operator on the first operand, and if that indicates that the first operand is false, then it will not bother to evaluate the second operand. If the first operand is not false, it will evaluate the second operand and then pass both into your custom & operator. The || operator works in much the same way but with the true and | operators, respectively.

You may be wondering why we need special true and false operators—couldn't we just define an implicit conversion to the bool type? In fact we can, and if we do that instead of providing &, |, true, and false, C# will use that to implement && and || for our type. However, some types may want to represent values that are neither true nor false—there may be a third value representing an unknown state. The true operator allows C# to ask the question "Is this definitely true?" and for the object to be able to answer "no" without implying that it's definitely false. A conversion to bool does not support that.

 The true and false operators have been present since the first version of C#, and their main application was to enable the implementation of types that support nullable Boolean values with similar semantics to those offered by many databases. The nullable type support added in C# 2.0 provides a better solution, so these operators are no longer particularly useful, but there are still some old parts of the runtime libraries that depend on them.

No other operators can be overloaded. For example, you cannot define custom meanings for the . operator used to access members of a method, or the conditional (? :) or null coalescing (??) operators.

Events

Structs and classes can declare *events*. This kind of member enables a type to provide notifications when interesting things happen, using a subscription-based model. For example, a UI object representing a button might define a Click event, and you can write code that subscribes to that event.

Events depend on delegates, and since Chapter 9 is dedicated to these topics, I won't go into any detail here. I'm mentioning them only because this section on type members would otherwise be incomplete.

Nested Types

The final kind of member we can define in a class, a struct, or a record is a nested type. You can define nested classes, records, structs, or any of the other types described later in this chapter. A nested type can do anything its normal counterpart would do, but it gets a couple of additional features.

When a type is nested, you have more choices for accessibility. A type defined at global scope can be only public or internal—private would make no sense, because that makes something accessible only from within its containing type, and there is no containing type when you define something at global scope. But a nested type does have a containing type, so if you define a nested type and make it private, that type can be used only from inside the type within which it is nested. Example 3-113 shows a private class.

Example 3-113. A private nested class

```
public static class FileSorter
{
    public static string[] GetByNameLength(string path)
    {
        string[] files = Directory.GetFiles(path);
        var comparer = new LengthComparer();
        Array.Sort(files, comparer);
        return files;
    }

    private class LengthComparer : IComparer<string>
    {
        public int Compare(string? x, string? y)
        {
            int diff = (x?.Length ?? 0) - (y?.Length ?? 0);
            return diff == 0
                ? StringComparer.OrdinalIgnoreCase.Compare(x, y)
                : diff;
        }
    }
}
```

Private classes can be useful in scenarios like this where you are using an API that requires an implementation of a particular interface, and either you don't want to make that interface part of your type or, as in this case, you couldn't even if you wanted to. (My FileSorter type is static, so I can't create an instance of it to pass to Array.Sort.) In this case, I'm calling Array.Sort to sort a list of files by the lengths of their names. (This is not useful, but it looks nice.) I'm providing the custom sort order in the form of an object that implements the IComparer<string> interface. I'll describe interfaces in detail in the next section, but this interface is just a description of what the Array.Sort method needs us to provide. I've written a custom class to implement this interface. This class is just an implementation detail of the rest of my code, so I don't want to make it public. A nested private class is just what I need.

Code in a nested type is allowed to use nonpublic members of its containing type. However, an instance of a nested type does not automatically get a reference to an instance of its containing type. If you need nested instances to have a reference to their container, then you will need to declare a field to hold that and arrange for it to be initialized, or define a suitable primary constructor; this would work in exactly the same way as any object that wants to hold a reference to another object. Obviously, it's an option only if the outer type is a reference type.

So far, we've looked only at classes, records, and structs, but there are some other ways to define custom types in C#. One of these is complicated enough to warrant getting its own chapter (Chapter 9), but there are a couple of simpler ones that I'll discuss here.

Interfaces

C#'s interface keyword defines a programming interface. Classes and structs can choose to implement interfaces. If you write code that works in terms of an interface, it will be able to work with anything that implements that interface, instead of being limited to working with one particular type.

For example, the .NET runtime libraries define an interface called IEnumerable<T>, which defines a minimal set of members for representing sequences of values. (It's a generic interface, so it can represent sequences of anything. For example, an IEnumerable<string> is a sequence of strings. Generic types are discussed in Chapter 4.) If a method has a parameter of type IEnumerable<string>, you can pass it a reference to an instance of any type that implements the interface, which means that a single method can work with arrays, various collection classes provided by the .NET runtime libraries, certain LINQ features, and many other things.

As Example 3-114 shows, an interface can declare methods, properties, and events. In most cases, it doesn't define their bodies. Properties indicate whether getters and/or setters should be present, but we typically have semicolons in place of the bodies. An interface is effectively a list of the members that a type will need to provide if it wants to implement the interface. Be aware that on .NET Framework, these method-like members are the only kinds of members interfaces can have. I'll discuss the additional member types available on .NET shortly, but the majority of interfaces you are likely to come across today only contain these kinds of members.

Example 3-114. An interface

```
public interface IDoStuff
{
    string this[int i] { get; set; }
    string Name { get; set; }
    int Id { get; }
    int SomeMethod(string arg);
    event EventHandler? Click;
}
```

Individual method-like members are not allowed accessibility modifiers—their accessibility is controlled at the level of the interface itself. (Like classes, interfaces are either public or internal, unless they are nested, in which case they can have any accessibility.) Interfaces cannot declare constructors—an interface only gets to say what services an object should supply once it has been constructed.

By the way, most interfaces in .NET follow the convention that their name starts with an uppercase I followed by one or more words in PascalCasing.

A class declares the interfaces that it implements in a list after a colon following the class name, as Example 3-115 shows. It must provide implementations of all the members listed in each interface it implements. You'll get a compiler error if you leave any out. When a type has a primary constructor, the colon and interface list come after the parameter list. Record types can also implement interfaces, using a similar syntax.

Example 3-115. Implementing an interface

```
public class DoStuff : IDoStuff
{
    public string this[int i] { get { return i.ToString(); } set { } }
    public string Name { get; set; }
    ...etc
}
```

When we implement an interface in C#, we typically define each of that interface's methods as a public member of our type. However, sometimes you may want to avoid this. Occasionally, some API may require you to implement an interface that you feel pollutes the purity of your class's API. Or, more prosaically, you may already have defined a member with the same name and signature as a member required by the interface, but that does something different from what the interface requires. Or worse, you may need to implement two different interfaces, both of which define members that have the same name and signature but require different behavior. You can solve any of these problems with a technique called *explicit implementation* to define members that implement a member of a specific interface without being public. Example 3-116 shows the syntax for this, with an implementation of one of the methods from the interface in Example 3-114. With explicit implementations, you do not specify the accessibility, and you prefix the member name with the interface name.

Example 3-116. Explicit implementation of an interface member

```
int IDoStuff.SomeMethod(string arg)
{
    ...
}
```

When a type uses explicit interface implementation, those members cannot be used through a reference of the type itself. They become visible only when referring to an object through an expression of the interface's type.

When a class implements an interface, it becomes implicitly convertible to that interface type. So you can pass any expression of type `DoStuff` from Example 3-115 as a method argument of type `IDoStuff`, for example.

Interfaces are reference types. Despite this, you can implement interfaces on both classes and structs. However, you need to be careful when doing so with a struct, because when you get hold of an interface-typed reference to a struct, it will be a reference to a *box*, which is effectively an object that holds a copy of a struct in a way that can be referred to via a reference. We'll look at boxing in Chapter 7.

Default Interface Implementation

Most interfaces only declare which members must be present, leaving the details to implementers. However, it doesn't have to be this way—an interface definition can include some implementation details. (This feature is available only on .NET, and not .NET Framework.) It can supply static fields, nested types, and bodies for methods, property accessors, and the `add` and `remove` methods for events (which I will describe in Chapter 9). Example 3-117 shows this in use to define a default implementation of a property.

Example 3-117. An interface with a default implementation of a property

```
public interface INamed
{
    int Id { get; }
    string Name => $"{this.GetType()}: {this.Id}";
}
```

If a class chooses to implement `INamed`, it will only be required to provide an implementation for this interface's `Id` property. It can also supply a `Name` property if it wants to, but this is optional. If the class does not define its own `Name`, the definition from the interface will be used instead.

When .NET added support for default interface implementations, this provided a partial solution to a long-standing limitation of interfaces: if you define an interface that you then make available for other code to use (e.g., via a class library), adding new members to that interface could cause problems for existing code that uses it. Code that invokes methods on the interface won't have a problem because it will be blissfully unaware that new members were added, but any class that implements your interface would be broken if you were to add new members without also supplying default implementations. A concrete class has to supply all the members of an interface it implements, so if the interface gets new members with no implementations, formerly complete implementations will now be incomplete. Unless you have some way of reaching out to everyone who has written types that implement your interface and getting them to add the missing members, you will cause them problems if they upgrade to the new version.

You might think that this would only be a problem if the authors of code that works with an interface deliberately upgraded to the library containing the updated interface, at which point they'd have an opportunity to fix the problem. However, library upgrades can sometimes be forced on code. If you write an application that uses multiple libraries, each of which was built against different versions of some common library, then at least one of those is going to end up getting a different version of that common library at runtime than the version it was compiled against. (Only one version is used at runtime, so they can't all have their expectations met.) This means that even if you use schemes such as semantic versioning, in which breaking changes are always accompanied by a change to the component's major version number, that might not be enough to avoid trouble: you might find yourself needing to use two components where one wants the v1.0 flavor of some interface, while another wants the v2.0 edition.

The upshot of this was that back before .NET added the ability to define default implementations for new members, interfaces were essentially frozen: you couldn't add new members over time, even across major version changes. But default interface implementations loosen this restriction: you can add a new member to an existing interface if you also provide a default implementation for it. That way, existing types that implement the older version will be able to supply a complete implementation of the updated definition, because they automatically pick up the default implementation of the newly added member without needing to be modified in any way. (There is a small fly in the ointment, making it still sometimes preferable to use the older solution to this problem, abstract base classes. Chapter 6 describes these issues. So although default interface implementation can provide a useful escape hatch, you should still avoid modifying published interfaces if at all possible.)

In addition to providing extra flexibility for backward compatibility, the default interface implementation feature adds seven more capabilities: interfaces can now define constants, static fields, static methods, static properties, custom operators, static events, and types. (Again, this is only on .NET, not .NET Framework.) Example 3-118 shows an interface that contains a nested constant and type.

Example 3-118. An interface with a `const` and a nested type

```
public interface IContainMultitudes
{
    public const string TheMagicWord = "Please";

    public enum Outcome
    {
        Yes,
        No
    }

    Outcome MayI(string request)
    {
        return request == TheMagicWord ? Outcome.Yes : Outcome.No;
    }
}
```

With non-method-like members such as these, we need to specify the accessibility, because in some cases you may want to introduce these nested members purely for the benefit of default method implementations, in which case you'd want them to be `private`. In this case, I want the relevant members to be accessible to all, since they form part of the API defined by this interface, so I have marked them as `public`. You might be looking at that nested `Outcome` type and wondering what's going on. I'll be discussing that in "Enums" on page 218, but first we need to look at the latest addition to interface types.

Static Virtual Members

C# 11.0 introduced a major new feature to interfaces: they can define *static virtual* members. These are the basis of one of the most prominent new features of .NET 7.0, *generic math*, which I'll cover in Chapter 4.

When an interface declares `static` methods, properties, events, or custom operators, these can now all be declared with either the `virtual` keyword (in which case a default implementation must be supplied) or the `abstract` keyword. (The `abstract` and `virtual` keywords were chosen for consistency with inheritance, the subject of Chapter 6.) Interface members declared in this way are static virtual members, and they indicate that any type implementing the interface will have a corresponding static member.

For example, any type implementing the `ITotalCount` shown in Example 3-119 is obliged to define a static property called `TotalCount`. The class shown earlier in Example 3-5 provides a `TotalCount` property of type `int`, so it could declare that it implements this interface.

Example 3-119. An interface with a static abstract property

```
public interface ITotalCount
{
    static abstract int TotalCount { get; }
}
```

If the interface had declared the member as `virtual`, it would have had to provide a default implementation, as the `IHanded` interface in Example 3-120 does. Any types implementing `IHanded` will have a static `Side` property. They are free to supply their own implementation, as `LeftHanded` does, but `DefaultHandedness` chooses not to, so it gets the default implementation that `IHanded` supplies.

Example 3-120. A static virtual property

```
public interface IHanded
{
    static virtual string Side => "Right";
}

public class LeftHanded : IHanded
{
    public static string Side => "Left";
}


public class DefaultHandedness : IHanded
{
}
```

But how do we use these properties? Since `LeftHanded` declared its own `Side` we can write `LeftHanded.Side`, but if we try writing `DefaultHandedness.Side`, that won't compile. This is consistent with nonstatic interface members: if a type just accepts a default interface implementation of some member, the type will have no corresponding public member (because it declared no such member). The member is visible only through the interface type. So if `Side` here were nonstatic, we could just cast an instance of `DefaultHandedness` to `IHanded`, e.g., `((IHanded)new DefaultHandedness()).Side`. But `Side` is declared as `static`, and you can't use a static member as though it were an instance member. How exactly are we supposed to get to the `DefaultHandedness` class's `IHanded.Side` member? It turns out that the only way to do this is through generic code. We won't be getting to that until Chapter 4, but Example 3-121 offers a preview.

Example 3-121. Using a static virtual member

```
public static void ShowHandedness<T>() where T : IHanded
{
    Console.WriteLine(T.Side);
}
```

ShowHandedness is a *generic method*. It happens to take no ordinary arguments, but the <T> after the method name declares a *type parameter* named T, meaning that we have to supply a *type argument* to invoke this method. We could write ShowHanded ness<LeftHanded>() for example. The where T : IHanded part defines a *constraint*, indicating that whatever type we supply, it must be one that implements IHanded. (We wouldn't be allowed to write ShowHandedness<int>() for example, because int doesn't implement IHanded.) Because we've stipulated that whatever type T ends up referring to, it will be a type that implements IHanded, the method can access any of IHanded's static members through T. When this method retrieves T.Side, that ends up accessing the Side static property for whichever type was specified. When we call ShowHandedness<LeftHanded>() this method displays Left, and when we call Show Handedness<DefaultHandedness>() it displays Right.

Since static virtual interface members can only be used by generic code, we will return to this in more detail in Chapter 4.

Enums

The enum keyword declares a very simple type that defines a set of named values. Example 3-122 shows an enum that defines a set of mutually exclusive choices. You could say that this *enumerates* the options, which is where the enum keyword gets its name.

Example 3-122. An enum with mutually exclusive options

```
public enum PorridgeTemperature
{
    TooHot,
    TooCold,
    JustRight
}
```

An enum can be used in most places you might use any other type—it could be the type of a local variable, a field, or a method parameter, for example. But one of the most common ways to use an enum is in a switch statement, as Example 3-123 shows.

Example 3-123. Switching with an enum

```
switch (porridge.Temperature)
{
case PorridgeTemperature.TooHot:
    GoOutsideForABit();
    break;

case PorridgeTemperature.TooCold:
    MicrowaveMyBreakfast();
    break;

case PorridgeTemperature.JustRight:
    NomNomNom();
    break;
}
```

As this illustrates, to refer to enumeration members, you must qualify them with the type name. In fact, an enum is really just a fancy way of defining a load of const fields. The members are all just int values under the covers. You can even specify the values explicitly, as Example 3-124 shows.

Example 3-124. Explicit enum values

```
[System.Flags]
public enum Ingredients
{
    Eggs          =        0b1,
    Bacon         =       0b10,
    Sausages      =      0b100,
    Mushrooms     =     0b1000,
    Tomato        =   0b1_0000,
    BlackPudding  =  0b10_0000,
    BakedBeans    = 0b100_0000,
    TheFullEnglish = 0b111_1111
}
```

This example also shows an alternative way to use an enum. The options in Example 3-124 are not mutually exclusive. I've used binary constants here, so you can see that each value corresponds to a particular bit position being set to 1. This makes it easy to combine them—Eggs and Bacon would be 3 (11 in binary), while Eggs, Bacon, Sausages, BlackPudding, and BakedBeans (my preferred combination) would be 103 (1100111 in binary, or 0x67 in hex).

When combining flag-based enumeration values, we normally use the bitwise OR operator. For example, you could write `Ingredients.Eggs|Ingredients.Bacon`. Not only is this significantly easier to read than using the numeric values, but it also works well with the search tools in IDEs—you can find all the places a particular symbol is used by right-clicking its definition and choosing Find All References or Go to References from the context menu. You might come across code that uses + instead of |. This works for some combinations; however, `Ingredients.The FullEnglish + Ingredients.Eggs` would be a value of 128, which does not correspond to anything, so it is safer to stick with |.

When you declare an `enum` that's designed to be combined in this way, you're supposed to annotate it with the `Flags` attribute, which is defined in the `System` namespace. (Chapter 14 will describe attributes in detail.) Example 3-124 does this, although in practice, it doesn't matter greatly if you forget, because the C# compiler doesn't care, and in fact, there are very few tools that pay any attention to it. The main benefit is that if you call `ToString` on an `enum` value, it will notice when the `Flags` attribute is present. For this `Ingredients` type, `ToString` would convert the value of 3 to the string `Eggs, Bacon`, which is also how the debugger would show the value, whereas without the `Flags` attribute, it would be treated as an unrecognized value, and you would just get a string containing the digit 3.

With this sort of flags-style enumeration, you can run out of bits fairly quickly. By default, `enum` uses `int` to represent the value, and with a set of mutually exclusive values, that's usually sufficient. It would be a fairly complicated scenario that needed billions of different values in a single enumeration type. However, with 1 bit per flag, an `int` provides space for just 32 flags. Fortunately, you can get a little more breathing room, because you can specify a different underlying type—you can use any built-in integer type, meaning that you can go up to 64 bits. As Example 3-125 shows, you can specify the underlying type after a colon following the `enum` type name.

Example 3-125. 64-bit enum

```
[Flags]
public enum TooManyChoices : long
{
    ...
}
```

All `enum` types are value types, incidentally, like the built-in numeric types or any struct. But they are very limited. You cannot define any members other than the constant values—no methods or properties, for example.

Enumeration types can sometimes enhance the readability of code. A lot of APIs accept a bool to control some aspect of their behavior but might often have done better to use an enum. Consider the code in Example 3-126. It constructs a StreamReader, a class for working with data streams that contain text. The second constructor argument is a bool.

Example 3-126. Unhelpful use of the bool type

```
using var rdr = new StreamReader(stream, true);
```

It's not remotely obvious what that second argument does. If you happen to be familiar with StreamReader, you may know that this argument determines whether byte ordering in a multibyte text encoding should be set explicitly from the code or determined from a preamble at the start of the stream. (Using the named argument syntax would help here.) And if you've got a really good memory, you might even know which of those choices true happens to select. But most mere mortal developers will probably have to reach for IntelliSense or even the documentation to work out what that argument does. Compare that experience with Example 3-127, which shows a different type.

Example 3-127. Clarity with an enum

```
using var fs = new FileStream(path, FileMode.Append);
```

This constructor's second argument uses an enumeration type, which makes for rather less opaque code. It doesn't take an eidetic memory to work out that this code intends to append data to an existing file.

As it happens, because this particular API has more than two options, it couldn't use a bool. So FileMode really had to be an enum. But these examples illustrate that even in cases where you're selecting between just two choices, it's well worth considering defining an enum for the job so that it's completely obvious which choice is being made when you look at the code.

Other Types

We're almost done with our survey of types and what goes in them. There's one kind of type that I'll not discuss until Chapter 9: delegates. We use delegates when we need a reference to a function, but the details are somewhat involved.

I've also not mentioned pointers. C# supports pointers that work in a pretty similar way to C-style pointers, complete with pointer arithmetic. For example, an int* points to an int. (If you're not familiar with these, they provide a reference to a particular location in memory. They are similar in concept to ref types but without the type safety rules.) These are a little weird, because they are slightly outside of the rest of the type system. For example, in Chapter 2, I mentioned that a variable of type `object` can refer to "almost anything." The reason I had to qualify that is that pointers are one of the two exceptions—`object` can work with any C# data type except a pointer or a `ref struct`. (Chapter 18 discusses the latter.)

But now we really are done. Some types in C# are special, including the fundamental types discussed in Chapter 2 and the records, structs, interfaces, enums, delegates, and pointers just described, but everything else looks like a class. There are a few classes that get special handling in certain circumstances—notably attribute classes (Chapter 14) and exception classes (Chapter 8)—but except for certain special scenarios, even those are otherwise completely normal classes. Even though we've seen all the kinds of types that C# supports, there's one way to define a class that I've not shown yet.

Anonymous Types

C# offers two mechanisms for grouping a handful of values together without explicitly defining a type for the job. You've already seen tuples, which were described in Chapter 2, but there is an alternative that has been in the language for much longer: Example 3-128 shows how to create an instance of an *anonymous type* and how to use it.

Example 3-128. An anonymous type

```
var x = new { Title = "Lord", Surname = "Voldemort" };

Console.WriteLine($"Welcome, {x.Title} {x.Surname}");
```

As you can see, we use the `new` keyword, but instead of the parentheses that would denote the constructor arguments (or an empty () if we want to invoke a zero-arguments constructor) we use the object initializer syntax. The C# compiler will generate code defining a type that has one read-only property for each entry inside the initializer. So in Example 3-128, the variable x will refer to an object that has two properties, `Title` and `Surname`, both of type `string`. (You do not state the property types explicitly in an anonymous type. The compiler infers each property's type from the initialization expression in the same way it does for the `var` keyword.) Since these are just normal properties, we can access them with the usual syntax, as the final line of the example shows.

The `with` syntax available for record types and `struct` types also works with anonymous types. The reason `with` is not available for all reference types is the lack of a general, universal cloning mechanism, but that's not a problem with anonymous types. They are always generated by the compiler, so the compiler knows exactly how to copy them.

The compiler generates a fairly ordinary class definition for each anonymous type. It is immutable, because all the properties are read-only. Much like a record, it overrides `Equals` so that you can compare instances by value, and it also provides a matching `GetHashCode` implementation. The only unusual thing about the generated class is that it's not possible to refer to the type by name in C#. Running Example 3-128 in the debugger, I find that the compiler has chosen the name `<>f__AnonymousType0'2`. This is not a legal identifier in C# because of those angle brackets (`<>`) at the start. C# uses names like this whenever it wants to create something that is guaranteed not to collide with any identifiers you might use in your own code, or that it wants to prevent you from using directly. This sort of identifier is called, rather magnificently, an *unspeakable name*.

Because you cannot write the name of an anonymous type, a method cannot declare that it returns one, or that it requires one to be passed as an argument (unless you use an anonymous type as an inferred generic type argument, something we'll see in Chapter 4). Of course, an expression of type `object` can refer to an instance of an anonymous type, but only the method that defines the type can use its properties (unless you use the `dynamic` type described in Chapter 2). So anonymous types are of somewhat limited value. They were added to the language for LINQ's benefit: they enable a query to select specific columns or properties from some source collection and also to define custom grouping criteria, as you'll see in Chapter 10.

These limitations provide a clue as to why Microsoft felt the need to add tuples in C# 7.0 when the language already had a pretty similar-looking feature. However, if the inability to use anonymous types as parameters or return types was the only problem, an obvious solution might have been to introduce a syntax enabling them to be identified. The syntax for referring to tuples could arguably have worked—we can now write (`string Name, double Age`) to refer to a tuple type, but why introduce a whole new concept? Why not just use that syntax to name anonymous types? (Obviously we'd no longer be able to call them anonymous types, but at least we wouldn't have ended up with two confusingly similar language features.) However, the lack of names isn't the only problem with anonymous types.

As C# has been used in increasingly diverse applications, and across a broader range of hardware, efficiency has become more of a concern. In the database access scenarios for which anonymous types were originally introduced, the cost of object allocations would have been a relatively small part of the picture, but the basic concept—a small bundle of values—is potentially useful in a much wider range of scenarios, some of which are more performance sensitive. However, anonymous types are all reference types, and while in many cases that's not a problem, it can rule them out in some hyper-performance-sensitive scenarios. Tuples, on the other hand, are all value types, making them viable even in code where you are attempting to minimize the number of allocations. (See Chapter 7 for more detail on memory management and garbage collection, and Chapter 18 for information about some of the newer language features that enable more efficient memory usage.) Also, since tuples are all based on a set of generic types under the covers, they may end up reducing the runtime overhead required to keep track of loaded types: with anonymous types, you can end up with a lot more distinct types loaded. For related reasons, anonymous types would have problems with compatibility across component boundaries.

Does this mean that anonymous types are no longer of any use? In fact, they still offer some advantages. The most significant one is that you cannot use a tuple in a lambda expression that will be converted into an expression tree. This issue is described in detail in Chapter 9, but the practical upshot is that you cannot use tuples in the kinds of LINQ queries mentioned earlier that anonymous types were added to support.

More subtle is the fact that with tuples, property names are a convenient fiction, whereas with anonymous types, they are real. This has two upshots. One regards equivalence: the tuples (X: 10, Y:20) and (W:10, H:20) are considered interchangeable, where any variable capable of holding one is capable of holding the other. That is not true for anonymous types: new { X = 10, Y = 20 } has a different type than new { W = 10, H = 20 }, and attempting to pass one to code that expects the other will cause a compiler error. This difference can make tuples more convenient, but it can also make them more error prone, because the compiler looks only at the shape of the data when asking whether you're using the right type. Anonymous types can still enable errors: if you have two types with exactly the same property names and types but that are semantically different, there's no way to express that with anonymous types. (In practice you'd probably just define two record types to deal with this.) The second upshot of anonymous types offering genuine properties is that you can pass them to code that inspects an object's properties. Many reflection-driven features such as certain serialization frameworks, or UI framework databinding, depend on being able to discover properties at runtime through reflection (see Chapter 13). Anonymous types may work better with these frameworks than tuples, in which the properties' real names are all things like Item1, Item2, etc.

Partial Types and Methods

There's one last topic I want to discuss relating to types. C# supports what it calls a *partial type declaration*. This just means that the type declaration might span multiple files. If you add the `partial` keyword to a type declaration, C# will not complain if another file defines the same type—it will simply act as though all the members defined by the two files had appeared in a single declaration in one file.

This feature exists to make it easier to write code-generation tools. For example, there are code generators built into the .NET SDK for regular expression processing and JSON serialization. These generate their code into partial types, enabling them to augment types that we have written. UI frameworks also often exploit this to generate the code that creates the objects that define the user interface layout. When generated parts are a separate file, they can be regenerated from scratch whenever needed without any risk of overwriting the code that you've written. Before partial types were introduced to C#, all the code for a class had to go in one file, and from time to time, code generation tools would get confused, leading to loss of code.

 Partial classes are not limited to code-generation scenarios, so you can of course use this to split your own class definitions across multiple files. However, if you've written a class so large and complex that you feel the need to split it into multiple source files just to keep it manageable, that's probably a sign that the class is too complex. A better response to this problem might be to change your design. However, it can be useful if you need to maintain code that is built in different ways for different target platforms: you can use partial classes to put target-specific parts in separate files.

Partial methods are also designed for code-generation scenarios, but they are slightly more complex. They allow one file, typically a generated file, to declare a method, and for another file to implement the method. (Strictly speaking, the declaration and implementation are allowed to be in the same file, but they usually won't be.) This may sound like the relationship between an interface and a class that implements that interface, but it's not quite the same. With partial methods, the declaration and implementation are in the same class—they're in different files only because the class has been split across multiple files.

If you do not provide an implementation of a partial method, then as long as the method definition does not specify any accessibility, has a `void` return type, and no `out` arguments, the compiler acts as though the method isn't there at all, and any code that invokes the method is ignored at compile time. The main reason for this is to support code-generation mechanisms that are able to offer many kinds of notifications but where you want zero runtime overhead for notifications that you don't need. Partial methods enable this by letting the code generator declare a partial method for each kind of notification it provides and to generate code that invokes all of these partial methods where necessary. All code relating to notifications for which you do not write a handler method will be stripped out at compile time.

It's an idiosyncratic mechanism, but it was driven by frameworks that provide extremely fine-grained notifications and extension points. There are some more obvious runtime techniques you could use instead, such as interfaces, or features that I'll cover in later chapters, such as callbacks or virtual methods. However, any of these would impose a relatively high cost for unused features. Unused partial methods get stripped out at compile time, reducing the cost of the bits you don't use to nothing, which is a considerable improvement.

Summary

You've now seen most of the kinds of types you can write in C# and the sorts of members they support. Classes are the most widely used, but structs are useful if you need value-like semantics for assignment and arguments; both support the same member types—namely, fields, constructors, methods, properties, indexers, events, custom operators, and nested types. Records provide a more convenient syntax for defining types that consist mostly of properties, especially if you want to be able to compare the values of such types. And while they do not have to be immutable, record types make it easier to define and work with immutable data. Interfaces are abstract, so at the instance level they support only methods, properties, indexers, and events. They can also provide static fields, nested types, and default implementations for other members and they can also require classes that implement them to provide certain static members. And enums are very limited, providing just a set of known values.

There's another feature of the C# type system that makes it possible to write very flexible types, called generic types. We'll look at these in the next chapter.

CHAPTER 4

Generics

In Chapter 3, I showed how to write types and described the various kinds of members they can contain. However, there's an extra dimension to classes, structs, interfaces, delegates, and methods that I did not show. They can define *type parameters*, placeholders that let you plug in different types at compile time. This allows you to write just one type and then produce multiple versions of it. A type that does this is called a *generic type*. For example, the runtime libraries define a generic class called List<T> that acts as a variable-length array. T is a type parameter here, and you can use almost any type as an argument, so List<int> is a list of integers, List<string> is a list of strings, and so on.[1] You can also write a *generic method*, which is a method that has its own type arguments, independently of whether its containing type is generic.

Generic types and methods are visually distinctive because they always have angle brackets (< and >) after the name. These contain a comma-separated list of parameters or arguments. The same parameter/argument distinction applies here as with methods: the declaration specifies a list of parameters, and then when you come to use the method or type, you supply arguments for those parameters. So List<T> defines a single type parameter, T, and List<int> supplies a *type argument*, int, for that parameter.

You can use any name you like for type parameters, within the usual constraints for identifiers in C#, but there are some popular conventions. It's common (but not universal) to use T when there's only one parameter. For multiparameter generics, you tend to see slightly more descriptive names. For example, the runtime libraries define the Dictionary<TKey, TValue> collection class. Sometimes you will see a descriptive

---

1 When saying the names of generic types, the convention is to use the word *of* as in "List of T" or "List of int."

name like that even when there's just one parameter, but in any case, you will tend to see a T prefix so that the type parameters stand out when you use them in your code.

Generic Types

Classes, structs, records, and interfaces can all be generic, as can delegates, which we'll be looking at in Chapter 9. Example 4-1 shows how to define a generic class. This happens to use C# 12.0's new primary constructor syntax, so after the type parameter list (<T>) this example also has a primary constructor parameter list.

Example 4-1. Defining a generic class

```
public class NamedContainer<T>(T item, string name)
{
    public T Item { get; } = item;
    public string Name { get; } = name;
}
```

The syntax for structs, records, and interfaces is much the same: the type name is followed immediately by a type parameter list. Example 4-2 shows how to write a generic record similar to the class in Example 4-1.

Example 4-2. Defining a generic record

```
public record NamedContainer<T>(T Item, string Name);
```

Inside the definition of a generic type, I can use the type parameter T anywhere you would normally see a type name. In the first two examples, I've used it as the type of a constructor argument and as the Item property's type. I could define fields of type T too. (In fact I have, albeit not explicitly. Automatic properties generate hidden fields, so my Item property will have an associated hidden field of type T.) You can also define local variables of type T. And you're free to use type parameters as arguments for other generic types. My NamedContainer<T> could declare members of type List<T>, for example.

The types that Examples 4-1 and 4-2 define are, like any generic type, not complete types. A generic type declaration is *unbound*, meaning that there are type parameters that must be filled in to produce a complete type. Basic questions, such as how much memory a NamedContainer<T> instance will require, cannot be answered without knowing what T is—the hidden field for the Item property would need 4 bytes if T were an int but 16 bytes if it were a decimal. The CLR cannot produce executable code for a type if it does not know how the contents will be arranged in memory. So to use this, or any other generic type, we must provide type arguments. Example 4-3 shows how. When type arguments are supplied, the result is sometimes called a *constructed type.* (This has nothing to do with constructors, the special kind of member we looked at in Chapter 3. In fact, Example 4-3 uses those too—it invokes the constructors of a couple of constructed types.)

Example 4-3. Using a generic class

```
var a = new NamedContainer<int>(42, "The answer");
var b = new NamedContainer<int>(99, "Number of red balloons");
var c = new NamedContainer<string>("Programming C#", "Book title");
```

You can use a constructed generic type anywhere you would use a normal type. For example, you can use them as the types for method parameters and return values, properties, or fields. You can even use one as a type argument for another generic type, as Example 4-4 shows.

Example 4-4. Constructed generic types as type arguments

```
// ...where a, and b come from Example 4-3.
List<NamedContainer<int>> namedInts = [a, b];
var namedNamedItem = new NamedContainer<NamedContainer<int>>(a, "Wrapped");
```

Each different type I supply as an argument to `NamedContainer<T>` constructs a distinct type. (And for generic types with multiple type arguments, each distinct combination of type arguments would construct a distinct type.) This means that `NamedContainer<int>` is a different type than `NamedContainer<string>`. That's why there's no conflict in using `NamedContainer<int>` as the type argument for another `NamedContainer`, as the final line of Example 4-4 does—there's no infinite recursion here.

Because each different set of type arguments produces a distinct type, in most cases there is no implied compatibility between different forms of the same generic type. You cannot assign a `NamedContainer<int>` into a variable of type `NamedContainer<string>` or vice versa. It makes sense that those two types are incompatible, because `int` and `string` are quite different types. But what if we used `object` as a type argument? As Chapter 2 described, you can put almost anything in an `object` variable. If you write a method with a parameter of type `object`, it's OK to pass a `string`, so you might expect a method that takes a `NamedContainer<object>` to be happy with a `NamedContainer<string>`. That won't work, but some generic types (specifically, interfaces and delegates) can declare that they want this kind of compatibility relationship. The mechanisms that support this (called *covariance* and *contravariance*) are closely related to the type system's inheritance mechanisms. Chapter 6 is all about inheritance and type compatibility, so I will discuss this aspect of generic types there.

The number of type parameters forms part of an unbound generic type's identity. This makes it possible to introduce multiple types with the same name as long as they have different numbers of type parameters. (The technical term for number of type parameters is *arity*.)

So you could define a generic class called, say, `Operation<T>`, and then another class, `Operation<T1, T2>`, and also `Operation<T1, T2, T3>`, and so on, all in the same namespace, without introducing any ambiguity. When you are using these types, it's clear from the number of arguments which type was meant—`Operation<int>` clearly uses the first, while `Operation<string, double>` uses the second, for example. And for the same reason, a nongeneric `Operation` class would be distinct from generic types of the same name.

My `NamedContainer<T>` example doesn't do anything to instances of its type argument, `T`—it never invokes any methods or uses any properties or other members of `T`. All it does is accept a `T` as a constructor argument, which it stores away for later retrieval. This is also true of many generic types in the runtime libraries—I've mentioned some collection classes (and we'll see more of these in Chapter 5), which are all variations on the same theme of containing data for later retrieval.

There is a reason for this: a generic class can find itself working with any type, so it can presume little about its type arguments. However, it doesn't have to be this way. You can specify *constraints* for your type arguments.

Constraints

C# allows you to state that a type argument must fulfill certain requirements. For example, suppose you want to be able to create new instances of the type on demand. Example 4-5 shows a simple class that provides deferred construction—it makes an instance available through a static property but does not attempt to construct that instance until the first time you read the property.

Example 4-5. Creating a new instance of a parameterized type

```
// For illustration only. Consider using Lazy<T> in a real program.
public static class Deferred<T>
    where T : new()
{
    private static T? _instance;

    public static T Instance => _instance ??= new T();
}
```

You wouldn't write a class like this in practice, because the runtime libraries offer Lazy<T>, which does the same job but with more flexibility. Lazy<T> can work correctly in multithreaded code, whereas Example 4-5 will not. Example 4-5 is just to illustrate how constraints work. Don't use it!

For this class to do its job, it needs to be able to construct an instance of whatever type is supplied as the argument for T. The get accessor uses the new keyword, and since it passes no arguments, it clearly requires T to provide a parameterless constructor. But not all types do, so what happens if we try to use a type without a suitable constructor as the argument for Deferred<T>?

The compiler will reject it, because it violates a constraint that this generic type has declared for T. Constraints appear just before the class's opening brace, and they begin with the where keyword. The new() constraint in Example 4-5 states that T is required to supply a zero-argument constructor.

If that constraint had not been present, the class in Example 4-5 would not compile—you would get an error on the line that attempts to construct a new T. A generic type (or method) is allowed to use only features of its type parameters that it has specified through constraints, or that are defined by the base object type. (The object type defines a ToString method, for example, so you can invoke that on instances of any type without needing to specify a constraint.)

C# offers only a very limited suite of constraints. You cannot demand a constructor that takes arguments, for example. In fact, C# supports only seven kinds of constraints on a type argument: a type constraint, a reference type constraint, a value type constraint, default, notnull, unmanaged, and the new() constraint. The default constraint only applies in inheritance scenarios, so we'll look at that in Chapter 6, and we just saw how new() works, so now let's look at the remaining five.

Type Constraints

You can constrain the argument for a type parameter to be compatible with a particular type. For example, you could use this to demand that the argument type implements a certain interface. Example 4-6 shows the syntax.

Example 4-6. Using a type constraint

```
public class GenericComparer<T> : IComparer<T>
    where T : IComparable<T>
{
    public int Compare(T? x, T? y)
    {
        if (x == null) { return y == null ? 0 : -1; }
```

```
        return x.CompareTo(y);
    }
}
```

I'll just explain the purpose of this example before describing how it takes advantage of a type constraint. This class provides a bridge between two styles of value comparison that you'll find in .NET. Some data types provide their own comparison logic, but at times, it can be more useful for comparison to be a separate function implemented in its own class. These two styles are represented by the `IComparable<T>` and `IComparer<T>` interfaces, which are both part of the runtime libraries. (They are in the `System` and `System.Collections.Generics` namespaces, respectively.) I showed `IComparer<T>` in Chapter 3—an implementation of this interface can compare two objects or values of type `T`. The interface defines a single `Compare` method that takes two arguments and returns either a negative number, 0, or a positive number if the first argument is, respectively, less than, equal to, or greater than the second. `IComparable<T>` is very similar, but its `CompareTo` method takes just a single argument, because with this interface, you are asking an instance to compare *itself* to some other instance.

Some of the runtime libraries' collection classes require you to provide an `IComparer<T>` to support ordering operations such as sorting. They use the model in which a separate object performs the comparison, because this offers two advantages over the `IComparable<T>` model. First, it enables you to use data types that don't implement `IComparable<T>`. Second, it allows you to plug in different sorting orders. (For example, suppose you want to sort some strings with a case-insensitive order. The `string` type implements `IComparable<string>`, but it provides a case-sensitive, locale-specific order.) So `IComparer<T>` is the more flexible model. However, what if you are using a data type that implements `IComparable<T>`, and you're perfectly happy with the order that provides? What would you do if you're working with an API that demands an `IComparer<T>`?

Actually, the answer is that you'd probably just use the .NET feature designed for this very scenario: `Comparer<T>.Default`. If `T` implements `IComparable<T>`, that property will return an `IComparer<T>` that does precisely what you want. So in practice you wouldn't need to write the code in Example 4-6, because Microsoft has already written it for you. However, it's instructive to see how you'd write your own version, because it illustrates how to use a type constraint.

The line starting with the `where` keyword states that this generic class requires the argument for its type parameter `T` to implement `IComparable<T>`. Without this addition, the `Compare` method would not compile—it invokes the `CompareTo` method on an argument of type `T`. That method is not present on all objects, and the C# compiler allows this only because we've constrained `T` to be an implementation of an interface that does offer such a method.

Interface constraints are somewhat odd: at first glance, it may look like we really shouldn't need them. If a method needs a particular argument to implement a particular interface, you would normally just use that interface as the argument's type. However, Example 4-6 can't do this. You can demonstrate this by trying Example 4-7. It won't compile.

Example 4-7. Will not compile: interface not implemented

```
public class GenericComparer<T> : IComparer<T>
{
    public int Compare(IComparable<T>? x, T? y)
    {
        if (x == null) { return y == null ? 0 : -1; }
        return x.CompareTo(y);
    }
}
```

The compiler will complain that I've not implemented the IComparer<T> interface's Compare method. Example 4-7 has a Compare method, but its signature is wrong— that first argument should be a T. I could also try the correct signature without specifying the constraint, as Example 4-8 shows.

Example 4-8. Will not compile: missing constraint

```
public class GenericComparer<T> : IComparer<T>
{
    public int Compare(T? x, T? y)
    {
        if (x == null) { return y == null ? 0 : -1; }
        return x.CompareTo(y);
    }
}
```

That will also fail to compile, because the compiler can't find that CompareTo method I'm trying to use. It's the constraint for T in Example 4-6 that enables the compiler to know what that method really is.

Type constraints don't have to be interfaces, by the way. You can use any type. For example, you can require a particular type argument to derive from a particular base class. More subtly, you can also define one parameter's constraint in terms of another type parameter. Example 4-9 requires the first type argument to derive from the second, for example.

Example 4-9. Constraining one argument to derive from another

```
public class Foo<T1, T2>
    where T1 : T2
...
```

Type constraints are fairly specific—they require either a particular inheritance relationship, or the implementation of certain interfaces. However, you can define slightly less specific constraints.

Reference Type Constraints

You can constrain a type argument to be a reference type. As Example 4-10 shows, this looks similar to a type constraint. You just put the keyword `class` instead of a type name. If you are in an enabled nullable annotation context, the meaning of this annotation changes: it requires the type argument to be a non-nullable reference type. If you specify `class?`, that allows the type argument to be either a nullable or a non-nullable reference type.

Example 4-10. Constraint requiring a reference type

```
public class Bar<T>
    where T : class
...
```

This constraint prevents the use of value types such as `int`, `double`, or any `struct` as the type argument. Its presence enables your code to do three things that would not otherwise be possible. First, it means that you can write code that tests whether variables of the relevant type are `null`.[2] If you've not constrained the type to be a reference type, there's always a possibility that it's a value type, and those can't have `null` values. The second capability is that you can use it as the target type of the `as` operator, which we'll look at in Chapter 6. This is just a variation on the first feature—the `as` keyword requires a reference type because it can produce a `null` result.

Nullable types such as `int?` (or `Nullable<int>`, as the CLR calls it) add nullability to value types, so you might be wondering whether you can use these as the argument for a type parameter with a `class` constraint. You can't, because although types such as `int?` allow comparison with `null`, they work quite differently than reference types, so the compiler often generates quite different code for nullable types than it does for a reference type.

---

2 This is permitted even if you used the plain `class` constraint in an enabled nullable annotation context. This constraint does not provide watertight guarantees of non-nullness, so C# permits comparison with `null`.

The third feature that a reference type constraint enables is the ability to use certain other generic types. It's often convenient for generic code to use one of its type arguments as an argument for another generic type, and if that other type specifies a constraint, you'll need to put the same constraint on your own type parameter. So if some other type specifies a class constraint, this might require you to constrain one of your own arguments in the same way.

Of course, this does raise the question of why the type you're using needs the constraint in the first place. It might be that it simply wants to test for null or use the as operator, but there's another reason for applying this constraint. Sometimes, you just need a type argument to be a reference type—there are situations in which a generic method might be able to compile without a class constraint, but it will not work correctly if used with a value type.

One common scenario in which this comes up is with libraries that can create fake objects to be used as part of a test by generating code at runtime. Using faked stand-in objects can often reduce the amount of code any single test has to exercise, which can make it easier to verify the behavior of the object being tested. For example, a test might need to verify that my code sends messages to a server at the right moment. I don't want to have to run a real server during a unit test, so I could provide an object that implements the same interface as the class that would transmit the message but that won't really send the message. Since this combination of an object under test plus a fake is a common pattern, I might choose to write a reusable base class embodying the pattern. Using generics means that the class can work for any combination of the type being tested and the type being faked. Example 4-11 shows a simplified version of this kind of helper class.

Example 4-11. Constrained by another constraint

```
using Microsoft.VisualStudio.TestTools.UnitTesting;
using Moq;

public class TestBase<TSubject, TFake>
    where TSubject : new()
    where TFake : class
{
    public TSubject? Subject { get; private set; }
    public Mock<TFake>? Fake { get; private set; }

    [TestInitialize]
    public void Initialize()
    {
        Subject = new TSubject();
        Fake = new Mock<TFake>();
    }
}
```

There are various ways to build fake objects for test purposes. You could just write new classes that implement the same interface as your real objects, but there are also third-party libraries that can generate them. One such library is called Moq (an open source project (*https://github.com/Moq*)), and that's where the Mock<T> class in Example 4-11 comes from. It's capable of generating a fake implementation of any interface or of any nonsealed class. (Chapter 6 describes the sealed keyword.) It will provide empty implementations of all members by default, and you can configure more interesting behaviors if necessary. You can also verify whether the code under test used the fake object in the way you expected.

How is that relevant to constraints? The Mock<T> class specifies a reference type constraint on its own type argument, T. This is due to the way in which it creates dynamic implementations of types at runtime; it's a technique that can work only for reference types. Moq generates a type at runtime, and if T is an interface, that generated type will implement it, whereas if T is a class, the generated type will derive from it.[3] There's nothing useful it can do if T is a struct, because you cannot derive from a value type. That means that when I use Mock<T> in Example 4-11, I need to make sure that the type argument I pass is not a struct (i.e., it must be a reference type). But the type argument I'm using is one of my class's type parameters: TFake. So I don't know what type that will be—that'll be up to whoever is using my TestBase class.

For my class to compile without error, I have to ensure that I have met the constraints of any generic types that I use. I have to guarantee that Mock<TFake> is valid, and the only way to do that is to add a constraint on my own type that requires TFake to be a reference type. And that's what I've done on the third line of the class definition in Example 4-11. Without that, the compiler would report errors on the two lines that refer to Mock<TFake>.

To put it more generally, if you want to use one of your own type parameters as the type argument for a generic that specifies a constraint, you'll need to specify the same constraint on your own type parameter.

Value Type Constraints

Just as you can constrain a type argument to be a reference type, you can instead constrain it to be a value type. As shown in Example 4-12, the syntax is similar to that for a reference type constraint but with the struct keyword.

---

3 Moq relies on the *dynamic proxy* feature from the Castle Project to generate this type. If you would like to use something similar in your code, you can find this at the Castle Project (*http://castleproject.org*).

Example 4-12. Constraint requiring a value type

```
public class Quux<T>
    where T : struct
...
```

Before now, we've seen the struct keyword only in the context of custom value types, but despite how it looks, this constraint permits bool, enum types, and any of the built-in numeric types such as int, as well as custom structs.

.NET's Nullable<T> type imposes this constraint. Recall from Chapter 3 that Nullable<T> provides a wrapper for value types that allows a variable to hold either a value or no value. (We normally use the special syntax C# provides, so we'd write, say, int? instead of Nullable<int>.) The only reason this type exists is to provide nullability for types that would not otherwise be able to hold a null value. So it only makes sense to use this with a value type—reference type variables can already be set to null without needing this wrapper. The value type constraint prevents you from using Nullable<T> with types for which it is unnecessary.

Value Types All the Way Down with Unmanaged Constraints

You can specify unmanaged as a constraint, which requires that the type argument be a value type but also that it contains no references. All of the type's fields must be value types, and if any of those fields is not a built-in primitive type, then its type must in turn contain only fields that are value types, and so on all the way down. In practice this means that all the actual data needs to be either one of a fixed set of built-in types (essentially, all the numeric types, bool, or a pointer) or an enum type. This is mainly of interest in interop scenarios, because types that match the unmanaged constraint can be passed safely and efficiently to unmanaged code. It can also be important if you are writing high-performance code that takes control of exactly where memory is allocated and when it is copied, using the techniques described in Chapter 18.

Not Null Constraints

If you use the nullable references feature described in Chapter 3 (which is enabled by default when you create new projects), you can specify a notnull constraint. This allows either value types or non-nullable reference types but not nullable reference types.

Other Special Type Constraints

Chapter 3 described various special kinds of types, including enumeration types (enum) and delegate types (covered in detail in Chapter 9). It is sometimes useful to constrain type arguments to be one of these kinds of types. There's no special trick to this, though: you can just use type constraints. All delegate types derive from `System.Delegate`, and all enumeration types derive from `System.Enum`. As Example 4-13 shows, you can just write a type constraint requiring a type argument to derive from either of these.

Example 4-13. Constraints requiring delegate and enum types

```
public class RequireDelegate<T>
    where T : Delegate
{
}

public class RequireEnum<T>
    where T : Enum
{
}
```

Multiple Constraints

If you'd like to impose multiple constraints for a single type argument, you can just put them in a list, as Example 4-14 shows. There are some restrictions. You cannot combine the `class`, `struct`, `notnull`, or `unmanaged` constraints—these are mutually exclusive. If you do use one of these keywords, it must come first in the list. If the `new()` constraint is present, it must be last.

Example 4-14. Multiple constraints

```
public class Spong<T>
    where T : IEnumerable<T>, IDisposable, new()
...
```

When your type has multiple type parameters, you write one `where` clause for each type parameter you wish to constrain. In fact, we saw this earlier—Example 4-11 defines constraints for both of its parameters.

Zero-Like Values

There are certain features that all types support and that therefore do not require a constraint. This includes the set of methods defined by the `object` base class, covered in Chapters 3 and 6. But there's a more basic feature that can sometimes be useful in generic code.

Variables of any type can be initialized to a default value. As you have seen in the preceding chapters, there are some situations in which the CLR does this for us. For example, all the fields in a newly constructed object will have a known value even if we don't write field initializers and don't supply values in the constructor. Likewise, a new array of any type will have all of its elements initialized to a known value. The CLR does this by filling the relevant memory with zeros. The exact meaning of this depends on the data type. For any of the built-in numeric types, the value will quite literally be the number 0, but for nonnumeric types, it's something else. For `bool`, the default is `false`, and for a reference type, it is `null`.

Sometimes, it can be useful for generic code to be able to obtain this initial default zero-like value for one of its type parameters. But you cannot use a literal expression to do this in most situations. You cannot assign `null` into a variable whose type is specified by a type parameter unless that parameter has been constrained to be a reference type. And you cannot assign the literal 0 into any such variable (although .NET 7.0's generic math feature makes it possible to constrain a type argument to be a numeric type, in which case you can write `T.Zero`).

Instead, you can request the zero-like value for any type using the `default` keyword. (This is the same keyword we saw inside a `switch` statement in Chapter 2 but used in a completely different way. C# keeps up the C-family tradition of defining multiple, unrelated meanings for each keyword.) If you write `default(SomeType)`, where *Some Type* is either a specific type or a type parameter, you will get the default initial value for that type: 0 if it is a numeric type, and the equivalent for any other type. For example, the expression `default(int)` has the value 0, `default(bool)` is `false`, and `default(string)` is `null`. You can use this with a generic type parameter to get the default value for the corresponding type argument, as Example 4-15 shows.

Example 4-15. Getting the default (zero-like) value of a type argument

```
static void ShowDefault<T>()
{
    Console.WriteLine(default(T));
}
```

Inside a generic type or method that defines a type parameter T, the expression `default(T)` will produce the default, zero-like value for T—whatever T may be—without requiring constraints. So you could use the generic method in Example 4-15 to verify that the defaults for `int`, `bool`, and `string` are the values I stated.

 When the nullable references feature (described in Chapter 3) is enabled, the compiler will consider a `default(T)` to be a potentially null value, unless you've ruled out the use of reference types by applying the `struct` constraint.

In cases where the compiler is able to infer what type is required, you can use a simpler form. Instead of writing `default(T)`, you can just write `default`. That wouldn't work in Example 4-15. `Console.WriteLine` can accept pretty much anything, so the compiler can't narrow it down to one option, but it will work in Example 4-16. There, the compiler can see that the generic method's return type is T?, so this must need a `default(T)`. Since it can infer that, it's enough for us to write just `default`.

Example 4-16. Getting the default (zero-like) value of an inferred type

```
static T? GetDefault<T>() => default;
```

And since I've just shown you an example of one, this seems like a good time to talk about generic methods.

Generic Methods

As well as generic types, C# also supports generic methods. In this case, the generic type parameter list follows the method name and precedes the method's normal parameter list. Example 4-17 shows a method with a single type parameter, T. It uses that parameter as its return type and also as the element type for an array to be passed in as the method's argument. This method returns the final element in the array, and because it's generic, it will work for any array element type.

Example 4-17. A generic method

```
public static T GetLast<T>(T[] items) => items[^1];
```

> You can define generic methods inside either generic types or non-generic types. If a generic method is a member of a generic type, all of the type parameters from the containing type are in scope inside the method, as well as the type parameters specific to the method.

Just as with a generic type, you can use a generic method by specifying its name along with its type arguments, as Example 4-18 shows.

Example 4-18. Invoking a generic method

```
int[] values = [1, 2, 3];
int last = GetLast<int>(values);
```

Generic methods work in a similar way to generic types but with type parameters that are only in scope within the method declaration and body. You can specify constraints in much the same way as with generic types. The constraints appear after the method's parameter list and before its body, as Example 4-19 shows.

Example 4-19. A generic method with a constraint

```
public static T MakeFake<T>()
    where T : class
{
    return new Mock<T>().Object;
}
```

There's one significant way in which generic methods differ from generic types, though: you don't always need to specify a generic method's type arguments explicitly.

Type Inference

The C# compiler is often able to infer the type arguments for a generic method. I can modify Example 4-18 by removing the type argument list from the method invocation, as Example 4-20 shows. This doesn't change the meaning of the code in any way.

Example 4-20. Generic method type argument inference

```
int[] values = [1, 2, 3];
int last = GetLast(values);
```

When presented with this sort of ordinary-looking method call, if there's no nongeneric method of that name available, the compiler starts looking for suitable generic methods. If the method in Example 4-17 is in scope, it will be a candidate, and the compiler will attempt to deduce the type arguments. This is a pretty simple case. The method expects an array of some type T, and we've passed an array with elements of type int, so it's not a massive stretch to work out that this code should be treated as a call to GetLast<int>.

It gets more complex with more intricate cases. The C# specification dedicates many pages to the type inference algorithm, but it's all to support one goal: letting you leave out type arguments when they would be redundant. By the way, type inference is always performed at compile time, so it's based on the static type of the method arguments.

With APIs that make extensive use of generics (such as LINQ, which is the topic of Chapter 10), explicitly listing every type argument can make the code very hard to follow, so it is common to rely on type inference. And if you use anonymous types, then type argument inference becomes essential because it is not possible to supply the type arguments explicitly.

Generic Math

One of the most significant new capabilities in C# 11.0 and .NET 7.0 is called *generic math*. This makes it possible to write generic methods that perform mathematical operations on variables declared with type parameters. To show why this required new language and runtime features, Example 4-21 shows a naive attempt to perform arithmetic in a generic method.

Example 4-21. A technique that doesn't work in C# generics

```
public static T Add<T>(T x, T y)
{
    return x + y;  // Will not compile
}
```

The compiler will complain about the use of addition here because nothing stops someone from using this method with a type parameter that does not support addition. What should happen if we called this method passing arguments of type `bool`? We'd probably like the answer to be that such attempts would be blocked: we should only be allowed to call this `Add<T>` method if we use a type argument that supports addition.

This is exactly the kind of scenario that constraints are meant for. All we need to do is constrain the type parameter `T` to types that *do* implement addition. But up until C# 11.0, it was not possible to specify such a constraint. We can require a type argument to provide certain members by using an interface type constraint, but interfaces used to be unable to require implementations to define particular operators. When types implement operators such as `+`, these are static members. (They have a distinctive syntax but they are really just static methods.) And it wasn't possible for an interface to define static `virtual` or `abstract` members. These keywords indicate, respectively, that a type either can or must define its own version of a particular member, and used to be applicable only in inheritance scenarios (described in Chapter 6) with nonstatic methods.

As you saw in Chapter 3, .NET 7.0 has extended the type system so that it is now possible for interfaces to require implementers to provide specific static members. C# 11.0 supports this with its new `static abstract` and `static virtual` syntax. This means that it is now possible to define interfaces that require implementers to offer, say, the + operator. The .NET runtime libraries now define such interfaces, meaning that we can define a constraint for a type parameter that requires it to support arithmetic. Example 4-22 does this, enabling it to use the + operator.

Example 4-22. Using generic math

```
public static T Add<T>(T x, T y)
    where T : INumber<T>
{
    return x + y; // No error, because INumber<T> requires + to be available
}
```

The INumber<T> interface is defined in the System.Numerics namespace and is implemented by all of the built-in numeric types. You can think of INumber<T> as saying that any type implementing this interface provides all common mathematical operations for type T. So int implements INumber<int>, float implements INumber<float>, and so on. The interface needs to be generic—it couldn't just be INumber because it needs to specify the input and output types for operators. Example 4-23 shows the problem that would occur if we tried to define this kind of constraint interface without a generic type argument.

Example 4-23. Why operator constraint interfaces need to be generic

```
public interface IAdd
{
    static abstract int operator +(int x, int y); // Won't compile
}
```

This hypothetical IAdd interface attempts to state that any implementing type must support the addition operator by defining it as abstract. But operator declarations need to state their input and output types. This example chooses int, so this would be of no use for any other type. In fact, it won't even compile—C# imposes a rule that when a type defines an operator member, at least one of the arguments must either have the same type as the declaring type, or it must derive from or implement that defining type. So MyType can define addition for a pair of MyType inputs, and it can also define addition for a MyType and an int, but it doesn't get to define addition for a pair of int values. (That would create ambiguity—if MyType could define that, C# wouldn't know whether to use that or the normal built-in behavior when adding two int values together.) The same rules apply to interfaces—at least one of the arguments in Example 4-23 would need to be IAdd. But as you'll see in Chapter 7, declaring these arguments with an interface type would result in boxing when the underlying types are value types, which would result in heap allocations each time you performed basic arithmetic.

This is why INumber<T> takes a type argument. It plugs this in as the input and output types of the + operator. In fact, it doesn't do that directly—each of the different operators is separated out into a distinct interface, and INumber<T> inherits them all. For example, INumber<T> inherits from IAdditionOperators<T,T,T>, and as

Example 4-24 shows, that's the interface that actually defines the operator members. The operator arguments here don't use interface types, they use the actual type parameter (avoiding any boxing overhead), but the compiler is satisfied because a constraint on this type parameter requires it to implement the interface.

Example 4-24. The `IAdditionOperators<TSelf, TOther, TResult>` interface

```
public interface IAdditionOperators<TSelf, TOther, TResult>
    where TSelf : IAdditionOperators<TSelf, TOther, TResult>?
{
    static abstract TResult operator +(TSelf left, TOther right);
    static virtual TResult operator checked +(TSelf left, TOther right)
        => left + right;
}
```

This is more complex than the hypothetical `IAdd` shown in Example 4-23. It is generic for the reasons just described, but it has three type arguments, not just one. This is to make it possible to define constraints requiring addition with mixed inputs. There are some mathematical objects that are more complex than individual values (e.g., vectors, matrices) and which support common arithmetic operations (e.g., you can add two matrices together), and in some cases you might be able to apply operations with different input types. For example, you can multiply a matrix by an ordinary number (a scalar) and the result is a new matrix. The operator interfaces are able to represent this because they take separate type arguments for the inputs and outputs, so a mathematical library that wanted to represent this capability could represent it as `IMultiplyOperators<double, Matrix, Matrix>`.

You'll notice that `INumber<T>` takes only one type argument. While the individual operator interfaces are able to represent hybrid operations, `INumber<T>` chooses not to exploit this—it passes its single type parameter in as all three type arguments to operator interfaces. So any type implementing `INumber<T>` implements `IAdditionOperators<T, T, T>`, `IMultiplyOperators<T, T, T>`, and so on.

The other feature making Example 4-24 more complex is that it enables types to provide different implementations of addition for checked and unchecked contexts. As Chapter 2 described, C# does not emit code detecting arithmetic overflow by default, but inside blocks or expressions marked with the checked keyword, arithmetic operations producing results too large to fit in the target type will cause exceptions. Types providing custom implementations of arithmetic operators can supply a different method to be used in a checked context so that they can offer the same feature. This is optional, which is why `IAdditionOperators<TSelf, TOther, TResult>` defines the checked + operator as virtual (not abstract): it provides a default implementation that just calls the unchecked version. This is a suitable default for types that do not overflow, such as `BigInteger`. Types that can overflow tend to need specialized code to detect this, in which case they will override the `checked` operator.

Generic Math Interfaces

As you've just seen, `System.Numerics` defines multiple interfaces representing various mathematical capabilities. Very often we'll just specify a constraint of `INumber<T>`, but sometimes we will need to be a bit more specific. Our code might need to be able to represent negative numbers, in which case `INumber<T>` is too broad: it is implemented by signed (e.g., `int`) and unsigned types (e.g., `uint`) types alike. If we specify `ISigned Number<T>` as a constraint, that will prevent the use of unsigned types. Generic math defines four groups of interfaces representing different kinds of characteristics we might require:

- Numeric category (e.g., `INumber<T>`, `ISignedNumber<T>`, `IFloatingPoint<T>`)
- Operator (e.g., `IAdditionOperators<TSelf, TOther, TResult>`, `IMultiply Operators<TSelf, TOther, TResult>`)
- Function (e.g., `IExponentialFunctions<TSelf, TOther, TResult>` or `ITrigono metricFunctions<TSelf, TOther, TResult>`)
- Parsing and formatting

The following sections describe each of these groups.

Numeric Category Interfaces

The various numeric category interfaces represent certain kinds of characteristics that we might want from numeric types, not all of which are universal to all kinds of numbers. Some methods, such as the generic `Add<T>` method shown in Example 4-22, will be able to work with more or less any numeric type, so a constraint of `INumber<T>` is a reasonable choice. But some code might be able to work only with whole numbers, while other code might absolutely require floating point. Figure 4-1 shows the category interfaces that let us express various capabilities that our generic code might require. Each of .NET's numeric types implements some but not all of these interfaces.

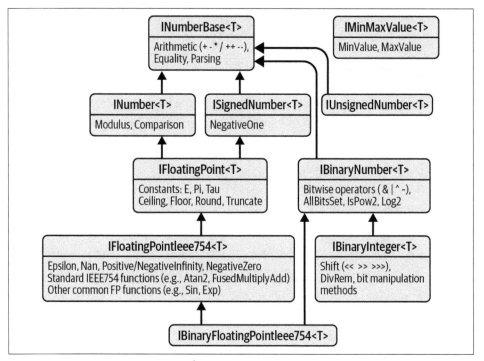

Figure 4-1. Numeric category interfaces

This figure shows inheritance relationships that define fixed relationships between some of the category interfaces. Chapter 6 describes inheritance in detail, but with interfaces it's fairly straightforward: any type that implements an interface is required also to implement any inherited interfaces. For example, if a number implements IFloatingPoint<T>, it must also implement INumber<T>. There are other relationships that, while not strictly required, exist in practice in .NET's numeric types. For example, although there is no absolute requirement that types implementing ISigned Number<T> must also implement INumber<T>, all the types built into the .NET runtime libraries that implement the former implement the latter. (For example, int, double, and decimal all implement both.)

The .NET documentation generally encourages you to use INumber<T> as the constraint in code where you need common arithmetic operations but don't have any particular requirements about the kind of number in use. However, you can see from Figure 4-1 that there is an even more general interface: INumberBase<T>. All of the interfaces in that diagram except for IMinMaxValue<T> inherit directly or indirectly from INumberBase<T> (and in practice, types that implement IMinMaxValue<T> usually implement INumberBase<T>), so if you want to write code that can work with the absolute widest range of types possible, INumberBase<T> is a better choice than

INumber<T>. Example 4-22 could be modified to specify INumberBase<T> as a constraint, for example, and it would still work, because the basic arithmetic operators are available.

So what's the difference? If you're using the numeric types built into .NET, the only impact of specifying INumber<T> as a constraint instead of INumberBase<T> is that you won't be able to use the Complex type. Complex numbers are two-dimensional, which means that for any two complex numbers, we can't necessarily say which is larger—for any particular complex number there will be infinitely many other complex numbers with different values but the same magnitude. INumberBase<T> requires types to support comparison for equality (is x equal to y?) but does not require types to support comparison for ordering (is x greater than y?). INumber<T> requires types to support both. So Complex implements INumberBase<T> but cannot implement INumber<T>. Also, Complex does not provide a way to get the remainder of a division operation, and this is similarly absent from the INumberBase<T> interface (but it is present in INumber<T>). These are the only two differences between these two interfaces. So unless you need your numbers to be sortable, or you need to calculate remainders (with the % operator), using INumberBase<T> as a constraint is the simplest way to work with the widest possible range of numeric types.

INumberBase<T> doesn't just define the basic arithmetic operators. It also defines properties called One and Zero. Example 4-25 uses Zero to provide an initial value for calculating the sum total of an array of values. Why not just write the literal 0? IL (the compiler's output) uses different representations for literals of different types, and since T here is a generic type argument, it's not possible for the compiler to generate code that creates a literal of type T.

Example 4-25. Using INumberBase<T>.Zero

```
static T Sum<T>(T[] values)
    where T : INumberBase<T>
{
    T total = T.Zero;
    foreach (T value in values)
    {
        total += value;
    }
    return total;
}
```

The Zero and One properties are available on any INumber<T>, but the interface also makes it possible to attempt conversions from other values. It defines a static Create Checked<TOther>(TOther value) method, so instead of T.Zero, we could have written T.CreateChecked(0). This is a generic method, and it constrains the TOther type argument to implement INumberBase<TOther> so you can pass any numeric type, but the compiler won't let you call T.CreateChecked("banana"), for example. However, not all conversions are guaranteed to succeed—if code passes a value to Create Checked of some type with a larger range than the target type, the value could exceed the target type's range, in which case the method will throw an OverflowException. For example, T.CreateChecked(uint.MaxValue) would fail if the generic method is invoked with a type argument of int. (This is why I've used T.Zero: that won't throw exceptions under any circumstances.) INumber<T> also defines CheckedSaturating, which handles out-of-range values by returning the largest or smallest available value (depending on the direction in which you exceeded the range). For example, if the target is int, and you pass a value that is too high, CreateSaturating will return int.MaxValue. If you pass too large a negative number it will return int.MinValue. There is also CreateTruncating, which just discards higher-order bits. For example, if the input is a long and the target is int, CreateTruncating will use the bottom 32 bits of the value and will simply ignore the top 32 bits. (This is the same as the behavior when casting a long to an int in an unchecked context.)

INumberBase<T> also provides various utility methods you can use to ask about certain characteristics. For example, it requires all implementing types to define IsPositive, IsNegative, and IsInteger static methods.

The IBinaryNumber<T> interface is implemented by all types that have a defined binary representation. In practice, this means all of .NET's native numeric types (integers and floating point) except for decimal, and it also includes BigInteger. It makes bitwise operators (such as & and |) available, and it defines IsPow2 and Log2 methods. IsPow2 enables you to discover whether the value has just a single nonzero binary digit (meaning it will be some power of two). Log2 essentially tells you how many binary digits are required to represent the value. IBinaryInteger<T> is more specialized, being implemented only by integer types (built-in and also BigInteger). It adds bit-shift and rotation operators, conversion to and from byte sequences in either big or little endian form, and some bit-counting functions.

There are various interfaces representing floating-point. One reason we can't have a one-size-fits-all definition is that decimal is technically a kind of floating-point number, but it is very different from float, double, and System.Half, each of which implements the IEEE754 international standard for floating-point arithmetic. That means those types have a well-defined binary structure, and support a particular set of standard operations besides basic arithmetic. decimal does not have those features, but if all you need is the ability to represent non-whole numbers, it may be sufficient, and if you specify a constraint of IFloatingPoint<T>, that will allow any of the floating-point types, including decimal. You would specify IFloatingPoint Ieee754<T> if you need the special values IEEE754 defines (such as NaN, the *not a number* value that can arise from some calculations, or its representations for positive and negative infinity) or if you need access to some of the standard IEEE754 operations such as trigonometric functions or exponentiation. Or you might specify this in order to exclude `decimal` because it has some very different characteristics around precision and error. It would be fairly rare to need the more specialized `IBinary FloatingPointIeee754<T>`. This is implemented by all of the native .NET types that implement `IFloatingPointIeee754<T>`, and it makes it possible to use bitwise operations, but it's relatively unusual to perform bit twiddling on floating-point values. In most cases, `IFloatingPointIeee754<T>` will be the most specific floating-point constraint you will need.

Figure 4-1 has one interface apparently sitting all on its own: `IMinMaxValue<T>`. In fact, almost all of the numeric types implement this—it makes `MinValue` and `Max Value` properties available, reporting the highest and lowest values the type can represent. It only looks so isolated because none of the other numeric category interfaces *requires* `IMinMaxValue<T>`; it's almost ubiquitous in practice. One exception is the `Com plex` type, which does not implement this because, as already discussed, it doesn't fully order its numbers, so there isn't one single, highest value. `BigInteger` also does not implement this, because its defining feature is that it has no fixed upper limit.

There are two more interfaces that the .NET documentation puts in the numeric category group: `IAdditiveIdentity<TSelf, TResult>` and `IMultiplicativeIden tity<TSelf, TResult>`. I did not include these in Figure 4-1 because they are slightly different from the other category interfaces. These are closely associated with two of the operator interfaces described in the next section. Every type in the .NET runtime libraries that implements `IAdditionOperators<TSelf, TOther, TResult>` also implements `IAdditiveIdentity<TSelf, TResult>`, and likewise for `IMultiplyOpera tors<TSelf, TOther, TResult>` and `IMultiplicativeIdentity<TSelf, TResult>`. These each define a single property, `AdditiveIdentity` and `MultiplicativeIden tity`, respectively. If you use these values as one of the operands of their corresponding operation, the result will be the other operand. (In other words, `x + T.AdditiveIdentity` and `x * T.MultiplicativeIdentity` are both equal to x.) In practice, that means `AdditiveIdentity` is zero and `MultiplicativeIdentity` is one for all of the numeric types .NET supplies. So why not just use `T.Zero` and `T.One`? It's because there are some less conventional mathematical objects that behave like numbers in certain ways, but which don't correspond directly to normal numbers like one or zero. For example, some mathematicians like to do math with shapes, using rotation and reflection, and in some cases there may be behavior that is addition-like, but where the additive identity isn't a simple number. Although none of the built-in numeric types enter this sort of territory, generic math was designed to make it possible to write libraries that do this kind of math.

Example 4-26 uses `IAdditiveIdentity<TSelf, TResult>` to implement an alternative to the `Sum<T>` method shown in Example 4-25. In theory this makes this method less constrained: it is able to work with any addable type, and does not require `INumberBase<T>`. All of the .NET runtime library types that are addable also implement `INumberBase<T>`, so this is of doubtful benefit, but if you are using a library representing more exotic mathematical objects, it might contain types that do not implement `INumberBase<T>` but which would work with this more precisely constrained method.

Example 4-26. Using `AdditiveIdentity`

```
public static T Sum<T>(T[] values)
    where T : IAdditionOperators<T, T, T>, IAdditiveIdentity<T, T>
{
    T total = T.AdditiveIdentity;
    foreach (T value in values)
    {
        total += value;
    }
    return total;
}
```

The somewhat complex and intricate taxonomy of numeric types represented by the numeric category interfaces makes it possible to define very specific constraints, which can enable generic code to work with the widest possible range of numeric types. However, as Example 4-26 shows, this comes at the cost of some complexity. The version of this code in Example 4-25 that used a constraint of `INumberBase<T>` is simpler, and doesn't require developers reading the code to have committed Figure 4-1 to memory, or to be sufficiently familiar with mathematical terminology to understand exactly what an additive identity is. And since all of .NET's numeric types implement `INumberBase<T>`, using that as a constraint will normally strike a better balance between ultimate flexibility and readability.

Operator Interfaces

You've already seen `IAdditionOperators<TSelf, TOther, TResult>`, which we can use as a constraint requiring the + operator to be available for a generic type parameter. This is one of a family of interfaces defining the availability of operators. Table 4-1 lists all the interfaces of this kind and shows which operators each interface defines.

Table 4-1. Operator interfaces

Interface	Operations	Available through
IAdditionOperators<TSelf,TOther,TResult>	x + y	INumberBase<T>
IBitwiseOperators<TSelf,TOther,TResult>	x & y, x | y, x ^ y, and ~x	IBinaryNumber<T>
IComparisonOperators<TSelf,TOther, TResult>	x < y, x > y, x <= y, and x >= y	INumber<T>
IDecrementOperators<TSelf>	--x and x--	INumberBase<T>
IDivisionOperators<TSelf,TOther,TResult>	x / y	INumberBase<T>
IEqualityOperators<TSelf,TOther,TResult>	x == y and x != y	INumberBase<T>
IIncrementOperators<TSelf>	++x and x++	INumberBase<T>
IModulusOperators<TSelf,TOther,TResult>	x % y	INumber<T>
IMultiplyOperators<TSelf,TOther,TResult>	x * y	INumberBase<T>
IShiftOperators<TSelf,TOther,TResult>	x << y, x >> y and x >>> y	IBinaryInteger<T>
ISubtractionOperators<TSelf,TOther,TResult>	x - y	INumberBase<T>
IUnaryNegationOperators<TSelf,TResult>	-x	INumberBase<T>
IUnaryPlusOperators<TSelf,TResult>	+x	INumberBase<T>

In practice we rarely express constraints directly in terms of these operator interfaces, because the various numeric category interfaces inherit from them and are less verbose. The final column of the table shows the most general category interface that inherits from that row's operator interface. When a type implements an operator interface, it will usually also implement that corresponding numeric category interface. As the preceding section just discussed, although you could specify a constraint of IAdditionOperators<T, T, T>, all of the types in the runtime libraries that implement that also implement INumberBase<T>. Unless you're using an unusual library that implements some operator interfaces but not the corresponding category interface, there's no benefit in practice to being more specific, so when you need a particular operator, you'll normally use the corresponding interface in the third column of Table 4-1 as the constraint.

Function Interfaces

Many common mathematical operations are expressed not as operators, but as functions. For most of .NET's history, we have used the methods defined by the System.Math class, but that type predates generics. Generic math makes features such as trigonometric functions and exponentiation available through static abstract methods defined by the interfaces listed in Table 4-2.

Table 4-2. Function interfaces

Interface	Operations
`IExponentialFunctions<TSelf>`	Exponential functions such as `T.Exp` (e^x) and `T.Exp2` (2^x)
`IHyperbolicFunctions<TSelf>`	Hyperbolic functions such as `T.Sinh`, `T.Cosh`, `T.Asinh`, and `T.Acosh`
`ILogarithmicFunctions<TSelf>`	Logarithmic functions such as `T.Log` and `T.Log2`
`IPowerFunctions<TSelf>`	Power function: `T.Pow` (x^y)
`IRootFunctions<TSelf>`	Root functions such as `T.Sqrt` and `T.Cbrt` (square and cube roots)
`ITrigonometricFunctions<TSelf>`	Trigonometric functions such as `T.Sin`, `T.Cos`, `T.Asin`, and `T.Acos`

As with the operator interfaces, we don't normally need to refer to these interfaces directly in constraints, because they are accessible through a numeric category. All of the .NET runtime library types that implement any of these interfaces also implement `IFloatingPointIeee754<T>`.

Parsing and Formatting

The final set of interfaces associated with generic math enables us to work with text representations of numbers. Strictly speaking, these four interfaces are not limited to working with just numeric types—`DateTimeOffset` implements all of them, for example. However, `INumberBase<T>` inherits from all of these, so they are available on types that support generic math.

`IParsable<T>` defines `Parse` and `TryParse` methods that enable you to convert a `string` to the target numeric type. There is also `ISpanParsable<T>`, which offers similar methods that can work with `ReadOnlySpan<char>`. Span types, which Chapter 18 describes in detail, make it possible to work with ranges of characters that are not necessarily full `string` objects in their own right. `ISpanParsable<T>` can parse text in subsections of an existing `string`, a `char[]`, memory allocated on the stack, or even in a block of memory allocated by mechanisms outside of the .NET runtime's control (e.g., through a system call, or by some external non-.NET library). There is also an `IUtf8SpanParsable<T>`, which can work directly with data encoded in UTF-8 format.

`IFormattable<T>`, `ISpanFormattable<T>`, and `IUtf8SpanFormattable<T>` go in the other direction: they are able to produce text representations of values. (These aren't new—they have been around since .NET 6.0—but they are now associated with generic math because `INumberBase<T>` inherits from them.) `IFormattable<T>` defines an overload of `ToString` accepting the same kind of composite formatting as `string.Format`, along with an optional `IFormatProvider` argument controlling details that vary by language and culture (such as conventions for digit separators). `ISpanFormattable<T>` defines `TryFormat`, which provides the same service, but instead of returning a newly allocated string, it writes its output directly into a

`Span<char>`, which may enable more complex strings to be built up with fewer allocations, reducing pressure on the garbage collector.

Generics and Tuples

C#'s lightweight tuples have a distinctive syntax, but as far as the runtime is concerned, there is nothing special about them. They are all just instances of a set of generic types. Look at Example 4-27. This uses (`int, int`) as the type of a local variable to indicate that it is a tuple containing two `int` values.

Example 4-27. Declaring a tuple variable in the normal way

```
(int, int) p = (42, 99);
```

Now look at Example 4-28. This uses the `ValueTuple<int, int>` type in the `System` namespace. But this is exactly equivalent to the declaration in Example 4-27. In Visual Studio or VS Code, if you hover the mouse over the `p2` variable, it will report its type as (`int, int`).

Example 4-28. Declaring a tuple variable with its underlying type

```
ValueTuple<int, int> p2 = (42, 99);
```

One thing that C#'s special syntax for tuples adds is the ability to name the tuple elements. The `ValueTuple` family names its elements `Item1`, `Item2`, `Item3`, etc., but in C# we can pick other names. When you declare a local variable with named tuple elements, those names are a fiction maintained by C#—they have no runtime representation at all. However, when a method returns a tuple, as in Example 4-29, it's different: the names need to be visible so that code consuming this method can use the same names. Even if this method is in some library component that my code has referenced, I want to be able to write `Pos().X`, instead of having to use `Pos().Item1`.

Example 4-29. Returning a tuple

```
public static (int X, int Y) Pos() => (10, 20);
```

To make this work, the compiler applies an attribute named `TupleElementNames` to the method's return value, and this contains an array listing the property names to use. (Chapter 14 describes attributes.) You can't actually write code that does this yourself: if you write a method that returns a `ValueTuple<int, int>` and you try to apply the `TupleElementNamesAttribute` as a `return` attribute, the compiler will produce an error telling you not to use this attribute directly and to use the tuple syntax instead. But that attribute is how the compiler reports the tuple element names.

Be aware that there's another family of tuple types in the runtime libraries, `Tuple<T>`, `Tuple<T1, T2>`, and so on. These look almost identical to the `ValueTuple` family. The difference is that the `Tuple` family of generic types are all classes, whereas all the `ValueTuple` types are structs. The C# lightweight tuple syntax only uses the `ValueTuple` family. The `Tuple` family has been around in the runtime libraries for much longer, though, so you often see them used in older code that needed to bundle a set of values together without defining a new type just for that job.

Summary

Generics enable us to write types and methods with type parameters, which can be filled in at compile time to produce different versions of the types or methods that work with particular types. One of the most important use cases for generics back when they were first introduced was to make it possible to write type-safe collection classes such as `List<T>`. We will look at some of these collection types in the next chapter.

CHAPTER 5

Collections

Most programs need to deal with multiple pieces of data. Your code might have to iterate through some transactions to calculate the balance of an account, for example, or display recent messages in a social media web application, or update the positions of characters in a game. In most kinds of applications, the ability to work with collections of information is likely to be important.

C# offers a simple kind of collection called an *array*. The CLR's type system supports arrays intrinsically, so they are efficient, but for some scenarios they can be too basic. The runtime libraries build on the fundamental services provided by arrays to provide more powerful and flexible collection types. I'll start with arrays, because they are the foundation of most of the collection classes.

Arrays

An array is an object that contains multiple *elements* of a particular type. Each element is a storage location similar to a field, but whereas with fields we give each storage slot a name, array elements are simply numbered. The number of elements is fixed for the lifetime of the array, so you must specify the size when you create it. Example 5-1 shows the syntax for creating new arrays.

Example 5-1. Creating arrays

```
int[] numbers = new int[10];
string[] strings = new string[numbers.Length];
```

As with all objects, we construct an array with the new keyword followed by a type name, but instead of parentheses with constructor arguments, we put square brackets containing the array size. As the example shows, the expression defining the size can be a constant, but it doesn't have to be—the second array's size will be determined by evaluating numbers.Length at runtime. In this case, the second array will have 10 elements because we're using the first array's Length property. All arrays have this read-only property, and it returns the total number of elements in the array.

The Length property's type is int, which means it can cope with arrays of up to about 2.1 billion elements. In a 32-bit process, the limiting factor on array size is likely to be available address space, but in 64-bit processes, larger arrays are possible, so there's also a LongLength property of type long. However, you don't see that used much, because the runtime does not currently support creation of arrays with more than 2,147,483,591 (0x7FFFFFC7) elements in any single dimension. So only rectangular multidimensional arrays (described later in this chapter) can contain more elements than Length can report. And even those have an upper limit of 4,294,967,295 (0xFFFFFFFF) elements on the current version of .NET.

In Example 5-1, I've broken my normal rule of avoiding redundant type names in variable declarations. The initializer expressions make it clear that the variables are arrays of int and string, respectively, so I'd normally use var for this sort of code, but I've made an exception here so that I can show how to write the name of an array type. Array types are distinct types in their own right, and if we want to refer to the type that is a single dimensional array of some particular element type, we put [] after the element type name.

All array types derive from a common base class called System.Array. This defines the Length and LongLength properties and various other members we'll be looking at in due course. You can use array types in all the usual places you can use other types. So you could declare a field, or a method parameter of type string[]. You can also use an array type as a generic type argument. For example, IEnumerable<int[]> would be a sequence of arrays of integers (each of which could be a different size).

An array type is always a reference type, regardless of the element type. Nonetheless, the choice between reference type and value type elements makes a significant difference in an array's behavior. As discussed in Chapter 3, when an object has a field with a value type, the value itself lives inside the memory allocated for the object. The same is true for arrays—when the elements are value types, the value lives in the array element itself, but with a reference type, elements contain only references. Each instance of a reference type has its own identity, and since multiple variables may all end up referring to that instance, the CLR needs to manage its lifetime independently of any other object, so it will end up with its own distinct block of memory. So while an array of 1,000 int values can all live in one contiguous memory block, with reference types, the array just contains the references, not the actual instances. An array of 1,000 different strings would need 1,001 heap blocks—one for the array and one for each string.

When using reference type elements, you're not obliged to make every element in an array of references refer to a distinct object. You can leave as many elements as you like set to null, and you're also free to make multiple elements refer to the same object. This is just another variation on the theme that references in array elements work in much the same way as they do in local variables and fields.

To access an element in an array, we use square brackets containing the index of the element we'd like to use. The index is zero-based. Example 5-2 shows a few examples.

Example 5-2. Accessing array elements

```
// Continued from Example 5-1
numbers[0] = 42;
numbers[1] = numbers.Length;
numbers[2] = numbers[0] + numbers[1];
numbers[numbers.Length - 1] = 99;
```

As with the array's size at construction, the array index can be a constant, but it can also be a more complex expression, calculated at runtime. In fact, that's also true of the part that comes directly before the opening bracket. In Example 5-2, I've just used a variable name to refer to an array, but you can use brackets after any array-typed expression. Example 5-3 retrieves the first element of an array returned by a method call. (The details of the example aren't strictly relevant, but in case you're wondering, it finds the copyright message associated with the component that defines an object's type. For example, if you pass a string to the method, it will return "© Microsoft Corporation. All rights reserved." This uses the reflection API and custom attributes, the topics of Chapters 13 and 14.)

Example 5-3. Convoluted array access

```
public static string GetCopyrightForType(object o)
{
    Assembly asm = o.GetType().Assembly;
    var copyrightAttribute = (AssemblyCopyrightAttribute)
        asm.GetCustomAttributes(typeof(AssemblyCopyrightAttribute), true)[0];
    return copyrightAttribute.Copyright;
}
```

Expressions involving array element access are special, in that C# considers them to be a kind of variable. This means that as with local variables and fields, you can use them on the lefthand side of an assignment statement, whether they're simple, like the expressions in Example 5-2, or more complex, like those in Example 5-3. You can also use them with the ref keyword (as described in Chapter 3) to pass a reference to a particular element to a method, to store it in a `ref` local variable, or to return it from a method with a `ref` return type.

The CLR always checks the index against the array size. If you try to use either a negative index or an index greater than or equal to the length of the array, the runtime will throw an `IndexOutOfRangeException`.

Although the size of an array is invariably fixed, its contents are always modifiable—there is no such thing as a read-only array. (As we'll see in "ReadOnlyCollection<T>" on page 287, .NET provides a class that can act as a read-only façade for an array.) You can, of course, create an array with an immutable element type, and this will prevent you from modifying the element in place. So Example 5-4, which uses the immutable `Complex` value type provided by .NET, will not compile.

Example 5-4. How not to modify an array with immutable elements

```
var values = new Complex[10];
// These lines both cause compiler errors:
values[0].Real = 10;
values[0].Imaginary = 1;
```

The compiler complains because the `Real` and `Imaginary` properties are read-only; `Complex` does not provide any way to modify its values. Nevertheless, you can modify the array: even if you can't modify an existing element in place, you can always overwrite it by supplying a different value, as Example 5-5 shows.

Example 5-5. Modifying an array with immutable elements

```
var values = new Complex[10];
values[0] = new Complex(10, 1);
```

Read-only arrays wouldn't be much use in any case, because all arrays start out filled with a default value that you don't get to specify. The CLR fills the memory for a new array with zeros, so you'll see `0`, `null`, or `false`, depending on the array's element type.

 If you write a zero-argument constructor for a `struct`, you might have expected array creation to invoke constructors of this kind automatically. It does not.

For some applications, all-zero (or equivalent) content might be a useful initial state for an array, but in some cases, you'll want to set some other content before starting to work.

Array Initialization

The most straightforward way to initialize an array is to assign values into each element in turn. Example 5-6 creates a `string` array, and since `string` is a reference type, creating a five-element array doesn't create five strings. Our array starts out with five nulls. (This is true even if you've enabled C#'s nullable references feature, as described in Chapter 3. Unfortunately, array initialization is one of the holes that make it impossible for that feature to offer absolute guarantees of non-nullness.) So the example goes on to populate each array element with a reference to a string.

Example 5-6. Laborious array initialization

```
var workingWeekDayNames = new string[5];
workingWeekDayNames[0] = "Monday";
workingWeekDayNames[1] = "Tuesday";
workingWeekDayNames[2] = "Wednesday";
workingWeekDayNames[3] = "Thursday";
workingWeekDayNames[4] = "Friday";
```

This works, but it is unnecessarily verbose. C# supports a shorter syntax that achieves the same thing, shown in Example 5-7. The compiler turns this into code that works like Example 5-6. With arrays of numbers (e.g., an `int[]`) the shorter syntax can generate more efficient code: instead of emitting a series of assignments, it can embed the array's values as a chunk of raw data in the compiled output, enabling it to initialize the entire array from that data with a single call to a .NET runtime library helper function. (The embedded data is read-only, and will be copied into a new array each time the code runs, so the effect is equivalent to sequence of assignments. It's just faster, and it results in more compact compiled code.)

Example 5-7. Initializing an array with a collection expression

```
string[] workingWeekDayNames =
    ["Monday", "Tuesday", "Wednesday", "Thursday", "Friday"];
```

The syntax in Example 5-7 is called a *collection expression*, and it is new in C# 12.0. As you'll see later, you can also use it with other collection types. It is now the preferred way to initialize sequence-like collections because it is more compact than the older approaches, it supports a wider range of collection types, and the compiler strives to generate the most efficient initialization code possible for whichever collection type you have chosen. (If you upgrade an older project to .NET 8.0, you will typically see several messages from the compiler suggesting that you move over to this new syntax.)

Collection expressions can copy data from other collections using the *spread* syntax illustrated in Example 5-8. This example creates a new array by copying the elements from the array in Example 5-7 into a new array with additional elements at the start and end. Spread elements are not required to be of precisely the same type—although this example spreads one `string[]` into a new `string[]`, I could have incorporated any collection representing a sequence of `string` elements, such as the `List<string>` type described later in this chapter.

Example 5-8. Using a spread element to copy an array as part of a collection expression

```
string[] weekDayNames = ["Sunday", .. workingWeekDayNames, "Saturday"];
```

Collection expressions are designed to resemble the list patterns you saw in Chapter 2, which is why spreads use the same `..` syntax as the slices that can appear in list patterns. However, while a list pattern can contain at most one slice, we're not limited to a single spread: a collection expression may contain any number of spread expressions.

Since collection expressions are new in C# 12.0, you are likely to come across existing code that uses the older *array initializer* syntax shown in Example 5-9. That particular example is more verbose, because it explicitly states that we want a new array of type `string[]`. This means that there are still uses for this older syntax: if the compiler is unable to infer the required collection type, you can't use a collection expression because it's not clear whether you want an array, a `List<string>`, an `Immutable List<string>`, or something else—all of those are potential target types for the collection expression to the right of the = in Example 5-7. That example avoids ambiguity by stating the type explicitly in the variable declaration, but if we had used `var`, the compiler would have complained that it couldn't determine which collection type we want. The more verbose initializer in Example 5-9 avoids this.

Example 5-9. Array initializer syntax

```
var workingWeekDayNames = new string[]
    { "Monday", "Tuesday", "Wednesday", "Thursday", "Friday" };
```

As it happens, C# has long supported one special case in which the older collection initializer syntax can omit the `new string[]` part. Example 5-10 shows that if you specify the type explicitly in the variable declaration, you can write just the initializer list, leaving out the `new` keyword. This works only in variable initializer expressions, by the way; you can't use this syntax to create an array in other expressions, such as assignments or method arguments. (The newer collection expression syntax works in all those contexts, as does the more verbose initializer expression in Example 5-9.) There's no practical difference between Example 5-10 and the newer syntax in Example 5-7, but since collection expressions offer additional flexibility in other contexts, and they are the most efficient way to initialize other collection types, they are likely to become the preferred idiomatic choice in these cases.

Example 5-10. Shorter array initializer syntax

```
string[] workingWeekDayNames =
    { "Monday", "Tuesday", "Wednesday", "Thursday", "Friday" };
```

The array initializer syntax offers yet another variation: if all the expressions inside the array initializer list are of the same type, the compiler can infer the array type, so we can write just new[] without an explicit element type. Example 5-11 does this.

Example 5-11. Array initializer syntax with element type inference

```
var workingWeekDayNames = new[]
    { "Monday", "Tuesday", "Wednesday", "Thursday", "Friday" };
```

That was actually slightly longer than Example 5-10. However, as with collection expressions and the other more verbose kinds of array initializers, this style is not limited to variable initialization. You can also use it when you need to pass an array as an argument to a method, for example. If the array you are creating will only be passed into a method and never referred to again, you may not want to declare a variable to refer to it. It might be neater to write the array directly in the argument list. Example 5-12 passes an array of strings to a method using this technique.

Example 5-12. Array as argument

```
SetHeaders(new[] { "Monday", "Tuesday", "Wednesday", "Thursday", "Friday" });
```

In most cases, the new collection expression syntax is likely to be a better choice, but there are some circumstances where its flexibility works against it. If the SetHeaders method invoked by Example 5-12 takes a first argument of type string[], then a collection expression would be a more succinct choice. However, it would be different if its first argument's type was IEnumerable<string> (a type we'll be looking at shortly, which would indicate that SetHeader can work with many different collection types). In that case, using a collection expression causes the compiler to generate code that creates a read-only wrapper around an array. This ensures that if SetHeaders were to try casting its input to an IList<T> it would be prevented from modifying it. That would make it safe to reuse the same collection each time the code ran, although as it happens the current compiler doesn't seem to do that. (The C# language specification gives the compiler some latitude here, so there may be situations in which it will cache and reuse the collection.) In situations where this protection is unnecessary (e.g., because you control the code to which the collection is passed, and know it does not attempt any such modifications) just passing an array would be more efficient. To do that, you could use an array initializer as Example 5-12 does, and not a collection expression, or you could cast a collection expression to an array type so that the compiler knows what type you require.

 If you write code that initializes an array with a fixed set of contents, like some of the preceding examples, you should consider putting the array into a `static readonly` field. That way, the array is created just once and reused. Unless you really need a new array instance every time the code runs (e.g., because you go on to modify the array, or because the contents aren't the same every time), or the method in question will be invoked only once, it can be more efficient to reuse the same array object each time.

Searching and Sorting

Sometimes, you will not know the index of the array element you need. For example, suppose you are writing an application that shows a list of recently used files. Each time the user opens a file in your application, you would want to bring that file to the top of the list, and you'd need to detect when the file was already in the list to avoid having it appear multiple times. If the user happened to use your recent file list to open the file, you would already know it's in the list and at what offset. But what if the user opens the file some other way? In that case, you've got a filename, and you need to find out where that appears in your list, if it's there at all.

Arrays can help you find the item you want in this kind of scenario. There are methods that examine each element in turn, stopping at the first match, and there are also methods that can work considerably faster if your array stores its elements in a particular order. To help with that, there are also methods for sorting the contents of an array into whichever order you require.

The static `Array.IndexOf` method provides the most straightforward way to search for an element. It does not need your array elements to be in any particular order: you just pass it the array in which to search and the value you're looking for, and it will walk through the elements until it finds a value equal to the one you want. It returns the index at which it found the first matching element, or −1 if it reached the end of the array without finding a match. Example 5-13 shows how you might use this method as part of the logic for updating a list of recently opened files.

Example 5-13. Searching with IndexOf

```
int recentFileListIndex = Array.IndexOf(myRecentFiles, openedFile);
if (recentFileListIndex < 0)
{
    AddNewRecentEntry(openedFile);
}
```

```
else
{
    MoveExistingRecentEntryToTop(recentFileListIndex);
}
```

That example starts its search at the beginning of the array, but you have other options. The IndexOf method is overloaded, and you can pass an index from which to start searching and optionally a second number indicating how many elements you want it to look at before it gives up. There's also a LastIndexOf method, which works in reverse. If you do not specify an index, it starts from the end of the array and works backward. As with IndexOf, you can provide one or two more arguments, indicating the offset at which you'd like to start and the number of elements to check.

These methods are fine if you know precisely what value you're looking for, but often, you'll need to be a bit more flexible: you may want to find the first (or last) element that meets some particular criteria. For example, suppose you have an array representing the bin values for a histogram. It might be useful to find out which is the first nonempty bin. So rather than searching for a particular value, you'd want to find the first element with any value other than zero. Example 5-14 shows how to use the FindIndex method to locate the first such entry.

Example 5-14. Searching with FindIndex

```
public static int GetIndexOfFirstNonEmptyBin(int[] bins)
    => Array.FindIndex(bins, IsNonZero);

private static bool IsNonZero(int value) => value != 0;
```

My IsNonZero method contains the logic that decides whether any particular element is a match, and I've passed that method as an argument to FindIndex. You can pass any method with a suitable signature—FindIndex requires a method that takes an instance of the array's element type and returns a bool. (Strictly speaking, it takes a Predicate<T>, which is a kind of delegate, something I'll discuss in Chapter 9.) Since any method with a suitable signature will do, we can make our search criteria as simple or as complex as we like.

By the way, the logic for this particular example is so simple that writing a separate method for the condition is probably overkill. For simple cases such as these, you'd almost certainly use the lambda syntax (using => to indicate that an expression represents an inline function) instead. That's also something I'll be discussing in Chapter 9, so this is jumping ahead, but I'll just show how it looks because it's more concise. Example 5-15 has exactly the same effect as Example 5-14 but doesn't require us to declare and write a whole extra method explicitly.

Example 5-15. Using a lambda with FindIndex

```
public static int GetIndexOfFirstNonEmptyBin(int[] bins)
    => Array.FindIndex(bins, value => value != 0);
```

As with `IndexOf`, `FindIndex` provides overloads that let you specify the offset at which to start searching and the number of elements to check before giving up. The `Array` class also provides `FindLastIndex`, which works backward—it corresponds to `LastIndexOf`, much as `FindIndex` corresponds to `IndexOf`.

When you're searching for an array entry that meets some particular criteria, you might not be all that interested in the index of the matching element—you might need to know only the value of the first match. Obviously, it's pretty easy to get that: you can just use the value returned by `FindIndex` in conjunction with the array index syntax. However, you don't need to, because the `Array` class offers `Find` and `FindLast` methods that search in precisely the same way as `FindIndex` and `FindLastIndex` but that return the first or last matching value instead of returning the index at which that value was found.

An array could contain multiple items that meet your criteria, and you might want to find all of them. You could write a loop that calls `FindIndex`, adding one to the index of the previous match and using that as the starting point for the next search, repeating until either reaching the end of the array or getting a result of −1, indicating that no more matches were found. And that would be the way to go if you needed to know the index of each match. But if you are interested only in knowing all of the matching values, and do not need to know exactly where those values were in the array, you could use the `FindAll` method shown in Example 5-16 to do all the work for you.

Example 5-16. Finding multiple items with FindAll

```
public static T[] GetNonNullItems<T>(T[] items) where T : class
    => Array.FindAll(items, value => value != null);
```

This takes any array with reference type elements and returns an array that contains only the non-null elements in that array.

All of the search methods I've shown so far run through an array's elements in order, testing each element in turn. This works well enough, but with large arrays it may be unnecessarily expensive, particularly in cases where comparisons are relatively complex. Even for simple comparisons, if you need to deal with arrays with millions of elements, this sort of search can take long enough to introduce visible delays. However, we can do much better. For example, given an array of values sorted into ascending order, a *binary search* can perform many orders of magnitude better. Example 5-17 shows two methods. The first, `Sort`, sorts an array of numbers into ascending order. And if we have such a sorted array, we can then pass it to Find, which uses the Array.BinarySearch method.

Example 5-17. Sorting an array, and BinarySearch

```
void Sort(int[] numbers)
{
    Array.Sort(numbers);
}

int Find(int[] numbers, int searchFor)
{
    return Array.BinarySearch(numbers, searchFor);
}
```

Binary search is a widely used algorithm that exploits the fact that its input is sorted to be able to rule out half of the array at each step. It starts with the element in the middle of the array. If that happens to be the value required, it can stop, but otherwise, depending on whether the value it found is higher or lower than the value we want, it can know instantly which half of the array the value will be in (if it's present at all). It then leaps to the middle of the remaining half, and if that's not the right value, again it can determine which quarter will contain the target. At each step, it narrows the search down by half, and after halving the size a few times, it will be down to a single item. If that's not the value it's looking for, the item it wants is missing.

 BinarySearch produces negative numbers when the value is not found. In these cases, this binary chop process will finish at the value nearest to the one we are looking for, and that might be useful information. So a negative number still tells us the search failed, but that number is the negation of the index of the closest match.

A binary search is more complex than a simple linear search, but with large arrays, it pays off because far fewer iterations are needed. Given an array of 100,000,000 elements, it has to perform only 27 steps instead of 100,000,000. Obviously, with smaller arrays, the improvement is reduced, and there will be some minimum size of array at which the relative complexity of a binary search outweighs the benefit. If your array contains only 10 values, a linear search may well be faster. But a binary search is certainly the clear winner with 100,000,000 int elements. The cases that require the most work are where it finds no match (producing a negative result), and in these cases, BinarySearch determines that an element is missing around 20,000 times faster than the linear search performed by Array.IndexOf does. However, you need to take care: a binary search works only for data that is already ordered, and the cost of getting your data into order could well outweigh the benefits. With an array of 100,000,000 ints, you would need to do about 500 searches before the cost of sorting was outweighed by the improved search speed, and, of course, that would work only if nothing changed in the meantime that forced you to redo the sort. With performance tuning, it's always important to look at the whole scenario and not just the microbenchmarks.

Incidentally, `Array.BinarySearch` offers overloads for searching within some subsection of the array, similar to those we saw for the other search methods. It also lets you customize the comparison logic. This works with the comparison interfaces I showed in earlier chapters. By default, it will use the `IComparable<T>` implementation provided by the array elements themselves, but you can provide a custom `IComparer<T>` instead. The `Array.Sort` method I used to put the elements into order also supports narrowing down the range and using custom comparison logic.

There are other searching and sorting methods besides the ones provided by the `Array` class itself. All arrays implement `IEnumerable<T>` (where `T` is the array's element type), which means you can also use any of the operations provided by .NET's *LINQ to Objects* functionality. This offers a much wider range of features for searching, sorting, grouping, filtering, and generally working with collections of objects; Chapter 10 will describe these features. Arrays have been in .NET for longer than LINQ, which is one reason for this overlap in functionality, but where arrays provide their own equivalents of standard LINQ operators, the array versions can sometimes be more efficient because LINQ is a more generalized solution.

Multidimensional Arrays

The arrays I've shown so far have all been one-dimensional, but C# supports two multidimensional forms: *jagged arrays* and *rectangular arrays.*

Jagged arrays

A jagged array is simply an array of arrays. The existence of this kind of array is a natural upshot of the fact that arrays have types that are distinct from their element type. Because `int[]` is a type, you can use that as the element type of another array. Example 5-18 shows how to create an array of arrays of integers.

Example 5-18. Creating a jagged array with collection expressions

```
int[][] arrays =
[
    [1, 2],
    [1, 2, 3, 4, 5, 6],
    [1, 2, 4],
    [1],
    [1, 2, 3, 4, 5]
];
```

I've used the collection expression syntax to initialize this array. As mentioned earlier, collection expressions are new in C# 12.0. Example 5-19 shows how to create an identical array with the older array initialization syntax.

Example 5-19. Creating a jagged array with array initializers

```
var arrays = new int[5][]
{
    new[] { 1, 2 },
    new[] { 1, 2, 3, 4, 5, 6 },
    new[] { 1, 2, 4 },
    new[] { 1 },
    new[] { 1, 2, 3, 4, 5 }
};
```

I've done something that wasn't strictly necessary here because I want to show a slightly odd feature of the jagged array constructor syntax. When using either collection expressions or array initializers, you don't have to specify the size explicitly, because the compiler will work it out for you. I've exploited that for the nested arrays in Example 5-19, but I've set the size (5) explicitly for the outer array. I could have omitted it, but I wanted to show where the size appears, because it might not be where you would expect, particularly once you think about what the type name for an array really means.

In general, array types have the form `ElementType[]`, so if the element type is `int[]`, we'd expect the resulting array type to be written as `int[][]`, and that's what we see. The constructor syntax is a bit more peculiar. It declares an array of five arrays, and at a first glance, `new int[5][]` seems like a perfectly reasonable way to express that. It is consistent with array index syntax for jagged arrays; we can write `arrays[1][3]`, which fetches the second of those five arrays and then retrieves the fourth element from that second array. This is not a specialized syntax, by the way—there is no need for special handling here, because any expression that evaluates to an array can be followed by the index in square brackets. The expression `arrays[1]` evaluates to an `int[]` array, and so we can follow that with `[3]`.

However, the new keyword *does* treat jagged arrays specially. It makes them look consistent with array element access syntax, but it has to twist things a little to do that. With a one-dimensional array, the pattern for constructing a new array is `new ElementType[length]`, so for creating an array of five things, you'd expect to write `new ElementType[5]`. If the things you are creating are arrays of `int`, wouldn't you expect to see `int[]` in place of `ElementType`? That would imply that the syntax should be `new int[][5]`.

That would be logical, but it looks like it's the wrong way around, and that's because the array type syntax itself is effectively reversed. Arrays are constructed types, like generics. With generics, the name of the generic type from which we construct the actual type comes before the type argument (e.g., `List<int>` takes the generic `List<T>` type and constructs it with a type argument of `int`). If arrays had generic-like syntax, we might expect to see `array<int>` for a one-dimensional array, `array<array<int>>` for two dimensions, and so on—the element type would come *after* the part that signifies that we want an array. But array types do it the other way around—the arrayness is signified by the `[]` characters, so the element type comes first. This is why the hypothetical logically correct syntax for array construction looks weird. C# avoids the weirdness by not getting overly stressed about logic here and just puts the size where most people expect it to go rather than where it arguably should go.

 The syntax extends in the obvious way—for example, `int[][][]` for the type and `new int[5][][]` for construction. C# does not define particular limits to the number of dimensions, but there are some implementation-specific runtime limits. (Microsoft's compiler didn't flinch when I asked for a 4,000-dimensional jagged array, but the CLR refused to load the resulting program. In fact, it wouldn't load anything with more than 2,816 dimensions.)

Examples 5-18 and 5-19 both initialize an array with five one-dimensional `int[]` arrays. The layout of the code should make it fairly clear why this sort of array is referred to as *jagged*: each row has a different length. With arrays of arrays, there is no requirement for a rectangular layout. I could go further. Arrays are reference types, so I could have set some rows to `null`. If I abandoned both the collection expression and array initializer syntaxes and initialized the array elements individually, I could have decided to make some of the one-dimensional `int[]` arrays appear in more than one row.

Because each row in this jagged array contains an array, I've ended up with six objects here—the five `int[]` arrays and then the `int[][]` array that contains references to them. If you introduce more dimensions, you'll get yet more arrays. For certain kinds of work, the nonrectangularity and the large numbers of objects can be problematic, which is why C# supports another kind of multidimensional array.

Rectangular arrays

A rectangular array is a single array object that supports multidimensional indexing. If C# didn't offer multidimensional arrays, we could build something a bit like them by convention. If you want an array with 10 rows and 5 columns, you could construct a one-dimensional array with 50 elements, and then use code like `myArray[i + (5 * j)]` to access it, where `i` is the column index and `j` is the row index. That would be an array that you had chosen to think of as being two-dimensional, even though it's really just one big contiguous block. A rectangular array is essentially the same idea, but where C# does the work for you. Example 5-20 shows how to declare and construct rectangular arrays. (This is one scenario in which we can't use the new collection expression syntax, because that only knows how to create one-dimensional collections. It works for jagged arrays because those are one-dimensional arrays of one-dimensional arrays: each object constructed has just a single dimension. With rectangular arrays, we have a single multidimensional object.)

 Rectangular arrays are not just about convenience. There's a type safety aspect too: int[,] is a different type than int[] or int[,,], so if you write a method that expects a two-dimensional rectangular array, C# will not allow anything else to be passed.

Example 5-20. A rectangular array

```
int[,] grid = new int[5, 10];
var smallerGrid = new int[,]
{
    { 1, 2, 3, 4 },
    { 2, 3, 4, 5 },
    { 3, 4, 5, 6 }
};
```

Rectangular array type names use only a single pair of square brackets, no matter how many dimensions they have. The number of commas inside the brackets denotes the number of dimensions, so this example with one comma is two-dimensional. The runtime seems to impose a much lower limit on the number of dimensions than for a jagged array. .NET 8.0 won't load a program that tries to use more than 32 dimensions in a rectangular array.

The multidimensional initializer syntax is very similar to the older initializer syntax for multidimensional arrays (see Example 5-19), except I do not start each row with new[], because this is one big array, not an array of arrays. The numbers in Example 5-20 form a shape that is clearly rectangular, and if you attempt to make things jagged (with different row sizes), the compiler will report an error. This extends to higher dimensions. If you wanted a three-dimensional "rectangular" array, it would need to be a *cuboid*. Example 5-21 shows a cuboid array. You could think of the initializer as being a list of two rectangular slices making up the cuboid. And you can go higher, with *hypercuboid* arrays (although they are still known as rectangular arrays, regardless of how many dimensions you use).

Example 5-21. A 2 × 3 × 5 cuboid "rectangular" array

```
var cuboid = new int[,,]
{
    {
        { 1, 2, 3, 4, 5 },
        { 2, 3, 4, 5, 6 },
        { 3, 4, 5, 6, 7 }
    },
    {
        { 2, 3, 4, 5, 6 },
        { 3, 4, 5, 6, 7 },
        { 4, 5, 6, 7, 8 }
    }
};
```

The syntax for accessing rectangular arrays is predictable enough. If the second variable from Example 5-20 is in scope, we could write smallerGrid[2, 3] to access the final item in the array; as with single-dimensional arrays, indices are zero-based, so this refers to the third row's fourth item.

Remember that an array's Length property returns the total number of elements in the array. Since rectangular arrays have all the elements in a single array (rather than being arrays that refer to some other arrays), this will return the product of the sizes of all the dimensions. A rectangular array with 5 rows and 10 columns would have a Length of 50, for example. If you want to discover the size along a particular dimension at runtime, use the GetLength method, which takes a single int argument indicating the dimension for which you'd like to know the size.

Copying and Resizing

Sometimes you will want to move chunks of data around in arrays. You might want to insert an item in the middle of an array, moving the items that follow it up by one position (and losing one element at the end, since array sizes are fixed). Or you might want to move data from one array to another, perhaps one of a different size.

The static Array.Copy method takes two references to arrays, along with a number indicating how many elements to copy. It offers overloads so that you can specify the positions in the two arrays at which to start the copy. (The simpler overload starts at the first element of each array.) You are allowed to pass the same array as the source and destination, and it will handle overlap correctly: the copy acts as though the elements were first all copied to a temporary location before starting to write them to the target.

As well as the static `Copy` method, the `Array` class defines a non-static `CopyTo` method, which copies the entire array into a target array, starting at the specified offset. This method is present because all arrays implement certain collection interfaces, including `ICollection<T>` (where `T` is the array's element type), which defines this `CopyTo` method. It is less flexible than `Copy`—`CopyTo` cannot copy a subrange of the array. In cases where either method would work, the documentation recommends using `Array.Copy`—`CopyTo` is just for the benefit of general-purpose code that can work with any implementation of a collection interface.

Copying elements from one array to another can become necessary when you need to deal with variable amounts of data. You would typically allocate an array larger than initially necessary, and if this eventually fills up, you'll need a new, larger array, and you'd need to copy the contents of the old array into the new one. In fact, the `Array` class can do this for you for one-dimensional arrays with its `Resize` method. The method name is slightly misleading, because arrays cannot be resized, so it allocates a new array and copies the data from the old one into it. `Resize` can build either a larger or a smaller array, and if you ask it for a smaller one, it will just copy as many elements as will fit.

While I'm talking about methods that copy the array's data around, I should mention `Reverse`, which simply reverses the order of the array's elements. Also, while this isn't strictly about copying, the `Array.Clear` method is often useful in scenarios where you're juggling array sizes—it allows you to reset some range of the array to its initial zero-like state.

These methods for moving data around within arrays are useful for building more flexible data structures on top of the basic services offered by arrays. But you often won't need to use them yourself, because the runtime libraries provide several useful collection classes that do this for you.

List<T>

The `List<T>` class, defined in the `System.Collections.Generic` namespace, contains a variable-length sequence of elements of type `T`. It provides an indexer that lets you get and set elements by number, so a `List<T>` behaves like a resizable array. It's not completely interchangeable—you cannot pass a `List<T>` as the argument for a parameter that expects a `T[]` array—but both arrays and `List<T>` implement various common generic collection interfaces that we'll be looking at later. For example, if you write a method that accepts an `IList<T>`, it will be able to work with either an array or a `List<T>`.

Although code that uses an indexer resembles array element access, it is not quite the same thing. An indexer is a kind of property, so it has the same issues with mutable value types that I discussed in Chapter 3. Given a variable pointList of type List<Point> (where Point is the mutable value type in the System.Windows namespace), you cannot write pointList[2].X = 2, because pointList[2] returns a copy of the value, and this code is effectively asking to modify that temporary copy. This would lose the update, so C# forbids it. But this does work with arrays. If pointArray is of type Point[], pointArray[2] does not *get* an element, it *identifies* an element, making it possible to modify an array element's value in situ by writing pointArray[2].X = 2. (Since ref return values were added to C#, it has become possible to write indexers that work this way, but List<T> and IList<T> were created long before that.) With immutable value types such as Complex, this distinction is moot, because you cannot modify their values in place in any case—you would have to overwrite an element with a new value whether using an array or a list.

Unlike an array, a List<T> provides methods that change its size. The Add method appends a new element to the end of the list, while AddRange can add several. Insert and InsertRange add elements at any point in the list, shuffling all the elements after the insertion point down to make space. These four methods all make the list longer, but List<T> also provides Remove, which removes the first instance of the specified value; RemoveAt, which removes an element at a particular index; and RemoveRange, which removes multiple elements starting at a particular index. These all shuffle elements back down, closing up the gap left by the removed element or elements, making the list shorter.

List<T> uses an array internally to store its elements. This means all the elements live in a single block of memory, and it stores them contiguously. This makes normal element access very efficient, but it is also why insertion needs to shift elements up to make space for the new element, and removal needs to shift them down to close up the gap.

Example 5-22 shows one way to create a List<T>. It's just a class, so we can use the normal constructor syntax. It shows how to add and remove entries and also how to access elements using the array-like indexer syntax. This also shows that List<T> provides its size through a Count property. This name may seem needlessly different than the Length provided by arrays, but there is a reason: this property is defined by ICollection<T>, which List<T> implements. Not all ICollection<T> implementations are sequences, so Length would in some cases be a misnomer. (As it happens, arrays also offer Count, because they also implement ICollection and ICollection<T>. However, they use explicit interface implementation, meaning that you can see an array's Count property only through a reference of one of these interface types.)

Example 5-22. Using a `List<T>`

```
var numbers = new List<int>();
numbers.Add(123);
numbers.Add(99);
numbers.Add(42);
Console.WriteLine(numbers.Count);
Console.WriteLine($"{numbers[0]}, {numbers[1]}, {numbers[2]}");

numbers[1] += 1;
Console.WriteLine(numbers[1]);

numbers.RemoveAt(1);
Console.WriteLine(numbers.Count);
Console.WriteLine($"{numbers[0]}, {numbers[1]}");
```

Because a `List<T>` can grow and shrink as required, you don't need to specify its size at construction. However, if you want to, you can specify its *capacity*. A list's capacity is the amount of space it currently has available for storing elements, and this will often be larger than the number of elements it contains. To avoid allocating a new internal array every time you add or remove an element, it keeps track of how many elements are in use independently of the size of the array. When it needs more space, it will overallocate, creating a new array that is larger than needed by an amount proportional to the size. This means that, if your program repeatedly adds items to a list, the larger it gets, the less frequently it needs to allocate a new array, but the proportion of spare capacity after each reallocation will remain about the same.

If you know up front that you will eventually store a specific number of elements in a list, you can pass that number to the constructor, and it will allocate exactly that much capacity, meaning that no further reallocation will be required. If you get this wrong, it won't cause an error—you're just requesting an initial capacity, and it's OK to change your mind later.

If the idea of unused memory going to waste in a list offends you, but you don't know exactly how much space will be required before you start, you could call the `TrimEx cess` method once you know the list is complete. This reallocates the internal storage to be exactly large enough to hold the list's current contents, eliminating waste. This will not always be a win. To ensure that it is using exactly the right amount of space, `TrimExcess` has to create a new array of the right size, leaving the old, oversized one to be reclaimed by the garbage collector later on, and in some scenarios, the overhead of forcing an extra allocation just to trim things down to size may be higher than the overhead of having some unused capacity.

Lists have a third constructor. Besides the default constructor, and the one that takes a capacity, you can also pass in a collection of data with which to initialize the list. You can pass any `IEnumerable<T>`.

You can provide initial content for lists in the same way as with an array, by writing a collection expression. Example 5-23 loads the same three values into a new list as at the start of Example 5-22.

Example 5-23. Initializing a list with a collection expression

```
List<int> numbers = [123, 99, 42];
```

As with arrays, the collection expression syntax was introduced in C# 12.0, and there is an older, slightly more verbose syntax. Example 5-24 has the same effect as Example 5-23.

Example 5-24. List initializer

```
var numbers = new List<int> { 123, 99, 42 };
```

If you're not using var, you can omit the type name after the new keyword, as Example 5-25 shows. But in contrast to arrays, you cannot omit the new keyword entirely. I've used a target-typed new() expression here to avoid writing out the type name a second time.

Example 5-25. List initializer with target-typed new

```
List<int> numbers = new() { 123, 99, 42 };
```

Examples 5-24 and 5-25 are equivalent, and each compile into code that calls Add once for each item in the list. You can use this syntax with any type that has a suitable Add method and implements the IEnumerable interface. This works even if Add is an extension method. (So if some type implements IEnumerable, but does not supply an Add method, you are free to use this initializer syntax if you provide your own Add.)

Example 5-23 generates marginally more efficient code. The collection expression syntax not only recognizes the same pattern as the initializer syntax (an IEnumerable implementation and an Add method), but it also has some additional tricks. If the collection type offers a constructor with a single argument of type int named capacity, it will use that to construct the collection, passing in the number of elements that will be in the list once initialization is complete. List<T> has such a constructor, and this enables it to allocate exactly the right amount of memory to hold its values. Examples 5-24 and 5-25 won't do this, and will just invoke the zero-arguments constructor, forcing List<T> to guess how many elements it will be asked to hold. The current implementation allocates enough space to hold four elements, which is slightly more than this example requires. In cases that end up with more than four elements, List<T> ends up discarding the original four element array it created and replacing it with a larger one (twice as large as before in the current implementation). It would be possible to avoid this mismatch of size and capacity in the initializer syntax examples by passing an argument of 3 to the constructor, but in Example 5-23 the compiler does that for us automatically. (The compiler can also generate code that efficiently loads all of the data into the list at once, instead of generating multiple calls to Add.) If we've used the spread syntax to copy elements from one or more other collections, it will attempt to determine the total number of elements before constructing the List<T>. It is possible to create situations where it can't do this (because not all collection types know in advance how many elements they will eventually produce), but in cases where it's possible to do so, the C# compiler will generate code that optimizes memory allocation when you use the collection expression syntax. The older initializer syntax does not do this.

List<T> provides IndexOf, LastIndexOf, Find, FindLast, FindAll, Sort, and Binary Search methods for finding and sorting list elements. These provide the same services as their array namesakes, although List<T> chooses to provide these as instance methods rather than statics.

We've now seen two ways to represent a list of values: arrays and lists. Fortunately, interfaces make it possible to write code that can work with either, so you won't need to write two sets of functions if you want to support both lists and arrays.

List and Sequence Interfaces

The runtime libraries define several interfaces representing collections. Three of these are relevant to simple linear sequences of the kind you can store in an array or a list: IList<T>, ICollection<T>, and IEnumerable<T>, all defined in the System. Collections.Generics namespace. There are three interfaces because different code makes different demands. Some methods need random access to any numbered element in a collection, but not everything does, and not all collections can support that —some sequences produce elements gradually, and there may be no way to leap straight to the nth element. Consider a sequence representing keypresses, for example —each item will emerge only as the user presses the next key. Your code can work with a wider range of sources if you opt for less demanding interfaces.

IEnumerable<T> is the most general of the collection interfaces because it demands the least from its implementers. I've mentioned it a few times already because it's an important interface that crops up a lot, but I've not shown the definition until now. As Example 5-26 shows, it declares just a single method.

Example 5-26. IEnumerable<T> and IEnumerable

```
public interface IEnumerable<out T> : IEnumerable
{
    IEnumerator<T> GetEnumerator();
}

public interface IEnumerable
{
    IEnumerator GetEnumerator();
}
```

Using inheritance, IEnumerable<T> requires its implementers also to implement IEnumerable, which appears to be almost identical. It's a nongeneric version of IEnumerable<T>, and its GetEnumerator method will typically do nothing more than invoke the generic implementation. The reason we have both forms is that the nongeneric IEnumerable has been around since .NET 1.0, which didn't support generics. The arrival of generics in .NET 2.0 made it possible to express the intent behind IEnumerable more precisely, but the old interface had to remain for compatibility. So these two interfaces effectively require the same thing: a method that returns an enumerator. What's an enumerator? Example 5-27 shows both the generic and nongeneric interfaces.

Example 5-27. IEnumerator<T> and IEnumerator

```
public interface IEnumerator<out T> : IDisposable, IEnumerator
{
    T Current { get; }
}

public interface IEnumerator
{
    bool MoveNext();
    object Current { get; }
    void Reset();
}
```

The usage model for an IEnumerable<T> (and also IEnumerable) is that you call GetEnumerator to obtain an enumerator, which can be used to iterate through all the items in the collection. You call the enumerator's MoveNext(); if it returns false, it means the collection was empty. Otherwise, the Current property will now provide the first item from the collection. Then you call MoveNext() again to move to the next item, and for as long as it keeps returning true, the next item will be available in Current. (The Reset method is a historical artifact added to help compatibility with COM, the Windows pre-.NET cross-language object model. The documentation allows implementations to throw a NotSupportedException from Reset, so you will not normally use this method.)

 Notice that IEnumerator<T> implementations are required to implement IDisposable. You must call Dispose on enumerators once you're finished with them, because many of them rely on this.

The foreach loop in C# does all of the work required to iterate through an enumerable collection for you,[1] including generating code that calls Dispose even if the loop terminates early due to a break statement, an error, or, perish the thought, a goto statement. Chapter 7 will describe the uses of IDisposable in more detail.

IEnumerable<T> is at the heart of LINQ to Objects, which I'll discuss in Chapter 10. LINQ operators are available on any object that implements this interface. The runtime libraries define a related interface, IAsyncEnumerable<T>. Conceptually, this is identical to IEnumerable<T>: it represents the ability to provide a sequence of items. The difference is that it enables items to be enumerated asynchronously. As Example 5-28 shows, this interface and its counterpart, IAsyncEnumerator<T>, resemble IEnumerable<T> and IEnumerator<T>. The main difference is the use of the asynchronous programming features ValueTask<T> and CancellationToken, which Chapter 16 will describe. There are also some minor differences: there are no nongeneric versions of these interfaces, and also, there's no facility to reset an existing asynchronous enumerator (although as noted earlier, many synchronous enumerators throw a NotSupportedException if you call Reset).

Example 5-28. IAsyncEnumerable<T> and IAsyncEnumerator<T>

```
public interface IAsyncEnumerable<out T>
{
    IAsyncEnumerator<T> GetAsyncEnumerator(
        CancellationToken cancellationToken = default);
}

public interface IAsyncEnumerator<out T> : IAsyncDisposable
{
```

---

1 Surprisingly, foreach doesn't require any particular interface; it will use anything with a GetEnumerator method that returns an object providing a MoveNext method and a Current property. Before generics, this was the only way to enable iteration through collections of value-typed elements without boxing every item. Chapter 7 describes boxing. Even though generics have fixed that, non-interface-based enumeration continues to be useful because it enables collection classes to provide an extra GetEnumerator that returns a struct, avoiding an additional heap allocation when the foreach loop starts. List<T> does this.

```
    T Current { get; }

    ValueTask<bool> MoveNextAsync();
}
```

You can consume an IAsyncEnumerable<T> with a specialized form of foreach loop, in which you prefix it with the await keyword. This can only be used in a method marked with the async keyword. Chapter 17 describes the async and await keywords in detail, and also the use of await foreach.

Although IEnumerable<T> is important and widely used, it's pretty restrictive. You can ask it only for one item after another, and it will hand them out in whatever order it sees fit. It does not provide a way to modify the collection, or even to find out how many items the collection contains without having to iterate through the whole lot. For these jobs, we have ICollection<T>, which is shown in Example 5-29.

Example 5-29. ICollection<T>

```
public interface ICollection<T> : IEnumerable<T>, IEnumerable
{
    void Add(T item);
    void Clear();
    bool Contains(T item);
    void CopyTo(T[] array, int arrayIndex);
    bool Remove(T item);

    int Count { get; }
    bool IsReadOnly { get; }
}
```

This requires implementers also to provide IEnumerable<T>, but notice that this does not inherit the nongeneric ICollection. There is such an interface, but it represents a different abstraction: it's missing all of the methods except CopyTo. When introducing generics, Microsoft reviewed how the nongeneric collection types were used and concluded that the one extra method that the old ICollection added didn't make it noticeably more useful than IEnumerable. Worse, it also included a property called SyncRoot that was intended to help manage certain multithreaded scenarios but that turned out to be a poor solution to that problem in practice. So the abstraction represented by ICollection did not get a generic equivalent and has not been greatly missed. During the review, Microsoft also found that the absence of a general-purpose interface for modifiable collections was a problem, and so it made ICollec tion<T> fit that bill. It was not entirely helpful to attach this old name to a different abstraction, but since almost nobody was using the old nongeneric ICollection, it doesn't seem to have caused much trouble.

The third interface for sequential collections is IList<T>, and all types that implement this are required to implement ICollection<T>, and therefore also IEnumerable<T>. As you'd expect, List<T> implements IList<T>. Arrays implement it too, using their element type as the argument for T. Example 5-30 shows how the interface looks.

Example 5-30. IList<T>

```
public interface IList<T> : ICollection<T>, IEnumerable<T>, IEnumerable
{
    int IndexOf(T item);
    void Insert(int index, T item);
    void RemoveAt(int index);

    T this[int index] { get; set; }
}
```

Again, although there is a nongeneric IList, this interface has no direct relationship to it, even though both interfaces represent similar concepts—the nongeneric IList has equivalents to the IList<T> members, and it also includes equivalents to most of ICollection<T>, including all the members missing from ICollection. So it would have been possible to require IList<T> implementations to implement IList, but that would have forced implementations to provide two versions of most members, one working in terms of the type parameter T and the other using object, because that's what the old nongeneric interfaces had to use. It would also force collections to provide the nonuseful SyncRoot property. The benefits would not outweigh these inconveniences, and so IList<T> implementations are not obliged to implement IList. They can if they want to, and List<T> does, but it's up to the individual collection class to choose.

One unfortunate upshot of the way these three generic interfaces are related is that they do not provide an abstraction representing indexed collections that are read-only, or even ones that are fixed-size. While IEnumerable<T> is a read-only abstraction, it's an in-order one with no way to go directly to the *n*th value. IList<T> provides indexed access, but it also defines methods for insertion and indexed removal, as well as mandating an implementation of ICollection<T> with its addition and value-based removal methods. You might be wondering how arrays can implement these interfaces, given that all arrays are fixed-size.

Arrays mitigate this problem by using explicit interface implementation to hide the IList<T> methods that can change a list's length, discouraging you from trying to use them. (As you saw in Chapter 3, this technique enables you to provide a full implementation of an interface but to be selective about which members are directly visible.) However, you can store a reference to an array in a variable of type IList<T>, making those methods visible—Example 5-31 uses this to call an array's IList<T>. Add method. However, this results in a runtime error.

Example 5-31. Trying (and failing) to enlarge an array

```
IList<int> array = new[] { 1, 2, 3 };
array.Add(4);  // Will throw an exception
```

The Add method throws a NotSupportedException, with an error message stating that the collection has a fixed size. If you inspect the documentation for IList<T> and ICollection<T>, you'll see that all the members that would modify the collection are allowed to throw this error. You can discover at runtime whether this will happen for *all* modifications with the ICollection<T> interface's IsReadOnly property. However, that won't help you discover up front when a collection allows only certain changes. (For example, an array's size is fixed, but you can still modify elements.)

This causes an irritating problem: if you're writing code that does in fact require a modifiable collection, there's no way to advertise that fact. If a method takes an IList<T>, it's hard to know whether that method will attempt to resize that list or not. Mismatches cause runtime exceptions, and those exceptions may well appear in code that isn't doing anything wrong, and where the mistake—passing the wrong sort of collection—was made by the caller. These problems are not showstoppers; in dynamically typed languages, this degree of compile-time uncertainty is in fact the norm, and it doesn't stop you from writing good code. It just shows that we can't rely on the type system to detect all mistakes.

There is a ReadOnlyCollection<T> class, but as we'll see later, that solves a different problem—it's a wrapper class, not an interface, so there are plenty of things that are fixed-size collections that do not present a ReadOnlyCollection<T>. If you were to write a method with a parameter of type ReadOnlyCollection<T>, it would not be able to work directly with certain kinds of collections (including arrays). In any case, it's not even the same abstraction—read-only is a tighter restriction than fixed-size.

.NET defines IReadOnlyList<T>, an interface that provides a better solution for representing read-only indexed collections (although it still doesn't help with modifiable fixed-size ones such as arrays). Like IList<T>, it requires an implementation of IEnumerable<T>, but it does not require ICollection<T>. It defines two members: Count, which returns the size of the collection (just like ICollection<T>.Count), and a read-only indexer. This solves most of the problems associated with using IList<T> for read-only collections. One minor problem is that because it's newer than most of the other interfaces I've described here it is not universally supported. (It was introduced in .NET Framework 4.5 in 2012, seven years after IList<T>.) So if you come across an API that requires an IReadOnlyList<T>, you can be sure it will not attempt to modify the collection, but if an API requires IList<T>, it's difficult to know whether that's because it intends to modify the collection or merely because it was written before IReadOnlyList<T> was invented.

 Collections do not need to be read-only to implement IReadOnly List<T>—a modifiable list can easily present a read-only façade. So this interface is implemented by all arrays and also List<T>.

The issues and interfaces I've just discussed raise a question: When writing code or classes that work with collections, what type should you use? With private implementation details (e.g., private fields, or inside methods) you will typically specify concrete types, not interfaces, because you don't need the flexibility to deal with different kinds of collections. But when it comes to the public-facing parts of your code (e.g., properties or method arguments) you will typically get the most flexibility if your API demands the least specific type it can work with. For example, if an IEnumerable<T> suits your needs, don't demand an IList<T>. Likewise, interfaces are usually better than concrete types, so you should prefer IList<T> over either List<T> or T[]. Just occasionally, there may be performance arguments for using a more specific type; if you have a tight loop critical to the overall performance of your application that works through the contents of a collection, you may find such code runs faster if it works only with array types, because the CLR may be able to perform better optimizations when it knows exactly what to expect. But in many cases, the difference will be too small to measure and will not justify the inconvenience of being tied to a particular implementation, so you should never take such a step without measuring the performance for the task at hand to see what the benefit might be. (And if you're considering such a performance-oriented change, you should also look at the techniques described in Chapter 18.) If you find that there is a possible performance win, but you're writing a shared library in which you want to provide both flexibility and the best possible performance, there are a couple of options for having it both ways. You could offer overloads so callers can pass in either an interface or a specific type. Alternatively, you could write a single public method that accepts the interface but that tests for known types and chooses between different internal code paths based on what the caller passes.

The interfaces we've just examined are not the only generic collection interfaces, because simple linear lists are not the only kind of collection. But before moving on to the others, I want to show enumerables and lists from the flip side: How do we implement these interfaces?

Implementing Lists and Sequences

It is often useful to provide information in the form of either an IEnumerable<T> or an IList<T>. The former is particularly important because .NET provides a powerful toolkit for working with sequences in the form of LINQ to Objects, which I'll show in Chapter 10. LINQ to Objects provides various operators that all work in terms of IEnumerable<T>. IList<T> is a useful abstraction anywhere that random access to any element by index is required. Some frameworks expect an IList<T>. If you want to bind a collection of objects to some kind of list control, for example, some UI frameworks will expect either an IList or an IList<T>.

You could implement these interfaces by hand, as none of them is particularly complicated. However, C# and the runtime libraries can help. There is direct language-level support for implementing IEnumerable<T>, and the runtime libraries provide support for the generic and nongeneric list interfaces.

Implementing IEnumerable<T> with Iterators

C# supports a special form of method called an *iterator*. An iterator is a method that produces enumerable sequences using the yield keyword. Example 5-32 shows a simple iterator and some code that uses it. This will display numbers counting down from 5 to 1.

Example 5-32. A simple iterator

```
static IEnumerable<int> Countdown(int start, int end)
{
    for (int i = start; i >= end; --i)
    {
        yield return i;
    }
}

foreach (int i in Countdown(5, 1))
{
    Console.WriteLine(i);
}
```

An iterator looks much like any normal method, but the way it returns values is different. The iterator in Example 5-32 has a return type of IEnumerable<int>, and yet it does not appear to return anything of that type. Instead of a normal return statement, it uses a yield return statement, and that returns a single int, not a collection. Iterators produce values one at a time with yield return statements, and unlike with a normal return, the method can continue to execute after returning a value—it's only when the method either runs to the end or decides to stop early with a yield break statement or by throwing an exception that it is complete. Example 5-33 shows this rather more starkly. Each yield return causes a value to be emitted from the sequence, so this one will produce the numbers 1–3.

Example 5-33. A very simple iterator

```
public static IEnumerable<int> ThreeNumbers()
{
    yield return 1;
    yield return 2;
    yield return 3;
}
```

Although this is fairly straightforward in concept, the way it works is somewhat involved because code in iterators does not run in the same way as other code. Remember, with IEnumerable<T>, the caller is in charge of when the next value is retrieved; a foreach loop will get an enumerator and then repeatedly call MoveNext() until that returns false, and expect the Current property to provide the current value. So how do Examples 5-32 and 5-33 fit into that model? You might think that perhaps C# stores all the values an iterator yields in a List<T>, returning that once the iterator is complete, but it's easy to demonstrate that that's not true by writing an iterator that never finishes, such as the one in Example 5-34.

Example 5-34. An infinite iterator

```
public static IEnumerable<BigInteger> Fibonacci()
{
    BigInteger v1 = 1;
    BigInteger v2 = 1;

    while (true)
    {
        yield return v1;
        BigInteger tmp = v2;
        v2 = v1 + v2;
        v1 = tmp;
    }
}
```

This iterator runs indefinitely; it has a while loop with a true condition, and it contains no break statement, so this will never voluntarily stop. If C# tried to run an iterator to completion before returning anything, it would get stuck here. (The numbers grow, so if it ran for long enough, the method would eventually terminate by throwing an OutOfMemoryException.) But if you try this, you'll find it starts returning values from the Fibonacci series immediately and will continue to do so for as long as you continue to iterate through its output. Clearly, C# is not simply running the whole method before returning.

C# performs some serious surgery on your code to make this work. If you examine the compiler's output for an iterator using a tool such as ILDASM (the disassembler for .NET code, provided with the .NET SDK), you'll find it generates a private nested class that acts as the implementation for both the IEnumerable<T> that the method returns and also the IEnumerator<T> that the IEnumerable<T>'s GetEnumerator method returns. The code from your iterator method ends up inside this class's Move Next method, but it is barely recognizable, because the compiler splits it up in a way that enables each yield return to return to the caller, but for execution to continue from where it left off the next time MoveNext is called. Where necessary, it will store local variables inside this generated class so that their values can be preserved across multiple calls to MoveNext. Perhaps the easiest way to get a feel for what C# has to do when compiling an iterator is to write the equivalent code by hand. Example 5-35 provides the same Fibonacci sequence as Example 5-34 without the aid of an iterator. It's not precisely what the compiler does, but it illustrates some of the challenges.

Example 5-35. Implementing IEnumerable<T> by hand

```
public class FibonacciEnumerable :
    IEnumerable<BigInteger>, IEnumerator<BigInteger>
{
    private BigInteger v1;
    private BigInteger v2;
    private bool first = true;

    public BigInteger Current => v1;

    public void Dispose() { }

    object IEnumerator.Current => Current;

    public bool MoveNext()
    {
        if (first)
        {
            v1 = 1;
            v2 = 1;
            first = false;
        }
        else
        {
            BigInteger tmp = v2;
            v2 = v1 + v2;
            v1 = tmp;
        }
```

```
        return true;
    }

    public void Reset()
    {
        first = true;
    }

    public IEnumerator<BigInteger> GetEnumerator() =>
        new FibonacciEnumerable();

    IEnumerator IEnumerable.GetEnumerator() => GetEnumerator();
}
```

This is not a particularly complex example, because its enumerator is essentially in either of two states—either it is running for the first time and therefore needs to run the code that comes before the loop or it is inside the loop. Even so, this code is much harder to read than Example 5-34, because the mechanics of supporting enumeration have obscured the essential logic.

The code would get even more convoluted if we needed to deal with exceptions. You can write using blocks and finally blocks, which enable your code to behave correctly in the face of errors, as I'll show in Chapters 7 and 8, and the compiler can end up doing a lot of work to preserve the correct semantics for these when the method's execution is split up over multiple iterations.[2] You wouldn't need to write too many enumerations by hand this way before being grateful that C# can do it for you.

Iterator methods don't have to return an IEnumerable<T>, by the way. If you prefer, you can return an IEnumerator<T> instead. And, as you saw earlier, objects that implement either of these interfaces also always implement the nongeneric equivalents, so if you need a plain IEnumerable or IEnumerator, you don't need to do extra work—you can pass an IEnumerable<T> to anything that was expecting a plain IEnumerable, and likewise for enumerators. If for some reason you want to provide one of these nongeneric interfaces and you don't wish to provide the generic version, you are allowed to write iterators that return the nongeneric forms directly.

One thing to be careful of with iterators is that they run very little code until the first time the caller calls MoveNext. So if you were to single-step through code that calls the Fibonacci method in Example 5-34, the method call would appear not to do anything at all. If you try to step into the method at the point at which it's invoked, none

---

2 Some of this cleanup work happens in the call to Dispose. Remember, IEnumerator<T> implementations all implement IDisposable. The foreach keyword calls Dispose after iterating through a collection (even if iteration was terminated by an error). If you're not using foreach and are performing iteration by hand, it's vitally important to remember to call Dispose.

of the code in the method runs. It's only when iteration begins that you'd see your iterator's body execute. This has a couple of consequences.

The first thing to bear in mind is that if your iterator method takes arguments, and you want to validate those arguments, you may need to do some extra work. By default, the validation won't happen until iteration begins, so errors will occur later than you might expect. If you want to validate arguments immediately, you will need to write a wrapper. Example 5-36 shows an example—it provides a normal method called Fibonacci that doesn't use yield return and will therefore not get the special compiler behavior for iterators. This normal method validates its argument before going on to call a nested iterator method. (This also illustrates that local methods can use yield return.)

Example 5-36. Iterator argument validation

```
public static IEnumerable<BigInteger> Fibonacci(int count)
{
    ArgumentOutOfRangeException.ThrowIfNegative(count);
    return Core(count);

    static IEnumerable<BigInteger> Core(int count)
    {
        BigInteger v1 = 1;
        BigInteger v2 = 1;

        for (int i = 0; i < count; ++i)
        {
            yield return v1;
            BigInteger tmp = v2;
            v2 = v1 + v2;
            v1 = tmp;
        }
    }
}
```

The second thing to remember is that iterators may execute several times. IEnumerable<T> provides a GetEnumerator that can be called many times over, and your iterator body will run from the start each time. So even though your iterator method may only have been called once, it could run multiple times.

Collection<T>

If you look at types in the runtime libraries, you'll find that when they offer properties that expose an implementation of IList<T>, they often do so indirectly. Instead of an interface, properties often provide some concrete type, although it's usually not List<T> either. List<T> is designed to be used as an implementation detail of your code, and if you expose it directly, you may be giving users of your class too much control. Do you want them to be able to modify the list? And even if you do, mightn't your code need to know when that happens?

The runtime libraries provide a Collection<T> class that is designed to be used as the base class for collections that a type will make publicly available. It is similar to List<T>, but there are two significant differences. First, it has a smaller API—it offers IndexOf, but all the other searching and sorting methods available for List<T> are missing, and it does not provide ways to discover or change its capacity independently of its size. Second, it provides a way for derived classes to discover when items have been added or removed. List<T> does not, on the grounds that it's your list so you presumably know when you add and remove items. Notification mechanisms are not free, so List<T> avoids unnecessary overhead by not offering them. But Collec tion<T> assumes that external code will have access to your collection and that you will therefore not be in control of every addition and removal, justifying the overhead involved in providing a way for you to find out when the list is modified. (This is only available to the code deriving from Collection<T>. If you want code using your collection to be able to detect changes, the ObservableCollection<T> type is designed for that exact scenario. For example, if you use this type as the source for a list in desktop and mobile UI frameworks such as WPF or MAUI, they will be able to update the displayed list automatically when you modify the collection.)

You typically derive a class from Collection<T>, and you can override the virtual methods it defines to discover when the collection changes. (Chapter 6 will discuss inheritance and overriding.) Collection<T> implements both IList and IList<T>, so you could present a Collection<T>-based collection through an interface type property, but it's common to make a derived collection type public and to use that instead of an interface as the property type.

ReadOnlyCollection<T>

If you want to provide a nonmodifiable collection, then instead of using Collec tion<T>, you can use ReadOnlyCollection<T>. This goes further than the restrictions imposed by arrays, by the way: not only can you not add, remove, or insert items, you cannot even replace elements. This class implements IList<T>, which requires an indexer with both a get and a set, but the set throws an exception. (Of course, it also implements IReadOnlyCollection<T>.)

If your collection's element type is a reference type, making the collection read-only does not prevent the objects to which the elements refer from being modified. I can retrieve, say, the 12th element from a read-only collection, and it will hand me back a reference. Fetching a reference counts as a read-only operation, but now that I have got that reference, the collection object is out of the picture, and I am free to do whatever I like with the reference. C# does not offer any concept of a read-only reference for reference types,[3] so the only way to present a truly read-only collection is to use an immutable type in conjunction with an `IReadOnlyCollection<T>` implementation.

There are two ways to use `ReadOnlyCollection<T>`. You can use it directly as a wrapper for an existing list—its constructor takes an `IList<T>`, and it will provide read-only access to that. (`List<T>` provides a method called `AsReadOnly` that constructs a read-only wrapper for you, by the way.) Alternatively, you could derive a class from it. As with `Collection<T>`, some classes do this for collections they wish to expose via properties, and it's usually because they want to define additional methods specific to the collection's purpose. Even if you derive from this class, you will still be using it to wrap an underlying list, because the only constructor it provides is the one that takes a list.

Addressing Elements with Index and Range Syntax

Whether using arrays, `List<T>`, `IList<T>`, or the various related types and interfaces just discussed, we've identified elements using simple examples such as `items[0]`, and more generally, expressions of the form `arrayOrListExpression[indexExpression]`. So far, all the examples have used an expression of type `int` for the index, but that is not the only choice. Example 5-37 accesses the final element of an array using an alternative syntax.

Example 5-37. Accessing the last element of an array with an end-relative index

```
char[] letters = ['a', 'b', 'c', 'd'];
char lastLetter = letters[^1];
```

This demonstrates one of two operators for use in indexers: the `^` operator. The other, shown in Example 5-38, is the *range operator*. It consists of a pair of periods (`..`), and it is used to identify subranges of arrays, strings, or any indexable type that implements a certain pattern. (Although this resembles the spread syntax we saw earlier, and also the slice syntax shown in Chapter 2, those appear only in collection expressions and list patterns, respectively. This range syntax is something else.)

Example 5-38. Getting a subrange of an array with the range operator

```
int[] numbers = [1, 2, 3, 4, 5, 6, 7];
// Gets 4th and 5th (but not the 3rd or 6th, for reasons explained shortly)
int[] theFourthTheFifth = numbers[3..5];
```

---

3 You might be wondering about `ref readonly`, described in Chapter 3, but that's a different kind of reference. A `ref readonly` to some reference-type variable only means you can't change the variable; it won't stop you making changes to whatever that variable refers to.

Expressions using the ^ and .. operators are of type `Index` and `Range`, respectively. These types are available in .NET but not .NET Framework, meaning that you can only use these language features on newer runtimes.

System.Index

You can put the ^ operator in front of any `int` expression. It produces a `Sys tem.Index`, a value type that represents a position. When you create an index with ^, it is end-relative, but you can also create start-relative indexes. There's no special operator for that, but since `Index` offers an implicit conversion from `int`, you can just assign `int` values directly into variables of type `Index`, as Example 5-39 shows. You can also explicitly construct an index, as the line with `var` shows. The final `bool` argument is optional—it defaults to `false`—but I'm showing it to illustrate how `Index` knows which kind you want.

Example 5-39. Some start-relative and end-relative Index values

```
Index first = 0;
Index second = 1;
Index third = 2;
var fourth = new Index(3, fromEnd: false);

Index antePenultimate = ^3;
Index penultimate = ^2;
Index last = ^1;
Index directlyAfterTheLast = ^0;
```

As Example 5-39 shows, end-relative indexes exist independently of any particular collection. (Internally, `Index` stores end-relative indexes as negative numbers. This means that an `Index` is the same size as an `int`. It also means that negative start- or end-relative values are illegal—you'll get an exception if you try to create one.) C# generates code that determines the actual element position when you use an index. If `small` and `big` are arrays with 3 and 30 elements, respectively, `small[last]` would return the third, and `big[last]` would return the 30th. C# will turn these into `small[last.GetOffset(small.Length)]` and `big[last.GetOffset(big.Length)]`, respectively.

It has often been said that three of the hardest problems in computing are picking names for things and off-by-one errors. At first glance, Example 5-39 makes it look like `Index` might be contributing to these problems. It may be vexing that the index for the third item is two, not three, but that at least is consistent with how arrays have always worked in C# and is normal for any zero-based indexing system. But given that zero-based convention, why on earth do the end-relative indexes appear to be one-based? We denote the first element with 0 but the last element with ^1!

There are some good reasons for this. The fundamental insight is that in C#, indexes have always specified distances. When programming language designers choose a zero-based indexing system, this is not really a decision to call the first element 0: it is a decision to interpret an index as a distance from the start of an array. An upshot of this is that an index doesn't really refer to an item. Figure 5-1 shows a collection with four elements and indicates where various index values would point in that collection. Notice that the indexes all refer to the boundaries between the items. This may seem like splitting hairs, but it's the key to understanding all zero-based index systems, and it is behind the apparent inconsistency in Example 5-39.

Figure 5-1. Where Index values point

When you access an element of a collection by index, you are asking for the element that *starts* at the position indicated by the index. So array[0] retrieves the single element that starts at the beginning of the array, the element that fills the space between indexes 0 and 1. Likewise, array[1] retrieves the element between indexes 1 and 2. What would array[^0] mean?[4] That would be an attempt to fetch the element that *starts* at the very end of the array. Since elements all take up a certain amount of space, an element that starts at the very end of the array would necessarily finish one position after the end of the array. In this four-element array, array[^0] is equivalent to array[4], so we're asking for the element occupying the space that starts four elements from the start and that ends five elements from the start. And since this is a four-element array, that's obviously not going to work.

The apparent discrepancy—the fact that array[0] gets the first, but we need to write array[^1] to get the last—occurs because elements sit between two indexes, and array indexers always retrieve the element between the index specified and the index after that. The fact that they do this even when you've specified an end-relative index is the reason those appear to be one-based. This language feature could have been designed differently: you could imagine a rule in which end-relative indexes always access the element that *ends* at the specified distance from the end and that starts one position earlier than that. There would have been a pleasing symmetry to this, because it would have made array[^0] refer to the final element, but this would have caused more problems than it solved.

---

4 Since end-relative indexes are stored as negative numbers, you might be wondering whether ^0 is even legal, given that the int type does not distinguish between positive and negative zero. It is allowed because, as you'll soon see, ^0 is useful when using ranges, so Index is able to make the distinction.

It would be confusing to have indexers interpret an index in two different ways—it would mean that two different indexes might refer to the same position and yet fetch different elements. In any case, C# developers have long been used to things working this way. As Example 5-40 shows, the way to access the final element of an array before the ^ index operator was added was to use an index calculated by subtracting one from the length. And if you wanted the element before last, you subtracted two from the length, and so on. As you can see, the new end-relative syntax is entirely consistent with the older approach.

Example 5-40. End-relative indexing without and with `Index`

```
int lastOld = numbers[numbers.Length - 1];
int lastNew = numbers[^1];

int penultimateOld = numbers[numbers.Length - 2];
int penultimateNew = numbers[^2];
```

One more way to think of this is to wonder what it might look like if we accessed arrays by specifying ranges. The first element is in the range 0–1, and the last is in the range ^1–^0. Expressed this way, there is clearly symmetry between the start-relative and end-relative forms. And speaking of ranges...

System.Range

As I said earlier, C# has two operators useful for working with arrays and other indexable types. We've just looked at ^ and the corresponding `Index` type. The other is called the *range operator*, and it has a corresponding type, `Range`, also in the `System` namespace. A `Range` is a pair of `Index` values, which it makes available through `Start` and `End` properties. `Range` offers a constructor taking two `Index` values, but in C# the idiomatic way to create one is with the range operator, as Example 5-41 shows.

Example 5-41. Various ranges

```
Range everything = 0..^0;
Range alsoEverything = 0..;
Range everythingAgain = ..^0;
Range everythingOneMoreTime = ..;
var yetAnotherWayToSayEverything = Range.All;

Range firstThreeItems = 0..3;
Range alsoFirstThreeItems = ..3;

Range allButTheFirstThree = 3..^0;
Range alsoAllButTheFirstThree = 3..;

Range allButTheLastThree = 0..^3;
```

```
Range alsoAllButTheLastThree = ..^3;

Range lastThreeItems = ^3..^0;
Range alsoLastThreeItems = ^3..;
```

As you can see, if you do not put a start index before the .., it defaults to 0, and if you omit the end, it defaults to ^0 (i.e., the very start and end, respectively). The example also shows that the start can be either start-relative or end-relative, as can the end.

 The default value for Range—the one you'll get in a field or array element that you do not explicitly initialize—is 0..0. This denotes an empty range. While this is a natural upshot of the fact that value types are always initialized to zero-like values by default, it might not be what you'd expect given that .. is equivalent to Range.All.

Since Range works in terms of Index, the start and end denote offsets, not elements. For example, consider what the range 1..3 would mean for the elements shown in Figure 5-1. In this case, both indexes are start-relative. The start index, 1, is the boundary between the first and second elements (a and b), and the end index, 3, is the boundary between the third and fourth elements (c and d). So this is a range that starts at the beginning of b and ends at the end of c, as Figure 5-2 shows. So this identifies a two-element range (b and c).

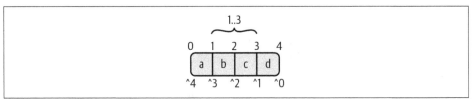

Figure 5-2. A range

The interpretation of ranges sometimes surprises people when they first see it: some expect 1..3 to represent the first, second, and third elements (or, if they take into account C#'s zero-based indexing, perhaps the second, third, and fourth elements). It can seem inconsistent at first that the start index appears to be inclusive while the end index is exclusive. But once you remember that an index refers not to an item but to an offset, and therefore the boundary between two items, it all makes sense. If you draw the positions represented by a range's indexes, as Figure 5-2 does, it becomes perfectly obvious that the range identified by 1..3 covers just two elements.

So what can we do with a Range? As Example 5-38 showed, we can use one to get a subrange of an array. That creates a new array of the relevant size and copies the values from the range into it. This same syntax also works for getting substrings, as Example 5-42 shows.

Example 5-42. Getting a substring with a range

```
string t1 = "dysfunctional";
string t2 = t1[3..6];
Console.WriteLine($"Putting the {t2} in {t1}");
```

You can also use `Range` with `ArraySegment<T>`, a value type that refers to a range of elements within an array. Example 5-43 makes a slight modification to Example 5-38. Instead of passing the range to the array's indexer, this first creates an `Array Segment<int>` that represents the entire array, and then uses a range to get a second `ArraySegment<int>` representing the fourth and fifth elements. The advantage of this is that it does not need to allocate a new array—both `ArraySegment<int>` values refer to the same underlying array; they just point to different sections of it, and since `ArraySegment<int>` is a value type, this can avoid allocating new heap blocks. (`Array Segment<int>` has no direct support for range, by the way. The compiler turns this into a call to the segment's `Slice` method.)

Example 5-43. Getting a subrange of an `ArraySegment<T>` with the range operator

```
int[] numbers = [1, 2, 3, 4, 5, 6, 7];
ArraySegment<int> wholeArrayAsSegment = numbers;
ArraySegment<int> theFourthTheFifth = wholeArrayAsSegment[3..5];
```

The `ArraySegment<T>` type has been around since .NET 2.0 (and has been in .NET Standard since 1.0). It's a useful way to avoid extra allocations, but it's limited: it only works with arrays. What about strings? All current versions of .NET support types offering a more general form of this concept, `Span<T>` and `ReadOnlySpan<T>`. (On .NET Framework, these are available through the `System.Memory` NuGet package. They are built into other .NET versions.) Just like `ArraySegment<T>`, `Span<T>` represents a subsequence of items inside something else, but it is much more flexible about what that "something else" might be. It could be an array, but it can also be a string, memory in a stack frame, or memory allocated by some library or system call entirely outside of .NET. The `Span<T>` and `ReadOnlySpan<T>` types are discussed in more detail in Chapter 18, but for now, Example 5-44 illustrates their basic use.

Example 5-44. Getting a subrange of a span with the range operator

```
int[] numbers = [1, 2, 3, 4, 5, 6, 7];
Span<int> wholeArrayAsSpan = numbers;
Span<int> theFourthTheFifth = wholeArrayAsSpan[3..5];
ReadOnlySpan<char> textSpan = "dysfunctional";
ReadOnlySpan<char> such = textSpan[3..6];
```

These last two examples have much the same logical meaning as the preceding examples, but they avoid making copies of the underlying data.

We've now seen that we can use ranges with several types: arrays, strings, `Array Segment<T>`, `Span<T>`, and `ReadOnlySpan<T>`. This raises a question: Does C# have a list of types that get special handling, or can we support indexers and ranges in our own types? The answers are, respectively, yes and yes. C# has some baked-in handling for arrays and strings: it knows to call specific runtime library methods to produce subarrays and substrings. However, there is no special range handling for array segments or spans: they work because they conform to a pattern. There is also a pattern to enable use of `Index`. If you support these same patterns, you can make `Index` and `Range` work with your own types.

Supporting Index and Range in Your Own Types

The array type does not define an indexer that accepts an argument of type `Index`. Nor do any of the generic array-like types shown earlier in this chapter—they all just have ordinary `int`-based indexers; however, you can use `Index` with them nonetheless. And as I explained earlier, code of the form `a[index]` will expand to `a[index.GetOffset(a.Length)]`.[5] So all you need is an `int`-based indexer and a property of type `int` called either `Length` or `Count`. Example 5-45 shows about the least amount of work you can possibly do to enable code to pass an `Index` to your type's indexer. It's not a very useful implementation, but it's enough to keep C# happy.

Example 5-45. Minimally enabling Index

```
public class Indexable
{
    public char this[int index] => (char)('0' + index);

    public int Length => 10;
}
```

There's an even simpler way: just define an indexer that takes an argument of type `Index`. However, most indexable types supply an `int`-based indexer, so in practice you'd be overloading your indexer, offering both forms. That is not simpler, but it would enable your code to distinguish between start- and end-relative indexes. If we use either 1 or `^9` with Example 5-45, its indexer sees 1 in either case, because C# generates code that converts the `Index` to a start-based `int`, but if you write an indexer with an `Index` parameter, C# will pass the `Index` straight in. If you overload the indexer so that both `int` and `Index` forms are available, it will never generate code

---

5 In cases where you use ^ directly against an `int` inside an array indexer (e.g., `a[^i]` where `i` is an `int`), the compiler generates marginally simpler code. Instead of converting `i` to an `Index`, then calling `GetOffset`, it will generate code equivalent to `a[a.Length - i]`.

that converts an Index to an int in order to call the int indexer: the pattern only kicks in if no Index-specific indexer is available.

IList<T> meets the pattern's requirements (as do types that implement it, such as List<T>), so you can pass an Index to the indexer of anything that implements this. (It supplies a Count property instead of Length, but the pattern accepts either.) This is a widely implemented interface, so in practice, many types automatically get support for Index despite having been written before Index was introduced. This is an example of how the pattern-based support for Index means libraries that target older .NET versions (such as .NET Standard 2.0) where Index is not available can nonetheless define types that will work with Index when used with newer versions of .NET.

The pattern for supporting Range is different: if your type supplies an instance method called Slice that takes two integer arguments, C# will allow code to supply a Range as an indexer argument. Example 5-46 shows the least a type can do to enable this, although it's not a very useful implementation. (As with Index, you can alternatively just define an indexer overload that accepts a Range directly. But again, an advantage to the pattern approach is that you can use it when targeting older versions that do not offer the Range or Index types—such as .NET Standard 2.0—while still supporting ranges for code that targets newer versions.)

Example 5-46. Minimally enabling Range

```
public class Rangeable
{
    public int Length => 10;

    public Rangeable Slice(int offset, int length) => this;
}
```

You might have noticed that this type doesn't define an indexer. That's because this pattern-based support for expressions of the form x[1..^1] doesn't need one. It may look like that expression uses an indexer, but this just calls the Slice method. (Likewise, the earlier range examples with string and arrays compile into method calls.) You need the Length property (or Count) because the compiler generates code that relies on this to resolve the range's indexes. Example 5-47 shows roughly how the compiler uses types that support this pattern.

Example 5-47. How range indexing expands

```
Rangeable r1 = new();
Range r = 2..^2;

Rangeable r2;
```

```
r2 = r1[r];
// is equivalent to
int startIndex = r.Start.GetOffset(r1.Length);
int endIndex = r.End.GetOffset(r1.Length);
r2 = r1.Slice(startIndex, endIndex - startIndex);
```

So far, all of the collections we've looked at have been linear: I've shown only simple sequences of objects or values, some of which offer indexed access. However, .NET provides other kinds of collections.

Dictionaries

One of the most useful kinds of collections is a dictionary. .NET offers the `Diction ary<TKey, TValue>` class, and there's a corresponding interface called, predictably, `IDictionary<TKey, TValue>`, and also a read-only version, `IReadOnlyDiction ary<TKey, TValue>`. These represent collections of key/value pairs, and their most important capability is to look up a value based on its key, making dictionaries useful for representing associations.

Suppose you are writing a UI for an application that supports online discussions. When displaying a message, you might want to show certain things about the user who sent it, such as their name and picture, and you'd probably want to avoid fetching these details from a persistent store every time; if the user is in conversation with a few friends, the same people will crop up repeatedly, so you'd want some sort of cache to avoid duplicate lookups. You might use a dictionary as part of this cache. Example 5-48 shows an outline of this approach. (It omits application-specific details of how the data is actually fetched and when old data is removed from memory.)

Example 5-48. Using a dictionary as part of a cache

```
public class UserCache
{
    private readonly Dictionary<string, UserInfo> _cachedUserInfo = new();

    public UserInfo GetInfo(string userHandle)
    {
        RemoveStaleCacheEntries();
        if (!_cachedUserInfo.TryGetValue(userHandle, out UserInfo? info))
        {
            info = FetchUserInfo(userHandle);
            _cachedUserInfo.Add(userHandle, info);
        }
        return info;
    }

    private UserInfo FetchUserInfo(string userHandle)
    {
```

```
        // fetch info...
    }

    private void RemoveStaleCacheEntries()
    {
        // application-specific logic deciding when to remove old entries...
    }
}

public class UserInfo
{
    // application-specific user information...
}
```

The first type argument, TKey, is used for lookups, and in this example, I'm using a string that identifies the user in some way. The TValue argument is the type of value associated with the key—information previously fetched for the user and cached locally in a UserInfo instance, in this case. The GetInfo method uses TryGetValue to look in the dictionary for the data associated with a user handle. There is a simpler way to retrieve a value. As Example 5-49 shows, dictionaries provide an indexer. However, that throws a KeyNotFoundException if there is no entry with the specified key. That would be fine if your code always expects to find what it's looking for, but in our case, the key will be missing for any user whose data is not already in the cache. This will probably happen rather a lot, which is why I'm using TryGetValue. As an alternative, we could have used the ContainsKey method to see if the entry exists before retrieving it, but that's inefficient if the value is present—the dictionary would end up looking up the entry twice, once in the call to ContainsKey and then again when we use the indexer. TryGetValue performs the test and the lookup as a single operation.

Example 5-49. Dictionary lookup with indexer

```
UserInfo info = _cachedUserInfo[userHandle];
```

As you might expect, we can also use the indexer to set the value associated with a key. I've not done that in Example 5-48. Instead, I've used the Add method, because it has subtly different semantics: by calling Add, you are indicating that you do not think any entry with the specified key already exists. Whereas the dictionary's indexer will silently overwrite an existing entry if there is one, Add will throw an exception if you attempt to use a key for which an entry already exists. In situations where the presence of an existing key would imply that something is wrong, it's better to call Add so that the problem doesn't go undetected.

The IDictionary<TKey, TValue> interface requires its implementations also to provide the ICollection<KeyValuePair<TKey, TValue>> interface, and therefore also

IEnumerable<KeyValuePair<TKey, TValue>>. The read-only counterpart requires the latter but not the former. These interfaces depend on a generic struct, KeyValue Pair<TKey, TValue>, which is a simple container that wraps a key and a value in a single instance. This means you can iterate through a dictionary using foreach, and it will return each key/value pair in turn.

The presence of an IEnumerable<T> and an Add method also means that we can use the collection initializer syntax. It's not quite the same as with a simple list, because a dictionary's Add takes two arguments: the key and value. However, the collection initializer syntax can cope with multiargument Add methods. You wrap each set of arguments in nested braces, as Example 5-50 shows.

Example 5-50. Collection initializer syntax with a dictionary

```
var textToNumber = new Dictionary<string, int>
{
    { "One", 1 },
    { "Two", 2 },
    { "Three", 3 },
};
```

As you saw in Chapter 3, there's an alternative way to populate a dictionary: instead of using a collection initializer, you can use the object initializer syntax. As you may recall, this syntax lets you set properties on a newly created object. Indexers are just a special kind of property, so it makes sense to be able to set them with an object initializer. Although Chapter 3 showed this already, it's worth comparing object initializers with collection initializers, so Example 5-51 shows the alternative way to initialize a dictionary.

Example 5-51. Object initializer syntax with a dictionary

```
var textToNumber = new Dictionary<string, int>
{
    ["One"] = 1,
    ["Two"] = 2,
    ["Three"] = 3
};
```

Although the outcome is the same here with Examples 5-50 and 5-51, the compiler generates slightly different code for each. With Example 5-50, it populates the collection by calling Add, whereas Example 5-51 uses the indexer. In these examples the result is the same, so there's no objective reason to choose one over the other, but the difference could matter in some cases. For example, if you are using a class that has an indexer but no Add method, only the index-based code would work. And even with Dictionary<TKey, TValue>, which offers both, Add throws an exception if you supply duplicate keys, whereas the indexer does not, so the collection initializer syntax has the benefit of checking that your keys are unique.

 You can use the collection expression syntax added in C# 12.0 to initialize an empty dictionary, but it does not provide a way to add entries. Currently, only the older initializer syntax can do this.

The Dictionary<TKey, TValue> collection class relies on hashes to offer fast lookup. Chapter 3 described the GetHashCode method, and you should ensure that whatever type you are using as a key provides a good hash implementation. The string class overrides GetHashCode so that it works well as a key, for example. The default GetHashCode method is viable only if different instances of a type are always considered to have different values, but types for which that is true function well as keys. Alternatively, the dictionary class provides constructors that accept an IEqualityComparer<TKey>, which allows you to provide an implementation of GetHashCode and Equals to use instead of the one supplied by the key type itself. Example 5-52 uses this to make a case-insensitive version of Example 5-50.

Example 5-52. A case-insensitive dictionary

```
var textToNumber =
    new Dictionary<string, int>(StringComparer.InvariantCultureIgnoreCase)
{
    { "One", 1 },
    { "Two", 2 },
    { "Three", 3 },
};
```

This uses the StringComparer class, which provides various implementations of IComparer<string> and IEqualityComparer<string>, offering different comparison rules. Here, I've chosen an ordering that ignores case, so textToNumber["tHrEe"] would have the same effect as textToNumber["three"]. This particular comparer also ignores the configured locale, ensuring consistent behavior in different regions. If I were using strings to be displayed, I'd probably use one of its culture-aware comparisons.

Sorted Dictionaries

Dictionary<TKey, TValue> does not guarantee to provide elements in any particular order when you iterate over its contents. In simple cases, it might return items in the order in which they were added, but you should not depend on this.

Sometimes, it's useful to be able to retrieve the contents of a dictionary in some meaningful order. You could always get the contents into an array and then sort them, but the System.Collections.Generic namespace contains two more implementations of the IDictionary<TKey, TValue> interface that keep their contents permanently in order. There's SortedDictionary<TKey, TValue> and the more confusingly titled SortedList<TKey, TValue>, which—despite the name—implements the IDictionary<TKey, TValue> interface and does not directly implement IList<T>.

These classes do not use hash codes. They still provide reasonably fast lookup, but they do it by keeping their contents sorted. They maintain the order every time you add a new entry, which makes addition rather slower for both these classes than with the hash-based dictionary, but it means that when you iterate over the contents, they come out in order. As with array and list sorting, you can specify custom comparison logic, but if you don't supply that, these dictionaries require the key type to implement IComparable<T>.

The ordering maintained by a SortedDictionary<TKey, TValue> is apparent only when you use its enumeration support (e.g., with foreach). SortedList<TKey, TValue> also enumerates its contents in order, but it additionally provides numerically indexed access to the keys and values. This does not work through the object's indexer—that expects to be passed a key just like any dictionary. Instead, the sorted list dictionary defines two properties, Keys and Values, which provide all the keys and values as IList<TKey> and IList<TValue>, respectively, sorted so that the keys will be in ascending order. (The Values are in key order as well as the Keys.)

Inserting and removing objects is relatively expensive for the sorted list because it has to shuffle the key and value list contents up or down. (This means a single insertion has $O(n)$ complexity.) The sorted dictionary, on the other hand, uses a tree data structure to keep its contents sorted. The exact details are not specified, but insertion and removal performance are documented as having $O(\log n)$ complexity, which is much better than for the sorted list.[6] However, this more complex data structure gives a sorted dictionary a significantly larger memory footprint. This means that neither is definitively faster or better than the other—it all depends on the usage pattern, which is why the runtime libraries supply both.

In most cases, the hash-based Dictionary<TKey, Value> will provide better insertion, removal, and lookup performance than either of the sorted dictionaries, and much lower memory consumption than a SortedDictionary<TKey, TValue>, so you should use these sorted dictionary collections only if you need to access the dictionary's contents in order.

---

6 The usual complexity analysis caveats apply—for small collections, the simpler data structure might well win, with the sorted list's theoretical advantage only coming into effect with larger collections.

Sets

The `System.Collections.Generic` namespace defines an `ISet<T>` interface. This offers a simple model: a particular value is either a member of the set or not. You can add or remove items, but a set does not keep track of how many times you've added an item, nor does `ISet<T>` require items to be stored in any particular order.

All set types implement `ICollection<T>`, which provides the methods for adding and removing items. In fact, it also defines the method for determining membership: although I've not drawn attention to it before now, you can see in Example 5-29 that `ICollection<T>` defines a `Contains` method. This takes a single value and returns `true` if that value is in the collection.

Given that `ICollection<T>` already provides the defining operations for a set, you might wonder why we need `ISet<T>`. But it does add a few things. Although `ICollection<T>` defines an `Add` method, `ISet<T>` defines its own subtly different version, which returns a `bool`, so you can find out whether the item you just added was already in the set. Example 5-53 uses this to detect duplicates in a method that displays each string in its input once. (This illustrates the usage, but in practice it would be simpler to use the `Distinct` LINQ operator described in Chapter 10.)

Example 5-53. Using a set to determine what's new

```
public static void ShowEachDistinctString(IEnumerable<string> strings)
{
    var shown = new HashSet<string>();  // Implements ISet<T>
    foreach (string s in strings)
    {
        if (shown.Add(s))
        {
            Console.WriteLine(s);
        }
    }
}
```

`ISet<T>` also defines some operations for combining sets. The `UnionWith` method takes an `IEnumerable<T>` and adds to the set all the values from that sequence that were not already in the set. The `ExceptWith` method removes from the set items that are also in the sequence you pass. The `IntersectWith` method removes from the set items that are not also in the sequence you pass. And `SymmetricExceptWith` also takes a sequence and removes from the set elements that are in the sequence, but also adds to the set values in the sequence that were not previously in the set.

There are also some methods for comparing sets. Again, these all take an `IEnumerable<T>` argument representing the other set with which the comparison is to be performed. `IsSubsetOf` and `IsProperSubsetOf` both let you check whether the set on which you invoke the method contains only elements that are also present in the sequence, with the latter method additionally requiring the sequence to contain at least one item not present in the set. `IsSupersetOf` and `IsProperSupersetOf` perform the same tests in the opposite direction. The `Overlaps` method tells you whether the two sets share at least one element in common.

Mathematical sets do not define an order for their contents, so it's not meaningful to refer to the 1st, 10th, or *n*th element of a set—you can ask only whether an element is in the set or not. In keeping with this feature of mathematical sets, .NET sets do not support indexed access, so `ISet<T>` does not demand support for `IList<T>`. Sets are free to produce the members in whatever order they like in their `IEnumerable<T>` implementation.

The runtime libraries offer classes that provide this interface with different implementation strategies, including: `HashSet` and `SortedSet`. As you may have guessed from the names, one of these does in fact choose to keep its elements in order; `SortedSet` keeps its contents sorted at all times and presents items in this order through its `IEnumerable<T>` implementation. The documentation does not describe the exact strategy used to maintain the order, but it appears to use a balanced binary tree to support efficient insertion and removal, and to offer fast lookup when trying to determine whether a particular value is already in the list.

`HashSet` works more like `Dictionary<TKey, TValue>`. It uses hash-based lookup, which can often be faster than the ordered approach, but if you enumerate through the collection with `foreach`, the results will not be in any useful order. (So the relationship between `HashSet` and `SortedSet` is much like that between the hash-based dictionary and the sorted dictionaries.)

Queues and Stacks

A *queue* is a list where you can only add items to the end of the list, and you can only remove the first item (at which point the second item, if there was one, becomes the new first item). This style of list is often called a first-in, first-out (FIFO) list. This makes it less useful than a `List<T>`, because you can read, write, insert, or remove items at any point in a `List<T>`. However, the constraints make it possible to implement a queue with considerably better performance characteristics for insertion and removal. When you remove an item from a `List<T>`, it has to shuffle all the items after the one removed to close up the gap, and insertions require a similar shuffle. Insertion and removal at the end of a `List<T>` is efficient, but if you need FIFO semantics, you can't work entirely at the end—you'll need to do either insertions or removals at the start, making `List<T>` a bad choice. `Queue<T>` can use a much more efficient strategy because it needs only to support queue semantics. (It uses a circular buffer internally, although that's an undocumented implementation detail.)

To add a new item to the end of a queue, call the Enqueue method. To remove the item at the head of the queue, call Dequeue, or use Peek if you want to look at the item without removing it. Both operations will throw an InvalidOperationException if the queue is empty. You can find out how many items are in the queue with the Count property.

Although you cannot insert, remove, or change items in the middle of the list, you can inspect the whole queue, because Queue<T> implements IEnumerable<T> and also provides a ToArray method that returns an array containing a copy of the current queue contents. It also implements ICollection<T>, so you could instead call the CopyTo method, which copies the queue contents into an array that you supply.

A *stack* is similar to a queue, except you retrieve items from the same end as you insert them—so this is a last-in, first-out (LIFO) list. Stack<T> looks very similar to Queue<T> except instead of Enqueue and Dequeue, the methods for adding and removing items use the traditional names for stack operations: Push and Pop. (Other methods, such as Peek and ToArray, remain the same.)

The runtime libraries do not offer a double-ended queue. However, linked lists can offer a superset of that functionality.

Linked Lists

The LinkedList<T> class provides an implementation of the classic doubly linked list data structure, in which each item in the sequence is wrapped in an object (of type LinkedListNode<T>) that provides a reference to its predecessor and its successor. The advantage of a linked list is that insertion and removal is inexpensive—it does not require elements to be moved around in arrays and does not require binary trees to be rebalanced. It just requires a few references to be swapped around. The downsides are that linked lists have fairly high memory overheads, requiring an extra object on the heap for every item in the collection, and it's also relatively expensive for the CPU to get to the nth item because you have to go to the start and then traverse n nodes.

The first and last nodes in a LinkedList<T> are available through the predictably named First and Last properties. You can insert items at the start or end of the list with AddFirst and AddLast, respectively. To add items in the middle of a list, call either AddBefore or AddAfter, passing in the LinkedListNode<T> before or after which you'd like to add the new item.

The list also provides RemoveFirst and RemoveLast methods and two overloads of a Remove method that allow you to remove either the first node that has a specified value or a particular LinkedListNode<T>.

The LinkedListNode<T> itself provides a Value property of type T containing the actual item for this node's point in the sequence. Its List property refers back to the containing LinkedList<T>, and the Previous and Next properties allow you to find the previous or next node.

To iterate through the contents of a linked list, you could retrieve the first node from the First property and then follow each node's Next property until you get a null. However, LinkedList<T> implements IEnumerable<T>, so it's easier just to use a for each loop. If you want to get the elements in reverse order, start with Last and follow each node's Previous. If the list is empty, First and Last will be null.

Concurrent Collections

The collection classes described so far are designed for single-threaded usage. You are free to use different instances on different threads simultaneously, but a particular instance of any of these types must be used only from one thread at any one time.[7] But some types are designed to be used by many threads simultaneously, without needing to use the synchronization mechanisms discussed in Chapter 16. These are in the System.Collections.Concurrent namespace.

The concurrent collections do not offer equivalents for every nonconcurrent collection type. Some classes are designed to solve specific concurrent programming problems. Even with the ones that do have nonconcurrent counterparts, the need for concurrent use without locking can mean that they present a somewhat different API than any of the normal collection classes.

The ConcurrentQueue<T> and ConcurrentStack<T> classes are the ones that look most like the nonconcurrent collections we've already seen, although they are not identical. The queue's Dequeue and Peek have been replaced with TryDequeue and Try Peek, because in a concurrent world, there's no reliable way to know in advance whether attempting to get an item from the queue will succeed. (You could check the queue's Count, but even if that is nonzero, some other thread may get in there and empty the queue between when you check the count and when you attempt to retrieve an item.) So the operation to get an item has to be atomic with the check for whether an item is available, hence the Try forms that can fail without throwing an exception. Likewise, the concurrent stack provides TryPop and TryPeek.

---

7 There's an exception to this rule: you can use a collection from multiple threads as long as none of the threads attempts to modify it.

ConcurrentDictionary<TKey, TValue> looks fairly similar to its nonconcurrent cousin, but it adds some extra methods to provide the atomicity required in a concurrent world. For example, the GetOrAdd method combines the test for the presence of a key with the addition of a new entry as a single atomic operation. It returns the existing value if there is one, and it can invoke a function to get the new value when required.

There is no concurrent list, because you tend to need more coarse-grained synchronization to use ordered, indexed lists successfully in a concurrent world. But if you just want a bunch of objects, there's ConcurrentBag<T>, which does not maintain any particular order. (Although the lack of ordering makes this sound similar to a set, there's one important difference: a bag can contain multiple copies of the same item.)

There's also BlockingCollection<T>, which acts like a queue but allows threads that want to take items off the queue to choose to block until an item is available. You can also set a limited capacity and make threads that put items onto the queue block if the queue is currently full, waiting until space becomes available.

Immutable Collections

Microsoft provides a set of collection classes that guarantee immutability and yet provide a lightweight way to produce a modified version of the collection without having to make an entire new copy. (These are built into .NET, but in .NET Framework, you will need a reference to the System.Collections.Immutable NuGet package to use these.)

Immutability can be a very useful characteristic in multithreaded environments, because if you know that the data you are working with cannot change, you don't need to take special precautions to synchronize your access to it. (This is a stronger guarantee than you get with IReadOnlyList<T>, which merely prevents you from modifying the collection; it could just be a façade over a collection that some other thread is able to modify.) But what do you do if your data needs to be updated occasionally? It seems a shame to give up on immutability and to take on the overhead of traditional multithreaded synchronization in cases where you expect conflicts to be rare.

A low-tech approach is to build a new copy of all of your data each time something changes (e.g., when you want to add an item to a collection, create a whole new collection with a copy of all the old elements and also the new one, and use that new collection from then on). The built-in string type works in exactly the same way because it is also immutable—the methods that sound like they will change the value, such as Trim, actually return a new string. This works but can be extremely inefficient when working with large quantities of data. However, techniques exist that can effectively reuse parts of existing collections. The basic principle is that if you want to add an item to a collection, you build a new collection that just points to the data that is already there, along with some extra information to say what has changed. It is rather more complex in practice, but the key point is that there are well-established ways in which to implement various kinds of collections so that you can efficiently build what look like complete self-contained copies of the original data with some small modification applied, without either having to modify the original data or having to build a complete new copy of the collection. The immutable collections do all this for you, encapsulating the work behind some straightforward interfaces.

This enables a model where you're free to update your application's model without affecting code that was in the middle of using the current version of the data. Consequently, you don't need to hold locks while reading data—you might need some synchronization when getting the latest version of the data, but thereafter, you can process the data without any concurrency concerns. This can be especially useful when writing multithreaded code. The .NET Compiler Platform (often known by its codename, Roslyn) that is the basis of Microsoft's C# compiler uses this technique to enable compilation to exploit multiple CPU cores efficiently.

The `System.Collections.Immutable` namespace defines its own interfaces—`IImmutableList<T>`, `IImmutableDictionary<TKey, TValue>`, `IImmutableQueue<T>`, `IImmutableStack<T>`, and `IImmutableSet<T>`. These collections can't just implement the interfaces we saw earlier, because all operations that modify the collection in any way need to return a new collection. Example 5-54 shows what this means for adding entries to a dictionary.

Example 5-54. Creating immutable dictionaries

```
IImmutableDictionary<int, string> d = ImmutableDictionary.Create<int, string>();
d = d.Add(1, "One");
d = d.Add(2, "Two");
d = d.Add(3, "Three");
```

The whole point of immutable types is that code using an existing object can be certain that nothing will change, so additions, removals, or modifications necessarily mean creating a new object that looks just like the old one but with the modification applied. So in Example 5-54, the variable d refers successively to four different immutable dictionaries: an empty one, one with one value, one with two values, and finally one with all three values.

If you are adding a range of values like this, and you won't be making intermediate results available to other code, it is more efficient to add multiple values in a single operation, because it doesn't have to produce a separate `IImmutableDictionary<TKey, TValue>` for each entry you add. (You could think of immutable collections as working a bit like a source control system, with each change corresponding to a commit—for every commit you do, a version of the collection will exist that represents its contents immediately after that change.) It's more efficient to batch a bunch of related changes into a single "version" so the collections all have AddRange methods that let you add multiple items in one step.

When you're building a new collection from scratch, the same principle applies: it will be more efficient if you put all of the initial content into the first version of the collection, instead of adding items one at a time. Each immutable collection type offers a nested Builder class to make this easier, enabling you to add items one at a time but to defer the creation of the actual collection until you have finished. Example 5-55 shows how this is done.

Example 5-55. Creating an immutable dictionary with a builder

```
ImmutableDictionary<int, string>.Builder b =
    ImmutableDictionary.CreateBuilder<int, string>();
b.Add(1, "One");
b.Add(2, "Two");
b.Add(3, "Three");
IImmutableDictionary<int, string> d = b.ToImmutable();
```

The builder object is not immutable. Much like StringBuilder, it is a mutable object that provides an efficient way to build a description of an immutable object.

All of the immutable collection types except for dictionaries support the collection expression syntax introduced in C# 12.0. Example 5-56 uses this to create an immutable list.

Example 5-56. Creating an immutable list with a collection expression

```
ImmutableList<int> numbers = [1, 2, 3, 4, 5];
```

In addition to the immutable list, dictionary, queue, stack, and set types, there's one more immutable collection class that is a bit different than the rest: Immutable Array<T>. This is essentially a wrapper providing an immutable façade around an array. It implements IImmutableList<T>, meaning that it offers the same services as an immutable list, but it has quite different performance characteristics.

When you call Add on an immutable list, it will attempt to reuse most of the data that is already there, so if you have a million items in your list, the "new" list returned by Add won't contain a new copy of those items—it will mostly reuse the data that was already there. However, to achieve this, ImmutableList<T> uses a somewhat complex tree data structure internally. The upshot is that looking up values by index in an ImmutableList<T> is not nearly as efficient as using an array (or a List<T>). The indexer for ImmutableList<T> has $O(log\ n)$ complexity.

An `ImmutableArray<T>` is much more efficient for reads—being a wrapper around an array, it has *O(1)* complexity, i.e., the time taken to fetch an entry is constant, regardless of how large the collection may be. The trade-off is that all of the `IImmutableList<T>` methods for building a modified version of the list (`Add`, `Remove`, `Insert`, `SetItem`, etc.) build a complete new array, including a new copy of any data that needs to be carried over. (In other words, unlike all the other immutable collection types, `ImmutableArray<T>` employs the low-tech approach to immutability that I described earlier.) This makes modifications very much more expensive, but if you have some data you do not expect to modify after the initial creation of the array, this is an excellent trade-off, because you will only ever build one copy of the array. And if you need to make only very occasional modifications, the high cost of each change might still be worth it overall.

Frozen Collections

.NET 8.0 adds a new namespace, `System.Collection.Frozen`, which defines `FrozenDictionary<TKey, TValue>` and `FrozenSet<T>` types. These are immutable implementations of the dictionary and set interfaces, respectively, and they are optimized for a different usage model than the corresponding immutable collections shown in the preceding section. Whereas those offer methods that produce a modified version of the collection without having to make an entire new copy, the frozen collections are optimized for scenarios in which you decide up front what you want in your collection, and will not make any further changes.

Despite the name, the immutable collection types are designed to accommodate change; they just do this by providing snapshots, and there are overheads involved in enabling change while making each individual snapshot immutable. That makes these types suboptimal in cases where there will be no further changes. (`ImmutableArray<T>` is an exception.) The ordinary, modifiable collection types such as `Dictionary<TKey, TValue>`` also need to be able to accommodate change, which also comes at a cost—they typically preallocate extra memory in anticipation of more items being added, for example. The frozen collection types are free to optimize their internal storage for exactly one data set because they don't need to be able to support subsequent change. They can do more work during initialization to improve the performance of each lookup.

The runtime libraries define extension methods for creating instances of the frozen collection types from other collections. Example 5-57 shows how to obtain a frozen dictionary from a normal one. There's a similar `ToFrozenSet` extension method that can convert any `IEnumerable<T>` into a `FrozenSet<T>`.

Example 5-57. Creating a FrozenDictionary<TKey, TValue> from a Dictio nary<TKey, TValue>

```
Dictionary<int, string> ordinary = GetOrdinaryDictionary();
FrozenDictionary<int, string> frozen = ordinary.ToFrozenDictionary();
```

FrozenDictionary implements IDictionary<TKey, TValue> and IReadOnlyDiction ary<TKey, TValue>, so once you've created one you can use it like a normal dictionary. (It implements the mutable IDictionary<TKey, TValue> because some libraries require that interface even when they won't actually modify the dictionary, but its implementation will throw a NotSupportedException if you try to modify the collection.)

The frozen collection types won't always be faster. In scenarios where they are a good fit—when you can supply the entire contents up front—they will usually outperform the immutable collections, but they won't necessarily outperform the ordinary collection types such as Dictionary<TKey, TValue>. The frozen collections do extra work during initialization in exchange for making lookups faster, so they only offer an improvement if you perform enough lookups to offset that initial cost. As with any performance-oriented change you should always measure the performance impact of introducing the frozen collections. The number of lookups needed to make these worthwhile will depend on the collection size, and also the key and element types, so there are no fixed rules about when the frozen collections will offer a benefit, but to give you a rough idea, I ran some tests using dictionaries with 100,000 elements. (You should take this with a grain of salt because all of the factors I just mentioned can make significant differences.) Lookups in this particular test were around 25% faster with the frozen dictionary than with Dictionary<TKey, TValue>, but it took over two million lookups to offset the higher initialization costs.

Summary

In this chapter, we saw the intrinsic support for arrays offered by the runtime and also the various collection classes that .NET provides when you need more than a fixed-size list of items. Next, we'll look at a more advanced topic: inheritance.

CHAPTER 6

Inheritance

C# classes support *inheritance*, a popular object-oriented code reuse mechanism. When you write a class, you can optionally specify a base class. Your class will derive from this, meaning that everything in the base class will be present in your class, as well as any members you add.

Classes and class-based record types support only single inheritance (so you can only specify one base class). Interfaces offer a form of multiple inheritance. Value types, including `record struct` types, do not support inheritance at all. One reason for this is that value types are not normally used by reference, which removes one of the main benefits of inheritance: runtime polymorphism. Inheritance is not necessarily incompatible with value-like behavior—some languages manage it—but it often has problems. For example, assigning a value of some derived type into a variable of its base type ends up losing all of the fields that the derived type added, a problem known as *slicing*. C# sidesteps this by restricting inheritance to reference types. When you assign a variable of some derived type into a variable of a base type, you're copying a reference, not the object itself, so the object remains intact. Slicing is an issue only if the base class offers a method that clones the object and doesn't provide a way for derived classes to extend that (or it does, but some derived class neglects to extend it).

Classes specify a base class using the syntax shown in Example 6-1—the base type appears after a colon that follows the class name. When a class has a primary constructor, that colon and base type appear after the constructor parameter list. This example assumes that a class called `SomeClass` has been defined elsewhere in the project, or one of the libraries it uses.

Example 6-1. Specifying a base class

```
public class Derived : SomeClass
{
}

public class DerivedWithPrimaryConstructor(int value) : SomeClass
{
    public override string ToString() => value.ToString();
}

public class AlsoDerived : SomeClass, IDisposable
{
    public void Dispose() { }
}
```

As you saw in Chapter 3, if the class implements any interfaces, these are also listed after the colon. If you want to derive from a class, and you want to implement interfaces as well, the base class must appear first, as the third class in Example 6-1 illustrates.

You can derive from a class that in turn derives from another class. The MoreDerived class in Example 6-2 derives from Derived, which in turn derives from Base.

Example 6-2. Inheritance chain

```
public class Base
{
}

public class Derived : Base
{
}

public class MoreDerived : Derived
{
}
```

This means that MoreDerived technically has multiple base classes: it derives from both Derived (directly) and Base (indirectly, via Derived). This is not multiple inheritance because there is only a single chain of inheritance—any single class derives directly from at most one base class. (All classes derive either directly or indirectly from object, which is the default base class if you do not specify one.)

Since a derived class inherits everything the base class has—all its fields, methods, and other members, both public and private—an instance of the derived class can do anything an instance of the base class could do. This is the classic *is a* relationship that inheritance implies in many languages. Any instance of MoreDerived is a Derived and also a Base. C#'s type system recognizes this relationship.

Inheritance and Conversions

C# provides various built-in implicit conversions. In Chapter 2, we saw the conversions for numeric types, but there are also ones for reference types. If some type D derives from B (either directly or indirectly), then a reference of type D can be converted implicitly to a reference of type B. This follows from the *is a* relationship I described in the preceding section—any instance of D is a B. This implicit conversion enables polymorphism: code written to work in terms of B will be able to work with any type derived from B.

Implicit reference conversions are special. Unlike other conversions, they do not change the value in any way. (The built-in implicit numeric conversions all create a new value from their input, often involving a change of representation. The binary representation of the integer 1 looks different for the float and int types, for example.) In effect, they convert the interpretation of the reference, rather than converting the reference itself or the object it refers to. As you'll see later in this chapter, there are various places where the CLR will take the availability of an implicit reference conversion into account but will not consider other forms of conversion.

 A custom implicit conversion between two reference types doesn't count as an implicit reference conversion for these purposes, because a method needs to be invoked to effect such a conversion. The cases in which implicit reference conversions are special rely on the fact that the "conversion" requires no work at runtime.

There is no implicit conversion in the opposite direction—although a variable of type B could refer to an object of type D, there's no guarantee that it will. There could be any number of types derived from B, and a B variable could refer to an instance of any of them. Nevertheless, you will sometimes want to attempt to convert a reference from a base type to a derived type, an operation sometimes referred to as a *downcast*. Perhaps you know for a fact that a particular variable holds a reference of a certain type. Or perhaps you're not sure and would like your code to provide additional services for specific types. C# offers three ways to do this.

We can attempt a downcast using the cast syntax. This is the same syntax we use for performing nonimplicit numeric conversions, as Example 6-3 shows.

Example 6-3. Feeling downcast

```
public static void UseAsDerived(Base baseArg)
{
    var d = (Derived) baseArg;

    // ...go on to do something with d
}
```

This conversion is not guaranteed to succeed—that's why we can't use an implicit conversion. If you try this when the `baseArg` argument refers to something that's neither an instance of `Derived` nor something derived from `Derived`, the conversion will fail, throwing an `InvalidCastException`. (Exceptions are described in Chapter 8.)

A cast is therefore appropriate only if you're confident that the object really is of the type you expect, and you would consider it to be an error if it turned out not to be. This is useful when an API accepts an object that it will later give back to you. Many asynchronous APIs do this, because in cases where you launch multiple operations concurrently, you need some way of working out which particular one finished when you get a completion notification (although, as we'll see in later chapters, there are various ways to tackle that problem). Since these APIs don't know what sort of data you'll want to associate with an operation, they usually just take a reference of type `object`, and you would typically use a cast to turn it back into a reference of the required type when the reference is eventually handed back to you.

Sometimes, you will not know for certain whether an object has a particular type. In this case, you can use the `as` operator instead, as shown in Example 6-4. This allows you to attempt a conversion without risking an exception. If the conversion fails, this operator just returns `null`.

Example 6-4. The as operator

```
public static void MightUseAsDerived(Base b)
{
    var d = b as Derived;

    if (d != null)
    {
        // ...go on to do something with d
    }
}
```

Although this technique is widely used, the introduction of patterns back in C# 7.0 provided a more succinct alternative. Example 6-5 has the same effect as Example 6-4: the body of the `if` runs only if b refers to an instance of `Derived`, in which case it can be accessed through the variable d. The `is` keyword here indicates that we want to test b against a pattern. In this case we're using a declaration pattern, which performs the same runtime type test as the `as` operator. An expression that applies a pattern with `is` produces a `bool` indicating whether the pattern matches. We can use this as the `if` statement's condition expression, removing the need to compare with `null`. And since declaration patterns incorporate variable declaration and initialization, the work that needed two statements in Example 6-4 can all be rolled into the `if` statement in Example 6-5.

Example 6-5. The `is` operator with a declaration pattern

```
public static void MightUseAsDerived(Base b)
{
    if (b is Derived d)
    {
        // ...go on to do something with d
    }
}
```

In addition to being more compact, the `is` operator also has the benefit of working in one scenario where `as` does not: you can test whether a reference of type `object` refers to an instance of a value type such as an `int`. (This may seem like a contradiction—how could you have a reference to something that is not a reference type? Chapter 7 will show how this is possible.) The `as` operator wouldn't work because it returns `null` when the instance is not of the specified type, but of course it cannot do that for a value type—there's no such thing as a `null` of type `int`. Since the declaration pattern eliminates the need to test for `null`—we just use the `bool` result that the `is` operator produces—we are free to use value types.

 Occasionally you may want to detect when a particular type is present without needing to perform a conversion. Since `is` can be followed by any pattern, you can use a type pattern, e.g., `is Derived`. This performs the same test as a declaration pattern, without going on to introduce a new variable.

When converting with the techniques just described, you don't necessarily need to specify the exact type. These operations will succeed as long as an implicit reference conversion exists from the object's real type to the type you're looking for. For example, given the `Base`, `Derived`, and `MoreDerived` types that Example 6-2 defines, suppose you have a variable of type `Base` that currently contains a reference to an instance of `MoreDerived`. Obviously, you could cast the reference to `MoreDerived` (and both `as` and `is` would also succeed for that type), but as you'd probably expect, converting to `Derived` would work too.

These four mechanisms also work for interfaces. When you try to convert a reference to an interface type reference (or test for an interface type with a type pattern), it will succeed if the object referred to implements the relevant interface.

Interface Inheritance

Interfaces support inheritance, but it's not quite the same as class inheritance. The syntax is similar, but as Example 6-6 shows, an interface can specify multiple base interfaces. While .NET offers only single implementation inheritance, this limitation does not apply to interfaces because most of the complications and potential ambiguities that can arise with multiple inheritance do not apply to purely abstract types. The most vexing problems are around handling of fields, which means that even interfaces with default implementations support multiple inheritance, because those don't get to add either fields or public members to the implementing type. (When a class uses a default implementation for a member, that member is accessible only through references of the interface's type.)

Example 6-6. Interface inheritance

```
interface IBase1
{
    void Base1Method();
}

interface IBase2
{
    void Base2Method();
}

interface IBoth : IBase1, IBase2
{
    void Method3();
}
```

Although *interface inheritance* is the official name for this feature, it is a misnomer—whereas derived classes inherit all members from their base, derived interfaces do not. It may appear that they do—given a variable of type IBoth, you can invoke the Base1Method and Base2Method methods defined by its bases. However, the true meaning of interface inheritance is that any type that implements an interface is obliged to implement all inherited interfaces. So a class that implements IBoth must also implement IBase1 and IBase2. It's a subtle distinction, especially since C# does not require implementers to list the base interfaces explicitly. The class in Example 6-7 only declares that it implements IBoth. However, if you were to use .NET's reflection API to inspect the type definition, you would find that the compiler has added IBase1 and IBase2 to the list of interfaces the class implements as well as the explicitly declared IBoth.

Example 6-7. Implementing a derived interface

```
public class Impl : IBoth
{
    public void Base1Method()
    {
    }

    public void Base2Method()
    {
    }

    public void Method3()
    {
    }
}
```

Since implementations of a derived interface must implement all base interfaces, C# lets you access bases' members directly through a reference of a derived type, so a variable of type IBoth provides access to Base1Method and Base2Method, as well as that interface's own Method3. Implicit reference conversions exist from derived interface types to their bases. For example, a reference of type IBoth can be assigned to variables of type IBase1 and IBase2.

Generics

If you derive from a generic class, you must supply the type arguments it requires. If your derived type is also generic, it can use its own type parameters as arguments if you wish, as long as they meet any constraints the base class defines. Example 6-8 shows both techniques and also illustrates that when deriving from a class with multiple type parameters, you can use a mixture, specifying one type argument directly and punting on another. (By the way, I've used C# 11.0's new required keyword here because otherwise the compiler warns of possible nullable reference problems: if I constructed a GenericBase<string> without initializing Item, that property's value would be null, despite its type being string.)

Example 6-8. Deriving from a generic base class

```
public class GenericBase1<T>
{
    public required T Item { get; set; }
}
```

```
public class GenericBase2<TKey, TValue>
    where TValue : class
{
    public required TKey Key { get; set; }
    public required TValue Value { get; set; }
}

public class NonGenericDerived : GenericBase1<string>
{
}

public class GenericDerived<T> : GenericBase1<T>
{
}

public class MixedDerived<T> : GenericBase2<string, T>
    where T : class
{
}
```

Although you are free to use any of your type parameters as type arguments for a base class, you cannot derive from a type parameter. This is a little disappointing if you are used to languages that permit such things, but the C# language specification simply forbids it. However, you are allowed to use your own type as a type argument to your base class. And you can also specify a constraint on a type argument that requires it to derive from your own type. Example 6-9 shows each of these.

Example 6-9. Self-referential type arguments

```
public class SelfAsTypeArgument : IComparable<SelfAsTypeArgument>
{
    // ...implementation removed for clarity
}

public class Curious<T>
    where T : Curious<T>
{
}
```

As you saw in Chapter 4, the generic math interfaces use this kind of constraint. It means that the type INumber<SomeType> is valid only if SomeType does in fact implement INumber<SomeType> (either directly or through inheritance).

Covariance and Contravariance

In Chapter 4, I mentioned that generic types have special rules for type compatibility, referred to as *covariance* and *contravariance*. These rules determine whether references of certain generic types are implicitly convertible to one another when implicit conversions exist between their type arguments.

 Covariance and contravariance are applicable only to the generic type arguments of interfaces and delegates. (Delegates are described in Chapter 9.) You cannot define a covariant or contravariant class, struct, or record.

Consider the simple `Base` and `Derived` classes shown earlier in Example 6-2, and look at the method in Example 6-10, which accepts any `Base`. (It does nothing with it, but that's not relevant here—what matters is what its signature says it can use.)

Example 6-10. A method accepting any `Base`

```
public static void UseBase(Base b)
{
}
```

We already know that as well as accepting a reference to any `Base`, this can also accept a reference to an instance of any type derived from `Base`, such as `Derived`. Bearing that in mind, consider the method in Example 6-11.

Example 6-11. A method accepting any `IEnumerable<Base>`

```
public static void AllYourBase(IEnumerable<Base> bases)
{
}
```

This requires an object that implements the `IEnumerable<T>` generic interface described in Chapter 5, where `T` is `Base`. What would you expect to happen if we attempted to pass an object that did not implement `IEnumerable<Base>` but did implement `IEnumerable<Derived>`? Example 6-12 does this, and it compiles just fine.

Example 6-12. Passing an `IEnumerable<T>` of a derived type

```
IEnumerable<Derived> derivedItems = new[] { new Derived(), new Derived() };
AllYourBase(derivedItems);
```

Intuitively, this makes sense. The `AllYourBase` method expects its argument to supply a sequence of objects that are all of type `Base`. An `IEnumerable<Derived>` fits the bill because it supplies a sequence of `Derived` objects, and any `Derived` object is also a `Base`. However, what about the code in Example 6-13?

Example 6-13. A method accepting any `ICollection<Base>`

```
public static void AddBase(ICollection<Base> bases)
{
    bases.Add(new Base());
}
```

Recall from Chapter 5 that `ICollection<T>` derives from `IEnumerable<T>`, and it adds the ability to modify the collection in certain ways. This particular method exploits that by adding a new `Base` object to the collection. That would mean trouble for the code in Example 6-14.

Example 6-14. Error: trying to pass an `ICollection<T>` with a derived type

```
ICollection<Derived> derivedList = new List<Derived>();
AddBase(derivedList);  // Will not compile
```

Code that uses the `derivedList` variable will expect every object in that list to be of type `Derived` (or something derived from it, such as the `MoreDerived` class from Example 6-2). But the `AddBase` method in Example 6-13 attempts to add a plain `Base` instance. That cannot be correct, and the compiler does not allow it. The call to `AddBase` will produce a compiler error complaining that references of type `ICollection<Derived>` cannot be converted implicitly to references of type `ICollection<Base>`.

How does the compiler know that it's not OK to do this, while the very similar-looking conversion from `IEnumerable<Derived>` to `IEnumerable<Base>` is allowed? It's not because Example 6-13 contains code that would cause a problem, by the way. You'd get the same compiler error even if the `AddBase` method were completely empty. The reason we don't get an error in Example 6-12 is that the `IEnumerable<T>` interface declares its type argument `T` as covariant. You saw the syntax for this in Chapter 5, but I didn't draw attention to it, so Example 6-15 shows the relevant part from that interface's definition again.

Example 6-15. Covariant type parameter

```
public interface IEnumerable<out T> : IEnumerable
```

That out keyword does the job. (Again, C# keeps up the C-family tradition of giving each keyword multiple jobs—we first saw this keyword in the context of method parameters that can return information to the caller.) Intuitively, describing the type argument T as "out" makes sense, in that the IEnumerable<T> interface only ever *provides* a T—it does not define any members that *accept* a T. (The interface uses this type parameter in just one place: its read-only Current property.)

Compare that with ICollection<T>. This derives from IEnumerable<T>, so clearly it's possible to get a T out of it, but it's also possible to pass a T into its Add method. So ICollection<T> cannot annotate its type argument with out. (If you were to try to write your own similar interface, the compiler would produce an error if you declared the type argument as being covariant. Rather than just taking your word for it, it checks to make sure you really can't pass a T in anywhere.)

The compiler rejects the code in Example 6-14 because T is not covariant in ICollection<T>. This usage of the terms *covariant* and *contravariant* come from a branch of mathematics called *category theory*. The parameters that behave like IEnumerable<T>'s T are called covariant because implicit reference conversions for the generic type work in the same direction as conversions for the type argument: Derived is implicitly convertible to Base, and since T is covariant in IEnumerable<T>, IEnumerable<Derived> is implicitly convertible to IEnumerable<Base>.

Contravariance works the other way around, and as you might guess, we denote it with the in keyword. It's easiest to see this in action with code that uses members of types, so Example 6-16 shows a marginally more interesting pair of classes than the earlier examples.

Example 6-16. Class hierarchy with actual members

```
public class Shape
{
    public required Rect BoundingBox { get; set; }
}

public class RoundedRectangle : Shape
{
    public required double CornerRadius { get; set; }
}
```

Example 6-17 defines two classes that use these shape types. Both implement IComparer<T>, which I introduced in Chapter 4. The BoxAreaComparer compares two shapes based on the area of their bounding box—the shape whose bounding box covers the greater area will be deemed the larger by this comparison. The CornerSharp nessComparer, on the other hand, compares rounded rectangles by looking at how pointy their corners are.

Example 6-17. Comparing shapes

```
public class BoxAreaComparer : IComparer<Shape>
{
    public int Compare(Shape? x, Shape? y)
    {
        if (x is null)
        {
            return y is null ? 0 : -1;
        }
        if (y is null)
        {
            return 1;
        }

        double xArea = x.BoundingBox.Width * x.BoundingBox.Height;
        double yArea = y.BoundingBox.Width * y.BoundingBox.Height;

        return Math.Sign(xArea - yArea);
    }
}

public class CornerSharpnessComparer : IComparer<RoundedRectangle>
{
    public int Compare(RoundedRectangle? x, RoundedRectangle? y)
    {
        if (x is null)
        {
            return y is null ? 0 : -1;
        }
        if (y is null)
        {
            return 1;
        }

        // Smaller corners are sharper, so smaller radius is "greater" for
        // the purpose of this comparison, hence the backward subtraction.
        return Math.Sign(y.CornerRadius - x.CornerRadius);
    }
}
```

References of type RoundedRectangle are implicitly convertible to Shape, so what about IComparer<T>? Our BoxAreaComparer can compare any shapes and declares this by implementing IComparer<Shape>. The comparer's type argument T is only ever used in the Compare method, and that is happy to be passed any Shape. It will not be fazed if we pass it a pair of RoundedRectangle references, so our class is a perfectly adequate IComparer<RoundedRectangle>. An implicit conversion from IComparer <Shape> to IComparer<RoundedRectangle> therefore makes sense, and is in fact allowed. However, the CornerSharpnessComparer is fussier. It uses the CornerRadius property, which is available only on rounded rectangles, not on any old Shape.

Therefore, no implicit conversion exists from `IComparer<RoundedRectangle>` to `IComparer<Shape>`.

This is the reverse of what we saw with `IEnumerable<T>`. Implicit conversion is available from `IEnumerable<T1>` to `IEnumerable<T2>` when an implicit reference conversion from T1 to T2 exists. But implicit conversion from `IComparer<T1>` to `IComparer<T2>` is available when an implicit reference conversion exists in the other direction: from T2 to T1. That reversed relationship is called contravariance. Example 6-18 is an excerpt of the definition for `IComparer<T>` showing this contravariant type parameter.

Example 6-18. Contravariant type parameter

```
public interface IComparer<in T>
```

Most generic type parameters are neither covariant nor contravariant. (They are *invariant*.) `ICollection<T>` cannot be variant, because it contains some members that accept a T and some that return one. An `ICollection<Shape>` might contain shapes that are not `RoundedRectangles`, so you cannot pass it to a method expecting an `ICollection<RoundedRectangle>`, because such a method would expect every object it retrieves from the collection to be a rounded rectangle. Conversely, an `ICollection<RoundedRectangle>` cannot be expected to allow shapes other than rounded rectangles to be added, and so you cannot pass an `ICollection<RoundedRectangle>` to a method that expects an `ICollection<Shape>` because that method may try to add other kinds of shapes.

Arrays are covariant, just like `IEnumerable<T>`. This is rather odd, because we can write methods like the one in Example 6-19.

Example 6-19. Changing an element in an array

```
public static void UseBaseArray(Base[] bases)
{
    bases[0] = new Base();
}
```

If I were to call this with the code in Example 6-20, I would be making the same mistake as I did in Example 6-14, where I attempted to pass an `ICollection<Derived>` to a method that wanted to put something that was not `Derived` into the collection. But while Example 6-14 does not compile, Example 6-20 does, due to the surprising covariance of arrays.

Example 6-20. Passing an array with derived element type

```
Derived[] derivedBases = [new Derived(), new Derived()];
UseBaseArray(derivedBases);
```

This makes it look as though we could sneakily make this array accept a reference to an object that is not an instance of the array's element type—in this case, putting a reference to a non-`Derived` object, `Base`, in `Derived[]`. But that would be a violation of the type system. Does this mean the sky is falling?

In fact, C# correctly forbids such a violation, but it relies on the CLR to enforce this at runtime. Although a reference to an array of type `Derived[]` can be implicitly converted to a reference of type `Base[]`, any attempt to set an array element in a way that is inconsistent with the type system will throw an `ArrayTypeMismatchException`. So Example 6-19 would throw that exception when it tried to assign a reference to a `Base` into the `Derived[]` array.

The runtime check ensures that type safety is maintained, and this enables a convenient feature. If we write a method that takes an array and only reads from it, we can pass arrays of some derived element type. The downside is that the CLR has to do extra work at runtime when you modify array elements to ensure that there is no type mismatch. It may be able to optimize the code to avoid having to check every single assignment, but there is still some overhead, meaning that arrays are not quite as efficient as they might be.

This somewhat peculiar arrangement dates back to the time before .NET had formalized concepts of covariance and contravariance—these came in with generics, which were introduced in .NET 2.0. Perhaps if generics had been around from the start, arrays would be less odd, although having said that, even after .NET 2.0 for many years the runtime libraries did not provide any other way to pass a collection covariantly to a method that wanted to read from it using indexing. Until .NET Framework 4.5 introduced `IReadOnlyList<T>` (for which `T` is covariant), there was no read-only indexed collection interface in the framework, and therefore no standard indexed collection interface with a covariant type parameter. (`IList<T>` is read/write, so just like `ICollection<T>`, it cannot offer variance.)

While we are on the subject of type compatibility and the implicit reference conversions that inheritance makes available, there is one more type we should look at: `object`.

System.Object

The System.Object type, or object, as we usually call it in C#, is useful because it can act as a sort of universal container: a variable of this type can hold a reference to almost anything. I've mentioned this before, but I haven't yet explained why it's true. The reason this works is that almost everything derives from object.

If you do not specify a base class when writing a class or record, the C# compiler automatically uses object as the base. As we'll see shortly, it chooses different bases for certain kinds of types such as structs, but even those derive from object indirectly. (As ever, pointer types are an exception—these do not derive from object.)

The relationship between interfaces and objects is slightly more subtle. Interfaces do not derive from object, because an interface can specify only other interfaces as its bases. However, a reference of any interface type is implicitly convertible to a reference of type object. This conversion will always be valid, because all types that are capable of implementing interfaces ultimately derive from object. Moreover, C# chooses to make the object class's members available through interface references even though they are not, strictly speaking, members of the interface. This means that references of any kind always offer the following methods defined by object: ToString, Equals, GetHashCode, and GetType.

The Ubiquitous Methods of System.Object

I've mentioned ToString a few times already. The default implementation returns the object's type name, but many types provide their own implementation of ToString, returning a more useful textual representation of the object's current value. The numeric types return a decimal representation of their value, for example, while bool returns either "True" or "False".

I discussed Equals and GetHashCode in Chapter 3, but I'll provide a quick recap here. Equals allows an object to be compared with any other object. The default implementation just performs an identity comparison—that is, it returns true only when an object is compared with itself. Many types provide an Equals method that performs value-like comparison—for example, two distinct string objects may contain identical text, in which case they will report being equal to each other. (Should you need to perform an identity-based comparison of objects that provide value-based comparison, you can use the object class's static ReferenceEquals method.) Incidentally, object also defines a static version of Equals that takes two arguments. This checks whether the arguments are null, returning true if both are null and false if only one is null; otherwise, it defers to the first argument's Equals method. And, as discussed in Chapter 3, GetHashCode returns an integer that is a reduced representation of the object's value, which is used by hash-based mechanisms such as the

`Dictionary<TKey, TValue>` collection class. Any pair of objects for which `Equals` returns `true` must return the same hash codes.

The `GetType` method provides a way to discover things about the object's type. It returns a reference of type `Type`. That's part of the reflection API, which is the subject of Chapter 13.

Besides these public members, available through any reference, `object` defines two more members that are not universally accessible. An object has access to these members only on itself. They are `Finalize` and `MemberwiseClone`. The CLR calls the `Finalize` method to notify you that your object is no longer in use and the memory it occupies is about to be reclaimed. In C# we do not normally work directly with the `Finalize` method, because C# presents this mechanism through destructors, as I'll show in Chapter 7. `MemberwiseClone` creates a new instance of the same type as your object, initialized with copies of all of your object's fields. If you need a way to create a clone of an object, this may be easier than writing code that copies all the contents across by hand, although it is not very fast.

The reason these last two methods are available only from inside the object is that you might not want other people cloning your object, and it would be unhelpful if external code could call the `Finalize` method, fooling your object into thinking that it was about to be freed if in fact it wasn't. The `object` class limits the accessibility of these members. But they're not private—that would mean that only the `object` class itself could access them, because private members are not visible even to derived classes. Instead, `object` makes theses members *protected*, an accessibility specifier designed for inheritance scenarios.

Accessibility and Inheritance

By now, you will already be familiar with most of the accessibility levels available for types and their members. Elements marked as `public` are available to all, `private` members are accessible only from within the type that declared them, and `internal` members are available to code defined in the same component.[1] But with inheritance, we get three other accessibility options.

A member marked as `protected` is available inside the type that defined it and also inside any derived types. But for code using an instance of your type, `protected` members are not accessible, just like `private` members.

The next protection level for type members is `protected internal`. (You can write `internal protected` if you prefer; the order makes no difference.) This makes the

---

1 More precisely, the same assembly, and also friend assemblies. Chapter 12 describes assemblies.

member more accessible than either protected or internal on its own: the member will be accessible to all derived types *and* to all code that shares an assembly.

The third protection level that inheritance adds is protected private. Members marked with this (or the equivalent private protected) are available only to types that are both derived from *and* defined in the same component (or a friend assembly) as the defining type.

You can use protected, protected internal, or protected private for any member of a type, and not just methods. You can even define nested types with these accessibility specifiers.

While protected and protected internal (although not protected private) members are not available through an ordinary variable of the defining type, they are still part of the type's public API, in the sense that anyone who has access to your classes will be able to use these members. As with most languages that support a similar mechanism, protected members in C# are typically used to provide services that derived classes might find useful. If you write a public class that supports inheritance, then anyone can derive from it and gain access to its protected members. Removing or changing protected members would therefore risk breaking code that depends on your class just as surely as removing or changing public members would.

When you derive from a class, you cannot make your class more visible than its base. If you derive from an internal class, for example, you cannot declare your class to be public. Your base class forms part of your class's API, so anyone wishing to use your class will also in effect be using its base class; this means that if the base is inaccessible, your class will also be inaccessible, which is why C# does not permit a class to be more visible than its base. If you derive from a protected nested class, your derived class could be protected, private, or protected private but not public, internal, or protected internal.

> This restriction does not apply to the interfaces you implement. A public class is free to implement internal or private interfaces. However, it does apply to an interface's bases: a public interface cannot derive from an internal interface.

When defining methods, there's another keyword you can add for the benefit of derived types: virtual.

Virtual Methods

A *virtual method* is one that a derived type can replace. Several of the methods defined by object are virtual: the ToString, Equals, GetHashCode, and Finalize methods are all designed to be replaced. The code required to produce a useful textual representation of an object's value will differ considerably from one type to another, as will the logic required to determine equality and produce a hash code. Types typically define a finalizer only if they need to do some specialized cleanup work when they go out of use.

Not all methods are virtual. In fact, C# makes methods nonvirtual by default. The object class's GetType method is not virtual, so you can always trust the information it returns to you because you know that you're calling the GetType method supplied by .NET, and not some type-specific substitute designed to fool you. To declare that a method should be virtual, use the virtual keyword, as Example 6-21 shows.

Example 6-21. A class with a virtual method

```
public class BaseWithVirtual
{
    public virtual void ShowMessage()
    {
        Console.WriteLine("Hello from BaseWithVirtual");
    }
}
```

 You can also apply the virtual keyword to properties. Properties are just methods under the covers, so this has the effect of making the accessor methods virtual. The same is true for events, which are discussed in Chapter 9.

There's nothing unusual about the syntax for invoking a virtual method. As Example 6-22 shows, it looks just like calling any other method.

Example 6-22. Using a nonstatic virtual method

```
public static void CallVirtualMethod(BaseWithVirtual o)
{
    o.ShowMessage();
}
```

The difference between virtual and nonvirtual instance method invocations is that a virtual method call decides at runtime which method to invoke. The code in Example 6-22 will, in effect, inspect the object passed in, and if the object's type supplies its own implementation of ShowMessage, it will call that instead of the one defined in `BaseWithVirtual`. The method is chosen based on the actual type the target object turns out to have at runtime, and not the static type (determined at compile time) of the expression that refers to the target object.

Derived types are not obliged to replace virtual methods. Example 6-23 shows two classes that derive from the one in Example 6-21. The first leaves the base class's implementation of `ShowMessage` in place. The second overrides it. Note the `override` keyword—C# requires us to state explicitly that we are intending to override a non-static virtual method.

Example 6-23. Overriding virtual methods

```
public class DeriveWithoutOverride : BaseWithVirtual
{
}

public class DeriveAndOverride : BaseWithVirtual
{
    public override void ShowMessage()
    {
        Console.WriteLine("This is an override");
    }
}
```

We can use these types with the method in Example 6-22. Example 6-24 calls it three times, passing in a different type of object each time.

Example 6-24. Exploiting virtual methods

```
CallVirtualMethod(new BaseWithVirtual());
CallVirtualMethod(new DeriveWithoutOverride());
CallVirtualMethod(new DeriveAndOverride());
```

This produces the following output:

```
Hello from BaseWithVirtual
Hello from BaseWithVirtual
This is an override
```

Obviously, when we pass an instance of the base class, we get the output from the base class's `ShowMessage` method. We also get that with the derived class that has not supplied an override. It is only the final class, which overrides the method, that produces different output. This shows that virtual methods provide a way to write *polymorphic* code: Example 6-22 can use a variety of types.

When overriding a method, the method name and its parameter types must be an exact match. In most cases, the return type will also be identical, but it doesn't always need to be. If the `virtual` method's return type is not `void`, and is not a `ref` return, the overriding method may have a different type as long as an implicit reference conversion from that type to the `virtual` method's return type exists. To put that more informally, an override is allowed to be more specific about its return type. This means that examples such as Example 6-25 are legal.

Example 6-25. An override that narrows the return type

```csharp
public class Product { }
public class Book : Product { }

public class ProductSourceBase
{
    public virtual Product Get() { return new Product(); }
}

public class BookSource : ProductSourceBase
{
    public override Book Get() { return new Book(); }
}
```

The return type of the override of `Get` is `Book`, even though the `virtual` method it overrides returns a `Product`. This is fine because anything that invokes this method through a reference of type `ProductSourceBase` will expect to get back a reference of type `Product`, and thanks to inheritance, a `Book` is a `Product`. So users of the `Product SourceBase` type will be unaware of and unaffected by the change. This feature can sometimes be useful in cases where code working directly with a derived type needs to know the specific type that will be returned.

You might be wondering why we need virtual methods, given that interfaces also enable polymorphic code, but virtual methods do have some advantages. A default interface member implementation cannot define or access nonstatic fields, so it is somewhat limited compared to a class that defines a virtual function. (And since default interface implementations require runtime support, they are unavailable to code that needs to be able to run on .NET Framework, which includes any library targeting .NET Standard 2.0 or older.) However, there is a more subtle advantage available to virtual methods, but before we can look at it, we need to explore a feature of virtual methods that at first glance even more closely resembles the way interfaces work.

Abstract Methods

You can define a virtual method without providing a default implementation. C# calls this an *abstract method*. If a class contains one or more abstract methods, the class is incomplete, because it doesn't provide all of the methods it defines. Classes of this kind are also described as being abstract, and it is not possible to construct instances of an abstract class; attempting to use the new operator with an abstract class will cause a compiler error. Sometimes when discussing classes, it's useful to make clear that some particular class is *not* abstract, for which we normally use the term *concrete class*.

If you derive from an abstract class, then unless you provide implementations for all the abstract methods, your derived class will also be abstract. You must state your intention to write an abstract class with the abstract keyword; if this is absent from a class that has unimplemented abstract methods (either ones it has defined itself or ones it has inherited from its base class), the C# compiler will report an error. Example 6-26 shows an abstract class that defines a single abstract method. Abstract methods are virtual by definition; there wouldn't be much use in defining a method that has no body if there were no way for derived classes to supply a body.

Example 6-26. An abstract class

```
public abstract class AbstractBase
{
    public abstract void ShowMessage();
}
```

Abstract method declarations just define the signature and do not contain a body. Unlike with interfaces, each abstract member has its own accessibility—you can declare abstract methods as public, internal, protected internal, protected pri vate, or protected. (It makes no sense to make an abstract or virtual method pri vate, because the method will be inaccessible to derived types and therefore impossible to override.)

 Although classes that contain abstract methods are required to be abstract, the converse is not true. It is legal to define a class as abstract even if it would be a viable concrete class. This prevents the class from being constructed. A class that derives from this will be concrete without needing to override any abstract methods.

Abstract classes have the option to declare that they implement an interface without needing to provide a full implementation. You can't just omit the unimplemented members, though. You must explicitly declare all of its members, marking any that you want to leave unimplemented as being abstract, as Example 6-27 shows. This forces concrete derived types to supply the implementation.

Example 6-27. Abstract interface implementation

```
public abstract class MustBeComparable : IComparable<string>
{
    public abstract int CompareTo(string? other);
}
```

There's clearly some overlap between abstract classes and interfaces. Both provide a way to define an abstract type that code can use without needing to know the exact type that will be supplied at runtime. Each option has its pros and cons. Interfaces have the advantage that a single type can implement multiple interfaces, whereas a class gets to specify only a single base class. But abstract classes can define fields and can use these in any default member implementations they supply. However, there's a more subtle advantage available to virtual methods that comes into play when you release multiple versions of a library over time.

Inheritance and Library Versioning

Imagine what would happen if you had written and released a library that defined some public interfaces and abstract classes, and in the second release of the library, you decided that you wanted to add some new members to one of the interfaces. It's conceivable that this might not cause a problem for customers using your code. Certainly, any place where they use a reference of that interface type will be unaffected by the addition of new features. However, what if some of your customers have written types that implement your interface? Suppose, for example, that in a future version of .NET, Microsoft decided to add a new member to the IEnumerable<T> interface.

If the interface were not to supply a default implementation for the new member, it would be a disaster. This interface is widely used but also widely implemented. Classes that already implement IEnumerable<T> would become invalid because they would not provide this new member, so old code would fail to compile, and code already compiled would throw MissingMethodException errors at runtime. C#'s support for default member implementations in interfaces mitigates this: in the unlikely event that Microsoft did add a new member to IEnumerable<T>, it could supply a default implementation preventing these errors. This doesn't help anyone using .NET Framework, which does not support this feature, but for newer runtimes, it makes modification of existing interface definitions seem viable. However, there's a more subtle problem. Some classes might by chance already have had a member with the same name and signature as the newly added method. If that code is recompiled against the new interface definition, the compiler would treat that existing member as part of the implementation of the interface, even though the developer who wrote the method did not write it with that intention. So unless the existing code coincidentally happens to do exactly what the new member requires, we'd have a problem, and we wouldn't get compiler errors or warnings to alert us.

Consequently, the widely accepted rule is that you do not alter interfaces once they have been published. If you have complete control over all of the code that uses and implements an interface, you can get away with modifying the interface, because you can make any necessary modifications to the affected code. But once the interface has become available for use in codebases you do not control—that is, once it has been published—it's no longer possible to change it without risking breaking someone else's code. Default interface implementations mitigate this risk, but they cannot eliminate the problem of existing methods accidentally being misinterpreted when they get recompiled against the updated interface.

Abstract base classes do not have to suffer from this problem. Obviously, introducing new abstract members would cause exactly the same `MissingMethodException` failures, but introducing new virtual methods does not.

But what if, after releasing version 1.0 of a component, you add a new virtual method in version 1.1 that turns out to have the same name and signature as a method that one of your customers happens to have added in a derived class? Perhaps in version 1.0, your component defines the rather uninteresting base class shown in Example 6-28.

Example 6-28. Base type version 1.0

```
public class LibraryBase
{
}
```

If you release this library, perhaps on the NuGet package management website (*https://nuget.org*), or maybe as part of some Software Development Kit (SDK) for your application, a customer might write a derived type such as the one in Example 6-29. The `Start` method they have written is clearly not meant to override anything in the base class.

Example 6-29. Class derived from version 1.0 base

```
public class CustomerDerived : LibraryBase
{
    public void Start()
    {
        Console.WriteLine("Derived type's Start method");
    }
}
```

Since you won't necessarily get to see every line of code that your customers write, you might be unaware of this Start method. So in version 1.1 of your component, you might decide to add a new virtual method, also called Start, as Example 6-30 shows.

Example 6-30. Base type version 1.1

```
public class LibraryBase
{
    public virtual void Start() { }
}
```

Imagine that your system calls this method as part of an initialization procedure introduced in v1.1. You've defined a default empty implementation so that types derived from LibraryBase that don't need to take part in that procedure don't have to do anything. Types that wish to participate will override this method. But what happens with the class in Example 6-29? Clearly the developer who wrote that did not intend to participate in your new initialization mechanism, because that didn't exist when they wrote their code. It could be bad if your code calls the CustomerDerived class's Start method, because the developer presumably expects it to be called only when their code decides to call it. Fortunately, the compiler will detect this problem. If the customer attempts to compile Example 6-29 against version 1.1 of your library (Example 6-30), the compiler will warn them that something is not right:

```
warning CS0114: 'CustomerDerived.Start()' hides inherited member
'LibraryBase.Start()'. To make the current member override that implementation,
add the override keyword. Otherwise add the new keyword.
```

This is why the C# compiler requires the override keyword when we replace non-static virtual methods. It wants to know whether we were intending to override an existing method, so that if we weren't, it can warn us about naming collisions. (The absence of any equivalent keyword signifying the intention to implement an interface member is why the compiler cannot detect the same problem with default interface implementation. And the reason for this absence is that default interface implementation didn't exist prior to C# 8.0.)

We get a warning rather than an error, because the compiler provides a behavior that is likely to be safe when this situation has arisen due to the release of a new version of a library. The compiler guesses—correctly, in this case—that the developer who wrote the CustomerDerived type didn't mean to override the LibraryBase class's Start method. So rather than having the CustomerDerived type's Start method override the base class's virtual method, it *hides* it. A derived type is said to hide a member of a base class when it introduces a new member with the same name.

Hiding methods is quite different than overriding them. When hiding occurs, the base method is not replaced. Example 6-31 shows how the hidden Start method remains available. It creates a CustomerDerived object and places a reference to that object in two variables of different types: one of type CustomerDerived and one of type LibraryBase. It then calls Start through each of these.

Example 6-31. Hidden versus virtual method

```
var d = new CustomerDerived();
LibraryBase b = d;

d.Start();
b.Start();
```

When we use the d variable, the call to Start ends up calling the derived type's Start method, the one that has hidden the base member. But the b variable's type is Library Base, so that invokes the base Start method. If CustomerDerived had overridden the base class's Start method instead of hiding it, both of those method calls would have invoked the override.

When name collisions occur because of a new library version, this hiding behavior is usually the right thing to do. If the customer's code has a variable of type CustomerDerived, then that code will want to invoke the Start method specific to that derived type. However, the compiler produces a warning because it doesn't know for certain that this is the reason for the problem. It might be that you *did* mean to override the method, and you just forgot to write the override keyword.

Like many developers, I don't like to see compiler warnings, and I try to avoid committing code that produces them. But what should you do if a new library version puts you in this situation? The best long-term solution is probably to change the name of the method in your derived class so that it doesn't clash with the method in the new version of the library. However, if you're up against a deadline, you may want a more expedient solution. So C# lets you declare that you know that there's a name clash and that you definitely want to hide the base member, not override it. As Example 6-32 shows, you can use the new keyword to state that you're aware of the issue and definitely want to hide the base class member. The code will still behave in the same way, but you'll no longer get the warning, because you've assured the compiler that you know what's going on. But this is an issue you should fix at some point, because sooner or later the existence of two methods with the same name on the same type that mean different things is likely to cause confusion.

Example 6-32. Avoiding warnings when hiding members

```
public class CustomerDerived : LibraryBase
{
    public new void Start()
    {
        Console.WriteLine("Derived type's Start method");
    }
}
```

 C# does not let you use the new keyword to deal with the equivalent problem that arises with default interface implementations. There is no way to retain the default implementation supplied by an interface and also declare a public method with the same signature. This is slightly frustrating because it's possible at the binary level: it's the behavior you get if you do not recompile the code that implements an interface after adding a new member with a default implementation. You can still have separate implementations of, say, ILibrary .Start and CustomerDerived.Start, but you have to use explicit interface implementation.

Just occasionally, you may see the new keyword used in this way for reasons other than handling library versioning issues. For example, the ISet<T> interface that I showed in Chapter 5 uses it to introduce a new Add method. ISet<T> derives from ICollection<T>, an interface that already provides an Add method, which takes an instance of T and has a void return type. ISet<T> makes a subtle change to this, shown in Example 6-33.

Example 6-33. Hiding to change the signature

```
public interface ISet<T> : ICollection<T>
{
    new bool Add(T item);
    // ...other members omitted for clarity
}
```

The ISet<T> interface's Add method tells you whether the item you just added was already in the set, something the base ICollection<T> interface's Add method doesn't support. ISet<T> needs its Add to have a different return type—bool instead of void—so it defines Add with the new keyword to indicate that it should hide the ICol lection<T> one. Both methods are still available—if you have two variables, one of type ICollection<T> and the other of type ISet<T>, both referring to the same object, you'll be able to access the void Add through the former and the bool Add through the latter.

Microsoft didn't have to do this. It could have called the new `Add` method something else—`AddIfNotPresent`, for example. But it's arguably less confusing just to have the one method name for adding things to a collection, particularly since you're free to ignore the return value, at which point the new `Add` looks indistinguishable from the old one. And most `ISet<T>` implementations will implement the `ICollection<T>`. `Add` method by calling straight through to the `ISet<T>.Add` method, so it makes sense that they have the same name.

Aside from the preceding example, so far I've discussed method hiding only in the context of compiling old code against a new version of a library. What happens if you have old code *already compiled* against an old library but that ends up *running* against a new version? That's a scenario you are highly likely to run into when the library in question is in the .NET runtime libraries. Suppose you are using third-party components that you have only in binary form (e.g., ones you've licensed from a company that does not supply source code). The supplier will have built these to use some particular version of .NET. If you upgrade your application to run with a new version of .NET, you might not be able to get hold of newer versions of the third-party components—maybe the vendor hasn't released them yet, or perhaps it has gone out of business.

If the components you're using were compiled for, say, .NET Standard 1.2, and you use them in a project built for .NET 8.0, all of those older components will end up using the .NET 8.0 versions of the runtime libraries. .NET has a versioning policy that arranges for all the components that a particular program uses to get the same version of the runtime libraries, regardless of which version any individual component may have been built for. So it's entirely possible that some component, *OldControls.dll*, contains classes that derive from classes in .NET Standard 1.2, and that define members that collide with the names of members newly added in .NET 8.0.

This is more or less the same scenario as I described earlier, except that the code that was written for an older version of a library is not going to be recompiled. We're not going to get a compiler warning about hiding a method, because that would involve running the compiler, and we have only the binary for the relevant component. What happens now?

Fortunately, we don't need the old component to be recompiled. The C# compiler sets various flags in the compiled output for each method it compiles, indicating things like whether the method is virtual or not and whether the method was intended to override some method in the base class. When you put the `new` keyword on a method, the compiler sets a flag indicating that the method is not meant to override anything. The CLR calls this the *newslot* flag. When C# compiles a method such as the one in Example 6-29, which does not specify either `override` or `new`, it also sets this same newslot flag for that method, because at the time the method was compiled, there was no method of the same name on the base class. As far as both the developer and the compiler were concerned, the `CustomerDerived` class's `Start` was written as a brand-new method that was not connected to anything on the base class.

So when this old component gets loaded in conjunction with a new version of the library defining the base class, the CLR can see what was intended—it can see that, as far as the author of the `CustomerDerived` class was concerned, `Start` is not meant to override anything. It therefore treats `CustomerDerived.Start` as a distinct method from `LibraryBase.Start`—it hides the base method just like it did when we were able to recompile.

By the way, everything I've said about virtual methods can also apply to properties, because a property's accessors are just methods. So you can define virtual properties, and derived classes can override or hide these in exactly the same way as with methods. I won't be getting to events until Chapter 9, but those are also methods in disguise, so they can also be virtual.

Static Virtual Methods

Before C# 11.0, you couldn't declare static methods as virtual, but as you saw in Chapters 3 and 4, interfaces can now do this. (Only interfaces, though. You still can't write `static virtual` or `static abstract` in any other kind of type.) Example 6-34 shows an excerpt from the source for `INumberBase<T>` in the .NET runtime libraries. As you saw in Chapter 4, this defines various characteristics common to numeric types, including a `static abstract` property, `One`.

Example 6-34. A static virtual property in an interface

```
public interface INumberBase<TSelf>
    : IAdditionOperators<TSelf, TSelf, TSelf>,
      ...
{
    /// <summary>Gets the value <c>1</c> for the type.</summary>
    static abstract TSelf One { get; }
    ...
}
```

This requires each numeric type to implement its own `One` property. (The binary representation of the number 1 is not the same across all numeric types.) But how do we ensure that we get the right implementation? Instance virtual method invocation selects the method based on the type of the object on which you invoke the method. But what about static virtual methods? Since there's no target object on which a static method is invoked, how is the runtime to know which type's implementation to use? With static virtual methods, the runtime has to use a different mechanism: the target type is determined by a generic type argument. As you saw in earlier chapters, we can invoke an interface's static virtual members only in generic code. If we constrain a type parameter to implement some interface that defines static virtual members, we can use those members through the type parameter, as Example 6-35 shows.

Example 6-35. Invoking static virtual interface members

```
public static T Two<T>()
    where T : INumberBase<T>
{
    return T.One + T.One;
}
```

This `Two<T>` method returns the representation of the number 2 for any type that implements `INumberBase<T>`, relying on the fact that `INumberBase<T>` defines a static virtual property called `One`, along with a static virtual + operator. (It's not a very useful method, but it serves to illustrate how static virtual dispatch works.)

Since we're accessing this property with `T.One`, the specific implementation we get is determined by the type argument we supply for `T` when invoking this `Two<T>` method. When we write `Two<int>`, the CLR knows that `T.One` needs to invoke `int.One`. If we were to write `Two<Complex>`, it would invoke `Complex.One`. So the target of a virtual static invocation is determined at the point where we supply the generic type argument.

One consequence of this is that the invocation target for static virtual members becomes apparent earlier than it does for instance virtual members. This can sometimes make it easier for the CLR to optimize the code—when you instantiate a generic method with a value-typed type argument, the CLR usually generates code specific to that type, meaning that it can know exactly which method a static virtual invocation refers to when JIT (or AOT) compilation occurs, so it doesn't have to generate code that has to work out what to do at runtime. (There may be some cases where the CLR can do this for instance members too—if I write `"x".ToString()` there's no doubt that I'm invoking `string.ToString`, for example—but it often won't be able to.) The fact that virtual static method targets are known at JIT compile time for value types helps to enable code that exploits generic math to perform just as well as code that performs arithmetic more conventionally.

Default Constraints

The section "Constraints" on page 230 described all but one of the ways in which you can define constraints for generic type parameters. It left the `default` constraint to this chapter, because that is used only in inheritance scenarios. It exists to deal with code like Example 6-36.

Example 6-36. A base type with overloads distinguished only by a value type constraint

```
public class Base
{
    public virtual void F<T>(T? t) where T : struct { }
    public virtual void F<T>(T? t) { }
}
```

At first glance, this looks like it should not compile: this class defines two methods with the same name, and what would appear to be the same signature: they both return nothing, and both take an argument of T?. This seems ambiguous, but it's not, because the first method's T is constrained to be a struct. In general, the presence of a constraint is not enough to distinguish otherwise-identical method signatures for overloading purposes, but it is in this particular case. Since T is constrained to be a value type, T? means something different than it does for an unconstrained type. Example 6-37 shows a different way to write the same code that makes it easier to see that these methods do have different signatures.

Example 6-37. Spelling out the effect of the struct constraint

```
public class BaseWithSignaturesMadeClear
{
    public virtual void F<T>(Nullable<T> t) where T : struct { }
    public virtual void F<T>(T? t) { }
}
```

That makes it possible for the compiler to distinguish between them. Example 6-38 shows various ways to call these two methods.

Example 6-38. Invoking the two methods

```
Base b = new();
int? nullInt = null;
int? nonNullNullableInt = 42;

// These call the 1st overload.
b.F(nullInt);
b.F(nonNullNullableInt);
b.F(default(int?));

// These call the 2nd overload.
b.F(42);
b.F("Hello");
b.F(default(int));

// This would cause a compiler error.
// b.F(null);
```

Types deriving from this class may be in for a surprise. Of the two F methods in Base, which would you expect Example 6-39 to override? It has been declared in exactly the same way as the second one, in which the type argument is unconstrained, so you might expect it to override that. In fact, it overrides the first.

Example 6-39. Overriding one of two ambiguous-looking methods

```
public class DerivedOverrideStructMethod : Base
{
    public override void F<T>(T? t) { }
}
```

The reason for this is that in older versions of C# you weren't allowed to write Example 6-36. It used to be illegal to write T? when T is an unconstrained type argument. (The rationale was that nullable value types work very differently than reference types, and since the compiler has to generate quite different code for each, it's not possible to support nullability unless T has been constrained so that the compiler knows whether it's a value type.) However, this turned out to be an onerous restriction, so as a compromise, the compiler now allows it. The behavior with value types is slightly surprising—if you supply int as the argument for an unconstrained type parameter T, the effective type of T? is int, and not, as you might expect, int?—but it does at least mean things work as you'd expect for reference types.

C# allows us to omit the type constraint on overrides in cases where there's no ambiguity (e.g., if the base defined only one F method, there would be absolutely no doubt as to which method Example 6-39 means to override) because it would be annoying to have to duplicate the constraints. This means that in cases where the base class defines a single F<T> method with T constrained to be a struct, Example 6-39 would unambiguously override that method, and would implicitly impose the same constraint.

Now imagine you're using some library that defined such a Base type, with just the one F method, and you had written a class such as the one in Example 6-39. Imagine now that some time later, the library gets updated to take advantage of the fact that we can now write T? for an unconstrained type, i.e., it changes the base class to look like Example 6-36 by adding that second F<T> overload. We would not want the meaning of our code to be changed by this. Our override in Example 6-39 has a first argument of type T?, but that's really Nullable<T> because when we wrote it, it was unambiguously overriding the struct-constrained form, and that shouldn't change just because a new version of the base class added a new overload.

To maintain backward compatibility, Example 6-39 carries on meaning what it always meant. That's how we end up with the slightly surprising result that given a base type like Example 6-36, Example 6-39 overrides the version of F where T is constrained to be a struct, and not the one it looks like it should override.

So what if you actually wanted to override the unconstrained method? This historical baggage means that the obvious syntax (not specifying a constraint in the override, matching the absence of a constraint in the base class) doesn't work. And this is why the default constraint exists. It is effectively a way to say explicitly that you mean to override the method where there are no constraints. Example 6-40 shows how we can use this to override each method defined in Example 6-36 independently.

Example 6-40. Using the default constraint

```
public class Derived : Base
{
    // This overrides the method with the "where T : struct" constraint
    public override void F<T>(T? t) { }

    // This overrides the method where T is unconstrained.
    public override void F<T>(T? t) where T : default { }
}
```

It's very rare to need to use this. Defining pairs of virtual methods like those in Example 6-36 is likely to cause confusion and it is best avoided. The language needs to offer default constraints so that you don't end up with a virtual method that you simply can't override, but if you find yourself having to use it, it would be better to see if you can revisit your design to avoid this.

Sealed Methods and Classes

Virtual methods are deliberately open to modification through inheritance. A sealed method is the opposite—it is one that cannot be overridden. Methods are sealed by default in C#: methods cannot be overridden unless declared virtual. But when you override a virtual method, you can seal it, closing it off for further modification. Example 6-41 uses this technique to provide a custom ToString implementation that cannot be further overridden by derived classes.

Example 6-41. A sealed method

```
public class FixedToString
{
    public sealed override string ToString() => "Arf arf!";
}
```

You can also seal an entire class, preventing anyone from deriving from it. As Example 6-42 shows, you put `sealed` before the `class` keyword. You can also put it before the `record` keyword in a class record type.

Example 6-42. A sealed class

```
public sealed class EndOfTheLine
{
}
```

Some types are inherently sealed. Value types, for example, do not support inheritance, so structs, record structs, and enums are effectively sealed. The built-in `string` class is also sealed.

There are two normal reasons for sealing either classes or methods. One is that you want to guarantee some particular invariant, and if you leave your type open to modification, you will not be able to guarantee that invariant. For example, instances of the `string` type are immutable. The `string` type itself does not provide a way to modify an instance's value, and because nobody can derive from `string`, you can guarantee that if you have a reference of type `string`, you have a reference to an immutable object. This makes it safe for you to use in scenarios where you do not want the value to change—for example, when you use an object as a key to a dictionary (or anything else that relies on a hash code), you need the value not to change, because if the hash code changes while the item is in use as a key, the container will malfunction.

The other usual reason for leaving things sealed is that designing types that can successfully be modified through inheritance is hard, particularly if your type will be used outside of your own organization. Simply opening things up for modification is not sufficient—if you decide to make all your methods virtual, it might make it easy for people using your type to modify its behavior, but you will have made a rod for your own back when it comes to maintaining the base class. Unless you control all of the code that derives from your class, it will be almost impossible to change anything in the base without breaking backward compatibility, because you will never know which methods may have been overridden in derived classes, making it hard to ensure that your class's internal state is consistent at all times. Developers writing derived types will doubtless do their best not to break things, but they will inevitably rely on aspects of your class's behavior that are undocumented. So in opening up every aspect of your class for modification through inheritance, you rob yourself of the freedom to change your class.

You should be very selective about which methods, if any, you make virtual. And you should also document whether callers are allowed to replace the method completely or whether they are required to call the base implementation as part of their override. Speaking of which, how do you do that?

Accessing Base Members

Everything that is in scope in a base class and is not private will also be in scope and accessible in a derived type. If you want to access some member of the base class, you typically just access it as if it were a normal member of your class. You can either access members through the this reference or just refer to them by name without qualification.

However, there are some situations in which you need to state explicitly that you mean to refer to a base class member. In particular, if you have overridden a method, calling that method by name will invoke your override recursively. If you want to call back to the original method that you overrode, there's a special keyword for that, shown in Example 6-43.

Example 6-43. Calling the base method after overriding

```
public class CustomerDerived : LibraryBase
{
    public override void Start()
    {
        Console.WriteLine("CustomerDerived starting");
        base.Start();
    }
}
```

By using the base keyword, we are opting out of the normal virtual method dispatch mechanism. If we had written just Start(), that would have been a recursive call, which would be undesirable here. By writing base.Start(), we get the method that would have been available on an instance of the base class, the method we overrode.

What if the inheritance chain is deeper? Suppose CustomerDerived derives from IntermediateBase and that IntermediateBase derives from LibraryBase and also overrides the Start method. In that case, writing base.Start() in our Customer Derived type will call the override defined by IntermediateBase. There's no way to bypass that and call the original LibraryBase.Start directly.

In this example, I have called the base class's implementation after completing my work. C# does not care when you call the base—you could call it as the first thing the method does, as the last, or halfway through the method. You could even call it several times, or not at all. It is up to the author of the base class to document whether and when the base class implementation of the method should be called by an override.

You can use the base keyword for other members too, such as properties and events. However, access to base constructors works a bit differently.

Inheritance and Construction

Although a derived class inherits all the members of its base class, this does not mean the same thing for constructors as it does for everything else. Most public members of the base class will be public members of the derived class too, accessible to anyone who uses your derived class. Constructors are the exception: someone using your class cannot construct it by using one of the constructors defined by its base class.

There is a straightforward reason for this: if you want an instance of some type D, then you'll want it to be a full-fledged D with everything in it properly initialized. Suppose that D derives from B. If you were able to use one of B's constructors directly, it wouldn't do anything to the parts specific to D. A base class's constructor won't know about any of the fields defined by a derived class, so it cannot initialize them. If you want a D, you'll need a constructor that knows how to initialize a D. So with a derived class, you can use only the constructors offered by that derived class, regardless of what constructors the base class might provide.

In the examples I've shown so far in this chapter, I've been able to ignore this because of the default constructor that C# provides. As you saw in Chapter 3, if you don't write a constructor, C# writes one for you that takes no arguments. It does this for derived classes too, and the generated constructor will invoke the no-arguments constructor of the base class. But this changes if I start writing my own constructors. Example 6-44 defines a pair of classes, where the base defines an explicit no-arguments constructor, and the derived class defines one that requires an argument.

Example 6-44. No default constructor in derived class

```
public class BaseWithZeroArgCtor
{
    public BaseWithZeroArgCtor()
    {
        Console.WriteLine("Base constructor");
    }
}

public class DerivedNoDefaultCtor : BaseWithZeroArgCtor
{
    public DerivedNoDefaultCtor(int i)
    {
        Console.WriteLine("Derived constructor");
    }
}
```

Because the base class has a zero-argument constructor, I can construct it with new BaseWithZeroArgCtor(). But I cannot do this with the derived type: I can construct that only by passing an argument—for example, new DerivedNoDefaultCtor(123).

So as far as the publicly visible API of DerivedNoDefaultCtor is concerned, the derived class appears not to have inherited its base class's constructor.

In fact, it has inherited it, as you can see by looking at the output you get if you construct an instance of the derived type:

```
Base constructor
Derived constructor
```

When constructing an instance of DerivedNoDefaultCtor, the base class's constructor runs immediately before the derived class's constructor. Since the base constructor ran, clearly it was present. All of the base class's constructors are available to a derived type, but they can be invoked only by constructors in the derived class. Example 6-44 invoked the base constructor implicitly: all constructors are required to invoke a constructor on their base class, and if you don't specify which to invoke, the compiler invokes the base's zero-argument constructor for you.

What if the base doesn't define a parameterless constructor? In that case, you'll get a compiler error if you derive a class that does not specify which constructor to call. Example 6-45 shows a base class without a zero-argument constructor. (The presence of explicit constructors disables the compiler's normal generation of a default constructor, and since this base class supplies only a constructor that takes arguments, this means there is no zero-argument constructor.) It also shows a derived class with two constructors, both of which call into the base constructor explicitly, using the base keyword.

Example 6-45. Invoking a base constructor explicitly

```
public class BaseNoDefaultCtor
{
    public BaseNoDefaultCtor(int i)
    {
        Console.WriteLine($"Base constructor: {i}");
    }
}

public class DerivedCallingBaseCtor : BaseNoDefaultCtor
{
    public DerivedCallingBaseCtor()
        : base(123)
    {
        Console.WriteLine("Derived constructor (default)");
    }

    public DerivedCallingBaseCtor(int i)
        : base(i)
    {
        Console.WriteLine($"Derived constructor: {i}");
```

```
    }
}
```

The derived class here decides to supply a parameterless constructor even though the base class doesn't have one—it supplies a constant value for the argument the base requires. The second just passes its argument through to the base.

Primary Constructors

If a base class has a primary constructor, this doesn't change anything for classes that derive from it. As Example 6-46 shows, we can invoke a base class's primary constructor in exactly the same way as we would any other base class constructor.

Example 6-46. Invoking a base class's default constructor explicitly

```
public class BasePrimaryCtor(int i)
{
    public override ToString() => $"Base {i}";
}

public class DerivedCallingBasePrimaryCtor : BasePrimaryCtor
{
    public DerivedCallingBasePrimaryCtor()
        : base(123)
    {
    }
}
```

But what if the derived class has a primary constructor? Example 6-1 already showed how this looks when using the base class's no-arguments constructor, but what if we need to pass arguments to a base constructor? In that case, we can supply an argument list after the base class name, as Example 6-47 shows.

Example 6-47. Invoking a base constructor from a primary constructor

```
public class DerivedWithPrimaryCallingBaseCtor(int i) : BaseNoDefaultCtor(i)
{
}
```

A type with a primary constructor can use this syntax to invoke any base class constructor requiring arguments. It doesn't matter whether the base class constructor is a primary constructor or an ordinary one.

In some cases, you might not want to pass a constructor argument through like this: sometimes a derived type will know what value to pass to the base record type, as Example 6-48 shows. (Incidentally, this also shows that record types can participate in inheritance. The syntax is the same as for ordinary classes.)

Example 6-48. Passing a constant to a base constructor

```
public abstract record Colorful(string Color);

public record FordModelT() : Colorful("Black");
```

Although the base `Colorful` record has a primary constructor requiring the `Color` property to be supplied, this derived type does not impose the same requirement. The popular story is that Ford's early car, the Model T, was only available in one color, so this particular derived type can just set the `Color` itself. Users of the `FordModelT` record do not need to supply the `Color`, even though it's a mandatory argument for the base `Colorful` type. Pedants will by now be itching to point out that this paint constraint applied only for 12 of the 19 years for which the Model T was produced. I would draw their attention to Example 6-49, which shows that although the `Ford ModelT` type does not require the `Color` property to be passed during construction, it can still be set with an object initializer. So this type enables the color to be specified just as it could with early and late Model Ts, but the default is aligned with the fact that the overwhelming majority of these cars were indeed black.

Example 6-49. Using a derived record that has made a mandatory base property optional

```
var commonModelT = new FordModelT();
var lateModelT = new FordModelT { Color = "Green" };
```

The syntax shown in Examples 6-47 and 6-48, where we put the arguments for the base constructor directly after the base type's name, is available only on types that define a primary constructor. If you look closely at Example 6-48, you'll see that after the `FordModelT` type name, there's an empty argument list, meaning that there is a no-arguments primary constructor. Although this may seem redundant, without it, we wouldn't be allowed to write `Colorful("Black")` after the colon. (We could have written an ordinary constructor instead, but that would have been more verbose.)

Developers often ask: *How do I provide all the same constructors as my base class, just passing the arguments straight through?* As you've now seen, the answer is: *write all the constructors by hand.* There is no way to get the C# compiler to generate constructors in a derived class that look identical to the ones that the base class offers. You need to do it the long-winded way. At least Visual Studio, VS Code, or JetBrains Rider can generate the code for you—if you click on a class declaration, and then click the Quick Actions icon that appears, it will offer to generate constructors with the same arguments as any nonprivate constructor in the base class, automatically passing all the arguments through for you. Even with such help, this can become onerous, especially in types with large numbers of properties that require values during construction.

Mandatory Properties

If a type defines properties that must always be supplied with values during construction, it can enforce this by defining one or more constructors that require their values as arguments. But as you saw in Chapter 3, C# 11.0 introduced an alternative: if we use the `required` keyword in a property declaration, this indicates that the property must be set even though there's no corresponding constructor argument. (We set it with the object initializer syntax.) The `required` keyword can be particularly useful when using inheritance because it can save us from repeating constructor parameter lists over and over. Example 6-50 shows how that sort of problem can start.

Example 6-50. Inheriting mandatory properties set with a constructor

```
public record PropertiesInCtor(int Id, string Name, double Width);

public record MoreCtorProps(int Id, string Name, double Width, int X)
    : PropertiesInCtor(Id, Name, Width);

public record YetMore(int Id, string Name, double Width, int X, int Y)
    : MoreCtorProps(Id, Name, Width, X);

public record EvenMore(int Id, string Name, double Width, int X, int Y, int Z)
    : YetMore(Id, Name, Width, X, Y);
```

This is an inheritance hierarchy with four types. (I'm using records because they provide the easiest way to define a type with properties that must be supplied to a constructor. A `class` can have same problem; it would just be a larger example.) As we get further down the inheritance chain, the constructor parameter list gets longer and longer because it has to include all of the base type's parameters, even though each derived type adds just one extra property. I've had to declare the base class's three arguments four times over, and then repeat their names another three times to pass them on to the base constructor—isn't inheritance supposed to help me avoid duplicating code? If the base `PropertiesInCtor` class had many more primary constructor arguments, this could become seriously inconvenient. Example 6-51 shows an alternative approach.

Example 6-51. Inheriting `required` properties

```
public record BaseWithManyRequiredProperties
{
    public required int Id { get; init; }
    public required string Name { get; init; }
    public required double Width { get; init; }
}

public record MoreRequiredProps : BaseWithManyRequiredProperties
```

```
{
    public required int X { get; init; }
}

public record YetMoreProps : MoreRequiredProps
{
    public required int Y { get; init; }
}

public record EvenMoreProps : MoreRequiredProps
{
    public required int Z { get; init; }
}
```

Admittedly, this has over twice as many lines of code, so you might not consider this to be an improvement. With this technique, you can't exploit record types' ability to generate properties automatically from a primary constructor (because we're trying to avoid constructors here). The upside is that the derived types no longer need to repeat the complete list of all properties. Constructors are inherited slightly differently from all other members, which is why we ended up repeating ourselves, but there's no such problem with properties. This wasn't a viable alternative before C# 11.0 added the `required` keyword because constructors used to be the only mechanism by which you could require particular properties to be supplied during construction. But now, if we construct an instance of `EvenMoreProps`, the compiler will report an error unless we write an object initializer that sets all five properties.

Even in this example, where the relatively small number of properties on the base types mean the benefits are offset by the verbosity of ordinary property syntax, this approach still offers another advantage. It is much easier to see that each derived type adds just a single new property. In a type hierarchy where base types have many more properties than this, the primary constructor syntax becomes increasingly unwieldy, because every derived type needs to repeat all of the base's parameters *twice* (once in its constructor parameter list, and again to pass them to the base constructor). You can rapidly reach a point where the ability to omit all of that means that even with the extra verbosity of explicit properties, `required` properties still end up looking more succinct overall.

Field Initialization

As Chapter 3 showed, a class's field initializers run before its constructor. The picture is more complicated once inheritance is involved, because there are multiple classes and multiple constructors. The easiest way to predict what will happen is to understand that although instance field initializers and constructors have separate syntax, C# ends up compiling all the initialization code for a particular class into the constructor. So a constructor performs the following steps: first, it runs field initializers specific to this class (so this step does not include base field initializers—the base class will take care of itself); next, it calls the base class constructor; and finally, it runs the body of the constructor. The upshot of this is that in a derived class, your instance field initializers will run before base class construction has occurred—not only before the base constructor body but even before the base's instance fields have been initialized. Example 6-52 illustrates this.

Example 6-52. Exploring construction order

```
public class BaseInit
{
    protected static int Init(string message)
    {
        Console.WriteLine(message);
        return 1;
    }

    private int b1 = Init("Base field b1");

    public BaseInit()
    {
        Init("Base constructor");
    }

    private int b2 = Init("Base field b2");
}

public class DerivedInit : BaseInit
{
    private int d1 = Init("Derived field d1");

    public DerivedInit()
    {
        Init("Derived constructor");
    }

    private int d2 = Init("Derived field d2");
}
```

I've put the field initializers on either side of the constructor just to show that their position relative to nonfield members is irrelevant. The order of the fields matters, but only with respect to one another. Constructing an instance of the DerivedInit class produces this output:

```
Derived field d1
Derived field d2
Base field b1
Base field b2
Base constructor
Derived constructor
```

This verifies that the derived type's field initializers run first, and then the base field initializers, followed by the base constructor body, and then finally the derived constructor body. In other words, although constructor bodies start with the base class, instance field initialization happens in reverse.

That's why you don't get to invoke instance methods in field initializers. Static methods are available, but instance methods are not, because the class is a long way from being ready. It could be problematic if one of the derived type's field initializers were able to invoke a method on the base class, because the base class has performed no initialization at all at that point—not only has its constructor body not run, but its field initializers haven't run either. If instance methods were available during this phase, we'd have to write all of our code to be very defensive, because we could not assume that our fields contain anything useful.

As you can see, the constructor bodies run relatively late in the process, which is why we are allowed to invoke methods from them. But there's still potential danger here. What if the base class defines a virtual method and invokes that method on itself in its constructor? If the derived type overrides that, we'll be invoking the method before the derived type's constructor body has run. (Its field initializers will have run at that point, though. In fact, this is the main reason field initializers run in what seems to be reverse order—it means that derived classes have a way of performing some initialization before the base class's constructor has a chance to invoke a virtual method.) If you're familiar with C++, you might hazard a guess that when the base constructor invokes a virtual method, it'll run the base implementation. But C# does it differently: a base class's constructor will invoke the derived class's override in that case. This is not necessarily a problem, and it can occasionally be useful, but it means you need to think carefully and document your assumptions clearly if you want your object to invoke virtual methods on itself during construction.

Record Types

When you define a record type (or you use the more explicit but functionally identical record class syntax), the resulting record type is, from the runtime's perspective, still a class. Record types can do most of the things that normal classes can—although they're typically all about the properties, you can add other members such as methods and constructors (either primary or conventional). And as you saw in Example 6-48, class-based records also support inheritance. (Since record struct types are value types, those do not support inheritance.)

There are some constraints on inheritance with record types. An ordinary class is not allowed to inherit from a record type—only record types can derive from record types. Similarly, a record type can inherit only from either another record type or the usual object base type. But within these constraints, inheritance with records works much as it does for classes.

When a record type defines a primary constructor, the compiler does a bit more work than it would for an ordinary class. Each constructor argument produces a property with the same name, and the compiler also generates a deconstructor. You are free to write an ordinary constructor in a record but you will no longer get either of these features. There's one inheritance scenario in which you might want deconstruction, but you won't be able to get the compiler to provide it for you. This happens when the base type has no primary constructor and defines a property explicitly. A derived type might want to make that mandatory by making it a constructor argument. You can do this, but you can't write a primary constructor, because primary constructors can only pass arguments to base constructors—they can't set base properties directly. You have to write the constructor in full, as Example 6-53 shows.

Example 6-53. Making an optional base property class positional

```
public abstract record OptionallyLabeled
{
    public string? Label { get; init; }
}

public record LabeledDemographic : OptionallyLabeled
{
    public LabeledDemographic(string label)
    {
        Label = label;
    }

    public void Deconstruct(out string? label) => label = Label;
}
```

Although this is not a primary constructor, it has a similar effect. The presence of the constructor in Example 6-53 will prevent the compiler from generating a default zero-argument constructor, meaning that code using LabeledDemographic will be obliged to provide the Label property during construction, just as if it had a primary constructor. You automatically get a deconstructor when a record type has a primary constructor, but I've had to write my own here. The compiler doesn't generate one because deconstruction ends up being a little odd when attempting to impose positional behavior in a type deriving from a nonpositional record (i.e., one without a primary constructor). The base class defines Label as optional, and even though we've defined a constructor that requires a non-null argument, it would be possible to follow the constructor with an object initializer that sets it back to null. (That would be weird but not illegal.) So our deconstructor ends up not quite matching our constructor—they specify different nullability.

Records, Inheritance, and the with Keyword

Chapter 3 showed how you can create modified copies of record types using a with expression. This builds a new instance that has all the same properties as the original except for any new property values you specify in the braces following the with keyword. This mechanism has been designed with inheritance in mind: the instance produced by the with keyword will always have the same type as its input, even in cases where the code is written in terms of the base type, like Example 6-54.

Example 6-54. Using with on a base record type

```
OptionallyLabeled Discount(OptionallyLabeled item)
{
    return item with
    {
        Label = "60% off!"
    };
}
```

This uses the abstract OptionallyLabeled record type from Example 6-53. We can call this passing in any concrete type derived from that abstract base. Example 6-55 calls it twice with two different types.

Example 6-55. Testing how with interacts with inheritance

```
Console.WriteLine(Discount(new OptionallyLabeledItem()));
Console.WriteLine(Discount(new Product("Sweater")));
```

Running that code produces this output:

```
OptionallyLabeledItem { Label = 60% off! }
Product { Label = 60% off!, Name = Sweater }
```

Console.WriteLine calls ToString on its input, and record types implement this by reporting their name and then their property values. So you can see from this that when the Discount method produced modified copies of its inputs, it successfully preserved the type. So even though Discount knows nothing about the Product record type or its Name property, when it created a copy with the new Label value, that Name property was correctly carried over.

This works because of code that the compiler generates for record types. I already described the copy constructor in Chapter 3, but that alone would not make this possible—the Discount method doesn't know about the OptionallyLabeledItem or Product types, so it wouldn't know to invoke their copy constructors. So records also get a hidden virtual method with an unspeakable name, <Clone>$. The with expression in Example 6-54 invokes this (before going on to set the Label property). The compiler-generated `<Clone>$` method invokes its own copy constructor. Since derived record types override `<Clone>$`, a `with` expression will always get a full copy of the input record no matter what its type is, even when the code is written in terms of a base type.

Special Base Types

The .NET runtime libraries define a few base types that have special significance in C#. The most obvious is `System.Object`, which I've already described in some detail.

There's also `System.ValueType`. This is the abstract base type of all value types, so any `struct` or `record struct` you define—and also all of the built-in value types, such as `int` and `bool`—derive from `ValueType`. Ironically, `ValueType` itself is a reference type; only types that derive from `ValueType` are value types. Like most types, `ValueType` derives from `System.Object`. There is an obvious conceptual difficulty here: in general, derived classes are everything their base class is, plus whatever functionality they add. So, given that `object` and `ValueType` are both reference types, it may seem odd that types derived from `ValueType` are not. And for that matter, it's not obvious how an `object` variable can hold a reference to an instance of something that's not a reference type. I will resolve all of these issues in Chapter 7.

C# does not permit you to write a type that derives explicitly from `ValueType`. If you want to write a type that derives from `ValueType`, that's what the `struct` keyword is for. You can declare a variable of type `ValueType`, but since the type doesn't define any public members, a `ValueType` reference doesn't enable anything you can't do with an `object` reference. The only observable difference is that with a variable of that type, you can assign instances of any value type into it but not instances of a reference type. Aside from that, it's identical to `object`. Consequently, it's fairly rare to see `ValueType` mentioned explicitly in C# code.

Enumeration types also all derive from a common abstract base type: `System.Enum`. Since enums are value types, you won't be surprised to find out that `Enum` derives from `ValueType`. As with `ValueType`, you would never derive from `Enum` explicitly—you use the `enum` keyword for that. Unlike `ValueType`, `Enum` does add some useful members. For example, its static `GetValues` method returns an array of all the enumeration's values, while `GetNames` returns an array with all those values converted to strings. It also offers `Parse`, which converts from the string representation back to the enumeration value.

As Chapter 5 described, arrays all derive from a common base class, `System.Array`, and you've already seen the features that offers.

The `System.Exception` base class is special: when you throw an exception, C# requires that the object you throw be of this type or a type that derives from it. (Exceptions are the topic of Chapter 8.)

Delegate types all derive from a common base type, `System.MulticastDelegate`, which in turn derives from `System.Delegate`. I'll discuss these in Chapter 9.

Those are all the base types that the CTS treats as being special. There's one more base type to which the C# compiler assigns particular significance, and that's `System.Attribute`. In Chapter 1, I applied certain annotations to methods and classes to tell the unit test framework to treat them specially. These attributes all correspond to types, so when I applied the `[TestClass]` attribute to a class, I was using a type called `TestClassAttribute`. Types designed to be used as attributes are all required to derive from `System.Attribute`. Some of them are recognized by the compiler—for example, there are some that control the version numbers that the compiler puts into the file headers of the EXE and DLL files it produces. In Chapter 14 I'll show all of this.

Summary

C# supports single implementation inheritance, and only with classes or reference type records—you cannot derive from a struct at all. However, interfaces can declare multiple bases, and a class can implement multiple interfaces. Implicit reference conversions exist from derived types to base types, and generic interfaces and delegates can choose to offer additional implicit reference conversions using either covariance or contravariance. All types derive from `System.Object`, guaranteeing that certain standard members are available on all variables. We saw how virtual methods allow derived classes to modify selected members of their bases, and how sealing can disable that. We also looked at the relationship between a derived type and its base when it comes to accessing members, and constructors in particular.

Our exploration of inheritance is complete, but it has raised some new issues, such as the relationship between value types and references and the role of finalizers. So, in the next chapter, I'll talk about the connection between references and an object's life cycle, along with the way the CLR bridges the gap between references and value types.

CHAPTER 7

Object Lifetime

One benefit of .NET's managed execution model is that the runtime can automate most of your application's memory management. I have shown numerous examples that create objects with the new keyword, and none has explicitly freed the memory consumed by these objects.

In most cases, you do not need to take any action to reclaim memory. The runtime provides a *garbage collector* (GC),[1] a mechanism that automatically discovers when objects are no longer in use and recovers the memory they had been occupying so that it can be used for new objects. However, there are certain usage patterns that can cause performance issues or even defeat the GC entirely, so it's useful to understand how it works. This is particularly important with long-running processes that could run for days (short-lived processes may be able to tolerate a few memory leaks).

The GC is designed to manage memory efficiently, but memory is not the only limited resource you may need to deal with. Some things have a small memory footprint in the CLR but represent something relatively expensive, such as a database connection or a handle from an OS API. The GC doesn't always deal with these effectively, so I'll explain IDisposable, the interface designed for dealing with things that need to be freed more urgently than memory.

Value types often have completely different rules governing their lifetime—some local variable values live only for as long as their containing method runs, for example. Nonetheless, value types sometimes end up acting like reference types and being managed by the GC. I will discuss why that can be useful, and I will explain the *boxing* mechanism that makes it possible.

---

1 The acronym GC is used throughout this chapter to refer to both the *garbage collector* mechanism and also *garbage collection*, which is what the garbage collector does.

Garbage Collection

The CLR maintains a *heap*, a service that provides memory for the objects and values whose lifetime is managed by the GC. Each time you construct an instance of a class with new, or you create a new array object, the CLR allocates a new heap block. The GC decides when to deallocate that block.

 If you are writing a .NET application that runs on an Android device using .NET's Xamarin tools, there will be two garbage collected heaps: one for .NET and one for Java. Normal C# activity in Xamarin applications uses the .NET heap, so Java's heap only enters the picture if you write C# code that uses Xamarin's services for manipulating Java objects. This is a .NET book, so I will be focusing on the .NET GC.

A heap block contains all the nonstatic fields for an object, or all the elements if it's an array. The CLR also adds a header, which is not directly visible to your program. This includes a pointer to a structure describing the object's type. This supports operations that depend on the real type of an object. For example, if you call GetType on a reference, the runtime uses this pointer to find out the type. (The type is often not completely determined by the static type of the reference, which could be an interface type or a base class of the actual type.) It's also used to work out which method to use when you invoke a virtual method or an interface member. The CLR also uses this to know how large the heap block is—the header does not include the block size, because the runtime can work that out from the object's type. (Most types are fixed size. There are only two exceptions, strings and arrays, which the CLR handles as special cases.) The header contains one other field, which is used for a variety of diverse purposes, including multithreaded synchronization and default hash code generation. Heap block headers are just an implementation detail, and different runtimes could choose different strategies.[2] However, it's useful to know what the overhead is. On a 32-bit system, the header is 8 bytes long, and if you're running in a 64-bit process, it takes 16 bytes. So an object that contained just one field of type double (an 8-byte type) would consume 16 bytes in a 32-bit process, and 24 bytes in a 64-bit process.

Although objects (i.e., instances of a class) always live on the heap, instances of value types are different: some live on the heap, and some don't.[3] The CLR stores some value-typed local variables on the stack, for example, but if the value is in an instance

---

2 The Mono runtime's GC shares no code with the .NET GC, even though both now live in the same GitHub repository. Nonetheless, they both use the same approach here.

3 Value types defined with ref struct are an exception: they always live on the stack. Chapter 18 discusses these.

field of a class, the class instance will live on the heap, and that value will therefore live inside that object on the heap. And in some cases, a value will have an entire heap block to itself.

If you're using something through a reference type variable, then you are accessing something on the heap. It's important to clarify exactly what I mean by a reference type variable, because unfortunately, the terminology is a little confusing here: C# uses the term *reference* to describe two quite different things. For the purposes of this discussion, a reference is something you can store in a variable of a type that derives from `object` (but not from `ValueType`) or that is an interface type. This does not include every `in`-, `out`-, or `ref`-style method argument, nor `ref` variables or returns. Although those are references of a kind, a `ref int` argument is a reference to a value type, and that's not the same thing as a reference type. (The CLR actually uses a different term than C# for the mechanism that supports `ref`, `in`, and `out`: it calls these *managed pointers*, making it clear that they are rather different from object references.)

The managed execution model used by C# (and all .NET languages) means the CLR knows about every heap block your code creates, and also about every field, variable, and array element in which your program stores references. This information enables the runtime to determine at any time which objects are *reachable*—that is, those that the program could conceivably get access to in order to use its fields and other members. If an object is not reachable, then by definition the program will never be able to use it again. To illustrate how the CLR determines reachability, I've written a simple method, shown in Example 7-1, that fetches web pages from my employer's website. (This is just meant to illustrate GC behavior, so it is slightly unrealistic: as explained in "Optional Disposal" on page 395, you wouldn't normally create a new `HttpClient` for each request.)

Example 7-1. Using and discarding objects

```
public static string FetchUrl(string relativeUri)
{
    var baseUri = new Uri("https://endjin.com/");
    var fullUri = new Uri(baseUri, relativeUri);
    var w = new HttpClient();
    HttpResponseMessage response = w.Send(
        new HttpRequestMessage(HttpMethod.Get, fullUri));
    return new StreamReader(response.Content.ReadAsStream()).ReadToEnd();
}
```

The CLR analyzes the way in which we use local variables and method arguments. For example, although the `relativeUri` argument is in scope for the whole method, we use it just once as an argument when constructing the second `Uri` and then never use it again. A variable is described as *live* from the first point at which it receives a value up until the last point at which it is used. Method arguments are live from the start of the method until their final usage, unless they are unused, in which case they are never live. Local variables become live later; baseUri becomes live once it has been assigned its initial value and then ceases to be live with its final usage, which in this example, happens at the same point as relativeUri. Liveness is an important property in determining whether a particular object is still in use.

To see the role that liveness plays, suppose that when Example 7-1 reaches the line that constructs the HttpClient, the CLR doesn't have enough free memory to hold the new object. It could request more memory from the OS at this point, but it also has the option to try to free up memory from objects that are no longer in use, meaning that our program wouldn't need to consume more memory than it's already using.[4] The next section describes the process that the CLR uses when it takes that second option.

Determining Reachability

.NET's basic approach is to determine which of the objects on the heap are reachable. If there's no way for a program to get hold of some object, it can safely be discarded. The CLR starts by determining all of the *root references* in your program. A *root* is a storage location, such as a local variable, that could contain a reference and is known to have been initialized, and that your program could use at some point in the future without needing to go via some other object reference. Not all storage locations are considered to be roots. If an object contains an instance field of some reference type, that field is not a root, because before you can use it, you'd need to get hold of a reference to the containing object, and it's possible that the object itself is not reachable. However, a reference type static field is a root reference, because the program can read the value in that field at any time—the only situation in which that field will become inaccessible in the future is when the component that defines the type is unloaded, which in most cases will be when the program exits.

Local variables and method arguments are more interesting. Sometimes they are roots but sometimes not. It depends on exactly which part of the method is currently executing. A local variable or argument can be a root only if the flow of execution is currently inside the region in which that variable or argument is live. So, in Example 7-1, baseUri is a root reference only after it has had its initial value assigned and before the call to construct the second Uri, which is a rather narrow window. The fullUri variable is a root reference for slightly longer, because it becomes live after receiving its initial value and continues to be live during the construction of the

---

4 The CLR doesn't always wait until it runs out of memory. I will discuss the details later. For now, the important point is that from time to time, it will try to free up some space.

`HttpClient` on the following line; its liveness ends only once `HttpRequestMessage` constructor has been called.

 When a variable's last use is as an argument in a method or constructor invocation, it ceases to be live when the method call begins. At that point, the method being called takes over—its own arguments are live at the start (except for arguments it does not use). However, they will typically cease to be live before the method returns. This means that in Example 7-1, the object referred to by `fullUri` may cease to be accessible through root references before the `HttpRequestMessage` constructor returns.

Since the set of live variables changes as the program executes, the set of root references also evolves. To guarantee correct behavior in the face of this moving target, the CLR can suspend all threads that are running managed code when necessary during garbage collection.

Live variables and static fields are not the only kinds of roots. Evaluation of expressions sometimes creates temporary objects, which need to stay alive for as long as necessary to complete the evaluation, so there can be some root references that don't correspond directly to any named entities in your code. And there are other types of root. For example, the `GCHandle` class lets you create new roots explicitly, which can be useful in interop scenarios to enable some unmanaged code to get access to a particular object. There are also situations in which roots are created implicitly. Certain kinds of applications can interoperate with non-.NET object-based systems (e.g., COM in Windows applications, or Java on Android), which can establish root references without explicit use of `GCHandle`—if the CLR needs to generate a wrapper making one of your .NET objects available to some other runtime, that wrapper will effectively be a root reference. Calls into unmanaged code may also involve passing pointers to memory on the heap, which will mean that the relevant heap block needs to be treated as reachable for the duration of the call. The broad principle is that roots will exist where necessary to ensure that objects that are still in use remain reachable.

Having built up a complete list of current root references for all threads, the GC works out which objects can be reached from these references. It looks at each reference in turn, and if non-null, the GC knows that the object it refers to is reachable. There may be duplicates—multiple roots may refer to the same object, so the GC keeps track of which objects it has already seen. For each newly discovered object, the GC adds all of the instance fields of reference type in that object to the list of references it needs to look at, again discarding duplicates. (This includes hidden fields generated by the compiler, such as those for automatic properties, which I described in Chapter 3.) It does the same for each element of any reference-typed arrays it discovers. This means that if an object is reachable, so are all the objects to which it holds references. The GC repeats this process until it runs out of new references to examine. Any objects that it has *not* discovered to be reachable must be unreachable, because the GC is simply doing what the program does: a program can use only objects that are accessible either directly or indirectly through its variables, temporary local storage, static fields, and other roots.

Going back to Example 7-1, what would all this mean if the CLR decides to run the GC when we construct the HttpClient? The fullUri variable is still live, so the Uri it refers to is reachable, but the baseUri is no longer live. We did pass a copy of baseUri into the constructor for the second Uri, and if that had stored a copy of the reference in a field, then it wouldn't matter that baseUri is not live; as long as there's some way to get to an object by starting from a root reference, then the object is reachable. But as it happens, the second Uri won't do that, so the first Uri the example allocates would be deemed to be unreachable, and the CLR would be free to recover the memory it had been using.

One important upshot of how reachability is determined is that the GC is unfazed by circular references. This is one reason .NET uses GC instead of reference counting (another popular approach for automating memory management). If you have two objects that refer to each other, a reference counting scheme will consider both objects to be in use, because each is referred to at least once. But the objects may be unreachable—if there are no other references to the objects, the application will not have any way to use them. Reference counting fails to detect this, so it could cause memory leaks, but with the scheme used by the CLR's GC, the fact that they refer to each other is irrelevant—the GC will never get to either of them, so it will correctly determine that they are no longer in use.

Accidentally Defeating the Garbage Collector

Although the GC can discover ways that your program could reach an object, it has no way to prove that it necessarily will. Take the impressively idiotic piece of code in Example 7-2. Although you'd never write code this bad, it makes a common mistake. It's a problem that usually crops up in more subtle ways, but I want to show it in a more obvious example first. Once I've shown how it prevents the GC from freeing objects that we're not going to be using, I'll describe a less straightforward but more realistic scenario in which this same problem often occurs.

Example 7-2. An appallingly inefficient piece of code

```
static void Main()
{
    var numbers = new List<string>();
    long total = 0;
    for (int i = 1; i < 100_000; ++i)
    {
```

```
        numbers.Add(i.ToString());
        total += i;
    }
    Console.WriteLine("Total: {total}, average: {total / numbers.Count}");
}
```

This adds together the numbers from 1 to 100,000 and then displays their average. The first mistake here is that we don't even need to do the addition in a loop, because there's a simple and very well-known closed-form solution for this sort of sum: n*(n+1)/2, with n being 100,000 in this case. That mathematical gaffe notwithstanding, this code does something even more stupid: it builds up a list containing every number it adds, but all it does with that list is retrieve its Count property to calculate an average at the end. Just to make things worse, the code converts each number into a string before putting it in the list. It never actually uses those strings. (I've shown the Main method declaration here to make it clear that numbers isn't used later on.) Obviously, this is a contrived example. Real examples of this kind of mistake tend to be better obfuscated. The purpose of this example is to show how you can run into a limitation of the GC.

Suppose the loop in Example 7-2 has been running for a while—perhaps it's on its 90,000th iteration and is trying to add an entry to the numbers list. Suppose that the List<string> has used up its spare capacity, and the Add method will therefore need to allocate a new, larger internal array. The CLR may decide at this point to run the GC to see if it can free up some space. What will happen?

Example 7-2 creates three kinds of objects: it constructs a List<string> at the start, it creates a new string each time around the loop by calling ToString() on an int, and more subtly, the List<string> will allocate a string[] to hold references to those strings. Because we keep adding new items, it will have to allocate larger and larger arrays. (That array is an implementation detail of List<string>, so we can't see it directly.) So the question is: Which of these objects can the GC discard to make space for a larger array in the call to Add?

Our numbers variable remains live until the program's final statement, and we're looking at an earlier point in the code, so the List<string> object it refers to is reachable. The string[] array object it is currently using must also be reachable: it's allocating a newer, larger one, but it will need to copy the contents of the old one across to the new one, so the list must still have a reference to that current array stored in one of its fields. Since that array is still reachable, every string the array refers to will also be reachable. Our program has created 90,000 strings so far, and the GC will find all of them by starting at our numbers variable, looking at the fields of the List<string> object that refers to, and then looking at every element in the array that one of the list's private fields refers to.

The only allocated items that the GC might be able to collect are old `string[]` arrays that the `List<string>` created back when the list was smaller and that it no longer has a reference to. By the time we've added 90,000 items, the list will probably have resized itself quite a few times. So depending on when the GC last ran, it will probably be able to find a few of these now-unused arrays. But more interesting here is what it cannot free.

The program will never use any of the 90,000 strings it has created, so ideally, we'd like the GC to free up the memory they occupy—they will be taking up a few megabytes. We can see very easily that these strings are not used, because this is such a short program. But the GC will not know that; it bases its decisions on reachability, and it correctly determines that all 90,000 strings are reachable by starting at the `num bers` variable. And as far as the GC is concerned, it's entirely possible that the list's `Count` property, which we use after the loop finishes, will look at the contents of the list.

You and I happen to know that it won't, because it doesn't need to, but that's because we know what the `Count` property means. For the GC to infer that our program will never use any of the list's elements directly or indirectly, it would need to know what `List<string>` does inside its `Add` and `Count` methods. This would mean analysis with a level of detail far beyond the mechanisms I've described, which could make GCs considerably more expensive. Moreover, even with the serious step up in complexity required to detect which reachable objects this example will never use, in more realistic scenarios the GC is unlikely to be able to make predictions that were significantly better than relying on reachability alone.

For example, a much more plausible way to run into this problem is in a cache. If you write a class that caches data that is expensive to fetch or calculate, imagine what would happen if your code only ever added items to the cache and never removed them. All of the cached data would be reachable for as long as the cache object itself is reachable. The problem is that your cache will consume more and more space, and unless your computer has sufficient memory to hold every piece of data that your program could conceivably need to use, it will eventually run out of memory.

A naive developer might complain that this is supposed to be the GC's problem. The whole point of GC is meant to be that I don't need to think about memory management, so why am I running out of memory all of a sudden? But, of course, the problem is that the GC has no way of knowing which objects are safe to remove.

Not being clairvoyant, it cannot accurately predict which cached items your program may need in the future—if the code is running in a server, future cache usage could depend on what requests the server receives, something the GC cannot predict. So although it's possible to imagine memory management smart enough to analyze something as simple as Example 7-2, in general, this is not a problem the GC can solve. Thus, if you add objects to collections and keep those collections reachable, the

GC will treat everything in those collections as being reachable. It's your job to decide when to remove items.

Collections are not the only mechanism where certain usage patterns can mislead the GC. As I'll show in Chapter 9, there's a common scenario in which careless use of events can cause memory leaks. More generally, if your program makes it possible for an object to be reached, the GC has no way of working out whether you're going to use that object again, so it has to be conservative.

That said, there is a technique for mitigating this with a little help from the GC.

Weak References

Although the GC will follow ordinary references in a reachable object's fields, it is possible to hold a *weak reference*. The GC does not follow weak references, so if the only way to reach an object is through weak references, the GC behaves as though the object is not reachable and will remove it. A weak reference provides a way of telling the CLR, "Do not keep this object around on my account, but for as long as something else needs it, I would like to be able to get access to it." Example 7-3 shows a cache that uses WeakReference<T>.

Example 7-3. Using weak references in a cache

```
public class WeakCache<TKey, TValue>
    where TKey : notnull
    where TValue : class
{
    private readonly Dictionary<TKey, WeakReference<TValue>> _cache = new();

    public void Add(TKey key, TValue value)
    {
        _cache.Add(key, new WeakReference<TValue>(value));
    }

    public bool TryGetValue(
        TKey key, [NotNullWhen(true)] out TValue? cachedItem)
    {
        if (_cache.TryGetValue(key, out WeakReference<TValue>? entry))
        {
            bool isAlive = entry.TryGetTarget(out cachedItem);
            if (!isAlive)
            {
                _cache.Remove(key);
            }
            return isAlive;
        }
        else
        {
            cachedItem = null;
```

```
            return false;
        }
    }
}
```

This cache stores all values via a WeakReference<T>. Its Add method passes the object to which we'd like a weak reference as the constructor argument for a new WeakReference<T>. The TryGetValue method attempts to retrieve a value previously stored with Add. It first checks to see if the dictionary contains a relevant entry. If it does, that entry's value will be the WeakReference<T> we created earlier. My code calls that weak reference's TryGetTarget method, which will return true if the object is still available and false if it has been collected.

 Availability doesn't necessarily imply reachability. The object may have become unreachable since the most recent GC. Or there may not even have been a GC since the object was allocated. TryGet Target can tell you only whether the GC has detected that it is eligible for collection.

If the object is available, TryGetTarget provides it through an out parameter, and this will be a strong reference. So, if this method returns true, we don't need to worry about any race condition in which the object becomes unreachable moments later—the fact that we've now stored that reference in the variable the caller supplied via the cachedItem argument will keep the target alive. If TryGetTarget returns false, my code removes the relevant entry from the dictionary, because it represents an object that no longer exists. That's important because although a weak reference won't keep its target alive, the WeakReference<T> is an object in its own right, and the GC can't free it until I've removed it from this dictionary. (In real application code you would also want to scan the whole dictionary periodically to remove all such entries instead of just checking individual entries only when something asks for them.) Example 7-4 tries this code out, forcing a couple of garbage collections so we can see it in action. (This splits each stage into separate methods with inlining disabled because otherwise, .NET's JIT compiler will inline these methods, and it ends up creating hidden temporary variables that can cause the array to remain reachable longer than it should, distorting the results of this test.)

Example 7-4. Exercising the weak cache

```
internal class Program
{
    private static readonly WeakCache<string, byte[]> cache = new();
    private static byte[]? data = new byte[100];

    private static void Main(string[] args)
```

```
{
    AddData();
    CheckStillAvailable();

    GC.Collect();
    CheckStillAvailable();

    SetOnlyRootToNull();
    GC.Collect();
    CheckNoLongerAvailable();
}

[MethodImpl(MethodImplOptions.NoInlining)]
private static void AddData()
{
    cache.Add("d", data!);
}

[MethodImpl(MethodImplOptions.NoInlining)]
private static void CheckStillAvailable()
{
    Console.WriteLine("Retrieval: " +
        cache.TryGetValue("d", out byte[]? fromCache));
    Console.WriteLine("Same ref?  " +
        object.ReferenceEquals(data, fromCache));
}

[MethodImpl(MethodImplOptions.NoInlining)]
private static void SetOnlyRootToNull()
{
    data = null;
}

[MethodImpl(MethodImplOptions.NoInlining)]
private static void CheckNoLongerAvailable()
{
    byte[]? fromCache;
    Console.WriteLine("Retrieval: " + cache.TryGetValue("d", out fromCache));
    Console.WriteLine("Null?  " + (fromCache == null));
}
}
```

This begins by adding a reference to a 100-byte array to the cache. It also stores a reference to the same array in a static field called data, keeping the array reachable until the code calls SetOnlyRootToNull, which sets data to null. The example tries to retrieve the value from the cache immediately after adding it and also uses object.ReferenceEquals just to check that the value we get back really refers to the same object that we put in. Then I force a garbage collection and try again. (This sort of artificial test code is one of the few situations in which you'd want to do this—see the section "Forcing Garbage Collections" on page 383.) Since the data field still holds a reference to the array, the array is still reachable, so we would expect the value still to be available from the cache. Next I set `data` to `null`, so my code is no longer keeping that array reachable. The only remaining reference is a weak one, so when I force another GC, we expect the array to be collected and the final lookup in the cache to fail. To verify this, I check both the return value, expecting `false`, and the value returned through the `out` parameter, which should be `null`. And that is exactly what happens when I run the program, as you can see:

```
Retrieval: True
Same ref?  True
Retrieval: True
Same ref?  True
Retrieval: False
Null?  True
```

 Writing code to illustrate GC behavior means entering treacherous territory. The principles of operation remain the same, but the exact behavior of small examples changes over time, often due to optimizations performed during JIT compilation. It's entirely possible that if you try these examples, you might see different behavior due to changes in the runtime since going to press.

Later, I will describe finalization, which complicates matters by introducing a twilight zone in which the object has been determined to be unreachable but has not yet gone. Objects that are in this state are typically of little use, so by default, a weak reference will treat objects waiting for finalization as though they have already gone. This is called a *short weak reference*. If, for some reason, you need to know whether an object has really gone (rather than merely being on its way out), the `WeakReference<T>` class's constructor has overloads, some of which can create a *long weak reference*, which provides access to the object even in this zone between unreachability and final removal.

Reclaiming Memory

So far, I've described how the CLR determines which objects are no longer in use but not what happens next. Having identified the garbage, the runtime must then collect it. The CLR uses different strategies for small and large objects. (By default, the .NET CLR defines a large object as one bigger than 85,000 bytes. Mono sets the bar lower at 8,000 bytes.) Most allocations involve small objects, so I'll write about those first.

The CLR tries to keep the heap's free space contiguous. That's easy when the application first starts up, because there's nothing but free space, and it can keep things contiguous by allocating memory for each new object directly after the last one. But after the first GC occurs, the heap is unlikely to look so neat. Most objects have short lifetimes, and it's common for the majority of objects allocated after any one GC to be unreachable by the time the next GC runs. However, some will still be in use. From time to time, applications create objects that hang around for longer, and whatever work was in progress when the GC ran will probably be using some objects, so the most recently allocated heap blocks are likely still to be in use. This means that the end of the heap might look something like Figure 7-1, where the shaded rectangles are the reachable blocks, and the white ones show blocks that are no longer in use.

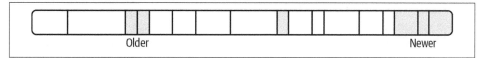

Figure 7-1. Section of heap with some reachable objects

One possible allocation strategy would be to start using these empty blocks as new memory is required, but there are a couple of problems with that approach. First, it tends to be wasteful, because the blocks the application requires will probably not fit precisely into the holes available. Second, finding a suitable empty block can be somewhat expensive, particularly if there are lots of gaps and you're trying to pick one that will minimize waste. It's not impossibly expensive, of course—lots of heaps work this way—but it's a lot costlier than the initial situation where each new block could be allocated directly after the last one because all the spare space was contiguous. The expense of heap fragmentation is nontrivial, so the CLR typically tries to get the heap back into a state where the free space is contiguous. As Figure 7-2 shows, it moves all the reachable objects toward the start of the heap so that all the free space is at the end, which puts it back in the favorable situation of being able to allocate new heap blocks one after another in the contiguous lump of free space.

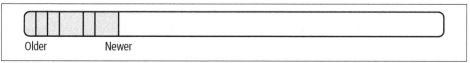

Figure 7-2. Section of heap after compaction

The runtime has to ensure that references to these relocated blocks continue to work after the blocks have moved. The CLR happens to implement references as pointers (although nothing requires this—a reference is just a value that identifies some particular instance on the heap). It already knows where all the references to any particular block are because it had to find them to discover which blocks were reachable. It adjusts all these pointers when it moves the block.

Besides making heap block allocation a relatively cheap operation, compaction offers another performance benefit. Because blocks are allocated into a contiguous area of free space, objects that were created in quick succession will typically end up right next to each other in the heap. This is significant, because the caches in modern CPUs tend to favor locality (i.e., they perform best when related pieces of data are stored close together).

The low cost of allocation and the high likelihood of good locality can sometimes mean that garbage-collected heaps offer better performance than traditional heaps that require the program to free memory explicitly. This may seem surprising, given that the GC appears to do a lot of extra work that is unnecessary in a noncollecting heap. Some of that "extra" work is nothing of the sort, however—something has to keep track of which objects are in use, and traditional heaps just push that house-keeping overhead into our code. However, relocating existing memory blocks comes at a price, so the CLR uses some tricks to minimize the amount of copying it needs to do.

The older an object is, the more expensive it will be for the CLR to compact the heap once it finally becomes unreachable. If the most recently allocated object is unreachable when the GC runs, compaction is free for that object: there are no more objects after it, so nothing needs to be moved. Compare that with the first object your program allocates—if that becomes unreachable, compaction would mean moving every reachable object on the heap. More generally, the older an object is, the more objects will be put after it, so the more data will need to be moved to compact the heap. Copying 20 MB of data to save 20 bytes does not sound like a great trade-off. So the CLR will often defer compaction for older parts of the heap.

To decide what counts as "old," the .NET runtime divides the heap into *generations*.[5] The boundaries between generations move around at each GC, because generations are defined in terms of how many GCs an object has survived. Any object allocated after the most recent GC is in generation 0, because it has not yet survived any collections. When the GC next runs, generation 0 objects that are still reachable will be moved as necessary to compact the heap and will then be deemed to be in generation 1.

Objects in generation 1 are not yet considered to be old. A GC will typically occur while the code is right in the middle of doing things—after all, it runs when space on the heap is being used up, and that won't happen if the program is idle. So there's a high chance that some of the recently allocated objects represent work in progress, and although they are currently reachable, they will become unreachable shortly. Generation 1 acts as a sort of holding zone while we wait to see which objects are short-lived and which are longer-lived.

As the program continues to execute, the GC will run from time to time, promoting new, surviving objects into generation 1. Some of the objects in generation 1 will

---

5 The Mono runtime uses a slightly simpler scheme, but it still relies on the basic principle of treating new and old objects differently.

become unreachable. However, the GC does not necessarily compact this part of the heap immediately—it may allow a few generation 0 collections and compactions in between each generation 1 compaction, but it will happen eventually. Objects that survive this stage are moved into generation 2, which is the oldest generation.

The CLR attempts to recover memory from generation 2 much less frequently than from other generations. Research shows that in most applications, objects that survive into generation 2 are likely to remain reachable for a long time, so when one of those objects does eventually become unreachable, it's likely to be very old, as will be the objects around it. This means that compacting this part of the heap to recover the memory is costly for two reasons: not only will this old object probably be followed by a large number of other objects (requiring a large volume of data to be copied), but also the memory it occupied might not have been used for a long time, meaning it's probably no longer in the CPU's cache, slowing down the copy even further. And the caching costs will continue after collection, because if the CPU has had to shift megabytes of data around in old areas of the heap, this will probably have the side effect of flushing other data out the CPU's cache. Cache sizes can be as small as 512 KB at the low-power, low-cost end of the spectrum, and can be over 90 MB in high-end, server-oriented chips, but in the midrange, anything from 2 MB to 16 MB of cache is typical, and many .NET applications' heaps will be larger than that. Most of the data the application had been using would have been in the cache right up until the generation 2 GC but would be gone once the GC has finished. So when the GC completes and normal execution resumes, the code will run in slow motion for a while until the data the application needs is loaded back into the cache.

Generations 0 and 1 are sometimes referred to as the *ephemeral* generations, because they mostly contain objects that exist only for a short while. (The part of Mono's heap that serves a similar purpose is called the *nursery*, because it's for young objects.) The contents of these parts of the heap will often be in the CPU's cache because they will have been accessed recently, so compaction is not particularly expensive for these sections. Moreover, because most objects have a short lifetime, the majority of memory that the GC is able to collect will be from objects in these first two generations, so these are likely to offer the greatest reward (in terms of memory recovered) in exchange for the CPU time expended. So it's common to see several ephemeral collections per second in a busy program, but it's also common for several minutes to elapse between successive generation 2 collections.

The CLR has another trick up its sleeve for generation 2 objects. They often don't change much, so there's a high likelihood that during the first phase of a GC—in which the runtime detects which objects are reachable—it would be repeating some work it did earlier, because it will follow exactly the same references and produce the same results for significant subsections of the heap. The CLR employs mechanisms to detect when older heap blocks are modified. This enables it to rely on summarized results from earlier GC operations instead of having to redo all of the work every time.

How does the GC decide whether to collect just from generation 0 or also from 1 or even 2? Collections for all three generations are triggered by using up a certain amount of memory. So, for generation 0 allocations, once you have allocated some particular number of bytes since the last GC, a new GC will occur. The objects that survive this will move into generation 1, and the CLR keeps track of the number of bytes added to generation 1 since the last generation 1 collection; if that number exceeds a threshold, generation 1 will be collected too. Generation 2 works in the same way. The thresholds are not documented, and in fact they're not even constant; the CLR monitors your allocation patterns and modifies these thresholds to try to find a good balance for making efficient use of memory, minimizing the CPU time spent in the GC and avoiding the excessive latency that could arise if the CLR waited a very long time between collections, leaving huge amounts of work to do when the collection finally occurs.

 This explains why, as mentioned earlier, the CLR doesn't necessarily wait until it has actually run out of memory before triggering a GC. It may be more efficient to run one sooner.

You may be wondering how much of the preceding information is of practical significance. After all, the bottom line would appear to be that the CLR ensures that heap blocks are kept around for as long as they are reachable, and that sometime after they become unreachable, it will eventually reclaim their memory, and it employs a strategy designed to do this efficiently. Are the details of this generational optimization scheme relevant to a developer? They are insofar as they tell us that some coding practices are likely to be more efficient than others.

The most obvious upshot of the process is that the more objects you allocate, the harder the GC will have to work. But you'd probably guess that without knowing anything about the implementation. More subtly, larger objects cause the GC to work harder—collections for each generation are triggered by the amount of memory your application uses. So bigger objects don't just increase memory pressure, they also end up consuming more CPU cycles as a result of triggering more frequent GCs.

Perhaps the most important fact to emerge from an understanding of the generational nature of the collector is that the length of an object's lifetime has an impact on how hard the GC must work. Objects that live for a very short time are handled efficiently, because the memory they use will be recovered quickly in a generation 0 or 1 collection, and the amount of data that needs to be moved to compact the heap will be small. Objects that live for an extremely long time are also OK, because they will end up in generation 2. They will not be moved about often, because collections are infrequent for that part of the heap. However, although very short-lived and very long-lived objects are handled efficiently, objects that live long enough to get into generation 2 but not much longer are a problem. Microsoft occasionally describes this occurrence as a *midlife crisis*.

If your application regularly creates lots of objects making it into generation 2 that go on to become unreachable, the CLR will need to perform collections on generation 2 more often than it otherwise might. (In fact, generation 2 is collected only during a *full collection*, which also collects free space previously used by large objects.) These are usually significantly more expensive than other collections. Compaction requires more work with older objects, but also, more housekeeping is required when disrupting the generation 2 heap. The picture the CLR has built up about reachability within this section of the heap may need to be rebuilt, which incurs a cost. There's a good chance that most of this part of the heap will not be in the CPU's cache either, so working with it can be slow.

Full GCs consume significantly more CPU time than collections in the ephemeral generations. In UI applications, this can cause delays long enough to be irritating for the user, particularly if parts of the heap had been paged out by the OS. In server applications, full collections may cause significant blips in the typical time taken to service a request. Such problems are not the end of the world, and as I'll describe later, the CLR offers some mechanisms to mitigate these kinds of issues. Even so, minimizing the number of objects that survive to generation 2 is good for performance. You would need to consider this when designing code that caches interesting data in memory—a cache aging policy that failed to take the GC's behavior into account could easily behave inefficiently, and if you didn't know about the perils of middle-aged objects, it would be hard to work out why. Also, as I'll show later in this chapter, the midlife crisis issue is one reason you might want to avoid C# destructors where possible.

I have left out some heap operational details, by the way. For example, I've not talked about how the GC typically dedicates sections of the address space to the heap in fixed-size chunks, nor the details of how it commits and releases memory. Interesting though these mechanisms are, they have much less relevance to how you design your code than an awareness of the assumptions that a generational GC makes about typical object lifetimes. The details also tend to change—recent releases of .NET have made significant modifications to the details of GC operation to improve performance, but the basic principles have remained the same.

There's one last thing to talk about on the topic of collecting memory from unreachable objects. As mentioned earlier, large objects work differently. There's a separate heap called, appropriately enough, the *large object heap* (LOH), and the .NET runtime uses this for any object larger than 85,000 bytes;[6] Mono's runtime uses an 8,000-byte threshold, because it is often used in more memory-constrained environments. That's just the object itself, not the sum total of all the memory an object allocates during construction. An instance of the GreedyObject class in Example 7-5 would be tiny—it needs only enough space for a single reference, plus the heap block overhead. In a 32-bit process, that would be 4 bytes for the reference and 8 bytes of overhead, and in a 64-bit process, it would be twice as large. However, the array to which it refers is 400,000 bytes long, so that would go on the LOH, while the GreedyObject itself would go on the ordinary heap.

Example 7-5. A small object with a large array

```
public class GreedyObject
{
    public int[] MyData = new int[100_000];
}
```

It's technically possible to create a class whose instances are large enough to require the LOH, but it's unlikely to happen outside of generated code or highly contrived examples. In practice, most LOH heap blocks will contain arrays and possibly strings.

The biggest difference between the LOH and the ordinary heap is that the GC does not usually compact the LOH, because copying large objects is expensive. (Applications can request that the LOH be compacted at the next full GC. But applications that do not explicitly request this will never have their LOH compacted in current CLR implementations.) It works more like a traditional C heap: the CLR maintains a list of free blocks and decides which block to use based on the size requested. However, the list of free blocks is populated by the same unreachability mechanism as is used by the rest of the heap.

Lightening the Load with Inline Arrays

The more objects we create, the more work the GC needs to do. C# 12.0 adds a new mechanism that can help us to allocate fewer objects. If we have written a type that always has an associated array (e.g., List<T> uses an array internally), that normally means that each instance of that type requires two allocations on the heap, one for itself and another for its array. However, in cases where the array always has the same number of elements, C# 12.0 gives us the option to define that as an *inline array*, meaning that the array elements can live inside another type's memory (just like a value-typed field) instead of requiring their own heap block.

---

6 .NET provides an application configuration setting that lets you change this threshold.

Inline arrays are intended for highly performance-sensitive scenarios. They add some complexity, they do not work on .NET Framework, and they are not as flexible as normal arrays. You should use them only in scenarios where performance profiling demonstrates that they make a useful difference.

To enable this capability without adding a whole new feature to the .NET type system, inline arrays are essentially just a particular kind of `struct`. It has always been possible to write code such as Example 7-6. Historically, performance-sensitive libraries have often used exactly this sort of type to avoid allocating small fixed-size arrays.

Example 7-6. Emulating fixed-size arrays before C# 12.0

```
public struct ThreeIntegersPseudoArray
{
    public int Element0;
    public int Element1;
    public int Element2;
}
```

The main problem with that approach is that it is cumbersome. We need to define a field for each "array" element. We can't use the normal array indexer syntax unless we define a custom indexer, and since we need to write a different type for each array size, we most likely won't want to write custom indexers for all of them.

C# 12.0's new inline array feature provides a better way to write this kind of type. The `ThreeIntegers` type shown in Example 7-7 serves the same purpose as the one in Example 7-6: because it is annotated with the `InlineArray(3)` attribute it will contain exactly three `int` values, and since it is a `struct`, it does not require its own heap block. I haven't had to declare all three elements explicitly. I have defined a single field, but in an inline array type this field doesn't exist at runtime—it is only there to indicate the element type. And this type automatically supports array indexer syntax.

Example 7-7. A fixed-size inline array type

```
[System.Runtime.CompilerServices.InlineArray(3)]
public struct ThreeIntegers
{
    private int _element0;
}
```

Example 7-8 declares a local variable of type `ThreeIntegers`. Since this is a value type, we don't need to use `new`—the `default` keyword here initializes all elements to zero. It won't need its own heap block. Where possible, the compiler will store these values on the stack as with any other value-typed local variables. And in cases where it can't do that (e.g., iterators or `async` methods), this variable would live inside the same heap-allocated type that holds all the other local variables, so we can use it without causing more allocations than would have happened in any case. If I declare a field of type `ThreeIntegers`, then just as with any other value type, its elements will live inside the containing type.

Example 7-8. Using a fixed-size inline array type

```
ThreeIntegers t = default;
t[0] += 1;
Console.WriteLine(t[0]);
Console.WriteLine(t[1] + t[2]);
```

It may seem odd to have to define a type for each different array size. You might be wondering why we don't apply the `InlineArray` attribute to a field instead. The downside with that approach is that it would have been a more disruptive change. It would either have required a change to the long-established fact that value types always have a fixed size, or it would have meant not using value types at all for this feature, and introducing some new way of embedding a value inside another type. So although it is a little cumbersome to have to define a distinct type for each array size, the big advantage is that it's a relatively small change to the type system—it's really just an easier way to do what people had already been doing for years with code like Example 7-6.

Garbage Collector Modes

Although the .NET runtime will tune some aspects of the GC's behavior at runtime (e.g., by dynamically adjusting the thresholds that trigger collections for each generation), it also offers a configurable choice between various modes designed to suit different kinds of applications. These fall into two broad categories—workstation and server, and then in each of these you can either use background or nonconcurrent collections. Background collection is on by default, but the default top-level mode depends on the project type: for console applications and applications using a GUI framework such as WPF, the GC runs in workstation mode, but ASP.NET Core web applications change this to server mode. You can control the GC mode explicitly by defining a `ServerGarbageCollection` property in your *.csproj* file, as Example 7-9 shows. This can go anywhere inside the root `Project` element.

Example 7-9. Enabling server GC in a project file

```
<PropertyGroup>
  <ServerGarbageCollection>true</ServerGarbageCollection>
</PropertyGroup>
```

This property makes the build system add a setting to the *YourApplication.runtimeconfig.json* file that it generates for your application. This contains a `configProperties` section, which can contain one or more *CLR host configuration knobs*. Enabling server GC in the project file sets the `System.GC.Server` knob to `true` in this configuration file. All GC settings are also controlled through configuration knobs, as are some other CLR behaviors, such as the JIT compiler mode.

The workstation modes are designed for the workloads that client-side code typically has to deal with, in which the process is usually working on either a single task or a small number of tasks at any one time. Workstation mode offers two variations: nonconcurrent and background.

In background mode (the default), the GC minimizes the amount of time for which it suspends threads during a GC. There are certain phases of the GC in which the CLR has to suspend execution to ensure consistency. For collections from the ephemeral generations, threads will be suspended for the majority of the operation. This is usually fine because these collections normally run very quickly. Full collections are the problem, and it's these that the background mode handles differently. Not all of the work done in a collection really needs to bring everything to a halt, and background mode exploits this, enabling full (generation 2) collections to proceed on a background thread without forcing other threads to block until that collection completes. This can enable machines with multiple processor cores (most machines, these days) to perform full GC collections on one core while other cores continue with productive work. It is especially useful in applications with a UI, because it reduces the likelihood of an application becoming unresponsive due to GCs.

The nonconcurrent mode is designed to optimize throughput on a single processor with a single core. It can be more efficient, because background GC uses slightly more memory and more CPU cycles for any particular workload than nonconcurrent GC in exchange for the lower latency. For some workloads, you may find your code runs faster if you set the `ConcurrentGarbageCollection` property to `false` in your project file. For most client-side code, the greatest concern is to avoid delays that are long enough to be visible to users. Users are more sensitive to unresponsiveness than they are to suboptimal average CPU utilization, so for interactive applications, using slightly more memory and CPU cycles in exchange for improved perceived performance is usually a good trade-off.

Server mode is significantly different than workstation mode. It is available only when you have multiple hardware threads; e.g., a multicore CPU or multiple physical CPUs. (If you have enabled server GC but your code ends up running on a single-core machine,[7] it falls back to using the workstation GC.) Its availability has nothing to do with which OS you're running, by the way—for example, server mode is available on nonserver and server editions of Windows alike if you have suitable hardware, and workstation mode is always available. Server mode is able to give each processor core its own section of the heap, so when a thread is working on its own problem independently of the rest of the process, it can allocate heap blocks with minimal contention. In server mode, the CLR creates several threads dedicated to GC, one for each logical CPU in the machine. These run with higher priority than normal threads, so when GCs do occur, all available CPU cores go to work on their own heaps, which can provide better throughput with large heaps than workstation mode.

 Objects created by one thread can still be accessed by others—logically, the heap is still a unified service. Server mode is just an implementation strategy optimized for workloads where each thread works on its own jobs mostly in isolation. Be aware that it works best if the jobs all have similar heap allocation patterns.

Until recently, these characteristics of server mode that enable it to make full use of a machine's resources could cause problems for some deployment models. If you have a server that does just one job, implemented as a single .NET process, you will want the available resources to be dedicated to that one process, so in these cases it's good that the GC tries to use all CPU cores simultaneously during collections, and that it has historically tended to be more eager to fully exploit the available memory than workstation mode. However, if a single server hosts a mix of workloads across multiple processes, you don't want them all acting that way, because contention for resources could reduce efficiency. .NET 8.0 made significant improvements in this area. It introduced a server GC feature called Dynamic Adaptation to Application Sizes (DATAS), in which server GC still makes full use of available resources if the application has high demands, but is more frugal when the usage doesn't justify this. This adaptation means that if a process has a highly variable workload, it can make full use of available resources during bursts of high activity, but when the load reduces it will relinquish these resources much sooner than in earlier .NET versions. It's now common practice to use container systems such as Docker to handle a mix of workloads efficiently on shared hardware, and this improved adaptability means server GC can now work better in those scenarios.

---

7 Rare though single-core CPUs are these days, it's still common to run in virtual machines that present only one core to the code they host. This is often the case if your application runs on a cloud-hosted service using a consumption-based tariff, for example.

DATAS is off by default. You can enable it by adding `<GarbageCollection AdaptationMode>1</GarbageCollectionAdaptationMode>` in a `PropertyGroup` in your *.csproj* file. This adds a `System.GC.DynamicAdaptationMode` property with a value of 1 to the `configProperties` section of your *.runtimeconfig.json* file.

Another feature of server GC is that it favors throughput over response time. In particular, collections happen less frequently, because this tends to increase the throughput benefits that multi-CPU collections can offer, but it also means that each individual collection takes longer.

As with workstation GC, the server GC uses background collection by default. In some cases, you may find you can improve throughput by disabling it, but be wary of the problems this can cause. The duration of a full collection in nonconcurrent server mode can cause serious delays in responsiveness on a website, for example, especially if the heap is large. You can mitigate this in a couple of ways. You can request notifications shortly before the collection occurs (using the `System.GC` class's `Register ForFullGCNotification`, `WaitForFullGCApproach`, and `WaitForFullGCComplete` methods), and if you have a server farm, a server that's running a full GC may be able to ask the load balancer to avoid passing it requests until the GC completes. The simpler alternative is to leave background collection enabled. Since background collections allow application threads to continue to run and even to perform generation 0 and 1 collections while the full collection proceeds in the background, it significantly improves the application's response time during collections while still delivering the throughput benefits of server mode.

Temporarily Suspending Garbage Collections

It is possible to ask .NET to disallow GC while a particular section of code runs. This is useful if you are performing time-sensitive work. Windows, macOS, and Linux are not real-time operating systems, so there are never any guarantees, but temporarily ruling out GCs at critical moments can nonetheless be useful for reducing the chances of things going slowly at the worst possible moment. Be aware that this mechanism works by bringing forward any GC work that might otherwise have happened in the relevant section of code, so this can cause GC-related delays to happen earlier than they otherwise would have. It only guarantees that once your designated region of code starts to run, there will be no further GCs if you meet certain requirements—in effect, it gets necessary delays out of the way before the time-sensitive work begins.

The `GC` class offers a `TryStartNoGCRegion` method, which you call to indicate that you want to begin some work that needs to be free from GC-related interruption. You must pass in a value indicating how much memory you will need during this work, and it will attempt to ensure that at least that much memory is available before proceeding (performing a GC to free up that space if necessary). If the method indicates success, then as long as you do not consume more memory than requested, your code will not be interrupted by the GC. You call `EndNoGCRegion` once you have finished the time-critical work, enabling the GC to return to its normal operation. If, before it calls `EndNoGCRegion`, your code uses more memory than you requested, the CLR may have to perform a GC, but it will only do so if it absolutely cannot avoid it until you call `EndNoGCRegion`.

Although the single-argument form of `TryStartNoGCRegion` will perform a full GC if necessary to meet your request, some overloads take a `bool`, enabling you to tell it that if a full blocking GC will be required to free up the necessary space, you'd prefer to abort. There are also overloads in which you can specify your memory requirements on the ordinary heap and the large object heap separately.

Accidentally Defeating Compaction

Heap compaction is an important feature of the CLR's GC, because it has a strong positive impact on performance. Certain operations can prevent compaction, and that's something you'll want to minimize, because fragmentation can increase memory use and reduce performance significantly.

To be able to compact the heap, the CLR needs to be able to move heap blocks around. Normally, it can do this because it knows all of the places in which your application refers to heap blocks, and it can adjust all the references when it relocates a block. But what if you're calling an OS API that works directly with the memory you provide? For example, if you read data from a file or a network socket, how will that interact with GC?

If you use system calls that read or write data using devices such as the hard drive or network interface, these normally work directly with your application's memory. If you read data from the disk, the OS may instruct the disk controller to put the bytes directly into the memory your application passed to the API. The OS will perform the necessary calculations to translate the virtual address into a physical address. (With virtual memory, the value your application puts in a pointer is only indirectly related to the actual address in your computer's RAM.) The OS will lock the pages into place for the duration of the I/O request to ensure that the physical address remains valid. It will then supply the disk system with that address. This enables the disk controller to copy data from the disk directly into memory, without needing further involvement from the CPU. This is very efficient but runs into problems when it encounters a compacting heap. What if the block of memory is a `byte[]` array on the heap? Suppose a GC occurs between us asking to read the data and the disk being able to supply the data. (The chances are fairly high; a mechanical disk with spinning platters can take 10 ms or more to start supplying data, which is an age in CPU terms.) If the GC decided to relocate our `byte[]` array to compact the heap, the physical memory address that the OS gave the disk controller would be out of date, so when the controller started putting data into memory, it would be writing to the wrong place.

There are three ways the CLR could deal with this. One would be to make the GC wait—heap relocations could be suspended while I/O operations are in progress. But that's a nonstarter in many scenarios; a busy server can run for days without ever entering a state in which no I/O operations are in progress. In fact, the server doesn't even need to be busy. It might allocate several byte[] arrays to hold the next few incoming network requests and would typically try to avoid getting into a state where it didn't have at least one such buffer available. The OS would have pointers to all of these and may well have supplied the network card with the corresponding physical address so that it can get to work the moment data starts to arrive. So even an idle server has certain buffers that cannot be relocated.

An alternative would be for the CLR to provide a separate nonmoving heap for these sorts of operations. Perhaps we could allocate a fixed block of memory for an I/O operation, and then copy the results into the byte[] array on the GC heap once the I/O has finished. But that's also not a brilliant solution. Copying data is expensive— the more copies you make of incoming or outgoing data, the slower your server will run, so you really want network and disk hardware to copy the data directly to or from its natural location. And if this hypothetical fixed heap were more than an implementation detail of the CLR—if it were available for application code to use directly to minimize copying—that might open the door to all the memory management bugs that GC is supposed to banish.

So the CLR uses a third approach: it selectively prevents heap block relocations. The GC is free to run while I/O operations are in progress, but certain heap blocks can be *pinned*. Pinning a block sets a flag that tells the GC that the block cannot currently be moved. So, if the GC encounters such a block, it will simply leave it where it is but will attempt to relocate everything around it.

There are five ways C# code normally causes heap blocks to be pinned. You can do so explicitly using the fixed keyword. This allows you to obtain a raw pointer to a storage location, such as a field or an array element, and the compiler will generate code that ensures that for as long as a fixed pointer is in scope, the heap block to which it refers will be pinned. A more common way to pin a block is through interop (i.e., calls into unmanaged code, such as an OS API). If you make an interop call to an API that requires a pointer to something, the CLR will detect when that points to a heap block, and it will automatically pin the block. By default, the CLR will unpin it automatically when the method returns. If you're calling an asynchronous API that will continue to use the memory after returning, you can use the GCHandle class mentioned earlier to pin a heap block until you explicitly unpin it; that's the third pinning technique.

The fourth and most common way to pin heap blocks is also the least direct: many runtime library APIs call unmanaged code on your behalf and will pin the arrays you pass in as a result. For example, the runtime libraries define a Stream class that represents a stream of bytes. There are several implementations of this abstract class. Some streams work entirely in memory, but some wrap I/O mechanisms, providing access to files or to the data being sent or received through a network socket. The abstract `Stream` base class defines methods for reading and writing data via `byte[]` arrays, and the I/O-based stream implementations will often pin the heap blocks containing those arrays for as long as necessary.

The fifth way is to use the `GC` class's `AllocateArray<T>` method. Instead of writing, say, `new byte[4096]`, you can write `GC.AllocateArray<byte>(4096, pinned: true)`. By passing `true` as that second argument, you are telling the CLR that you want this array to be pinned permanently. The CLR maintains an additional heap especially for this purpose called the *pinned object heap* (POH). As with the LOH, arrays in the POH will not be moved around, avoiding the overhead that pinning can otherwise cause. (The POH and corresponding `AllocateArray<T>` method do not exist on .NET Framework.)

If you are writing an application that does a lot of pinning (e.g., a lot of network I/O), you may need to think carefully about how you allocate the arrays that get pinned. Pinning does the most harm for objects allocated recently in the normal way (i.e., not using `AllocateArray<T>`) because these live in the area of the heap where most compaction activity occurs. Pinning recently allocated blocks tends to cause the ephemeral section of the heap to fragment. Memory that would normally have been recovered almost instantly must now wait for blocks to become unpinned, so by the time the collector can get to those blocks, a lot more other blocks will have been allocated after them, meaning that a lot more work is required to recover the memory.

If pinning is causing your application problems, there will be a few common symptoms. The percentage of CPU time spent in the GC will be relatively high—anything over 10% is considered to be bad. But that alone does not necessarily implicate pinning—it could be the result of middle-aged objects causing too many full collections. So you can monitor the number of pinned blocks on the heap[8] to see if these are the specific culprit. If it looks like excessive pinning is causing you pain, you can use `GC.AllocateArray<T>` to allocate the relevant blocks on the POH.

 Arrays allocated on the POH can be used exactly like any other kind of array, and are freed using the normal GC mechanisms. You don't need to do anything special in your code to work with arrays allocated in this way. The only difference is that their location is fixed.

---

8 Microsoft supplies various free tools that can explore GC activity including dotnet-trace, dotnet-counters, and PerfView.

The Span<T> and Memory<T> types discussed in Chapter 18 can sometimes provide an alternative way to avoid pinning problems. They make it much easier than it used to be to work with memory that does not live on the GC heap. So you could sidestep pinning entirely, although you'd be taking on the responsibility for managing the relevant memory.

.NET Framework has no POH, but there's still a way to minimize the impact of pinning: try to ensure that pinning mostly happens only to objects in generation 2. If you allocate a pool of buffers and reuse them for the duration of the application, this will mean that you're pinning blocks that the GC is fairly unlikely to want to move, keeping the ephemeral generations free to be compacted at any time. The earlier you allocate the buffers, the better, because the older an object is, the less likely the GC is to want to move it, so if you're going to use this approach, you should do it during your application startup if possible.

Forcing Garbage Collections

The System.GC class provides a Collect method that allows you to force a GC to occur. You can pass a number indicating the generation you would like to collect, and the overload that takes no arguments performs a full collection. You will rarely have good reason to call GC.Collect. I'm mentioning it here because it comes up a lot on the web, which could easily make it seem more useful than it is.

Forcing a GC can cause problems. The GC monitors its own performance and tunes its behavior in response to your application's allocation patterns. For this to work, it needs to allow enough time between collections to get an accurate picture of how well its current settings are working. If you force collections to occur too often, it will not be able to tune itself, and the outcome will be twofold: the GC will run more often than necessary, and when it does run, its behavior will be suboptimal. Both problems are likely to increase the amount of CPU time spent in the GC.

So when would you force a collection? If you happen to know that your application has just finished some work and is about to go idle, it might be worth considering forcing a collection. GCs are usually triggered by activity, so if you know that your application is about to go to sleep—perhaps it's a service that has just finished running a batch job and will not do any more work for another few hours—you know that it won't be allocating new objects and will therefore not trigger the GC automatically. So forcing a GC would provide an opportunity to return memory to the OS before the application goes to sleep. That said, if this is your scenario, it might be worth looking at mechanisms that would enable your process to exit entirely—there are various ways in which jobs or services that are only required from time to time can be unloaded completely when they are inactive. But if that technique is inapplicable for some reason—perhaps your process has high startup costs or needs to stay running to receive incoming network requests—a forced full collection might be the next best option.

It's worth being aware that there is one way that a GC can be triggered without your application needing to do anything. When the system is running low on memory, Windows broadcasts a message to all running processes. The CLR handles this message and forces a GC when it occurs. So even if your application does not proactively attempt to return memory, memory might be reclaimed eventually if something else in the system needs it. (This is a Windows-only feature.)

Destructors and Finalization

The CLR works hard on our behalf to find out when our objects are no longer in use. It's possible to get it to notify you of this—instead of simply removing unreachable objects, the CLR can first tell an object that it is about to be removed. The CLR calls this finalization, but C# presents it through a special syntax: to exploit finalization, you must write a destructor.

 If your background is in C++, do not be fooled by the name, or the similar syntax. As you will see, a C# destructor is different from a C++ destructor in some important ways.

Example 7-10 shows a destructor. This code compiles into an override of a method called Finalize, which as Chapter 6 mentioned, is a special method defined by the object base class. Finalizers are always required to call the base implementation of Finalize that they override. C# generates that call for us to prevent us from violating the rule, which is why it doesn't let us simply write a Finalize method directly. You cannot write code that invokes a finalizer—they are called by the CLR, so we do not specify an accessibility level for the destructor.

Example 7-10. Class with destructor

```
public class LetMeKnowMineEnd
{
    ~LetMeKnowMineEnd()
    {
        Console.WriteLine("Goodbye, cruel world");
    }
}
```

The CLR does not guarantee to run finalizers on any particular schedule. First of all, it needs to detect that the object has become unreachable, which won't happen until the GC runs. If your program is idle, that might not happen for a long time; the GC normally runs only when your program is doing something, or when system-wide memory pressure causes the GC to spring into life. It's entirely possible that minutes, hours, or even days could pass between your object becoming unreachable and the CLR noticing that it has become unreachable.

Even when the CLR does detect unreachability, it still doesn't guarantee to call the finalizer straightaway. Finalizers run on a dedicated thread. Because current versions of the CLR have only one finalization thread (regardless of which GC mode you choose), a slow finalizer will cause other finalizers to wait.

In most cases, the CLR doesn't even guarantee to run finalizers at all. When a process exits, if the finalization thread hasn't already managed to run all extant finalizers, it will exit without waiting for them all to finish.

In summary, finalizers can be delayed indefinitely if your program is either idle or busy, and are not guaranteed to run. But it gets worse—you can't actually do much that is useful in a finalizer.

You might think that a finalizer would be a good place to ensure that certain work is properly completed. For example, if your object writes data to a file but buffers that data so as to be able to write a small number of large chunks rather than writing in tiny dribs and drabs (because large writes are often more efficient), you might think that finalization is the obvious place to ensure that data in your buffers has been safely flushed out to disk. But think again.

During finalization, an object cannot trust the other objects it has references to. If your object's destructor runs, your object must have become unreachable. This means it's highly likely that any other objects yours refers to have also become unreachable. The CLR is likely to discover the unreachability of groups of related objects simultaneously—if your object created three or four objects to help it do its job, the whole lot will become unreachable at the same time. The CLR makes no guarantees about the order in which it runs finalizers. This means it's entirely possible that by the time your destructor runs, all the objects you were using have already been finalized. So, if they also perform any last-minute cleanup, it's too late to use them. For example, the FileStream class, which derives from Stream and provides access to a file, closes its file handle in its destructor. Thus, if you were hoping to flush your data out to the FileStream, it's too late—the file stream may well already be closed.

 To be fair, things are marginally less bad than I've made them sound so far. Although the CLR does not guarantee to run most finalizers, it will usually run them in practice. The absence of guarantees matters only in relatively extreme situations. Even so, this doesn't mitigate the fact that you cannot, in general, rely on other objects in your destructor.

Since destructors seem to be of remarkably little use—that is, you can have no idea if or when they will run, and you can't use other objects inside a destructor—then what are they for?

The main reason finalization exists at all is to make it possible to write .NET types that are wrappers for the sorts of entities that are traditionally represented by handles —things like files and sockets. These are created and managed outside of the CLR— files and sockets require the operating system to allocate resources; libraries may also provide handle-based APIs, and they will typically allocate memory on their own private heaps to store information about whatever the handle represents. The CLR cannot see these activities—all it sees is a .NET object with a field containing an integer, and it has no idea that the integer is a handle for some resource outside of the CLR. So it doesn't know that it's important that the handle be closed when the object falls out of use. This is where finalizers come in: they are a place to put code that tells something external to the CLR that the entity represented by the handle is no longer in use. The inability to use other objects is not a problem in this scenario.

 If you are writing code that wraps a handle, you should normally use one of the built-in classes that derive from SafeHandle or, if absolutely necessary, derive your own. This base class extends the basic finalization mechanism with some handle-oriented helpers. Furthermore, it gets special handling from the interop layer to avoid premature freeing of resources.

There are some other uses for finalization, although the unpredictability and unreliability already discussed mean there are limits to what it can do for you. Some classes contain a finalizer that does nothing other than check that the object was not abandoned in a state where it had unfinished work. For example, if you had written a class that buffers data before writing it to a file, as described previously, you would need to define some method that callers should use when they are done with your object (perhaps called Flush or Close), and you could write a finalizer that checks to see if the object was put into a safe state before being abandoned, raising an error if not. This would provide a way to discover when programs have forgotten to clean things up correctly.

If you write a finalizer, you should disable it when your object is in a state where it no longer requires finalization, because finalization has its costs. If you offer a Close or Flush method, finalization is unnecessary once these have been called, so you should call the System.GC class's SuppressFinalize method to let the GC know that your object no longer needs to be finalized. If your object's state subsequently changes, you can call the ReRegisterForFinalize method to reenable it.

The greatest cost of finalization is that it guarantees that your object will survive at least into the first generation and possibly beyond. Remember, all objects that survive from generation 0 make it into generation 1. If your object has a finalizer, and you have not disabled it by calling SuppressFinalize, the CLR cannot get rid of your object until it has run its finalizer. And since finalizers run asynchronously on a separate thread, the object has to remain alive even though it has been found to be unreachable. So the object is not yet collectable, even though it is unreachable. It therefore lives on into generation 1. It will usually be finalized shortly afterward, meaning that the object will then become a waste of space until a generation 1 collection occurs. Those happen rather less frequently than generation 0 collections. A finalized object therefore makes inefficient use of memory, which is a reason to avoid finalization, and a reason to disable it whenever possible in objects that do sometimes require it.

 Even though SuppressFinalize can save you from the most egregious costs of finalization, an object that uses this technique still has higher overheads than an object with no finalizer at all. The CLR does some extra work when constructing finalizable objects to keep track of those that have not yet been finalized. (Calling SuppressFinalize just takes your object back out of this tracking list.) So, although suppressing finalization is much better than letting it occur, it's better still if you don't ask for it in the first place.

A slightly weird upshot of finalization is that an object that the GC discovered was unreachable can make itself reachable again. It's possible to write a destructor that stores the this reference in a root reference, or perhaps in a collection that is reachable via a root reference. Nothing stops you from doing this, and the object will continue to work (although its finalizer will not run a second time if the object becomes unreachable again), but it's an odd thing to do. This is referred to as *resurrection*, and just because you can do it doesn't mean you should. It is best avoided.

I hope that by now, I have convinced you that destructors do not provide a general-purpose mechanism for shutting down objects cleanly. They are mostly useful only for dealing with handles for things that live outside of the CLR's control, and it's best to avoid relying on them. If you need timely, reliable cleanup of resources, there's a better mechanism.

IDisposable

The runtime libraries define an interface called IDisposable. The CLR does not treat this interface as being in any way special, but C# has some built-in support for it. IDisposable is a simple abstraction; as Example 7-11 shows, it defines just one member, the Dispose method.

Example 7-11. The IDisposable interface

```
public interface IDisposable
{
    void Dispose();
}
```

The idea behind IDisposable is straightforward. If your code creates an object that implements this interface, you should call Dispose once you've finished using that object (with the occasional exception—see "Optional Disposal" on page 395). This then provides the object with an opportunity to free up resources it may have allocated. If the object being disposed of was using resources represented by handles, it will typically close those handles immediately rather than waiting for finalization to kick in (and it should suppress finalization at the same time). If the object was using services on some remote machine in a stateful way—perhaps holding a connection open to a server to be able to make requests—it would immediately let the remote system know that it no longer requires the services, in whatever way is necessary (for example, by closing the connection).

 There is a persistent myth that calling Dispose causes the GC to do something. You may read on the web that Dispose finalizes the object, or even that it causes the object to be garbage collected. This is nonsense. The CLR does not handle IDisposable or Dispose differently than any other interface or method.

IDisposable is important because it's possible for an object to consume very little memory and yet tie up some expensive resources. For example, consider an object that represents a connection to a database. Such an object might not need many fields—it could even have just a single field containing a handle representing the connection. From the CLR's point of view, this is a pretty cheap object, and we could allocate hundreds of them without triggering a GC. But in the database server, things would look different—it might need to allocate a considerable amount of memory for each incoming connection. Connections might even be strictly limited by licensing terms. (This illustrates that "resource" is a fairly broad concept—it means pretty much anything that you might run out of.)

Relying on GC to notice when database connection objects are no longer in use is likely to be a bad strategy. The CLR will know that we've allocated, say, 50 of the things, but if that consumes only a few hundred bytes in total, it will see no reason to run the GC. And yet our application may be about to grind to a halt—if we have only 50 connection licenses for the database, the next attempt to create a connection will fail. And even if there's no licensing limitation, we could still be making highly inefficient use of database resources by opening far more connections than we need.

It's imperative that we close connection objects as soon as we can, without waiting for the GC to tell us which ones are out of use. This is where IDisposable comes in. It's not just for database connections, of course. It's critically important for any object that is a front for something that lives outside the CLR, such as a file or a network connection. Even for resources that aren't especially constrained, IDisposable provides a way to tell objects when we're finished with them so that they can shut down cleanly, solving the problem described earlier for objects that perform internal buffering.

If a resource is expensive to create, you may want to reuse it. This is often the case with database connections, so the usual practice is to maintain a pool of connections. Instead of closing a connection when you're finished with it, you return it to the pool, making it available for reuse. (Many of .NET's data access providers can do this for you.) The IDisposable model is still useful here. When you ask a resource pool for a resource, it usually provides a wrapper around the real resource, and when you dispose that wrapper, it returns the resource to the pool instead of freeing it. So calling Dispose is really just a way of saying, "I'm done with this object," and it's up to the IDisposable implementation to decide what to do next with the resource it represents.

Implementations of IDisposable are required to tolerate multiple calls to Dispose. Although this means consumers can call Dispose multiple times without harm, they should not attempt to use an object after it has been disposed. In fact, the runtime libraries define a special exception that objects can throw if you misuse them in this way: ObjectDisposedException. (I will discuss exceptions in Chapter 8.)

You're free to call Dispose directly, of course, but C# also supports IDisposable in three ways: foreach loops, using statements, and using declarations. A using statement is a way to ensure that you reliably dispose an object that implements IDispos able once you're done with it. Example 7-12 shows how to use it.

Example 7-12. A using statement

```
using (StreamReader reader = File.OpenText(@"C:\temp\File.txt"))
{
    Console.WriteLine(reader.ReadToEnd());
}
```

This is equivalent to the code in Example 7-13. The try and finally keywords are part of C#'s exception handling system, which I'll discuss in detail in Chapter 8. In this case, they're being used to ensure that the call to Dispose inside the finally block executes even if something goes wrong in the code inside the try block. This also ensures that Dispose gets called if you execute a return statement in the middle of the block. (It even works if you use a goto statement to jump out of it.)

Example 7-13. How using statements expand

```
{
    StreamReader reader = File.OpenText(@"C:\temp\File.txt");
    try
    {
        Console.WriteLine(reader.ReadToEnd());
    }
    finally
    {
        if (reader != null)
        {
            ((IDisposable) reader).Dispose();
        }
    }
}
```

If the variable type of the declaration in the `using` statement is a value type, C# will not generate the code that checks for `null` and will just invoke `Dispose` directly.

C# also offers a simpler alternative, a `using` declaration, shown in Example 7-14. The difference is that we don't need to provide a block. A `using` declaration disposes its variable when the variable goes out of scope. It still generates `try` and `finally` blocks, so in cases where a `using` statement's block happens to finish at the end of some other block (e.g., it finishes at the end of a method), you can change to a `using` declaration with no change of behavior. This reduces the number of nested blocks, which can make your code easier to read. (On the other hand, with an ordinary `using` block, it may be easier to see exactly when the object is no longer used. So each style has its pros and cons.)

Example 7-14. A using declaration

```
using StreamReader reader = File.OpenText(@"C:\temp\File.txt");
Console.WriteLine(reader.ReadToEnd());
```

If you need to use multiple disposable resources within the same scope, and you want to use a `using` statement, not a declaration (e.g., because you want to dispose the resources at the earliest opportunity instead of waiting for the relevant variables to go out of scope), you can nest them, but it might be easier to read if you stack multiple `using` statements in front of a single block. Example 7-15 uses this to copy the contents of one file to another.

Example 7-15. Stacking using statements

```
using (Stream source = File.OpenRead(@"C:\temp\File.txt"))
using (Stream copy = File.Create(@"C:\temp\Copy.txt"))
{
```

```
    source.CopyTo(copy);
}
```

Stacking using statements is not a special syntax; it's just an upshot of the fact that a using statement is always followed by a single embedded statement, which will be executed before Dispose gets called. Normally, that statement is a block, but in Example 7-15, the first using statement's embedded statement is the second using statement. If you use using declarations instead, stacking is unnecessary because these don't have an associated embedded statement.

A foreach loop generates code that will use IDisposable if the enumerator implements it. Example 7-16 shows a foreach loop that uses just such an enumerator.

Example 7-16. A foreach loop

```
foreach (string file in Directory.EnumerateFiles(@"C:\temp"))
{
    Console.WriteLine(file);
}
```

The Directory class's EnumerateFiles method returns an IEnumerable<string>. As you saw in Chapter 5, this has a GetEnumerator method that returns an IEnumerator <string>, an interface that inherits from IDisposable. Consequently, the C# compiler will produce code equivalent to Example 7-17.

Example 7-17. How foreach loops expand

```
{
    IEnumerator<string> e =
        Directory.EnumerateFiles(@"C:\temp").GetEnumerator();
    try
    {
        while (e.MoveNext())
        {
            string file = e.Current;
            Console.WriteLine(file);
        }
    }
    finally
    {
        if (e != null)
        {
            ((IDisposable) e).Dispose();
        }
    }
}
```

There are several variations the compiler can produce, depending on the collection's enumerator type. If it's a value type that implements IDisposable, the compiler won't generate the check for null in the finally block (just as in a using statement). If the static type of the enumerator does not implement IDisposable, the outcome depends on whether the type is open for inheritance. If it is sealed, or if it is a value type, the compiler will not generate code that attempts to call Dispose at all. If it is not sealed, the compiler generates code in the finally block that tests at runtime whether the enumerator implements IDisposable, calling Dispose if it does and doing nothing otherwise.

The IDisposable interface is easiest to consume when you obtain a resource and finish using it in the same method, because you can write a using statement (or where applicable, a foreach loop) to ensure that you call Dispose. But sometimes, you will write a class that creates a disposable object and puts a reference to it in a field, because it will need to use that object over a longer timescale. For example, you might write a logging class, and if a logger object writes data to a file, it might hold on to a StreamWriter object. C# provides no automatic help here, so it's up to you to ensure that any contained objects get disposed. You would write your own implementation of IDisposable that disposes the other objects, as Example 7-18 does. Note that this example sets _file to null, so it will not attempt to dispose the file twice. This is not strictly necessary, because the StreamWriter will tolerate multiple calls to Dispose. But it does give the Logger object an easy way to know that it is in a disposed state, so if we were to add some real methods, we could check _file and throw an ObjectDisposedException if it is null.

Example 7-18. Disposing a contained instance

```
public sealed class Logger(string filePath) : IDisposable
{
    private StreamWriter? _file = File.CreateText(filePath);

    public void Dispose()
    {
        if (_file != null)
        {
            _file.Dispose();
            _file = null;
        }
    }
    // A real class would go on to do something with the StreamWriter, of course
}
```

This example dodges an important problem. The class is sealed, which avoids the issue of how to cope with inheritance. If you write an unsealed class that implements IDisposable, you should provide a way for a derived class to add its own disposal logic. The most straightforward solution would be to make `Dispose` virtual so that a derived class can override it, performing its own cleanup in addition to calling your base implementation. However, there is a more complicated pattern that you will see from time to time in .NET.

Some objects implement `IDisposable` and also have a finalizer. Since the introduction of `SafeHandle` and related classes, it's relatively unusual for a class to need to provide both (unless it derives from `SafeHandle`). Only wrappers for handles normally need finalization, and classes that use handles now typically defer to a `SafeHandle` to provide that, rather than implementing their own finalizers. However, there are exceptions, and some library types implement a pattern designed to support both finalization and `IDisposable`, allowing you to provide custom behaviors for both in derived classes. For example, the `Stream` base class works this way.

 This pattern is called the *dispose pattern*, but do not take that to mean that you should normally use this when implementing `IDis posable`. On the contrary, it is extremely unusual to need this pattern. Even back when it was invented, few classes needed it, and now that we have `SafeHandle`, it is almost never necessary. (`Safe Handle` was introduced in .NET 2.0, so it has been a very long time since the dispose pattern was broadly useful.) Unfortunately, some people misunderstood the narrow utility of this pattern, so you will find a certain amount of well-intentioned but utterly wrong advice telling you that you should use this for all `IDisposable` implementations. Ignore it. The pattern's main relevance today is that you sometimes encounter it in old types such as `Stream`.

The pattern is to define a protected overload of `Dispose` that takes a single `bool` argument. The base class calls this from its public `Dispose` method and also its destructor, passing in `true` or `false`, respectively. That way, you have to override only one method, the protected `Dispose`. It can contain logic common to both finalization and disposal, such as closing handles, but you can also perform any disposal-specific or finalization-specific logic because the argument tells you which sort of cleanup is being performed. Example 7-19 shows how this might look. (This is for illustration only—the `MyCustomLibraryInteropWrapper` class has been made up for this example.)

Example 7-19. Custom finalization and disposal logic

```
public class MyFunkyStream : Stream
{
    // For illustration purposes only. Usually better to avoid this whole
    // pattern and to use some type derived from SafeHandle instead.
    private IntPtr _myCustomLibraryHandle;
```

```
    private Logger? _log;

    protected override void Dispose(bool disposing)
    {
        base.Dispose(disposing);

        if (_myCustomLibraryHandle != IntPtr.Zero)
        {
            MyCustomLibraryInteropWrapper.Close(_myCustomLibraryHandle);
            _myCustomLibraryHandle = IntPtr.Zero;
        }
        if (disposing)
        {
            if (_log != null)
            {
                _log.Dispose();
                _log = null;
            }
        }
    }

    // ...overloads of Stream's abstract methods would go here
}
```

This hypothetical example is a custom implementation of the Stream abstraction that uses some external non-.NET library that provides handle-based access to resources. We prefer to close the handle when the public Dispose method is called, but if that hasn't happened by the time our finalizer runs, we want to close the handle then. So the code checks to see if the handle is still open and closes it if necessary, and it does this whether the call to the Dispose(bool) overload happened as a result of the object being explicitly disposed or being finalized—we need to ensure that the handle is closed in either case. However, this class also appears to use an instance of the Logger class from Example 7-18. Because that's an ordinary object, we shouldn't attempt to use it during finalization, so we attempt to dispose it only if our object is being disposed. If we are being finalized, then although Logger itself is not finalizable, it uses a FileStream, which is finalizable; and it's quite possible that the FileStream finalizer will already have run by the time our MyFunkyStream class's finalizer runs, so it would be a bad idea to call methods on the Logger.

When a base class provides this virtual protected form of Dispose, it should call GC.SuppressFinalization in its public Dispose. The Stream base class does this. More generally, if you find yourself writing a class that offers both Dispose and a finalizer, then whether or not you choose to support inheritance with this pattern, you should in any case suppress finalization when Dispose is called.

Since I've recommended avoiding this pattern, what should code like Example 7-18 do if using sealed is unacceptable? The answer is straightforward: if you are writing a class that implements IDisposable and you want that class to be open for inheritance (i.e., not sealed), make your Dispose method virtual. That way, derived types can override it to add their own disposal logic (and these overrides should always call the base class's Dispose).

Optional Disposal

Although you should call Dispose at some point on most objects that implement IDisposable, there are a few exceptions. For example, the Reactive Extensions for .NET (described in Chapter 11) provide IDisposable objects that represent subscriptions to streams of events. You can call Dispose to unsubscribe, but some event sources come to a natural end, automatically shutting down any subscriptions. If that happens, you are not required to call Dispose. Also, the Task type, which is used extensively in conjunction with the asynchronous programming techniques described in Chapter 17, implements IDisposable but does not need to be disposed unless you cause it to allocate a WaitHandle, something that will not occur in normal usage. The way Task is generally used makes it particularly awkward to find a good time to call Dispose on it, so it's fortunate that it's not normally necessary.

The HttpClient class is another exception to the normal rules but in a different way. We rarely call Dispose on instances of this type, but in this case it's because we are encouraged to reuse instances. If you construct, use, and dispose an HttpClient each time you need one, you will defeat its ability to reuse existing connections when making multiple requests to the same server. This can cause two problems. First, opening an HTTP connection can sometimes take longer than sending the request and receiving the response, so preventing HttpClient from reusing connections to send multiple requests over time can cause significant performance problems. Connection reuse only works if you reuse the HttpClient.[9] Second, the TCP protocol (which underpins HTTP requests unless you're using HTTP/3) has characteristics that mean the OS cannot always instantly reclaim all the resources associated with a connection: it may need to keep the connection's TCP port reserved for a considerable time (maybe a few minutes) after you've told the OS to close the connection, and it's possible to run out of ports, preventing all further communication.

Such exceptions are unusual. It is only safe to omit calls to Dispose when the documentation for the class you're using explicitly states that it is not required.

---

9 Strictly speaking, it's the underlying MessageHandler that needs to be reused. If you obtain an HttpClient from an IHttpClientFactory, you normally dispose it because the factory holds on to the handler and reuses it across HttpClient instances.

Boxing

While I'm discussing GC and object lifetime, there's one more topic I should talk about in this chapter: *boxing*. Boxing is the process that enables a variable of type `object` to refer to a value type. An `object` variable is capable only of holding a reference to something on the heap, so how can it refer to an `int`? What happens when the code in Example 7-20 runs?

Example 7-20. Using an `int` as an object

```
static void Show(object o)
{
    Console.WriteLine(o.ToString());
}

int num = 42;
Show(num);
```

The `Show` method expects an object, and I'm passing it `num`, which is a local variable of the value type `int`. In these circumstances, C# generates a box, which is essentially a reference type wrapper for a value. The CLR can automatically provide a box for any value type, although if it didn't, you could write your own class that does something similar. Example 7-21 shows a hand-built box.

Example 7-21. Not actually how a box works

```
// Not a real box but similar in effect.
public class Box<T>(T v)
    where T : struct
{
    public readonly T Value = v;

    public override string? ToString() => Value.ToString();
    public override bool Equals(object? obj) => Value.Equals(obj);
    public override int GetHashCode() => Value.GetHashCode();
}
```

This is a fairly ordinary class that contains a single instance of a value type as its only field. If you invoke the standard members of `object` on the box, this class's overrides make it look as though you invoked them directly on the field itself. So, if I passed new `Box<int>(num)` as the argument to `Show` in Example 7-20, `Show` would receive a reference to that box. When `Show` called `ToString`, the box would call the `int` field's `ToString`, so you'd expect the program to display 42.

We don't need to write Example 7-21, because the CLR will build the box for us. It will create an object on the heap that contains a copy of the boxed value and forward the standard `object` methods to the boxed value. And it does some things that we can't. If you ask a boxed `int` its type by calling `GetType`, it will return the same `Type` object as you'd get if you called `GetType` directly on an `int` variable—I can't do that with my custom `Box<T>`, because `GetType` is not virtual. Also, getting back the underlying value is easier than it would be with a hand-built box, because unboxing is an intrinsic CLR feature.

If you have a reference of type `object`, and you cast it to `int`, the CLR checks to see if the reference does indeed refer to a boxed `int`; if it does, the CLR returns a copy of the boxed value. (If not, it throws an `InvalidCastException`.) So, inside the `Show` method of Example 7-20, I could write `(int) o` to get back a copy of the original value, whereas if I were using the class in Example 7-21, I'd need the more convoluted `((Box<int>) o).Value`.

I can also use pattern matching to extract a boxed value. Example 7-22 uses a declaration pattern to detect whether the variable o contains a reference to a boxed `int`, and if it does, it extracts that into the local variable i. As we saw in Chapter 2, when you use a pattern with the `is` operator like this, the resulting expression evaluates to `true` if the pattern matches and `false` if it does not. So the body of this `if` statement runs only if there was an `int` value there to be unboxed.

Example 7-22. Unboxing a value with a type pattern

```
if (o is int i)
{
    Console.WriteLine(i * 2);
}
```

Boxes are automatically available for all structs,[10] not just the built-in value types. If the struct implements any interfaces, the box will provide all the same interfaces. (That's another trick that Example 7-21 cannot perform.)

Some implicit conversions cause boxing. You can see this in Example 7-20. I have passed an expression of type `int` where `object` was required, without needing an explicit cast. Implicit conversions also exist between a value and any of the interfaces that value's type implements. For example, you can assign a value of type `int` into a variable of type `IComparable<int>` (or pass it as a method argument of that type) without needing a cast. This causes a box to be created, because variables of any interface type are like variables of type `object`, in that they can hold only a reference to an item on the garbage-collected heap.

---

10 Except for `ref struct` types, because those invariably live on the stack.

Implicit boxing conversions are not implicit reference conversions. This means that they do not come into play with covariance or contravariance. For example, IEnumerable<int> is not compatible with IEnumerable<object> despite the existence of an implicit conversion from int to object, because that is not an implicit reference conversion.

Implicit boxing can occasionally cause problems for one of two reasons. First, it makes it easy to generate extra work for the GC. The CLR does not attempt to cache boxes, so if you write a loop that executes 100,000 times, and that loop contains an expression that uses an implicit boxing conversion, you'll end up generating 100,000 boxes, which the GC will eventually have to clean up just like anything else on the heap. Second, each box operation (and each unbox) copies the value, which might not provide the semantics you were expecting. Example 7-23 illustrates some potentially surprising behavior.

Example 7-23. Illustrating the pitfalls of mutable structs

```
static void CallDispose(IDisposable o)
{
    o.Dispose();
}

DisposableValue dv = new ();
Console.WriteLine("Passing value variable:");
CallDispose(dv);
CallDispose(dv);
CallDispose(dv);

IDisposable id = dv;
Console.WriteLine("Passing interface variable:");
CallDispose(id);
CallDispose(id);
CallDispose(id);

Console.WriteLine("Calling Dispose directly on value variable:");
dv.Dispose();
dv.Dispose();
dv.Dispose();

Console.WriteLine("Passing value variable:");
CallDispose(dv);
CallDispose(dv);
CallDispose(dv);

public struct DisposableValue : IDisposable
{
    private bool _disposedYet;
```

```
    public void Dispose()
    {
        if (!_disposedYet)
        {
            Console.WriteLine("Disposing for first time");
            _disposedYet = true;
        }
        else
        {
            Console.WriteLine("Was already disposed");
        }
    }
}
```

The `DisposableValue` struct implements the `IDisposable` interface we saw earlier. It keeps track of whether it has been disposed already. The program contains a `CallDis pose` method that calls `Dispose` on any `IDisposable` instance. The program declares a single variable of type `DisposableValue` and passes this to `CallDispose` three times. Here's the output from that part of the program:

```
Passing value variable:
Disposing for first time
Disposing for first time
Disposing for first time
```

On all three occasions, the struct seems to think this is the first time we've called `Dis pose` on it. That's because each call to `CallDispose` created a new box—we are not really passing the dv variable; we are passing a newly boxed copy each time, so the `CallDispose` method is working on a different instance of the struct each time. This is consistent with how value types normally work—even when there's no boxing, when you pass one as an argument, you get a copy (unless you use the `ref` or `in` keywords).

The next part of the program ends up generating just a single box—it assigns the value into another local variable of type `IDisposable`. This uses the same implicit conversion as we did when passing the variable directly as an argument, so this creates yet another box, but it does so only once. We then pass the same reference to this particular box three times over, which explains why the output from this phase of the program looks different:

```
Passing interface variable:
Disposing for first time
Was already disposed
Was already disposed
```

These three calls to CallDispose all use the same box, which contains an instance of our struct, and so after the first call, it remembers that it has been disposed already. Next, our program calls Dispose directly on the local variable, producing this output:

```
Calling Dispose directly on value variable:
Disposing for first time
Was already disposed
Was already disposed
```

No boxing at all is involved here, so we are modifying the state of the local variable. Someone who only glanced at the code might not have expected this output—we have already passed the dv variable to a method that called Dispose on its argument, so it might be surprising to see that it thinks it hasn't been disposed the first time around. But once you understand that CallDispose requires a reference and therefore cannot use a value directly, it's clear that every call to Dispose before this point has operated on some boxed copy, and not the local variable.

Finally, we make three more calls passing the dv directly to CallDispose again. This is exactly what we did at the start of the code, so these calls generate yet more boxed copies. But this time, we are copying a value that's already in the state of having been disposed, so we see different output:

```
Passing value variable:
Was already disposed
Was already disposed
Was already disposed
```

The behavior is all straightforward when you understand what's going on, but it requires you to be mindful that you're dealing with a value type and to understand when boxing causes implicit copying. This is one of the reasons Microsoft discourages developers from writing value types that can change their state—if a value cannot change, then a boxed value of that type also cannot change. It matters less whether you're dealing with the original or a boxed copy, so there's less scope for confusion, although it is still useful to understand when boxing will occur to avoid performance penalties.

Boxing used to be a much more common occurrence in early versions of .NET. Before generics arrived in .NET 2.0, collection classes all worked in terms of object, so if you wanted a resizable list of integers, you'd end up with a box for each int in the list. Generic collection classes do not cause boxing—a List<int> is able to store unboxed values directly.

Boxing Nullable<T>

Chapter 3 described the `Nullable<T>` type, a wrapper that adds null value support to any value type. Remember, C# has special syntax for this, in which you can just put a question mark on the end of a value type name, so we'd normally write `int?` instead of `Nullable<int>`. The CLR has special support for `Nullable<T>` when it comes to boxing.

`Nullable<T>` itself is a value type, so if you attempt to get a reference to it, the compiler will generate code that attempts to box it, as it would with any other value type. However, at runtime, the CLR will not produce a box containing a copy of the `Null able<T>` itself. Instead, it checks to see if the value is in a null state (i.e., its `HasValue` property returns `false`), and if so, it just returns `null`. Otherwise, it boxes the contained value. For example, if a `Nullable<int>` has a value, boxing it will produce a box of type `int`. This will be indistinguishable from the box you'd get if you had started with an ordinary `int` value. (One upshot of this is that the pattern matching shown in Example 7-22 works whether the type of variable originally boxed was an `int` or an `int?`. You use `int` in the declaration pattern in either case.)

You can unbox a boxed `int` into variables of either type `int?` or `int`. So all three unboxing operations in Example 7-24 will succeed. They would also succeed if the first line were modified to initialize the `boxed` variable from a `Nullable<int>` that was not in the null state. (If you were to initialize `boxed` from a `Nullable<int>` in the null state, that would have the same effect as initializing it to `null`, in which case the final line of this example would throw a `NullReferenceException`.)

Example 7-24. Unboxing an `int` to nullable and non-nullable variables

```
object boxed = 42;
int? nv = boxed as int?;
int? nv2 = (int?) boxed;
int v = (int) boxed;
```

This is a runtime feature, and not simply the compiler being clever. The IL `box` instruction, which is what C# generates when it wants to box a value, detects `Nullable<T>` values; the `unbox` and `unbox.any` IL instructions are able to produce a `Nullable<T>` value from either a `null` or a reference to a boxed value of the underlying type. So, if you wrote your own wrapper type that looked like `Nullable<T>`, it would not behave in the same way; if you assigned a value of your type into an `object`, it would box your whole wrapper just like any other value. It's only because the CLR knows about `Nullable<T>` that it behaves differently.

Summary

In this chapter, I described the heap that the runtime provides. I showed the strategy that the CLR uses to determine which heap objects can still be reached by your code, and the generation-based mechanism it uses to reclaim the memory occupied by objects that are no longer in use. The GC is not clairvoyant, so if your program keeps an object reachable, the GC has to assume that you might use that object in the future. This means you will sometimes need to be careful to make sure you don't cause memory leaks by accidentally keeping hold of objects for too long. We looked at the finalization mechanism, and its various limitations and performance issues, and we also looked at `IDisposable`, which is the preferred system for cleaning up nonmemory resources. Finally, we saw how value types can act like reference types thanks to boxing.

In the next chapter, I will show how C# presents the error-handling mechanisms of the CLR.

CHAPTER 8

Exceptions

Some operations can fail. If your program is reading data from a file stored on an external drive, someone might disconnect the drive. Your application might try to construct an array only to discover that the system does not have enough free memory. Intermittent wireless network connectivity can cause network requests to fail. One widely used way for a program to discover these sorts of failures is for each API to return a value indicating whether the operation succeeded. This requires developers to be vigilant if all errors are to be detected, because programs must check the return value of every operation. This is certainly a viable strategy, but it can obscure the code; the logical sequence of work to be performed when nothing goes wrong can get buried by all of the error checking, making the code harder to maintain. C# supports another popular error-handling mechanism that can mitigate this problem: *exceptions.*

When an API reports failure with an exception, this disrupts the normal flow of execution, leaping straight to the nearest suitable error-handling code. This enables a degree of separation between error-handling logic and the code that tries to perform the task at hand. This can make code easier to read and maintain, although it does have the downside of making it harder to see all the possible ways in which the code may execute.

Exceptions can also report problems with operations where a return code might not be practical. For example, the runtime can detect and report problems for basic operations, even something as simple as using a reference. Reference type variables can contain null, and if you try to invoke a method on a null reference, it will fail. The runtime reports this with an exception.

Most errors in .NET are represented as exceptions. However, some APIs offer you a choice between return codes and exceptions. For example, the int type has a Parse method that takes a string and attempts to interpret its contents as a number, and if you pass it some nonnumeric text (e.g., `"Hello"`), it will indicate failure by throwing a `FormatException`. If you don't like that, you can call `TryParse` instead, which does exactly the same job, but if the input is nonnumeric, it returns `false` instead of throwing an exception. (Since the method's return value has the job of reporting success or failure, the method provides the integer result via an `out` parameter.) Numeric parsing is not the only operation to use this pattern, in which a pair of methods (`Parse` and `TryParse`, in this case) provides a choice between exceptions and return values. As you saw in Chapter 5, dictionaries offer a similar choice. The indexer throws an exception if you use a key that's not in the dictionary, but you can also look up values with `TryGetValue`, which returns `false` on failure, just like `TryParse`. Although this pattern crops up in a few places, for the majority of APIs, exceptions are the only choice.

If you are designing an API that could fail, how should it report failure? Should you use exceptions, a return value, or both? Microsoft's class library design guidelines contain instructions that seem unequivocal:

> Do not return error codes. Exceptions are the primary means of reporting errors in frameworks.
>
> —.NET Framework Design Guidelines

But how does that square with the existence of `int.TryParse`? The guidelines have a section on performance considerations for exceptions that says this:

> Consider the Try-Parse pattern for members that might throw exceptions in common scenarios to avoid performance problems related to exceptions.
>
> —.NET Framework Design Guidelines

Failing to parse a number is not necessarily an error. For example, you might want your application to allow the month to be specified numerically or as text. So there are certainly common scenarios in which the operation might fail, but the guideline has another criterion: it suggests using it for "extremely performance-sensitive APIs," so you should offer the `TryParse` approach only when the operation is fast compared to the time taken to throw and handle an exception.

Exceptions can typically be thrown and handled in a few microseconds, so they're not desperately slow—not nearly as slow as reading data over a network connection, for example—but they're not blindingly fast either. I find that on my computer, a single thread can parse five-digit numeric strings at a rate of roughly 100 million strings per second on .NET 8.0, and it's capable of rejecting nonnumeric strings at a similar speed if I use `TryParse`. The `Parse` method handles numeric strings just as fast, but it's roughly 500 times slower at rejecting nonnumeric strings than `TryParse`, thanks to the cost of exceptions. Of course, converting strings to integers is a pretty fast operation, so this makes exceptions look particularly bad, but that's why this pattern is most common on operations that are naturally fast.

Exceptions can be especially slow when debugging. This is partly because the debugger has to decide whether to break in, but it's particularly pronounced with the first unhandled exception your program hits. This can give the impression that exceptions are considerably more expensive than they really are. The numbers in the preceding paragraph are based on observed runtime behavior without debugging overheads. That said, those numbers slightly understate the costs, because handling an exception tends to cause the CLR to run bits of code and access data structures it would not otherwise need to use, which can have the effect of pushing useful data out of the CPU's cache. This can cause code to run slower for a short while after the exception has been handled, until the nonexceptional code and data can make their way back into the cache. The simplicity of my example reduces this effect.

Most APIs do not offer a *TryXxx* form, and will report all failures as exceptions, even in cases where failure might be common. For example, the file APIs do not provide a way to open an existing file for reading without throwing an exception if the file is missing. (You can use a different API to test whether the file is there first, but that's no guarantee of success. It's always possible for some other process to delete the file between your asking whether it's there and attempting to open it.) Since filesystem operations are inherently slow, the *TryXxx* pattern would not offer a worthwhile performance boost here even though it might make logical sense.

 If you do use the *TryXxx* pattern, be aware that in cases where there are multiple reasons the operation could fail, the `false` return value typically indicates just one particular kind of failure. So a method of this kind might still throw an exception for some failure modes.

Exception Sources

Class library APIs are not the only source of exceptions. They can be thrown in any of the following scenarios:

- Your own code detects a problem.
- Your program uses a class library API, which detects a problem (e.g., you're using a database client library, and the database rejects an attempt to modify a row because it violates a data integrity constraint).
- The runtime detects the failure of an operation (e.g., arithmetic overflow in a checked context, or an attempt to use a null reference, or an attempt to allocate an object for which there is not enough memory).

- The runtime detects a situation outside of your control that affects your code (e.g., the runtime tries to allocate memory for some internal purpose and finds that there is not enough free memory).

Although these all use the same exception-handling mechanisms, the places in which the exceptions emerge are different. When your own code throws an exception (which I'll show you how to do later), you'll know what conditions cause it to happen, but when do these other scenarios produce exceptions? I'll describe where to expect each sort of exception in the following sections.

Exceptions from APIs

With an API call, there are several kinds of problems that could result in exceptions. You may have provided arguments that make no sense, such as a null reference where a non-null one is required, or an empty string where the name of a file was expected. Or the arguments might look OK individually but not collectively. For example, you could call an API that copies data into an array, asking it to copy more data than will fit. You could describe these as "that will never work"–style errors, and they are usually the result of mistakes in the code. (One developer who used to work on the C# compiler team refers to these as *boneheaded* exceptions.)

A different class of problems arises when the arguments all look plausible but the operation turns out not to be possible given the current state of the world. For example, you might ask to open a particular file, but the file may not be present; or perhaps it exists, but some other program already has it open and has demanded exclusive access to the file. Yet another variation is that things may start well but conditions can change, so perhaps you opened a file successfully and have been reading data for a while, but then the file becomes inaccessible. As suggested earlier, someone may have unplugged a disk, or the drive could have failed due to overheating or age.

Software that communicates with external services over a network needs to take into account that an exception doesn't necessarily indicate that anything is really wrong—sometimes requests fail due to some temporary condition, and you may just need to retry the operation. This is particularly common in cloud environments, where individual servers often come and go as part of the load balancing that cloud platforms typically offer—it is normal for a few operations to fail for no particular reason.

 When using services via a library, you should find out whether it already handles this for you. For example, the Azure Storage libraries perform retries automatically by default and will only throw an exception if you disable this behavior or if problems persist after several attempts. You shouldn't normally add your own exception handling and retry loops for this kind of error around libraries that do this for you.

Asynchronous programming adds yet another variation. In Chapters 16 and 17, I'll show various asynchronous APIs—ones where work can progress after the method that started it has returned. Work that runs asynchronously can also fail asynchronously, in which case the library might have to wait until your code next calls into it before it can report the error.

Despite the variations, in all these cases the exception will come from some API that your code calls. (Even when asynchronous operations fail, exceptions emerge either when you try to collect the result of an operation or when you explicitly ask whether an error has occurred.) Example 8-1 shows some code where exceptions of this kind could emerge.

Example 8-1. Getting an exception from a library call

```
static void Main(string[] args)
{
    using (var r = new StreamReader(@"C:\Temp\File.txt"))
    {
        while (!r.EndOfStream)
        {
            Console.WriteLine(r.ReadLine());
        }
    }
}
```

There's nothing categorically wrong with this code, so we won't get any exceptions complaining about arguments being self-evidently wrong. (In the unofficial terminology, it makes no boneheaded mistakes.) If your computer's C: drive has a *Temp* folder, and if that contains a *File.txt* file, and if the user running the program has permission to read that file, and if nothing else on the computer has already acquired exclusive access to the file, and if there are no problems—such as disk corruption—that could make any part of the file inaccessible, and if no new problems (such as the drive catching fire) develop while the program runs, this code will work just fine: it will show each line of text in the file. But that's a lot of *ifs*.

If there is no such file, the `StreamReader` constructor will not complete. Instead, it will throw an exception. This program makes no attempt to handle that, so the application would terminate. If you ran the program outside of Visual Studio's debugger, you would see the following output:

```
Unhandled exception. System.IO.FileNotFoundException: Could not find file 'C:\
Temp\File.txt'.
File name: 'C:\Temp\File.txt'
   at Microsoft.Win32.SafeHandles.SafeFileHandle.CreateFile(String fullPath,
FileMode mode, FileAccess access, FileShare share, FileOptions options)
   at Microsoft.Win32.SafeHandles.SafeFileHandle.Open(String fullPath, FileMode
mode, FileAccess access, FileShare share, FileOptions options,
```

```
Int64 preallocationSize)
   at System.IO.Strategies.OSFileStreamStrategy..ctor(String path, FileMode mode
, FileAccess access, FileShare share, FileOptions options, Int64 preallocationSi
ze)
   at System.IO.Strategies.FileStreamHelpers.ChooseStrategyCore(String path, Fil
eMode mode, FileAccess access, FileShare share, FileOptions options, Int64 preall
ocationSize)
   at System.IO.Strategies.FileStreamHelpers.ChooseStrategy(FileStream fileStrea
m, String path,
FileMode mode, FileAccess access, FileShare share, Int32 bufferSize,
FileOptions options, Int64 preallocationSize)
   at System.IO.StreamReader.ValidateArgsAndOpenPath(String path, Encoding encod
ing, Int32 bufferSize)
   at System.IO.StreamReader..ctor(String path)
   at Exceptional.Program.Main(String[] args) in
c:\Examples\Ch08\Example1\Program.cs:line 10
```

This tells us what error occurred, and shows the full call stack of the program at the point at which the problem happened. On Windows, the system-wide error handling will also step in, so depending on how your computer is configured, you might see its error reporting dialog, and it may even report the crash to Microsoft's error reporting service. If you run the same program in a debugger, it will tell you about the exception and highlight the line on which the error occurred, as Figure 8-1 shows.

Figure 8-1. Visual Studio reporting an exception

What we're seeing here is the default behavior that occurs when a program does nothing to handle exceptions: if a debugger is attached, it will step in, and if not, the program just crashes. I'll show how to handle exceptions soon, but this illustrates that you cannot simply ignore them.

The call to the StreamReader constructor is not the only line that could throw an exception in Example 8-1, by the way. The code calls ReadLine multiple times, and any of those calls could fail. In general, any member access could result in an exception, even just reading a property, although class library designers usually try to minimize the extent to which properties throw exceptions. If you make an error of the "that will never work" (boneheaded) kind, then a property might throw an exception but usually not for errors of the "this particular operation didn't work" kind. For example, the documentation states that the `EndOfStream` property used in Example 8-1 would throw an exception if you tried to read it after having called `Dispose` on the `StreamReader` object—an obvious coding error—but if there are problems reading the file, `StreamReader` will throw exceptions only from methods or the constructor.

Failures Detected by the Runtime

Another source of exceptions is when the CLR itself detects that some operation has failed. Example 8-2 shows a method in which this could happen. As with Example 8-1, there's nothing innately wrong with this code (other than not being very useful). It is perfectly possible to use this without causing problems. However, if someone passes in 0 as the second argument, the code will attempt an illegal operation.

Example 8-2. A potential runtime-detected failure

```
static int Divide(int x, int y)
{
    return x / y;
}
```

The CLR will detect when this division operation attempts to divide by zero and will throw a `DivideByZeroException`. This will have the same effect as an exception from an API call: if the program makes no attempt to handle the exception, it will crash, or the debugger will break in.

 Division by zero is not always illegal in C#. Floating-point types support special values representing positive and negative infinity, which is what you get when you divide a positive or negative value by zero; if you divide zero by itself, you get the special Not a Number value. None of the integer types support these special values, so integer division by zero is always an error.

The final source of exceptions I described earlier is also the detection of certain failures by the runtime, but they work a bit differently. They are not necessarily triggered directly by anything that your code did on the thread on which the exception occurred. These are sometimes referred to as *asynchronous exceptions*, and in theory they can be thrown at literally any point in your code, making it hard to ensure that you can deal with them correctly. However, these tend to be thrown only in fairly catastrophic circumstances, often when your program is about to be shut down, so you can't normally handle them in a useful way. For example, `StackOverflow Exception` and `OutOfMemoryException` can in theory be thrown at any point (because the CLR may need to allocate memory for its own purposes even if your code didn't do anything that explicitly attempts this).

I've described the usual situations in which exceptions are thrown, and you've seen the default behavior, but what if you want your program to do something other than crash?

Handling Exceptions

When an exception is thrown, the CLR looks for code to handle the exception. The default exception-handling behavior comes into play only if there are no suitable handlers anywhere on the entire call stack. To provide a handler, we use C#'s `try` and `catch` keywords, as Example 8-3 shows.

Example 8-3. Handling an exception

```
try
{
    using (var r = new StreamReader(@"C:\Temp\File.txt"))
    {
        while (!r.EndOfStream)
        {
            Console.WriteLine(r.ReadLine());
        }
    }
}
catch (FileNotFoundException)
{
    Console.WriteLine("Couldn't find the file");
}
```

The block immediately following the `try` keyword is usually known as a *try block*, and if the program throws an exception while it's inside such a block, the CLR looks for matching *catch blocks*. Example 8-3 has just a single `catch` block, and in the parentheses following the `catch` keyword, you can see that this particular block is intended to handle exceptions of type `FileNotFoundException`.

You saw earlier that if there is no *C:\Temp\File.txt* file, the `StreamReader` constructor throws a `FileNotFoundException`. In Example 8-1, that caused our program to crash, but because Example 8-3 has a `catch` block for that exception, the CLR will run that `catch` block. At this point, it will consider the exception to have been handled, so the program does not crash. Our `catch` block is free to do whatever it wants, and in this case, my code just displays a message indicating that it couldn't find the file.

Exception handlers do not need to be in the method in which the exception originated. The CLR walks up the stack until it finds a suitable handler. If the failing `Stream Reader` constructor call were in some other method that was called from inside the `try` block in Example 8-3, our `catch` block would still run (unless that method provided its own handler for the same exception).

Exception Objects

Exceptions are objects, and their type derives from the `Exception` base class.[1] This defines properties providing information about the exception, and some derived types add properties specific to the problem they represent. Your `catch` block can get a reference to the exception if it needs information about what went wrong. Example 8-4 shows a modification to the `catch` block from Example 8-3. In the parentheses after the `catch` keyword, as well as specifying the exception type, we also provide an identifier (x) with which code in the `catch` block can refer to the exception object. This enables the code to read a property specific to the `FileNotFoundEx ception` class: `FileName`.

Example 8-4. Using the exception in a catch block

```
try
{
    // ...same code as Example 8-3...
}
catch (FileNotFoundException ex)
{
    Console.WriteLine($"File '{ex.FileName}' is missing");
}
```

This will display the name of the file that couldn't be found. With this simple program, we already knew which file we were trying to open, but you could imagine this property being helpful in a more complex program that deals with multiple files.

The general-purpose members defined by the base `Exception` class include the `Message` property, which returns a string containing a textual description of the problem. The default error handling for console applications displays this. The text `Could not find file 'C:\Temp\File.txt'` that we saw when first running Example 8-1 came from the `Message` property. So I could have just displayed that instead of

---

1 Strictly speaking, the CLR allows any type as an exception. However, C# can throw only `Exception`-derived types. Some languages let you throw other types, but it is strongly discouraged.

building my own message, although there will often be cases where your knowledge about what the code was trying to do when the problem occurs will enable you to produce a more informative message than the default. But the Message property is important when you're diagnosing unexpected exceptions.

 The Message property is intended for human consumption. It is therefore a bad idea to write code that attempts to interpret an exception by inspecting the Message property.

One reason you shouldn't rely on exact text appearing in Message is that some APIs localize these messages, so string comparisons could fail when your code runs on a computer configured to run in a region where the main spoken language is different than yours. Moreover, Microsoft doesn't treat exception message changes as breaking changes, so the text might change even within the same locale. It is best to rely on the actual exception type, although some exceptions such as IOException get used in ambiguous ways. So you sometimes need to inspect the HResult property, which will be set to an error code from the OS in such cases.

Exception also defines an InnerException property. This is often null, but it comes into play when one operation fails as a result of some other failure. Sometimes, exceptions that occur deep inside a library would make little sense if they were allowed to propagate all the way up to the caller. For example, .NET provides a library for parsing XAML files. (XAML—Extensible Application Markup Language—is used by various .NET UI frameworks, including WPF.) XAML is extensible, so it's possible that your code (or perhaps some third-party code) will run as part of the process of loading a XAML file, and this extension code could fail—suppose a bug in your code causes an IndexOutOfRangeException to be thrown while trying to access an array element. It would be somewhat mystifying for that exception to emerge from a XAML API, so regardless of the underlying cause of the failure, the library throws a XamlParseException. This means that if you want to handle the failure to load a XAML file, you know exactly which exception to handle, but the underlying cause of the failure is not lost: when some other exception caused the failure, it will be in the InnerException.

All exceptions contain information about where the exception was thrown. The StackTrace property provides the call stack as a string. As you've already seen, the default exception handler for console applications displays that. There's also a Target Site property, which tells you which method was executing. It returns an instance of the reflection API's MethodBase class. See Chapter 13 for details on reflection.

Multiple catch Blocks

A try block can be followed by multiple catch blocks. If the first catch does not match the exception being thrown, the CLR will then look at the next one, then the next, and so on. Example 8-5 supplies handlers for FileNotFoundException, Direc toryNotFoundException, and IOException.

Example 8-5. Handling multiple exception types

```
try
{
    using (var r = new StreamReader(@"C:\Temp\File.txt"))
    {
        while (!r.EndOfStream)
        {
            Console.WriteLine(r.ReadLine());
        }
    }
}
catch (FileNotFoundException ex)
{
    Console.WriteLine($"File '{ex.FileName}' is missing");
}
catch (DirectoryNotFoundException)
{
    Console.WriteLine($"The containing directory does not exist.");
}
catch (IOException ex)
{
    Console.WriteLine($"IO error: '{ex.Message}'");
}
```

An interesting feature of this example is that both FileNotFoundException and DirectoryNotFoundException derive from IOException. I could remove the first two catch blocks, and this would still handle these exceptions correctly (just with less-specific messages), because the CLR considers a catch block to be a match if it handles the base type of the exception. So Example 8-5 has two viable handlers for a FileNotFoundException and also two viable handlers for DirectoryNotFound Exception. (The third handler is still useful because the documentation tells us that for certain kinds of failure, StreamReader will throw an IOException, and not either of the more specific types.) In these cases, C# requires more specific handlers to come first. If I were to move the IOException handler above the other handlers, I'd get this compiler error for each of the more specific handlers:

```
error CS0160: A previous catch clause already catches all exceptions of this or
of a super type ('IOException')
```

If you write a catch block for the Exception base type, it will catch all exceptions. In most cases, this is the wrong thing to do. While it's good to handle the exceptions you can anticipate, if you don't know what an exception represents, you should normally let it pass. Otherwise, you risk masking a problem. If you let the exception carry on, it's more likely to get to a place where it will be noticed, increasing the chances that you will fix the problem properly at some point. A catchall handler would be appropriate if you intend to wrap all exceptions in another exception and throw that, like the XamlParseException described earlier. A catchall exception handler might also make sense if it's at a point where the only place left for the exception to go is the default handling supplied by the system. (That might mean the Main method for a console application, but for multithreaded applications, it might mean the code at the top of a newly created thread's stack.) It might be appropriate in these locations to catch all exceptions and write the details to a logfile or some similar diagnostic mechanism. Even then, once you've logged it, you would probably want to rethrow the exception, as described later in this chapter, or even terminate the process with a non-zero exit code.

For critically important services, you might be tempted to write code that swallows the exception so that your application can limp on. This is a bad idea. If an exception you did not anticipate occurs, your application's internal state may no longer be trustworthy, because your code might have been halfway through an operation when the failure occurred. If you cannot afford for the application to go offline, the best approach is to arrange for it to restart automatically after a failure. Most cloud providers' hosting services can be configured to do this automatically.

Exception Filters

You can make a catch block conditional: if you provide an *exception filter* for your catch block, it will only catch exceptions when the filter condition is true. Example 8-6 shows how this can be useful. It uses the client API for Azure Table Storage, a NoSQL storage service offered as part of Microsoft's Azure cloud computing platform. This API's TableClient class has an AddEntity method that will throw a RequestFailedException if something goes wrong. The problem is that "something goes wrong" is very broad and covers more than connectivity and authentication failures. You will also see this exception for situations such as an attempt to insert a row when another row with the same keys already exists. That is not necessarily an error—it can occur as part of normal usage in some optimistic concurrency models.

Example 8-6. catch block with exception filter

```
public static bool InsertIfDoesNotExist(MyEntity item, TableClient table)
{
    try
    {
        table.AddEntity(item);
        return true;
    }
    catch (RequestFailedException ex)
    when (x.Status == 409)
    {
        return false;
    }
}
```

Example 8-6 looks for that specific failure case and returns `false` instead of allowing the exception to continue propagating up the stack. It does this with a `when` clause containing a filter, which must be an expression of type `bool`. If the `Execute` method throws a `StorageException` that does not match the filter condition, the exception will propagate as usual—it will be as though the `catch` block were not there.

> When using exception filters, a single `try` block can have multiple `catch` blocks for the same exception. Normally that would cause a compiler error, because only the first such `catch` would do anything, but with filters, that's not necessarily the case, so the compiler allows it. You can even have one unfiltered `catch` for a particular exception type when there are also filtered `catch` blocks for the same type, but the unfiltered one must appear last.

An exception filter must be an expression that produces a `bool`. It can invoke external methods if necessary. Example 8-6 just fetches a property and performs a comparison, but you are free to invoke any method as part of the expression.[2] However, you should be careful to avoid doing anything in your filter that might cause another exception. If that happens, that second exception will be lost.

Nested try Blocks

If an exception occurs in a `try` block that does not provide a suitable handler, the CLR will keep looking. It will walk up the stack if necessary, but you can have multiple sets of handlers in a single method by nesting one `try/catch` inside another `try` block, as Example 8-7 shows. `ShowFirstLineLength` nests a `try/catch` pair inside the

---

2 Exception filters cannot use the `await` keyword, which is discussed in Chapter 17.

try block of another `try`/`catch` pair. Nesting can also be done across methods—the `Main` method will catch any `NullReferenceException` that emerges from the `Show FirstLineLength` method (which will be thrown if the file is completely empty—the call to `ReadLine` will return `null` in that case).

Example 8-7. Nested exception handling

```csharp
static void Main(string[] args)
{
    try
    {
        ShowFirstLineLength(@"C:\Temp\File.txt");
    }
    catch (NullReferenceException)
    {
        Console.WriteLine("NullReferenceException");
    }
}

static void ShowFirstLineLength(string fileName)
{
    try
    {
        using (var r = new StreamReader(fileName))
        {
            try
            {
                Console.WriteLine(r.ReadLine()!.Length);
            }
            catch (IOException ex)
            {
                Console.WriteLine("Error while reading file: {0}",
                    x.Message);
            }
        }
    }
    catch (FileNotFoundException ex)
    {
        Console.WriteLine("Couldn't find the file '{0}'", x.FileName);
    }
}
```

I nested the `IOException` handler here to make it apply to one particular part of the work: it handles only errors that occur while reading the file after it has been opened successfully. It might sometimes be useful to respond to that scenario differently than for an error that prevented you from opening the file in the first place.

The cross-method handling here is somewhat contrived. The `NullReferenceExcep` tion could be avoided by testing the return value of `ReadLine` for null. (The compiler would have pointed that out to me if I hadn't deliberately silenced it with the ! after ReadLine().) However, the underlying CLR mechanism this illustrates is extremely important. A particular try block can define catch blocks just for those exceptions it knows how to handle, allowing others to escape up to higher levels.

Letting exceptions carry on up the stack is often the right thing to do. Unless there is something useful your method can do in response to discovering an error, it's going to need to let its caller know there's a problem, so unless you want to wrap the exception in a different kind of exception, you may as well let it through.

 If you're familiar with Java, you may be wondering if C# has anything equivalent to checked exceptions. It does not. Methods do not formally declare the exceptions they throw, so there's no way the compiler can tell you if you have failed either to handle them or declare that your method might, in turn, throw them.

You can also nest a try block inside a catch block. This is important if there are ways in which your error handler itself can fail. For example, if your exception handler logs information about a failure to disk, that could fail if there's a problem with the disk.

Some try blocks never catch anything. It's illegal to write a try block that isn't followed directly by something, but that something doesn't have to be a catch block: it can be a *finally block*.

finally Blocks

A finally block contains code that always runs once its associated try block has finished. It runs whether execution left the try block simply by reaching the end, returning from the middle, or throwing an exception. The finally block will run even if you use a goto statement to jump right out of the try block. Example 8-8 shows a finally block in use.

Example 8-8. A finally block

```
using Microsoft.Office.Interop.PowerPoint;

...

[STAThread]
static void Main(string[] args)
{
    var pptApp = new Application();
    Presentation pres = pptApp.Presentations.Open(args[0]);
    try
    {
```

```
        ProcessSlides(pres);
    }
    finally
    {
        pres.Close();
    }
}
```

This is an excerpt from a utility I wrote to process the contents of a Microsoft Office PowerPoint file. This just shows the outermost code; I've omitted the actual detailed processing code, because it's not relevant here (although if you're curious, the full version in the downloadable examples for this book exports animated slides as video clips). I'm showing it because it uses `finally`. This example uses COM interop to control the PowerPoint application. This example closes the document once it has finished, and the reason I put that code in a `finally` block is that I don't want the program to leave things open if something goes wrong partway through. This is important because of the way COM automation works. It's not like opening a file, where the OS automatically closes everything when the process terminates. If this program exits suddenly, PowerPoint will not close whatever had been opened—it just assumes that you meant to leave things open. (You might do this deliberately when creating a new document that the user will then edit.) I don't want that, and closing the file in a `finally` block is a reliable way to avoid it.

Normally, you'd write a `using` statement for this sort of thing, but PowerPoint's COM-based automation API doesn't support .NET's `IDisposable` interface. In fact, as we saw in the previous chapter, the `using` statement works in terms of `finally` blocks under the covers, as does `foreach`, so you're relying on the exception-handling system's `finally` mechanism even when you write `using` statements and `foreach` loops.

 `finally` blocks run correctly when your exception blocks are nested. If some method throws an exception that is handled by a method that's, say, five levels above it in the call stack, and if some of the methods in between were in the middle of `using` statements, `foreach` loops, or `try` blocks with associated `finally` blocks, all of these intermediate `finally` blocks (whether explicit or generated implicitly by the compiler) will execute before the handler runs.

Handling exceptions is only half of the story, of course. Your code may well detect problems, and exceptions may be an appropriate mechanism for reporting them.

Throwing Exceptions

Throwing an exception is very straightforward. You simply construct an exception object of the appropriate type, and then use the throw keyword. Example 8-9 does this when its position argument is outside the range that makes sense.

Example 8-9. Throwing an exception

```
public static string GetCommaSeparatedEntry(string text, int position)
{
    string[] parts = text.Split(',');
    if (position < 0 || position >= parts.Length)
    {
        throw new ArgumentOutOfRangeException(nameof(position));
    }
    return parts[position];
}
```

The CLR does all of the work for us. It captures the information required for the exception to be able to report its location through properties like StackTrace and TargetSite. (It doesn't calculate their final values, because these are relatively expensive to produce. It just makes sure that it has the information it needs to be able to produce them if asked.) It then hunts for a suitable try/catch block, and if any finally blocks need to be run, it'll execute those.

Example 8-9 illustrates a common technique used when throwing exceptions that report a problem with a method argument. Exceptions such as ArgumentNull Exception, ArgumentOutOfRangeException, and their base class ArgumentException can all report the name of the offending argument. (This is optional because sometimes you need to report inconsistency across multiple arguments, in which case there isn't a single argument to be named.) It's a good idea to use C#'s nameof operator. You can use this with any expression that refers to a named item, such as an argument, a variable, a property, or a method. It compiles into a string containing the item's name.

I could have simply used the string literal "position" here instead, but the advantages of nameof are that it can avoid silly mistakes (if I type positon instead of posi tion, the compiler will tell me that there's no such symbol), and it can help avoid problems caused when renaming a symbol. If I were to rename the position argument in Example 8-9, I could easily forget to change a string literal to match. But by using nameof(position), I'll get an error if I change the name of the argument to, say, pos, without also changing nameof(position)—the compiler will report that there is no identifier called position. If I ask a C#-aware IDE (e.g., Visual Studio or JetBrains Rider) to rename the argument, it will automatically update all the places in the code that use the symbol, so it will replace the exception's constructor argument with nameof(input) for me.

We could use a similar technique with ArgumentNullException, but .NET offers a helper function that can simplify throwing this particular exception. As Example 8-10 shows, instead of having to write an if statement that tests the input, with a body that throws an exception identifying the correct parameter name, we can just call Argu mentNullException.ThrowIfNull.

Example 8-10. Throwing an ArgumentNullException

```
public static int CountCommas(string input)
{
    ArgumentNullException.ThrowIfNull(input);
    return input.Count(ch => ch == ',');
}
```

This tests whatever argument you pass and throws an ArgumentNullException if it is null. But how can this set the parameter name correctly? This ThrowIfNull method is annotated with the CallerArgumentExpression attribute. As Chapter 14 describes, this attribute enables the ThrowIfNull helper to discover the text of the expression that the caller used as the argument. Since we pass our input argument to this helper, it will be passed an additional hidden argument, the string "input". So this has all the same benefits as using nameof with other argument exceptions, but it also performs the relevant test for us.

Many exception types provide a constructor overload that lets you set the Message text. A more specialized message may make problems easier to diagnose, but there's one thing to be careful of. Exception messages often find their way into diagnostic logs and may also be sent automatically in emails by monitoring systems.

 You should be careful about what information you put in exception messages. This is particularly important if your software will be used in countries with data protection laws such as the General Data Protection Regulation (GDPR) that applies in EU nations. If an exception message contains information that refers in any way to a specific user, and this ends up in a log, this might contravene those laws.

Rethrowing Exceptions

Sometimes it is useful to write a `catch` block that performs some work in response to an error but allows the error to continue once that work is complete. There's an obvious but wrong way to do this, illustrated in Example 8-11.

Example 8-11. How not to rethrow an exception

```
try
{
    DoSomething();
}
catch (IOException ex)
{
    LogIOError(ex);
    // This next line is BAD!
    throw x;  // Do not do this
}
```

This will compile without errors, and it will even appear to work, but it has a serious problem: it loses the context in which the exception was originally thrown. The CLR treats this as a brand-new exception (even though you're reusing the exception object) and will reset the location information: the `StackTrace` and `TargetSite` will report that the error originated inside your `catch` block. This could make it hard to diagnose the problem, because you won't be able to see where it was originally thrown. Example 8-12 shows how you can avoid this problem.

Example 8-12. Rethrowing without loss of context

```
try
{
    DoSomething();
}
catch (IOException ex)
{
    LogIOError(ex);
    throw;
}
```

The only difference between this and Example 8-11 (aside from removing the warning comments) is that I'm using the `throw` keyword without specifying which object to use as the exception. You're allowed to do this only inside a `catch` block, and it rethrows whichever exception the `catch` block was in the process of handling. This means that the `Exception` properties that report the location from which the exception was thrown will still refer to the original throw location, not the rethrow.

There is another context-related issue to be aware of when handling exceptions that you might need to rethrow that arises from how the CLR supplies information to Windows Error Reporting (WER), the component that leaps into action when an application crashes on Windows. Depending on how your machine is configured, WER might show a crash dialog that can offer options including restarting the application, reporting the crash to Microsoft, debugging the application, or just terminating it. In addition to all that, when a Windows application crashes, WER captures several pieces of information to identify the crash location. For .NET applications, this includes the name, version, and timestamp of the component that failed, the exception type that was thrown, and information about the location from which the exception was thrown. These pieces of information are sometimes referred to as the *bucket* values. If the application crashes twice with the same values, those two crashes go into the same bucket, meaning that they are considered to be in some sense the same crash.

Retrieving this information from the Windows Event Log is all very well for code running on computers you control (or you might prefer to use more direct ways to monitor such applications, using systems such as Microsoft's Application Insights to collect telemetry, in which case WER is not very interesting). Where WER becomes more important is for applications that may run on other computers outside of your control, e.g., applications with a UI that run entirely locally or console applications. Computers can be configured to upload crash reports to an error reporting service, and usually, just the bucket values get sent, although the services can request additional data if the end user consents. Bucket analysis can be useful when deciding how to prioritize bug fixes: it makes sense to start with the largest bucket, because that's the crash your users are seeing most often. (Or, at least, it's the one seen most often by users who have not disabled crash reporting. I always enable this on my computers, because I want the bugs I encounter in the programs I use to be fixed first.)

 The way to get access to accumulated crash bucket data depends on the kind of application you're writing. For a line-of-business application that runs only inside your enterprise, you will probably want to run an error reporting server of your own, but if the application runs outside of your administrative control, you can use Microsoft's own crash servers. There's a certificate-based process for verifying that you are entitled to the data, but once you've jumped through the relevant hoops, Microsoft will show you all reported crashes for your applications, sorted by bucket size.

Certain exception-handling tactics can defeat the crash bucket system. If you write common error-handling code that gets involved with all exceptions, there's a risk that WER will think that your application only ever crashes inside that common handler, which would mean that crashes of all kinds would go into the same bucket. This is not inevitable, but to avoid it, you need to understand how your exception-handling code affects WER crash bucket data.

If an exception rises to the top of the stack without being handled, WER will get an accurate picture of exactly where the crash happened, but things may go wrong if you catch an exception before eventually allowing it (or some other exception) to continue up the stack. A bit surprisingly, .NET will successfully preserve the location for WER even if you use the bad approach shown in Example 8-11. (It's only from .NET's perspective inside that application that this loses the exception context—StackTrace will show the rethrow location. So WER does not necessarily report the same crash location as .NET code will see in the exception object.) It's a similar story when you wrap an exception as the InnerException of a new one: .NET will use that inner exception's location for the crash bucket values.

This means that it's relatively easy to preserve the WER bucket. The only ways to lose the original context are either to handle the exception completely (i.e., not to crash) or to write a catch block that handles the exception and then throws a new one without passing the original one in as an InnerException.

Although Example 8-12 preserves the original context, this approach has a limitation: you can rethrow the exception only from inside the block in which you caught it. But asynchronous programming is now very prevalent, so it is common for exceptions to occur on some random worker thread. We need a reliable way to capture the full context of an exception, and to be able to rethrow it with that full context some arbitrary amount of time later, possibly from a different thread.

The ExceptionDispatchInfo class solves these problems. If you call its static Capture method from a catch block, passing in the current exception, it captures the full context, including the information required by WER. The Capture method returns an instance of ExceptionDispatchInfo. When you're ready to rethrow the exception, you can call this object's Throw method, and the CLR will rethrow the exception with the original context fully intact. Unlike the mechanism shown in Example 8-12, you don't need to be inside a catch block when you rethrow. You don't even need to be on the thread from which the exception was originally thrown.

 If you use the async and await keywords described in Chapter 17, they use ExceptionDispatchInfo for you to ensure that exception context is preserved correctly.

Failing Fast

Some situations call for drastic action. If you detect that your application is in a hopelessly corrupt state, throwing an exception may not be sufficient, because there's always the chance that something may handle it and then attempt to continue. This risks corrupting persistent state—perhaps the invalid in-memory state could lead to your program writing bad data into a database. It may be better to bail out immediately before you do any lasting damage.

The `Environment` class provides a `FailFast` method. If you call this, the CLR will then terminate your application. (If you're running on Windows, it will also write a message to the Windows Event Log and provide details to WER.) If the `DOTNET_Dbg EnableMiniDump` environment variable is set to 1, this will create a *minidump*, a file that can subsequently be loaded by a debugger to inspect the program's state at the moment of failure. You can optionally supply a string and an exception. These details will be written to the standard error output, and will also be preserved in the minidump if one is created. On Windows, these details will also be written to the event log, including the WER bucket values for the point at which the exception was thrown.

Exception Types

When your code detects a problem and throws an exception, you need to choose which type of exception to throw. You can define your own exception types, but the runtime libraries define a large number of exception types, so in a lot of situations, you can just pick an existing type. There are hundreds of exception types, so a full list would be inappropriate here; if you want to see the complete set, the online documentation for the `Exception` class lists the derived types. However, there are certain ones that it's important to know about.

The runtime libraries define an `ArgumentException` class, which is the base of several exceptions that indicate when a method has been called with bad arguments. Example 8-9 used `ArgumentOutOfRangeException`, and Example 8-10 indirectly threw an `ArgumentNullException`, both of which derive from `ArgumentException`. It defines a `ParamName` property, which contains the name of the parameter that was supplied with a bad argument. This is important for multiargument methods, because the caller will need to know which one was wrong. All these exception types have constructors that let you specify the parameter name, and you can see one of these in use in Example 8-9. The base `ArgumentException` is a concrete class, so if the argument is wrong in a way that is not covered by one of the derived types, you can just throw the base exception, providing a textual description of the problem.

Besides the general-purpose types just described, some APIs define more specialized derived argument exceptions. For example, the `System.Globalization` namespace defines an exception type called `CultureNotFoundException` that derives from `ArgumentException`. You can do something similar, and there are two reasons you might want to. If there is additional information you can supply about why the argument is invalid, you will need a custom exception type so you can attach that information to the exception. (`CultureNotFoundException` provides three properties describing aspects of the culture information for which it was searching.) Alternatively, it might be that a particular form of argument error could be handled specially by a caller. Often, an argument exception implies a programming error, but in situations where it might indicate an environment or configuration problem (e.g., not having the right language packs installed), developers might want to handle that specific issue differently. Using the base `ArgumentException` would be unhelpful in that case, because it would be hard to distinguish between the particular failure they want to handle and any other problem with the arguments.

Some methods may want to perform work that could produce multiple errors. Perhaps you're running some sort of batch job, and if some individual tasks in the batch fail, you'd like to abort those but carry on with the rest, reporting all the failures at the end. For these scenarios, it's worth knowing about `AggregateException`. This extends the `InnerException` concept of the base `Exception`, adding an `InnerExceptions` property that returns a collection of exceptions.

 If you nest work that can produce an `AggregateException` (e.g., if you run a batch within a batch), you can end up with some of your inner exceptions also being of type `AggregateException`. This exception offers a `Flatten` method, which recursively walks through any such nested exceptions and produces a single flat list with all the nesting removed. It returns an `AggregateException` with that list as its `InnerExceptions`.

Another commonly used type is `InvalidOperationException`. You would throw this if someone tries to do something with your object that it cannot support in its current state. For example, suppose you have written a class that represents a request that can be sent to a server. You might design this in such a way that each instance can be used only once, so if the request has already been sent, trying to modify the request further would be a mistake, and this would be an appropriate exception to throw. Another important example is if your type implements `IDisposable` and someone tries to use an instance after it has been disposed. That's a sufficiently common case that there's a specialized type derived from `InvalidOperationException` called `ObjectDisposed Exception`.

You should be aware of the distinction between `NotImplementedException` and the similar-sounding but semantically different `NotSupportedException`. The latter should be thrown when an interface demands it. For example, the `IList<T>` interface defines methods for modifying collections but does not require collections to be modifiable—instead, it says that read-only collections should throw NotSupported Exception from members that would modify the collection. An implementation of IList<T> can throw this and still be considered to be complete, whereas Not ImplementedException means something is missing. You will most often see this in code generated by IDEs—these can create stub methods if you ask them to generate an interface implementation or provide an event handler. They generate this code to save you from having to type in the full method declaration, but it's still your job to implement the body of the method. The generated methods will throw this exception so that you do not accidentally leave empty methods in place.

You would normally want to remove all code that throws NotImplementedException before shipping, replacing it with appropriate implementations. However, there is a situation in which you might want to throw it. Suppose you've written a library containing an abstract base class, and your customers write classes that derive from this. When you release new versions of the library, you can add new methods to that base class. Now imagine that you want to add a new library feature for which it would seem to make sense to add a new abstract method to your base class. That would be a breaking change—existing code that successfully derives from the old version of the class would no longer work. You can avoid this problem by providing a virtual method instead of an abstract method, but what if there's no useful default implementation that you can provide? In that case, you might write a base implementation that throws a NotImplementedException. Code built against the old version of the library will not try to use the new feature, so it would never attempt to invoke the method. But if a customer tried to use the new library feature without overriding the relevant method in their class, they would then get this exception. In other words, this provides a way to enforce a requirement of the form: you must override this method if and only if you want to use the feature it represents. (You could use the same approach when adding new members to an interface with default implementations.)

There are, of course, other, more specialized exceptions in the framework, and you should always try to find an exception that matches the problem you wish to report. However, you will sometimes need to report an error for which the runtime libraries do not supply a suitable exception. In this case, you will need to write your own exception class.

Custom Exceptions

The minimum requirement for a custom exception type is that it should derive from Exception (either directly or indirectly). However, there are some design guidelines. The first thing to consider is the immediate base class: if you look at the built-in exception types, you'll notice that many of them derive only indirectly from Exception, through either ApplicationException or SystemException. You should avoid both of these. They were originally introduced with the intention of distinguishing between exceptions produced by applications and ones produced by .NET. However, this did not prove to be a useful distinction. Some exceptions could be thrown by both in different scenarios, and in any case, it was not normally useful to write a handler that caught all application exceptions but not all system ones, or vice versa. The class library design guidelines now tell you not to use these two base types.

Custom exception classes normally derive directly from `Exception`, unless they represent a specialized form of some existing exception. For example, we already saw that `ObjectDisposedException` is a special case of `InvalidOperationException`, and the runtime libraries define several more specialized derivatives of that same base class, such as `ProtocolViolationException` for networking code. If the problem you wish your code to report is clearly an example of some existing exception type, but it still seems useful to define a more specialized type, then you should derive from that existing type.

Although the `Exception` base class has a parameterless constructor, you should not normally use it. Exceptions should provide a useful textual description of the error, so your custom exception's constructors should all call one of the `Exception` constructors that take a string. You can either hardcode the message string[3] in your derived class or define a constructor that accepts a message, passing it on to the base class; it's common for exception types to provide both, although that might be a waste of effort if your code uses only one of the constructors. It depends on whether your exception might be thrown by other code or just yours.

It's also common to provide a constructor that accepts another exception, which will become the `InnerException` property value. Again, if you're writing an exception entirely for your own code's use, there's not much point in adding this constructor until you need it, but if your exception is part of a reusable library, this is a common feature. Example 8-13 shows a hypothetical example that offers various constructors, along with an enumeration type that is used by the property the exception adds.

Example 8-13. A custom exception

```
public class DeviceNotReadyException : InvalidOperationException
{
    public DeviceNotReadyException(DeviceStatus status)
        : this("Device status must be Ready", status)
    {
```

---

3 You could also consider looking up a localized string with the facilities in the `System.Resources` namespace instead of hardcoding it. The exceptions in the runtime libraries all do this. It's not mandatory, because not all programs run in multiple regions, and even for those that do, exception messages will not necessarily be shown to end users.

```
    }

    public DeviceNotReadyException(string message, DeviceStatus status)
        : base(message)
    {
        Status = status;
    }

    public DeviceNotReadyException(string message, DeviceStatus status,
                                    Exception innerException)
        : base(message, innerException)
    {
        Status = status;
    }

    public DeviceStatus Status { get; }
}

public enum DeviceStatus
{
    Disconnected,
    Initializing,
    Failed,
    Ready
}
```

The justification for a custom exception here is that this particular error has something more to tell us besides the fact that something was not in a suitable state. It provides information about the object's state at the moment at which the operation failed.

Unhandled Exceptions

Earlier, you saw the default behavior that a console application exhibits when your application throws an exception that it does not handle. It displays the exception's type, message, and stack trace and then terminates the process. This happens whether the exception went unhandled on the main thread or a thread you created explicitly, or even a thread pool thread that the CLR created for you.

The CLR provides a way to discover when unhandled exceptions reach the top of the stack. The AppDomain class provides an UnhandledException event, which the CLR raises when this happens on any thread.[4] I'll be describing events in Chapter 9, but jumping ahead a little, Example 8-14 shows how to handle this event. It also throws an unhandled exception to try the handler out.

---

4 Although .NET does not support the creation of new appdomains, it still provides the AppDomain class, because that exposes certain important features, such as this event. It will provide a single instance via AppDo main.CurrentDomain.

Example 8-14. Unhandled exception notifications

```
static void Main(string[] args)
{
    AppDomain.CurrentDomain.UnhandledException += OnUnhandledException;

    // Crash deliberately to illustrate the UnhandledException event
    throw new InvalidOperationException();
}

private static void OnUnhandledException(object sender,
    UnhandledExceptionEventArgs e)
{
    Console.WriteLine($"An exception went unhandled: {e.ExceptionObject}");
}
```

When the handler is notified, it's too late to stop the exception—the CLR will terminate the process shortly after calling your handler. The main reason this event exists is to provide a place to put logging code so that you can record some information about the failure for diagnostic purposes. In principle, you could also attempt to store any unsaved data to facilitate recovery if the program restarts, but you should be careful: if your unhandled exception handler gets called, then by definition your program is in a suspect state, so whatever data you save may be invalid.

There is one important scenario in which unhandled exceptions will not terminate the process by default. If you use the Task class (described in Chapter 16) to run concurrent work, it catches any exceptions that emerge from that work, and puts the associated Task into a *faulted* state. This means that exceptions in tasks are, strictly speaking, never unhandled. However, if nothing ever inspects the state of a faulted task, that's called an *unobserved* exception. By default, this doesn't terminate the process, but .NET provides a mechanism (described in Chapter 16) by which you can discover when it happens.

Some application frameworks provide their own ways to deal with unhandled exceptions. For example, UI frameworks (e.g., Windows Forms, WPF) for desktop applications for Windows do this, partly because the default behavior of writing details to the console is not very useful for applications that don't show a console window. These applications need to run a message loop to respond to user input and system messages. It inspects each message and may decide to call one or more methods in your code, in which case it wraps each call in a try block so that it can catch any exceptions your code may throw. The frameworks may show error information in a window instead. And web frameworks, such as ASP.NET Core, need a different mechanism: at a minimum, they should generate a response that indicates a server-side error in the way recommended by the HTTP specification.

This means that the `UnhandledException` event that Example 8-14 uses may not be raised when an unhandled exception escapes from your code, because it may be caught by a framework. If you are using an application framework, you should check to see if it provides its own mechanism for dealing with unhandled exceptions. For example, ASP.NET Core applications can supply a callback to a method called `Use ExceptionHandler` during application startup. WPF has its own `Application` class, and its `DispatcherUnhandledException` event is the one to use. Likewise, Windows Forms provides an `Application` class with a `ThreadException` member.

Even when you're using these frameworks, their unhandled exception mechanisms deal only with exceptions that occur on threads the frameworks control. If you create a new thread and throw an unhandled exception on that, it would show up in the `AppDomain` class's `UnhandledException` event, because frameworks don't control the whole CLR.

Summary

In .NET, errors are usually reported with exceptions, apart from in certain scenarios where failure is expected to be common and the cost of exceptions is likely to be high compared to the cost of the work at hand. Exceptions allow error-handling code to be separate from code that carries out work. They also make it hard to ignore errors—unexpected errors will propagate up the stack and eventually cause the program to terminate and produce an error report. `catch` blocks allow us to handle those exceptions that we can anticipate. (You can also use them to catch all exceptions indiscriminately, but that's usually a bad idea—if you don't know why a particular exception occurred, you cannot know for certain how to recover from it safely.) `finally` blocks provide a way to perform cleanup safely regardless of whether code executes successfully or encounters exceptions. The runtime libraries define numerous useful exception types, but if necessary, we can write our own.

In the chapters so far, we've looked at the basic elements of code, classes and other custom types, collections, and error handling. There's one last feature of the C# type system to look at: a special kind of object called a *delegate*.

CHAPTER 9

Delegates, Lambdas, and Events

The most common way to use an API is to invoke the methods and properties its classes provide, but sometimes things need to work in reverse—the API may need to call your code, an operation often described as a *callback*. In Chapter 5, I showed the search features offered by arrays and lists. To use these, I wrote a method that returned `true` when its argument met my criteria, and the relevant APIs called my method for each item they inspected. Not all callbacks are this immediate. Asynchronous APIs can call a method in our code when long-running work completes. In a client-side application, I want my code to run when the user interacts with certain visual elements in particular ways, such as clicking a button.

Interfaces and virtual methods can enable callbacks. In Chapter 4, I showed the `ICom parer<T>` interface, which defines a single `CompareTo` method. This is called by methods like `Array.Sort` when we want a customized sort ordering. You could imagine a UI framework that defined an `IClickHandler` interface with a `Click` method, and perhaps also `DoubleClick`. The framework could require us to implement this interface if we want to be notified of button clicks.

In fact, none of .NET's UI frameworks use the interface-based approach, because it gets cumbersome when you need multiple kinds of callback. Single- and double-clicks are the tip of the iceberg for user interactions—in WPF applications, each UI element can provide over 100 kinds of notifications. Most of the time, you need to handle only one or two events from any particular element, so an interface with 100 methods to implement would be annoying.

Splitting notifications across multiple interfaces could mitigate this inconvenience. Default interface implementations could help, because it would make it possible to provide default, empty implementations for all callbacks, meaning we'd need to override only the ones we were interested in. (Neither .NET Standard 2.0 nor .NET Framework support this language feature, but a library targeting those could supply a base class with virtual methods instead.) But even with these refinements, there's a serious drawback with this object-oriented approach. Imagine a UI with four buttons. In a hypothetical UI framework that used the approach I've just described, if you wanted each button to have its own click handler, you'd need four distinct implementations of the IClickHandler interface. A single class can implement any particular interface only once, so you'd need to write four classes. That seems very cumbersome when all we really want to do is tell a button to call a particular method when clicked.

C# provides a much simpler solution in the form of a *delegate*, which is a reference to a method. If you want a library to call your code back for any reason, you will normally just pass a delegate referring to the method you'd like it to call. I showed an example of that in Chapter 5, which I've reproduced in Example 9-1. This finds the index of the first element in an int[] array with a nonzero value.

Example 9-1. Searching an array using a delegate

```
public static int GetIndexOfFirstNonEmptyBin(int[] bins)
    => Array.FindIndex(bins, IsNonZero);

private static bool IsNonZero(int value) => value != 0;
```

At first glance, this seems straightforward: the second parameter to Array.FindIndex requires a method that it can call to ask whether a particular element is a match, so I passed my IsNonZero method as an argument. But what does it really mean to pass a method, and how does this fit in with .NET's type system, the CTS?

Delegate Types

Example 9-2 shows the declaration of the FindIndex method used in Example 9-1. The first parameter is the array to be searched, but it's the second one we're interested in—that's where I passed a method.

Example 9-2. Method with a delegate parameter

```
public static int FindIndex<T>(
    T[] array,
    Predicate<T> match)
```

The method's second parameter's type is Predicate<T>, where T is the array element type, and since Example 9-1 uses an int[], that will be a Predicate<int>. (In case you don't have a background in either formal logic or computer science, this type uses the word *predicate* in the sense of a function that determines whether something is true or false. For example, you could have a predicate that tells you whether a number is even. Predicates are often used in this kind of filtering operation.) Example 9-3 shows how this type is defined. This is the whole of the definition, not an excerpt; if you wanted to write a type that was equivalent to Predicate<T>, that's all you'd need to write.

Example 9-3. The Predicate<T> delegate type

```
public delegate bool Predicate<in T>(T obj);
```

Breaking Example 9-3 down, we begin as usual with the accessibility, and we can use all the same keywords we could for other types, such as public or internal. (Like any type, delegate types can optionally be nested inside some other type, in which case you can also use private or protected.) Next is the delegate keyword, which tells the C# compiler that we're defining a delegate type. The rest of the definition looks, not coincidentally, just like a method declaration. We have a return type of bool. You put the delegate type name where you'd normally see the method name. The angle brackets indicate that this is a generic type with a single type parameter T, and the in keyword indicates that T is contravariant. Finally, the method signature has a single parameter of that type.

 The use of contravariance here lets you use a predicate that is more general than would otherwise be required. For example, because all values of type string are compatible with the type object, all values of Predicate<object> are compatible with the type Predicate<string>. Or to put that informally, if an API needs a method that inspects a string, it will work perfectly well if you pass it a method that is able to inspect any object. Chapter 6 described contravariance in detail.

Delegate types are special in .NET, and they work quite differently than classes or structs. The compiler generates a superficially normal-looking type definition with various members that we'll look at in more detail later, but the members are all empty—C# produces no IL for any of them. The CLR provides the implementation at runtime.

A delegate type's parameter list can make arguments optional by defining default values, just like with a normal method declaration, as Example 9-4 shows. I'll show how to invoke a delegate shortly, but optional arguments are handled in exactly the same way as when invoking methods. Similarly, you can define a delegate type that has the params keyword on the final parameter (which must then be an array type) to enable variable numbers of arguments.

Example 9-4. A delegate type with one optional argument

```
public delegate void Log(string message, string? source = "");
```

Instances of delegate types are usually just called delegates, and they refer to methods. A method is compatible with (i.e., can be referred to by an instance of) a particular delegate type if its signature matches. The `IsNonZero` method in Example 9-1 takes an `int` and returns a `bool`, so it is compatible with `Predicate<int>`. The match does not have to be precise. If implicit reference conversions are available for parameter types, you can use a more general method. (Although this may sound very similar to the upshot of `T` being contravariant, this is a subtly different issue. `T` being contravariant in `Predicate<T>` determines what types an existing instance of `Predicate<T>` can be converted to. This is separate from the rules around whether you can construct a new delegate of some specific type from a particular method: the signature matching rules I'm now describing apply even for nongeneric delegates, and for generic delegates with invariant type parameters.) For example, a method with a return type of `bool`, and a single parameter of type `object`, would be compatible with `Predi cate<object>`, but because such a method can accept `string` arguments, it would also be compatible with `Predicate<string>`. (It would not be compatible with `Predi cate<int>`, because there's no implicit reference conversion from `int` to `object`. There's an implicit conversion, but it's a boxing conversion, not a reference conversion.)

Creating a Delegate

The simplest way to create a delegate is to write just the method name. Example 9-5 declares a variable, p, and initializes it with the `IsNonZero` method from Example 9-1. (This code requires `IsNonZero` to be in scope, so we could only write this inside the same class.)

Example 9-5. Creating a delegate

```
var p = IsNonZero;
```

This example says nothing about the particular delegate type required, which causes the compiler to pick from one of a couple of families of generic types that I'll be describing later in this chapter. In the unusual cases where you can't use those, it will define a type for you. In this case, it will use `Func<int, bool>`, reflecting the fact that `IsNonZero` is a method that takes an `int` and returns a `bool`. This is a reasonable choice, but what if I wanted to use the `Predicate<int>` type because I'm planning to pass it to `Array.FindIndex`, as in Example 9-1? If you don't want the compiler's default choice, you can use the `new` keyword, as Example 9-6 shows. This lets you state the type, and where you'd normally pass constructor arguments, you can supply the name of a compatible method.

Example 9-6. Constructing a delegate

```
var p = new Predicate<int>(IsNonZero);
```

In practice, we rarely use new for delegates. It's necessary only in cases where the compiler will not infer the right delegate type. Typically, the compiler can work it out from context. Example 9-7 declares a variable with an explicit type, so the compiler knows a Predicate<int> is required—we don't need to use new here. This has the same effect as Example 9-6, although thanks to a feature added in C# 11.0 it will be slightly more efficient in cases where the code runs many times. The compiler generates a hidden static field to hold the delegate, meaning construction only has to happen the first time this line of code runs; it will reuse the same delegate on all subsequent occasions.

Example 9-7. Implicit delegate construction

```
Predicate<int> p = IsNonZero;
```

That still mentions the delegate type name explicitly, but often we don't even need to do that. Example 9-1 correctly determined that IsNonZero needed to be turned into a Predicate<int> without us needing to say so. The compiler knows that the second argument to FindIndex is Predicate<T>, and because we supplied a first argument of type int[], it deduced that T is int, so it knows the second argument's full type is Predicate<int>. Having worked that out, it uses the same built-in implicit conversion rules to construct the delegate as Example 9-7. So when you pass a delegate to a method, the compiler can normally work out the right type by itself.

When code refers to a method by name like this, the name is technically called a *method group*, because multiple overloads may exist for a single name. The compiler narrows this down by looking for the best possible match in a similar way to how it chooses an overload when you invoke a method. As with method invocation, it is possible that there will be either no matches or multiple equally good matches, and in those cases the compiler will produce an error.

Method groups can take several forms. In the examples shown so far, I have used an unqualified method name, which works only when the method in question is in scope. If you want to refer to a static method defined in some other class, you would need to qualify it with the class name, as Example 9-8 shows.

Example 9-8. Delegates referring to methods in another class

```
internal static class Program
{
    static void Main()
    {
        Predicate<int> p1 = Tests.IsGreaterThanZero;
        Predicate<int> p2 = Tests.IsLessThanZero;
    }
}

internal class Tests
{
    public static bool IsGreaterThanZero(int value) => value > 0;

    public static bool IsLessThanZero(int value) => value < 0;
}
```

Delegates don't have to refer to static methods. They can refer to an instance method. There are a couple of ways you can make that happen. One is simply to refer to an instance method by name from a context in which that method is in scope. The `GetIs` `GreaterThanPredicate` method in Example 9-9 returns a delegate that refers to `IsGreaterThan`. Both are instance methods, so they can be used only with an object reference, but `GetIsGreaterThanPredicate` has an implicit `this` reference, and the compiler automatically provides that to the delegate that it implicitly creates. (This prevents the compiler from using the optimization introduced in C# 11.0—in these cases it can't create a hidden static field to cache the delegate because each delegate will refer to a specific instance of `ThresholdComparer`. In principle it could create a hidden nonstatic field instead, but it does not. Adding an extra field to every instance of a type has a higher cost than a single static field, so there's a significant risk that this would have a negative effect.)

Example 9-9. Implicit instance delegate

```
public class ThresholdComparer
{
    public required int Threshold { get; init; }

    public bool IsGreaterThan(int value) => value > Threshold;

    public Predicate<int> GetIsGreaterThanPredicate() => IsGreaterThan;
}
```

Alternatively, you can be explicit about which instance you want. Example 9-10 creates three instances of the `ThresholdComparer` class from Example 9-9, and then creates three delegates referring to the `IsGreaterThan` method, one for each instance.

Example 9-10. Explicit instance delegate

```
var zeroThreshold = new ThresholdComparer { Threshold = 0 };
var tenThreshold = new ThresholdComparer { Threshold = 10 };
var hundredThreshold = new ThresholdComparer { Threshold = 100 };

Predicate<int> greaterThanZero = zeroThreshold.IsGreaterThan;
Predicate<int> greaterThanTen = tenThreshold.IsGreaterThan;
Predicate<int> greaterThanOneHundred = hundredThreshold.IsGreaterThan;
```

You don't have to limit yourself to simple expressions of the form `variable Name.MethodName`. You can take any expression that evaluates to an object reference, and then just append `.MethodName`; if the object has one or more methods called `MethodName`, that will be a valid method group.

> You can define delegate types with any number of parameters. For example, the runtime libraries define `Comparison<T>`, which compares two items, and therefore takes two arguments (both of type `T`).

C# will not let you create a delegate that refers to an instance method without specifying either implicitly or explicitly which instance you mean, and it will always initialize the delegate with that instance.

> When you pass a delegate to some other code, that code does not need to know whether the delegate's target is a static or an instance method. And for instance methods, the code that uses the delegate does not supply the instance. Delegates that refer to instance methods always know which instance they refer to, as well as which method.

There's another way to create a delegate that can be useful if you do not necessarily know which method or object you will use until runtime: you can use the reflection API (which I will explain in detail in Chapter 13). First, you obtain a `MethodInfo`, an object representing a particular method. Then you call its `CreateDelegate<TDele gate>` method, specifying the delegate type as a type argument and, where required, passing the target object. (If you're creating a delegate referring to a static method, there is no target object, so there's an overload that takes only the delegate type.) This will create a delegate referring to whichever method the `MethodInfo` instance identifies. Example 9-11 uses this technique. It obtains a `Type` object (also part of the reflection API; it's a way to refer to a particular type) representing the `ThresholdComparer` class. Next, it asks it for a `MethodInfo` representing the `IsGreaterThan` method. On this, it calls the overload of CreateDelegate that takes the delegate type and the target instance.

Example 9-11. CreateDelegate

```
MethodInfo m = typeof(ThresholdComparer).GetMethod("IsGreaterThan")!;
var greaterThanZero = m.CreateDelegate<Predicate<int>>(zeroThreshold);
```

There is another way to perform the same job: the Delegate type has a static Create Delegate method, which avoids the need to obtain the MethodInfo. You pass it two Type objects—the delegate type and the type defining the target method—and also the method name. If you already have a MethodInfo in hand, you may as well use that, but if all you have is the name, this alternative is more convenient.

 Selecting a delegate target by name at runtime is likely not to work if you build a trimmed self-contained executable (e.g., if you're using Native AOT) as described in Chapter 12. Example 9-11 specifies the target type and method names directly, so the build tools can deduce that they must not remove the ThresholdCom parer.IsGreaterThan method in this case, but in general, code that uses these kinds of dynamic techniques to choose the target at runtime is typically incompatible with trimming.

To summarize what we've seen so far, a delegate identifies a specific function, and if that's an instance function, the delegate also contains an object reference. But some delegates do more.

Multicast Delegates

If you look at any delegate type with a reverse-engineering tool such as ILDASM,[1] you'll see that whether it's a type supplied by the runtime libraries or one you've defined yourself, it derives from a base type called MulticastDelegate. As the name suggests, this means delegates can refer to more than one method. This is mostly of interest in notification scenarios where you may need to invoke multiple methods when some event occurs. However, all delegates support this whether you need it or not.

Even delegates with non-void return types derive from MulticastDelegate. That doesn't usually make much sense. For example, code that requires a Predicate<T> will normally inspect the return value. Array.FindIndex uses it to find out whether

---

[1] ILDASM ships with Visual Studio. At the time of writing, Microsoft doesn't provide a cross-platform version, but you could use the open source project ILSpy (*https://oreil.ly/ILSpy*).

an element matches our search criteria. If a single delegate refers to multiple methods, what's `FindIndex` supposed to do with multiple return values? It just accepts the default behavior, which is to execute all the methods but to ignore the return values of all except the final method that runs. (It's possible to write code to provide special handling for multicast delegates, but `FindIndex` does not.)

The multicast feature is available through the `Delegate` class's static `Combine` method. This takes any two delegates and returns a single delegate. When the resulting delegate is invoked, it is as though you invoked the two original delegates one after the other. This works even when the delegates you pass to `Combine` already refer to multiple methods—you can chain together ever larger multicast delegates. If the same method is referred to in both arguments, the resulting combined delegate will invoke it twice.

 Delegate combination always produces a new delegate. And the `Combine` method doesn't modify either of the delegates you pass it.

In fact, we rarely call `Delegate.Combine` explicitly, because C# has built-in support for combining delegates. You can use the + or += operators. Example 9-12 shows both, combining the three delegates from Example 9-10 into a single multicast delegate. The two resulting delegates are equivalent—this just shows two ways of writing the same thing. Both cases compile into a couple of calls to `Delegate.Combine`.

Example 9-12. Combining delegates

```
Predicate<int> megaPredicate1 =
    greaterThanZero + greaterThanTen + greaterThanOneHundred;

Predicate<int> megaPredicate2 = greaterThanZero;
megaPredicate2 += greaterThanTen;
megaPredicate2 += greaterThanOneHundred;
```

You can also use the - or -= operators, which produce a new delegate that is a copy of the first operand but with its last reference to the method referred to by the second operand removed. As you might guess, this turns into a call to `Delegate.Remove`.

Invoking a Delegate

So far, I've shown how to create a delegate, but what if you're writing your own API that needs to call back into a method supplied by your caller? First, you would need to pick a delegate type. You could use one supplied by the runtime libraries, or, if necessary, you can define your own. Then, you can use this delegate type for a method parameter or a property. Example 9-13 shows what to do when you want to call the method (or methods) the delegate refers to.

Example 9-13. Invoking a delegate

```
public static void CallMeRightBack(Predicate<int> userCallback)
{
    bool result = userCallback(42);
    Console.WriteLine(result);
}
```

As this not terribly realistic example shows, you can use an argument of delegate type as though it were a function. This also works for local variables, fields, and properties. In fact, any expression that produces a delegate can be followed by an argument list in parentheses. The compiler will generate code that invokes the delegate. If the delegate has a non-`void` return type, the invocation expression's value will be whatever the underlying method returns (or, in the case of a delegate referring to multiple methods, whatever the final method returns).

Although delegates are special types with runtime-generated code, there is ultimately nothing magical about invoking them. Invoking a delegate with a single target method works as though your code had called the target method in the conventional way. Invoking a multicast delegate is just like calling each of its target methods in turn. In either case, calls happen on the same thread, and exceptions propagate out of methods that were invoked via a delegate in exactly the same way as they do when you invoke the method directly.

If you want to get all the return values from a multicast delegate, you can take control of the invocation process. Delegates offer a `GetInvocationList` method, which returns an array containing a single-method delegate for each of the methods to which the original multicast delegate refers. If you call this on a normal, nonmulticast delegate, this list will contain just that one delegate, but if the multicast feature is being exploited, you could then loop over the array, invoking each in turn.

There is one more way to invoke a delegate that is occasionally useful. The base `Dele gate` class provides a `DynamicInvoke` method. You can call this on a delegate of any type without needing to know at compile time exactly what arguments are required. It takes a `params` array of type `object[]`, so you can pass any number of arguments. It will verify the number and type of arguments at runtime. This can enable certain late-binding scenarios. The intrinsic language features enabled by the `dynamic` keyword (discussed in Chapter 2) are more comprehensive, but they are slightly more heavyweight due to the extra flexibility, so if `DynamicInvoke` does precisely what you need, it is the better choice. (As with the dynamic delegate creation mechanisms we saw earlier, this technique is not a good fit with trimming, so you should avoid this if you want to use Native AOT.)

Common Delegate Types

The runtime libraries provide several useful delegate types, and you will often be able to use these instead of needing to define your own. For example, there is a set of generic delegates named `Action` with varying numbers of type parameters. These all follow a common pattern: for each type parameter, there's a single method parameter of that type. Example 9-14 shows the first four, including the zero-argument form.

Example 9-14. The first few `Action` delegates

```
public delegate void Action();
public delegate void Action<in T1>(T1 arg1);
public delegate void Action<in T1, in T2 >(T1 arg1, T2 arg2);
public delegate void Action<in T1, in T2, in T3>(T1 arg1, T2 arg2, T3 arg3);
```

Although this is clearly an open-ended concept—you could imagine delegates of this form with any number of parameters—the CTS does not provide a way to define this sort of type as a pattern, so the runtime libraries have to define each form as a separate type. Consequently, there is no 200-parameter form of `Action`. The largest has 16 parameters.

The obvious limitation with `Action` is that these types have a `void` return type, so they cannot refer to methods that return values. But there's a similar family of delegate types, `Func`, that allows any return type. Example 9-15 shows the first few delegates in this family, and as you can see, they're pretty similar to `Action`. They just get an additional final type parameter, `TResult`, which specifies the return type. As with `Action<T>`, these go up to 16 parameters.

Example 9-15. The first few `Func` delegates

```
public delegate TResult Func<out TResult>();
public delegate TResult Func<in T1, out TResult>(T1 arg1);
public delegate TResult Func<in T1, in T2, out TResult>(T1 arg1, T2 arg2);
public delegate TResult Func<in T1, in T2, in T3, out TResult>(
    T1 arg1, T2 arg2, T3 arg3);
```

These `Action` and `Func` types are the ones C# will use as the *natural* type of a delegate expression, when possible. You saw this earlier in Example 9-5, when, in the absence of any other direction, the compiler picked `Func<int, bool>`. It will use the `Action` family for methods that have a `void` return type.

These two families of delegates would appear to have most requirements covered. Unless you're writing monster methods with more than 16 parameters, when would you ever need anything else? Well, there are some cases that cannot be expressed with generic type arguments. For example, if you need a delegate that can work with `ref`, in, or out parameters, you can't just write, say, `Func<bool, string, out int>`. This is because there is no such type as `out int` in .NET. When we use the `out` keyword in a method declaration, that's a statement about exactly how the argument works, so an `out int` parameter's type is still `int`. Generic type arguments only get to specify a type and cannot fully convey the distinction between `in`, `out`, and `ref` parameters.[2] So in these cases, you'll have to write a matching delegate type.

Another reason to define a custom delegate type is that you cannot use a `ref struct` as a generic type argument. (Chapter 18 discusses these types.) So if you try to instantiate the generic `Action<T>` type with the `ref struct` type `Span<int>`, by writing `Action<Span<int>>`, you will get a compiler error. This limitation exists because `ref struct` types can only be used in certain scenarios (they must always live on the stack), and there's no way to determine whether any particular generic type or method uses its type arguments only in the ways that are allowed. (You could imagine a new kind of type argument constraint that expressed this, but at the time of writing this, no such constraint exists.) So if you want a delegate type that can refer to a method that takes a `ref struct` argument, it needs to be a dedicated, nongeneric delegate.

 If you're relying on the compiler to determine a delegate expression's natural type (e.g., you write `var m = SomeMethod;`), these cases in which the `Func` and `Action` delegates cannot be used are the cases in which the compiler will generate a delegate type for you.

None of these restrictions explains why the runtime libraries define a separate `Predicate<T>` delegate type. `Func<T, bool>` would work perfectly well. Sometimes this kind of specialized delegate type exists as an accident of history: many delegate types have been around since before these general-purpose `Action` and `Func` types were added. But that's not the only reason—new delegate types continue to be added even now. The main reason is that sometimes it's useful to define a specialized delegate type to indicate particular semantics.

If you have a `Func<T, bool>`, all you know is that you've got a method that takes a `T` and returns a `bool`. But with a `Predicate<T>`, there's an implied meaning: it makes a decision about that `T` instance and returns `true` or `false` accordingly; not all methods that take a single argument and return a `bool` necessarily fit that pattern. By providing a `Predicate<T>`, you're not just saying that you have a method with a particular

---

2 Generic type *definitions* can use the `in` and `out` keywords, but that's different. It indicates when the type *parameter* is contra- or covariant in a generic type. You can't use `in` or `out` when you supply a specific *argument* for a type parameter.

signature; you're saying you have a method that serves a particular purpose. For example, `HashSet<T>` (described in Chapter 5) has an `Add` method that takes a single argument and returns a `bool`, so it matches the signature of `Predicate<T>` but not the semantics. `Add`'s main job is to perform an action with side effects, returning some information about what it did, whereas predicates just tell you something about a value or object.

The runtime libraries define many delegate types, most of them even more specialized than `Predicate<T>`. For example, the `System.IO` namespace and its descendants define several that relate to specific events, such as `SerialPinChangedEventHandler`, which is used only when you're working with old-fashioned serial ports such as the once-ubiquitous RS232 interface.

Type Compatibility

Delegate types do not derive from one another. Any delegate type you define in C# will derive directly from `MulticastDelegate`, as do all of the delegate types in the runtime libraries. However, the type system supports certain implicit reference conversions for generic delegate types through covariance and contravariance. The rules are very similar to those for interfaces. As the `in` keyword in Example 9-3 showed, the type parameter T in `Predicate<T>` is contravariant, which means that if an implicit reference conversion exists between two types, A and B, an implicit reference conversion also exists between the types `Predicate<B>` and `Predicate<A>`. Example 9-16 shows an implicit conversion that this enables.

Example 9-16. Delegate contravariance

```
public static bool IsLongString(object o)
{
    return o is string s && s.Length > 20;
}

static void Main(string[] args)
{
    Predicate<object> po = IsLongString;
    Predicate<string> ps = po;
    Console.WriteLine(ps("Too short"));
}
```

The `Main` method first creates a `Predicate<object>` referring to the `IsLongString` method. Any target method for this predicate type is capable of inspecting any `object` of any kind; thus, it's clearly able to meet the needs of code that requires a predicate capable of inspecting strings. It therefore makes sense that the implicit conversion to `Predicate<string>` should succeed—which it does, thanks to contravariance. Covariance also works in the same way as it does with interfaces, so it would typically be associated with a delegate's return type. (We denote covariant type parameters with the out keyword.) All of the built-in Func delegate types have a covariant type parameter representing the function's return type called TResult. The type parameters for the function's parameters are all contravariant, as are all of the type parameters for the Action delegate types.

 The variance-based delegate conversions are implicit reference conversions. This means that when you convert the reference, the result still refers to the same delegate instance. (All implicit *reference* conversions have this characteristic, but not all implicit conversions work this way. Implicit numeric conversions create a new instance of the target type; implicit boxing conversions create a new box on the heap.) So in Example 9-16, po and ps refer to the same delegate on the heap. This is subtly different from assigning IsLongString into both variables—that would create two delegates of different types.

You might also expect delegates that look the same to be compatible. For example, a Predicate<int> can refer to any method that a Func<int, bool> can use, and vice versa, so you might expect an implicit conversion to exist between these two types. You might be further encouraged by the "Delegate compatibility" section in the C# specification, which says that delegates with identical parameter lists and return types are compatible. (In fact, it goes further, saying that certain differences are allowed. For example, I mentioned earlier that argument types may be different as long as certain implicit reference conversions are available.) However, if you try the code in Example 9-17, it won't work.

Example 9-17. Illegal delegate conversion

```
Predicate<string> pred = IsLongString;
Func<string, bool> f = pred;  // Will fail with compiler error
```

Adding an explicit cast doesn't work either—it removes the compiler error, but you just get a runtime error instead. The CTS considers these to be incompatible types, so a variable declared with one delegate type cannot hold a reference to a different delegate type even if their method signatures are compatible (except for when the two delegate types in question are based on the same generic delegate type and are compatible thanks to covariance or contravariance). This is not the scenario for which C#'s delegate compatibility rules are designed—they are mainly used to determine whether a particular method can be the target for a particular delegate type.

The lack of type compatibility between "compatible" delegate types may seem odd, but structurally identical delegate types don't necessarily have the same semantics, as we've already seen with Predicate<T> and Func<T,bool>. If you find yourself needing to perform this sort of conversion, it may be a sign that something is not quite right in your code's design.[3]

Behind the Syntax

Although it takes just a single line of code to define a delegate type (as Example 9-3 showed), the compiler turns this into a type that defines three methods and a constructor. Of course, the type also inherits members from its base classes. All delegates derive from `MulticastDelegate`, although all of the interesting instance members come from its base class, `Delegate`. (`Delegate` inherits from `object`, so delegates all have the ubiquitous `object` methods too.) Even `GetInvocationList`, clearly a multicast-oriented feature, is defined by the `Delegate` base class.

The split between `Delegate` and `MulticastDelegate` is the meaningless and arbitrary result of a historical accident. The original plan was to support both multicast and unicast delegates, but toward the end of the prerelease period for .NET 1.0 this distinction was dropped, and now all delegate types support multicast instances. This happened sufficiently late in the day that Microsoft felt it was too risky to merge the two base types into one, so the split remained even though it serves no purpose.

I've already mentioned a couple of the public instance members that `Delegate` defines: the `DynamicInvoke` and `GetInvocationList` methods. There are two more. The `Method` property returns the `MethodInfo` representing the target method. (Chapter 13 describes the `MethodInfo` type.) The `Target` property returns the object that will be passed as the implicit `this` argument of the target method; if the delegate refers to a static method, `Target` will return `null`. Example 9-18 shows the signatures of the compiler-generated constructor and methods for a delegate type. The details vary from one type to the next; these are the generated members in the `Predicate<T>` type.

Example 9-18. The members of a delegate type

```
public Predicate(object target, IntPtr method);

public bool Invoke(T obj);

public IAsyncResult BeginInvoke(T obj, AsyncCallback callback, object state);
public bool EndInvoke(IAsyncResult result);
```

---

3 Alternatively, you may just be one of nature's dynamic language enthusiasts, with an allergy to expressing semantics through static types. If that's the case, C# may not be the language for you.

Any delegate type you define will have four similar members. After compilation, none of them will have bodies yet. The compiler generates only their declarations, because the CLR supplies their implementations at runtime.

The constructor takes the target object (which is `null` for static methods) and an `IntPtr` identifying the method.[4] Notice that this is not the `MethodInfo` returned by the `Method` property. Instead, this is a *function token*, an opaque binary identifier for the target method. The CLR can provide binary metadata tokens for all members and types, but there's no C# syntax for working with them, so we don't normally see them. When you construct a new instance of a delegate type, the compiler automatically generates IL that fetches the function token. The reason delegates use tokens internally is that they can be more efficient than working with reflection API types such as `MethodInfo`.

The `Invoke` method is the one that calls the delegate's target method (or methods). You can use this explicitly from C#, as Example 9-19 shows. It is almost identical to Example 9-13, the only difference being that the delegate variable is followed by `.Invoke`. This generates exactly the same code as Example 9-13, so whether you write `Invoke` or just use the syntax that treats delegate identifiers as though they were method names is a matter of style. As a former C++ developer, I've always felt at home with the Example 9-13 syntax, because it's similar to using function pointers in that language, but there's an argument that writing `Invoke` explicitly makes it easier to see that the code is using a delegate.

Example 9-19. Using Invoke explicitly

```
public static void CallMeRightBack(Predicate<int> userCallback)
{
    bool result = userCallback.Invoke(42);
    Console.WriteLine(result);
}
```

One benefit of this explicit form is that you can use the null-conditional operator to handle the case where the delegate variable is null. Example 9-20 uses this to attempt invocation only when a non-null argument is supplied.

4 `IntPtr` is a value type typically used for opaque handle values, or for working with pointers in low-level high-performance code.

Example 9-20. Using Invoke with the null-conditional operator

```
public static void CallMeMaybe(Action<int>? userCallback)
{
    userCallback?.Invoke(42);
}
```

The Invoke method is the home for a delegate type's method signature. When you define a delegate type, this is where the return type and parameter list you specify end up. When the compiler needs to check whether a particular method is compatible with a delegate type (e.g., when you create a new delegate of that type), the compiler compares the Invoke method with the method you've supplied.

As Example 9-18 shows, all delegate types also have BeginInvoke and EndInvoke methods. These used to provide a way to use the thread pool, but they are deprecated and don't work on the current version of .NET. (You'll get a PlatformNotSupported Exception if you call either method.) They still work on .NET Framework, but they are obsolete. You should ignore these outdated methods and use the techniques described in Chapter 16 instead. The main reason these methods used to be popular is that they provided an easy way to pass a set of values from one thread to another—you could just pass whatever you needed as the arguments for the delegate. However, C# now has a much better way to solve the problem: anonymous functions.

Anonymous Functions

C# lets you create delegates without needing to define a separate method explicitly. You can write a special kind of expression whose value is a method. You could think of them as *method expressions* or *function expressions*, but the official name is *anonymous functions*. Expressions can be passed directly as arguments or assigned directly into variables, so the methods these expressions produce don't have names. (At least, not in C#. The runtime requires all methods to have names, so C# generates hidden names for these things, but from a C# language perspective, they are anonymous.)

For simple methods, the ability to write them inline as expressions can remove a lot of clutter. And as we'll see in "Captured Variables" on page 454, the compiler exploits the fact that delegates are more than just a reference to a method to provide anonymous functions with access to any variables that were in scope in the containing method at the point at which the anonymous function appears.

For historical reasons, C# provides two ways to define an anonymous function. The older way involves the delegate keyword and is shown in Example 9-21. This form is known as an *anonymous method*.[5] I've put each argument for FindIndex on a separate line to make the anonymous function (the second argument) stand out, but C# does not require this.

Example 9-21. Anonymous method syntax

```
public static int GetIndexOfFirstNonEmptyBin(int[] bins)
{
    return Array.FindIndex(
        bins,
        delegate (int value) { return value > 0; }
    );
}
```

In some ways, this resembles the normal syntax for defining methods. The parameter list appears in parentheses and is followed by a block containing the body of the method (which can contain as much code as you like, by the way, and is free to contain nested blocks, local variables, loops, and anything else you can put in a normal method). But instead of a method name, we just have the keyword delegate. The compiler infers the return type. In this case, the FindIndex method's signature declares the second parameter to be a Predicate<T>, which tells the compiler that the return type has to be bool.

In fact, the compiler knows more than just the return type. I've passed FindIndex an int[] array, so the compiler will deduce that the type argument T is int, making the second argument a Predicate<int>. This means that in Example 9-21, I had to supply information—the type of the delegate's parameter—that the compiler already knew. A later version of C# introduced a more compact anonymous function syntax that takes better advantage of what the compiler can deduce, shown in Example 9-22.

Example 9-22. Lambda syntax

```
public static int GetIndexOfFirstNonEmptyBin(int[] bins)
{
    return Array.FindIndex(
        bins,
        value => value > 0
    );
}
```

---

5 Unhelpfully, there are two similar terms that mean almost but not quite the same thing. The C# documentation uses *anonymous function* as the general term for either kind of method expression. *Anonymous method* would be a better name for this because these are not all strictly functions—they can have a void return—but by the time Microsoft needed a general term for these things, that name was already taken.

This form of anonymous function is called a *lambda expression*, and it is named after a branch of mathematics that is the foundation of a function-based model for computation. There is no particular significance to the choice of the Greek letter lambda (λ). It was the accidental result of the limitations of 1930s printing technology. The inventor of lambda calculus, Alonzo Church, originally wanted a different notation, but when he published his first paper on the subject, the typesetting machine operator decided to print λ instead, because that was the closest approximation to Church's notation that the machine could produce. Despite these inauspicious origins, this arbitrarily chosen term has become ubiquitous. LISP, an early and influential programming language, used the name *lambda* for expressions that are functions, and since then, many languages have followed suit, including C#.

Example 9-22 is exactly equivalent to Example 9-21; I've just been able to leave various things out. The => token unambiguously marks this out as being a lambda, so the compiler does not need that cumbersome and ugly `delegate` keyword just to recognize this as an anonymous function. The compiler knows from the surrounding context that the method has to take an `int`, so there's no need to specify the parameter's type; I just provided the parameter's name: `value`. For simple methods that consist of just a single expression, the lambda syntax lets you omit the block and the `return` statement. This all makes for very compact lambdas, but in some cases, you might not want to omit quite so much, so as Example 9-23 shows, there are various optional features. Every lambda in this example is equivalent.

Example 9-23. Lambda variations

```
Predicate<int> p1 = value => value > 0;
Predicate<int> p2 = (value) => value > 0;
Predicate<int> p3 = (int value) => value > 0;
Predicate<int> p4 = value => { return value > 0; };
Predicate<int> p5 = (value) => { return value > 0; };
Predicate<int> p6 = (int value) => { return value > 0; };
Predicate<int> p7 = bool (value) => value > 0;
Predicate<int> p8 = bool (int value) => value > 0;
Predicate<int> p9 = bool (value) => { return value > 0; };
Predicate<int> pA = bool (int value) => { return value > 0; };
```

The first variation is that you can put parentheses around the parameter. This is optional with a single parameter, but it is mandatory for multiparameter lambdas. You can also be explicit about the parameters' types (in which case you will also need parentheses, even if there's only one parameter). And, if you like, you can use a block instead of a single expression, at which point you also have to use the `return` keyword if the lambda returns a value. The normal reason for using a block would be if you wanted to write multiple statements inside the method. The final four lines show that you can specify the return type explicitly, although that's only allowed when the parameter list is in parentheses.

You may be wondering why there are quite so many different forms—why not have just one syntax and be done with it? Although the final line of Example 9-23 shows the most general form, it's also a lot more cluttered than the first line. Since one of the goals of lambdas is to provide a more concise alternative to anonymous methods, C# supports these shorter forms where they can be used without ambiguity.

You can also write a lambda that takes no arguments. As Example 9-24 shows, we just put an empty pair of parentheses in front of the => token. (And, as this example also shows, lambdas that use the greater than or equals operator, >=, can look a bit odd due to the meaningless similarity between the => and >= tokens.)

Example 9-24. A zero-argument lambda

```
Func<bool> isAfternoon = () => DateTime.Now.Hour >= 12;
```

The flexible and compact syntax means that lambdas have all but displaced the older anonymous method syntax. However, the older syntax offers one advantage: it allows you to omit the parameter list entirely. In some situations where you provide a callback, you need to know only that whatever you were waiting for has now happened. This is particularly common when using the standard event pattern described later in this chapter, because that requires event handlers to accept arguments even in situations where they serve no purpose. For example, when a button is clicked, there's not much else to say beyond the fact that it was clicked, and yet all of the button types in .NET's various UI frameworks pass two arguments to the event handler. Example 9-25 successfully ignores this by using an anonymous method that omits the parameter list.

Example 9-25. Ignoring arguments in an anonymous method

```
EventHandler clickHandler = delegate { Debug.WriteLine("Clicked!"); };
```

EventHandler is a delegate type that requires its target methods to take two arguments, of type object and EventArgs. If our handler needed access to either, we could, of course, add a parameter list, but the anonymous method syntax lets us leave it out if we want. You cannot do this with a lambda. That said, lambdas offer a succinct way to ignore arguments, which Example 9-26 illustrates.

Example 9-26. A lambda discarding its arguments

```
EventHandler clickHandler = (_, _) => Debug.WriteLine("Clicked!");
```

This has exactly the same effect as Example 9-25 but using the lambda syntax. I've provided an argument list in parentheses, but because I don't want to use either argument, I've put an underscore in each position. This denotes a *discard*. You have seen the _ character in patterns in early chapters, and it's broadly similar in meaning here: it indicates that we know there's a value available; it's just that we don't care what it is and don't intend to use it.

 Before C# introduced support for this discard syntax, people would often use a similar-looking convention. The underscore symbol is a valid identifier, so for single-argument lambdas, nothing stops you from defining an argument named _ and choosing not to refer to it. It got weird with multiple arguments because you can't use the same name for two arguments, meaning Example 9-26 would not compile on older versions of C#. To work around this, people just used multiple underscores, so you might see a lambda starting (_, __, ___) =>. Thankfully, C# now allows us to use a single _ throughout.

Lambdas and Default Arguments

You saw earlier that a delegate type can define default argument values for some or all of its parameters. Prior to C# 12.0, you had to define your own delegate type explicitly to do this, but you can now also do it with the lambda syntax. Example 9-27 shows a delegate specifying a default argument of 10 for its only parameter.

Example 9-27. A lambda specifying a default argument value

```
var withDefault = (int x = 10) => x * 2;
```

I've used var here to demonstrate what happens when you get the compiler to infer the delegate type for a lambda with default arguments. Normally, a lambda like this that takes a single int argument and returns an int result would become a Func<int, int>, but the presence of the = 10 changes that. Func<int, int> represents a method with a single parameter that does not have a default argument. (Generic type parameters are always types, so although you could imagine some syntax like Impossible Type<int, 10, int> it's not possible to write a generic type that works this way—you can't pass a value as a generic type argument.) Since the runtime libraries do not define any type that can be used as the natural type for withDefault in Example 9-27, the compiler will generate an anonymous type similar to the one shown in Example 9-28, which shows how we might have achieved the same end result before C# 12.0.

In fact, the compiler puts this default argument value in two places. It becomes part of the generated generic type, but it also becomes part of the hidden method the compiler generates to hold the code for the lambda. You can see this in the following example, Example 9-28—that x = 10 shows up not only in the `WithDefaultDelegate` type but also in the `WithDefaultMethod`.

Example 9-28. The approximate effect of a lambda specifying a default argument value

```
public delegate int WithDefaultDelegate(int x = 10);

public static class EffectOfLambdaWithDefaultArg
{
    public static void UseLambda()
    {
        WithDefaultDelegate withDefault = WithDefaultMethod;
        Console.WriteLine($"Default arg: {withDefault()}");
        Console.WriteLine($"Supplied arg: {withDefault(42)}");
    }

    private static int WithDefaultMethod(int x = 10)
    {
        return x * 2;
    }
}
```

It's important that the compiler specifies the default value not just on the delegate type but also on the method itself, because it enables one of the main intended scenarios for this new C# 12.0 feature. Some frameworks, most notably the ASP.NET Core web framework, will detect when methods have default argument values, and modify their behavior accordingly. Example 9-29 shows a simple but complete web application that accepts requests just on the root URL (e.g., `https://localhost/`).

Example 9-29. Using a lambda with a default argument in ASP.NET Core

```
WebApplicationBuilder builder = WebApplication.CreateBuilder(args);
WebApplication app = builder.Build();

app.MapGet("/", (string name = "World") => $"Hello {name}!");

app.Run();
```

This supplies a lambda to `MapGet` to provide the code to run for any request for that URL. It defines a single argument, `name`, and if a client supplies a value for that in a query string, e.g., `https://localhost/?name=Ian`, the value will be passed to this code. But since the lambda has specified a default value, ASP.NET Core knows that this is optional, and it will pass in that default value of `"World"` if the client request did not supply something else.

ASP.NET Core looks at the target method (and not the delegate type) to determine whether there are any default arguments. It works that way because ASP.NET Core supported default values in earlier versions, before C# 12.0 made it possible for lambdas to specify default arguments. You used to have to write an explicit method as Example 9-30 does to have somewhere to put the default argument value. As it happens, with this example C# 12.0 will generate a delegate type that includes the default argument, but since earlier compilers didn't do that, ASP.NET Core had to look at the target method itself. It continues to do that in the current version to ensure compatibility.

Example 9-30. Specifying a default argument in ASP.NET Core without a lambda

```
static string HandleRootUrl(string name = "World")
{
    return $"Hello {name}!";
}
app.MapGet("/", HandleRootUrl);
```

Since the default argument goes in two places—the delegate type and the target method—it's possible to create situations in which these are mismatched. Example 9-31 does this, first by assigning two lambdas with different default arguments into the same variable, and then by assigning lambdas into variables whose explicit types do not match the default arguments supplied.

Example 9-31. Mismatched default arguments

```
// The compiler generates a delegate type with a default argument of 10.
var withDefault = (int x = 10) => x * 2;

// Warning because this has a different default value (20) than withDefault's
// compiler-generated delegate type.
withDefault = (int x = 20) => x + 2;

// The WithDefaultDelegate delegate defined in a previous example also
// specifies a default argument of 10 so this also generates a warning.
WithDefaultDelegate c = (int x = 20) => x - 1;

// Also warns, because the delegate type does not specify a default argument,
// but the lambda does.
Func<int, int> f = (int x = 20) => x + 3;
```

For all but the first assignment, the compiler generates warnings telling you that the target method's default argument value does not match the default value specified by the delegate type. (On the final line, the delegate type does not specify a default argument at all, but this too produces a warning when you use it with a lambda that does have a default argument.) The effect of these mismatches depends on how the resulting delegate is used. You've already seen that ASP.NET Core ignores any default in the delegate type, and looks only at the target method (to retain compatibility with pre-C# 12.0 behavior). But code that just invokes a delegate in the normal way will use the default value from the delegate type, ignoring any defaults specified by the target method itself. In practice it's best to avoid getting into a situation where you need to know which of the two defaults will be used, which is why C# warns you if you create a situation in which they will be different.

Captured Variables

While anonymous functions often take up much less space in your source code than a full, normal method, they're not just about conciseness. The C# compiler uses a delegate's ability to refer not just to a method but also to some additional context to provide an extremely useful feature: it can make variables from the containing method available to the anonymous function. Example 9-32 shows a method that returns a `Predicate<int>`. It creates this with a lambda that uses an argument from the containing method.

Example 9-32. Using a variable from the containing method

```
public static Predicate<int> IsGreaterThan(int threshold)
{
    return value => value > threshold;
}
```

This provides the same functionality as the `ThresholdComparer` class in Example 9-9, but instead of having to write an entire class, we need only a single, simple method. We can make this even more compact by using an expression-bodied method, as Example 9-33 shows. (This might be a bit *too* concise—two different uses of => in close proximity to > won't win any prizes for readability.)

Example 9-33. Using a variable from the containing method (expression-bodied)

```
public static Predicate<int> IsGreaterThan(int threshold) =>
    value => value > threshold;
```

In either form, the code is almost deceptively simple, so it's worth looking closely at what it does. The `IsGreaterThan` method returns a delegate instance. That delegate's target method performs a simple comparison—it evaluates the `value > threshold` expression and returns the result. The `value` variable in that expression is just the delegate's argument—the `int` passed by whichever code invokes the `Predicate<int>` that `IsGreaterThan` returns. The second line of Example 9-34 invokes that code, passing in 200 as the argument for `value`.

Example 9-34. Where the value argument comes from

```
Predicate<int> greaterThanTen = IsGreaterThan(10);
bool result = greaterThanTen(200);
```

The threshold variable in the expression is trickier. This is not an argument to the anonymous function. It's the argument of IsGreaterThan, and Example 9-34 passes a value of 10 as the threshold argument. However, IsGreaterThan has to return before we can invoke the delegate it returns. Since the method for which that threshold variable was an argument has already returned, you might think that the variable would no longer be available by the time we invoke the delegate. In fact, it's fine, because the compiler does some work on our behalf. If an anonymous function uses local variables that were declared by the containing method, or if it uses that method's parameters, the compiler generates a class to hold those variables so that they can outlive the method that created them. The compiler generates code in the containing method to create an instance of this class. (Remember, each invocation of a block gets its own set of local variables, so if any locals get pushed into an object to extend their lifetime, a new object will be required for each invocation.) This is one of the reasons why the popular myth that says local variables of value type always live on the stack is not true—in this case, the compiler copies the incoming threshold argument's value to a field of an object on the heap, and code that uses the threshold variable ends up using that field instead. Example 9-35 shows the generated code that the compiler produces for the anonymous function in Example 9-32.

Example 9-35. Code generated for an anonymous function

```
[CompilerGenerated]
private sealed class <>c__DisplayClass0_0
{
    public int threshold;

    public bool <IsGreaterThan>b__0(int value)
    {
        return (value > this.threshold);
    }
}
```

The class and method names all begin with characters that are illegal in C# identifiers, to ensure that this compiler-generated code cannot clash with anything we write—this is technically an *unspeakable name*. (The exact names are not fixed, by the way—you may find they are slightly different if you try this.) This generated code bears a striking resemblance to the ThresholdComparer class from Example 9-9, which is unsurprising, because the goal is the same: the delegate needs some method that it can refer to, and that method's behavior depends on a value that is not fixed. Anonymous functions are not a feature of the runtime's type system, so the compiler has to generate a class to provide this kind of behavior on top of the CLR's basic delegate functionality.

Once you know that this is what's really happening when you write an anonymous function, it follows naturally that the inner method is able not just to read the variable but also to modify it. This variable is just a field in an object that two methods—the anonymous function and the containing method—have access to. Example 9-36 uses this to maintain a count that is updated from an anonymous function.

Example 9-36. Modifying a captured variable

```
static void Calculate(int[] nums)
{
    int zeroEntryCount = 0;
    int[] nonZeroNums = Array.FindAll(
        nums,
        v =>
        {
            if (v == 0)
            {
                zeroEntryCount += 1;
                return false;
            }
            else
            {
                return true;
            }
        });
    Console.WriteLine($"Number of zero entries: {zeroEntryCount}");
    Console.WriteLine($"First nonzero entry: {nonZeroNums[0]}");
}
```

Everything in scope for the containing method is also in scope for anonymous functions. If the containing method is an instance method, this includes any instance members of the type, so your anonymous function could access fields, properties, and methods. (The compiler supports this by adding a field to the generated class to hold a copy of the this reference.) The compiler puts only what it needs to in generated classes of the kind shown in Example 9-35, and if you don't use variables or instance members from the containing scope, it might be able to generate a static method.

The FindAll method in the preceding examples does not hold on to the delegate after it returns—any callbacks will happen while FindAll runs. Not everything works that way, though. Some APIs perform asynchronous work and will call you back at some point in the future, by which time the containing method may have returned. This means that any variables captured by the anonymous function will live longer than the containing method. In general, this is fine, because all of the captured variables live in an object on the heap, so it's not as though the anonymous function is relying on a stack frame that is no longer present. The one thing you need to be careful of, though, is explicitly releasing resources before callbacks have finished. Example 9-37 shows an easy mistake to make. This uses an asynchronous, callback-based API to download the resource at a particular URL via HTTP. (This calls the `ContinueWith` method on the `Task<Stream>` returned by `HttpClient.GetStreamAsync`, passing a delegate that will be invoked once the HTTP response comes back. `ContinueWith` is part of the Task Parallel Library described in Chapter 16.)

Example 9-37. Premature disposal

```
HttpClient http = GetHttpClient();
using (FileStream file = File.OpenWrite(@"c:\temp\page.txt"))
{
    http.GetStreamAsync("https://endjin.com/")
        .ContinueWith((Task<Stream> t) => t.Result.CopyToAsync(file));
} // Will probably dispose FileStream before callback runs
```

The `using` statement in this example will dispose the `FileStream` as soon as execution reaches the point at which the `file` variable goes out of scope in the outer method. The problem is that this `file` variable is also used in an anonymous function, which will in all likelihood run after the thread executing that outer method has left that `using` statement's block. The compiler has no understanding of when the inner block will run—it doesn't know whether that's a synchronous callback like `Array.FindAll` uses or an asynchronous one. So it cannot do anything special here—it just calls `Dispose` at the end of the block, as that's what our code told it to do.

The asynchronous language features discussed in Chapter 17 can help avoid this sort of problem. When you use those to consume APIs that present this kind of `Task`-based pattern, the compiler can then know exactly how long things remain in scope. This enables the compiler to generate continuation callbacks for you, and as part of this, it can arrange for a `using` statement to call `Dispose` at the correct moment.

In performance-critical code, you may need to bear the costs of anonymous functions in mind. If the anonymous function uses variables from the outer scope, then in addition to the delegate object that you create to refer to the anonymous function, you may be creating an additional one: an instance of the generated class to hold shared local variables. The compiler will reuse these variable holders when it can—if one method contains two anonymous functions, they may be able to share an object, for example. Even with this sort of optimization, you're still creating additional objects, increasing the pressure on the GC. (And in some cases you can end up creating this object even if you never hit the code path that creates the delegate.) It's not particularly expensive—these are typically small objects—but if you're up against a particularly oppressive performance problem, you might be able to eke out some small improvements by writing things in a more long-winded fashion in order to reduce the number of object allocations.

 Local functions do not always incur this same overhead. When a local function uses its outer method's variables, it does not extend their lifetime. The compiler therefore doesn't need to create an object on the heap to hold the shared variables. It still creates a type to hold all the shared variables, but it defines this as a `struct` that it passes by reference as a hidden `in` argument, avoiding the need for a heap block. (If you create a delegate that refers to a local function, it can no longer use this optimization, and it reverts to the same strategy it uses for anonymous functions, putting shared variables in an object on the heap.)

More subtly, using an outer scope's local variables in an anonymous function will extend the liveness of those variables, which may mean the GC will take longer to detect when objects those variables refer to are no longer in use. As you may recall from Chapter 7, the CLR analyzes your code to work out when variables are in use so that it can free objects without waiting for the variables that refer to them to go out of scope. This enables the memory used by some objects to be reclaimed significantly earlier, particularly in methods that take a long time to complete. But liveness analysis applies only to conventional local variables. It cannot be applied for variables that are used in an anonymous function, because the compiler transforms those variables into fields. (From the CLR's perspective, they are not local variables at all.) Since C# typically puts all of these transformed variables for a particular scope into a single object, you will find that none of the objects these variables refer to can be reclaimed until the method completes and the object containing the variables becomes unreachable itself. This can mean that in some cases there may be a measurable benefit to setting a local variable to `null` when you're done with it, enabling that particular object's memory to be reclaimed at the next GC. (Normally, that would be bad advice, and even with anonymous functions it might not have a useful effect in practice. You should only do this if performance testing demonstrates a clear advantage. But it's worth investigating in cases where you're seeing GC-related performance problems and you make heavy use of long-running anonymous functions.)

You can easily avoid these potential performance downsides in anonymous functions: just don't use captured variables. If an anonymous function never tries to use anything from its containing scope, the C# compiler won't engage the corresponding mechanisms, completely avoiding all the overhead. You can tell the compiler that you are intending to avoid capturing variables by annotating it with the `static` keyword, as Example 9-38 shows. Just as an ordinary `static` method does not have implicit access to an instance of its defining type, a `static` anonymous function has no access to its containing scope. This use of `static` doesn't change how code is generated—any anonymous function that does not rely on capture will avoid all capture-related overheads, regardless of whether it was marked as `static`. This just asks the compiler to report errors if you inadvertently attempt to use variables from the function's containing scope.

Example 9-38. Opting out of variable capture with `static`

```
public static Predicate<int> IsGreaterThan10() => static value => value > 10;
```

Variable capture can also occasionally lead to bugs, particularly due to a subtle scope-related issue with `for` loops. (`foreach` loops don't have this problem.) Example 9-39 runs into this.

Example 9-39. Problematic variable capture in a `for` *loop*

```
public static void Caught()
{
    var greaterThanN = new Predicate<int>[10];
    for (int i = 0; i < greaterThanN.Length; ++i)
    {
        greaterThanN[i] = value => value > i; // Bad use of i
    }

    Console.WriteLine(greaterThanN[5](20));
    Console.WriteLine(greaterThanN[5](6));
}
```

This example initializes an array of `Predicate<int>` delegates, where each delegate tests whether the value is greater than some number. (You wouldn't have to use arrays to see the problem I'm about to describe, by the way. Your loop might instead pass the delegates it creates into one of the mechanisms described in Chapter 16 that enable parallel processing by running the code on multiple threads. But arrays make it easier to show the problem.) Specifically, it compares the value with `i`, the loop counter that decides where in the array each delegate goes, so you might expect the element at index 5 to refer to a method that compares its argument with 5. If that were so, this code would show `True` twice. In fact, it displays `True` and then `False`. It turns out that Example 9-39 produces an array of delegates where every single element compares its argument with 10.

This usually surprises people when they encounter it. With hindsight, it's easy enough to see why this happens when you know how the C# compiler enables an anonymous function to use variables from its containing scope. The `for` loop declares the `i` variable, and because it is used not only by the containing `Caught` method but also by each delegate the loop creates, the compiler will generate a class similar to the one in Example 9-35, and the variable will live in a field of that class. Since the variable comes into scope when the loop starts, and remains in scope for the duration of the loop, the compiler will create one instance of that generated class, and it will be shared by all of the delegates. So, as the loop increments i, this modifies the behavior of all of the delegates, because they all use that same i variable.

Fundamentally, the problem is that there's only one i variable here. You can fix the code by introducing a new variable inside the loop. Example 9-40 copies the value of i into another local variable, current, which does not come into scope until an iteration is under way, and goes out of scope at the end of each iteration. So, although there is only one i variable, which lasts for as long as the loop runs, we get what is effectively a new current variable each time around the loop. Because each delegate gets its own distinct current variable, this modification means that each delegate in the array compares its argument with a different value—the value that the loop counter had for that particular iteration.

Example 9-40. Modifying a loop to capture the current value

```
for (int i = 0; i < greaterThanN.Length; ++i)
{
    int current = i;
    greaterThanN[i] = value => value > current;
}
```

The compiler still generates a class similar to the one in Example 9-35 to hold the current variable that's shared by the inline and containing methods, but this time, it will create a new instance of that class each time around the loop in order to give each anonymous function a different instance of that variable. (When you use a foreach loop, the scoping rules are a little different: its iteration variable's scope is per iteration, meaning that it's logically a different instance of the variable each time around the loop, so there would be no need to add an extra variable inside the loop as we have to with for.)

You may be wondering what would happen if you wrote an anonymous function that used variables at multiple scopes. Example 9-41 declares a variable called offset before the loop, and the lambda uses both that and a variable whose scope lasts for only one iteration.

Example 9-41. Capturing variables at different scopes

```
int offset = 10;
for (int i = 0; i < greaterThanN.Length; ++i)
{
    int current = i;
    greaterThanN[i] = value => value > (current + offset);
}
```

In that case, the compiler would generate two classes, one to hold any per-iteration shared variables (`current`, in this example) and one to hold those whose scope spans the whole loop (`offset`, in this case). Each delegate's target object would contain inner scope variables, and that would contain a reference to the outer scope.

Figure 9-1 shows roughly how this would work, although it has been simplified to show just the first five items. The `greaterThanN` variable contains a reference to an array. Each array element contains a reference to a delegate. Each delegate refers to the same method, but each one has a different target object, which is how each delegate can capture a different instance of the `current` variable. Each of these target objects refers to a single object containing the `offset` variable captured from the scope outside of the loop.

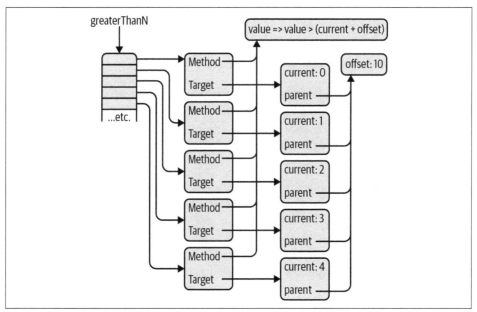

Figure 9-1. Delegates and captured scopes

Lambdas and Expression Trees

Lambdas have an additional trick up their sleeves beyond providing delegates. Some lambdas produce a data structure that represents code. This occurs when you use the lambda syntax in a context that requires an `Expression<T>`, where `T` is a delegate type. `Expression<T>` itself is not a delegate type; it is a special type in the runtime libraries (in the `System.Linq.Expressions` namespace) that triggers this alternative handling of lambdas in the compiler. Example 9-42 uses this type.

Example 9-42. A lambda expression

```
Expression<Func<int, bool>> greaterThanZero = value => value > 0;
```

This example looks similar to some of the lambdas and delegates I've shown already in this chapter, but the compiler handles this very differently. It will not generate a method—there will be no compiled IL representing the lambda's body. Instead, the compiler will produce code similar to that in Example 9-43.

Example 9-43. What the compiler does with a lambda expression

```
ParameterExpression valueParam = Expression.Parameter(typeof(int), "value");
ConstantExpression constantZero = Expression.Constant(0);
BinaryExpression comparison = Expression.GreaterThan(valueParam, constantZero);
Expression<Func<int, bool>> greaterThanZero =
    Expression.Lambda<Func<int, bool>>(comparison, valueParam);
```

This code calls various factory functions provided by the `Expression` class to produce an object for each subexpression in the lambda. This starts with the `value` parameter and the constant value `0`. These are fed into an object representing the "greater than" comparison expression, which in turn becomes the body of an object representing the whole lambda expression.

The ability to produce an object model for an expression makes it possible to write an API where the behavior is controlled by the structure and content of an expression. For example, some data access APIs can take an expression similar to the ones produced by Examples 9-42 and 9-43 and use it to generate part of a database query. I'll be talking about C#'s integrated query features in Chapter 10, but Example 9-44 gives a flavor of how a lambda expression can be used as the basis of a query.

Example 9-44. Expressions and database queries

```
var expensiveProducts = dbContext.Products.Where(p => p.ListPrice > 3000);
```

This example happens to use a Microsoft library called the Entity Framework, but various other data access technologies support the same approach. In this example, the `Where` method takes an argument of type `Expression<Func<Product,bool>>`.[6] `Product` is a class that corresponds to an entity in the database, but the important part here is the use of `Expression<T>`. That means that the compiler will generate code that creates a tree of objects whose structure corresponds to that lambda expression. The `Where` method processes this expression tree, generating a SQL query that includes this clause: `WHERE [Extent1].[ListPrice] > cast(3000 as decimal(18))`. So, although I wrote my query as a C# expression, the work required to find matching objects will all happen on my database server.

Expression trees were added to C# to enable this sort of query handling as part of the set of features known collectively as *LINQ* (which is the subject of Chapter 10). However, as with most LINQ-related features, it's possible to use them for other things. For example, a popular .NET library used in automated testing called Moq (*https:// github.com/moq*) exploits this. It creates fake implementations of interfaces for test purposes, and it uses lambda expressions to provide a simple API for configuring how those fakes should behave. Example 9-45 uses Moq's `Mock<T>` class to create a fake implementation of .NET's `IEqualityComparer<string>` interface. The code calls the `Setup` method, which takes an expression indicating a specific invocation we'd like to define special handling for—in this case, if the fake's implementation of `IEquality Comparer<string>.Equals` is called with the arguments of `"Color"` and `"Colour"`, we'd like it to return `true`.

Example 9-45. Use of lambda expressions by the Moq library

```
var fakeComparer = new Mock<IEqualityComparer<string>>();
fakeComparer
    .Setup(c => c.Equals("Color", "Colour"))
    .Returns(true);
```

If that argument to `Setup` were just a delegate, there would be no way for Moq to inspect it. But because it's an expression tree, Moq is able to delve into it and find out what we've asked for.

 Unfortunately, expression trees are an area of C# that have lagged behind the rest of the language. They were introduced in C# 3.0, and various language features added since then, such as support for tuples and asynchronous expressions, can't be used in an expression tree because the object model has no way to represent them.

---

6 You may be surprised to see `Func<Product,bool>` here and not `Predicate<Product>`. The `Where` method is part of a .NET feature called LINQ that makes extensive use of delegates. To avoid defining huge numbers of new delegate types, LINQ uses `Func` types, and for consistency across the API, it prefers `Func` even when other standard types would fit.

Events

Sometimes it is useful for objects to be able to provide notifications of when interesting things have happened—in a client-side UI framework, you will want to know when the user clicks one of your application's buttons, for example. Delegates provide the basic callback mechanism required for notifications, but there are many ways you could go about using them. Should the delegate be passed as a method argument, a constructor argument, or perhaps as a property? How should you support unsubscribing from notifications? The CTS formalizes the answers to these questions through a special kind of class member called an *event*, and C# has syntax for working with events. Example 9-46 shows a class with one event member.

Example 9-46. A class with an event

```csharp
public class Eventful
{
    public event Action<string>? Announcement;

    public void Announce(string message)
    {
        Announcement?.Invoke(message);
    }
}
```

As with all members, you can start with an accessibility specifier, and it will default to private if you leave that off. Next, the event keyword singles this out as an event. Then there's the event's type, which can be any delegate type. I've used Action<string>, although as you'll soon see, this is an unorthodox choice. Finally, we put the member name, so this example defines an event called Announcement.

To handle an event, you must provide a delegate of the right type, and you must use the += syntax to attach that delegate as the handler. Example 9-47 uses a lambda, but you can use any expression that produces, or is implicitly convertible to, a delegate of the type the event requires.

Example 9-47. Handling events

```csharp
var source = new Eventful();
source.Announcement += m => Console.WriteLine($"Announcement: {m}");
```

As well as defining an event, Example 9-46 also shows how to *raise* it—that is, how to invoke all the handlers that have been attached to the event. Its Announce uses the same syntax we would use if Announcement were a field containing a delegate that we wanted to invoke. In fact, as far as the code inside the class is concerned, that's exactly what an event looks like—it appears to be a field. I've chosen to use the delegate's

Invoke member explicitly here instead of writing Announcement(message) because this lets me use the null-conditional operator (?.). This causes the compiler to generate code that invokes the delegate only if it is not null. Otherwise I would have had to write an if statement verifying that the field is not null before invoking it.

So why do we need a special member type if this looks just like a field? Well, it looks like a field only from inside the defining class. Code outside of the class cannot raise the event, so the code shown in Example 9-48 will not compile.

Example 9-48. How not to raise an event

```
var source = new Eventful();
source.Announcement("Will this work?"); // No, this will not even compile
```

From the outside, the only things you can do to an event are to attach a handler using += and to remove one using -=. The syntax for adding and removing event handlers is unusual in that it's the only case in C# in which you get to use += and -= without the corresponding standalone + or - operators being available. The actions performed by += and -= on events both turn out to be method calls in disguise. Just as properties are really pairs of methods with a special syntax, so are events. They are similar in concept to the code shown in Example 9-49. (In fact, the real code includes some moderately complex lock-free, thread-safe code. I've not shown this because the multithreading obscures the basic intent.) This won't have quite the same effect, because the event keyword adds metadata to the type identifying the methods as being an event, so this is just for illustration.

Example 9-49. The approximate effect of declaring an event

```
private Action<string>? Announcement;

// Not the actual code.
// The real code is more complex, to tolerate concurrent calls.
public void add_Announcement(Action<string> handler)
{
    Announcement += handler;
}
public void remove_Announcement(Action<string> handler)
{
    Announcement -= handler;
}
```

Just as with properties, events exist mainly to offer a convenient, distinctive syntax and to make it easier for tools to know how to present the features that classes offer. Events are particularly important for UI elements. In most UI frameworks, the objects representing interactive elements can often raise a wide range of events, corresponding to various forms of input such as keyboard, mouse, or touch. There are also often events relating to behavior specific to a particular control, such as selecting a new item in a list. Because the CTS defines a standard idiom by which elements can expose events, visual UI designers, such as the ones built into Visual Studio, can display the available events and offer to generate handlers for you.

Standard Event Delegate Pattern

The event in Example 9-46 is unusual in that it uses the Action<T> delegate type. This is perfectly legal, but in practice, you will rarely see that, because almost all events use delegate types that conform to a particular pattern. This pattern requires the delegate's method signature to have two parameters. The first parameter's type is object, and the second's type is either EventArgs or some type derived from EventArgs. Example 9-50 shows the EventHandler delegate type in the System namespace, which is the simplest and most widely used example of this pattern.

Example 9-50. The EventHandler delegate type

```
public delegate void EventHandler(object sender, EventArgs e);
```

The first parameter is usually called sender, because the event source passes a reference to itself for this argument. This means that if you attach a single delegate to multiple event sources, that handler can always know which source raised any particular notification.

The second parameter provides a place to put information specific to the event. For example, WPF UI elements define various events for handling mouse input that use more specialized delegate types, such as MouseButtonEventHandler, with signatures that specify a corresponding specialized event parameter that offers details about the event. For example, MouseButtonEventArgs defines a GetPosition method that tells you where the mouse was when the button was clicked, and it defines various other properties offering further detail, including ClickCount and Timestamp.

Whatever the specialized type of the second parameter may be, it will always derive from the base EventArgs type. That base type is not very interesting—it does not add members beyond the standard ones provided by object. However, it does make it possible to write a general-purpose method that can be attached to any event that uses this pattern. The rules for delegate compatibility mean that even if the delegate type specifies a second parameter of type MouseButtonEventArgs, a method whose second parameter is of type EventArgs is an acceptable target. This can occasionally be useful for code generation or other infrastructure scenarios. However, the main benefit of the standard event pattern is simply one of familiarity—experienced C# developers generally expect events to work this way.

Custom Add and Remove Methods

Sometimes, you might not want to use the default event implementation generated by the C# compiler. For example, a class may define a large number of events, most of which will not be used on the majority of instances. UI frameworks often have this characteristic. A WPF UI can have thousands of elements, every one of which offers over 100 events, but you normally attach handlers only to a few of these elements, and even with these, you handle only a fraction of the events on offer. It is inefficient for every element to dedicate a field to every available event in this case.

Using the default field-based implementation for large numbers of rarely used events could add hundreds of bytes to the footprint of each element in a UI, which can have a discernible effect on performance. (In a typical WPF application, this could add up to a few hundred thousand bytes. That might not sound like much given modern computers' memory capacities, but it can put your code in a place where it is no longer able to make efficient use of the CPU's cache, causing a nosedive in application responsiveness. Even if the cache is several megabytes in size, the fastest parts of the cache are usually much smaller, and wasting a few hundred kilobytes in a critical data structure can make a world of difference to performance.)

Another reason you might want to eschew the default compiler-generated event implementation is that you may want more sophisticated semantics when raising events. For example, WPF supports *event bubbling*: if a UI element does not handle certain events, they will be offered to the parent element, then the parent's parent, and so on up the tree until a handler is found or it reaches the top. Although it would be possible to implement this sort of scheme with the standard event implementation C# supplies, much more efficient strategies are possible when event handlers are relatively sparse.

To support these scenarios, C# lets you provide your own add and remove methods for an event. It will look just like a normal event from the outside—anyone using your class will use the same += and -= syntax to add and remove handlers—and it won't be possible to tell that it provides a custom implementation. Example 9-51 shows a class with two such events, and it uses a single dictionary, shared across all instances of the class, to keep track of which events have been handled on which objects. The approach is extensible to larger numbers of events—the dictionary uses pairs of objects as the key, so each entry represents a particular (source, event) pair. (This is not production-quality code, by the way. It's not safe for multithreaded use, and it will also leak memory when a `ScarceEventSource` instance that still has event handlers attached falls out of use. This example just illustrates how custom event handlers look; it's not a fully engineered solution.)

Example 9-51. Custom add and remove for sparse events

```
public class ScarceEventSource
{
    // One dictionary shared by all instances of this class,
    // tracking all handlers for all events.
    // Beware of memory leaks - this code is for illustration only.
    private static readonly
     Dictionary<(ScarceEventSource, object), EventHandler> _eventHandlers
      = new();

    // Objects used as keys to identify particular events in the dictionary.
    private static readonly object EventOneId = new();
    private static readonly object EventTwoId = new();


    public event EventHandler EventOne
    {
        add => AddEvent(EventOneId, value);
        remove => RemoveEvent(EventOneId, value);
    }

    public event EventHandler EventTwo
    {
        add => AddEvent(EventTwoId, value);
        remove => RemoveEvent(EventTwoId, value);
    }

    public void RaiseBoth()
    {
        RaiseEvent(EventOneId, EventArgs.Empty);
        RaiseEvent(EventTwoId, EventArgs.Empty);
    }

    private (ScarceEventSource, object) MakeKey(object eventId) => (this, eventId);

    private void AddEvent(object eventId, EventHandler handler)
    {
        var key = MakeKey(eventId);
        _eventHandlers.TryGetValue(key, out EventHandler? entry);
        entry += handler;
        _eventHandlers[key] = entry;
    }

    private void RemoveEvent(object eventId, EventHandler handler)
    {
        var key = MakeKey(eventId);
        EventHandler? entry = _eventHandlers[key];
        entry -= handler;
        if (entry == null)
        {
            _eventHandlers.Remove(key);
```

```
        }
        else
        {
            _eventHandlers[key] = entry;
        }
    }

    private void RaiseEvent(object eventId, EventArgs e)
    {
        var key = MakeKey(eventId);
        if (_eventHandlers.TryGetValue(key, out EventHandler? handler))
        {
            handler(this, e);
        }
    }
}
```

The syntax for custom events is reminiscent of the full property syntax: we add a block after the member declaration that contains the two members, although they are called add and remove instead of get and set. (Unlike with properties, you must always supply both methods.) This disables the generation of the field that would normally hold the event, meaning that the ScarceEventSource class has no instance fields at all—instances of this type are as small as it's possible for an object to be.

The price for this small memory footprint is a considerable increase in complexity; I've written about 16 times as many lines of code as I would have needed with compiler-generated events, and we'd need even more to fix the shortcomings described earlier. Moreover, this technique provides an improvement only if the events really are not handled most of the time—if I attached handlers to both events for every instance of this class, the dictionary-based storage would consume more memory than simply having a field for each event in each instance of the class. So you should consider this sort of custom event handling only if you either need nonstandard event-raising behavior or are very sure that you really will be saving memory, and that the savings are worthwhile.

Events and the Garbage Collector

As far as the GC is concerned, delegates are normal objects like any other. If the GC discovers that a delegate instance is reachable, then it will inspect the Target property, and whichever object that refers to will also be considered reachable, along with whatever objects that object in turn refers to. Although there is nothing remarkable about this, there are situations in which leaving event handlers attached can cause objects to hang around in memory when you might have expected them to be collected by the GC.

There's nothing intrinsic to delegates and events that makes them unusually likely to defeat the GC. If you do get an event-related memory leak, it will have the same structure as any other .NET memory leak: starting from a root reference, there will be some chain of references that keeps an object reachable even after you've finished using it. Despite this, events often get special blame for memory leaks, and that's because they are often used in ways that can cause problems.

For example, suppose your application maintains some object model representing its state and that your UI code is in a separate layer that makes use of that underlying model, adapting the information it contains for presentation on screen. This sort of layering is usually advisable—it's a bad idea to intermingle code that deals with user interactions and code that implements the application's logic. But a problem can arise if the underlying model advertises changes in state that the UI needs to reflect. If these changes are advertised through events, your UI code will typically attach handlers to those events.

Now imagine that someone closes one of your application's windows. You would hope that the objects representing that window's UI would all be detected as unreachable the next time the GC runs. The UI framework is likely to have attempted to make that possible. For example, WPF ensures that each instance of its Window class is reachable for as long as the corresponding window is open, but once the window has been closed, it stops holding references to the window, to enable all of the UI objects for that window to be collected.

However, if you handle an event from your main application's model with a method in a Window-derived class, and if you do not explicitly remove that handler when the window is closed, you will have a problem. As long as your application is still running, something somewhere will presumably be keeping your application's underlying model reachable. This means that the target objects of any delegates held by your application model (e.g., delegates that were added as event handlers) will continue to be reachable, preventing the GC from freeing them. So, if a Window-derived object for the now-closed window is still handling events from your application model, that window—and all of the UI elements it contains—will still be reachable and will not be garbage collected.

There's a persistent myth that this sort of event-based memory leak has something to do with circular references. In fact, GC copes perfectly well with circular references. It's true that there are often circular references in these scenarios, but they're not the issue. The problem is caused by accidentally keeping objects reachable after you no longer need them. Doing that will cause problems regardless of whether circular references are present.

You can deal with this by ensuring that if your UI layer ever attaches handlers to objects that will stay alive for a long time, you remove those handlers when the relevant UI element is no longer in use. Alternatively, you could use weak references to ensure that if your event source is the only thing holding a reference to the target, it doesn't keep it alive. WPF can help you with this—it provides a `WeakEventManager` class that allows you to handle an event in such a way that the handling object is able to be garbage collected without needing to unsubscribe from the event. WPF uses this technique itself when databinding the UI to a data source that provides property change notification events.

 Although event-related leaks often arise in UIs, they can occur anywhere. As long as an event source remains reachable, all of its attached handlers will also remain reachable.

Events Versus Delegates

Some APIs provide notifications through events, while others just use delegates directly. How should you decide which approach to use? In some cases, the decision may be made for you because you want to support some particular idiom. For example, if you want your API to support the asynchronous features in C#, you will need to implement the pattern described in Chapter 17, which uses delegates, but not events, for completion callbacks. Events, on the other hand, provide a clear way to subscribe and unsubscribe, which will make them a better choice in some situations. Convention is another consideration: if you are writing a UI element, events will most likely be appropriate, because that's the predominant idiom.

In cases where constraints or conventions do not provide an answer, you need to think about how the callback will be used. If there will be multiple subscribers for a notification, an event could be the best choice. This is not absolutely necessary, because any delegate is capable of multicast behavior, but by convention, this behavior is usually offered through events. If users of your class will need to remove the handler at some point, events are also likely to be a good choice. That being said, the `IObservable` interface also supports multicast and unsubscription and might be a better choice if you need more advanced functionality. This interface is part of the Reactive Extensions for .NET and is described in Chapter 11.

You would typically pass a delegate as an argument to a method or constructor if it only makes sense to have a single target method. For example, if the delegate type has a non-`void` return value that the API depends on (such as the `bool` returned by the predicate passed to `Array.FindAll`), it makes no sense to have multiple targets or zero targets. An event is the wrong idiom here, because its subscription-oriented model considers it perfectly normal to attach either no handlers or multiple handlers.

Occasionally, scenarios arise in which it might make sense to have either zero handlers or one handler, but never more than one. For example, take WPF's `Collection View` class, which can sort, group, and filter data from a collection. You configure filtering by providing a `Predicate<object>`. This is not passed as a constructor argument, because filtering is optional, so instead, the class defines a `Filter` property. An event would be inappropriate here, partly because `Predicate<object>` does not fit the usual event delegate pattern, but mainly because the class needs an unambiguous answer of yes or no, so it does not want to support multiple targets. (The fact that all delegate types support multicast means that it's still possible to supply multiple targets, of course. But the decision to use a property rather than an event signals the fact that it's not useful to attempt to provide multiple callbacks here.)

Delegates Versus Interfaces

Back at the start of this chapter, I argued that delegates offer a less cumbersome mechanism for callbacks and notifications than interfaces do. So why do some APIs require callers to implement an interface to enable callbacks? Why do we have `IComparer<T>` and not a delegate? Actually, we have both—there's a delegate type called `Comparison<T>`, which is supported as an alternative by many of the APIs that accept an `IComparer<T>`. Arrays and `List<T>` have overloads of their `Sort` methods that take either.

There are some situations in which the object-oriented approach may be preferable to using delegates. An object that implements `IComparer<T>` could provide properties to adjust the way the comparison works (e.g., the ability to select between various sorting criteria). You may want to collect and summarize information across multiple callbacks, and although you can do that through captured variables, it may be easier to get the information back out again at the end if it's available through properties of an object.

This is really a decision for whoever is writing the code that is being called back, and not for the developer writing the code that makes the call. Delegates ultimately are more flexible, because they allow the consumer of the API to decide how to structure their code, whereas an interface imposes constraints. However, if an interface happens to align with the abstractions you want, delegates can seem like an irritating extra detail. This is why some APIs present both options, such as the sorting APIs that accept either an `IComparer<T>` or a `Comparison<T>`.

Interfaces might be preferable to delegates if you need to provide multiple related callbacks. The Reactive Extensions for .NET define an abstraction for notifications that includes the ability to know when you've reached the end of a sequence of events or when there has been an error, so in that model, subscribers implement an interface with three methods—`OnNext`, `OnCompleted`, and `OnError`. It makes sense to use an interface, because all three methods are typically required for a complete subscription.

Summary

Delegates are objects that provide a reference to a method, which can be either a static or an instance method. With instance methods, the delegate also holds a reference to the target object, so the code that invokes the delegate does not need to supply a target. Delegates can also refer to multiple methods, although that complicates matters if the delegate's return type is not void. While delegate types get special handling from the CLR, they are still just reference types, meaning that a reference to a delegate can be passed as an argument, returned from a method, and stored in a field, variable, or property. A delegate type defines a signature for the target method. This is represented through the type's Invoke method, but C# can hide this, offering a syntax in which you can invoke a delegate expression directly without explicitly referring to Invoke. You can construct a delegate that refers to any method with a compatible signature. You can also get C# to do more of the work for you—if you use the lambda syntax to create an anonymous function, C# will supply a suitable declaration for you and can also do work behind the scenes to make variables in the containing method available to the inner one. Delegates are the basis of events, which provide a formalized publish/subscribe model for notifications.

One C# feature that makes particularly extensive use of delegates is LINQ, which is the subject of the next chapter.

CHAPTER 10
LINQ

Language Integrated Query (LINQ) is a powerful collection of C# language features for working with sets of information. It is useful in any application that needs to work with multiple pieces of data (i.e., almost any application). Although one of its original goals was to provide straightforward access to relational databases, LINQ is applicable to many kinds of information. For example, it can also be used with in-memory object models, HTTP-based information services, JSON, and XML documents. And as we'll see in Chapter 11, it can work with live streams of data too.

LINQ is not a single feature. It relies on several language elements that work together. The most conspicuous LINQ-related language feature is the *query expression*, a form of expression that loosely resembles a database query but that can be used to perform queries against any supported source, including plain old objects. As you'll see, query expressions rely heavily on some other language features such as lambdas, extension methods, and expression object models.

Language support is only half the story. LINQ needs class libraries to implement a set of querying primitives called *LINQ operators*. Each different kind of data requires its own implementation, and a set of operators for any particular type of information is referred to as a *LINQ provider*. (These can also be used from Visual Basic and F#, by the way, because those languages support LINQ too.) Microsoft supplies several providers, some built into the runtime libraries and some available as separate NuGet packages. There is a provider for Entity Framework Core (EF Core) for example, an object/relational mapping system for working with databases. The Cosmos DB cloud database (a feature of Microsoft Azure) offers a LINQ provider. And the Reactive Extensions for .NET (Rx) described in Chapter 11 provide LINQ support for live streams of data. In short, LINQ is a widely supported idiom in .NET, and it's extensible, so you will also find open source and other third-party providers.

Most of the examples in this chapter use LINQ to Objects. This is partly because it avoids cluttering the examples with extraneous details such as database or service connections, but there's a more important reason. LINQ's introduction in 2007 significantly changed the way I write C#, and that's entirely because of LINQ to Objects. Although LINQ's query syntax makes it look like it's primarily a data access technology, I have found it to be far more valuable than that. Having LINQ's services available on any collection of objects makes it useful in every part of your code.

Query Expressions

The most visible feature of LINQ is the query expression syntax. It's not the most important—as we'll see later, it's entirely possible to use LINQ productively without ever writing a query expression. However, it's a very natural syntax for many kinds of queries.

At first glance, a query expression loosely resembles a relational database query, but the syntax works with any LINQ provider. Example 10-1 shows a query expression that uses LINQ to Objects to search for certain `CultureInfo` objects. (A `CultureInfo` object provides a set of culture-specific information, such as the symbol used for the local currency, what language is spoken, and so on. Some systems call this a *locale*.) This particular query looks at the character that denotes what would, in English, be called the decimal point. Many countries actually use a comma instead of a period, and in those countries, 100,000 would mean the number 100 written out to three decimal places; in English-speaking cultures, we would normally write this as 100.000. The query expression searches all the cultures known to the system and returns those that use a comma as the decimal separator.

Example 10-1. A LINQ query expression

```
IEnumerable<CultureInfo> commaCultures =
    from culture in CultureInfo.GetCultures(CultureTypes.AllCultures)
    where culture.NumberFormat.NumberDecimalSeparator == ","
    select culture;

foreach (CultureInfo culture in commaCultures)
{
    Console.WriteLine(culture.Name);
}
```

The `foreach` loop in this example shows the results of the query. The output will vary according to the language support installed on the system you run it on. On my system, this lists the names of 366 cultures, indicating that slightly under half of the 869 available cultures use a comma, not a decimal point. Of course, I could easily have achieved this without using LINQ. Example 10-2 will produce the same results.

Example 10-2. The non-LINQ equivalent

```
CultureInfo[] allCultures = CultureInfo.GetCultures(CultureTypes.AllCultures);
foreach (CultureInfo culture in allCultures)
{
    if (culture.NumberFormat.NumberDecimalSeparator == ",")
    {
        Console.WriteLine(culture.Name);
    }
}
```

Both examples have eight nonblank lines of code, although if you ignore lines that contain only braces, Example 10-2 contains just four, two fewer than Example 10-1. Then again, if we count statements, the LINQ example has just three, compared to four in the loop-based example. So it's difficult to argue convincingly that either approach is simpler than the other.

However, Example 10-1 has a significant advantage: the code that decides which items to choose is well separated from the code that decides what to do with those items. Example 10-2 intermingles these two concerns: the code that picks the objects is half outside and half inside the loop.

Another difference is that Example 10-1 has a more declarative style: it focuses on what we want, not how to get it. The query expression describes the items we'd like, without mandating that this be achieved in any particular way. For this very simple example, that doesn't matter much, but for more complex examples, and particularly when using a LINQ provider for database access, it can be very useful to allow the provider a free hand in deciding exactly how to perform the query. Example 10-2's approach of iterating over everything in a foreach loop and picking the item it wants would be a bad idea if we were talking to a database—you generally want to let the server do this sort of filtering work.

The query in Example 10-1 has three parts. All query expressions are required to begin with a from clause, which specifies the source of the query. In this case, the source is an array of type CultureInfo[], returned by the CultureInfo class's GetCul tures method. As well as defining the source for the query, the from clause contains a name, culture. This is called the *range variable*, and we can use it in the rest of the query to represent a single item from the source. Clauses can run many times—the where clause in Example 10-1 runs once for every item in the collection, so the range variable will have a different value each time. This is reminiscent of the iteration variable in a foreach loop. In fact, the overall structure of the from clause is similar—we have the variable that will represent an item from a collection, then the in keyword, then the source for which that variable will represent individual items. Just as a foreach loop's iteration variable is in scope only inside the loop, the range variable culture is meaningful only inside this query expression.

Although analogies with foreach can be helpful for understanding the intent of LINQ queries, you shouldn't take this too literally. For example, not all providers directly execute the expressions in a query. Some LINQ providers convert query expressions into database queries, in which case the C# code in the various expressions inside the query does not run in any conventional sense. So, although it is true to say that the range variable represents a single value from the source, it's not always true to say that clauses will execute once for every item they process, with the range value taking that item's value. It happens to be true for Example 10-1 because it uses LINQ to Objects, but it's not so for all providers.

The second part of the query in Example 10-1 is a where clause. This clause is optional, or if you want, you can have several in one query. A where clause filters the results, and the one in this example states that I want only the CultureInfo objects with a NumberFormat that indicates that the decimal separator is a comma.

The final part of the query is a select clause. All query expressions end with either a select clause or a group clause. This determines the final output of the query. This example indicates that we want each CultureInfo object that was not filtered out by the query. The foreach loop in Example 10-1 that shows the results of the query uses only the Name property, so I could have written a query that extracted only that. As Example 10-3 shows, if I do this, I also need to change the loop, because the resulting query now produces strings instead of CultureInfo objects.

Example 10-3. Extracting just one property in a query

```
IEnumerable<string> commaCultures =
    from culture in CultureInfo.GetCultures(CultureTypes.AllCultures)
    where culture.NumberFormat.NumberDecimalSeparator == ","
    select culture.Name;

foreach (string cultureName in commaCultures)
{
    Console.WriteLine(cultureName);
}
```

This raises a question: In general, what type do query expressions have? In Example 10-1, commaCultures is an IEnumerable<CultureInfo>; in Example 10-3, it's an IEnumerable<string>. The output item type is determined by the final clause of the query—the select or, in some cases, the group clause. However, not all query expressions result in an IEnumerable<T>. It depends on which LINQ provider you use—I've ended up with IEnumerable<T> because I'm using LINQ to Objects.

It's common to use the var keyword when declaring variables that hold LINQ queries. This is necessary if a select clause produces instances of an anonymous type, because there is no way to write the name of the resulting query's type. Even if anonymous types are not involved, var is still widely used, and there are two reasons. One is just a matter of consistency: some people feel that because you have to use var for some LINQ queries, you should use it for all of them. Another argument is that LINQ query types often have verbose and ugly names, and var results in less cluttered code. In this chapter I have used var where necessary.

How did C# know that I wanted to use LINQ to Objects? It's because I used an array as the source in the from clause. More generally, LINQ to Objects will be used when you specify any IEnumerable<T> as the source, unless a more specialized provider is available. However, this doesn't really explain how C# discovers the existence of providers in the first place and how it chooses between them. To understand that, you need to know what the compiler does with a query expression.

How Query Expressions Expand

The compiler converts all query expressions into one or more method calls. Once it has done that, the LINQ provider is selected through exactly the same mechanisms that C# uses for any other method call. The compiler does not have any built-in concept of what constitutes a LINQ provider. It just relies on convention. Example 10-4 shows what the compiler does with the query expression in Example 10-3.

Example 10-4. The effect of a query expression

```
IEnumerable<string> commaCultures =
    CultureInfo.GetCultures(CultureTypes.AllCultures)
    .Where(culture => culture.NumberFormat.NumberDecimalSeparator == ",")
    .Select(culture => culture.Name);
```

The Where and Select methods are examples of LINQ operators. A LINQ operator is nothing more than a method that conforms to one of the standard patterns. I'll describe these patterns later, in "Standard LINQ Operators" on page 486.

The code in Example 10-4 is all one statement, and I'm chaining method calls together—I call the Where method on the return value of GetCultures, and I call the Select method on the return value of Where. The formatting looks a little peculiar, but it's too long to go on one line; and, even though it's not terribly elegant, I prefer to put the . at the start of the line when splitting chained calls across multiple lines, because it makes it much easier to see that each new line continues from where the last one left off. Leaving the period at the end of the preceding line looks neater but also makes it much easier to misread the code.

The compiler has turned the `where` and `select` clauses' expressions into lambdas. Notice that the range variable ends up as a parameter in each lambda. This is one example of why you should not take the analogy between query expressions and `foreach` loops too literally. Unlike a `foreach` iteration variable, the range variable does not exist as a single conventional variable. In the query, it is just an identifier that represents an item from the source, and in expanding the query into method calls, C# may end up creating multiple real variables for a single range variable, like it has with the arguments for the two separate lambdas here.

All query expressions boil down to this sort of thing—chained method calls with lambdas. (This is why we don't strictly need the query expression syntax—you could write any query using method calls instead.) Some are more complex than others. The expression in Example 10-1 ends up with a simpler structure despite looking almost identical to Example 10-3. Example 10-5 shows how it expands. It turns out that when a query's `select` clause just passes the range variable straight through, the compiler interprets that as meaning that we want to pass the results of the preceding clause straight through without further processing, so it doesn't add a call to `Select`. (There is one exception to this: if you write a query expression that contains nothing but a `from` and a `select` clause, it will generate a call to `Select` even if the `select` clause is trivial.)

Example 10-5. How trivial select *clauses expand*

```
IEnumerable<CultureInfo> commaCultures =
    CultureInfo.GetCultures(CultureTypes.AllCultures)
    .Where(culture => culture.NumberFormat.NumberDecimalSeparator == ",");
```

The compiler has to work harder if you introduce multiple variables within the query's scope. You can do this with a `let` clause. Example 10-6 performs the same job as Example 10-3, but I've introduced a new variable called `numFormat` to refer to the number format. This makes my `where` clause shorter and easier to read, and in a more complex query that needed to refer to that format object multiple times, this technique could remove a lot of clutter.

Example 10-6. Query with a let *clause*

```
IEnumerable<string> commaCultures =
    from culture in CultureInfo.GetCultures(CultureTypes.AllCultures)
    let numFormat = culture.NumberFormat
    where numFormat.NumberDecimalSeparator == ","
    select culture.Name;
```

When you write a query that introduces additional variables like this, the compiler automatically generates an anonymous type with a property for each of the variables so that it can make them all available at every stage. To get the same effect with ordinary method calls, we'd need to do something similar, as Example 10-7 shows.

Example 10-7. How multivariable query expressions expand (approximately)

```
IEnumerable<string> commaCultures =
    CultureInfo.GetCultures(CultureTypes.AllCultures)
    .Select(culture => new { culture, numFormat = culture.NumberFormat })
    .Where(vars => vars.numFormat.NumberDecimalSeparator == ",")
    .Select(vars => vars.culture.Name);
```

No matter how simple or complex they are, query expressions are nothing more than a specialized syntax for method calls.

Deferred Evaluation

LINQ to Objects has been designed to work well with sequences like the one returned by the Fibonacci method in Example 10-8. That returns a never-ending sequence—it will keep providing numbers from the Fibonacci series for as long as the code keeps asking for them. I have used the IEnumerable<BigInteger> returned by this method as the source for a query expression.

Example 10-8. Query with an infinite source sequence

```
using System.Numerics;

static IEnumerable<BigInteger> Fibonacci()
{
    BigInteger n1 = 1;
    BigInteger n2 = 1;
    yield return n1;
    while (true)
    {
        yield return n2;
        BigInteger t = n1 + n2;
        n1 = n2;
        n2 = t;
    }
}

IEnumerable<BigInteger> evenFib = from n in Fibonacci()
                                  where n % 2 == 0
                                  select n;

foreach (BigInteger n in evenFib)
{
```

```
        Console.WriteLine(n);
    }
```

This will use the Where extension method that LINQ to Objects provides for IEnumerable<T>. You could imagine an implementation of Where that iterates through its source collection, putting items that match the criteria into a List<T> that it returns once it has worked through the whole input. But if it worked that way, this program would never make it as far as displaying a single number. Where can never work its way through the whole input here because my Fibonacci enumerator is infinite.

In fact, Example 10-8 works perfectly—it produces a steady stream of output consisting of the Fibonacci numbers that are divisible by 2. This means it can't be attempting to perform all of the filtering when we call Where. Instead, its Where method returns an IEnumerable<T> that filters items on demand. It won't try to fetch anything from the input sequence until something asks for a value, at which point it will start retrieving one value after another from the source until the filter delegate says that a match has been found. It then produces that and doesn't try to retrieve anything more from the source until it is asked for the next item. Example 10-9 shows how you could implement this behavior by taking advantage of C#'s yield return feature.

Example 10-9. A custom deferred Where operator

```
public static class CustomDeferredLinqProvider
{
    public static IEnumerable<T> Where<T>(this IEnumerable<T> src,
                                          Func<T, bool> filter)
    {
        foreach (T item in src)
        {
            if (filter(item))
            {
                yield return item;
            }
        }
    }
}
```

The real LINQ to Objects implementation of Where is somewhat more complex. It detects certain special cases, such as arrays and lists, and it handles them in a way that is slightly more efficient than the general-purpose implementation that it falls back to for other types. However, the principle is the same for Where and all of the other operators: these methods do not perform the specified work. Instead, they return objects that will perform the work on demand. It's only when you attempt to retrieve the results of a query that anything really happens. This is called *deferred evaluation*, or sometimes *lazy evaluation*.

Deferred evaluation has the benefit of not doing work until you need it, and it makes it possible to work with infinite sequences. However, it also has disadvantages. You may need to be careful to avoid evaluating queries multiple times. Example 10-10 makes this mistake, causing it to do much more work than necessary. This loops through several different numbers and writes out each one using the currency format of each culture that uses a comma as a decimal separator.

 If you run this on Windows, you may find that most of the lines this code displays will contain ? characters, indicating that the console cannot display most of the currency symbols. In fact, it can—it just needs permission. By default, the Windows console uses an 8-bit code page for backward-compatibility reasons. If you run the command chcp 65001 from a Command Prompt, it will switch that console window into a UTF-8 code page, enabling it to show any Unicode characters supported by your chosen console font. You might want to configure the console to use a font with comprehensive support for uncommon characters—Consolas or Lucida Console, for example—to take best advantage of that.

Example 10-10. Accidental reevaluation of a deferred query

```
IEnumerable<CultureInfo> commaCultures =
    from culture in CultureInfo.GetCultures(CultureTypes.AllCultures)
    where culture.NumberFormat.NumberDecimalSeparator == ","
    select culture;

object[] numbers = [1, 100, 100.2, 10000.2];

foreach (object number in numbers)
{
    foreach (CultureInfo culture in commaCultures)
    {
        Console.WriteLine(string.Format(culture, "{0}: {1:c}",
                        culture.Name, number));
    }
}
```

The problem with this code is that even though the commaCultures variable is initialized outside of the number loop, we iterate through it for each number. And because LINQ to Objects uses deferred evaluation, that means that the actual work of running the query is redone every time around the outer loop. So, instead of evaluating that where clause once for each culture (869 times on my system), it ends up running four times for each culture (3,476 times) because the whole query is evaluated once for each of the four items in the numbers array. It's not a disaster—the code still works correctly. But if you do this in a program that runs on a heavily loaded server, it will harm your throughput.

If you know you will need to iterate through the results of a query multiple times, consider using either the `ToList` or `ToArray` extension methods provided by LINQ to Objects. These immediately evaluate the whole query once, producing an `IList<T>` or a `T[]` array, respectively (so you shouldn't use these methods on infinite sequences, obviously). You can then iterate through that as many times as you like without incurring any further costs (beyond the minimal cost inherent in reading array or list elements). But in cases where you iterate through a query only once, it is usually better not to use these methods, as they'll consume more memory than necessary.

LINQ, Generics, and IQueryable<T>

LINQ providers use generic types. LINQ to Objects uses `IEnumerable<T>`. Several of the database providers use a type called `IQueryable<T>`. More broadly, the pattern is to have some generic type *Source*`<T>`, where *Source* represents some source of items, and `T` is the type of an individual item. A source type with LINQ support makes operator methods available on *Source*`<T>` for any `T`, and those operators also typically return *Source*`<TResult>`, where `TResult` may or may not be different than `T`.

`IQueryable<T>` is interesting because it is designed to be used by multiple providers. This interface, its base `IQueryable`, and the related `IQueryProvider` are shown in Example 10-11.

Example 10-11. IQueryable and IQueryable<T>

```
public interface IQueryable : IEnumerable
{
    Type ElementType { get; }
    Expression Expression { get; }
    IQueryProvider Provider { get; }
}

public interface IQueryable<out T> : IEnumerable<T>, IQueryable
{
}

public interface IQueryProvider
{
    IQueryable CreateQuery(Expression expression);
    IQueryable<TElement> CreateQuery<TElement>(Expression expression);
    object? Execute(Expression expression);
    TResult Execute<TResult>(Expression expression);
}
```

The most obvious feature of IQueryable<T> is that it adds no members to its bases. That's because it's designed to be used entirely via extension methods. The System. Linq namespace defines all of the standard LINQ operators for IQueryable<T> as extension methods provided by the Queryable class. However, all of these simply defer to the Provider property defined by the IQueryable base. So, unlike LINQ to Objects, where the extension methods on IEnumerable<T> define the behavior, an IQueryable<T> implementation is able to decide how to handle queries because it gets to supply the IQueryProvider that does the real work.

However, all IQueryable<T>-based LINQ providers have one thing in common: they interpret the lambdas as expression objects, not delegates. Example 10-12 shows the declaration of the Where extension methods defined for IEnumerable<T> and IQuery able<T>. Compare the predicate parameters.

Example 10-12. Enumerable versus Queryable

```
public static class Enumerable
{
    public static IEnumerable<TSource> Where<TSource>(
        this IEnumerable<TSource> source,
        Func<TSource, bool> predicate)
    ...
}

public static class Queryable
{
    public static IQueryable<TSource> Where<TSource>(
        this IQueryable<TSource> source,
        Expression<Func<TSource, bool>> predicate)
    ...
}
```

The Where extension for IEnumerable<T> (LINQ to Objects) takes a Func<TSource, bool>, and as you saw in Chapter 9, this is a delegate type. But the Where extension method for IQueryable<T> (used by numerous LINQ providers) takes Expression <Func<TSource, bool>>, and as you also saw in Chapter 9, this causes the compiler to build an object model of the expression and pass that as the argument.

A LINQ provider typically uses IQueryable<T> if it wants these expression trees. And that's usually because it's going to inspect your query and convert it into something else, such as a SQL query.

There are some other common generic types that crop up in LINQ. Some LINQ features guarantee to produce items in a certain order, and some do not. More subtly, a handful of operators produce items in an order that depends upon the order of their input. This can be reflected in the types for which the operators are defined and the types they return. LINQ to Objects defines IOrderedEnumerable<T> to represent ordered data, and there's a corresponding IOrderedQueryable<T> type for IQueryable<T>-based providers. (Providers that use their own types tend to do something similar—Parallel LINQ, described in Chapter 16, defines an Ordered ParallelQuery<T>, for example.) These derive from their unordered counterparts, such as IEnumerable<T> and IQueryable<T>, so all the usual operators are available, but they make it possible to define operators or other methods that need to take the existing order of their input into account. For example, in "Ordering" on page 497, I will show a LINQ operator called ThenBy, which is available only on sources that are already ordered.

When looking at LINQ to Objects, this ordered/unordered distinction may seem unnecessary, because IEnumerable<T> always produces items in some sort of order. But some providers do not necessarily do things in any particular order, perhaps because they parallelize query execution, or because they get a database to execute the query for them, and databases reserve the right to meddle with the order in certain cases if it enables them to work more efficiently.

Standard LINQ Operators

In this section, I will describe the standard operators that LINQ providers can supply. Where applicable, I will also describe the query expression equivalent, although many operators do not have a corresponding query expression form. Some LINQ features are available only through explicit method invocation. This is even true with certain operators that can be used in query expressions, because most operators are overloaded, and query expressions can't use some of the more advanced overloads.

 LINQ operators are not operators in the usual C# sense—they are not symbols such as + or &&. LINQ has its own terminology, and for this chapter, an operator is a query capability offered by a LINQ provider. In C#, it looks like a method.

All of these operators have something in common: they have all been designed to support composition. This means that you can combine them in almost any way you like, making it possible to build complex queries out of simple elements. To enable this, operators not only take some type representing a set of items (e.g., an IEnumerable<T>) as their input, but most of them also return something representing a set of items. As already mentioned, the item type is not always the same—an operator might take some IEnumerable<T> as input, and produce IEnumerable<TResult> as output, where TResult does not have to be the same as T. Even so, you can still chain the things together in any number of ways. Part of the reason this works is that LINQ operators are like mathematical functions in that they do not modify their inputs; rather, they produce a new result that is based on their operands. (Functional programming languages typically have the same characteristic.) This means that not only are you free to plug operators together in arbitrary combinations without fear of side effects, but you are also free to use the same source as the input to multiple queries, because no LINQ query will ever modify its input. Each operator returns a new query based on its input.

Nothing enforces this functional style. The compiler doesn't care what a method representing a LINQ operator does. It is only by convention that operators are functional, in order to support composition, but the built-in LINQ providers all work this way.

Not all providers offer complete support for all operators. The main providers Microsoft supplies—such as LINQ to Objects or the LINQ support in EF Core and Rx—are as comprehensive as they can be, but there are some situations in which certain operators will not make sense.

To demonstrate the operators in action, I need some source data. Many of the examples in the following sections will use the code in Example 10-13.

Example 10-13. Sample input data for LINQ queries

```
public record Course(
    string Title,
    string Category,
    int Number,
    DateOnly PublicationDate,
    TimeSpan Duration)
{
    public static readonly Course[] Catalog =
    [
        new Course(
            Title: "Elements of Geometry",
            Category: "MAT", Number: 101, Duration: TimeSpan.FromHours(3),
            PublicationDate: new DateOnly(2009, 5, 20)),
        new Course(
            Title: "Squaring the Circle",
            Category: "MAT", Number: 102, Duration: TimeSpan.FromHours(7),
            PublicationDate: new DateOnly(2009, 4, 1)),
        new Course(
            Title: "Recreational Organ Transplantation",
            Category: "BIO", Number: 305, Duration: TimeSpan.FromHours(4),
            PublicationDate: new DateOnly(2002, 7, 19)),
        new Course(
            Title: "Hyperbolic Geometry",
            Category: "MAT", Number: 207, Duration: TimeSpan.FromHours(5),
            PublicationDate: new DateOnly(2007, 10, 5)),
        new Course(
            Title: "Oversimplified Data Structures for Demos",
```

```
            Category: "CSE", Number: 104, Duration: TimeSpan.FromHours(2),
            PublicationDate: new DateOnly(2023, 11, 14)),
        new Course(
            Title: "Introduction to Human Anatomy and Physiology",
            Category: "BIO", Number: 201, Duration: TimeSpan.FromHours(12),
            PublicationDate: new DateOnly(2001, 4, 11)),
    ];
}
```

Filtering

One of the simplest operators is `Where`, which filters its input. You provide a predicate, which is a function that takes an individual item and returns a `bool`. `Where` returns an object representing the items from the input for which the predicate is true. (Conceptually, this is very similar to the `FindAll` method available on `List<T>` and array types, but using deferred execution.)

As you've already seen, query expressions represent this with a `where` clause. However, there's an overload of the `Where` operator that provides an additional feature not accessible from a query expression. You can write a filter lambda that takes two arguments: an item from the input and an index representing that item's position in the source. Example 10-14 uses this form to exclude every second item from the input, and it also drops courses shorter than three hours.

Example 10-14. Where operator with index

```
IEnumerable<Course> q = Course.Catalog.Where(
    (course, index) => (index % 2 == 0) && course.Duration.TotalHours >= 3);
```

Indexed filtering is meaningful only for ordered data. It always works with LINQ to Objects, because that uses `IEnumerable<T>`, which produces items one after another, but not all LINQ providers process items in sequence. For example, with EF Core, the LINQ queries you write in C# will be handled on the database. Unless a query explicitly requests some particular order, a database is usually free to process items in whatever order it sees fit, possibly in parallel. In some cases, a database may have optimization strategies that enable it to produce the results a query requires using a process that bears little resemblance to the original query. So it might not even be meaningful to talk about, say, the 14th item handled by a `WHERE` clause. Consequently, if you were to write a query similar to Example 10-14 using EF Core, executing the query would cause an exception, complaining that the indexed `Where` operator is not available. If you're wondering why the overload is even present if the provider doesn't support it, it's because EF Core uses `IQueryable<T>`, so all the standard operators are available at compile time; providers that choose to use `IQueryable<T>` can only report the nonavailability of operators at runtime.

LINQ providers that implement some or all of the query logic on the server side usually limit what you can do in a query's lambdas. Conversely, LINQ to Objects runs queries in process, so it lets you invoke any method from inside a filter lambda—if you want to call `Console.WriteLine` or read data from a file in your predicate, LINQ to Objects can't stop you. But LINQ providers for databases need to be able to translate your lambdas into something the server can process, so they will reject expressions that use methods with no server-side equivalent.

Even so, you might have expected the exception to emerge when you invoke `Where`, instead of when you try to execute the query (i.e., when you first try to retrieve one or more items). However, providers that convert LINQ queries into some other form, such as a SQL query, typically defer all validation until you execute the query. This is because some operators may be valid only in certain scenarios, meaning that the provider may not know whether any particular operator will work until you've finished building the whole query. It would be inconsistent if errors caused by nonviable queries sometimes emerged while building the query and sometimes when executing it, so even in cases where a provider could determine earlier that a particular operator will fail, it will usually wait until you execute the query to tell you.

The filter lambda you supply to the `Where` operator must take an argument of the item type (the `T` in `IEnumerable<T>`, for example), and it must return a `bool`. You may remember from Chapter 9 that the runtime libraries define a suitable delegate type called `Predicate<T>`, but I also mentioned in that chapter that LINQ avoids this, and we can now see why. The indexed version of the `Where` operator cannot use `Predicate<T>`, because there's an additional argument, so that overload uses `Func<T, int, bool>`. There's nothing stopping the unindexed form of `Where` from using `Predicate<T>`, but LINQ providers tend to use `Func` across the board to ensure that operators with similar meanings have similar-looking signatures. Most providers therefore use `Func<T, bool>` instead, to be consistent with the indexed version. (C# doesn't care which you use—query expressions still work if the provider uses `Predicate<T>`, but none of Microsoft's providers do this.)

The C# compiler's nullability analysis doesn't understand what LINQ operators do. Given an `IEnumerable<string?>`, writing `xs.Where(s => s is not null)` removes any null items, but `Where` will still return an `IEnumerable<string?>`. The compiler has no expectations around what `Where` will do, so it doesn't understand that the output is effectively an `IEnumerable<string>`.

LINQ defines another filtering operator: OfType<T>. This is useful if your source contains a mixture of different item types—perhaps the source is an IEnumerable <object> and you'd like to filter this down to only the items of type string. Example 10-15 shows how the OfType<T> operator can do this.

Example 10-15. The OfType<T> operator

```
public static void ShowAllStrings(IEnumerable<object> src)
{
    foreach (string s in src.OfType<string>())
    {
        Console.WriteLine(s);
    }
}
```

When you use the OfType<T> operator with a reference type, it will filter out any null values. If you've enabled nullable reference types, OfType avoids the problems that Where(s => s is not null) encounters: if you call OfType<string> on a sequence of type IEnumerable<string?>, the resulting type will be IEnumerable<string>. But that's not because OfType was designed with nullable reference types in mind. On the contrary, it effectively ignores the nullability when you use a reference type as the type argument. It happens to do what we want in this case because it's always looking for a positive match. (It effectively performs the same test as patterns like o is string.) The surprising corollary is that OfType<string?> will also filter out null items, with the slightly peculiar result that it returns an IEnumerable<string?> that will never produce a null.

Both Where and OfType<T> will produce empty sequences if none of the objects in the source meets the requirements. This is not considered to be an error—empty sequences are quite normal in LINQ. Many operators can produce them as output, and most operators can cope with them as input.

One last way to filter items is to remove duplicates, for which LINQ defines the Distinct operator. Example 10-16 contains a query that extracts the category names from all the courses and then feeds that into the Distinct operator to ensure that each unique category name appears just once.

Example 10-16. Removing duplicates with Distinct

```
IEnumerable<string> categories =
    Course.Catalog.Select(c => c.Category).Distinct();
```

Select

When writing a query, we may want to extract only certain pieces of data from the source items. The `select` clause at the end of most queries lets us supply a lambda that will be used to produce the final output items, and there are a couple of reasons we might want to make our `select` clause do more than simply pass each item straight through. We might want to pick just one specific piece of information from each item, or we might want to transform it into something else entirely.

You've seen several `select` clauses already, and I showed in Example 10-3 that the compiler turns them into a call to `Select`. However, as with many LINQ operators, the version accessible through a query expression is not the only option. There's one other overload, which provides not just the input item from which to generate the output item but also the index of that item. Example 10-17 uses this to generate a numbered list of course titles.

Example 10-17. `Select` operator with index

```
IEnumerable<string> nonIntro = Course.Catalog.Select((course, index) =>
    $"Course {index}: {course.Title}");
```

Be aware that the zero-based index passed into the lambda will be based on what comes into the `Select` operator and will not necessarily represent the item's original position in the underlying data source. This might not produce the results you were hoping for in code such as Example 10-18.

Example 10-18. Indexed `Select` downstream of `Where` operator

```
IEnumerable<string> nonIntro = Course.Catalog
    .Where(c => c.Number >= 200)
    .Select((course, index) => $"Course {index}: {course.Title}");
```

This code will select the courses found at indexes 2, 3, and 5, respectively, in the `Course.Catalog` array, because those are the courses whose `Number` property satisfies the `Where` expression. However, this query will number the three courses as 0, 1, and 2, because the `Select` operator sees only the items the `Where` clause let through, so the `Select` clause never had access to the original source. As far as it is concerned, there are only three items. If you wanted the indexes relative to the original collection, you'd need to extract those upstream of the `Where` clause, as Example 10-19 shows.

Example 10-19. Indexed Select upstream of Where operator

```
IEnumerable<string> nonIntro = Course.Catalog
    .Select((course, index) => new { course, index })
    .Where(vars => vars.course.Number >= 200)
    .Select(vars => $"Course {vars.index}: {vars.course.Title}");
```

You may be wondering why I've used an anonymous type here and not a tuple. I could replace `new { course, index }` with just `(course, index)`, and the code would work equally well. (It might even be more efficient, because tuples are value types, but anonymous types are reference types. Tuples would create less work for the GC here.) However, in general, tuples will not always work in LINQ. The lightweight tuple syntax was introduced in C# 7.0, so they weren't around when expression trees were added back in C# 3.0. The expression object model has not been updated to support this language feature, so if you try to use a tuple with an `IQueryable<T>`-based LINQ provider, you will get compiler error CS8143, telling you that `An expression tree may not contain a tuple literal`. So I tend to use anonymous types in this chapter because they work with query-based providers. But if you're using a purely local LINQ provider (e.g., Rx or LINQ to Objects), feel free to use tuples.

The indexed `Select` operator is similar to the indexed `Where` operator. So, as you would probably expect, not all LINQ providers support it in all scenarios.

Data shaping and anonymous types

If you are using a LINQ provider to access a database, the `Select` operator can offer an opportunity to reduce the quantity of data you fetch, which could reduce the load on your servers. When you use a data access technology such as EF Core to execute a query that returns a set of objects representing persistent entities, there's a trade-off between doing too much work up front and having to do lots of extra deferred work. Should those frameworks fully populate all of the object properties that correspond to columns in various database tables? Should they also load related objects? In general, it's more efficient not to fetch data you're not going to use, and data that is not fetched up front can always be loaded later on demand. However, if you try to be too frugal in your initial request, you may ultimately end up making a lot of extra requests to fill in the gaps, which could outweigh any benefit from avoiding unnecessary work.

When it comes to related entities, EF Core allows you to configure which related entities should be prefetched and which should be loaded on demand, but for any particular entity that gets fetched, all properties relating to columns are typically fully populated. This means queries that request whole entities end up fetching all the columns for any row that they touch.

If you needed to use only one or two columns, fetching them all is relatively expensive. Example 10-20 uses this somewhat inefficient approach. It shows a fairly typical EF Core query.

Example 10-20. Fetching more data than is needed

```
IQueryable<Product> pq = from product in dbCtx.Product
                         where product.ListPrice > 3000
                         select product;
foreach (var prod in pq)
{
    Console.WriteLine($"{prod.Name} ({prod.Size}): {prod.ListPrice}");
}
```

This LINQ provider translates the `where` clause into an efficient SQL equivalent. However, the SQL `SELECT` clause retrieves all the columns from the table. Compare that with Example 10-21. This modifies only one part of the query: the LINQ `select` clause now returns an instance of an anonymous type that contains only those properties we require. (The loop that follows the query can remain the same. It uses `var` for its iteration variable, which will work fine with the anonymous type, which provides the three properties that loop requires.)

Example 10-21. A select clause with an anonymous type

```
var pq = from product in dbCtx.Product
         where product.ListPrice > 3000
         select new { product.Name, product.ListPrice, product.Size };
```

The code produces exactly the same results, but it generates a much more compact SQL query that requests only the `Name`, `ListPrice`, and `Size` columns. If you're using a table with many columns, this will produce a significantly smaller response because it's no longer dominated by data we don't need. This reduces the load on the network connection to the database server and also results in faster processing because the data will take less time to arrive. This technique is called *data shaping*.

This approach will not always be an improvement. For one thing, it means you are working directly with data in the database instead of using entity objects. This might mean working at a lower level of abstraction than would be possible if you use the entity types, which might increase development costs. Also, in some environments, database administrators do not allow ad hoc queries, forcing you to use stored procedures, in which case you won't have the flexibility to use this technique.

Projecting the results of a query into an anonymous type is not limited to database queries, by the way. You are free to do this with any LINQ provider, such as LINQ to Objects. It can sometimes be a useful way to get structured information out of a query without needing to define a class specially. (As I mentioned in Chapter 3, anonymous types can be used outside of LINQ, but this is one of the main scenarios for which they were designed. Grouping by composite keys is another, as I'll describe in "Grouping" on page 512.)

Projection and mapping

The Select operator is sometimes referred to as *projection*, and it is the same operation that many languages call *map*, which provides a slightly different way to think about the Select operator. So far, I've presented Select as a way to choose what comes out of a query, but you can also look at it as a way to apply a transformation to every item in the source. Example 10-22 uses Select to produce modified versions of a list of numbers. It variously doubles the numbers, squares them, and turns them into strings.

Example 10-22. Using Select to transform numbers

```
int[] numbers = [0, 1, 2, 3, 4, 5];

IEnumerable<int> doubled = numbers.Select(x => 2 * x);
IEnumerable<int> squared = numbers.Select(x => x * x);
IEnumerable<string> numberText = numbers.Select(x => x.ToString());
```

SelectMany

The SelectMany LINQ operator is used in query expressions that have multiple from clauses. It's called SelectMany because, instead of selecting a single output item for each input item, you provide it with a lambda that produces a whole collection for each input item. The resulting query produces all of the objects from all of these collections, as though all of the collections your lambda returns were merged into one. (This won't remove duplicates. Sequences can contain duplicates. If you want to remove them, you can use the Distinct operator shown earlier.) There are a couple of ways of thinking about this operator. One is that it provides a means of flattening two levels of hierarchy—a collection of collections—into a single level. Another way to look at it is as a Cartesian product—that is, a way to produce every possible combination from some input sets.

Example 10-23 shows how to use this operator in a query expression. This code highlights the Cartesian-product-like behavior. It shows every combination of the letters A, B, and C with a single digit from 1 to 5—that is, A1, B1, C1, A2, B2, C2, etc. (If you're wondering about the apparent incompatibility of the two input sequences, the select clause of this query relies on the fact that if you use the + operator to add a string and some other type, C# generates code that calls ToString on the nonstring operand for you.)

Example 10-23. Using SelectMany from a query expression

```
int[] numbers = [1, 2, 3, 4, 5];
string[] letters = ["A", "B", "C"];

IEnumerable<string> combined = from number in numbers
                              from letter in letters
                              select letter + number;
foreach (string s in combined)
{
    Console.WriteLine(s);
}
```

Example 10-24 shows how to invoke the operator directly. This is equivalent to the query expression in Example 10-23.

Example 10-24. SelectMany operator

```
IEnumerable<string> combined = numbers.SelectMany(
    number => letters,
    (number, letter) => letter + number);
```

Example 10-23 uses two fixed collections—the second from clause returns the same letters collection every time. However, you can make the expression in the second from clause return a value based on the current item from the first from clause. You can see in Example 10-24 that the first lambda passed to SelectMany (which actually corresponds to the second from clause's final expression) receives the current item from the first collection through its number argument, so you can use that to choose a different collection for each item from the first collection. I can use this to exploit SelectMany's flattening behavior.

I've copied a jagged array from Example 5-18 in Chapter 5 into Example 10-25, which then processes it with a query containing two from clauses. Note that the expression in the second from clause is now row, the range variable of the first from clause.

Example 10-25. Flattening a jagged array

```
int[][] arrays =
[
    [1, 2],
    [1, 2, 3, 4, 5, 6],
    [1, 2, 4],
    [1],
    [1, 2, 3, 4, 5]
];
```

```
IEnumerable<int> flattened = from row in arrays
                             from number in row
                             select number;
```

The first from clause asks to iterate over each item in the top-level array. Each of these items is also an array, and the second from clause asks to iterate over each of these nested arrays. This nested array's type is int[], so the range variable of the second from clause, number, represents an int from that nested array. The select clause just returns each of these int values.

The resulting sequence provides every number in the arrays in turn. It has flattened the jagged array into a simple linear sequence of numbers. This behavior is conceptually similar to writing a nested pair of loops, one iterating over the outer int[][] array, and an inner loop iterating over the contents of each individual int[] array.

The compiler uses the same overload of SelectMany for Example 10-25 as it does for Example 10-24, but there's an alternative in this case. The final select clause is simpler in Example 10-25—it just passes on items from the second collection unmodified, which means the simpler overload shown in Example 10-26 does the job equally well. With this overload, we just provide a single lambda, which chooses the collection that SelectMany will expand for each of the items in the input collection.

Example 10-26. SelectMany without item projection

```
IEnumerable<int> flattened = arrays.SelectMany(row => row);
```

That's a somewhat terse bit of code, so in case it's not clear quite how that could end up flattening the array, Example 10-27 shows how you might implement SelectMany for IEnumerable<T> if you had to write it yourself.

Example 10-27. One implementation of SelectMany

```
public static IEnumerable<T2> MySelectMany<T, T2>(
    this IEnumerable<T> src, Func<T, IEnumerable<T2>> getInner)
{
    foreach (T itemFromOuterCollection in src)
    {
        IEnumerable<T2> innerCollection = getInner(itemFromOuterCollection);
        foreach (T2 itemFromInnerCollection in innerCollection)
        {
            yield return itemFromInnerCollection;
        }
    }
}
```

Why does the compiler not use the simpler option shown in Example 10-26? The C#
language specification defines how query expressions are translated into method
calls, and it mentions only the overload shown in Example 10-23. Perhaps the reason
the specification doesn't mention the simpler overload is to reduce the demands C#
makes of types that want to support this double-from query form—you'd need to
write only one method to enable this syntax for your own types. However, .NET's various LINQ providers are more generous, providing this simpler overload for the benefit of developers who choose to use the operators directly. In fact, some providers
define two more overloads: there are versions of both the SelectMany forms we've
seen so far that also pass an item index to the first lambda. (The usual caveats about
indexed operators apply, of course.)

Although Example 10-27 gives a reasonable idea of what LINQ to Objects does in
SelectMany, it's not the exact implementation. There are optimizations for special
cases. Moreover, other providers may use very different strategies. Databases often
have built-in support for Cartesian products, so some providers may implement
SelectMany in terms of that.

Ordering

In general, LINQ queries do not guarantee to produce items in any particular order
unless you explicitly define the order you require. You can do this in a query expression with an orderby clause. As Example 10-28 shows, you specify the expression that
defines how to order the items and a direction—so this will produce a collection of
courses ordered by ascending publication date. As it happens, ascending is the
default, so you can leave off that qualifier without changing the meaning. As you've
probably guessed, you can specify descending to reverse the order.

Example 10-28. Query expression with orderby clause

```
IOrderedEnumerable<Course> q = from course in Course.Catalog
                               orderby course.PublicationDate ascending
                               select course;
```

The compiler transforms the orderby clause in Example 10-28 into a call to the
OrderBy method, and it would use OrderByDescending if you had specified a descend
ing sort order. With source types that make a distinction between ordered and
unordered collections, these operators return the ordered type (for example, IOrder
edEnumerable<T> for LINQ to Objects, and IOrderedQueryable<T> for IQuery
able<T>-based providers).

With LINQ to Objects, these operators have to retrieve every element from their input before they can produce any output elements. An ascending OrderBy can determine which item to return first only once it has found the lowest item, and it won't know for certain which is the lowest until it has seen all of them. It still uses deferred evaluation—it won't do anything until you ask it for the first item. But as soon as you do ask it for something, it has to do all the work at once. Some providers will have additional knowledge about the data that can enable more efficient strategies. (For example, a database may be able to use an index to return values in the order required.)

LINQ to Objects' OrderBy and OrderByDescending operators each have two overloads, only one of which is available from a query expression. If you invoke the methods directly, you can supply an additional parameter of type IComparer<TKey>, where TKey is the type of the expression by which the items are being sorted. This is likely to be important if you sort based on a string property, because there are several different orderings for text, and you may need to choose one based on your application's locale, or you may want to specify a culture-invariant ordering to ensure consistency across all environments.

The expression that determines the order in Example 10-28 is very simple—it just retrieves the PublicationDate property from the source item. You can write more complex expressions if you want to. If you're using a provider that translates a LINQ query into something else, there may be limitations. If the query runs on the database, you may be able to refer to other tables—the provider might be able to convert an expression such as product.ProductCategory.Name into a suitable join. However, you will not be able to run any old code in that expression, because it must be something that the database can execute. But LINQ to Objects just invokes the expression once for each object, so you really can put in there whatever code you like.

You may want to sort by multiple criteria. You should *not* do this by writing multiple orderby clauses. Example 10-29 makes this mistake.

Example 10-29. How not to apply multiple ordering criteria

```
IOrderedEnumerable<Course> q =
    from course in Course.Catalog
    orderby course.PublicationDate ascending
    orderby course.Duration descending // BAD! Could discard previous order
    select course;
```

This code orders the items by publication date and then by duration but does so as two separate and unrelated steps. The second orderby clause guarantees only that the results will be in the order specified in that clause and does not guarantee to preserve anything about the order in which the elements originated. If what you actually wanted was for the items to be in order of publication date, and for any items with the same publication date to be ordered by descending duration, you would need to write the query in Example 10-30.

Example 10-30. Multiple ordering criteria in a query expression

```
IOrderedEnumerable<Course> q =
    from course in Course.Catalog
    orderby course.PublicationDate ascending, course.Duration descending
    select course;
```

LINQ defines separate operators for this multilevel ordering: ThenBy and ThenBy Descending. Example 10-31 shows how to achieve the same effect as the query expression in Example 10-30 by invoking the LINQ operators directly. For LINQ providers whose types make a distinction between ordered and unordered collections, the ThenBy and ThenByDescending operators will be available only on the ordered form, such as IOrderedQueryable<T> or IOrderedEnumerable<T>. If you were to try to invoke ThenBy directly on Course.Catalog, the compiler would report an error.

Example 10-31. Multiple ordering criteria with LINQ operators

```
IOrderedEnumerable<Course> q = Course.Catalog
    .OrderBy(course => course.PublicationDate)
    .ThenByDescending(course => course.Duration);
```

.NET 7.0 added two new ordering operators: Order and OrderDescending, which can be convenient if you have a collection of items that are inherently comparable. For example, if you had an IEnumerable<int>, OrderBy looks slightly clunky because it requires a lambda even though you want to sort by the int values themselves, and not by some property of these values. You used to have to write numbers.OrderBy (n => n), but now, you can write numbers.Order() (or numbers.OrderDescend ing()).

You will find that some LINQ operators preserve some aspects of ordering even if you do not ask them to. For example, LINQ to Objects will typically produce items in the same order in which they appeared in the input unless you write a query that causes it to change the order. But this is simply an artifact of how LINQ to Objects works, and you should not rely on it in general. In fact, even when you are using that particular LINQ provider, you should check with the documentation to see whether the order you're getting is guaranteed or is just an accident of implementation. In most cases, if you care about the order, you should write a query that makes that explicit.

Containment Tests

LINQ defines various standard operators for discovering things about what the collection contains. Some providers may be able to implement these operators without needing to inspect every item. (For example, a database-based provider might use a WHERE clause, and the database could be able to use an index to evaluate that without needing to look at every element.) However, there are no restrictions—you can use these operators however you like, and it's up to the provider to discover whether it can exploit a shortcut.

 Unlike most LINQ operators, in the majority of providers these return neither a collection nor an item from their input. They generally just return true or false, or in some cases, a count. Rx is a notable exception: its implementations of these operators wrap the bool or int in a single-element IObservable<T> that produces the result. It does this to preserve the reactive nature of processing in Rx.

Contains

> Takes a single item, and returns true if the source contains the specified item and false if it does not.

Any

> Takes an optional predicate, and returns true if the predicate is true for at least one item in the source. If you do not provide the predicate, this returns true if the source contains at least one item.

Count *and* LongCount

> Take an optional predicate, and return the number of elements in the source for which the predicate is true. If you do not provide the predicate, these return the number of elements in the source. Count returns an int, so you would use Long Count only when dealing with very large collections. (LongCount is likely to be overkill for most LINQ to Objects applications, but it could matter when the collection lives in a database.)

All

> Takes a predicate, and it returns true if and only if the source contains no items that do not match the predicate. (I've used this slightly awkward phrasing for a reason: this returns true for an empty sequence. This is consistent with the mathematical logical operator that All represents: the *universal quantifier*, usually written as an upside-down A ($\forall$) and pronounced "for all." Mathematicians long ago agreed on the convention that applying the universal quantifier to an empty set yields the value true.)

You should be wary of code such as if (q.Count() > 0). Calculating the exact count may require the entire source query (q in this case) to be evaluated, and in any case, it is likely to require more work than simply answering the question, *Is this empty?* If q refers to a LINQ query, writing if (q.Any()) is likely to be more efficient. That said, outside of LINQ, this is not the case for list-like collections. If q were an IList<T>, for example, retrieving an element count would be cheap and may actually be more efficient than the Any operator.

There are some situations in which you might want to use a count only if one can be calculated efficiently. (For example, a user interface might want to show the total number of items available if this is easy to determine, but could easily choose not to show it for cases where that would be too expensive.) For these scenarios, you can use the TryGetNonEnumeratedCount method. This will return true if the count can be determined without having to iterate through the whole collection, and false if not. When it returns true, it passes the count back through its single argument of type out int.

Asynchronous Immediate Evaluation

Although most LINQ operators defer execution, as you've now seen there are some exceptions. With most LINQ providers, the Contains, Any, and All operators do not produce a wrapped result. (E.g., in LINQ to Objects, these return a bool, not an IEnumerable<bool>.) This sometimes means that these operators need to do some slow work. For example, EF Core's LINQ provider will need to send a query to the database and wait for the response before being able to return the bool result. The same goes for ToArray and ToList, which produce fully populated collections, instead of an IEnumerable<T> or IQueryable<T> that have the potential to produce results in the future.

As Chapter 16 describes, it is common for slow operations like these to implement the Task-based Asynchronous Pattern (TAP), enabling us to use the await keyword described in Chapter 17. Some LINQ providers therefore choose to offer asynchronous versions of these operators. For example, EF Core offers SingleAsync, ContainsAsync, AnyAsync, AllAsync, ToArrayAsync, and ToListAsync, and equivalents for the other operators we'll see that perform immediate evaluation.

Specific Items and Subranges

It can be useful to write a query that produces just a single item. Perhaps you're looking for the first object in a list that meets certain criteria, or maybe you want to fetch information in a database identified by a particular key. LINQ defines several operators that can do this and some related ones for working with a subrange of the items a query might return.

Use the `Single` operator when you have a query that you believe should produce exactly one result. Example 10-32 shows just such a query—it looks up a course by its category and number, and in my sample data, this uniquely identifies a course.

Example 10-32. Applying the `Single` operator to a query

```
IEnumerable<Course> q = from course in Course.Catalog
                        where course.Category == "MAT" && course.Number == 101
                        select course;

Course geometry = q.Single();
```

Because LINQ queries are built by chaining operators together, we can take the query built by the query expression and add on another operator—the `Single` operator, in this case. While most operators would return an object representing another query (an `IEnumerable<T>` here, since we're using LINQ to Objects), `Single` is different. Like `ToArray` and `ToList`, the `Single` operator evaluates the query immediately, but it then returns the one and only object that the query produced. If the query fails to produce exactly one object—perhaps it produces no items, or two—this will throw an `InvalidOperationException`. (Since this is another of the operators that produces a result immediately, some providers offer `SingleAsync` as described in the sidebar "Asynchronous Immediate Evaluation" on page 501.)

There's an overload of the `Single` operator that takes a predicate. As Example 10-33 shows, this allows us to express the same logic as the whole of Example 10-32 more compactly. (As with the `Where` operator, all the predicate-based operators in this section use `Func<T, bool>`, not `Predicate<T>`.)

Example 10-33. The `Single` operator with predicate

```
Course geometry = Course.Catalog.Single(
    course => course.Category == "MAT" && course.Number == 101);
```

The `Single` operator is unforgiving: if your query does not return exactly one item, it will throw an exception. There's a slightly more flexible variant called `SingleOrDefault`, which allows a query to return either one item or no items. If the query returns nothing, this method returns the default value for the item type (i.e., `null` if it's a reference type, `0` if it's a numeric type, etc.). Multiple matches still cause an exception. As with `Single`, there are two overloads: one with no arguments for use on a source that you believe contains no more than one object, and one that takes a predicate lambda.

LINQ defines two related operators, `First` and `FirstOrDefault`, each of which offers overloads taking no arguments or a predicate. For sequences containing zero or one matching items, these behave in exactly the same way as `Single` and `SingleOr Default`: they return the item if there is one; if there isn't, `First` will throw an exception, while `FirstOrDefault` will return `null` or an equivalent value. However, these operators respond differently when there are multiple results—instead of throwing an exception, they just pick the first result and return that, discarding the rest. This might be useful if you want to find the most expensive item in a list—you could order a query by descending price and then pick the first result. Example 10-34 uses a similar technique to pick the longest course from my sample data.

Example 10-34. Using `First` to select the longest course

```
IOrderedEnumerable<Course> q = from course in Course.Catalog
                               orderby course.Duration descending
                               select course;
Course longest = q.First();
```

If you have a query that doesn't guarantee any particular order for its results, these operators will pick one item arbitrarily.

 Do not use `First` or `FirstOrDefault` unless you expect there to be multiple matches and you want to process only one of them. Some developers use these when they expect only a single match. The operators will work, of course, but the `Single` and `SingleOr Default` operators more accurately express your expectations. They will let you know when your expectations were misplaced, throwing an exception when there are multiple matches. If your code embodies incorrect assumptions, it's usually best to know about it instead of plowing on regardless.

The existence of `First` and `FirstOrDefault` raises an obvious question: Can I pick the last item? The answer is yes; there are also `Last` and `LastOrDefault` operators, and again, each offers two overloads—one taking no arguments and one taking a predicate.

The `SingleOrDefault`, `FirstOrDefault`, and `LastOrDefault` operators each offer an overload enabling you to supply a value to return as the default, instead of the usual zero-like value. Example 10-35 shows how to use this `SingleOrDefault` overload to get a value of −1 when the list is empty, making it possible to distinguish between an empty list and a list containing a single zero value. (Of course, if all possible values for `int` are valid in your application, this doesn't help you, and you'd need to detect an empty collection in some other way. But in cases where you can designate some special value to represent *not here* [e.g., −1 in this case], these overloads are helpful.)

Example 10-35. SingleOrDefault with explicit default value

```
int valueOrNegative = numbers.SingleOrDefault(-1);
```

The next obvious question is: What if I want a particular element that's neither the first nor the last? Your wish is, in this particular instance, LINQ's command, because it offers `ElementAt` and `ElementAtOrDefault` operators, both of which take just an index. This provides a way to access elements of any `IEnumerable<T>` by index. You can specify the index as an `int`. Alternatively, some providers define overloads taking an `Index`, which, as you may recall from "Addressing Elements with Index and Range Syntax" on page 288, enables the use of end-relative positions. For example, `^2` denotes the second-from-last element.

You need to be careful with `ElementAt` and `ElementAtOrDefault` because they can be surprisingly expensive. If you ask for the 10,000th element, these operators may need to request and discard the first 9,999 elements to get there. If you specify an end-relative position by writing, say, `source.ElementAt(^500)`, the operator may need to read every single element to find out which is the last, and with that particular example, it may also have to hang on to the last 500 elements it has seen because until it gets to the end, it doesn't know which element will be the one it ultimately has to return.

As it happens, LINQ to Objects detects when the source object implements `IList<T>`, in which case it uses the indexer to retrieve the element directly instead of going the slow way around. But not all `IEnumerable<T>` implementations support random access, so these operators can be very slow. In particular, even if your source implements `IList<T>`, once you've applied one or more LINQ operators to it, the output of those operators will typically not support indexing. So it would be particularly disastrous to use `ElementAt` in a loop of the kind shown in Example 10-36.

Example 10-36. How not to use ElementAt

```
IEnumerable<Course> mathsCourses =
    Course.Catalog.Where(c => c.Category == "MAT");
for (int i = 0; i < mathsCourses.Count(); ++i)
{
    // Never do this!
    Course c = mathsCourses.ElementAt(i);
    Console.WriteLine(c.Title);
}
```

Even though `Course.Catalog` is an array, I've filtered its contents with the `Where` operator, which returns a query of type `IEnumerable<Course>` that does not implement `IList<Course>`. The first iteration won't be too bad—I'll be passing `ElementAt` an index of 0, so it just returns the first match, and with my sample data, the very first item `Where` inspects will match. But the second time around the loop, we're calling `ElementAt` again. The query that `mathsCourses` refers to does not keep track of where we got to in the previous loop—it's an `IEnumerable<T>`, not an `IEnumerator<T>`—so this will start again. `ElementAt` will ask that query for the first item, which it will promptly discard, and then it will ask for the next item, and that becomes the return value. So the `Where` query has now been executed twice—the first time, `ElementAt` asked it for only one item, and then the second time it asked it for two, so it has processed the first course twice now. The third time around the loop (which happens to be the final time), we do it all again, but this time, `ElementAt` will discard the first two matches and will return the third, so now it has looked at the first course three times, the second one twice, and the third and fourth courses once. (The third course in my sample data is not in the `MAT` category, so the `Where` query will skip over this when asked for the third item.) So, to retrieve three items, I've evaluated the `Where` query three times, causing it to evaluate my filter lambda seven times.

In fact, it's worse than that, because the `for` loop will also invoke that `Count` method each time, and with a nonindexable source such as the one returned by `Where`, `Count` has to evaluate the entire sequence—the only way the LINQ to Objects `Where` operator can tell you how many items match is to look at all of them. So this code fully evaluates the query returned by `Where` three times in addition to the three partial evaluations performed by `ElementAt`. We get away with it here because the collection is small, but if I had an array with 1,000 elements, all of which turned out to match the filter, we'd be fully evaluating the `Where` query 1,000 times and performing partial evaluations another 1,000 times. Each full evaluation calls the filter predicate 1,000 times, and the partial evaluations here will do so on average 500 times, so the code would end up executing the filter 1,500,000 times. Iterating through the `Where` query with the `foreach` loop would evaluate the query just once, executing the filter expression 1,000 times, and would produce the same results.

So be careful with both `Count` and `ElementAt`. If you use them in a loop that iterates over the collection on which you invoke them, the resulting code will have $O(n^2)$ complexity (i.e., the cost of running the code rises proportionally to the number of items squared).

All of the operators I've just described return a single item from the source. There are four more operators that also get selective about which items to use but can return multiple items: `Skip`, `Take`, `SkipLast`, and `TakeLast`. Each of these takes a single `int` argument. As the name suggests, `Skip` discards the specified number of elements from the beginning of the sequence and then returns everything else from its source. `Take` returns the specified number of elements from the start of the sequence and then discards the rest (so it is similar to `TOP` in SQL). `SkipLast` and `TakeLast` do the same except they work at the end, e.g., you could use `TakeLast` to get the final five items from the source, or `SkipLast` to omit the final five items.

Some providers (including LINQ to Objects) supply an overload of Take that accepts a Range, enabling the use of the range syntax described in "Addressing Elements with Index and Range Syntax" on page 288. For example, source.Take(10..^10) is equivalent to source.Skip(10).SkipLast(10), skipping the first 10 and also the last 10 items. Since the range syntax lets you use either start- or end-relative indexes for both the start and end of the range, we can express other combinations with this overload of Take. For example, source.Take(10..20) has the same effect as source.Skip(10).Take(10); source.Take(^10..^2) is equivalent to source.Take Last(10).SkipLast(2).

There are also predicate-driven versions, SkipWhile and TakeWhile. SkipWhile will discard items from the sequence until it finds one that does not match the predicate, at which point it will return that and every item that follows for the rest of the sequence (whether or not the remaining items match the predicate). Conversely, Take While returns items until it encounters the first item that does not match the predicate, at which point it discards that and the remainder of the sequence.

Although Skip, Take, SkipLast, TakeLast, SkipWhile, and TakeWhile are all clearly order-sensitive, they are not restricted to just the ordered types, such as IOrdered Enumerable<T>. They are also defined for IEnumerable<T>, which is reasonable, because even though there may be no particular order guaranteed, an IEnumerable<T> always produces elements in some order. (The only way you can extract items from an IEnumerable<T> is one after another, so there will always be an order, even if it's arbitrary. It might not be the same every time you enumerate the items, but for any single evaluation, the items must come out in some order.) Moreover, IOrderedEnumerable<T> is not widely implemented outside of LINQ, so it's quite common to have non-LINQ-aware objects that produce items in a known order but that implement only IEnumerable<T>. These operators are useful in these scenarios, so the restriction is relaxed. Slightly more surprisingly, IQueryable<T> also supports these operations, but that's consistent with the fact that many databases support TOP (roughly equivalent to Take) even on unordered queries. As always, individual providers may choose not to support individual operations, so in scenarios where there's no reasonable interpretation of these operators, they will just throw an exception.

Whole-Sequence, Order-Preserving Operations

LINQ defines certain operators whose output includes every item from the source, and that preserve or reverse the order. Not all collections necessarily have an order, so these operators will not always be supported. However, LINQ to Objects supports all of them:

Concat

Combines two sequences, producing all of the elements from the first sequence (in whatever order that sequence returns them), followed by all of the elements from the second sequence (again, preserving the order).

DefaultIfEmpty

Returns all of the elements from the source. However, if the source is empty, it returns a single element. If you don't pass the value to return as the default, this uses default(TElement).

Prepend *and* Append

Returns all the same elements as the source sequence but with one additional element at start or end, respectively.

Reverse

Reverses the order of the elements.

SequenceEqual

Compares two sequences. Returns true if they are the same length and contain the same values in the same order.

Zip

Combines two sequences, pairing elements. The first item it returns will be based on both the first item from the first sequence and the first item from the second sequence. The second item in the zipped sequence will be based on the second items from each of the sequences, and so on. (The name Zip is meant to bring to mind how a zipper in an article of clothing brings two things together in perfect alignment. It's not an exact analogy. When a zipper brings together the two parts, the teeth from the two halves interlock in an alternating fashion. But the Zip operator does not interleave its inputs like a physical zipper's teeth. It brings items from the two sources together in pairs.) Some providers also define an overload for combining three lists.

Aggregation

The Sum and Average operators add together the values of all the source items. Sum returns the total, and Average returns the total divided by the number of items. LINQ providers that support these typically make them available for collections of items of these numeric types: decimal, double, float, int, and long. There are also overloads that work with any item type in conjunction with a lambda that takes an item and returns one of those numeric types. That allows us to write code such as Example 10-37, which works with a collection of Course objects and calculates the average of a particular value extracted from the object: the course length in hours.

Example 10-37. Average operator with projection

```
Console.WriteLine("Average course length in hours: {0}",
    Course.Catalog.Average(course => course.Duration.TotalHours));
```

LINQ also defines Min and Max operators. You can apply these to any type of sequence, although it is not guaranteed to succeed—the particular provider you're using may report an error if it doesn't know how to compare the types you've used. For example, LINQ to Objects requires the objects in the sequence to implement IComparable.

Min and Max both have overloads that accept a lambda that gets the value to use from the source item. Example 10-38 uses this to find the date on which the most recent course was published.

Example 10-38. Max with projection

```
DateOnly m = mathsCourses.Max(c => c.PublicationDate);
```

Notice that this does not return the course with the most recent publication date; it returns that course's publication date. If you want to select the object for which a particular property has the maximum value, you can use MaxBy. Example 10-39 will find the course with the highest PublicationDate, but unlike Example 10-38, it returns the relevant course, instead of the date. (As you might expect, there's also a MinBy.)

Example 10-39. MaxBy with projection for criteria but not for result

```
Course? mostRecentlyPublished = mathsCourses.MaxBy(c => c.PublicationDate);
```

You may have spotted the ? in that example, indicating that MaxBy might return a null result. This happens with both Max and MaxBy in cases where the input collection is empty and the output type is either a reference type or a nullable form of one of the supported numeric types (e.g., int? or double?). When the output is a non-nullable struct (e.g., DateOnly, as with Example 10-38), these operators cannot return null and will throw an InvalidOperationException instead. If you are working with a reference type and you want an exception for an empty input like you would get if the output were a value type, the only way to do that is to check for a null result yourself and throw an exception. Example 10-40 shows one way to do this.

Example 10-40. MaxBy with projection for criteria but not for result, with error on empty input

```
Course mostRecentlyPublished = mathsCourses.MaxBy(c => c.PublicationDate)
    ?? throw new InvalidOperationException("Collection must not be empty");
```

LINQ to Objects defines specialized overloads of Min and Max for sequences that return the same numeric types that Sum and Average deal with (i.e., decimal, double, float, int, and long and their nullable forms). It also defines similar specializations for the form that takes a lambda. These overloads exist to improve performance by avoiding boxing. The general-purpose form relies on IComparable, and getting an interface type reference to a value always involves boxing that value. For large collections, boxing every single value would put considerable extra pressure on the GC.

LINQ defines an operator called Aggregate, which generalizes the pattern that Min, Max, Sum, and Average all use, which is to produce a single result with a process that involves taking every source item into consideration. It's possible to implement all four of these operators (and their ...By counterparts) in terms of Aggregate. Example 10-41 uses the Sum operator to calculate the total duration of all courses, and then shows how to use the Aggregate operator to perform the exact same calculation.

Example 10-41. Sum and equivalent with Aggregate

```
double t1 = Course.Catalog.Sum(course => course.Duration.TotalHours);
double t2 = Course.Catalog.Aggregate(
    0.0, (hours, course) => hours + course.Duration.TotalHours);
```

Aggregation works by building up a value that represents what we know about all the items inspected so far, referred to as the *accumulator*. The type we use depends on the knowledge we want to accumulate. Here, I'm just adding all the numbers together, so I've used a double (because the TimeSpan type's TotalHours property is also a double).

Initially we have no knowledge, because we haven't looked at any items yet. We need to provide an accumulator value to represent this starting point, so the Aggregate operator's first argument is the *seed*, an initial value for the accumulator. In Example 10-41, the accumulator is just a running total, so the seed is 0.0.

The second argument is a lambda that describes how to update the accumulator to incorporate information for a single item. Since my goal here is simply to calculate the total time, I just add the duration of the current course to the running total.

Once Aggregate has looked at every item, this particular overload returns the accumulator directly. It will be the total number of hours across all courses in this case. We can implement Max if we use a different accumulation strategy. Instead of maintaining a running total, the value representing everything we know so far about the data is simply the highest value seen yet. Example 10-42 shows the rough equivalent of Example 10-38. (It's not exactly the same, because Example 10-42 makes no attempt to detect an empty source. Max will throw an exception if this source is empty, but this will just return the date 0/0/0000.)

Example 10-42. Implementing Max with Aggregate

```
DateOnly m = mathsCourses.Aggregate(
    new DateOnly(),
    (date, c) => date > c.PublicationDate ? date : c.PublicationDate);
```

This illustrates that `Aggregate` does not impose any single meaning for the value that accumulates knowledge—the way you use it depends on what you're doing. Some operations require an accumulator with a bit more structure. Example 10-43 calculates the average course duration with `Aggregate`.

Example 10-43. Implementing Average with Aggregate

```
double average = Course.Catalog.Aggregate(
    new { TotalHours = 0.0, Count = 0 },
    (totals, course) => new
    {
        TotalHours = totals.TotalHours + course.Duration.TotalHours,
        Count = totals.Count + 1
    },
    totals => totals.Count > 0
        ? totals.TotalHours / totals.Count
        : throw new InvalidOperationException("Sequence was empty"));
```

The average duration requires us to know two things: the total duration and the number of items. So, in this example, my accumulator uses a type that can contain two values, one to hold the total and one to hold the item count. I've used an anonymous type because as already mentioned, that is sometimes the only option in LINQ, and I want to show the most general case. However, it's worth mentioning that in this particular case, a tuple might be better. It will work because this is LINQ to Objects, and since lightweight tuples are value types whereas anonymous types are reference types, a tuple would reduce the number of objects being allocated.

 Example 10-43 relies on the fact that when two separate methods in the same component create instances of two identical anonymous types, the compiler generates a single type that is used for both. The seed produces an instance of an anonymous type consisting of a `double` called `TotalHours` and an `int` called `Count`. The accumulation lambda also returns an instance of an anonymous type with the same member names and types in the same order. The C# compiler deems that these will be the same type, which is important, because `Aggregate` requires the lambda to accept and also return an instance of the accumulator type.

Example 10-43 uses a different overload than the earlier example. It takes an extra lambda, which is used to extract the return value from the accumulator—the accumulator builds up the information I need to produce the result, but the accumulator itself is not the result in this example.

Of course, if all you want to do is calculate the sum, maximum, or average values, you wouldn't use Aggregate—you'd use the specialized operators designed to do those jobs. Not only are they simpler, but they're often more efficient. (For example, a LINQ provider for a database might be able to generate a query that uses the database's built-in features to calculate the minimum or maximum value.) I just wanted to show the flexibility, using examples that are easily understood. But now that I've done that, Example 10-44 shows a particularly concise example of Aggregate that doesn't correspond to any other built-in operator. This takes a collection of rectangles and returns the bounding box that contains all of those rectangles.

Example 10-44. Aggregating bounding boxes

```
public static Rect GetBounds(IEnumerable<Rect> rects) =>
    rects.Aggregate(Rect.Union);
```

The Rect structure in this example is from the System.Windows namespace. This is part of WPF, and it's a very simple data structure that just contains four numbers—X, Y, Width, and Height—so you can use it in non-WPF applications if you like.[1] Example 10-44 uses the Rect type's static Union method, which takes two Rect arguments and returns a single Rect that is the bounding box of the two inputs (i.e., the smallest rectangle that contains both of the input rectangles).

I'm using the simplest overload of Aggregate here. It does the same thing as the one I used in Example 10-41, but it doesn't require me to supply a seed—it just uses the first item in the list. Example 10-45 is equivalent to Example 10-44 but makes the steps more explicit. I've provided the first Rect in the sequence as an explicit seed value, using Skip to aggregate over everything except that first element. I've also written a lambda to invoke the method, instead of passing the method itself. If you're using this sort of lambda that just passes its arguments straight on to an existing method with LINQ to Objects, you can just pass the method name instead, and it will call the target method directly rather than going through your lambda. (You can't do that with expression-based providers, because they require a lambda.)

Using the method directly is more succinct, but it also makes for slightly obscure code, which is why I've spelled it out in Example 10-45.

---

1 If you do so, be careful not to confuse it with another WPF type, Rectangle. That's an altogether more complex beast that supports animation, styling, layout, user input, databinding, and various other WPF features. Do not attempt to use Rectangle outside of a WPF application.

Example 10-45. More verbose and less obscure bounding box aggregation

```
public static Rect GetBounds(IEnumerable<Rect> rects)
{
    IEnumerable<Rect> theRest = rects.Skip(1);
    return theRest.Aggregate(rects.First(), (r1, r2) => Rect.Union(r1, r2));
}
```

These two examples work the same way. They start with the first rectangle as the seed. For the next item in the list, `Aggregate` will call `Rect.Union`, passing in the seed and the second rectangle. The result—the bounding box of the first two rectangles— becomes the new accumulator value. And that then gets passed to `Union` along with the third rectangle, and so on. Example 10-46 shows what the effect of this `Aggregate` operation would be if performed on a collection of four `Rect` values. (I've represented the four values here as `r1`, `r2`, `r3`, and `r4`. To pass them to `Aggregate`, they'd need to be inside a collection such as an array.)

Example 10-46. The effect of Aggregate

```
Rect bounds = Rect.Union(Rect.Union(Rect.Union(r1, r2), r3), r4);
```

`Aggregate` is LINQ's name for an operation some other languages call *reduce*. You also sometimes see it called *fold*. LINQ went with the name `Aggregate` for the same reason it calls its projection operator `Select` instead of *map* (the more common name in functional programming languages): LINQ's terminology is more influenced by SQL than it is by functional programming languages.

Grouping

Sometimes you will want to process all items that have something in common as a group. Example 10-47 uses a query to group courses by category, writing out a title for each category before listing all the courses in that category.

Example 10-47. Grouping query expression

```
IEnumerable<IGrouping<string, Course>> subjectGroups =
    from course in Course.Catalog
    group course by course.Category;

foreach (IGrouping<string, Course> group in subjectGroups)
{
    Console.WriteLine($"Category: {group.Key}");
    Console.WriteLine();

    foreach (Course course in group)
    {
```

```
        Console.WriteLine(course.Title);
    }
    Console.WriteLine();
}
```

A group clause takes an expression that determines group membership—in this case, any courses whose Category properties return the same value will be deemed to be in the same group. A group clause produces a collection in which each item implements a type representing a group. Since I am using LINQ to Objects, and I am grouping by category string, the type of the subjectGroup variable in Example 10-47 will be IEnu merable<IGrouping<string, Course>>. This particular example produces three group objects, depicted in Figure 10-1.

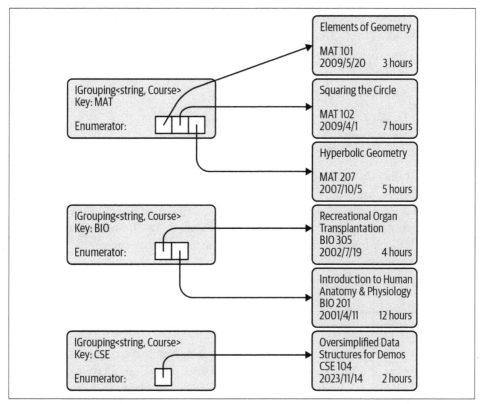

Figure 10-1. Result of evaluating a grouping query

Each of the IGrouping<string, Course> items has a Key property, and because the query groups items by the course's Category property, each key contains a string value from that property. There are three different category names in the sample data in Example 10-13: MAT, BIO, and CSE, so these are the Key values for the three groups.

The IGrouping<TKey, TItem> interface derives from IEnumerable<TItem>, so each group object can be enumerated to find the items it contains. So in Example 10-47, the outer foreach loop iterates over the three groups returned by the query, and then the inner foreach loop iterates over the Course objects in each of the groups.

The query expression turns into the code in Example 10-48.

Example 10-48. Expanding a simple grouping query

```
IEnumerable<IGrouping<string, Course>> subjectGroups =
    Course.Catalog.GroupBy(course => course.Category);
```

Query expressions offer some variations on the theme of grouping. With a slight modification to the original query, we can arrange for the items in each group to be something other than the original Course objects. In Example 10-49, I've changed the expression immediately after the group keyword from just course to course.Title.

Example 10-49. Group query with item projection

```
IEnumerable<IGrouping<string, string>> subjectGroups =
    from course in Course.Catalog
    group course.Title by course.Category;
```

This still has the same grouping expression, course.Category, so this produces three groups as before, but now it's of type IGrouping<string, string>. If you were to iterate over the contents of one of the groups, you'd find each group offers a sequence of strings, containing the course names. As Example 10-50 shows, the compiler expands this query into a different overload of the GroupBy operator.

Example 10-50. Expanding a group query with an item projection

```
IEnumerable<IGrouping<string, string>> subjectGroups = Course.Catalog
    .GroupBy(course => course.Category, course => course.Title);
```

Query expressions are required to have either a select or a group as their final clause. However, if a query contains a group clause, that doesn't have to be the last clause. In Example 10-49, I modified how the query represents each item within a group (i.e., the boxes on the right of Figure 10-1), but I'm also free to customize the objects representing each group (the items on the left). By default, I get the IGroup ing<TKey, TItem> objects (or the equivalent for whichever LINQ provider the query is using), but I can change this. Example 10-51 uses the optional into keyword in its group clause. This introduces a new range variable, which iterates over the group objects, which I can go on to use in the rest of the query. I could follow this with other clause types, such as orderby or where, but in this case, I've chosen to use a select clause.

Example 10-51. Group query with group projection

```
IEnumerable<string> subjectGroups =
    from course in Course.Catalog
    group course by course.Category into category
    select $"Category '{category.Key}' contains {category.Count()} courses";
```

The result of this query is an IEnumerable<string>, and if you display all the strings it produces, you get this:

```
Category 'MAT' contains 3 courses
Category 'BIO' contains 2 courses
Category 'CSE' contains 1 courses
```

As Example 10-52 shows, this expands into a call to the same GroupBy overload that Example 10-48 uses, and then uses the ordinary Select operator for the final clause.

Example 10-52. Expanded group query with group projection

```
IEnumerable<string> subjectGroups = Course.Catalog
    .GroupBy(course => course.Category)
    .Select(category =>
        $"Category '{category.Key}' contains {category.Count()} courses");
```

LINQ to Objects defines some more overloads for the GroupBy operator that are not accessible from the query syntax. Example 10-53 shows an overload that provides a slightly more direct equivalent to Example 10-51.

Example 10-53. GroupBy with key and group projections

```
IEnumerable<string> subjectGroups = Course.Catalog.GroupBy(
    course => course.Category,
    (category, courses) =>
        $"Category '{category}' contains {courses.Count()} courses");
```

This overload takes two lambdas. The first is the expression by which items are grouped. The second is used to produce each group object. Unlike the previous examples, this does not use the IGrouping<TKey, TItem> interface. Instead, the final lambda receives the key as one argument and then a collection of the items in the group as the second. This is exactly the same information that IGrouping<TKey, TItem> encapsulates, but because this form of the operator can pass these as separate arguments, it removes the need for the operator to create objects to represent the groups.

There's yet another version of this operator shown in Example 10-54. It combines the functionality of all the other flavors.

Example 10-54. GroupBy operator with key, item, and group projections

```
IEnumerable<string> subjectGroups = Course.Catalog.GroupBy(
    course => course.Category,
    course => course.Title,
    (category, titles) =>
        $"Category '{category}' contains {titles.Count()} courses: " +
            string.Join(", ", titles));
```

This overload takes three lambdas. The first is the expression by which items are grouped. The second determines how individual items in a group are represented—this time I've chosen to extract the course title. The third lambda is used to produce each group object, and as with Example 10-53, this final lambda is passed the key as one argument, and its other argument gets the group items, as transformed by the second lambda. So, rather than the original `Course` items, this second argument will be an `IEnumerable<string>` containing the course titles, because that's what the second lambda in this example requested. The result of this `GroupBy` operator is once again a collection of strings, but now it looks like this:

```
Category 'MAT' contains 3 courses: Elements of Geometry, Squaring the Circle, Hy
perbolic Geometry
Category 'BIO' contains 2 courses: Recreational Organ Transplantation, Introduc
tion to Human Anatomy and Physiology
Category 'CSE' contains 1 courses: Oversimplified Data Structures for Demos
```

I've shown four versions of the `GroupBy` operator. All four take a lambda that selects the key to use for grouping, and the simplest overload takes nothing else. The others let you control the representation of individual items in the group, or the representation of each group, or both. There are four more versions of this operator. They offer all the same services as the four I've shown already but also take an `IEqualityCom parer<T>`, which lets you customize the logic that decides whether two keys are considered to be the same for grouping purposes.

Sometimes it is useful to group by more than one value. For example, suppose you want to group courses by both category and publication year. You could chain the operators, grouping first by category and then by year within the category (or vice versa). But you might not want this level of nesting—instead of groups of groups, you might want to group courses under each unique combination of `Category` and publication year. You do this by putting both values into the key, and you can do that by using an anonymous type, as Example 10-55 shows.

Example 10-55. Composite group key

```
var bySubjectAndYear =
    from course in Course.Catalog
    group course by new { course.Category, course.PublicationDate.Year };
foreach (var group in bySubjectAndYear)
{
    Console.WriteLine($"{group.Key.Category} ({group.Key.Year})");
    foreach (Course course in group)
    {
        Console.WriteLine(course.Title);
    }
}
```

This takes advantage of the fact that anonymous types implement Equals and GetHashCode for us. It works for all forms of the GroupBy operator. With LINQ providers that don't treat their lambdas as expressions (e.g., LINQ to Objects), you could use a tuple instead, which would be slightly more succinct while having the same effect.

Conversion

Sometimes you will need to convert a query of one type to some other type. For example, you might have ended up with a collection where the type argument specifies some base type (e.g., object), but you have good reason to believe that the collection actually contains items of some more specific type (e.g., Course). When dealing with individual objects, you can just use the C# cast syntax to convert the reference to the type you believe you're dealing with. Unfortunately, this doesn't work for types such as IEnumerable<T> or IQueryable<T>.

Although covariance means that an IEnumerable<Course> is implicitly convertible to an IEnumerable<object>, you cannot convert in the other direction even with an explicit downcast. If you have a reference of type IEnumerable<object>, attempting to cast that to IEnumerable<Course> will succeed only if the object implements IEnumerable<Course>. It's quite possible to end up with a sequence that consists entirely of Course objects but that does not implement IEnumerable<Course>. Example 10-56 creates just such a sequence, and it will throw an exception when it tries to cast to IEnumerable<Course>.

Example 10-56. How not to cast a sequence

```
IEnumerable<object> sequence = Course.Catalog.Select(c => (object) c);
var courseSequence = (IEnumerable<Course>)sequence; // InvalidCastException
```

This is a contrived example, of course. I forced the creation of an IEnumerable <object> by casting the Select lambda's return type to object. However, it's easy enough to end up in this situation for real, in only slightly more complex circumstances. Fortunately, there's an easy solution. You can use the `Cast<T>` operator, shown in Example 10-57.

Example 10-57. How to cast a sequence

```
IEnumerable<Course> courseSequence = sequence.Cast<Course>();
```

This returns a query that produces every item in its source in order, but it casts each item to the specified target type as it does so. This means that although the initial `Cast<T>` might succeed, it's possible that you'll get an `InvalidCastException` some point later when you try to extract values from the sequence. After all, in general, the only way the `Cast<T>` operator can verify that the sequence you've given it really does only ever produce values of type `T` is to extract all those values and attempt to cast them. It can't evaluate the whole sequence up front because you might have supplied an infinite sequence. If the first billion items your sequence produces will be of the right type, but after that you return one of an incompatible type, the only way `Cast<T>` can discover this is to try casting items one at a time.

 `Cast<T>` and `OfType<T>` look similar, and developers sometimes use one when they should have used the other (usually because they didn't know both existed). `OfType<T>` does almost the same thing as `Cast<T>`, but it silently filters out any items of the wrong type instead of throwing an exception. If you expect and want to ignore items of the wrong type, use `OfType<T>`. If you do not expect items of the wrong type to be present at all, use `Cast<T>`, because if you turn out to be wrong, it will let you know by throwing an exception, reducing the risk of allowing a potential bug to remain hidden.

LINQ to Objects defines an `AsEnumerable<T>` operator. This just returns the source without modification—it has no effect at runtime. Its purpose is to force the use of LINQ to Objects even if you are dealing with something that might have been handled by a different LINQ provider. For example, suppose you have something that implements `IQueryable<T>`. That interface derives from `IEnumerable<T>`, but the extension methods that work with `IQueryable<T>` will take precedence over the LINQ to Objects ones. If your intention is to execute a particular query on a database, and then use further client-side processing of the results with LINQ to Objects, you can use `AsEnumerable<T>` to draw a line that says, "This is where we move things to the client side."

Conversely, there's also `AsQueryable<T>`. This is designed to be used in scenarios where you have a variable of static type `IEnumerable<T>` that you believe might contain a reference to an object that also implements IQueryable<T>, and you want to ensure that any queries you create use that instead of LINQ to Objects. If you use this operator on a source that does not in fact implement IQueryable<T>, it returns a wrapper that implements IQueryable<T> but uses LINQ to Objects under the covers.

Yet another operator for selecting a different flavor of LINQ is AsParallel. This returns a ParallelQuery<T>, which lets you build queries to be executed by Parallel LINQ, a LINQ provider that can execute certain operations in parallel to improve performance when multiple CPU cores are available.

There are some operators that convert the query to other types and also have the effect of executing the query immediately rather than building a new query chained off the back of the previous one. ToArray, ToList, and ToHashSet return an array, list, or hash set, respectively, containing the complete results of executing the input query. ToDictionary and ToLookup do the same, but rather than producing a straightforward list of the items, they both produce results that support associative lookup. ToDictionary returns a Dictionary<TKey, TValue>, so it is intended for scenarios where a key corresponds to exactly one value. ToLookup is designed for scenarios where a key may be associated with multiple values, so it returns a different type, ILookup<TKey, TValue>.

I did not mention this lookup interface in Chapter 5 because it is specific to LINQ. It is essentially the same as a read-only dictionary interface, except the indexer returns an IEnumerable<TValue> instead of a single TValue.

While the array and list conversions take no arguments, the dictionary and lookup conversions need to be told what value to use as the key for each source item. You tell them by passing a lambda, as Example 10-58 shows. This uses the course's Category property as the key.

Example 10-58. Creating a lookup

```
ILookup<string, Course> categoryLookup =
    Course.Catalog.ToLookup(course => course.Category);
foreach (Course c in categoryLookup["MAT"])
{
    Console.WriteLine(c.Title);
}
```

The ToDictionary operator offers an overload that takes the same argument but returns a dictionary instead of a lookup. It would throw an exception if you called it in the same way that I called ToLookup in Example 10-58, because multiple course objects share categories, so they would map to the same key. ToDictionary requires each object to have a unique key. To produce a dictionary from the course catalog, you'd either need to group the data by category first and have each dictionary entry refer to an entire group or need a lambda that returned a composite key based on both the course category and number, because that combination is unique to a course.

Both operators also offer an overload that takes a pair of lambdas—one that extracts the key and a second that chooses what to use as the corresponding value (you are not obliged to use the source item as the value). Finally, there are overloads that also take an IEqualityComparer<T>.

You've now seen the most important standard LINQ operators, but since that has taken quite a few pages, you may find it useful to have a concise summary. Table 10-1 lists the operators and describes briefly what each is for. For completeness, this includes some additional less widely used operators.

Table 10-1. Summary of LINQ operators

Operator	Purpose
Aggregate	Combines all items through a user-supplied function to produce a single result.
All	Returns true if the predicate supplied is false for no items.
Any	Returns true if the predicate supplied is true for at least one item.
Append	Returns a sequence with all the items from its input sequence with one item added to the end.
AsEnumerable	Returns the sequence as an IEnumerable<T>. (Useful for forcing use of LINQ to Objects.)
AsParallel	Returns a ParallelQuery<T> for parallel query execution.
AsQueryable	Ensures use of IQueryable<T> handling where available.
Average	Calculates the arithmetic mean of the items.
Cast	Casts each item in the sequence to the specified type.
Chunk	Splits a sequence into equal-sized batches.
Concat	Forms a sequence by concatenating two sequences.
Contains	Returns true if the specified item is in the sequence.
Count, LongCount	Return the number of items in the sequence.
DefaultIfEmpty	Produces the source sequence's elements, unless there are none, in which case it produces a single element with a default value.
Distinct	Removes duplicate values.
DistinctBy	Removes values for which a projection produces duplicate values.
ElementAt	Returns the element at the specified position (throwing an exception if out of range).
ElementAtOrDefault	Returns the element at the specified position (producing the element type's default value if out of range).
Except	Filters out items that are in the other collection provided.
First	Returns the first item, throwing an exception if there are no items.
FirstOrDefault	Returns the first item, or a default value if there are no items.
GroupBy	Gathers items into groups.

Operator	Purpose
GroupJoin	Groups items in another sequence by how they relate to items in the input sequence.
Intersect	Filters out items that are not in the other collection provided.
IntersectBy	Same as Intersect but using a projection for comparison.
Join	Produces an item for each matching pair of items from the two input sequences.
Last	Returns the final item, throwing an exception if there are no items.
LastOrDefault	Returns the final item, or a default value if there are no items.
Max	Returns the highest value.
MaxBy	Returns the item for which a projection produces the highest value.
Min	Returns the lowest value.
MinBy	Returns the item for which a projection produces the lowest value.
OfType	Filters out items that are not of the specified type.
Order	Produces items in an ascending order based on the value of the items themselves.
OrderBy	Produces items in an ascending order based on the value selected by a projection.
OrderDescending	Produces items in a descending order based on the value of the items themselves.
OrderByDescending	Produces items in a descending order based on the value selected by a projection.
Prepend	Returns a sequence starting with a specified single item, followed by all the items from its input sequence.
Reverse	Produces items in the opposite order than the input.
Select	Projects each item through a function.
SelectMany	Combines multiple collections into one.
SequenceEqual	Returns true only if all items are equal to those in the other sequence provided.
Single	Returns the only item, throwing an exception if there are no items or more than one item.
SingleOrDefault	Returns the only item, or a default value if there are no items; throws an exception if there is more than one item.
Skip	Filters out the specified number of items from the start.
SkipLast	Filters out the specified number of items from the end.
SkipWhile	Filters out items from the start for as long as the items match a predicate.
Sum	Returns the result of adding all the items together.
Take	Produces the specified number or range of items, discarding the rest.
TakeLast	Produces the specified number of items from the end of the input (discarding all items before that).
TakeWhile	Produces items as long as they match a predicate, discarding the rest of the sequence as soon as one fails to match.
ToArray	Returns an array containing all of the items.
ToDictionary	Returns a dictionary containing all of the items.
ToHashSet	Returns a HashSet<T> containing all of the items.
ToList	Returns a List<T> containing all of the items.

Operator	Purpose
ToLookup	Returns a multivalue associative lookup containing all of the items.
Union	Produces all items that are in either or both of the inputs.
UnionBy	Same as Union but using a projection for comparison.
Where	Filters out items that do not match the predicate provided.
Zip	Combines items at the same position from two or three inputs.

Sequence Generation

The Enumerable class defines the extension methods for IEnumerable<T> that constitute LINQ to Objects. It also offers a few additional (nonextension) static methods that can be used to create new sequences. Enumerable.Range takes two int arguments and returns an IEnumerable<int> that produces a sequentially increasing series of numbers, starting from the value of the first argument and containing as many numbers as the second argument. For example, Enumerable.Range(15, 10) produces a sequence containing the numbers 15 to 24 (inclusive).

Enumerable.Repeat<T> takes a value of type T and a count. It returns a sequence that will produce that value the specified number of times.

Enumerable.Empty<T> returns an IEnumerable<T> that contains no elements. This may not sound very useful, because there's a much less verbose alternative. You could write new T[0], which creates an array that contains no elements. (Arrays of type T implement IEnumerable<T>.) However, the advantage of Enumerable.Empty<T> is that for any given T, it returns the same instance every time. This means that if for any reason you end up needing an empty sequence repeatedly in a loop that executes many iterations, Enumerable.Empty<T> is more efficient, because it puts less pressure on the GC.

Other LINQ Implementations

Most of the examples I've shown in this chapter have used LINQ to Objects, except for a handful that have referred to EF Core. In this final section, I will provide a quick description of some other LINQ-based technologies. This is not a comprehensive list, because anyone can write a LINQ provider.

Entity Framework Core

The database examples I have shown have used the LINQ provider that is part of Entity Framework Core (EF Core). EF Core is a data access technology that ships in a NuGet package, Microsoft.EntityFrameworkCore. (EF Core's predecessor, the Entity Framework, is still built into .NET Framework but is not in newer versions of .NET.)

EF Core can map between a database and an object layer. It supports multiple database vendors.

EF Core relies on IQueryable<T>. For each persistent entity type in a data model, the EF can provide an object that implements IQueryable<T> and that can be used as the starting point for building queries to retrieve entities of that type and of related types. Since IQueryable<T> is not unique to the EF, you will be using the standard set of extension methods provided by the Queryable class in the System.Linq namespace, but that mechanism is designed to allow each provider to plug in its own behavior.

Because IQueryable<T> defines the LINQ operators as methods that accept Expression<T> arguments and not plain delegate types, any expressions you write in either query expressions or as lambda arguments to the underlying operator methods will turn into compiler-generated code that creates a tree of objects representing the structure of the expression. The EF relies on this to be able to generate database queries that fetch the data you require. This means that you are obliged to use lambdas; unlike with LINQ to Objects, you cannot use anonymous methods or delegates with an EF query.

Because IQueryable<T> derives from IEnumerable<T>, it's possible to use LINQ to Objects operators on any EF source. You can do this explicitly with the AsEnumerable<T> operator, but it could also happen accidentally if you used an overload that's supported by LINQ to Objects and not IQueryable<T>. For example, if you attempt to use a delegate instead of a lambda as, say, the predicate for the Where operator, this will fall back to LINQ to Objects. The upshot here is that EF will end up downloading the entire contents of the table and then evaluating the Where operator on the client side. This is unlikely to be a good idea.

Parallel LINQ (PLINQ)

Parallel LINQ is similar to LINQ to Objects in that it is based on objects and delegates rather than expression trees and query translation. But when you start asking for results from a query, it will use multithreaded evaluation where possible, using the thread pool to try to use the available CPU resources fully and efficiently. Chapter 16 will show multithreading in action.

LINQ to XML

LINQ to XML is not a LINQ provider. I'm mentioning it here because its name makes it sound like one. It's really an API for creating and parsing XML documents. It's called *LINQ to XML* because it was designed to make it easy to execute LINQ queries against XML documents, but it achieves this by presenting XML documents through a .NET object model. The runtime libraries provide two separate APIs that do this: as well as LINQ to XML, it also offers the XML Document Object Model (DOM). The DOM is based on a platform-independent standard, and thus, it's not a brilliant match for .NET idioms and feels unnecessarily quirky compared with most of the runtime libraries. LINQ to XML was designed purely for .NET, so it integrates better with normal C# techniques. This includes working well with LINQ, which it does by providing methods that extract features from the document in terms of `IEnumerable<T>`. This enables it to defer to LINQ to Objects to define and execute the queries.

IAsyncEnumerable<T>

As Chapter 5 described, .NET defines the `IAsyncEnumerable<T>` interface, which is an asynchronous equivalent to `IEnumerable<T>`. Chapter 17 will describe the language features that enable you to use this. A full set of LINQ operators is available, although they are not built into the .NET runtime libraries. They are available in a NuGet package called `System.Linq.Async`.

Reactive Extensions

The Reactive Extensions for .NET (or Rx, as they're often abbreviated) are the subject of the next chapter, so I won't say too much about them here, but they are a good illustration of how LINQ operators can work on a variety of types. Rx inverts the model shown in this chapter where we ask a query for items once we're good and ready. So, instead of writing a `foreach` loop that iterates over a query, or calling one of the operators that evaluates the query such as `ToArray` or `SingleOrDefault`, an Rx source calls us when it's ready to supply data.

Despite this inversion, there is a LINQ provider for Rx that supports most of the standard LINQ operators.

Summary

In this chapter, I showed the query syntax that supports some of the most commonly used LINQ features. This lets us write queries in C# that resemble database queries but can query any LINQ provider, including LINQ to Objects, which lets us run queries against our object models. I showed the standard LINQ operators for querying, all of which are available with LINQ to Objects, and most of which are available with database providers. I also provided a quick roundup of some of the common LINQ providers for .NET applications.

The last provider I mentioned was Rx. But before we look at Rx's LINQ provider, the next chapter will begin by looking at how Rx itself works.

CHAPTER 11

Rx: Reactive Extensions

The Reactive Extensions for .NET (usually shortened to *Rx*) are designed for working with asynchronous and event-based information sources. Rx provides services that help you orchestrate and synchronize the way your code reacts to data from these kinds of sources. We already saw how to define and subscribe to events in Chapter 9, but Rx offers much more than these basic features. It provides an abstraction that has a steeper learning curve than events, but it comes with a powerful set of operators that makes it far easier to combine and manage multiple streams of events than is possible with the free-for-all that delegates and .NET events provide. Microsoft has also made an associated set of libraries called Reaqtor available that builds on the foundation of Rx to provide a framework for reliable, stateful, distributed, scalable, high-performance event processing in services. (The q in Reaqtor is a nod to the `IQuerable<T>` interface described in the preceding chapter.)

Rx's fundamental abstraction, `IObservable<T>`, represents a sequence of items, and its operators are defined as extension methods for this interface. This might sound a lot like LINQ to Objects, and there are similarities—not only does `IObservable<T>` have a lot in common with `IEnumerable<T>`, but Rx also supports almost all of the standard LINQ operators. If you are familiar with LINQ to Objects, you will also feel at home with Rx. The difference is that in Rx, sequences are less passive. Unlike `IEnumerable<T>`, Rx sources do not wait to be asked for their items, nor can the consumer of an Rx source demand to be given the next item. Instead, Rx uses a *push* model in which the source notifies its recipients when items are available.

For example, if you're writing an application that deals with live financial information, such as stock market price data, `IObservable<T>` is a much more natural model than `IEnumerable<T>`. Because Rx implements standard LINQ operators, you can write queries against a live source—you could narrow down the stream of events with a `where` clause or group them by stock symbol. Rx goes beyond standard LINQ, adding its own operators that take into account the temporal nature of a live event source. For example, you could write a query that provides data only for stocks that are changing price more frequently than some minimum rate.

Rx's push-oriented approach makes it a better match than `IEnumerable<T>` for event-like sources. But why not just use events, or even plain delegates? Rx addresses four shortcomings of those alternatives. First, it defines a standard way for sources to report errors. Second, it is able to deliver items in a well-defined order, even in multi-threaded scenarios involving numerous sources. Third, Rx provides a clear way to signal when there are no more items. Fourth, because a traditional event is represented by a special kind of member, not a normal object, there are significant limits on what you can do with an event—you can't pass a .NET event as an argument to a method, store it in a field, or offer it in a property.

You can do these things with a delegate, but that's not the same thing—delegates can handle events but cannot represent a source of them. There's no way to write a method that subscribes to some .NET event that you pass as an argument, because you can't pass the actual event itself. Rx fixes this by representing event sources as objects, instead of a special distinctive element of the type system that doesn't work like anything else.

We get all four of these features for free back in the world of `IEnumerable<T>`, of course. A collection can throw an exception when its contents are being enumerated, but with callbacks, it's less obvious when and where to deliver exceptions. `IEnumerable<T>` makes consumers retrieve items one at a time, so the ordering is unambiguous, but with plain events and delegates, nothing enforces that. And `IEnumerable<T>` tells consumers when the end of the collection has been reached, but with a simple callback, it's not necessarily clear when you've had the last call. `IObservable<T>` handles all of these eventualities, bringing the things we can take for granted with `IEnumerable<T>` into the world of events.

By providing a coherent abstraction that addresses these problems, Rx is able to bring all of the benefits of LINQ to event-driven scenarios. Rx does not replace events; I wouldn't have dedicated one-fifth of Chapter 9 to them if it did. In fact, Rx can integrate with events. It can bridge between its own abstractions and several others, not just ordinary events but also `IEnumerable<T>` and various asynchronous programming models. Far from deprecating events, Rx raises their capabilities to a new level. It's considerably harder to get your head around Rx than events, but it offers much more power once you do.

Two interfaces form the heart of Rx. Sources that present items through this model implement `IObservable<T>`. Subscribers are required to supply an object that implements `IObserver<T>`. These two interfaces are built into .NET. The other parts of Rx are in the `System.Reactive` NuGet package. That package is an open source project (*https://github.com/dotnet/reactive*) that was originally written by Microsoft (hence the `System` namespace), but which is now a community-maintained .NET Foundation project.

Fundamental Interfaces

There are two essential types in Rx: the `IObservable<T>` and `IObserver<T>` interfaces. These are important enough to be in the `System` namespace. Example 11-1 shows their definitions.

Example 11-1. IObservable<T> and IObserver<T>

```
public interface IObservable<out T>
{
    IDisposable Subscribe(IObserver<T> observer);
}

public interface IObserver<in T>
{
    void OnCompleted();
    void OnError(Exception error);
    void OnNext(T value);
}
```

The fundamental abstraction in Rx, `IObservable<T>`, is implemented by event sources. Instead of using the `event` keyword, it models events as a sequence of items. An `IObservable<T>` can have any number of subscribers, and it provides them with items as and when it's ready to.

As you can see from the `out` keyword, the type argument for `IObservable<T>` is covariant, meaning that if you have a type `Base` that is the base type of another type `Derived`, then just as you can pass a `Derived` to any method expecting a `Base`, you can pass an `IObservable<Derived>` to anything expecting an `IObservable<Base>`. It makes sense intuitively to see the `out` keyword here, because like `IEnumerable<T>`, this is a source of information—items come out of it. Conversely, items go into a subscriber's `IObserver<T>` implementation, so that has the `in` keyword, which denotes contravariance—you can pass an `IObserver<Base>` to anything expecting an `IObserver<Derived>`. (I described variance in Chapter 6.)

We can subscribe to a source by passing an implementation of `IObserver<T>` to the `Subscribe` method. The source will invoke `OnNext` when it wants to report events. Rx has a basic rule that the source is required to wait until `OnNext` returns before either calling `OnNext` again, or calling `OnError` or `OnComplete`. This rule keeps things simple for observers: even in multithreaded applications, any single observer will only ever have to deal with one thing at a time. (More subtly, it may also require a source to detect re-entrancy: if the observer's `OnNext` performs some action that indirectly causes the source to emit another item, the source is not allowed to make a recursive call into the observer. It has to wait until the `OnNext` in progress returns. This can make things complex for sources, but as you'll see, the Rx libraries can help with that.) The source can call `OnCompleted` to indicate that there will be no further activity, and if it wants to report an error, it can call `OnError`. Both `OnCompleted` and `On Error` indicate the end of the stream, so another basic Rx rule is that an observable should not call any further methods on the observer after that.

 You will not necessarily get an exception immediately if you break these rules. If you use the NuGet `System.Reactive` library to help implement and consume these interfaces, there are certain circumstances in which it can detect this kind of mistake. But in general it is the responsibility of code calling the `IObserver<T>` methods to stick to the rules.

There's a visual convention for representing Rx activity. It's sometimes called a *marble diagram*, because it consists mainly of small circles that look a bit like marbles. Figure 11-1 uses this convention to represent two sequences of events. The horizontal lines represent subscriptions to sources, with the vertical bar on the left indicating the start of the subscription, and the horizontal position indicating when something occurred (with elapsed time increasing from left to right). The circles indicate calls to `OnNext` (i.e., events being reported by the source). An arrow on the righthand end indicates that the subscription was still active by the end of the time the diagram represents. A vertical bar on the right indicates the end of the subscription—either due to a call to `OnError` or `OnCompleted` or because the subscriber unsubscribed.

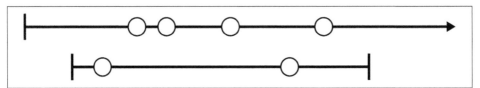

Figure 11-1. Simple marble diagram

When you call `Subscribe` on an observable, it returns an object that implements `IDisposable`, which provides a way to unsubscribe. If you call `Dispose`, the observable will not deliver any more notifications to your observer. This can be more convenient than the mechanism for unsubscribing from an event. To unsubscribe from an event, you must pass in an equivalent delegate to the one you used for subscription. If you're using anonymous methods, that can be surprisingly awkward, because often the only way to do that is to keep hold of a reference to the original delegate. With Rx, any subscription to a source is represented as an `IDisposable`, making it easier to handle in a uniform way. In fact, you often do not need to unsubscribe anyway—this is necessary only if you want to stop receiving notifications before the source completes (making this an example of something that is relatively unusual in .NET: optional disposability).

IObserver<T>

As you'll see, in practice we often don't call a source's Subscribe method directly, nor do we usually need to implement IObserver<T> ourselves. Instead, it's common to use one of the delegate-based extension methods that Rx provides and that attaches an Rx-supplied implementation. However, those extension methods are not part of Rx's fundamental types, and they are in the optional System.Reactive NuGet package, not the .NET runtime libraries. So for now I'll show what you'd need to write if these interfaces are all you've got. Example 11-2 shows a simple but complete observer.

Example 11-2. Simple IObserver<T> implementation

```
class MySubscriber<T> : IObserver<T>
{
    public void OnNext(T value) => Console.WriteLine("Received: " + value);
    public void OnCompleted() => Console.WriteLine("Complete");
    public void OnError(Exception ex) => Console.WriteLine("Error: " + ex);
}
```

Observers can often be very simple thanks to the guarantees that Rx sources (i.e., implementations of IObservable<T>) are required to make about how they call an observer's methods. Observers can safely assume that the calls will happen in a certain order: OnNext is called for each item that the source provides, and once either OnCompleted or OnError is called, there will be no further calls to any of the three methods. Furthermore, the observer can count on the fact that calls are not allowed to overlap—when an observable source calls one of our observer's methods, it must wait for that method to return before calling again. When we write an observer, we don't need to worry about multithreaded calls, and even in a single-threaded world, it's not our problem to detect and prevent re-entrant calls—that's the source's job.

This makes life simple for the observer. Rx always provides events as a sequence. So, although IObservable<T> may look like the simpler interface, having just one method, it's the more demanding one to implement. As you'll see later, it's usually easiest to let the Rx libraries implement this for you, but it's still important to know how observable sources work, so I'll implement it by hand to begin with.

IObservable<T>

Rx makes a distinction between *hot* and *cold* observable sources. A hot observable produces each value as and when something of interest happens, and if no subscribers are attached at that moment, that value will be lost. A hot observable typically represents something live, such as mouse input, keypresses, or data reported by a sensor, which is why the values it produces are independent of how many subscribers, if any, are attached. Hot sources typically have broadcast-like behavior—they send each item to all of their subscribers. These can be the more complex kind of source to implement, so I'll discuss cold sources first.

Implementing cold sources

Whereas hot sources report items as and when they want to, cold observables work differently. They start pushing values when an observer subscribes, and they provide values to each subscriber separately, rather than broadcasting. This means that a subscriber won't miss anything by being too late, because the source starts providing items when you subscribe. Example 11-3 shows a very simple cold source.

Example 11-3. A simple cold observable source

```
public class SimpleColdSource : IObservable<string>
{
    public IDisposable Subscribe(IObserver<string> observer)
    {
        observer.OnNext("Hello,");
        observer.OnNext("World!");
        observer.OnCompleted();
        return EmptyDisposable.Instance;
    }

    private class EmptyDisposable : IDisposable
    {
        public readonly static EmptyDisposable Instance = new();
        public void Dispose() { }
    }
}
```

The moment an observer subscribes, this source will provide two values, the strings "Hello," and "World!", and will then indicate the end of the sequence by calling OnCompleted. It does all that inside Subscribe, so this doesn't really look like a subscription—the sequence is already over by the time Subscribe returns, so there's nothing meaningful to do to support unsubscription. That's why this returns a trivial implementation of IDisposable. (I've chosen an extremely simple example so I can show the basics. Real sources will be more complex.)

To show this in action, we need to create an instance of SimpleColdSource, and also an instance of my observer class from Example 11-2, and use that to subscribe to the source, as Example 11-4 does.

Example 11-4. Attaching an observer to an observable

```
var source = new SimpleColdSource();
var sub = new MySubscriber<string>();
source.Subscribe(sub);
```

Predictably, this produces the following output:

```
Received: Hello,
Received: World!
Complete
```

In general, a cold observer will have access to some underlying source of information, which it can push to a subscriber on demand. In Example 11-3, that "source" was just two hardcoded values. Example 11-5 shows a slightly more interesting cold observable, which reads the lines out of a file and provides them to a subscriber.

Example 11-5. A cold observable representing a file's contents

```
public class FilePusher : IObservable<string>
{
    private readonly string _path;
    public FilePusher(string path)
    {
        _path = path;
    }

    public IDisposable Subscribe(IObserver<string> observer)
    {
        using (var sr = new StreamReader(_path))
        {
            while (sr.ReadLine() is string line) // Repeats until null returned
            {
                observer.OnNext(line);
            }
        }
        observer.OnCompleted();
        return EmptyDisposable.Instance;
    }

    private class EmptyDisposable : IDisposable
    {
        public static EmptyDisposable Instance = new();
        public void Dispose() { }
    }
}
```

As before, this does not represent a live source of events, and it leaps into action only when something subscribes, but it's a little more interesting than Example 11-3. This calls into the observer as and when it retrieves each line from a file, so although the point at which it starts doing its work is determined by the subscriber, this source is in control of the rate at which it provides values. Just like Example 11-3, this delivers all the items to the observer on the caller's thread inside the call to Subscribe, but it would be a relatively small conceptual leap from Example 11-5 to one in which the code reading from the file either ran on a separate thread or used asynchronous techniques (such as those described in Chapter 17), thus enabling Subscribe to return before the work is complete (at which point you'd need to write a more interesting IDisposable implementation to enable callers to unsubscribe). This would still be a cold source, because it represents some underlying set of data that it can enumerate from the start for the benefit of each individual subscriber.

Example 11-5 is not quite complete—it fails to handle errors that occur while reading from the file. We need to catch these and call the observer's OnError method. Unfortunately, it's not quite as simple as wrapping the whole loop in a try block, because that would also catch exceptions that emerged from the observer's OnNext method. If that throws an exception, we should allow it to carry on up the stack—we should handle only exceptions that emerge from the places we expect in our code. Unfortunately, this rather complicates the code. Example 11-6 puts all the code that uses FileStream inside a try block but will allow any exceptions thrown by the observer to propagate up the stack, because it's not up to us to handle those.

Example 11-6. Handling filesystem errors but not observer errors

```
public IDisposable Subscribe(IObserver<string> observer)
{
    StreamReader? sr = null;
    string? line = null;

    try
    {
        while (true)
        {
            try
            {
                sr ??= new StreamReader(_path);
                line = sr.ReadLine();
            }
            catch (IOException ex)
            {
                observer.OnError(ex);
                break;
            }
```

```
            if (line is not null)
            {
                observer.OnNext(line);
            }
            else
            {
                observer.OnCompleted();
                break;
            }
        }
    }
    finally
    {
        sr?.Dispose();
    }
    return EmptyDisposable.Instance;
}
```

If I/O exceptions occur while reading from the file, this reports them to the observer's OnError method—so this source uses all three of the IObserver<T> methods.

Implementing hot sources

Hot sources notify all current subscribers of values as they become available. This means that any hot observable must keep track of which observers are currently subscribed. Subscription and notification are separated out with hot sources in a way that they usually aren't with cold ones.

Example 11-7 is an observable source that reports a single item for each keypress, and it's a particularly simple source as hot ones go. It's single-threaded, so it doesn't need to do anything special to avoid overlapping calls. It doesn't report errors, so it never needs to call observers' OnError methods. And it never stops, so it doesn't need to call OnCompleted either. Even so, it's quite involved. (Things will get much simpler once I introduce the Rx library support—this example is relatively complex because for now, I'm sticking with just the two fundamental interfaces.)

Example 11-7. IObservable<T> for monitoring keypresses

```
public class KeyWatcher : IObservable<char>
{
    private readonly List<Subscription> _subscriptions = new();

    public IDisposable Subscribe(IObserver<char> observer)
    {
        var sub = new Subscription(this, observer);
        _subscriptions.Add(sub);
        return sub;
    }
```

```
public void Run()
{
    while (true)
    {
        // Passing true here stops the console from showing the character
        char c = Console.ReadKey(true).KeyChar;

        // ToArray duplicates the list, enabling us to iterate over a
        // snapshot of our subscribers. This avoids errors when an
        // observer unsubscribes from inside its OnNext method.
        foreach (Subscription sub in _subscriptions.ToArray())
        {
            sub.Observer.OnNext(c);
        }
    }
}

private class Subscription(KeyWatcher parent, IObserver<char> observer)
    : IDisposable
{
    private KeyWatcher? _parent = parent;

    public IObserver<char> Observer { get; } = observer;

    public void Dispose()
    {
        if (_parent is not null)
        {
            _parent._subscriptions.Remove(this);
            _parent = null;
        }
    }
}
}
```

This defines a nested class called `Subscription` to keep track of each observer that subscribes, and this also provides the implementation of `IDisposable` that our `Sub scribe` method is required to return. The observable creates a new instance of this nested class and adds it to a list of current subscribers during `Subscribe`, and then if `Dispose` is called, it removes itself from that list.

As a general rule in .NET, you should `Dispose` any `IDisposable` resources allocated on your behalf when you've finished using them. However, in Rx, it is common not to call `Dispose` on objects representing subscriptions, so if you implement such an object, you should not count on it being disposed. It's typically unnecessary, because Rx can clean up for you. Unlike with ordinary .NET events or delegates, observables can unambiguously come to an end, at which point any resources allocated to subscribers can be freed. (Some run indefinitely, but in that case, subscriptions usually remain active for the life of the program.) Admittedly, the examples I've shown so far

---

don't clean up automatically, because I've provided my own implementations that are simple enough not to need to, but the Rx libraries do if you use their source and subscriber implementations. The only time you'd normally dispose of a subscription in Rx is if you want to unsubscribe before the source completes.

> Subscribers are not obliged to ensure that the object returned by Subscribe remains reachable. You can ignore it if you don't need the ability to unsubscribe early, and it won't matter if the garbage collector frees the object, because none of the IDisposable implementations that Rx supplies to represent subscriptions have finalizers. (And although you don't normally implement these yourself—I'm doing so here only to illustrate how it works—if you do write your own, you should take the same approach: do not implement a finalizer on a class that represents a subscription.)

The KeyWatcher class in Example 11-7 has a Run method. That's not a standard Rx feature; it's just a loop that sits and waits for keyboard input—this observable won't actually produce any notifications unless something calls that method. Each time this loop receives a key, it calls the OnNext method on every currently subscribed observer. Notice that I'm building a copy of the subscriber list (by calling ToArray—that's a simple way to get a List<T> to duplicate its contents), because there's every possibility that a subscriber might choose to unsubscribe in the middle of a call to OnNext. If I had passed the subscriber list directly to foreach, I would get an exception in this scenario, because a List<T> doesn't allow items to be added and removed if you're in the middle of iterating through one.

> This example only guards against re-entrant calls on the same thread; handling multithreaded unsubscription would be altogether more complex. In fact, even building a copy is not sufficiently paranoid. I should really be checking that each observer in my snapshot is still currently subscribed before calling its OnNext, because it's possible that one observer might choose to unsubscribe some other observer. This also makes no attempt to deal with unsubscription from another thread. Later on, I'll replace all of this with a much more robust implementation from the Rx library.

In use, this hot source is very similar to my cold sources. We need to create an instance of the KeyWatcher and also another instance of my observer class (with a type argument of char this time, because this source produces characters instead of strings). Because this source does not generate items until its monitoring loop runs, I need to call Run to kick it off, as Example 11-8 does.

Example 11-8. Attaching an observer to an observable

```
var source = new KeyWatcher();
var sub = new MySubscriber<char>();
source.Subscribe(sub);
source.Run();
```

Running that code, the application will wait for keyboard input, and if you press, say, the *m* key, the observer (Example 11-2) will display the message `Received: m`. (And since my source never ends, the `Run` method will never return.)

You might need to deal with a mixture of hot and cold observables. Also, some cold sources have some hot characteristics. For example, you could imagine a source that represented alert messages, and it might make sense to implement that in such a way that it stored alerts, to make sure you didn't miss anything that happens in between creating the source and attaching a subscriber. So it would be a cold source—any new subscriber would get all the events so far—but once a subscriber has caught up, the ongoing behavior would look more like a hot source, because any new events would be broadcast to all current subscribers. As you'll see, the Rx libraries provide various ways to mix and adapt between the two types of sources.

While it's useful to see what observers and observables need to do, it's more productive to let Rx take care of the grunt work, so now I'll show how you would write sources and subscribers if you were using the `System.Reactive` NuGet library instead of just the two fundamental interfaces.

Publishing and Subscribing with Delegates

If you use the `System.Reactive` NuGet package, you do not need to implement either `IObservable<T>` or `IObserver<T>` directly. The library provides several implementations. Some of these are adapters, bridging between Rx and other representations of asynchronously generated sequences. Some wrap existing observable streams. But the helpers aren't just for adapting existing things. They can also help if you want to write code that originates new items or that acts as the final destination for items. The simplest of these helpers provide delegate-based APIs for creating and consuming observable streams.

Creating an Observable Source with Delegates

Some of the preceding examples have shown that although `IObservable<T>` is a simple interface, sources that implement it may have to do a fair amount of work to track subscribers. And we've not even seen the whole story yet. As you'll see in "Schedulers" on page 565, a source often needs to take extra measures to ensure that it integrates well with Rx's threading mechanisms. Fortunately, the Rx libraries can do some of that work for us. Example 11-9 shows how to use the `Observable` class's static

`Create` method to implement a cold source. (Each call to `GetFilePusher` will create a new source, so this is effectively a factory method.) `Observable` is defined in the `System.Reactive.Linq` namespace.

Example 11-9. Delegate-based observable source

```
public static IObservable<string> GetFilePusher(string path)
{
    return Observable.Create<string>(async (observer, cancel) =>
    {
        using (var sr = new StreamReader(path))
        {
            while (await sr.ReadLineAsync(cancel) is string line)
            {
                observer.OnNext(line);
            }
        }
        observer.OnCompleted();
    });
}
```

This serves the same purpose as Example 11-5—it provides an observable source that supplies each line in a file in turn to subscribers. The heart of the code is the same, but I've been able to write just a single method instead of a whole class. Each time an observer subscribes to the observable that `GetFilePusher` returns, Rx invokes the callback I passed to `Create`, and that just has to provide the items. Rx supplies the `IObservable<T>` implementation, and also the `IDisposable` returned for each call to `Subscribe`.

I've also been able to use C#'s asynchronous language features (specifically, the `async` and `await` keywords, the subject of Chapter 17), which is helpful because this code does file I/O. If you don't need this, `Create` offers overloads that work with non-async callbacks.

I've written rather less code than in Example 11-5, but as well as simplifying my implementation, `Observable.Create` does three more subtle things for us that are not immediately apparent from the code.

First, this handles errors, even though this looks more like the non-error-aware Example 11-5 than the more complex Example 11-6. Rx will automatically handle exceptions that emerge from the callback and will report them to subscribers by calling `OnError`. The earlier example was complicated by the possibility of errors emerging from the subscriber's `OnNext`, but now we don't need to worry about that, because Rx does not pass the real `IObserver<T>` directly to our callback. The `observer` argument in the nested method in Example 11-9 refers to an Rx-supplied wrapper that detects when the underlying `OnNext` throws an exception, and automatically shuts down the subscription before allowing the exception to propagate. This wrapper will ignore all further calls to any of the IObserver<T> methods, freeing us from the convoluted error handling we needed in Example 11-6.

Second, this code handles unsubscription, unlike the earlier examples. The Create method passes a CancellationToken to notify us if the subscriber calls Dispose on the object returned by Subscribe. (Cancellation is described in "Cancellation" on page 750.) Example 11-9 passes that to ReadLineAsync, which means that work will stop immediately upon unsubscription. (ReadLineAsync will throw a TaskCancel edException, but Rx will handle that, and everything will come to a halt.) More subtly, Rx has our back even if we don't pay full attention to the CancellationToken. The wrapper Rx supplies for the observer automatically stops forwarding notifications upon unsubscription. So even if the loop here hadn't passed cancel to ReadLine Async, and carried on running through the file even after the subscriber stopped listening, the subscriber wouldn't receive items after it has asked to stop.

The third thing Observable.Create does for us under the covers is that in certain circumstances, it will use Rx's scheduler system to call our code via a work queue instead of invoking it directly. This avoids deadlocks that could otherwise occur in cases where you've chained multiple observables together. I will be describing schedulers later in this chapter.

Observable.Create is good for cold sources such as Example 11-9. Hot sources work differently, broadcasting live events to all subscribers, and Observable.Create does not cater to them directly because it invokes the delegate you pass once for each subscriber. However, the Rx libraries can still help.

Rx provides a Publish extension method for any IObservable<T>, defined by the Observable class in the System.Reactive.Linq namespace. This method is designed to wrap a source whose subscription method (i.e., the delegate you pass to Observable.Create) supports being run only once but to which you want to attach multiple subscribers—it handles the multicast logic for you. Strictly speaking, a source that supports only a single subscription has not fulfilled the IObservable<T> interface's contract, but as long as you hide it behind Publish, it doesn't matter. The purpose of Publish is to let you write a source that falls short in this particular way, and to turn it into a proper a hot source. Example 11-10 shows how to create a source that provides the same functionality as the KeyWatcher in Example 11-7. I've also hooked up two subscribers, just to illustrate the point that this supports multiple subscribers.

Example 11-10. Delegate-based hot source

```
IObservable<char> singularHotSource = Observable.Create(
    (Func<IObserver<char>, IDisposable>) (observer =>
```

```
{
    while (true)
    {
        observer.OnNext(Console.ReadKey(true).KeyChar);
    }
}));

IConnectableObservable<char> keySource = singularHotSource.Publish();

keySource.Subscribe(new MySubscriber<char>());
keySource.Subscribe(new MySubscriber<char>());

keySource.Connect();
```

The Publish method does not call Subscribe on the source immediately. Nor does it do so when you first attach a subscriber to the source it returns. I have to tell the published source when I want it to start. Notice that Publish returns an IConnectableOb servable<T>. This derives from IObservable<T> and adds a single extra method, Connect. This interface represents a source that doesn't start until it's told to, and it's designed to let you hook up all the subscribers you need before you set it running. Calling Connect on the source returned by Publish causes it to subscribe to my original source, invoking the subscription callback I passed to Observable.Create, which runs my loop. This causes the Connect method to have the same effect as calling Run on my original Example 11-7.

Connect returns an IDisposable. This provides a way to disconnect at some later point—that is, to unsubscribe from the underlying source. (If you don't call this, the connectable observable returned by Publish will remain subscribed to your source even if you Dispose each of the individual downstream subscriptions.) In this particular example, the call to Connect will never return, because the code I passed to Observable.Create also never returns. Most observable sources don't do this. Typically, they avoid it by using either asynchronous or scheduler-based techniques, which I will show later in this chapter.

The combination of the delegate-based Observable.Create and the multicasting offered by Publish has enabled me to throw away everything in Example 11-7 except for the loop that actually generates items, and even that has become simpler. Being able to remove about 80% of the code isn't the whole story, either. This will work better—Publish lets Rx handle my subscribers, which will deal correctly with the awkward situations in which subscribers unsubscribe while being notified.

Of course, the Rx libraries don't just help with implementing sources. They can simplify subscribers too.

Subscribing to an Observable Source with Delegates

Just as you don't have to implement IObservable<T>, it's also not necessary to provide an implementation of IObserver<T>. You won't always care about all three methods—the KeyWatcher observable in Example 11-7 never even calls the OnCompleted or OnError methods, because it runs indefinitely and has no error detection. Even when you do need to provide all three methods, you won't necessarily want to write a whole separate type to provide them. So the Rx libraries provide extension methods to simplify subscription, defined by the ObservableExtensions class in the System namespace. Most C# source files include a using System; directive, or are in a project with an implicit global using directive for System, so the extensions it offers will usually be available as long as your project has a reference to the System .Reactive NuGet package. There are several overloads for the Subscribe method available for any IObservable<T>. Example 11-11 uses one of them.

Example 11-11. Subscribing without implementing IObserver<T>

```
var source = new KeyWatcher();
source.Subscribe(value => Console.WriteLine("Received: " + value));
source.Run();
```

This example has the same effect as Example 11-8. However, by using this approach, we no longer need to write a whole class implementing IObserver<T> like Example 11-2. With this Subscribe extension method, Rx provides the IObserver<T> implementation for us, and we provide methods only for the notifications we want.

The Subscribe overload used by Example 11-11 takes an Action<T>, where T is the item type of the IObservable<T>, which in this case is char. Although my source doesn't provide error notifications or use OnCompleted to indicate the end of the items, plenty of sources do, so there are three overloads of Subscribe to handle that. One takes an extra delegate of type Action<Exception> to handle errors. Another takes a second delegate of type Action (i.e., one that takes no arguments) to handle the completion notification. The third overload takes three delegates—the same per-item callback that they all take, and then an exception handler and a completion handler.

If you do not provide an exception handler when using delegate-based subscription, but the source calls OnError, the IObserver<T> Rx supplies throws the exception to keep the error from going unnoticed. Example 11-5 calls OnError in the catch block where it handles I/O exceptions, and if you subscribed using the technique in Example 11-11, you'd find that the call to OnError throws the IOException right back out again—the same exception is thrown twice in a row, once by the StreamReader and then again by the Rx-supplied IObserver<T> implementation. Since we'd already be in the catch block in Example 11-5 by this time (and not the try block), this second throw would cause the exception to emerge from the Subscribe method, either to be handled farther up the stack or crashing the application.

There's one more overload of the Subscribe extension method, taking no arguments. This subscribes to a source and then does nothing with the items it receives. (It will throw any errors back to the source, just like the other overloads that don't take an error callback.) This would be useful if you have a source that does something important as a side effect of subscription, although it's probably best to avoid designs where that's necessary.

Sequence Builders

Rx defines several methods that create new sequences from scratch, without requiring either custom types or callbacks. These are designed for certain simple scenarios such as single-element sequences, empty sequences, or particular patterns. These are all static methods defined by the Observable class.

Empty

The Observable.Empty<T> method is similar to the Enumerable.Empty<T> method from LINQ to Objects that I showed in Chapter 10: it produces an empty sequence. (The difference, of course, is that it implements IObservable<T>, not IEnumerable <T>.) As with the LINQ to Objects method, this is useful when you're working with APIs that demand an observable source and you have no items to provide.

Any observer that subscribes to an Observable.Empty<T> sequence will have its OnCompleted method called immediately.

Never

The Observable.Never<T> method produces a sequence that never does anything—it produces no items, and unlike an empty sequence, it never even completes. (The Rx team considered calling this Infinite<T> to emphasize the fact that as well as never producing anything, it also never ends.) There is no counterpart in LINQ to Objects. If you wanted to write an IEnumerable<T> equivalent of Never, it would be one that blocked indefinitely when you first tried to retrieve an item. In the pull-based world of LINQ to Objects, this would not be at all useful—it would cause the calling thread to freeze for the lifetime of the process. (An IAsyncEnumerable<T> equivalent would return a ValueTask<bool> that never completes from the first call to MoveNextAsync. This does not need to block a thread, but you still end up with a logical operation in progress that never completes.) But in Rx's reactive world, sources don't block progress just because they are in a state where they're not currently producing items, so Never is a less disastrous idea. It can be helpful with some of the operators I'll show later that can use an IObservable<T> to represent duration. Never can represent an activity you want to run indefinitely.

Return

The Observable.Return<T> method takes a single argument and returns an observable sequence that immediately produces that one value and then completes. Just as Empty is useful when something requires a sequence and you have no items, this is useful when something requires a sequence and you have exactly one item. This is a cold source—you can subscribe to it any number of times, and each subscriber will receive the same value. There is no exact equivalent in LINQ to Objects, although the Rx team provides a library called the Interactive Extensions for .NET (or Ix for short, available in the System.Interactive NuGet package) that provides IEnumerable<T> versions of this and several of the other operators described in this chapter that are in Rx but not LINQ to Objects.

Throw

The Observable.Throw<T> method takes a single argument of type Exception and returns an observable sequence that passes that exception to OnError immediately for any subscriber. Like Return, this is also a cold source that can be subscribed to any number of times, and it will do the same thing to each subscriber.

Range

The Observable.Range method generates a sequence of numbers. (It always returns an IObservable<int>, which is why it does not take a type argument.) Like the Enumerable.Range method, it takes a starting number and a count. This is a cold source that will produce the entire range for each subscriber.

Repeat

The `Observable.Repeat<T>` method takes an input and produces a sequence that repeatedly produces that input over and over again. The input can be a single value, but it can also be another observable sequence, in which case it will forward items until that input completes and will then resubscribe to produce the whole sequence repeatedly. (That means that this will only genuinely repeat the data if you pass it a cold observable.)

If you pass no other arguments, the resulting sequence will produce values indefinitely—the only way to stop it is to unsubscribe. You can also pass a count, saying how many times you would like the input to repeat.

Generate

The `Observable.Generate<TState, TResult>` method can produce more complex sequences than the other methods I've just described. You provide `Generate` with an object or value representing the generator's initial state. This can be any type you like —it's one of the method's generic type arguments. You must also supply three functions: one that inspects the current state to decide whether the sequence is complete yet, one that advances the state in preparation for producing the next item, and one that determines the value to produce for the current state. Example 11-12 uses this to create a source that produces random numbers until the sum total of all the numbers produced exceeds 10,000.

Example 11-12. Generating items

```
IObservable<int> src = Observable.Generate(
    (Current: 0, Total: 0, Random: new Random()),
    state => state.Total <= 10000,
    state =>
    {
        int value = state.Random.Next(1000);
        return (value, state.Total + value, state.Random);
    },
    state => state.Current);
```

This always produces 0 as the first item, illustrating that `Generate` calls the function that determines the current value (the final lambda in Example 11-12) before making the first call to the function that iterates the state.

You could achieve the same effect as this example by using `Observable.Create` and a loop. However, `Generate` inverts the flow of control: instead of your code sitting in a loop telling Rx when to produce the next item, Rx asks your functions for the next item. This gives Rx more flexibility over scheduling of the work. For example, it enables `Generate` to offer overloads that bring timing into the picture. Example 11-13 produces items in a similar way but passes an extra function as the final argument that tells Rx to delay the delivery of each item by a random amount.

Example 11-13. Generating timed items

```
IObservable<int> src = Observable.Generate(
    (Current: 0, Total: 0, Random: new Random()),
    state => state.Total < 10000,
    state =>
    {
        int value = state.Random.Next(1000);
        return (value, state.Total + value, state.Random);
    },
    state => state.Current,
    state => TimeSpan.FromMilliseconds(state.Random.Next(1000)));
```

For this to work, Rx needs to be able to schedule work to happen at some point in the future. I'll explain how this works in "Schedulers" on page 565.

LINQ Queries

One of the greatest benefits of using Rx is that it has a LINQ implementation, enabling you to write queries to process asynchronous streams of items such as events. Example 11-14 illustrates this. It begins by producing an observable source representing `MouseMove` events from a UI element. I'll talk about this technique in more detail in "Adaptation" on page 571, but for now it's enough to know that Rx can wrap any .NET event as an observable source. Each event produces an item that provides two properties containing the values normally passed to event handlers as arguments (i.e., the sender and the event arguments).

Example 11-14. Filtering items with a LINQ query

```
IObservable<EventPattern<MouseEventArgs>> mouseMoves =
    Observable.FromEventPattern<MouseEventHandler, MouseEventArgs>(
        h => background.MouseMove += h, h => background.MouseMove -= h);

IObservable<Point> dragPositions =
    from move in mouseMoves
    where Mouse.Captured == background
    select move.EventArgs.GetPosition(background);

dragPositions.Subscribe(point => { line.Points.Add(point); });
```

The where clause in the LINQ query filters the events so that we process only those events that were raised while a specific UI element (background) has captured the mouse. This particular example is based on WPF (and that background variable comes from a XAML file that you can find in the full examples for this book), but in general, Windows desktop applications that want to support dragging *capture* the mouse when the mouse button is pressed and *release* it afterward. This ensures that the capturing element receives mouse move events for as long as the drag is in progress, even if the mouse moves over other UI elements. Typically, UI elements receive mouse move events when the mouse is over them even if they have not captured the mouse. So I need that where clause in Example 11-14 to ignore those events, leaving only mouse movements that occur while a drag is in progress. So, for the code in Example 11-14 to work, you'd need to attach event handlers such as those in Example 11-15 to the relevant element's MouseDown and MouseUp events.

Example 11-15. Capturing the mouse

```
private void OnBackgroundMouseDown(object sender, MouseButtonEventArgs e)
{
    background.CaptureMouse();
}

private void OnBackgroundMouseUp(object sender, MouseButtonEventArgs e)
{
    if (Mouse.Captured == background)
    {
        background.ReleaseMouseCapture();
    }
}
```

The select clause in Example 11-14 works in Rx just like it does in LINQ to Objects, or with any other LINQ provider. It allows us to extract information from the source items to use as the output. In this case, mouseMoves is an observable sequence of Event Pattern<MouseEventArgs> objects, but what I really want is an observable sequence of mouse locations. So the select clause in Example 11-14 asks for the position relative to a particular UI element.

The upshot of this query is that dragPositions refers to an observable sequence of Point values, which will report each change of mouse position that occurs while a particular UI element in my application has captured the mouse. This is a hot source, because it represents something that's happening live: mouse input. The LINQ filtering and projection operators do not change the nature of the source, so if you apply them to a hot source, the resulting query will also be hot, and if the source is cold, the filtered result will be too.

Operators do not detect the hotness of the source. The Where and Select operators just pass this aspect straight through. Each time you subscribe to the final query produced by the Select operator, it will subscribe to its input. In this case, the input was the observable returned by the Where operator, which will in turn subscribe to the source produced by adapting the mouse move events. If you subscribe a second time, you'll get a second chain of subscriptions. The hot event source will broadcast every event to both chains, so each item will go through the filtering and projection process twice. So be aware that attaching multiple subscribers to a complex query of a hot source will work but may incur unnecessary expense. If you need to do this, it may be better to call Publish on the query, which as you've seen, can make a single subscription to its input and then multicast each item to all its subscribers.

The final line of Example 11-14 subscribes to the filtered and projected source and adds each Point value it produces to the Points collection of another UI element called line. That's a Polyline element, not shown here,[1] and the upshot of this is that you can scrawl on the application's window with the mouse. (If you've been doing Windows development for long enough, you may remember the Scribble examples—the effect here is much the same.)

Rx provides most of the standard query operators described in Chapter 10.[2] Most of these work in Rx exactly as they do with other LINQ implementations. However, some work in ways that may seem slightly surprising at first glance, as I will describe in the next few sections.

Grouping Operators

The standard grouping operator, GroupBy, produces a sequence of sequences. With LINQ to Objects, it returns IEnumerable<IGrouping<TKey, TSource>>, and as you saw in Chapter 10, IGrouping<TKey, TSource> itself derives from IEnumerable<TSource>. The GroupJoin is similar in concept: although it returns a plain IEnumerable<T>, that T is the result of a projection function that is passed a sequence as input. So, in either case, you get what is logically a sequence of sequences.

In the world of Rx, grouping produces an observable sequence of observable sequences. This is perfectly consistent but can seem a little surprising because Rx introduces a temporal aspect: the observable source that represents all the groups produces a

---

1 You can download the full WPF example to which this snippet belongs as part of the examples for this book (*https://oreil.ly/prog-cs-12-repo*).

2 It is missing the OrderBy and ThenBy operators, because these make little sense in a push-based world. They cannot produce any items until they have seen all of their input items.

new item (a new observable source) at the instant it discovers each new group. Example 11-16 illustrates this by watching for changes in the filesystem and then forming them into groups based on the folder in which each occurred. For each group, we get an `IGroupedObservable<TKey, TSource>`, which is the Rx equivalent of `IGrouping<TKey, TSource>`.

Example 11-16. Grouping events

```
string path = Environment.GetFolderPath(Environment.SpecialFolder.MyDocuments);
var w = new FileSystemWatcher(path);
IObservable<EventPattern<FileSystemEventArgs>> changes =
    Observable.FromEventPattern<FileSystemEventHandler, FileSystemEventArgs>(
        h => w.Changed += h, h => w.Changed -= h);
w.IncludeSubdirectories = true;
w.EnableRaisingEvents = true;

IObservable<IGroupedObservable<string, string>> folders =
    from change in changes
    group Path.GetFileName(change.EventArgs.FullPath)
      by Path.GetDirectoryName(change.EventArgs.FullPath);

folders.Subscribe(f =>
{
    Console.WriteLine("New folder ({0})", f.Key);
    f.Subscribe(file =>
        Console.WriteLine("File changed in folder {0}, {1}", f.Key, file));
});
```

The lambda that subscribes to the grouping source, `folders`, subscribes to each group that the source produces. The number of folders from which events could occur is endless, as new ones could be added while the program is running. So the `folders` observable will produce a new observable source each time it detects a change in a folder it hasn't seen before, as Figure 11-2 shows.

Notice that the production of a new group doesn't mean that any previous groups are now complete, which is different than how we typically consume groups in LINQ to Objects. When you run a grouping query on an `IEnumerable<T>`, as it produces each group you can enumerate the contents entirely before moving on to the next one. But you can't do that with Rx, because each group is represented as an observable, and observables aren't finished until they tell you they're complete—instead, each group subscription remains active. In Example 11-16, it's entirely possible that a folder for which a group had already started will be dormant for a long time while activity occurs in other folders, only for it to start up again later. And more generally, Rx's grouping operators have to be prepared for that to happen with any source.

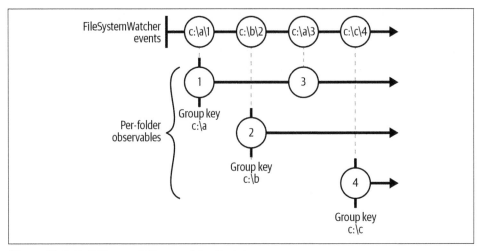

Figure 11-2. Splitting an IObservable<T> into groups

Join Operators

Rx provides the standard Join and GroupJoin operators. However, they work a bit differently than how LINQ to Objects or most database LINQ providers handle joins. In those worlds, items from two input sets are typically joined based on having some value in common. However, Rx does not base joins on values. Instead, items are joined if they are contemporaneous—if their durations overlap, then they are joined.

But hang on a minute. What exactly is an item's duration? Rx deals in instantaneous events; producing an item, reporting an error, and finishing a stream are all things that happen at a particular moment. So the join operators use a convention: for each source item, you can provide a function that returns an IObservable<T>. The duration for that source item starts when the item is produced and finishes when the corresponding IObservable<T> first reacts (i.e., it either completes or generates an item). Figure 11-3 illustrates this idea. At the top is an observable source, beneath which is a series of sources that define each item's duration. At the bottom, I've shown the duration that the per-item observables establish for their source items.

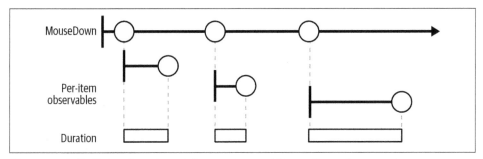

Figure 11-3. Defining duration with an IObservable<T> for each source item

Although you can use a different IObservable<T> for each source item, you don't have to—it's valid to use the same source every time. We could use a single source representing MouseUp events for all of the duration-defining observables in Figure 11-3. A source can even define its own duration. For example, if you provide an observable source representing MouseDown events, you might want each item's duration to end when the next item begins. This would mean that the items had contiguous durations—after the first item arrives, there is always exactly one current item, and it is the last one that occurred.

Now that we know how Rx decides what constitutes an item's duration for the purposes of a join, how does it use that information? Remember, join operators combine two inputs. (The duration-defining sources do not count as an input. They provide additional information about one of the inputs.) Rx considers a pair of items from the two input streams to be related if their durations overlap. The way it presents related items in the output depends on whether you use the Join or the GroupJoin operator. The Join operator's output is a stream containing one item for each pair of related items. (You provide a projection function that will be passed each pair, and it's up to you what to do with them. This function gets to decide the output item type for the joined stream.) Figure 11-4 shows two input streams based on the events MouseDown and MouseMove (with durations defined by MouseUp and MouseMove, respectively). At the bottom of the diagram is the observable the Join operator would produce for these two streams.

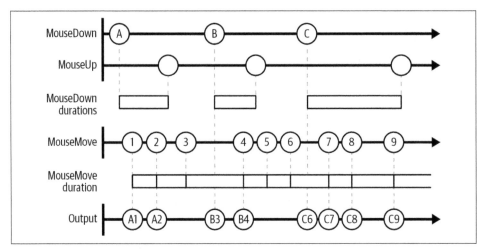

Figure 11-4. Join operator

As you can see, any place where the durations of two items from the input streams overlap, we get an output item combining the two inputs. If the overlapping items started at different times (which will normally be the case), the output item is produced whenever the later of the two inputs started. The MouseDown event A starts before the MouseMove event 1, so the resulting output, A1, occurs where the overlap begins (i.e., when MouseMove event 1 occurs). But event 3 occurs before event B, so the joined output B3 occurs when B starts.

Event 5's duration does not overlap with any MouseDown items' durations, so we do not see any items for that in the output stream. Conversely, it would be possible for a MouseMove event to appear in multiple output items (just like each MouseDown event does). If there had been no 3 event, event 2 would have a duration that started inside A and finished inside B, so as well as the A2 shown in Figure 11-4, there would be a B2 event at the same time as B starts. Example 11-17 shows code that performs the join illustrated in Figure 11-4.

Example 11-17. Joining observables

```
IObservable<EventPattern<MouseEventArgs>> downs =
    Observable.FromEventPattern<MouseButtonEventHandler, MouseEventArgs>(
        h => background.MouseDown += h, h => background.MouseDown -= h);
IObservable<EventPattern<MouseEventArgs>> ups =
    Observable.FromEventPattern<MouseButtonEventHandler, MouseEventArgs>(
        h => background.MouseUp += h, h => background.MouseUp -= h);
IObservable<EventPattern<MouseEventArgs>> allMoves =
    Observable.FromEventPattern<MouseEventHandler, MouseEventArgs>(
        h => background.MouseMove += h, h => background.MouseMove -= h);
```

```
IObservable<Point> dragPositions = downs.Join(
    allMoves,
    down => ups,
    move => allMoves,
    (down, move) => move.EventArgs.GetPosition(background));
```

We can use the `dragPositions` observable source produced by either of these examples to replace the one in Example 11-14. Unlike some earlier examples that needed to filter based on whether the `background` element has captured the mouse, Rx is now providing us only those move events whose duration overlaps with the duration of a `MouseDown` event. Any moves that happen in between mouse presses will either be ignored or, if they are the last move to occur before a mouse down, we'll receive that position at the moment the mouse button is pressed. The effect is that `dragPositions` reports all the mouse locations from the start to end of any drag operation.

`GroupJoin` combines items in a similar way, but instead of producing a single observable output, it produces an observable of observables. For the current example, that would mean that its output would produce a new observable source for each `Mouse Down` input. This would consist of all the pairs containing that input, and it would have the same duration as that input.

SelectMany Operator

As you saw in Chapter 10, the `SelectMany` operator effectively flattens a collection of collections into a single one. This operator gets used when a query expression has multiple `from` clauses, and with LINQ to Objects, its operation is similar to having nested `foreach` loops. With Rx, it still has this flattening effect—it lets you take an observable source where each item it produces is also an observable source (or can be used to generate one), and the result of the `SelectMany` operator will be a single observable sequence that contains all of the items from all of the child sources. However, as with grouping, things may be less orderly than in LINQ to Objects. The push-driven nature of Rx, with its potential for asynchronous operation, makes it possible for all of the observable sources involved to be pushing new items at once, including the original source that is used as a source of nested sources. (The `SelectMany` operator still ensures that only one event will be delivered at a time—when it calls on `OnNext`, it waits for that to return before making another call. The potential for chaos only goes as far as mixing up the order in which events are delivered.)

When you use LINQ to Objects to iterate through a jagged array, everything happens in a straightforward order. It will retrieve the first nested array and then iterate through all the elements in that array before moving to the next nested array and iterating through that, and so on. But this orderly flattening only occurs because with

IEnumerable<T>, the consumer controls when it retrieves items. With Rx, subscribers receive items when sources provide them.

Despite the free-for-all, the behavior is straightforward enough: the output stream produced by SelectMany just provides items as and when the sources provide them.

Aggregation and Other Single-Value Operators

Several of the standard LINQ operators reduce an entire sequence of values to a single value. These include the aggregation operators, such as Min, Sum, and Aggregate; the quantifiers Any and All; and the Count operator. It also includes selective operators, such as ElementAt. These are available in Rx, but unlike most LINQ implementations, the Rx implementations do not return plain single values. They all return an IObservable<T>, just like operators that produce sequences as outputs.

 The First, Last, FirstOrDefault, LastOrDefault, Single, and SingleOrDefault operators should all work the same way, but for historical reasons, they do not. Introduced in v1 of Rx, they returned single values that were not wrapped in an IObservable <T>, which meant they would block until the source provided what they needed. This doesn't fit well with a push-based model and risks introducing deadlock, so these are now deprecated, and there are new asynchronous versions that work the same way as the other single-value operators in Rx. These all just append Async to the original operators' names (e.g., FirstAsync, LastAsync, etc.).

Each of these operators still produces a single value, but they all present that value as an observable source. The reason is that unlike LINQ to Objects, Rx cannot enumerate its input to calculate the aggregate value or to find the value being selected. The source is in control, so the Rx versions of these operators have to wait for the source to provide its values—like all operators, the single-value operators have to be reactive, not proactive. Operators that need to see every value, such as Average, cannot produce their result until the source says it has finished. Even an operator that doesn't need to wait until the very end of the input, such as FirstAsync or ElementAt, still cannot do anything until the source decides to provide the value the operator is waiting for. As soon as a single-value operator is able to provide a value, it does so and then completes.

The ToArray, ToList, ToDictionary, and ToLookup operators work in a similar way. Although these all produce the entire contents of the source, they do so as a single output object, which is wrapped as a single-item observable source.

If you really want to sit and wait for the value of any of these items, you can use C#'s `await` keyword on any observable source. Logically, it does the same kind of thing as the old deprecated `First`, `Last`, etc. methods but it does so with an efficient non-blocking asynchronous wait of the kind described in Chapter 17. (If you use it on a source that returns multiple items, it waits until the source completes and then returns the final item. It throws an exception if the source completes without producing any items.) And if you are truly determined to risk deadlock by blocking your thread while waiting for value, you can use `Wait`, a nonstandard operator specific to Rx available on any `IObservable<T>`. So the nonasynchronous "sit and wait" behavior of the deprecated `First`, `Last`, etc., operators is still available; it's just no longer the default.

Concat Operator

Rx's `Concat` operator shares the same concept as other LINQ implementations: it combines two input sequences to produce a sequence that will produce every item in its first input, followed by every item in its second input. (In fact, Rx goes further than some LINQ providers and can accept a collection of inputs and will concatenate them all.) This is useful only if the first stream eventually completes—that's true in LINQ to Objects too, of course, but infinite sources are more common in Rx. Also, be aware that this operator does not subscribe to the second stream until the first has finished. This is because cold streams typically start producing items when you subscribe, and the `Concat` operator does not want to have to buffer the second source's items while it waits for the first to complete. This means that `Concat` may produce nondeterministic results when used with hot sources. (If you want an observable source that contains all the items from two hot sources, use `Merge`, which I'll describe shortly.)

Rx is not satisfied with merely providing standard LINQ operators. It defines many more of its own operators.

Rx Query Operators

One of Rx's main goals is to simplify working with multiple potentially independent observable sources that produce items asynchronously. Rx's designers sometimes refer to "orchestration and synchronization," meaning that your system may have many things going on at once, but you need to achieve some kind of coherency in how your application reacts to events. Many of Rx's operators are designed with this goal in mind.

Not everything in this section is driven by the unique requirements of Rx. A few of Rx's nonstandard operators (e.g., Scan) would make perfect sense in other LINQ providers. And versions of many of these are available for IEnumerable<T> in the Interactive Extensions for .NET (Ix), which, as mentioned earlier, are to be found in the System.Interactive NuGet package.

Rx has such a large repertoire of operators that to do them all justice would roughly quadruple the size of this chapter, which is already on the long side. Since this is not a book about Rx, and because some of the operators are very specialized, I will just pick some of the most useful. I recommend browsing through the source (*https://github.com/dotnet/reactive*) or the Rx documentation (*https://introtorx.com*) to discover the full and remarkably comprehensive set of operators it provides.

Merge

The Merge operator combines all of the elements from two or more observable sequences into a single observable sequence. I can use this to fix a problem that occurs in Example 11-14. This processes mouse input, and if you've done much Windows UI programming, you know that you will not necessarily get a mouse move notification corresponding to the points at which the mouse button was pressed and released. The notifications for these button events include mouse location information, so Windows sees no need to send a separate mouse move message providing these locations, because it would just be sending you the same information twice. This is perfectly logical, and also rather annoying.[3] These start and end locations are not in the observable source that represents mouse positions in those examples. I can fix that by merging the positions from all three events. Example 11-18 shows how to fix Example 11-14.

Example 11-18. Merging observables

```
IObservable<EventPattern<MouseEventArgs>> dragMoves =
    from move in allMoves
    where Mouse.Captured == background
    select move;

IObservable<EventPattern<MouseEventArgs>> allDragPositionEvents =
    Observable.Merge(downs, ups, dragMoves);

IObservable<Point> dragPositions =
```

---

3 Like some developers.

```
from move in allDragPositionEvents
select move.EventArgs.GetPosition(background);
```

This uses the three observables from earlier examples representing the three relevant events: MouseDown, MouseUp, and MouseMove. Since all three of these need to share the same projection (the select clause), but only one needs to filter events, I've restructured things a bit. Only mouse moves need filtering, so I've written a separate query for that. I've then used the Observable.Merge method to combine all three event streams into one.

 Merge is available both as an extension method and a nonextension static method. If you use the extension methods available on a single observable, the only Merge overloads available combine it with a single other source (optionally specifying a scheduler). In this case, I had three sources, which is why I used the nonextension method form. However, if you have an expression that is either an enumerable of observable sources or an observable source of observable sources, you'll find that there are also Merge extension methods for these. So I could have written new[] { downs, ups, dragMoves }.Merge().

My allDragPositionEvents variable refers to a single observable stream that will report all the mouse moves I need. Finally, I run this through a projection to extract the mouse position for each item. Again, the result is a hot source. As before, it will produce a position any time the mouse moves while the background element has captured the mouse, but it will also produce a position each time either the MouseDown or MouseUp event occurs. I could subscribe to this with the same call shown in the final line of Example 11-14 to keep my UI up to date, and this time, I wouldn't be missing the start and end positions.

In the example I've just shown, the sources are all endless, but that will not always be the case. What should a merged observable do when one of its inputs stops? If one stops due to an error, that error will be passed on by the merged observable, at which point it will be complete—an observable is not allowed to continue producing items after reporting an error. However, although an input can unilaterally terminate the output with an error, if inputs complete normally, the merged observable doesn't complete until all of its inputs are complete.

Windowing Operators

Rx defines two operators, Buffer and Window, that both produce an observable output where each item is based on multiple adjacent items from the source. (The name Window has nothing to do with UIs, by the way.) Figure 11-5 shows three ways in which you could use the Buffer operator. I've numbered the circles representing items in the input, and below this are blobs representing the items that will emerge from the observable source produced by Buffer, with lines and numbers indicating which input items are associated with each output item. Window works in a very similar way, as you'll see shortly.

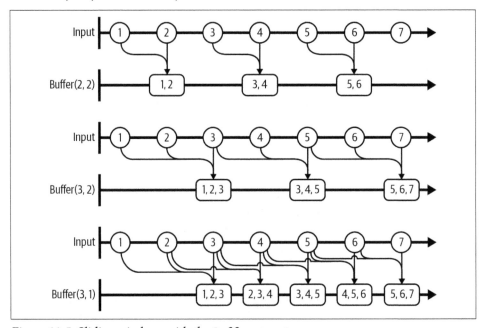

Figure 11-5. Sliding windows with the Buffer operator

In the first case, I've passed arguments of (2, 2), indicating that I want each output item to correspond to two input items and that I want to start a new buffer on every second input item. That may sound like two different ways of saying the same thing until you look at the second example in Figure 11-5, in which arguments of (3, 2) indicate that each output item corresponds to three items from the input, but I still want the buffers to begin on every other input. This means that each *window*—the set of items from the input used to build an output item—overlaps with its neighbors. This will happen whenever the second argument, the *skip*, is smaller than the window. The first output item's window contains the first, second, and third input. The second output's window contains the third, fourth, and fifth, so the third item appears in both.

The final example in the figure shows a window size of three, but this time I've asked for a skip size of one—so in this case, the window moves along by only one input item at a time, but it incorporates three items from the source each time. I could also specify a skip that is larger than the window, in which case the input items that fell between windows would simply be ignored.

The Buffer operator tends to introduce a lag. In the second and third cases, the window size of three means that the input observable needs to produce its third value before the whole window can be provided for the output item. With Buffer, this always means a delay of the size of the window, but as you'll see, with the Window operator, each window can get under way before it is full.

 Buffer offers an overload that takes a single number, which has the same effect as passing the same number twice. (E.g., instead of Buffer(2, 2), you could write just Buffer(2).) This is logically equivalent to LINQ to Objects' Chunk operator. As discussed in Chapter 10, the main reason Rx didn't use the same name is that Rx implemented Buffer about a decade before LINQ to Objects added Chunk.

The difference between the Buffer and Window operators is the way in which they present the windowed items. Buffer is the most straightforward. It provides an IObservable<IList<T>>, where T is the input item type. In other words, if you subscribe to the output of Buffer, for each window produced, your subscriber will be passed a list containing all the items in the window. Example 11-19 uses this to produce a smoothed-out version of the mouse locations from Example 11-14.

Example 11-19. Smoothing input with Buffer

```
IObservable<Point> smoothed = from points in dragPositions.Buffer(5, 2)
                              let x = points.Average(p => p.X)
                              let y = points.Average(p => p.Y)
                              select new Point(x, y);
```

The first line of this query states that I want to see groups of five consecutive mouse locations, and I want one group for every other input. The rest of the query calculates the average mouse position within the window and produces that as the output item. Figure 11-6 shows the effect. The top line is the result of using the raw mouse positions. The line immediately beneath it uses the smoothed points generated by Example 11-19 from the same input. As you can see, the top line is rather ragged, but the bottom line has smoothed out a lot of the lumps.

Figure 11-6. Smoothing in action

Example 11-19 uses a mixture of LINQ to Objects and Rx's LINQ implementation. The query expression itself uses Rx, but the range variable, points, is of type IList<Point> (because Buffer returns an IObservable<IList<Point>> in this example). So the nested queries that invoke the Average operator on points will get the LINQ to Objects implementation.

If the Buffer operator's input is hot, it will produce a hot observable as a result. So you could subscribe to the observable in the smoothed variable in Example 11-19 with similar code to the final line of Example 11-14, and it would show the smoothed line in real time as you drag the mouse. As discussed, there will be a slight lag—the code specifies a skip of two, so it will update the screen only for every other mouse event. Averaging over the last five points will also increase the gap between the mouse pointer and the end of the line. With these parameters, the discrepancy is small enough not to be too distracting, but with more aggressive smoothing, it could get annoying.

Window versus Buffer

The Window operator is very similar to the Buffer operator, but instead of presenting each window as an IList<T>, it provides an IObservable<T>. If you used Window on dragPositions in Example 11-19, the result would be IObservable<IObservable<Point>>. Figure 11-7 shows how the Window operator would work in the last of the scenarios illustrated in Figure 11-5, and as you can see, it can start each window sooner. It doesn't have to wait until all of the items in the window are available; instead of providing a fully populated list containing the window, each output item is an IObservable<T> that will produce the window's items as and when they become available. Each observable produced by Window completes immediately after supplying the final item (i.e., at the same instant at which Buffer would have provided the whole window). So, if your processing depends on having the whole window, Window can't get it to you any faster, because it's ultimately governed by the rate at which input items arrive, but it will start to provide values earlier.

One potentially surprising feature of the observables produced by Window in this example is their start times. Whereas they end immediately after producing their final item, they do not start immediately before producing their first. The observable representing the very first window starts right away—you will receive that observable as soon as you subscribe to the observable of observables the operator returns. So the first window will be available immediately, even if the `Window` operator's input hasn't done anything yet. Then each new window starts as soon as all the input items it needs to skip have been received. In this example, I'm using a skip count of one, so the second window starts after the input has produced one item, the third after two have been produced, and so on.

As you'll see later in this section, and also in "Timed Sequences" on page 577, `Window` and `Buffer` support some other ways to define when each window starts and stops. The general pattern is that as soon as the `Window` operator gets to a point where a new item from the source would go into a new window, the operator creates that window, anticipating the window's first item rather than waiting for it (see Figure 11-7).

Figure 11-7. Window operator

If the input completes, all currently open windows will also complete. This means that it's possible to see empty windows. (In fact, with a skip size of one, you're guaranteed to get one empty window if the source completes.) In Figure 11-7, one window right at the bottom has started but has not yet produced any items. If the input were to complete without producing any more items, the three observable sources still in progress would also complete, including that final one that hasn't yet produced anything.

Because `Window` delivers items into windows as soon as the source provides them, it might enable you to get started with processing sooner than you can with `Buffer`, perhaps improving overall responsiveness. The downside of `Window` is that it tends to be more complex—your subscribers will start receiving output values before all the items for the corresponding input window are available. Whereas `Buffer` provides you with a list that you can inspect at your leisure, with `Window`, you'll need to continue working in Rx's world of sequences that produce items only when they're good and ready. To perform the same smoothing as Example 11-19 with `Window` requires the code in Example 11-20.

Example 11-20. Smoothing with Window

```
IObservable<Point> smoothed =
    from points in dragPositions.Window(5, 2)
    from totals in points.Aggregate(
      new { X = 0.0, Y = 0.0, Count = 0 },
      (acc, point) => new
        { X = acc.X + point.X, Y = acc.Y + point.Y, Count = acc.Count + 1 })
    where totals.Count > 0
    select new Point(totals.X / totals.Count, totals.Y / totals.Count);
```

This is more complicated because I've been unable to use the `Average` operator, due to the need to cope with the possibility of empty windows. (Strictly speaking, that doesn't matter in these examples where I have one `Polyline` that keeps getting longer and longer. But a real application would likely want to group the points by drag operation, to create a new line for each drag. Since each individual observable source of points would complete at the end of the drag, empty windows would be possible, and in general any use of `Window` will need to cope with that.) The `Average` operator produces an error if you provide it with an empty sequence, so I've used the `Aggregate` operator instead, which lets me add a `where` clause to filter out empty windows instead of crashing. But that's not the only aspect that is more complex.

As I mentioned earlier, all of Rx's aggregation operators—`Aggregate`, `Min`, `Max`, and so on—work differently than with most LINQ providers. LINQ requires these operators to reduce the stream down to a single value, so they normally return a single value.

For example, if I were to call the LINQ to Objects version of `Aggregate` with the arguments shown in Example 11-20, it would return a single value of the anonymous type I'm using for my accumulator. But in Rx, the return type is `IObservable<T>` (where `T` is that accumulator type in this case). It still produces a single value, but it presents that value through an observable source. Unlike LINQ to Objects, which can enumerate its input to calculate, say, an average, the Rx operator has to wait for the source to provide its values, so it can't produce an aggregate of those values until the source says it has finished.

Because the `Aggregate` operator returns an `IObservable<T>`, I've had to use a second `from` clause. This passes that source to the `SelectMany` operator, which extracts all values and makes them appear in the final stream—in this case, there is just one value (per window), so `SelectMany` is effectively unwrapping the averaged point from its single-item stream.

The code in Example 11-20 is more complex than Example 11-19, and I think it's considerably harder to understand how it works. Worse, it doesn't even offer any benefit. The `Aggregate` operator will begin its work as soon as inputs become available, but the code cannot produce the final result—the average—until it has seen every point in the window. If I'm going to have to wait until the end of the window before I can update the UI, I may as well stick with `Buffer`.

So, in this particular case, `Window` was a lot more work for no benefit. However, if the work being done on the items in the window was less trivial, or if the volumes of data involved were so large that you didn't want to buffer the entire window before starting to process it, the extra complexity could be worth the benefit of being able to start the aggregation process without having to wait for the whole input window to become available.

Demarcating windows with observables

The `Window` and `Buffer` operators provide some other ways of defining when windows should start and finish. Just as the join operators can specify duration with an observable, you can supply a function that returns a duration-defining observable for each window. Example 11-21 uses this to break keyboard input into words. The `keySource` variable in this example is the observable sequence from Example 11-10 that produces an item for each keypress.

Example 11-21. Breaking text into words with windows

```
IObservable<IObservable<char>> wordWindows = keySource.Window(
    () => keySource.FirstAsync(char.IsWhiteSpace));

IObservable<string> words = from wordWindow in wordWindows
                            from chars in wordWindow.ToArray()
```

```
                      select new string(chars).Trim();

words.Subscribe(word => Console.WriteLine("Word: " + word));
```

The `Window` operator will immediately create a new window in this example, and it will also invoke the lambda I've supplied to find out when that window should end. It will keep it open until the observable source the lambda returns either produces a value or completes. When that happens, `Window` will immediately open the next window, invoking the lambda again to get another observable to determine the length of the second window, and so on. The lambda here produces the next whitespace character from the keyboard, so the window will close on the next space. In other words, this breaks the input sequence into a series of windows where each window contains zero or more nonwhitespace characters followed by one whitespace character.

The observable sequence the `Window` operator returns presents each window as an `IObservable<char>`. The second statement in Example 11-21 is a query that converts each window to a string. (This will produce empty strings if the input contains multiple adjacent whitespace characters. That's consistent with the behavior of the `string` type's `Split` method, which performs the pull-oriented equivalent of this partitioning. If you don't like it, you can always filter out the blanks with a `where` clause.)

Because Example 11-21 uses `Window`, it will start making characters for each word available as soon as the user types them. But because my query calls `ToArray` on the window, it will end up waiting until the window completes before producing anything. This means `Buffer` would be equally effective. It would also be simpler. As Example 11-22 shows, I don't need a second `from` clause to collect the completed window if I use `Buffer`, because it provides me with windows only once they are complete.

Example 11-22. Word breaking with `Buffer`

```
IObservable<IList<char>> wordWindows = keySource.Buffer(
    () => keySource.FirstAsync(char.IsWhiteSpace));

IObservable<string> words = from wordWindow in wordWindows
                            select new string(wordWindow.ToArray()).Trim();
```

The Scan Operator

The `Scan` operator is very similar to the standard `Aggregate` operator, with one difference. Instead of producing a single result after its source completes, it produces a sequence containing each accumulator value in turn. To illustrate this, I will first introduce a record type that will act as a very simple model for a stock trade. This type, shown in Example 11-23, also defines a static method that provides a randomly generated stream of trades for test purposes.

Example 11-23. Simple stock trade with test stream

```
public record Trade(string StockName, decimal UnitPrice, int Number)
{
    public static IObservable<Trade> GetTestStream()
    {
        return Observable.Create<Trade>(observer =>
        {
            string[] names = { "MSFT", "GOOGL", "AAPL" };
            var r = new Random(0);
            for (int i = 0; i < 100; ++i)
            {
                var t = new Trade(
                    StockName: names[r.Next(names.Length)],
                    UnitPrice: r.Next(1, 100),
                    Number: r.Next(10, 1000));
                observer.OnNext(t);
            }
            observer.OnCompleted();
            return Disposable.Empty;
        });
    }
}
```

Example 11-24 shows the normal `Aggregate` operator being used to calculate the total number of stocks traded, by adding up the `Number` property of every trade. (You'd normally just use the `Sum` operator, but I'm showing this for comparison with `Scan`.)

Example 11-24. Summing with Aggregate

```
IObservable<Trade> trades = Trade.GetTestStream();

IObservable<long> tradeVolume = trades.Aggregate(
    0L, (total, trade) => total + trade.Number);
tradeVolume.Subscribe(Console.WriteLine);
```

This displays a single number, because the observable produced by `Aggregate` provides only a single value. Example 11-25 shows almost exactly the same code but using `Scan` instead.

Example 11-25. Running total with Scan

```
IObservable<Trade> trades = Trade.GetTestStream();
```

```
IObservable<long> tradeVolume = trades.Scan(
    0L, (total, trade) => total + trade.Number);
tradeVolume.Subscribe(Console.WriteLine);
```

Instead of producing a single output value, this produces one output item for each input, which is the running total for all items the source has produced so far. Scan is particularly useful if you need aggregation-like behavior in an endless stream, such as one based on an event source. Aggregate is no use in that scenario because it will not produce anything if its input never completes.

The Amb Operator

Rx defines an operator with the somewhat cryptic name of Amb. (See the sidebar, "Why Amb?") This takes any number of observable sequences and waits to see which one does something first. (The documentation talks about which of the inputs "reacts" first. This means that it calls any of the three IObserver<T> methods.) Whichever input jumps into action first effectively becomes the Amb operator's output—it forwards everything the chosen stream does, immediately unsubscribing from the other streams. (If any of them manage to produce elements after the first stream does, but before the operator has had time to unsubscribe, those elements will be ignored.)

Why Amb?

The Amb operator's name is short for *ambiguous*. This seems like a violation of Microsoft's own class library design guidelines, which forbid abbreviations unless the shortened form is more widely used than the full name and likely to be understood even by nonexperts. This operator's name is well established—it was introduced in 1963 in a paper by John McCarthy (inventor of the LISP programming language). However, it's not all that widely used, so the name fails the test of being instantly understandable by nonexperts.

However, the expanded name isn't really any more transparent. If you're not already familiar with the operator, the name Ambiguous wouldn't be much more help in trying to guess what it does than just Amb. If you are familiar with it, you will already know that it's called Amb. So there is no obvious downside to using the abbreviation, and there's a benefit for people who already know it.

Another reason the Rx team used this name was to pay homage to John McCarthy, whose work was profoundly influential for computing in general, and for the LINQ and Rx projects in particular. (McCarthy's work had a direct impact on many of the features discussed in this chapter and Chapter 10.)

You might use this operator to optimize a system's response time by sending a request to multiple machines in a server pool and using the result from whichever responds first. (There are dangers with this technique, not least of which is that it could increase the overall load on your system so much that the effect is to slow everything down, including the operations you were hoping to speed up. Nevertheless, careful selective application of this technique can sometimes be successful.)

DistinctUntilChanged

The final operator I'm going to describe in this section is very simple but rather useful. The `DistinctUntilChanged` operator removes adjacent duplicates. Suppose you have an observable source that produces items on a regular basis but tends to produce the same value multiple times in a row. You might need to take action only when a different value emerges. `DistinctUntilChanged` is for exactly this scenario—when its input produces an item, it will be passed on only if it was different from the previous item (or if it was the first item).

I've not yet shown all of the Rx operators I want to introduce. However, the remaining ones, which I'll discuss in "Timed Sequences" on page 577, are all time sensitive. And before I can show those, I need to describe how Rx handles timing.

Schedulers

Rx performs certain work through *schedulers*. A scheduler is an object that provides three services:

1. Deciding when to execute a particular piece of work. For example, when an observer subscribes to a cold source, should the source's items be delivered to the subscriber immediately, or should that work be deferred to reduce the risk of re-entrancy problems?

2. Running work in a particular context. A scheduler might decide always to execute work on a specific thread, for example.

3. Keeping track of time. Some Rx operations are time dependent; to ensure predictable behavior and to enable testing, schedulers provide a virtualized model for time, so Rx code does not have to depend on the current time of day reported by .NET's `DateTimeOffset` class.

The scheduler's first two roles are sometimes interdependent. For example, Rx supplies a few schedulers for use in UI applications. For example, there's `Dispatcher Scheduler` for WPF applications and `Control Scheduler` for Windows Forms programs. There's no specific support today for MAUI, but there is a more generic one called `SynchronizationContextScheduler`, which will work in all .NET UI frameworks, albeit with slightly less control over the details than the framework-specific ones. All of these have a common characteristic: they ensure that work executes in a suitable context for accessing UI objects, which typically means running the work on a particular thread. If code that schedules work is running on some other thread, the scheduler may have no choice but to defer the work, because it will not be able to run it until the UI framework is ready. This might mean waiting for a particular thread to finish whatever it is doing. In this case, running the work in the right context necessarily also has an impact on when the work is executed.

This isn't always the case, though. Rx provides two schedulers that use the current thread. One of them, `ImmediateScheduler`, is extremely simple: it runs work the instant it is scheduled. When you give this scheduler some work, it won't return until the work is complete. The other, `CurrentThreadScheduler`, maintains a work queue, which gives it some flexibility with ordering. For example, if some work is scheduled in the middle of executing some other piece of work, it can allow the work item in progress to finish before starting on the next. If no work items are queued or in progress, `CurrentThreadScheduler` runs work immediately, just like `Immediate Scheduler`. When a work item it has invoked completes, the `CurrentThreadSched uler` inspects the queue and will invoke the next item if it's not empty. So it attempts to complete all work items as quickly as possible, but unlike `ImmediateScheduler`, it will not start to process a new work item before the previous one has finished.

Specifying Schedulers

Rx operations often do not go through schedulers. Many observable sources invoke their subscribers' methods directly. Sources that can generate a large number of items in quick succession are typically an exception. For example, the `Range` and `Repeat` methods for creating sequences use a scheduler to govern the rate at which they provide items to new subscribers. You can pass in an explicit scheduler or let them pick a default one. You can also get a scheduler involved explicitly even when using sources that don't accept one as an argument.

ObserveOn

A common way to specify a scheduler is with one of the `ObserveOn` extension methods defined by various static classes in the `System.Reactive.Linq` namespace.[4] This is useful if you want to handle events in a specific context (such as the UI thread) even though they may originate from somewhere else.

---

4 The overloads are spread across multiple classes because some of these extension methods are technology specific. WPF gets `ObserveOn` overloads that work directly with its `Dispatcher` class instead of `IScheduler`, for example.

You can invoke ObserveOn on any IObservable<T>, passing in an IScheduler, and it returns another IObservable<T>. If you subscribe to the observable that returns, your observer's OnNext, OnCompleted, and OnError methods will all be invoked through the scheduler you specified. Example 11-26 uses this to ensure that it's safe to update the UI in the item handler callback.

Example 11-26. ObserveOn specific scheduler

```
IObservable<Trade> trades = GetTradeStream();
IObservable<Trade> tradesInUiContext =
    trades.ObserveOn(DispatcherScheduler.Current);
tradesInUiContext.Subscribe(t =>
{
    tradeInfoTextBox.AppendText(
        $"{t.StockName}: {t.Number} at {t.UnitPrice}\r\n");
});
```

In this example, I used the DispatcherScheduler class's static Current property, which returns a scheduler that executes work via the current thread's Dispatcher. (Dispatcher is the class that manages the UI message loop in WPF applications.) Rx's DispatcherObservable class defines various extension methods providing WPF-specific overloads, and instead of passing in a scheduler, I can call ObserveOn passing just a Dispatcher object. I could use this in the codebehind for a UI element with code such as that in Example 11-27.

Example 11-27. ObserveOn WPF Dispatcher

```
IObservable<Trade> tradesInUiContext = trades.ObserveOn(this.Dispatcher);
```

The advantage of this approach is that I don't need to be on the UI thread at the point at which I call ObserveOn. The Current property used in Example 11-26 works only if you are on the thread for the dispatcher you require. If I'm already on that thread, there's an even simpler way to set this up. I can use the ObserveOnDispatcher extension method, which obtains a DispatcherScheduler for the current thread's dispatcher, as shown in Example 11-28.

Example 11-28. Observing on the current dispatcher

```
IObservable<Trade> tradesInUiContext = trades.ObserveOnDispatcher();
```

SubscribeOn

Most of the various `ObserveOn` extension methods have corresponding `SubscribeOn` methods. (There's also `SubscribeOnDispatcher`, the counterpart of `ObserveOn Dispatcher`.) Instead of arranging for each call to an observer's methods to be made through the scheduler, `SubscribeOn` performs the call to the source observable's `Sub scribe` method through the scheduler. And if you unsubscribe by calling `Dispose`, that will also be delivered through the scheduler. This can be important for cold sources, because many perform significant work in their `Subscribe` method, some even delivering all of their items immediately.

> In general, there's no guarantee of any correspondence between the context in which you subscribe to a source and the context in which the items it produces will be delivered to a subscriber. Some sources will notify you from their subscription context, but many won't. If you need to receive notifications in a particular context, then unless the source provides some way to specify a scheduler, use `ObserveOn`.

Passing schedulers explicitly

Some operations accept a scheduler as an argument. You will tend to find this in operations that can generate many items. The `Observable.Range` method that generates a sequence of numbers optionally takes a scheduler as a final argument to control the context from which these numbers are generated. This also applies to the APIs for adapting other sources, such as `IEnumerable<T>` to observable sources, as described in "Adaptation" on page 571.

Another scenario in which you can usually provide a scheduler is when using an observable that combines inputs. Earlier, you saw how the `Merge` operator combines the output of multiple sequences. You can provide a scheduler to tell the operator to subscribe to the sources from a specific context.

Finally, timed operations all depend on a scheduler. I will show some of these in "Timed Sequences" on page 577.

Built-in Schedulers

I've already described UI-oriented schedulers such as `DispatcherScheduler` (for WPF), `ControlScheduler` (for Windows Forms), and `SynchronizationContext Scheduler`, and also the two schedulers for running work on the current thread, `Cur rentThreadScheduler` and `ImmediateScheduler`. But there are some others worth being aware of.

EventLoopScheduler runs all work items on a specific thread. It can create a new thread for you, or you can provide it with a callback method that it will invoke when it wants you to create the thread. You might use this in a UI application to process incoming data. It lets you move work off the UI thread to keep the application responsive but ensures that all processing happens on a single thread, which can simplify concurrency issues.

NewThreadScheduler creates a new thread for each top-level work item it processes. (If that work item spawns further work items, those will run on the same thread, rather than creating new ones.) This is appropriate only if you need to do a lot of work for each item, because threads have relatively high startup and teardown costs in Windows. You are normally better off using a thread pool if you need concurrent processing of work items.

TaskPoolScheduler uses the Task Parallel Library's (TPL) thread pool. The TPL, described in Chapter 16, provides an efficient pool of threads that can reuse a single thread for multiple work items, amortizing the startup costs of creating the thread.

ThreadPoolScheduler uses the CLR's thread pool to run work. This is similar in concept to the TPL thread pool, but it's a somewhat older piece of technology. (The TPL was introduced in .NET 4.0, but the CLR thread pool has existed since v1.0.) This is a bit less efficient in certain scenarios. Rx introduced this scheduler because early versions of Rx supported old versions of .NET that didn't have the TPL. It retains it for backward-compatibility reasons.

HistoricalScheduler is useful when you want to test time-sensitive code without needing to execute your tests in real time. All schedulers provide a time-keeping service, but the HistoricalScheduler lets you decide the exact rate at which you want the scheduler to behave as though time is elapsing. So, if you need to test what happens if you wait 30 seconds, you can just tell the HistoricalScheduler to act as though 30 seconds have passed, without having to actually wait.

Subjects

Rx defines various *subjects*, classes that implement both IObserver<T> and IObservable<T>. These can sometimes be useful if you need Rx to provide a robust implementation of either of these interfaces, but the usual Observable.Create or Subscribe methods are not convenient. For example, perhaps you need to provide an observable source, and there are several different places in your code from which you want to provide values for that source to produce. This is awkward to fit into the Create method's subscription callback model and can be easier to handle with a subject. Some of the subject types provide additional behavior, but I'll start with the simplest.

Subject<T>

Subject<T> relays calls to all observers that have subscribed using its IObservable<T> interface. So, if you subscribe one or more observables to a Subject<T> and then call OnNext, the subject will call OnNext on each of its subscribers. It's the same for the other methods, OnCompleted and OnError. This multicast relay behavior is very similar to the facility provided by the Publish operator[5] I used in Example 11-10, so Subject<T> provides an alternative way for me to remove all of the code for tracking subscribers from my KeyWatcher source, as Example 11-29 shows.

Example 11-29. Implementing IObservable<T> with a Subject<T>

```
public class KeyWatcher
{
    private readonly Subject<char> _subject = new();

    public IObservable<char> Keys => _subject;

    public void Run()
    {
        while (true)
        {
            _subject.OnNext(Console.ReadKey(true).KeyChar);
        }
    }
}
```

This is much simpler than the original in Example 11-7. The combination of Observable.Create and the Publish operator in Example 11-10 is arguably simpler still, but Subject<T> does offer two advantages. First, it's easier to see when the loop that generates keypress notifications runs. Example 11-10 behaves in a very similar way, but unless you're familiar with how Publish works, it is not obvious how. Second, if I wanted to, I could call _subject.OnNext from anywhere inside my KeyWatcher class, whereas Example 11-10 can only produce items inside the callback function invoked by Observable.Create. As it happens, this example doesn't need that flexibility, but in scenarios that do, a Subject<T> is helpful.

BehaviorSubject<T>

BehaviorSubject<T> works almost exactly like Subject<T>, with one difference: it immediately notifies any observer that subscribes. If you have already completed the subject, it'll just call OnComplete immediately on any new subscribers. Otherwise,

---

5 In fact, Publish uses Subject<T> internally in the current version of Rx.

BehaviorSubject<T> remembers the last item it received and hands that out to new subscribers. When you construct a BehaviorSubject<T>, you have to supply an initial value that it will provide to new subscribers until the first call to OnNext.

BehaviorSubject<T> is like a variable: it has a value that you can retrieve at any time, and which might change. Being reactive, you subscribe to retrieve its value, and your observer will be notified of any further changes. BehaviorSubject<T> has a mix of hot and cold characteristics. It provides a value instantly to any subscriber, making it seem like a cold source, but it broadcasts new values to all current subscribers, more like a hot source.

ReplaySubject<T>

ReplaySubject<T> records the values it receives so that it can replay old items to each new subscriber. Once it has provided a particular subscriber with all recorded items, it transitions into more hot-like behavior for that subscriber, forwarding all new incoming items. So, in the long run, every subscriber to a ReplaySubject<T> will, by default, see every item that the ReplaySubject<T> receives from its source, regardless of how early or late that subscriber subscribed to the subject.

ReplaySubject<T> is like BehaviorSubject<T> but with a longer memory. In its default configuration, it will consume ever more memory for as long as it is subscribed to a source. However, you can limit this. ReplaySubject<T> offers various constructor overloads specifying an upper limit on either the number of items to replay or the time for which it will hold on to items. Obviously, if you do this, new subscribers can no longer depend on getting all of the items previously received.

AsyncSubject<T>

AsyncSubject<T> remembers the final value it receives. If you subscribe to an AsyncSubject<T> before its source has completed, your observer receives nothing until the source completes. But once the source has completed, the AsyncSubject<T> acts as a cold source that provides a single value, unless the source completed without providing a value, in which case this subject will complete all new subscribers immediately.

Adaptation

Interesting and powerful though Rx is, it would not be much use if it existed in a vacuum. If you are working with asynchronous notifications, it's possible that they will be supplied by an API that does not support Rx. Although IObservable<T> and IObserver<T> have been around for a long time (since .NET 4.0, which was released in 2010), not every API that could support these interfaces does. Also, because Rx's fundamental abstraction is a sequence of items, there's a good chance that at some point you might need to convert between Rx's push-oriented IObservable<T> and the pull-oriented equivalents IEnumerable<T> and IAsyncEnumerable<T>. Rx provides ways to adapt these and other kinds of sources into IObservable<T>, and in some cases, it can adapt in either direction.

IEnumerable<T> and IAsyncEnumerable<T>

Any IEnumerable<T> can easily be brought into the world of Rx thanks to the ToObservable extension methods. These are defined by the Observable static class in the System.Reactive.Linq namespace. Example 11-30 shows the simplest form, which takes no arguments.

Example 11-30. Converting an IEnumerable<T> to an IObservable<T>

```
public static void ShowAll(IEnumerable<string> source)
{
    IObservable<string> observableSource = source.ToObservable();
    observableSource.Subscribe(Console.WriteLine);
}
```

The ToObservable method itself does not enumerate its input—it just returns a wrapper that implements IObservable<T>. This wrapper is a cold source, and each time you subscribe an observer to it, only then does it iterate through the input, passing each item to the observer's OnNext method and calling OnCompleted at the end. If the source throws an exception, this adapter will call OnError. Example 11-31 shows how ToObservable might work if it weren't for the fact that it needs to use a scheduler.

Example 11-31. How ToObservable might look without scheduler support

```
public static IObservable<T> MyToObservable<T>(this IEnumerable<T> input)
{
    return Observable.Create((IObserver<T> observer) =>
        {
            bool inObserver = false;
            try
            {
                foreach (T item in input)
                {
                    inObserver = true;
                    observer.OnNext(item);
                    inObserver = false;
                }
                inObserver = true;
                observer.OnCompleted();
            }
```

```
            catch (Exception ex)
            {
                if (inObserver)
                {
                    throw;
                }
                observer.OnError(ex);
            }
            return () => { };
        });
}
```

This is not how it really works. (A full implementation would have been much harder to read, defeating the purpose of the example, which was to show the basic idea behind ToObservable.) The real method uses a scheduler to manage the iteration process, enabling subscription to occur asynchronously if required. It also supports stopping the work if the observer's subscription is canceled early. There's an overload that takes a single argument of type IScheduler, which lets you tell it to use a particular scheduler; if you don't provide one, it'll use CurrentThreadScheduler.

When it comes to going in the other direction—that is, when you have an IObservable<T>, but you would like to treat it as an IEnumerable<T>—you can call the ToEnumerable extension methods, also provided by the Observable class. Example 11-32 wraps an IObservable<string> as an IEnumerable<string> so that it can iterate over the items in the source using an ordinary foreach loop.

Example 11-32. Using an IObservable<T> as an IEnumerable<T>

```
public static void ShowAll(IObservable<string> source)
{
    foreach (string s in source.ToEnumerable())
    {
        Console.WriteLine(s);
    }
}
```

The wrapper subscribes to the source on your behalf. If the source provides items faster than you can iterate over them, the wrapper will store the items in a queue so you can retrieve them at your leisure. If the source does not provide items as fast as you can retrieve them, the wrapper will just wait until items become available. You should be wary of ToEnumerable though, because if no items are available, it will block your thread until the source produces an item. This risks deadlock—if a thread is stuck inside ToEnumerable that could prevent whatever progress was required for the source to produce its next item.

The IAsyncEnumerable<T> interface provides the same model as IEnumerable<T> but in a way that enables efficient, nonblocking asynchronous operation using the techniques discussed in Chapter 17. Rx offers a `ToObservable` extension method for this and also a `ToAsyncEnumerable` method extension method for `IObservable<T>`. These both come from the `AsyncEnumerable` class, and to use that you will need a reference to a separate NuGet package called `System.Linq.Async`.

.NET Events

Rx can wrap a .NET event as an `IObservable<T>` using the `Observable` class's static `FromEventPattern` method. Earlier, in Example 11-16, I used a `FileSystemWatcher`, a class from the `System.IO` namespace that raises various events when files are added, deleted, renamed, or otherwise modified in a particular folder. I needed to bring its events into Rx's world of `IObservable<T>`.

Example 11-33 uses the same technique as the first part of that example, which I glossed over last time. This code uses the `Observable.FromEventPattern` static method to produce an observable source representing the watcher's `Created` event.

Example 11-33. Wrapping an event in an `IObservable<T>`

```
string path = Environment.GetFolderPath(Environment.SpecialFolder.MyDocuments);
var w = new FileSystemWatcher(path);
IObservable<EventPattern<FileSystemEventArgs>> changes =
    Observable.FromEventPattern<FileSystemEventHandler, FileSystemEventArgs>(
        h => w.Changed += h, h => w.Changed -= h);
w.IncludeSubdirectories = true;
w.EnableRaisingEvents = true;

changes.Subscribe(evt => Console.WriteLine(evt.EventArgs.FullPath));
```

This is significantly more complicated than just subscribing to the event in the normal way shown in Chapter 9, and this particular example gains nothing from it. However, one benefit of using Rx is that if you were writing a UI application, you could use `ObserveOn` with a suitable scheduler to ensure that your handler was always invoked on the right thread, regardless of which thread raised the event. Another benefit—and the usual reason for doing this—is that you can use any of Rx's query operators to process the events. (That's why the original Example 11-16 did this.)

The element type of the observable source that Example 11-33 produces is `Event Pattern<FileSystemEventArgs>`. Rx defines the generic `EventPattern<T>` type specifically for representing the raising of an event where the event's delegate type conforms to the standard pattern described in Chapter 9 (i.e., it takes two arguments, the first being of type `object`, representing the object that raised the event, and the second being some type derived from `EventArgs`, containing information about the event). `EventPattern<T>` has two properties, `Sender` and `EventArgs`, corresponding to the two arguments that an event handler would receive. In effect, this is an object that represents what would normally be a method call to an event handler.

`Observable.FromEventPattern` is somewhat fiddly to use: Example 11-33 has had to pass in a pair of lambdas, one to subscribe from the event and one to unsubscribe. This is due to a shortcoming of events: you can't pass an event as an argument. This is one of the ways in which Rx improves on events—once you're in the world of Rx, event sources and subscribers are both represented as objects (implementing `IObserv able<T>` and `IObserver<T>`, respectively), making it straightforward to pass them into methods as arguments. But that doesn't help us at the point where we're dealing with an event that's not yet in Rx's world.

There is an alternative overload that seems slightly simpler: instead of a pair of lambdas, you can pass just the name of the event. However, this forces Rx to use reflection (described in Chapter 13) to discover the event's type and locate its add and remove methods at runtime. This causes a couple of problems. First, it can prevent the use of ahead-of-time (AOT) compilation, because AOT depends on being able to work out what our code will do at compile time. Second, it means the compiler can't help you with types—if you attach handlers to a .NET event directly with a lambda, the compiler can determine the argument types from the event definition, and you'll get a compiler error if you try to use the delegate-based `Observable.FromEventPattern` with the wrong type arguments. But if you pass the event name as a string, the compiler doesn't know which event you're using, meaning it can't tell you about certain kinds of mistakes. So it's usually best to use the approach shown in Example 11-33.

Asynchronous APIs

.NET supports various asynchronous patterns, which I'll be describing in detail in Chapters 16 and 17. The first to be introduced in .NET was the Asynchronous Programming Model (APM). However, this pattern is not supported directly by the new C# asynchronous language features, so most .NET APIs now use the TPL, and for older APIs the TPL offers adapters that can provide a task-based wrapper for an APM-based API. Rx can represent any TPL task as an observable source.

The basic model for all of .NET's asynchronous patterns is that you start some work that will eventually complete, optionally producing a result. So it may seem odd to translate this into Rx, where the fundamental abstraction is a sequence of items, not a single result. In fact, one useful way to understand the difference between Rx and the TPL is that `IObservable<T>` is analogous to `IEnumerable<T>`, while `Task<T>` is analogous to a property of type `T`. Whereas with `IEnumerable<T>` and properties, the caller decides when to fetch information from the source, with `IObservable<T>` and `Task<T>`, the source provides the information when it's ready. The choice of which party decides when to provide information is separate from the question of whether the information is singular or a sequence of items. So a mapping between singular asynchronous APIs and IObservable<T> seems a little mismatched. But then we can cross similar boundaries in the nonasynchronous world—LINQ defines various standard operators that produce a single item from a sequence, such as First or Last. Rx supports those operators, but it additionally supports going in the other direction: bringing singular asynchronous sources into a stream-like world. The upshot is an IObservable<T> source that produces just a single item (or reports an error if the operation fails). The analogy in the nonasynchronous world would be taking a single value and wrapping it in an array so that you can pass it to an API that requires an IEnumerable<T>.

Example 11-34 uses this facility to produce an IObservable<string> that will either produce a single value containing the text downloaded from a particular URL or report a failure should the download fail.

Example 11-34. Wrapping a Task<T> as an IObservable<T>

```
public static IObservable<string> GetWebPageAsObservable(
    Uri pageUrl, IHttpClientFactory cf)
{
    async Task<string> GetPageAsync()
    {
        using HttpClient web = cf.CreateClient();
        return await web.GetStringAsync(pageUrl).ConfigureAwait(false);
    }
    return GetPageAsync().ToObservable();
}
```

The ToObservable method used in this example is an extension method defined for Task by Rx. For this to be available, you'll need the System.Reactive.Thread ing.Tasks namespace to be in scope.

One potentially unsatisfactory feature of Example 11-34 is that it will attempt the download only once, no matter how many observers subscribe to the source. Depending on your requirements, that might be fine, but in some scenarios, it might make sense to attempt to download a fresh copy every time. If you want that, you should use the Observable.FromAsync method, because you pass that a lambda that it invokes each time a new observer subscribes. Your lambda returns a task that will then be wrapped as an observable source. Example 11-35 uses this to start a new download for each subscriber.

Example 11-35. Creating a new task for each subscriber

```
public static IObservable<string> GetWebPageAsObservable(
    Uri pageUrl, IHttpClientFactory cf)
{
    return Observable.FromAsync(async () =>
```

```
        {
            using HttpClient web = cf.CreateClient();
            return await web.GetStringAsync(pageUrl);
        });
}
```

This might be suboptimal if you have many subscribers. On the other hand, it's more efficient when nothing attempts to subscribe at all. Example 11-34 starts the asynchronous work immediately without even waiting for any subscribers. That may be a good thing—if the stream will definitely have subscribers, kicking off slow work without waiting for the first subscriber will reduce your overall latency. However, if you are writing a class in a library that presents multiple observable sources, which might not all be used, deferring work until the first subscription might be better.

Timed Sequences

Because Rx can work with live streams of information, you may need to handle items in a time-sensitive way. For example, the rate at which items arrive might be important, or you may wish to group items based on when they were provided. In this final section, I'll describe some of the time-based operators that Rx offers.

Since schedulers play a central role with how Rx handles timing, all of the methods and operators described in this section offer overloads enabling you to specify the IScheduler they should use.

Timed Sources

The methods described in this section do not require an existing IObservable<T> as input. They create new IObservable<long> sequences from scratch.

Observable.Interval
: Regularly produces values at the interval specified by an argument of type Time Span. The items are of type long. It produces values of zero, one, two, and so on. Interval handles each subscriber independently (i.e., it is a cold source), so although each subscriber will receive items at the same interval, they won't generally receive them at the same time.

Observable.Timer
: The simplest overload waits for the duration specified with a TimeSpan argument then produces a single item. There are also overloads that accept an extra Time Span, which will repeatedly produce the value just like Interval. In fact, Inter val is just a wrapper for Timer, offering a simpler API.

Timed Operators

The operators described in this section are all extension methods, taking an existing observable sequence as input and returning an IObservable<T> based on the input:

Timestamp

> Reports the time at which each element entered the operator. This can be useful in cases where there may be a significant delay in between the item being produced and your code getting to handle it. (For example, if you have used ObserveOn to ensure that your handler always runs on the UI thread, delays occur when the UI thread may be busy.) Example 11-36 uses this to show the times at which an Interval produces its items. As you can see, this turns the IObservable<long> returned by Interval into a sequence of Timestamped <long> elements. Timestamped<T> defines two properties, Value and Timestamp, providing the input element and the time it arrived at this operator, respectively.

Example 11-36. Timestamped items

```
IObservable<Timestamped<long>> src =
    Observable.Interval(TimeSpan.FromSeconds(1)).Timestamp();
src.Subscribe(i => Console.WriteLine(
    $"Event {i.Value} at {i.Timestamp.ToLocalTime():T}"));
```

TimeInterval

> Whereas Timestamp records the current time at which items are produced, its relative counterpart TimeInterval records the time between successive items. Given an IObservable<T>, this returns an IObservable<TimeInterval<T>>.

Throttle

> Lets you limit the rate at which you process items. You pass a TimeSpan that specifies the minimum time interval you want between any two items. If the underlying source produces items faster than this, Throttle will just discard them. If the source is slower than the specified rate, Throttle just passes everything straight through. Surprisingly (or at least, I found this surprising), once the source exceeds the specified rate, Throttle drops *everything* until the rate drops back down below the specified level. So, if you specify a rate of 10 items a second, and the source produces 100 per second, it won't simply return every 10th item— it'll return nothing until the source slows down.

Sample

Produces items from its input at the interval specified by its TimeSpan argument, regardless of the rate at which the input observable is generating items. If the underlying source produces items faster than the chosen rate, Sample drops items to limit the rate. However, if the source is running slower, the Sample operator will just repeat the last value to ensure a constant supply of notifications.

Timeout

Passes everything through from its source observable unless the source leaves too large a gap either between the subscription time and the first item or between two subsequent calls to the observer. You specify the minimum acceptable gap with a TimeSpan argument. If no activity occurs within that time, the Timeout operator completes by reporting a TimeoutException to OnError.

Delay

Time-shifts an observable source. You can pass a TimeSpan, in which case the operator will delay everything by the specified amount, or you can pass a Date TimeOffset, indicating a specific time at which you would like it to start replaying its input. Alternatively, you can pass an observable, and whenever that observable first produces something or completes, the Delay operator will start producing the values it has stored. The Delay operator attempts to maintain the same spacing between inputs. So, if the underlying source produces an item immediately, then another item after three seconds, and then a third item after a minute, the observable produced by Delay will produce items separated by the same time intervals.

The fidelity with which Delay can reproduce the exact timing of the items is determined by the nature of the scheduler you're using and the available CPU capacity on the machine. For example, if you use one of the UI-based schedulers, it will be limited by the availability of the UI thread and the rate at which that can dispatch work.

DelaySubscription

Time-shifts subscription to an observable source. DelaySubscription offers a similar set of overloads to the Delay operator, but the way it tries to effect a delay is different. When you subscribe to an observable source produced by Delay, it will immediately subscribe to the underlying source and start buffering items, forwarding each item only when the required delay has elapsed.

The strategy employed by DelaySubscription is simply to delay the subscription to the underlying source and then forward each item immediately. This typically works well for cold sources, because with those, delaying the start of work will typically time-shift the entire process. But for a hot source, DelaySubscription will cause you to miss any events that occurred during the delay, and after that, you'll start getting events with no time shift. So `Delay` is more dependable—by time-shifting each item individually, it works for both hot and cold sources. However, it has to do more work—it needs to buffer everything it receives for the delay duration. For busy sources or long delays, this could consume a lot of memory. And the attempt to reproduce the original timings with a time shift is considerably more complicated than just passing items straight on. So, in scenarios where it is viable, `DelaySubscription` is more efficient.

Timed Windowing Operators

I described the `Buffer` and `Window` operators earlier, but I didn't show their time-based overloads. As well as being able to specify a window size and skip count, or to mark window boundaries with an ancillary observable source, you can also specify time-based windows.

If you pass just a `TimeSpan`, both operators will break the input into adjacent windows at the specified interval. Example 11-37 applies `Buffer` this way to the `words` observable defined in Example 11-22 to estimate the words per minute.

Example 11-37. Timed windows with `Buffer`

```
IObservable<int> wordGroupCounts =
    from wordGroup in words.Buffer(TimeSpan.FromSeconds(6))
    select wordGroup.Count * 10;
wordGroupCounts.Subscribe(c => Console.WriteLine($"Words per minute: {c}"));
```

There are also overloads accepting both a `TimeSpan` and an `int`, enabling you to close the current window (thus starting the next window) either when the specified interval elapses or when the number of items exceeds a threshold. In addition, there are overloads accepting two `TimeSpan` arguments. These support the time-based equivalent of the combination of a window size and a skip count. The first `TimeSpan` argument specifies the window duration, while the second specifies the interval at which to start new windows. This means the windows do not need to be strictly adjacent—you can have gaps between them, or they can overlap. Example 11-38 uses this to provide more frequent estimates of the word rate while still using a six-second window.

Example 11-38. Overlapping timed windows

```
IObservable<int> wordGroupCounts =
    from wordGroup in words.Buffer(TimeSpan.FromSeconds(6),
                                   TimeSpan.FromSeconds(1))
    select wordGroup.Count * 10;
```

Reaqtor—Rx as a Service

Although Rx is now a fully community-supported project,[6] it was originally created by Microsoft. The same team also produced a set of components that makes it possible to host long-running Rx queries in a service. Microsoft has been using this internally for years to provide event-driven functionality in a variety of its online services, including the Bing search engine and the online versions of Office. It enables features such as setting up alerts that tell you when you'll need to leave to get to an appointment on time given current traffic conditions, for example. It has a proven track record of being able to maintain millions of active queries. For many years this was an internal project, but it is now an open source project called Reaqtor. The code for the core libraries that make this possible is hosted at the Reaqtor source repository (*https://github.com/reaqtive/reaqtor*), and there is a site with documentation and supporting information (*https://reaqtive.net*).[7]

Reaqtor takes the programming model of Rx—observable sequences, subjects, and operators—and exploits .NET's expression tree features described in Chapter 9 to enable queries to be stored or sent across the network. It also provides versions of standard LINQ operators that are able to persist their state, enabling queries with stateful operators (e.g., `Aggregate`, `DistinctUntilChanged`, or anything else that needs to remember something about what it has already seen) to survive beyond the lifetime of any single process. This enables an application to define a LINQ query to some observable source of data and set up a subscription to that query that will be hosted in a server pool, persisting with an arbitrarily long lifetime. Reaqtor is designed to offer the same kind of durability as a database, so some of Microsoft's applications have Rx queries that have been running uninterrupted for several years.

The relationship between Rx and Reaqtor is not unlike the relationship between LINQ to Objects and Entity Framework (EF) Core. As you saw in Chapter 10, LINQ to Objects is built on `IEnumerable<T>`, and it works entirely in-memory, with no persistence or cross-process capability. EF Core takes the same basic concepts and offers most of the same operators, but by building on the expression-tree-based `IQuery able<T>`, EF Core is able to send representations of an application's queries over to a database server so that they can be executed remotely—EF Core brings LINQ into a world of durable persistence and distributed execution. Similarly, whereas Rx is built on `IObservable<T>` and runs entirely in-memory, Reaqtor uses an expression-tree-based interface `IQbservable<T>`. (Note the Q instead of an O, denoting its similarity in concept to `IQueryable<T>`.) `IQbservable<T>` looks very similar to `IObserv able<T>` and offers all of the same operators, but because it works in the world of

---

6 I became the primary Rx project maintainer in January 2023 by the way.

7 I am the primary maintainer for Reaqtor too.

expression trees, it is possible for Reaqtor to convert queries into a form that can be sent over the network to a server farm, which can then reconstitute runnable versions of those queries hosted inside the server farm. It exploits the serializability to store the queries, enabling them to be migrated from one machine to another within the server farm, providing persistence and durability in the face of individual server failures. Reaqtor brings Rx into a world of durable persistence and distributed execution.

At the time of writing, there isn't an off-the-shelf hosted version of Reaqtor freely available, so it takes quite a lot of work to build something real from the Reaqtor libraries. But I've built a couple of applications on top of this with my employer, so I can say with confidence that it is certainly possible.

Summary

As you've now seen, the Reactive Extensions for .NET provide a lot of functionality. The concept underpinning Rx is a well-defined abstraction for sequences of items where the source decides when to provide each item, and a related abstraction representing a subscriber to such a sequence. By representing both concepts as objects, event sources and subscribers both become first-class entities, meaning you can pass them as arguments, store them in fields, and generally do anything with them that you can do with any other data type in .NET. While you can do all of that with a delegate too, .NET events are not first class. Moreover, Rx provides a clearly defined mechanism for notifying a subscriber of errors, something that neither delegates nor events handle well. As well as defining a first-class representation for event sources, Rx defines a comprehensive LINQ implementation, which is why Rx is sometimes described as LINQ to Events. In fact, it goes well beyond the set of standard LINQ operators, adding numerous operators that exploit and help to manage the live and potentially time-sensitive world that event-driven systems occupy. Rx also provides various services for bridging between its basic abstractions and those of other worlds, including standard .NET events, IEnumerable<T>, and various asynchronous models.

CHAPTER 12

Assemblies and Deployment

So far in this book, I've used the term *component* to describe either a library or an executable. It's now time to look more closely at exactly what that means. In .NET the smallest unit of deployment for a software component is called an *assembly*, and it is typically a *.dll* file. Assemblies are an important aspect of the type system, because each type is identified not just by its name and namespace but also by its containing assembly. Assemblies provide a kind of encapsulation that operates at a larger scale than individual types, thanks to the `internal` accessibility specifier, which works at the assembly level.

.NET assemblies can't run on their own—they rely on the .NET runtime, and we have a few options for ensuring that a suitable runtime is available when we deploy our applications. The runtime provides an *assembly loader*, which automatically finds and loads the assemblies a program needs. To ensure that the loader can find the right components, assemblies have structured names that include version information, and they can optionally contain a globally unique element to prevent ambiguity.

Most of the C# project types in Visual Studio's "Create a new project" dialog produce a single assembly as their main output, as do most of the project templates available from the command line with `dotnet new`. When you build a project, it will often put additional files in the output folder too, such as copies of any assemblies that your code relies on that are not built into the .NET runtime, and other files needed by your application. (For example, a website project will typically need to produce CSS and script files in addition to server-side code.) But there will usually be a particular assembly that is the build target of your project, containing all of the types your project defines along with the code those types contain.

Anatomy of an Assembly

Assemblies use the Win32 Portable Executable (PE) file format, the same format that executables (EXEs) and dynamic link libraries (DLLs) have always used in modern versions of Windows.[1] It is "portable" in the sense that the same basic file format is used across different CPU architectures. Non-.NET PE files are generally architecture-specific, but .NET assemblies often aren't. Even if you're running .NET on Linux or macOS, it'll still use this Windows-based format—most .NET assemblies can run on all supported operating systems, so we use the same file format everywhere.

The C# compiler produces an assembly as its output, usually with an extension of *.dll*. Tools that understand the PE file format will recognize a .NET assembly as a valid, but rather dull, PE file. The CLR essentially uses PE files as containers for a .NET-specific data format, so to classic Win32 tools, a C# DLL will not appear to export any APIs. Remember that C# compiles to a binary intermediate language (IL), which is not directly executable. The normal Windows mechanisms for loading and running the code in an executable or DLL won't work with IL, because that can run only with the help of the CLR. Similarly, .NET defines its own format for encoding metadata and does not use the PE format's native capability for exporting entry points or importing the services of other DLLs.

> Later, we'll look at the ahead-of-time (AOT) compilation tools in the .NET SDK. These can incorporate native executable code into your build output, but if you enable this through the *Ready to Run* feature, even this embedded native code is loaded and executed under the control of the CLR and is directly accessible only to managed code. Native AOT is different, but we'll get to that.

In most cases, you won't build .NET assemblies with an extension of *.exe*. Even project types that produce directly runnable outputs (such as console or WPF applications) produce a *.dll* as their primary output. They also generate an executable file, but it's not a .NET assembly. It's just a *host* (sometimes referred to as a bootstrapper) that starts the runtime and then loads and executes your application's main assembly. By default, the type of host you get depends on what OS you build on—for example, if you build on Windows, you'll get a Windows *.exe* host, whereas on Linux it will be an executable in the ELF format.[2] (The exception to this is when you target the .NET Framework. Since that supports only Windows, it doesn't need different hosts for

---

1 I'm using *modern* in a very broad sense here—Windows NT introduced PE support in 1993.

2 With suitable build settings you can produce host executables for all supported targets regardless of which OS you build on.

different operating systems, so these projects produce a .NET assembly with an extension of *.exe* that incorporates the bootstrapper.)

.NET Metadata

As well as containing the compiled IL, an assembly contains *metadata*, which provides a full description of all of the types it defines, whether public or private. The CLR needs to have complete knowledge of all the types your code uses to be able to make sense of the IL and turn it into running code—the binary format for IL frequently refers to the containing assembly's metadata and is meaningless without it. The reflection API, which is the subject of Chapter 13, makes the information in this metadata available to your code.

Resources

You can embed binary resources in a DLL alongside the code and metadata. Client-side applications might do this with bitmaps, for example. To embed a file, you can add it to a project, select it in Solution Explorer, and then use the Properties panel to set its Build Action to Embedded Resource. This embeds a copy of the entire file into the component. To extract the resource at runtime, you use the `Assembly` class's `Get ManifestResourceStream` method, which is part of the reflection API described in Chapter 13. However, in practice, you wouldn't normally use this facility directly—most applications use embedded resources through a localizable mechanism that I'll describe later in this chapter.

So, in summary, an assembly contains a comprehensive set of metadata describing all the types it defines; it holds all of the IL for those types' methods, and it can optionally embed any number of binary streams. This is typically all packaged up into a single PE file. However, that is not always the whole story.

Multifile Assemblies

The old (but still supported) Windows-only .NET Framework allows an assembly to span multiple files. You can split the code and metadata across multiple *modules*, and it is also possible for some binary streams that are logically embedded in an assembly to be put in separate files. This feature is rarely used, and only .NET Framework supports it. However, it's necessary to know about it because some of its consequences persist. In particular, parts of the design of the reflection API (Chapter 13) make no sense unless you know about this feature.

With a multifile assembly, there's always one main file that represents the assembly. This will be a PE file, and it contains a particular element of the metadata called the *assembly manifest*. This is not to be confused with the Win32-style manifest that most executables contain. The assembly manifest is just a description of what's in the assembly, including a list of any additional modules or other external files; in a multi-module assembly, the manifest describes which types are defined in which files.

Other PE Features

Although C# does not use the classic Win32 mechanisms for representing code or exporting APIs in EXEs and DLLs, there are still a couple of old-school features of the PE format that assemblies can use.

Win32-style resources

.NET defines its own mechanism for embedding binary resources, and a localization API built on top of that, so for the most part it makes no use of the PE file format's intrinsic support for embedding resources. Nonetheless, there's nothing stopping you from putting classic Win32-style resources into a .NET component—the C# compiler offers various command-line switches that do this. However, there's no .NET API for accessing these resources at runtime from within your application, which is why you'd normally use .NET's own resource system. But there are some exceptions.

Windows expects to find certain resources in executables. For example, it defines a way to embed version information as an unmanaged resource. C# assemblies normally do this, but you don't need to define a version resource explicitly. The compiler can generate one for you, as I show in "Version" on page 608. This ensures that if an end user looks at your assembly's properties in Windows File Explorer, they will be able to see the version number. (By convention, .NET assemblies typically contain this Win32-style version information whether they target just Windows or can run on any platform.)

Windows *.exe* files typically contain two additional Win32 resources. You may want to define a custom icon for your application to control how it appears on the task bar or in Windows File Explorer. This requires you to embed the icon in the Win32 way, because File Explorer doesn't know how to extract .NET resources. You can do this by adding an <ApplicationIcon> property to your *.csproj* file. If you're using Visual Studio, it provides a way to set this through the project's properties pages. Also, if you're writing a classic Windows desktop application or console application (whether written with .NET or not), it should supply an application manifest. Without this, Windows will presume that your application was written before 2006[3] and will modify or disable certain OS features for backward compatibility. The manifest also needs to be present if you are writing a desktop application and you want it to pass certain Microsoft certification requirements. This kind of manifest has to be embedded as a Win32 resource. The .NET SDK will add a basic manifest by default, but if you need to

---

3 This was the year Windows Vista shipped. Application manifests existed before then, but this was the first version of Windows to treat their absence as signifying legacy code.

customize it (e.g., because you're writing a console application that will need to run with elevated privileges), you can specify a manifest with an `<ApplicationManifest>` property in your *.csproj* file (or again, with the project properties pages in Visual Studio).

Remember that unless you're targeting the old .NET Framework, the main assembly is a *.dll,* even for Windows desktop applications, and when you target Windows, the build process produces a separate *.exe* that launches the .NET runtime and then loads that assembly. As far as Windows is concerned, this host executable is your application, so the icon and manifest resources will end up in that file. But if you target the .NET Framework, there will be no separate host executable, so these resources end up in the main assembly.

Console versus GUI

Windows makes a distinction between console applications and Windows applications. To be precise, the PE format requires a *.exe* file to specify a *subsystem,* and back in the old days of Windows NT, this enabled the use of multiple operating system *personalities*—early versions included a POSIX subsystem, for example. These days, PE files target one of just three subsystems, and one of those is for kernel-mode device drivers. The two user-mode options used today select between Windows graphical user interface (GUI) and Windows console applications. The principal difference is that Windows will show a console window when running the latter (or if you run it from a command prompt, it will just use the existing console window), but a Windows GUI application does not get a console window.

You can select between these subsystems with an `<OutputType>` property in your project file set to `Exe` or `WinExe`, or in Visual Studio you can use the "Output type" drop-down list in the project properties. (The output type defaults to `Library`, or "Class Library" in Visual Studio's UI. This builds a DLL, but since the subsystem is determined when a process launches, it makes no difference whether a DLL targets the Windows Console or Windows GUI subsystem. The `Library` setting always targets the former.) If you target the .NET Framework, this subsystem setting applies to the *.exe* file that is built as your application's main assembly, and with newer versions of .NET, it will apply to the host *.exe.* (As it happens, it will also apply to the main assembly *.dll* that the host loads, but this has no effect because the subsystem is determined by the *.exe* for which the process is launched.)

Type Identity

As a C# developer, your first point of contact with assemblies will usually be the fact that they form part of a type's identity. When you write a class, it will end up in an assembly. When you use a type from the runtime libraries or from some other library, your project will need a reference to the assembly that contains the type before you can use it.

This is not always obvious when using system types. The build system automatically adds references to various runtime library assemblies, so most of the time, you will not need to add a reference before you can use a runtime library type, and since you do not normally refer to a type's assembly explicitly in the source code, it's not immediately obvious that the assembly is a mandatory part of what it takes to pinpoint a type. But despite not being explicit in the code, the assembly has to be part of a type's identity, because there's nothing stopping you or anyone else from defining new types that have the same name as existing types. For example, you could define a class called System.String in your project. This is a bad idea, and the compiler will warn you that this introduces ambiguity, but it won't stop you. And even though your class will have the exact same fully qualified name as the built-in string type, the compiler and the runtime can still distinguish between these types.

Whenever you use a type, either explicitly by name (e.g., in a variable or parameter declaration) or implicitly through an expression, the C# compiler knows exactly what type you're referring to, meaning it knows which assembly defined the type. So it is able to distinguish between the System.String intrinsic to .NET and a System .String unhelpfully defined in your own component. The C# scoping rules mean that an explicit reference to System.String identifies the one that you defined in your own project, because local types effectively hide ones of the same name in external assemblies. If you use the string keyword, that always refers to the built-in type. You'll also be using the built-in type when you use a string literal, or if you call an API that returns a string. Example 12-1 illustrates this—it defines its own System.String and then uses a generic method that displays the type and assembly name for the static type of whatever argument you pass it. (This uses the reflection API, which is described in Chapter 13.)

Example 12-1. What type is a piece of string?

```
using System;

// Never do this!
namespace System
{
    public class String
    {
    }
}

class Program
{
    static void Main()
    {
```

```
        System.String? s = null;
        ShowStaticTypeNameAndAssembly(s);
        string? s2 = null;
        ShowStaticTypeNameAndAssembly(s2);
        ShowStaticTypeNameAndAssembly("String literal");
        ShowStaticTypeNameAndAssembly(Environment.OSVersion.VersionString);
    }

    static void ShowStaticTypeNameAndAssembly<T>(T item)
    {
        Type t = typeof(T);
        Console.WriteLine(
            $"Type: {t.FullName}. Assembly: {t.Assembly.FullName}.");
    }
}
```

The Main method in this example tries each of the ways of working with strings I just described, and it writes out the following:

```
Type: System.String. Assembly TypeIdentity, Version=1.0.0.0, Culture=neutral,
 PublicKeyToken=null.
Type: System.String. Assembly System.Private.CoreLib, Version=8.0.0.0,
 Culture=neutral, PublicKeyToken=7cec85d7bea7798e.
Type: System.String. Assembly System.Private.CoreLib, Version=8.0.0.0,
 Culture=neutral, PublicKeyToken=7cec85d7bea7798e.
Type: System.String. Assembly System.Private.CoreLib, Version=8.0.0.0,
 Culture=neutral, PublicKeyToken=7cec85d7bea7798e.
```

The explicit use of System.String ended up with my type, and the rest all used the system-defined string type. This demonstrates that the C# compiler can cope with multiple types with the same name. This also shows that IL is able to make that distinction. IL's binary format ensures that every reference to a type identifies the containing assembly. But just because you can create and use multiple identically named types doesn't mean you should. You do not usually name the containing assembly explicitly in C#, so it's a particularly bad idea to introduce pointless collisions by defining, say, your own System.String class. (As it happens, in a pinch you can resolve this sort of collision if you really need to—see the sidebar "Extern Aliases" on page 590 for details—but it's better to avoid it.)

By the way, if you run Example 12-1 on .NET Framework, you'll see mscorlib in place of System.Private.CoreLib. .NET changed which assemblies many runtime library types live in. You might be wondering how this can work with .NET Standard, which enables you to write a single DLL that can run on .NET Framework and .NET. How could a .NET Standard component correctly identify a type that lives in different assemblies on different targets? The answer is that .NET has a *type forwarding* feature in which references to types in one assembly can be redirected to some other assembly at runtime. (A type forwarder is just an assembly-level attribute that describes where the real type definition can be found. Attributes are the subject of

Chapter 14.) .NET Standard components reference neither mscorlib nor System.Private.CoreLib—they are built as though runtime library types are defined in an assembly called netstandard. Each .NET runtime supplies a netstandard implementation that forwards to the appropriate types at runtime. In fact, even code built directly for .NET often ends up using type forwarding. If you inspect the compiled output, you'll find that it expects most runtime library types to be defined in an assembly called System.Runtime, and it's only through type forwarding that these end up using types in System.Private.CoreLib.

Extern Aliases

When multiple types with the same name are in scope, C# normally uses the one from the nearest scope, which is why a locally defined System.String can hide the built-in type of the same name. It's unwise to introduce this sort of name clash, but this problem occasionally occurs when external libraries that you depend on have made bad naming decisions. If that's where you are, C# offers a mechanism that lets you specify the assembly you want. You can define an *extern alias*.

In Chapter 1, I showed type aliases defined with the using keyword that make it easier to refer to types that have the same simple name but different namespaces. An extern alias makes it possible to distinguish between types with the same fully qualified name in different assemblies.

To define an extern alias, you need to add an Aliases element inside the relevant element in your *.csproj* file. Depending on whether the target component is a NuGet package, another project, or a plain DLL, that will be a PackageReference, Project Reference, or Reference element, respectively. As a child of that element, add an Aliases element containing the name (or a comma-separated list of names) to use, e.g., <Aliases>A1</Aliases>. If you're using Visual Studio, it can do this for you: expand the Dependencies list in Solution Explorer and then expand either the Packages, Projects, or Assemblies section and select a reference. You can then set the alias for that reference in the Properties panel. If you define an alias of A1 for one assembly and A2 for another, you can then declare that you want to use these aliases by putting the following at the top of a C# file:

```
extern alias A1;
extern alias A2;
```

With these in place, you can qualify type names with A1:: or A2:: followed by the fully qualified name. This tells the compiler that you want to use types defined by the assembly (or assemblies) associated with that alias, even if some other type of the same name would otherwise have been in scope.

If it's a bad idea to have multiple types with the same name, why does .NET make it possible in the first place? In fact, supporting name collisions was not the goal; it's just a side effect of the fact that .NET makes the assembly part of the type. The assembly needs to be part of the type definition so that the CLR can know which assembly to load for you at runtime when you first use some feature of that type.

Deployment

To run the code in the assemblies that constitute our application, we need to ensure that they are copied to the computer that will host that application, along with any other supporting files necessary for successful execution. This process is called *deployment*. There are several ways to deploy a .NET application.

The first question we will need to ask when choosing a deployment strategy is: How will we ensure that a suitable .NET runtime is available on the target system? There are two possible answers: either the runtime is installed at the system level,[4] or the application will need to bring its own copy of the runtime. So we can choose between *framework-dependent* and *self-contained* deployment models, respectively.

Framework-Dependent

The framework-dependent approach, where we rely on the .NET runtime being installed at the system level, has some advantages over a self-contained deployment. If you don't need to ship a copy of the .NET runtime, your deployable package will be much smaller because it needs to include only files specific to your application. It might also offer servicing advantages: assuming your host machines have mainte-nance procedures in place to install updates to the .NET runtime, you won't need to deploy new versions of your application just to receive these runtime updates. The downside, of course, is that something has to ensure that a suitable version of the .NET runtime is in fact installed.

There are some scenarios in which you can take the presence of the runtime for gran-ted. For example, cloud platforms often preinstall it in the virtual machines or con-tainers that will host your code. In corporate environments, the .NET runtime might be part of standard OS images rolled out across the organization.

There are some scenarios in which you will need to take steps to ensure that the .NET runtime is installed, but for which a framework-dependent approach still makes sense. If you are using a containerization technology such as Docker, for example, Microsoft makes standard images available in which .NET is preinstalled. If you use

---

4 On a conventional machine or VM this would mean running the .NET runtime installer. If you're using containers, it would mean selecting an image that includes the runtime.

one of these images as a starting point, your application image needs to add only the files for a framework-dependent deployment of your application.

There are two variations on the framework-dependent model. If you run this command:

```
dotnet publish
```

the SDK will build a *framework-dependent executable* deployment. This includes an executable file that makes your application runnable, sometimes referred to as the *host*. This executable's main job is to discover which .NET runtimes are installed on the target system, and to choose the most appropriate one to run your application (or to report an error if it can't find a suitable runtime). Executable files are inherently platform-specific: if you run the preceding command on Windows, you'll get a *.exe* file, but on Linux you'll get an executable that can run on Linux, and likewise with macOS. The executable's name will be the same as the name of the assembly your project produces (except the assembly has a *.dll* extension, regardless of target platform), and by default this will be the same as your project filename. So *MyApp.csproj* will build a *MyApp.dll* and an executable, which on Windows will be called *MyApp.exe*, whereas on Linux and macOS, it will be called *MyApp*.

Although publication defaults to producing an executable suitable for the OS and CPU architecture of the machine on which you run `dotnet publish`, you can ask for other targets. This command builds a framework-dependent executable where the executable file runs on macOS, and is built for the x64 processor architecture:

```
dotnet publish -r osx-x64
```

The value following the `-r` argument is a *runtime identifier* (RID). It starts with an operating system identifier (e.g., `win`, `osx`, `ios`, `linux`, or `android`; OS X has been rebranded as macOS, but the .NET SDK's Mac support predates that change). This is optionally followed by more detail, typically including the CPU architecture (e.g., `win-x86`). In Linux RIDs, it can also indicate which distribution is expected, e.g., `linux-musl-arm64`, because that will determine which system libraries are available.

This choice of RID might affect more than just the host executable. Your code could use conditional compilation (`#if` directives) to include platform-specific sections. Also, some NuGet packages support only specific RIDs, or provide RID-specific files. However, it's fairly common for everything in your deployable output to be completely portable across OS and CPU type except for the host executable.

It is possible to ask the SDK to omit the executable entirely:

```
dotnet publish -p:UseAppHost=false
```

This is the other framework-dependent style, and it is called a *framework-dependent deployment*. (That's a slightly confusing name because it's not obvious that this is distinct from a framework-dependent executable. It sounds more like the name for the broader category that includes both styles.) This produces output that does not include a host executable, but is otherwise identical to what you would get without that final argument.

How do you run your application if there's no executable? If a computer has the .NET runtime installed, the dotnet command-line interface (sometimes called the *dotnet CLI*) will be available on the system path. You can use dotnet run MyApp.dll where *MyApp.dll* is your application's main assembly, and it will run the application in exactly the same way as the host executable would have done (including working out which of the .NET runtimes installed on the system is the best choice).

The host executable adds a couple of advantages. First, it makes it easier to run the application. If you've written a command-line tool in .NET, it would be inconvenient for users of that tool to have to type dotnet run "C:\Program Files\MyTools \MyCommand.dll" instead of just MyCommand. Second, when you use system tools that monitor processes (such as the Windows Task Manager, or the ps command on Linux) the process will be listed as MyCommand if launched with a host executable. Programs launched using dotnet run all show up as dotnet, making it hard to tell which application is which if more than one program is using .NET.

There are two advantages to not using the host executable. First, as long as none of your code and none of the components you depend on require a particular OS or CPU type, a framework-dependent deployment is completely portable: the same files will work on any target platform. Second, even if you target a specific OS and CPU, omitting the application host makes your deployment slightly smaller. (The host executable for Windows on x64 processors is about 138 KB.) In some cloud platforms, minimizing the size of a deployment can reduce the startup time, so if you don't need the host executable, you may as well omit it.

Self-Contained

For scenarios where you can't presume that a suitable runtime will be installed as part of your environment, and you don't want to add any separate prerequisite procedures to install one at a system-wide level, you could choose .NET's self-contained deployment model. This bundles a complete copy of the .NET runtime (the CLR, the libraries—everything needed to run a .NET application) in the deployable output of your application. As you might expect, this makes for a much larger deployable package.

A framework-dependent deployment of a simple "Hello, World" application takes about 5.2 KB. (I'm not including the 10 KB file containing debug symbol information in that figure.) The exact size of a self-contained deployment depends on the RID, but if I build the same application with this command:

```
dotnet publish -r win-x64 --self-contained true
```

The deployable output is 70 MB in size. That's about four orders of magnitude larger than the smallest possible framework-dependent deployment of the same code. With real applications, the difference will not be as large—as the amount of code in your application grows, and the more NuGet packages it depends on, the larger a framework-dependent deployment would grow. However, it takes a hefty application to outweigh the 70 MB of the .NET runtime.

Trimming

Once you've discovered just how large self-contained deployments are, you might well ask: Can I make them smaller? You can, although this creates some constraints. You can enable *trimming*, which omits code that we're not using, whether that code resides in libraries obtained from NuGet, or the runtime libraries themselves. Enabling trimming is straightforward enough: you just add a single property to your project file, as Example 12-2 shows.

Example 12-2. Enabling trimming in project file

```
<PropertyGroup>
  <PublishTrimmed>true</PublishTrimmed>
</PropertyGroup>
```

> The `PublishTrimmed` setting affects only self-contained deployment (which includes Native AOT if you're using that). It has no impact on any other build outputs.

Enabling trimming on a "Hello, World" application targeting `win-x64` gets the size down from 70 MB to about 17.5 MB. That's a substantial improvement, although it's still much larger than a framework-dependent deployment. A trimmed self-contained deployment still includes a copy of the CLR because we need basic services such as JIT compilation and garbage collection. Since the runtime makes use of its own libraries internally, a significant subset of the runtime libraries will be included even when you don't use them directly.

Trimming can be particularly important when we use the Mono CLR. Remember, .NET offers more than one CLR. The default one most applications use offers sophisticated mechanisms to deliver high performance, but these aren't always a good fit in memory-constrained environments. The Mono CLR was, for many years, optimized for mobile platforms, and now also supports in-browser execution by targeting Web Assembly (WASM). This CLR is significantly smaller, meaning that assemblies (application-specific, runtime library components, and NuGet packages) typically account for the majority of the size of a deployment. If you are building for WASM in order to run .NET code inside a web browser (e.g., when using the Blazor framework) trimming can improve page load speeds considerably.

It is not always straightforward for the build system to work out which library code is in use. For most of .NET's existence, it was safe to assume that the whole of the runtime library was available, because either .NET is installed or it is not, and so some libraries have come to depend on dynamic mechanisms such as runtime code generation. These make it tricky for the build process to work out what is safe to omit—your application code might have no direct references to a particular library type, but that type might end up being loaded via reflection, or used by code emitted at runtime.

 Trimming is often incompatible with mechanisms that rely on discovering type information at runtime using reflection (see Chapter 13). For example, certain ways of using the serialization features described in Chapter 15 do this, although they also offer trimming-friendly modes of operation.

The runtime libraries include annotations to help the compiler understand how to trim the code, and so that it can warn you when you are using non-trim-compatible features. Before .NET 7.0, components that had no such annotations were treated as untrimmable by default, but now the SDK will analyze components that are not annotated to detect the use of non-trim-friendly features. If it can determine that a component does not use such features (or that your application doesn't use the parts of that component that do), it can safely trim code.

Ahead-of-Time (AOT) Compilation

As you know, the C# compiler emits code in a non-CPU-specific form called IL, and this is normally compiled into machine code at runtime at the first moment that it is required, a process called *just-in-time* (JIT) compilation. However, you can instruct the .NET SDK to generate machine language (or, where applicable, WASM) at build time. This is known as ahead-of-time (AOT) compilation. .NET offers two forms of AOT: *ReadyToRun* and *Native AOT*.

ReadyToRun

ReadyToRun (R2R) is a hybrid model in which native code gets generated at build time and is added to the assembly alongside everything else that would normally be included. All of the IL and type information remain present. R2R is a conservative option: it will never prevent anything from working. Even if your compiled code ends up running on a different CPU architecture than the native code was generated for, it will still work because the IL is still present, so the CLR can just fall back to JIT compilation.

The main benefit of R2R is that it can improve application startup time. As long as the native code embedded in the assembly matches the target architecture, the CLR can use that instead of JIT compiling code. You can enable R2R by adding a property to your project file, as Example 12-3 shows.

Example 12-3. Enabling R2R in a project file

```
<PropertyGroup>
  <PublishReadyToRun>true</PublishReadyToRun>
</PropertyGroup>
```

The R2R code generation occurs only when you publish—it's relatively slow, so you won't generally want to wait for it to happen during normal development and debugging. You will need to specify a RID so that the build tools know which OS and CPU architecture to build native code for:

```
dotnet publish -r win-x64
```

Even when the R2R code is a match for the target system, the CLR might choose to replace it after a while. The runtime keeps track of which methods are used most often, and for heavily used methods, it may decide to regenerate the code to better match usage patterns (a mechanism called *tiered JIT*). For example, it might notice that although a method has an argument with an interface type, in practice the same concrete type seems to be passed every time, and so it can generate a version of the method optimized for that type (while still being able to fall back to more general code in case some other type is ever passed in).

R2R does not radically change the way that code runs. It just enables the CLR to avoid having to JIT compile methods in some circumstances. Consequently, R2R code needs the .NET runtime to be present. You can use it with either self-contained or framework-dependent deployment.

Native AOT

The second form of AOT compilation is Native AOT. This is a self-contained model, and it works much more like traditional compilation of the kind used by languages such as C and C++: all machine code is generated at build time. The resulting executable contains everything it needs to run, so you can just copy the file onto a target machine and run it. (This is, in effect, a kind of self-contained deployment.) The IL is not copied into the build output, and type information will be included only where the build tools detect that it is required. JIT compilation is not available. It is enabled with a project file setting, as Example 12-4 shows.

Example 12-4. Enabling Native AOT in a project file

```
<PropertyGroup>
  <PublishAot>true</PublishAot>
</PropertyGroup>
```

As with R2R, Native AOT code generation occurs only when you publish the application. And again we need to specify a RID so the tools know what kind of native code is required. For example:

```
dotnet publish -r win-x64
```

Native AOT is a more radical option than R2R. Code built this way can't run on an OS or processor architecture other than the one it was built for because the IL is not included, meaning that there's no way for the CLR to fall back to JIT compilation. The version of the CLR that gets embedded in a Native AOT application does not include the JIT compiler. (This also means that tiered JIT compilation is not available, so the performance can sometimes be lower.) Native AOT trims code, so the constraints that apply to trimming also apply here—certain dynamic techniques such as runtime code generation are unavailable.

Native AOT can produce the smallest self-contained programs. (This is an area in which .NET 8.0 has made significant improvements.) Earlier, we saw that a self-contained, trimmed "Hello, world" application was 17.5 MB in size when built for win-x64. With Native AOT this comes down to about 1.4 MB. Those of us old enough to remember floppy disks might raise an eyebrow at the idea that the simplest possible command-line program might barely fit on a removable storage disk, but remember that this does include a CLR. (There's a garbage collector in there, for example.) Compared to conventional self-contained deployment's 70 MB (17.5 MB trimmed), 1.4 MB looks positively frugal. Native AOT enables you to produce completely self-contained executables whose size is in the same ballpark as with languages such as Go and Rust.

An application will typically start up more quickly when you use Native AOT than it will with the other deployment options. That's partly down to the small file size—smaller files can be loaded into memory more quickly. The Native AOT CLR is much smaller than the normal .NET CLR, so it loads quickly too. You also don't need to wait for JIT compilation, but there's even an advantage over R2R deployment. With R2R, the CLR still has to decide whether the available native code is suitable, and because it needs to be able to substitute JIT compiled code where appropriate, it must add a level of indirection that Native AOT can avoid. So Native AOT applications typically have faster startup times even than R2R applications. This can make Native AOT a good choice in cloud environments that provision execution environments dynamically—systems such as AWS Lambda or Azure Functions might wait until a network request comes into a service before actually loading your code into memory and may shut it down after only a very short period of inactivity, and in these cases, startup time can have a particularly significant effect on average performance.

Loading Assemblies

You may have been alarmed earlier when I said that the build system automatically adds references to all the runtime library components available on your target framework. Perhaps you wondered how you might go about removing some of these in the name of efficiency. As far as runtime overhead is concerned, you do not need to worry. The C# compiler effectively ignores any references to built-in assemblies that your project never uses, so there's no danger of loading DLLs that you don't need. (If you're not using trimming, however, it's worth avoiding references to unused components that are *not* built into .NET to avoid copying unneeded DLLs when you deploy the app—there's no sense in making deployments larger than they need to be. So you shouldn't add references to NuGet packages that you're not using. But unused references to DLLs that are already installed as part of .NET cost you nothing.)

Even if C# didn't strip out unused references at compile time, there would still be no risk of unnecessary loading of unused DLLs. The CLR does not attempt to load assemblies until your application first needs them. Most applications do not exercise every possible code path each time they execute, so it's fairly common for significant portions of the code in your application not to run. Your program might finish its work having left entire classes unused—perhaps classes that get involved only when an unusual error condition arises. If the only place you use a particular assembly is inside a method of such a class, that assembly won't get loaded.

 Native AOT works differently because it produces a single executable file containing not just your application's code, but also all of the code it uses from libraries. We don't deploy assemblies when using Native AOT, so the assembly loading mechanisms described in this section don't apply. Instead, it just relies on the usual operating system mechanisms for demand-loading of code.

The CLR has some discretion for deciding exactly what it means to "use" a particular assembly. If a method contains any code that refers to a particular type (e.g., it declares a variable of that type or it contains expressions that use the type implicitly), then the CLR may consider that type to be used when that method first runs even if you don't get to the part that really uses it. Consider Example 12-5.

Example 12-5. Type loading and conditional execution

```
static IComparer<string> GetComparer(bool useStandardOrdering)
{
    if (useStandardOrdering)
```

```
    {
        return StringComparer.CurrentCulture;
    }
    else
    {
        return new MyCustomComparer();
    }
}
```

Depending on its argument, this function returns either an object provided by the runtime libraries' `StringComparer` or a new object of type `MyCustomComparer`. The `StringComparer` type is defined in the same assembly as core types such as `int` and `string`, so that will have been loaded when our program started. But suppose the other type, `MyCustomComparer`, was defined in a separate assembly from my application, called `ComparerLib`. Obviously, if this `GetComparer` method is called with an argument of `false`, the CLR will need to load `ComparerLib` if it hasn't already. But what's slightly more surprising is that it will probably load `ComparerLib` the first time this method is called even if the argument is `true`. To be able to JIT compile this `GetComparer` method, the CLR will need access to the `MyCustomComparer` type definition—for one thing it will need to check that the type really has a zero-argument constructor. (Obviously Example 12-5 wouldn't compile in that case, but it's possible that code was compiled against a different version of `ComparerLib` than is present at runtime.) The JIT compiler's operation is an implementation detail, so it's not fully documented and could change from one version to the next, but it seems to operate one method at a time. So simply invoking this method is likely to be enough to trigger the loading of the `ComparerLib` assembly.

This raises the question of how .NET finds assemblies. If assemblies can be loaded implicitly as a result of running a method, we don't necessarily have a chance to tell the runtime where to find them. So .NET has a mechanism for this.

Assembly Resolution

When the runtime needs to load an assembly, it goes through a process called *assembly resolution*. In some cases you will tell .NET to load a particular assembly (e.g., when you first run an application), but the majority are loaded implicitly. The exact mechanism depends on whether your application is self-contained.

In a self-contained deployment, assembly resolution is pretty straightforward because everything—your application's own assemblies, any external libraries you depend on, all of the system assemblies built into .NET, and the CLR itself—ends up in one folder. So unless the application directs the CLR to look elsewhere, everything will load from the application folder, including all the .NET runtime library assemblies.

Framework-dependent applications necessarily use a more complex resolution mechanism than self-contained ones. When such an application starts up, it will first determine exactly which version of .NET to run. This won't necessarily be the version your application was built against, and there are various options to configure exactly which is chosen. By default, if the same *Major.Minor* version is available, that will be used. E.g., if a framework-dependent application built for .NET 7.0 runs on a system with .NET versions 6.0.24, 7.0.12, and 8.0.0 installed, it will run on 7.0.12. It is also possible to run on a higher major version number than the app was built against (e.g., build for 7.0 but run on 8.0) but only by explicitly requesting this through configuration. (The build tools automatically produce a file called *YourApp.runtimeconfig.json* in your build output declaring which version you are using, and this file can include settings to enable *roll-forward*.)

The chosen runtime version selects not just the CLR but also the assemblies making up the .NET runtime libraries. You can typically find all the installed runtime versions in the *C:\Program Files\dotnet\shared\Microsoft.NETCore.App* folder on Windows, */usr/local/share/dotnet/shared/Microsoft.NETCore.App* on macOS, or */usr/share/dotnet/shared/Microsoft.NETCore.App* on Linux, with version-based subfolders such as *8.0.0*. (You should not rely on these paths—the files may move in future versions of .NET.) The assembly resolution process will look in this version-specific folder, and this is how framework-dependent applications get to use built-in .NET assemblies.

If you poke around these folders, you may notice other folders under *shared*, such as *Microsoft.AspNetCore.App*. It turns out that the shared component mechanism is not just for the runtime libraries built into .NET—it is also possible to install the assemblies for whole frameworks. .NET applications declare that they are using a particular application framework. (The *YourApp.runtimeconfig.json* file in your build output declares not just the .NET version, but also the framework you are using. Console apps specify Microsoft.NETCore.App, whereas a web application will specify Micro soft.AspNetCore.App, and WPF or Windows Forms apps specify Microsoft.Win dowsDesktop.App. The build tools automatically work out what to put in there based on what's in your project file, so you normally don't need to configure this yourself.) This enables applications that target specific Microsoft frameworks not to have to include a complete copy of all of the framework's DLLs even though that framework is not part of .NET itself.

If you install the plain .NET runtime, you will get just Microsoft.NETCore.App and none of the application frameworks. So applications that target frameworks such as ASP.NET Core or WPF will be unable to run if they are built for framework-dependent deployment (which is the default) because that presumes that those frameworks will be preinstalled on target systems, and the assembly resolution process will fail to find framework-specific components. The .NET SDK installs these additional framework components, so you won't see this problem on your development machine, but you might see it when deploying at runtime. You can tell the build tools to include the framework's components, but this is not normally necessary. If you run your application on a public cloud service such as Azure, these generally preinstall relevant framework components, so in practice you will usually only run into this situation if you are configuring a server yourself or when deploying desktop applications. For those cases, Microsoft offers installers for the .NET runtime (*https://dotnet.microsoft.com*) that also include the components for web or desktop frameworks.

The *shared* folder in the *dotnet* installation folder is not one you should modify yourself. It is intended only for Microsoft's own frameworks. However, it is possible to install additional system-wide components if you want, because .NET also supports something called the *runtime package store*. This is an additional directory structured in much the same way as the *shared* folder just described. You can build a suitable directory layout with the `dotnet store` command, and if you set the `DOTNET_SHARED_STORE` environment variable, the CLR will look in there during assembly resolution. This enables you to play the same trick as is possible with Microsoft's frameworks: you can build applications that depend on a set of components without needing to include them in your build output, as long as you've arranged for those components to be preinstalled on the target system.

Aside from looking in these two locations for common frameworks, the CLR will also look in the application's own directory during assembly resolution, just as it would for a self-contained application. Also, the CLR has some mechanisms for enabling updates to be applied. For example, on Windows, it is possible for Microsoft to push out critical updates to .NET components via Windows Update.

But broadly speaking, the basic process of assembly resolution for framework-dependent applications is that implicit assembly loading occurs either from your application directory or from a shared set of components installed on the system. This is also true for applications running on the older .NET Framework, although the mechanisms are a bit different. It has something called the *Global Assembly Cache* (GAC), which effectively combines the functionality provided by both of the shared stores in .NET. It is less flexible, because the store location is fixed; .NET's use of an environment variable opens up the possibility of different shared stores for different applications.

Explicit Loading

Although the CLR will load assemblies automatically, you can also load them explicitly. For example, if you are creating an application that supports plug-ins, during development you will not know exactly what components you will load at runtime. The whole point of a plug-in system is that it's extensible, so you'd probably want to load all the DLLs in a particular folder. (You would need to use reflection to discover and make use of the types in those DLLs, as Chapter 13 describes.)

 Native AOT has no JIT compiler, so you can use only those assemblies that were compiled to native code during the build. Some of the APIs discussed in this section will work, but only for assemblies your project depends on in the conventional way, and only if trimming hasn't discarded the relevant code. This doesn't support scenarios that need truly dynamic loading, such as plug-in systems.

If you know the full path of an assembly, loading it is very straightforward: you call the `Assembly` class's static `LoadFrom` method, passing the path of the file. (This method is completely unsupported in Native AOT.) The path can be relative to the current directory, or it can be absolute. This static method returns an instance of the `Assembly` class, which is part of the reflection API. It provides ways of discovering and using the types defined by the assembly.

Occasionally, you might want to load a component explicitly (e.g., to use it via reflection) without wanting to specify the path. For example, you might want to load a particular assembly from the runtime libraries. You should never hardcode the location for a system component—they tend to move from one version of .NET to the next. If your project has a reference to the relevant assembly and you know the name of a type it defines, you can write `typeof(TheType).Assembly`. But if that's not an option, you should use the `Assembly.Load` method, passing the name of the assembly.

`Assembly.Load` uses exactly the same mechanism as implicitly triggered loading. So you can refer to either a component that you've installed alongside your application or a system component. In either case, you should specify a full name (see "Assembly Names" on page 605) e.g., `ComparerLib, Version=1.0.0.0, Culture=neutral, PublicKeyToken=null`.

 If you've enabled trimming, this approach might not work if you use a particular type only through dynamic loading and reflection, because the trimmer might not understand that you are using a particular type.

The .NET Framework version of the CLR remembers which assemblies were loaded with `LoadFrom`. If an assembly loaded in this way triggers the implicit loading of further assemblies, the CLR will search the location from which that assembly was loaded. This means that if your application keeps plug-ins in a separate folder that the CLR would not normally look in, those plug-ins could install other components that they depend on in that same plug-in folder. The CLR will then find them without needing further calls to `LoadFrom`, even though it would not normally have looked in that folder for an implicitly triggered load. However, .NET does not support this behavior. It provides a different mechanism to support plug-in scenarios.

Isolation and Plug-ins with AssemblyLoadContext

.NET provides a type called `AssemblyLoadContext`. It enables a degree of isolation between groups of assemblies within a single application.[5] This solves a problem that can arise in applications that support a plug-in model.

If a plug-in depends on some component that the hosting application also uses, but wants a different version than the host, this can cause problems if you use the simple mechanisms described in the preceding section. Typically, the .NET runtime *unifies* these references, meaning that it loads just a single version. In any cases where the types in that shared component are part of the plug-in interface, this is exactly what you need: if an application requires plug-ins to implement some interface that relies on types from, say, the `Newtonsoft.Json` library, it's important that the application and the plug-ins all agree on which version of that library is in use.

But unification can cause problems with components used as implementation details, and not as part of the API between the application and its plug-ins. If the host application uses, say, v6.0 of `Microsoft.Extensions.Logging` internally, and a plug-in uses v8.0 of the same component, there's no particular need to unify this to a single version choice at runtime—there would be no harm in the application and plug-in each using the version they require. Unification could cause problems: forcing the plug-in to use v6.0 would cause exceptions at runtime if it attempted to use features only present in v8.0. Forcing the application to use v8.0 could also cause problems because major version number changes often imply that a breaking change was introduced.

To avoid these kinds of problems, you can introduce custom assembly load contexts. You can write a class that derives from `AssemblyLoadContext`, and for each of these that you instantiate, the .NET runtime creates a corresponding load context that supports loading of different versions of assemblies than may already have been loaded by the application. You can define the exact policy you require by overloading the `Load` method, as Example 12-6 shows.

Example 12-6. A custom `AssemblyLoadContext` for plug-ins

```
using System.Reflection;
using System.Runtime.Loader;
```

---

5 This is not available in .NET Framework or .NET Standard. Isolation was typically managed with *appdomains* on .NET Framework, an older mechanism that is not supported in .NET.

```
namespace HostApp;

public class PlugInLoadContext(
    string pluginPath,
    ICollection<string> plugInApiAssemblyNames) : AssemblyLoadContext
{
    private readonly AssemblyDependencyResolver _resolver = new(pluginPath);
    private readonly ICollection<string> _plugInApiAssemblyNames =
        plugInApiAssemblyNames;

    protected override Assembly Load(AssemblyName assemblyName)
    {
        if (!_plugInApiAssemblyNames.Contains(assemblyName.Name!))
        {
            string? assemblyPath = _resolver.ResolveAssemblyToPath(assemblyName);
            if (assemblyPath != null)
            {
                return LoadFromAssemblyPath(assemblyPath);
            }
        }

        return AssemblyLoadContext.Default.LoadFromAssemblyName(
            assemblyName);
    }
}
```

This takes the location of the plug-in DLL, along with a list of the names of any special assemblies where the plug-in must use the same version as the host application. (This would include assemblies defining types used in your plug-in interface. You don't need to include assemblies that are part of .NET itself—these are always unified, even if you use custom load contexts.) The runtime will call this class's Load method each time an assembly is loaded in this context. This code checks to see whether the assembly being loaded is one of the special ones that must be common to plug-ins and the host application. If not, this looks in the plug-in's folder to see if the plug-in has supplied its own version of that assembly. In cases where it will not use an assembly from the plug-in folder (either because the plug-in hasn't supplied this particular assembly or because it is one of the special ones), this context defers to AssemblyLoad Context.Default, meaning that the application host and plug-in use the same assemblies in these cases. Example 12-7 shows this in use.

Example 12-7. Using the plug-in load context

```
Assembly[] plugInApiAssemblies =
[
    typeof(IPlugIn).Assembly,
    typeof(JsonReader).Assembly
];
var plugInAssemblyNames = new HashSet<string>(
```

```
    plugInApiAssemblies.Select(a => a.GetName().Name!));

var ctx = new PlugInLoadContext(plugInDllPath, plugInAssemblyNames);
Assembly plugInAssembly = ctx.LoadFromAssemblyPath(plugInDllPath);
```

This builds a list of assemblies that the plug-in and application must share, and passes their names into the plug-in context, along with a path to the plug-in DLL. Any DLLs that the plug-in depends on and that are copied into the same folder as the plug-in will be loaded, unless they are in that list, in which case the plug-in will use the same assembly as the host application itself.

Assembly Names

Assembly names are structured. They always include a *simple name*, which is the name by which you would normally refer to the DLL, such as *MyLibrary* or *System.Runtime*. This is usually the same as the filename but without the extension. It doesn't technically have to be,[6] but the assembly resolution mechanism assumes that it is. Assembly names always include a version number. There are also some optional components, including the *public key token*, a string of hexadecimal digits, which makes it possible to give an assembly a unique name.

Strong Names

If an assembly's name includes a public key token, it is said to be a *strong name*. Microsoft advises that any .NET component that targets .NET Framework and is published for shared use (e.g., made available via NuGet) should have a strong name. However, if you are writing a new component that will only run on .NET, there are no benefits to strong naming, because these newer runtimes never validate the public key token.

Since the purpose of strong naming is to make the name unique, you may be wondering why assemblies do not simply use a Globally Unique Identifier (GUID). The answer is that historically, strong names also did another job: they were designed to provide some degree of assurance that the assembly has not been tampered with. Early versions of .NET checked strongly named assemblies for tampering at runtime, but these checks were removed because they imposed a considerable runtime overhead, often for little or no benefit. Microsoft's documentation now explicitly advises against treating strong names as a security feature. However, in order to understand and use strong names, you need to know how they were originally meant to work.

As the terminology suggests, an assembly name's public key token has a connection with cryptography. It is the hexadecimal representation of a 64-bit hash of a public

---

6 If you use `Assembly.LoadFrom`, the CLR does not care whether the filename matches the simple name.

key. Strongly named assemblies are required to contain a copy of the full public key from which the hash was generated. The assembly file format also provides space for a digital signature, generated with the corresponding private key.

Asymmetric Encryption

If you're not familiar with asymmetric encryption, this is not the place for a thorough introduction, but here's a very rough summary. Strong names use an encryption algorithm called RSA, which works with a pair of keys: the public key and the private key. Messages encrypted with the public key can be decrypted only with the private key, and vice versa. This enables the creation of a digital signature for an assembly: to sign an assembly, you calculate a hash of its contents and then encrypt that hash with the private key. This signature is then copied into the assembly, and its validity can be verified by anyone with access to the public key—they can calculate the hash of the assembly's contents themselves, and they can decrypt your signature with the public key, and if the results are different, the signature is invalid, implying either that it was not produced by the owner of the private key or that the file has been modified since the signature was generated, so the file is suspect. The mathematics of encryption are such that it is thought to be essentially impossible to create a valid-looking signature unless you have access to the private key, and it's also essentially impossible to modify the assembly without modifying the hash. And in cryptography, "essentially impossible" means "theoretically possible but too computationally expensive to be practical, unless some major unexpected breakthrough in number theory or perhaps quantum computing emerges, rendering most current cryptosystems useless."

The uniqueness of a strong name relies on the fact that key generation systems use cryptographically secure random-number generators, and the chances of two people generating two key pairs with the same public key token are vanishingly small. The assurance that the assembly has not been tampered with comes from the fact that a strongly named assembly must be signed, and only someone in possession of the private key can generate a valid signature. Any attempt to modify the assembly after signing it will invalidate the signature.

The signature associated with a strong name is independent of Authenticode, a longer-established code signing mechanism in Windows. These serve different purposes. Authenticode provides traceability, because the public key is wrapped in a certificate that tells you something about where the code came from. With a strong name's public key token, all you get is a number, so unless you happen to know who owns that token, it tells you nothing. Authenticode lets you ask, "Where did this component come from?" A public key token lets you say, "This is the component I want." It's common for a single .NET component to use both mechanisms.

If an assembly's private key becomes public knowledge, anyone can generate valid-looking assemblies with the corresponding key token. Some open source projects deliberately publish both keys so that anyone can build the components from source. This completely abandons any security the key token could offer, but that's fine because Microsoft now recommends that we not treat strong names as a security feature. The practice of publishing your strong naming private key recognizes that it is useful to have a unique name, even without a guarantee of authenticity. .NET took this one step further, by making it possible for components to have a strong name without needing to use a private key at all. In keeping with Microsoft's adoption of open source development, this means you can now build and use your own versions of Microsoft-authored components that have the same strong name, even though Microsoft has not published its private key. See the sidebar, "Strong Name Keys and Public Signing," for information on how to work with keys.

Strong Name Keys and Public Signing

There are three popular approaches for working with strong names. The simplest is to use the real names throughout the development process and to copy the public and private keys to all developers' machines so that they can sign the assemblies every time they build. This approach is viable only if you don't want to keep the private key secret, because it's easy for developers to compromise the secrecy of the private key either accidentally or deliberately. Since strong names no longer offer security, there's nothing wrong with this. Some organizations nonetheless attempt to keep their private keys secret as a matter of policy, so you may encounter other ways of working.

Another approach is to use a completely different set of keys during development, switching to the real name only for designated release builds. This avoids the need for all developers to have a copy of the real private key, but it can cause confusion, because developers may end up with two sets of components on their machines, one with development names and one with real names.

The third approach is to use the real names across the board, but instead of signing every build, just filling the part of the file reserved for the signature with 0 values. .NET calls this *Public Signing*, and it's more of a convention than a feature: it works because these runtimes never check the signatures of strongly named assemblies. (.NET Framework does still check signatures in certain cases. For example, to install an assembly in the GAC, it must have a strong name with a valid signature. It has a slightly more complex mechanism called *Delay Signing*, which makes you jump through a few more hoops, but the effect is the same: developers can compile assemblies that have the real strong names without then needing to generate signatures.)

You can generate a key file for a strong name with a command-line utility called *sn* (short for *strong name*).

Microsoft uses the same token on most of the assemblies in the runtime libraries. (Many groups at Microsoft produce .NET components, so this token is common only to the components that are part of .NET, not for Microsoft as a whole.) Here's the full name of mscorlib, a system assembly that offers definitions of various core types such as System.String:

```
mscorlib, Version=4.0.0.0, Culture=neutral, PublicKeyToken=b77a5c561934e089
```

By the way, that's the right name even for the latest versions of .NET at the time of writing. The Version is 4.0.0.0 even though .NET Framework is now on v4.8.1, and .NET on 8.0. (In .NET, mscorlib contains nothing but type forwarders, because the relevant types have moved, mostly to System.Private.CoreLib. And while that real home of these types is now on version 8.0.0.0, the mscorlib version number remains the same.) Assembly version numbers have technical significance, so Microsoft does not always update the version number in the names of library components in step with the marketing version numbers.

While the public key token is an optional part of an assembly's name, the version is mandatory.

Version

All assembly names include a four-part version number. When an assembly name is represented as a string (e.g., when you pass one as an argument to Assembly.Load), the version consists of four decimal integers separated by dots (e.g., 4.0.0.0). The binary format that IL uses for assembly names and references limits the range of these numbers—each part must fit in a 16-bit unsigned integer (a ushort), and the highest allowable value in a version part is actually one less than the maximum value that would fit, making the highest legal version number 65534.65534.65534.65534.

Each of the four parts has a name. From left to right, they are the *major version*, the *minor version*, the *build*, and the *revision*. However, there's no particular significance to any of these names. Some developers use certain conventions, but nothing checks or enforces them. A common convention is that any change in the public API requires a change to either the major or minor version number, and a change likely to break existing code should involve a change of the major number. (Marketing is another popular reason for a major version change.) If an update is not intended to make any visible changes to behavior (except, perhaps, fixing a bug), changing the build number is sufficient. The revision number could be used to distinguish between two components that you believe were built against the same source but not at the same time. Alternatively, some people relate the version numbers to branches in source control, so a change in just the revision number might indicate a patch applied to a version that has long since stopped getting major updates. However, you're free to make up your own meanings. As far as the CLR is concerned, there's really only one interesting thing you can do with a version number, which is to compare it with some other version number—either they match or one is higher than the other.

 NuGet packages also have version numbers, and these do not need to be connected in any way to assembly versions. Many package authors make them similar by convention, but this is not universal. NuGet *does* treat the components of a package version number as having particular significance: it has adopted the widely used *semantic versioning* rules. This uses versions with three parts, named major, minor, and patch.

Version numbers in runtime library assembly names ignore all the conventions I have just described. Most of the components had the same version number (2.0.0.0) across four major updates. With .NET 4.0, everything changed to 4.0.0.0, which is still in use with the latest version of .NET Framework (4.8). In .NET 8.0, many of these components now have a matching major version of 8, but as you've seen with its copy of mscorlib, that's not universal.

You typically specify the version number by adding a <Version> element inside a <PropertyGroup> of your *.csproj* file. (Visual Studio also offers a UI for this: if you open the Properties page for the project, its Package section lets you configure various naming-related settings. The "Package version" field sets the version.) The build system uses this in two ways: it sets the version number on the assembly, but, if you generate a NuGet package for your project, by default it will also use this same version number for the package, and since NuGet version numbers have three parts, you normally specify just three numbers here, and the fourth part of the assembly version will default to zero. (If you really want to specify all four digits, consult the documentation for how to set the assembly and NuGet versions separately.)

The build system tells the compiler which version number to use for the assembly name via an assembly-level attribute. I'll describe attributes in more detail in Chapter 14, but this one's pretty straightforward. If you want to find it, the build system typically generates a file called *ProjectName.AssemblyInfo.cs* in a subfolder of your project's *obj* folder. This contains various attributes describing details about the assembly, including an AssemblyVersion attribute, such as the one shown in Example 12-8.

Example 12-8. Specifying an assembly's version

```
[assembly: System.Reflection.AssemblyVersion("1.0.0.0")]
```

The C# compiler provides special handling for this attribute—it does not apply it blindly as it would most attributes. It parses the version number and embeds it in the way required by .NET's metadata format. It also checks that the string conforms to the expected format and that the numbers are in the allowed range.

By the way, the version that forms part of an assembly's name is distinct from the one stored using the standard Win32 mechanism for embedding versions. Most .NET files contain both kinds. By default, the build system will use the `<Version>` setting for both, but it's common for the file version to change more frequently. This was particularly important with .NET Framework, in which only a single instance of any major version can be installed at once—if a system has .NET Framework 4.7.2 installed and you install .NET Framework 4.8.1, that will replace version 4.7.2. (.NET doesn't do this—you can install any number of versions side by side on a single computer.) This in-place updating combined with Microsoft's tendency to keep assembly versions the same across releases could make it hard to work out exactly what is installed, at which point the file version becomes important. On a computer with .NET Framework 4.0 sp1 installed, its version of *mscorlib.dll* had a Win32 version number of `4.0.30319.239`. If you've installed .NET 4.8.1, this changes to `4.8.9181.0`, but the assembly version remains at `4.0.0.0`. (As service packs and other updates are released, the file version will keep climbing.)

By default, the build system will use the `<Version>` for both the assembly and Windows file versions, but if you want to set the file version separately, you can add a `<FileVersion>` to your project file. (Visual Studio's project properties Package section also lets you set this.) Under the covers, this works with another attribute that gets special handling from the compiler, `AssemblyFileVersion`. It causes the compiler to embed a Win32 version resource in the file, so this is the version number users see if they right-click your assembly in Windows Explorer and show the file properties.

This file version is usually a more appropriate place to put a version number that identifies the build provenance than the version that goes into the assembly name. The latter is really a declaration of the supported API version, and any updates that are designed to be fully backward compatible should probably leave it unaltered and should change only the file version.

Version Numbers and Assembly Loading

Since version numbers are part of an assembly's name (and therefore its identity), they are also, ultimately, part of a type's identity. The `System.String` in `mscorlib` version `2.0.0.0` is not the same thing as the type of the same name in `mscorlib` version `4.0.0.0`.

The handling of assembly version numbers changed with .NET. In .NET Framework, when you load a strongly named assembly by name (either implicitly by using types it defines or explicitly with `Assembly.Load`), the CLR requires the version number to be an exact match.[7] .NET relaxed this, so if the version on disk has a version number equal to or higher than the version requested, it will use it. There are two factors behind this change. The first is that the .NET development ecosystem has come to rely on NuGet (which didn't even exist for most of the first decade of .NET's existence), meaning that it has become increasingly common to depend on fairly large numbers of external components. Second, the rate of change has increased—in the early days we would often need to wait for years between new releases of .NET components. (Security patches and other bug fixes might turn up more often, but new functionality would tend to emerge slowly, and typically in big chunks, as part of a whole wave of updates to the runtime, frameworks, and development tools.) But today, it can be rare for an application to go for as long as a month without the version of some component somewhere changing. .NET Framework's strict versioning policy now looks unhelpful. (In fact, there are parts of the build system dedicated to digging through your NuGet dependencies, working out the specific versions of each component you're using, and picking the best version to use when different components want different versions of some shared component. When you target .NET Framework, by default it will automatically generate a configuration file with a vast number of version substitution rules telling the CLR to use those versions no matter which version any single assembly says it wants. So even if you target the .NET Framework, the build system will, by default, effectively disable strict versioning.)

Another change is that .NET Framework only takes assembly versions into account for strongly named assemblies. .NET checks that the version number of the assembly on disk is equal to or greater than the required version regardless of whether the target assembly is strongly named.

Culture

So far we've seen that assembly names include a simple name, a version number, and optionally a public key token. They also have a *culture* component. (A culture represents a language and a set of conventions, such as currency, spelling variations, and date formats.) This is not optional, although the most common value for this is the default: neutral, indicating that the assembly contains no culture-specific code or data. The culture is usually set to something else only on assemblies that contain culture-specific resources. The culture of an assembly's name is designed to support localization of resources such as images and strings. To show how, I'll need to explain the localization mechanism that uses it.

All assemblies can contain embedded binary streams. (You can put text in these streams, of course. You just have to pick a suitable encoding.) The Assembly class in

---

7 It's possible to configure the CLR to substitute a specific different version, but even then, the loaded assembly has to have the exact version specified by the configuration.

the reflection API provides a way to work directly with these, but it's more common to use the `ResourceManager` class in the `System.Resources` namespace. This is far more convenient than working with the raw binary streams, because the `ResourceManager` defines a container format that allows a single stream to hold any number of strings, images, sound files, and other binary items, and Visual Studio has a built-in editor for working with this container format. The reason I'm mentioning all of this in the middle of a section that's ostensibly about assembly names is that `ResourceManager` also provides localization support, and the assembly name's culture is part of that mechanism. To demonstrate how this works, I'll walk you through a quick example.

The easiest way to use the `ResourceManager` is to add a resource file in the *.resx* format to your project. (This is not the format used at runtime. It's an XML format that gets compiled into the binary format required by `ResourceManager`. It's easier to work with text than binary in most source control systems. It also makes it possible to work with these files if you're using an editor without built-in support for the format.) To add one of these from Visual Studio's Add New Item dialog, select the Visual C#→General category, and then choose Resources File. I'll call mine *MyResources.resx*. Visual Studio will show its resource editor, which opens in string editing mode, as Figure 12-1 shows. As you can see, I've defined a single string with a name of `ColString` and a value of `Color`.

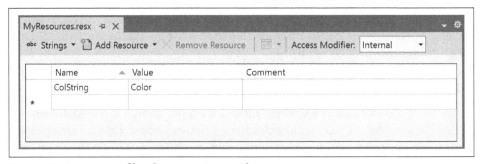

Figure 12-1. Resource file editor in string mode

I can retrieve this value at runtime. The build system generates a wrapper class for each *.resx* file you add, with a static property for each resource you define. This makes it very easy to look up a string resource, as Example 12-9 shows.

Example 12-9. Retrieving a resource with the wrapper class

```
string colText = MyResources.ColString;
```

The wrapper class hides the details, which is usually convenient, but in this case, the details are the whole reason I'm demonstrating a resource file, so I've shown how to use the `ResourceManager` directly in Example 12-10. I've included the entire source for the file, because namespaces are significant here—the build tools prepend your project's default namespace to the embedded resource stream name, so I've had to ask for `ResourceExample.MyResources` instead of just `MyResources`. (If I had put the resources in a subfolder, the tools would also include the name of that folder in the resource stream name.)

Example 12-10. Retrieving a resource at runtime

```
using System.Resources;

namespace ResourceExample;

class Program
{
    static void Main()
    {
        var rm = new ResourceManager(
            "ResourceExample.MyResources", typeof(Program).Assembly);
        string colText = rm.GetString("ColString")!;
        Console.WriteLine($"And now in {colText}");
    }
}
```

So far, this is just a rather long-winded way of getting hold of the string `"Color"`. However, now that we've got a `ResourceManager` involved, I can define some localized resources. Being British, I have strong opinions on the correct way to spell the word *color*. They are not consistent with O'Reilly's editorial policy, and in any case I'm happy to adapt my work for my predominantly American readership. But a program can do better—it should be able to provide different spellings for different audiences. (And taking it a step further, it should be able to change the language entirely for countries in which some form of English is not the predominant language.) In fact, my program already contains all the code it needs to support localized spellings of the word *color*. I just need to provide it with the alternative text.

I can do this by adding a second resource file with a carefully chosen name: *MyResources.en-GB.resx*. That's almost the same as the original but with an extra *.en-GB* before the *.resx* extension. That is short for English-Great Britain, and it is the standardized (albeit politically tone-deaf) name of the culture for my home. (The name for the culture that denotes English-speaking parts of the US is *en-US*.) Having added such a file to my project, I can add a string entry with the same name as before, `ColString`, but this time with the correct (where I'm sitting[8]) value of `Colour`. If you run the application on a system configured with a British locale, it will use the British spelling. The odds are that your machine is not configured for this locale, so if you want to try this, you can add the code in Example 12-11 at the very start of the `Main` method in Example 12-10 to force .NET to use the British culture when looking up resources.

Example 12-11. Forcing a nondefault culture

```
Thread.CurrentThread.CurrentUICulture =
    new System.Globalization.CultureInfo("en-GB");
```

How does this relate to assemblies? Well, if you look at the compiled output, you'll see that, as well as the usual executable file and related debug files, the build process has created a subdirectory called *en-GB*, which contains an assembly file called *Resource Example.resources.dll*. (*ResourceExample* is the name of my project. If you created a project called *SomethingElse*, you'd see *SomethingElse.resources.dll*.) That assembly's name will look like this:

```
ResourceExample.resources, Version=1.0.0.0, Culture=en-GB, PublicKeyToken=null
```

The version number and public key token will match those for the main project—in my example, I've left the default version number, and I've not given my assembly a strong name. But notice the `Culture`. Instead of the usual `neutral` value, I've got `en-GB`, the same culture string I specified in the filename for the second resource file I added. If you add more resource files with other culture names, you'll get a folder containing a culture-specific assembly for each culture you specify. These are called *satellite resource assemblies*.

When you first ask a `ResourceManager` for a resource, it will look for a satellite resource assembly with the same culture as the thread's current UI culture. So it would attempt to load an assembly using the name shown a couple of paragraphs ago. If it doesn't find that, it tries a more generic culture name—if it fails to find `en-GB` resources, it will look for a culture called just `en`, denoting the English language without specifying any particular region. Only if it finds neither (or if it finds matching assemblies, but they do not contain the resource being looked up) does it fall back to the neutral resource built into the main assembly.

The CLR's assembly loader looks in different places when a nonneutral culture is specified. It looks in a subdirectory named for the culture. That's why the build process placed my satellite resource assembly in an *en-GB* folder.

---

8 Hove, England.

Since this localization mechanism depends on loading a culture-specific assembly at runtime you might expect this not to work on Native AOT. In fact, .NET makes special provisions to support this localization mechanism on Native AOT, although this is disabled by default because it adds runtime overheads: the `InvariantGlobalization` build variable defaults to `true` for Native AOT projects, so you'll need to set this to `false` in your project file to use `ResourceManager` for localization.

The search for culture-specific resources incurs some runtime costs. These are not large, but if you're writing an application that will never be localized, you might want to avoid paying the price for a feature you're not using. As just mentioned it's disabled by default for Native AOT, but you can use that same setting to disable it in any .NET application. More subtly, if the majority of your users are in one particular locale, you can embed the resources for one particular culture directly into your main assembly, avoiding the need to load a satellite assembly but still supporting localization in other regions. You do this by putting those resources not in a culture-specific file such as *MyResources.en-US.resx*, but in a file with no culture name, such as *MyResources.resx*. You can then indicate that these are in fact the right resources for a particular locale by applying the assembly-level attribute shown in Example 12-12.

Example 12-12. Specifying the culture for built-in resources

```
[assembly: NeutralResourcesLanguage("en-US")]
```

When an application with that attribute runs on a system in the usual US locale, the `ResourceManager` will not attempt to search for resources. It will just go straight for the ones compiled into your main. assembly

Protection

In Chapter 3, I described some of the accessibility specifiers you can apply to types and their members, such as `private` or `public`. In Chapter 6, I showed some of the additional mechanisms available when you use inheritance. It's worth quickly revisiting these features, because assemblies play a part.

Also in Chapter 3, I introduced the `internal` keyword and said that classes and methods with this accessibility are available only within the same *component*, a slightly vague term that I chose because I had not yet introduced assemblies. Now that it's clear what an assembly is, it's safe for me to say that a more precise description of the `internal` keyword is that it indicates that a member or type should be accessible only to code in the same assembly.[9] Likewise, `protected internal` members are available to code in derived types, and also to code defined in the same assembly, and the similar but more restrictive `protected private` protection level makes members available only to code that is in a derived type that is defined in the same assembly.

Target Frameworks and .NET Standard

One of the decisions you need to make for each assembly that you build is the target framework or frameworks you will support. Each *.csproj* file will have either a `<Tar getFramework>` element indicating the target or a `<TargetFrameworks>` element containing a list of frameworks. The particular target is indicated with a *target framework moniker* (TFM). For example, `net6.0`, `net7.0`, and `net8.0` represent .NET 6.0, .NET 7.0, and .NET 8.0, respectively. For the .NET Framework 4.6.2, 4.7.2, and 4.8, the TFMs are `net462`, `net472`, and `net48`, respectively. When you list multiple target frameworks, you will get multiple assemblies when you build, each in its own subfolder named for the TFM. The SDK effectively builds the project multiple times.

If you need access to some OS-specific functionality, there are OS-specific variants of .NET TFMs, such as `net8.0-ios` or `net8.0-windows`. (.NET Framework is inherently Windows-only.) You can incorporate an OS version number too: `net8.0-windows10.0.22621` indicates that you will be using API features introduced in Windows SDK 10.0.22621, meaning that your application can use functionality introduced in Windows 11. This doesn't mean that your component absolutely requires that version or later. It's possible to detect that you're on an older version of Windows and gracefully downgrade functionality appropriately. The OS version in the TFM determines only which APIs you can *attempt* to use.

If you need to provide different code for each target platform (perhaps because you can only implement certain functionality on newer target versions), you might need to use conditional compilation (described in "Compilation Symbols" on page 56). But in cases where the same code works for all targets, it might make sense to build for a single target, .NET Standard. As I described in Chapter 1, the various versions of .NET Standard define common subsets of the .NET runtime libraries that are available across multiple versions of .NET. I said that if you need to target both .NET and .NET Framework, the best choice today is typically .NET Standard 2.0 (which has a TFM of `netstandard2.0`). However, it's worth being aware of the other options, particularly if you're looking to make your component available to the widest possible audience.

---

9 Internal items are also available to *friend assemblies*, meaning any assemblies referred to with an `InternalsVisibleTo` attribute, as described in Chapter 14.

.NET libraries published on NuGet may decide to target the lowest version of .NET Standard that they can if they want to ensure the broadest reach. Versions 1.1 through 1.6 gradually added more functionality in exchange for supporting a smaller range of targets. (For example, if you want to use a .NET Standard 1.3 component on .NET Framework, it needs to be .NET Framework 4.6 or later; targeting .NET Standard 1.4 requires .NET Framework 4.6.1 or later.) .NET Standard 2.0 was a larger leap forward and marked an important point in .NET Standard's evolution: according to Microsoft's current plans, this will be the highest version number able to run on .NET Framework. Versions of .NET Framework from 4.7.2 onward fully support it, but .NET Standard 2.1 will not run on any version of .NET Framework now or in the future. It will run on all supported versions of .NET. Mono v6.4 and later support it too. But this is the end of the road for the classic .NET Framework. In practice, .NET Standard 2.0 is currently a popular choice with component authors because it enables the component to run on all recently released versions of .NET while providing access to a very broad set of features.

All of this has caused a certain amount of confusion, and you might be pleased to know that newer versions of .NET simplify things. If you don't need to support .NET Framework, you can just target .NET 6.0 or later, ignoring .NET Standard. Mono and Native AOT can run components that target .NET 6.0, so targeting .NET 6.0 will cover most runtimes. You can target later versions of .NET such as 8.0 of course; the significance of .NET 6.0 is that it was the first .NET version with long-term support in which a single target framework was available on the mobile device targets that Mono supports as well as Windows, Linux, and macOS. (Components that target .NET 6.0 run just fine on .NET 8.0 by the way. And that will continue to be true even after .NET 6.0 is out of support: as long as you're using a supported .NET runtime, it doesn't matter if your application includes components specifying a target framework that is now out of support. .NET 8.0 can happily load any component that targets any version in the .NET lineage all the way back to .NET Core 1.0.)

What does this all mean for C# developers? If you are writing code that will never be used outside of a particular project, you will normally just target the latest version of .NET. You will be able to use any NuGet package that targets .NET Standard, up to and including v2.1, and also any package that targets any version of .NET (which means the overwhelming majority of what's on NuGet will be available to you).

If you are writing libraries that you intend to share, and if you want your components to be available to the largest audience possible, you should target .NET Standard unless you absolutely need some feature that is only available in a particular runtime. .NET Standard 2.0 is a reasonable choice—you could open your library up to a wider audience by dropping to a lower version, but today, the versions of .NET that support .NET Standard 2.0 are widely available, so you would only contemplate targeting older versions if you need to support developers still using older .NET Frameworks. (Microsoft does this in most of its NuGet libraries, but you don't necessarily have to tie yourself to the same regime of support for older versions.) Microsoft provides a useful guide to which versions of the various .NET implementations support the various .NET Standard versions (*https://oreil.ly/ok1ay*). If you want to use certain newer features (such as the memory-efficient types described in Chapter 18), you may need to target a more recent version of .NET Standard, with 2.1 being the latest at the time of writing, but be aware that this rules out running on .NET Framework. At that point, you might as well just target .NET 6.0 or a later version of .NET, because .NET Standard has little to offer in the unified post-.NET-Framework world. In any case, the development tools will ensure that you only use APIs available in whichever version of .NET or .NET Standard you declare support for.

Summary

An assembly is a deployable unit, almost always a single file, typically with a *.dll* or *.exe* extension. It is a container for types and code, and may also embed binary resource streams. A type belongs to exactly one assembly, and that assembly forms part of the type's identity—the .NET runtime can distinguish between two types with the same name in the same namespace if they are defined in different assemblies. Assemblies have a composite name consisting of a simple textual name, a four-part version number, a culture string, and optionally a public key token. Assemblies with a public key token are called strongly named assemblies, giving them a globally unique name. Assemblies can either be deployed alongside the application that uses them or stored in a system-wide repository. (In .NET Framework, that repository is the Global Assembly Cache, and assemblies must be strongly named to use this. .NET provides shared copies of built-in assemblies, and depending on how you install these newer runtimes, they may also have shared copies of frameworks such as ASP.NET Core and WPF. And you can optionally set up a separate runtime package store containing other shared assemblies to avoid having to include them in application folders.)

The runtime can load assemblies automatically on demand, which typically happens the first time you run a method that contains some code that depends on a type defined in the relevant assembly. You can also load assemblies explicitly if you need to.

As I mentioned earlier, every assembly contains comprehensive metadata describing the types it contains. In the next chapter, I'll show how you can get access to this metadata at runtime.

CHAPTER 13
Reflection

The CLR knows a great deal about the types our programs define and use. It requires all assemblies to provide detailed metadata, describing each member of every type, including private implementation details. It relies on this information to perform critical functions, such as JIT compilation and garbage collection. However, it does not keep this knowledge to itself. The *reflection* API grants access to this detailed type information, so your code can discover everything that the runtime can see. Moreover, you can use reflection to make things happen. For example, a reflection object representing a method not only describes the method's name and signature, but it also lets you invoke the method. And you can go further still and generate code at runtime.

Reflection is particularly useful in extensible frameworks, because they can use it to adapt their behavior at runtime based on the structure of your code. For example, Visual Studio's Properties panel uses reflection to discover what public properties a component offers, so if you write a component that can appear on a design surface, such as a UI element, you do not need to do anything special to make its properties available for editing—Visual Studio will find them automatically.

 Many reflection-based frameworks that can automatically discover what they need to know also allow components to enrich that information explicitly. For example, although you don't need to do anything special to support editing in the Properties panel, you can customize the categorization, description, and editing mechanisms if you want to. This is normally achieved with *attributes*, which are the topic of Chapter 14.

As you saw in the preceding chapter, .NET offers some deployment mechanisms that can limit the use of reflection. Trimming a self-contained deployment reduces its size by omitting code that your application does not use. This leaves out unused types entirely, but even with types you do use, individual members will be trimmed if your code doesn't use them directly or indirectly. Trimming removes type information as well as code, so reflection can provide an incomplete picture of a type in a trimmed application. Native AOT takes this further: it will often trim metadata even for members that are in use, retaining only executable code and the most basic information required to make GC work. This helps to reduce the size of the compiled output—if you won't be using reflection for the majority of the code in your project, there's no need to copy that information into the output. (This is possible because Native AOT never performs JIT compilation. Normally, .NET applications include full type information for all untrimmed code regardless of whether it will be used through reflection because the JIT compiler needs it.) In straightforward cases where trim analysis can determine that you will definitely be using reflection against particular members of a particular type, Native AOT will include the necessary metadata, but in general you should assume that reflection-based functionality might encounter limitations if you use Native AOT, and you will need to test carefully. (Be aware that when you enable trimming or Native AOT in a project, trimming occurs only when you ask the .NET SDK to *publish* your application—launching the code directly from the development environment typically doesn't apply either trimming or native code generation. This can make it easy to miss differences in behavior that occur once trimming has been applied.)

If you try to use a .NET runtime library feature that depends on reflection in an application that uses trimming, the compiler will warn you when you use it in a way that might not produce the behavior you wanted. Reflection-based methods in the runtime libraries have annotations that supply the trimmer with information that guides its operation, enabling it to determine either that it will need to include specific members, or that certain methods are essentially incompatible with trimming. In some cases you might need to add similar annotations to your own code to enable the analysis to fully understand your requirements. (The compiler will tell you when this is necessary.) Even then, there are some situations that can defeat this analysis, so you may find that reflection-driven features don't initially work correctly when using trimming or Native AOT. Normally, adding your own annotations will enable you to deal with this. Alternatively, some parts of the runtime library that use reflection by default, such as the JSON serialization features described in Chapter 15, offer reflection-free ways of using the APIs.

Not all .NET libraries have trimming annotations, because trimming is a relatively new feature. If you use a NuGet package that has no such annotations, trimming will have to rely entirely on analyzing the code to work out if and how it's using reflection. This can mean the warnings you get may be less helpful—you might get a warning when there isn't really a problem—or the trimmer may have to be conservative, and trim less code than it could.

Reflection Types

The reflection API defines various classes in the `System.Reflection` namespace. These classes have a structural relationship that mirrors the way that assemblies and the type system work. For example, a type's containing assembly is part of its identity, so the reflection class that represents a type (`Type`[1]) has an `Assembly` property that returns its containing `Assembly` object. And you can navigate this relationship in both directions—you can discover all of the types in an assembly from the `Assembly` class's `DefinedTypes` property. An application that can be extended by loading plug-in DLLs would typically use this to find the types each plug-in provides.

Figure 13-1 shows the reflection types that correspond to .NET types, their members, and the components that contain them. The arrows represent containment relationships. (As with assemblies and types, these are all navigable in both directions.)

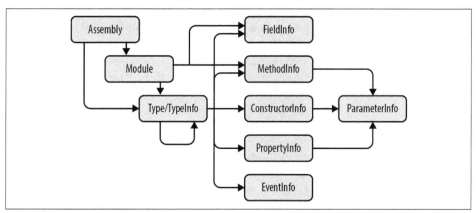

Figure 13-1. Reflection containment hierarchy

Figure 13-2 illustrates the inheritance hierarchy for these types. This shows a couple of extra abstract types, `MemberInfo` and `MethodBase`, which are shared by various reflection classes that have a certain amount in common. For example, constructors and methods both have parameter lists, and the mechanism for inspecting these is provided by their shared base class, `MethodBase`. All members of types have certain common features, such as accessibility, so anything that is (or can be) a member of a type is represented in reflection by an object that derives from `MemberInfo`.

---

1 For historical reasons discussed later, a subset of this functionality is in a derived type called `TypeInfo`. But the base `Type` class is the one you most often encounter.

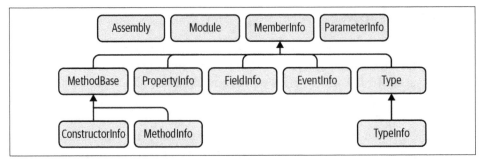

Figure 13-2. Reflection inheritance hierarchy

Assembly

The `Assembly` class represents, predictably enough, a single assembly. If you're writing a plug-in system, or some other sort of framework that needs to load user-supplied DLLs and use them (such as a unit test runner), the `Assembly` type will be your starting point. As Chapter 12 showed, the static `Assembly.Load` method takes an assembly name and returns the object for that assembly. (That method will load the assembly if necessary, but if it has already been loaded, it just returns a reference to the relevant `Assembly` object.) But there are some other ways to get hold of objects of this kind.

The `Assembly` class defines three context-sensitive static methods that each return an `Assembly`. The `GetEntryAssembly` method returns the object representing the EXE file containing your program's `Main` method. The `GetExecutingAssembly` method returns the assembly that contains the method from which you called it. `GetCalling Assembly` walks up the stack by one level and returns the assembly containing the code that called the method that called `GetCallingAssembly`.

> The JIT compiler's optimizations can sometimes produce surprising results with `GetExecutingAssembly` and `GetCallingAssembly`. Method inlining and tail call optimizations can both cause these methods to return the assembly for methods that are one stack frame farther back than you would expect. You can prevent inlining optimizations by annotating a method with the `MethodImpl` `Attribute`, passing the `NoInlining` flag from the `MethodImpl` `Options` enumeration. (Attributes are described in Chapter 14.) There's no way to disable tail call optimizations explicitly, but those will be applied only when a particular method call is the last thing a method does before returning.

`GetCallingAssembly` can be useful in diagnostic logging, because it provides information about the code that called your method. The `GetExecutingAssembly` method is less useful: you presumably already know which assembly the code will be in because you're the developer writing it. It may still be useful to get hold of the Assem bly object for the component you're writing, but there are other ways. The Type object described in the next section provides an Assembly property. Example 13-1 uses that to get the Assembly via the containing class. Empirically, this seems to be faster, which is not entirely surprising because it's doing less work—both techniques need to retrieve reflection objects, but one of them also has to inspect the stack.

Example 13-1. Obtaining your own Assembly via a Type

```
class Program
{
    static void Main()
    {
        Assembly me = typeof(Program).Assembly;
        Console.WriteLine(me.FullName);
    }
}
```

If you want to use an assembly from a specific place on disk, you can use the LoadFrom method described in Chapter 12. Alternatively, you can use the System .Reflection.MetadataLoadContext NuGet package's MetadataLoadContext class. This loads the assembly in such a way that you can inspect its type information, but no code in the assembly will execute, nor will any assemblies it depends on be loaded automatically. This is an appropriate way to load an assembly if you're writing a tool that displays or otherwise processes information about a component but does not want to run its code. There are a few reasons it can be important to avoid loading an assembly in the usual way with such a tool. Loading an assembly and inspecting its types can sometimes trigger the execution of code (such as static constructors) in that assembly. Also, if you load for reflection purposes only, the processor architecture is not significant, so you could load a 32-bit-only DLL into a 64-bit process, or you could inspect an ARM-only assembly in an x86 process.

Having obtained an Assembly from any of the aforementioned mechanisms, you can discover various things about it. The FullName property provides the display name, for example. Or you can call GetName, which returns an AssemblyName object, providing easy programmatic access to all of the components of the assembly's name.

You can retrieve a list of all of the other assemblies on which a particular Assembly depends by calling GetReferencedAssemblies. If you call this on an assembly you've written, it will not necessarily return all of the assemblies you can see in the Dependencies node in Visual Studio's Solution Explorer, because the C# compiler strips out unused references.

Assemblies contain types, so you can find `Type` objects representing those types by calling an `Assembly` object's `GetType` method, passing in the name of the type you require, including its namespace. This will return `null` if the type is not found, unless you call one of the overloads that additionally accept a `bool`—with these, passing `true` produces an exception if the type is not found. There's also an overload that takes two `bool` arguments, the second of which lets you pass `true` to request a case-insensitive search. All of these methods will return either `public` or `internal` types. You can also request a nested type, by specifying the name of the containing type, then a + symbol, then the nested type name. Example 13-2 gets the `Type` object for a type called `Inside` nested inside a type called `ContainingType` in the `MyLib` namespace. This works even if the nested type is private.

Example 13-2. Getting a nested type from an assembly

```
Type? nt = someAssembly.GetType("MyLib.ContainingType+Inside");
```

The `Assembly` class also provides a `DefinedTypes` property that returns a collection containing a `TypeInfo` object for every type (top-level or nested) the assembly defines, and also `ExportedTypes`, which returns only public types, and it returns `Type` objects and not full `TypeInfo` objects. (The distinction is described in "Type and TypeInfo" on page 629.) That will also include any `public` nested types. It will not include `protected` types nested inside `public` types, which is perhaps a bit surprising because such types are accessible from outside the assembly (albeit only to classes that derive from the containing type).

Besides returning types, `Assembly` can also create new instances of them with the `CreateInstance` method. If you pass just the fully qualified name of the type as a string, this will create an instance if the type is public and has a no-arguments constructor. There's an overload that lets you work with nonpublic types and types with constructors that require arguments; however, it is rather more complex to use, because it also takes arguments that specify whether you want a case-insensitive match for the type name, along with a `CultureInfo` object that defines the rules to use for case-insensitive comparisons—different countries have different ideas about how such comparisons work. It also has arguments for controlling more advanced scenarios. However, you can pass `null` for most of these, as Example 13-3 shows.

Example 13-3. Dynamic construction

```
object? o = asm.CreateInstance(
    "MyApp.WithConstructor",
    false,
    BindingFlags.Public | BindingFlags.Instance,
    null,
    ["Constructor argument"],
```

```
null,
null);
```

This creates an instance of a type called `WithConstructor` in the `MyApp` namespace in the assembly to which `asm` refers. The `false` argument indicates that we want an exact match on the name, not a case-insensitive comparison. The `BindingFlags` indicate that we are looking for a public instance constructor. (See the sidebar "Binding Flags.") The first `null` argument is where you could pass a `Binder` object, which allows you to customize the behavior when the arguments you have supplied do not exactly match the types of the required arguments. By leaving this out, I'm indicating that I expect the ones I've supplied to match exactly. (I'll get an exception if they don't.) The array argument contains the list of arguments I'd like to pass to the constructor—a single string, in this case. The penultimate `null` is where I'd pass a culture if I were using either case-insensitive comparisons or automatic conversions between numeric types and strings, but since I'm doing neither, I can leave it out. And the final argument once supported scenarios that have now been deprecated, so it should always be `null`.

BindingFlags

Many of the reflection APIs take an argument of the `BindingFlags` enumeration type to determine which members to return. For example, you can specify `Binding Flags.Public` to indicate that you want only public members or types, or `Binding Flags.NonPublic` to indicate that you want only items that are not public, or you can combine both flags to indicate that you'd like either.

Be aware that it's possible to specify combinations that will return nothing. When working with members, you must include either `BindingFlags.Instance`, `Binding Flags.Static`, or both, for example, because all type members are one or the other (likewise for `BindingFlags.Public` and `BindingFlags.NonPublic`).

Often, methods that can accept `BindingFlags` offer an overload that does not. This typically defaults to specifying public members, both instance and static (i.e., `Binding Flags.Public | BindingFlags.Static | BindingFlags.Instance`).

`BindingFlags` defines numerous options, but not all are applicable in every scenario. For example, it defines a `FlattenHierarchy` value, which is used for reflection APIs that return type members: if this flag is present, members defined by the base class will be considered, as well as those defined by the class specified. This option is not applicable to `Assembly.CreateInstance` because you cannot use a base class constructor directly to construct a derived type.

Module

Figure 13-1 shows `Assembly` as a container of `Module` objects. As Chapter 12 discussed, .NET Framework supports splitting the contents of one assembly across multiple files (*modules*), but this rarely used feature is not supported in .NET. In most cases, you can ignore the `Module` type—you can normally do everything you need with the other types in the reflection API. One exception is that the APIs for generating code at runtime require you to identify which module should contain the generated code, even when you're creating just one module. (.NET's APIs for generating code at runtime are beyond the scope of this book.)

The `Module` class provides one other service: surprisingly, it defines `GetField`, `GetFields`, `GetMethod`, and `GetMethods` properties. These provide access to globally scoped methods and fields. You never see these in C#, because the language requires all fields and methods to be defined within a type, but the CLR allows globally scoped methods and fields, so the reflection API has to be able to present them. These are exposed through `Module`, and not `Assembly`, so even in modern .NET's one-module-per-assembly world, you can only get to them through the `Module` type. You can retrieve that from an `Assembly` object's `Modules` property, or you can use any of the API types described in the following sections that derive from `MemberInfo`. (Figure 13-2 shows which types do so.) This defines a `Module` property that returns the `Module` in which the relevant member is defined.

MemberInfo

Like all the classes I'm describing in this section, `MemberInfo` is abstract. However, unlike the rest, it does not correspond to one particular feature of the type system. It is a shared base class providing common functionality for all of the types that represent items that can be members of other types. So this is the base class of `Constructor Info`, `MethodInfo`, `FieldInfo`, `PropertyInfo`, `EventInfo`, and `Type`, because all of those can be members of other types. In fact, in C#, all except `Type` are *required* to be members of some other type (although, as you just saw in the preceding section, some languages allow methods and fields to be scoped to a module instead of a type).

`MemberInfo` defines common properties required by all type members. There's a `Name` property, of course, and also a `DeclaringType`, which refers to the `Type` object for the item's containing type; this returns `null` for nonnested types and module-scoped methods and fields. `MemberInfo` also defines a `Module` property that refers to the containing module, regardless of whether the item in question is module-scoped or a member of a type.

As well as `DeclaringType`, `MemberInfo` defines a `ReflectedType`, which indicates the type from which the `MemberInfo` was retrieved, which won't always be the declaring type when inheritance is involved. This should be an obscure area of the reflection

API that could mostly be ignored, but unfortunately it has an unhelpful consequence. Example 13-4 shows the problem.

Example 13-4. DeclaringType versus ReflectedType

```
class Base
{
    public void Foo()
    {
    }
}

class Derived : Base
{
}

class Program
{
    static void Main()
    {
        MemberInfo bf = typeof(Base).GetMethod("Foo")!;
        MemberInfo df = typeof(Derived).GetMethod("Foo")!;

        Console.WriteLine("Base    Declaring: {0}, Reflected: {1}",
                          bf.DeclaringType, bf.ReflectedType);
        Console.WriteLine("Derived Declaring: {0}, Reflected: {1}",
                          df.DeclaringType, df.ReflectedType);
        Console.WriteLine("Same:   {0}", bf == df);
    }
}
```

This gets the MethodInfo for the Base.Foo and Derived.Foo methods. (MethodInfo derives from MemberInfo.) These are just different ways of describing the same method—Derived does not define its own Foo, so it inherits the one defined by Base. However, the program produces this output:

```
Base    Declaring: Base, Reflected: Base
Derived Declaring: Base, Reflected: Derived
Same:   False
```

When retrieving the information for Foo via the Base class's Type object, the DeclaringType and ReflectedType are, unsurprisingly, both Base. However, when we retrieve the Foo method's information via the Derived type, the DeclaringType tells us that the method is defined by Base, while the ReflectedType tells us that we obtained this method via the Derived type.

Because a MemberInfo remembers which type you retrieved it from, comparing two MemberInfo objects is not a reliable way to detect whether they refer to the same thing. When Example 13-4 compares bf and df, the result is false despite the fact that they both refer to Base.Foo. If you had been unaware of the ReflectedType property, you might not have expected this behavior.

Slightly surprisingly, MemberInfo does not provide any information about the visibility of the member it describes. This may seem odd, because in C#, all of the constructs that correspond to the types that derive from MemberInfo (such as constructors, methods, or properties) can be prefixed with public, private, etc. The reflection API does make this information available but not through the MemberInfo base class. This is because the CLR handles visibility for certain member types a little differently from how C# presents it. From the CLR's perspective, properties and events do not have an accessibility of their own. Instead, their accessibility is managed at the level of the individual methods. This enables a property's get and set to have different accessibility levels, and likewise for an event's accessors. We can control property accessor accessibility independently in C# if we want to, but where C# misleads us is that it lets us specify a single accessibility level for the entire property. This is really just shorthand for setting both accessors to the same level. The confusing part is that it lets us specify the accessibility for the property and then a different accessibility for one of the members, as Example 13-5 does.

Example 13-5. Property accessor accessibility

```
public int Count
{
    get;
    private set;
}
```

This is a bit misleading because, despite how it looks, that public accessibility does not apply to the whole property. This property-level accessibility simply tells the compiler what to use for accessors that don't specify their own accessibility level. The first version of C# required both property accessors to have the same accessibility, so it made sense to state it for the whole property. (It still has an equivalent restriction for events.) But this was an arbitrary restriction—the CLR has always allowed each accessor to have a different accessibility. C# now supports this, but because of the history, the syntax for exploiting this is deceptively asymmetric. From the CLR's point of view, Example 13-5 just says to make the get public and the set private. Example 13-6 would be a better representation of what's really going on.

Example 13-6. How the CLR sees property accessibility

```
// Won't compile but arguably should
int Count
{
    public get;
    private set;
}
```

But we can't write it that way, because C# demands that the accessibility for the more visible of the two accessors be stated at the property level. This makes the syntax simpler when both properties have the same accessibility, but it makes things a bit weird when they're different. Moreover, the syntax in Example 13-5 (i.e., the syntax the compiler actually supports) makes it look like we should be able to specify accessibility in three places: the property and both of the accessors. The CLR does not support that, so the compiler will produce an error if you try to specify accessibility for both of the accessors. So there is no accessibility for the property or event itself. (Imagine if there were—what would it even mean if a property had `public` accessibility but its `get` were `internal` and its `set` were `private`?) Consequently, not everything that derives from `MemberInfo` has a particular accessibility, so the reflection API provides properties representing accessibility farther down in the class hierarchy.

Type and TypeInfo

The `Type` class represents a particular type. It is more widely used than any of the other classes in this chapter, which is why it alone lives in the `System` namespace while the rest are defined in `System.Reflection`. It's the easiest to get hold of because C# has an operator designed for just this job: `typeof`. I've shown this in a few examples already, but Example 13-7 shows it in isolation. As you can see, you can use either a built-in name, such as `string`, or an ordinary type name, such as `IDisposable`. You could also include the namespace, but that's not necessary when the type's namespace is in scope.

Example 13-7. Getting a Type with typeof

```
Type stringType = typeof(string);
Type disposableType = typeof(IDisposable);
```

Also, as I mentioned in Chapter 6, the `System.Object` type (or `object`, as we usually write it in C#) provides a `GetType` instance method that takes no arguments. You can call this on any reference type variable to retrieve the type of the object that variable refers to. This will not necessarily be the same type as the variable itself, because the variable may refer to an instance of a derived type. You can also call this method on any value type variable, and because value types do not support inheritance, it will always return the Type object for the variable's static type.

So all you need is an object, a value, or a type identifier (such as string), and it is trivial to get a Type object. And, there are many other places Type objects can come from.

In addition to Type, we also have TypeInfo. This was introduced in early versions of .NET (called .NET Core at the time, to distinguish it from the .NET Framework) with the intention of enabling Type to serve purely as a lightweight identifier, and for TypeInfo to be the mechanism by which you reflect against a type. This was a departure from how Type had always worked in .NET Framework, where it performs both roles. This dual role was arguably a mistake because if you only need an identifier, Type is unnecessarily heavyweight. .NET Core was originally envisaged as having a separate existence from .NET Framework with no need for strict compatibility, so it seemed to provide an opportunity to fix historical design problems. However, once Microsoft made the decision that .NET Core would be the basis of all future versions of .NET, it became necessary to bring it back into line with how .NET Framework had always worked. However, by this time, .NET Framework had also introduced TypeInfo, and for a while, new type-level reflection features were added to that instead of Type to minimize incompatibilities with .NET Core 1. .NET Core 2.0 realigned with .NET Framework, but this meant that the split of functionality between Type and TypeInfo is now just an upshot of what was added when. TypeInfo contains members added during the brief period between its introduction and the decision to revert to the old way. In cases where you have a Type but you need to use a feature specific to TypeInfo, you can get this from a Type by calling GetTypeInfo.

As you've already seen, you can retrieve Type objects from an Assembly, either by name or as a comprehensive list. The reflection types that derive from MemberInfo also provide a reference to their containing type through DeclaringType. (Type derives from MemberInfo, so it also offers this property, which is relevant when dealing with nested types.)

You can also call the Type class's own static GetType method. If you pass just a namespace-qualified string, it will search for the named type in a system assembly called mscorlib, and also in the assembly from which you called the method. However, you can pass an *assembly-qualified name*, which combines an assembly name and a type name. A name of this form starts with the namespace-qualified type name, followed by a comma and the assembly name. For example, this is the assembly-qualified name of the System.String class in .NET Framework 4.8.1 (split across two lines to fit in this book):

```
System.String, mscorlib, Version=4.0.0.0, Culture=neutral,
    PublicKeyToken=b77a5c561934e089
```

You can discover a type's assembly-qualified name through the `Type.Assembly QualifiedName` property. Be aware that this won't always match what you asked for. If you pass the preceding type name into `Type.GetType` on .NET 8.0, it will work, but if you then ask the returned `Type` for its `AssemblyQualifiedName`, it will return this instead:

```
System.String, System.Private.CoreLib, Version=8.0.0.0, Culture=neutral,
    PublicKeyToken=7cec85d7bea7798e
```

The only reason it works when you pass either the first string or just `System.String` is because `mscorlib` still exists for backward compatibility purposes. I described this in the preceding chapter, but to summarize, in .NET Framework, the `mscorlib` assembly contains the core types of the runtime libraries, but in .NET, the code has moved elsewhere. `mscorlib` still exists, but it contains only type forwarding entries indicating which assembly each class now lives in. For example, it forwards `Sys tem.String` to its new home, which, at the time of this writing, is the `System.Pri vate.CoreLib` assembly.

As well as the standard `MemberInfo` properties, such as `Module` and `Name`, the `Type` and `TypeInfo` classes add various properties of their own. The inherited `Name` property contains the unqualified name, so `Type` adds a `Namespace` property. All types are scoped to an assembly, so `Type` defines an `Assembly` property. (You could, of course, get there via `Module.Assembly`, but it's more convenient to use the `Assembly` property.) It also defines a `BaseType` property, although that will be `null` for some types (e.g., nonderived interfaces and the type object for the `System.Object` class).

Since `Type` can represent all sorts of types, there are properties you can use to determine exactly what you've got: `IsArray`, `IsClass`, `IsEnum`, `IsInterface`, `IsPointer`, and `IsValueType`. (You can also get `Type` objects for non-.NET types in interop scenarios, so there's also an `IsCOMObject` property.) If it represents a class, there are some properties that tell you more about what kind of class you've got: `IsAbstract`, `IsSealed`, and `IsNested`. That last one is applicable to value types as well as classes.

`Type` also defines numerous properties providing information about the type's visibility. For nonnested types, `IsPublic` tells you whether it's `public` or `internal`, but things are more complex for nested types. `IsNestedAssembly` indicates an `internal` nested type, while `IsNestedPublic` and `IsNestedPrivate` indicate `public` and `private` nested types. Instead of the usual C-family "protected" terminology, the CLR uses the term *family*, so we have `IsNestedFamily` for `protected`, `IsNestedFamOR Assem` for `protected internal`, and `IsNestedFamANDAssem` for `protected private`.

There is no IsRecord property. As far as the runtime is concerned, record types are classes or structs. Records are a feature of the C# type system but not of the .NET runtime's type system, the CTS. Reflection is a runtime feature, so it presents the CTS perspective.

The `TypeInfo` class also provides methods to discover related reflection objects. (The properties in this paragraph are all defined on `TypeInfo`, not `Type`. As previously discussed, this is just an accident of when they were defined.) Most of these come in two forms: one where you want a complete list of all the items of the specified kind and one where you know the name of the thing you're looking for. For example, we have `DeclaredConstructors`, `DeclaredEvents`, `DeclaredFields`, `DeclaredMethods`, `DeclaredNestedTypes`, and `DeclaredProperties` along with their counterparts, `Get DeclaredConstructor`, `GetDeclaredEvent`, `GetDeclaredField`, `GetDeclaredMethod`, `GetDeclaredNestedType`, and `GetDeclaredProperty`.

The `Type` class lets you discover type compatibility relationships. You can ask whether one type derives from another type by calling the type's `IsSubclassOf` method. Inheritance is not the only reason one type may be compatible with a reference of a different type—a variable whose type is an interface can refer to an instance of any type that implements that interface, regardless of its base class. The `Type` class therefore offers a more general method called `IsAssignableFrom`, shown in Example 13-8, which tells you whether an implicit reference conversion exists.

Example 13-8. Testing type compatibility

```
Type stringType = typeof(string);
Type objectType = typeof(object);
Console.WriteLine(stringType.IsAssignableFrom(objectType));
Console.WriteLine(objectType.IsAssignableFrom(stringType));
```

This shows `False` and then `True`, because you cannot take a reference to an instance of type `object` and assign it into a variable of type `string`, but you can take a reference to an instance of type `string` and assign it into a variable of type `object`.

As well as telling you things about a type and its relationships to other types, the `Type` class provides the ability to use a type's members at runtime. It defines an `InvokeMem ber` method, the exact meaning of which depends on what kind of member you invoke—it could mean calling a method, or getting or setting a property or field, for example. Since some member types support multiple kinds of invocation (e.g., both get and set), you need to specify which particular operation you want. Example 13-9 uses `InvokeMember` to invoke a method identified by its name (the `member` string argument) on an instance of a type, also identified by name, that it instantiates dynamically. This illustrates how reflection can be used to work with types and members whose identities are not known until runtime.

Example 13-9. Invoking a method with `InvokeMember`

```
public static object? CreateAndInvokeMethod(
  string typeName, string member, params object[] args)
{
    Type t = Type.GetType(typeName)
        ?? throw new ArgumentException(
            $"Type {typeName} not found", nameof(typeName));
    object instance = Activator.CreateInstance(t)!;
    return t.InvokeMember(
      member,
      BindingFlags.Instance | BindingFlags.Public | BindingFlags.InvokeMethod,
      null,
      instance,
      args);
}
```

This example first creates an instance of the specified type—this uses a slightly different approach to dynamic creation than the one I showed earlier with `Assembly.CreateInstance`. Here I'm using `Type.GetType` to look up the type, and then I'm using a class I've not mentioned before, `Activator`. This class's job is to create new instances of objects whose type you have determined at runtime. Its functionality overlaps somewhat with `Assembly.CreateInstance`, but in this case, it's the most convenient way to get from a `Type` to a new instance of that type. Then I've used the `Type` object's `InvokeMember` to invoke the specified method. As with Example 13-3, I've had to specify binding flags to indicate what kind of member I'm looking for and also what to do with it—here I'm looking to call a method (as opposed to, say, setting a property value). As with Example 13-3, the `null` argument is a place where I would have specified a `Binder` if I had wanted to support automatic coercion of the method argument types.

Generic Types

.NET's support for generics complicates the role of the `Type` class. As well as representing an ordinary nongeneric type, a `Type` can represent a particular instance of a generic type (e.g., `List<int>`) but also an unbound generic type (e.g., `List<>`, although that's an illegal type identifier in all but one very specific scenario). Example 13-10 shows how to obtain both kinds of `Type` objects.

Example 13-10. Type objects for generic types

```
Type bound = typeof(List<int>);
Type unbound = typeof(List<>);
```

The typeof operator is the only place in which you can use an unbound generic type identifier in C#—in all other contexts, it would be an error not to supply type arguments. By the way, if the type takes multiple type arguments, you must provide commas—for example, typeof(Dictionary<,>). This is necessary to avoid ambiguity when there are multiple generic types with the same names, distinguished only by the number of type parameters (also known as the *arity*)—for example, typeof(Func<,>) versus typeof(Func<,,,>). You cannot specify a partially bound generic type. For example, typeof(Dictionary<string,>) would fail to compile.

You can tell when a Type object refers to a generic type—the IsGenericType property will return true for both bound and unbound from Example 13-10. You can also determine whether or not the type arguments have been supplied by using the IsGeneric TypeDefinition property, which would return false and true for bound and unbound, respectively. If you have a bound generic type and you'd like to get the unbound type from which it was constructed, you use the GetGenericType Def inition method—calling that on bound would return the same type object that unbound refers to.

Given a Type object whose IsGenericTypeDefinition property returns true, you can construct a new bound version of that type by calling MakeGenericType, passing an array of Type objects, one for each type argument.

If you have a generic type, you can retrieve its type arguments from the Generic TypeArguments property. Perhaps surprisingly, this even works for unbound types, although it behaves differently than with a bound type. If you get GenericType Arguments from bound from Example 13-10, it will return an array containing a single Type object, which will be the same one you would get from typeof(int). If you get unbound.GenericTypeArguments, you will also get an array containing a single Type, but this time, it will be a Type object that does not represent a specific type—its IsGen ericParameter property will be true, indicating that this represents a placeholder. Its name in this case will be T. In general, the name will correspond to whatever placeholder name the generic type chooses. For example, with typeof(Diction ary<,>), you'll get two Type objects called TKey and TValue, respectively. You will encounter similar generic argument placeholder types if you use the reflection API to look up members of generic types. For example, if you retrieve the MethodInfo for the Add method of the unbound List<> type, you'll find that it takes a single argument of a type named T, which returns true from its IsGenericParameter property.

When a Type object represents an unbound generic parameter, you can find out whether the parameter is covariant or contravariant (or neither) through its Generic ParameterAttributes method.

MethodBase, ConstructorInfo, and MethodInfo

Constructors and methods have a great deal in common. The same accessibility options are available for both kinds of members, they both have argument lists, and they can both contain code. Consequently, the MethodInfo and ConstructorInfo reflection types share a base class, MethodBase, which defines properties and methods for handling these common aspects.

To obtain a MethodInfo or ConstructorInfo, besides using the Type class properties I mentioned earlier, you can also call the MethodBase class's static GetCurrentMethod method. This inspects the calling code to see if it's a constructor or a normal method and returns either a MethodInfo or ConstructorInfo accordingly.

As well as the members it inherits from MemberInfo, MethodBase defines properties specifying the member's accessibility. These are similar in concept to those I described earlier for types, but the names are marginally different, because unlike Type, MethodBase does not define accessibility properties that make a distinction between nested and nonnested members. So with MethodBase, we find IsPublic, IsPrivate, IsAssembly, IsFamily, IsFamilyOrAssembly, and IsFamilyAndAssembly for public, private, internal, protected, protected internal, and protected private, respectively.

In addition to accessibility-related properties, MethodBase defines properties that tell you about aspects of the method, such as IsStatic, IsAbstract, IsVirtual, IsFinal, and IsConstructor.

There are also properties for dealing with generic methods. IsGenericMethod and IsGenericMethodDefinition are the method-level equivalents of the type-level IsGenericType and IsGenericTypeDefinition properties. As with Type, there's a GetGenericMethodDefinition method to get from a bound generic method to an unbound one, and a MakeGenericMethod to produce a bound generic method from an unbound one. You can retrieve type arguments by calling GetGenericArguments, and as with generic types, this will return specific types when called on a bound method and will return placeholder types when used with an unbound method.

You can inspect the implementation of the method by calling GetMethodBody. This returns a MethodBody object that provides access to the IL (as an array of bytes) and also to the local variable definitions used by the method.

The `MethodInfo` class derives from `MethodBase` and represents only methods (and not constructors). It adds a `ReturnType` property that provides a `Type` object indicating the method's return type. (There's a special system type, `System.Void`, whose `Type` object is used here when a method returns nothing.)

The `ConstructorInfo` class does not add any properties beyond those it inherits from `MethodBase`. It does define two read-only static fields, though: `ConstructorName` and `TypeConstructorName`. These contain the strings `".ctor"` and `".cctor"`, respectively, which are the values you will find in the `Name` property for `ConstructorInfo` objects for instance and static constructors. As far as the CLR is concerned, these are the real names—although in C# constructors appear to have the same name as their containing type, that's true only in your C# source files, and not at runtime.

You can invoke the method or constructor represented by a `MethodInfo` or `ConstructorInfo` by calling the `Invoke` method. This does the same thing as `Type.InvokeMember`—Example 13-9 used that to call a method. However, because `Invoke` is specialized for working with just methods and constructors, it's rather simpler to use. With a `ConstructorInfo`, you need to pass only an array of arguments. With `MethodInfo`, you also pass the object on which you want to invoke the method, or `null` if you want to invoke a static method. Example 13-11 performs the same job as Example 13-9 but using `MethodInfo`.

Example 13-11. Invoking a method

```
public static object? CreateAndInvokeMethod(
    string typeName, string member, params object[] args)
{
    Type t = Type.GetType(typeName)
        ?? throw new ArgumentException(
            $"Type {typeName} not found", nameof(typeName));
    MethodInfo m = t.GetMethod(member)
        ?? throw new ArgumentException(
            $"Method {member} not found", nameof(member));
    object instance = Activator.CreateInstance(t)!;
    return m.Invoke(instance, args);
}
```

For either methods or constructors, you can call `GetParameters`, which returns an array of `ParameterInfo` objects representing the method's parameters.

ParameterInfo

The `ParameterInfo` class represents parameters for methods or constructors. Its `ParameterType` and `Name` properties provide the basic information you'd see from looking at the method signature. It also defines a `Member` property that refers back to the method or constructor to which the parameter belongs. The `HasDefaultValue` property will tell you whether the parameter is optional, and if it is, `DefaultValue` provides the value to be used when the argument is omitted.

If you are working with members defined by unbound generic types, or with an unbound generic method, be aware that the `ParameterType` of a `ParameterInfo` could refer to a generic type argument, and not a real type. This is also true of any `Type` objects returned by the reflection objects described in the next three sections.

FieldInfo

`FieldInfo` represents a field in a type. You typically obtain it from a `Type` object with `GetField` or `GetFields`, or if you're using code written in a language that supports global fields, you can retrieve those from the containing `Module`.

`FieldInfo` defines a set of properties representing accessibility. These look just like the ones defined by `MethodBase`. Additionally, there's `FieldType`, representing the type a field can contain. (As always, if the member belongs to an unbound generic type, this might refer to a type argument rather than a specific type.) There are also some properties providing further information about the field, including `IsStatic`, `IsInitOnly`, and `IsLiteral`. These correspond to `static`, `readonly`, and `const` in C#, respectively. (Fields representing values in enumeration types will also return `true` from `IsLiteral`.)

`FieldInfo` defines `GetValue` and `SetValue` methods that let you read and write the value of the field. These take an argument specifying the instance to use, or `null` if the field is static. As with the `MethodBase` class's `Invoke`, these do not do anything you couldn't do with the `Type` class's `InvokeMember`, but these methods are typically more convenient.

PropertyInfo

The `PropertyInfo` type represents a property. You can obtain these from the containing `Type` object's `GetProperty` or `GetProperties` methods. As I mentioned earlier, `PropertyInfo` does not define any properties for accessibility, because the accessibility is determined at the level of the individual get and set methods. You can retrieve those with the `GetGetMethod` and `GetSetMethod` methods, which both return `Method Info` objects.

Much like with `FieldInfo`, the `PropertyInfo` class defines `GetValue` and `SetValue` methods for reading and writing the value. Properties are allowed to take arguments—C# indexers are properties with arguments, for example. So there are overloads of `GetValue` and `SetValue` that take arrays of arguments. Also, there is a `GetIndexParameters` method that returns an array of `ParameterInfo` objects, representing the arguments required to use the property. The property's type is available through the `PropertyType` property.

EventInfo

Events are represented by `EventInfo` objects, which are returned by the `Type` class's `GetEvent` and `GetEvents` methods. Like `PropertyInfo`, this does not have any accessibility properties, because the event's add and remove methods each define their own accessibility. You can retrieve those methods with `GetAddMethod` and `GetRemove Method`, which both return a `MethodInfo`. `EventInfo` defines an `EventHandlerType`, which returns the type of delegate that event handlers are required to supply.

You can attach and remove handlers by calling the `AddEventHandler` and `Remove EventHandler` methods. As with all other dynamic invocation, these just offer a more convenient alternative to the `Type` class's `InvokeMember` method.

Reflection Contexts

.NET has a feature called *reflection contexts*. These enable reflection to provide a virtualized view of the type system. By writing a custom reflection context, you can modify how types appear—you can cause a type to look like it has extra properties, or you can add to the set of attributes that members and parameters appear to offer. (Chapter 14 will describe attributes.)

Reflection contexts are useful because they make it possible to write reflection-driven frameworks that enable individual types to customize how they are handled but without forcing every type that participates into providing explicit support. Prior to the introduction of custom reflection contexts in .NET Framework 4.5, this was handled with various ad hoc systems. Take the Properties panel in Visual Studio, for example. This can automatically display every public property defined by any .NET object that ends up on a design surface (e.g., any UI component you write). It's great to have automatic editing support even for components that do not provide any explicit handling for that, but components should have the opportunity to customize how they behave at design time.

Because the Properties panel predates .NET Framework 4.5, it uses one of the ad hoc solutions: the `TypeDescriptor` class. This is a wrapper on top of reflection, which allows any class to augment its design-time behavior by implementing `ICustomType Descriptor`. This enables a class to customize the set of properties it offers for editing and also to control how they are presented, even offering custom editing UIs. This is flexible, but has the downside of coupling the design-time code with the runtime code—components that use this model cannot easily be shipped without also supplying the design-time code. So Visual Studio introduced its own virtualization mechanisms for separating the two.

To avoid having each framework define its own virtualization system, custom reflection contexts add virtualization directly into the reflection API. If you want to write code that can consume type information provided by reflection but can also support design-time augmentation or modification of that information, it's no longer necessary to use some sort of wrapper layer. You can use the usual reflection types described earlier in this chapter, but it's now possible to ask reflection to give you different implementations of these types, providing different virtualized views.

You do this by writing a custom reflection context that describes how you want to modify the view that reflection provides. Example 13-12 shows a particularly boring type followed by a custom reflection context that makes that type look like it has a property.

Example 13-12. A simple type, enhanced by a reflection context

```
class NotVeryInteresting
{
}

class MyReflectionContext : CustomReflectionContext
{
    protected override IEnumerable<PropertyInfo> AddProperties(Type type)
    {
        if (type == typeof(NotVeryInteresting))
        {
            var fakeProp = CreateProperty(
                MapType(typeof(string).GetTypeInfo()),
                "FakeProperty",
                o => "FakeValue",
                (o, v) => Console.WriteLine($"Setting value: {v}"));

            return new[] { fakeProp };
        }
        else
        {
            return base.AddProperties(type);
        }
    }
}
```

Code that uses the reflection API directly will see the NotVeryInteresting type exactly as it is, with no properties. However, we can map that type through MyReflectionContext, as Example 13-13 shows.

Example 13-13. Using a custom reflection context

```
var ctx = new MyReflectionContext();
TypeInfo mappedType = ctx.MapType(typeof(NotVeryInteresting).GetTypeInfo());

foreach (PropertyInfo prop in mappedType.DeclaredProperties)
{
    Console.WriteLine($"{prop.Name} ({prop.PropertyType.Name})");
}
```

The `mappedType` variable holds a reference to the resulting mapped type. It still looks like an ordinary reflection `TypeInfo` object, and we can iterate through its properties in the usual way with `DeclaredProperties`, but because we've mapped the type through my custom reflection context, we see the modified version of the type. This code's output will show that the type appears to define one property called `Fake Property`, of type `string`.

Summary

The reflection API makes it possible to write code whose behavior is based on the structure of the types it works with. This might involve deciding which values to present in a UI grid based on the properties an object offers, or it might mean modifying the behavior of a framework based on what members a particular type chooses to define. For example, parts of the ASP.NET Core web framework will detect whether your code is using synchronous or asynchronous programming techniques and adapt appropriately. These techniques require the ability to inspect code at runtime,[2] which is what reflection enables. All of the information in an assembly required by the type system is available to our code. Furthermore, you can present this through a virtualized view by writing a custom reflection context, making it possible to customize the behavior of reflection-driven code.

Code that inspects the structure of types to drive its behavior often needs additional information. For example, the `System.Text.Json` namespace includes types described in Chapter 15 that can convert between .NET objects and JSON documents. These typically rely on reflection, but you can take more precise control over the purpose by supplying extra information in the form of *attributes*. These are the topic of the next chapter.

---

2 ASP.NET Core 8.0 has introduced an alternate mechanism that uses Roslyn, the C# compiler API, enabling it to inspect the code at build time instead. It generates code embedding the relevant information to avoid the need for reflection, enabling use of Native AOT. Reflection is still used by default if you don't target Native AOT.

CHAPTER 14

Attributes

In .NET, you can annotate components, types, and their members with *attributes*. An attribute's purpose is to control or modify the behavior of a framework, a tool, the compiler, or the CLR. For example, in Chapter 1, I showed a class annotated with the [TestClass] attribute. This told a unit testing framework that the annotated class contains some tests to be run as part of a test suite.

Attributes are passive containers of information that do nothing on their own. To draw an analogy with the physical world, if you print out a shipping label containing an address and tracking information and attach it to a package, that label will not in itself cause the package to make its way to a destination. Such a label is useful only once the package is in the hands of a shipping company. When the company picks up your parcel, it'll expect to find the label and will use it to work out how to route your package. So the label is important, but ultimately, its only job is to provide information that some system requires. .NET attributes work the same way—they have an effect only if something goes looking for them. Some attributes are handled by the CLR or the compiler, but these are in the minority. The majority of attributes are consumed by frameworks, libraries, tools (such as a unit test runner), or your own code.

Applying Attributes

To avoid having to introduce an extra set of concepts into the type system, .NET models attributes as instances of .NET types. To be used as an attribute, a type must derive from the System.Attribute class, but it can otherwise be entirely ordinary. To apply an attribute, you put the type's name in square brackets, and this usually goes directly before the attribute's target. (Since C# mostly ignores whitespace, attributes don't have to be on a separate line, but that is the convention when the target is a type or a member.) Example 14-1 shows some attributes from Microsoft's test framework. I've applied one to the class to indicate that this contains tests I'd like to run, and I've also applied attributes to individual methods, telling the test framework which ones represent tests and which contain initialization code to be run before each test.

Example 14-1. Attributes in a unit test class

```
using Microsoft.VisualStudio.TestTools.UnitTesting;

namespace ImageManagement.Tests;

[TestClass]
public class WhenPropertiesRetrieved
{
    private ImageMetadataReader? _reader;

    [TestInitialize]
    public void Initialize()
    {
        _reader = new ImageMetadataReader(TestFiles.GetImage());
    }

    [TestMethod]
    public void ReportsCameraMaker()
    {
        Assert.AreEqual(_reader!.CameraManufacturer, "Fabrikam");
    }

    [TestMethod]
    public void ReportsCameraModel()
    {
        Assert.AreEqual(_reader!.CameraModel, "Fabrikam F450D");
    }
}
```

If you look at the documentation for most attributes, you'll find that their real name ends with `Attribute`. If there's no class with the name you specify in the brackets, the C# compiler tries appending `Attribute`, so in Example 14-1 the [TestClass] attribute refers to the `TestClassAttribute` class. If you really want to, you can spell the class name out in full—for example, [TestClassAttribute]—but it's more common to use the shorter version.

If you want to apply multiple attributes, you have two options. You can either provide multiple sets of brackets or put multiple attributes inside a single pair of brackets, separated by commas.

Some attribute types can take constructor arguments. For example, Microsoft's test framework includes a `TestCategoryAttribute`. When running tests, you can choose to execute only those in a certain category. This attribute requires you to pass the category name as a constructor argument, because there would be no point in applying this attribute without specifying the name. As Example 14-2 shows, the syntax for specifying an attribute's constructor arguments is unsurprising.

Example 14-2. Attribute with constructor argument

```
[TestCategory("Property Handling")]
[TestMethod]
public void ReportsCameraMaker()
{
    ...
```

You can also specify property or field values. Some attributes have features that can be controlled only through properties or fields, and not constructor arguments. (If an attribute has lots of optional settings, it's usually easier to present these as properties or fields, instead of defining a constructor overload for every conceivable combination of settings.) The syntax for this is to write one or more *PropertyOrField Name=Value* entries after the constructor arguments (or instead of them, if there are no constructor arguments). Example 14-3 shows another attribute used in unit testing, ExpectedExceptionAttribute, which allows you to specify that when your test runs, you expect it to throw a particular exception. The exception type is mandatory, so we pass that as a constructor argument, but this attribute also allows you to state whether the test runner should accept exceptions of a type derived from the one specified. (By default, it will accept only an exact match.) This is controlled with the AllowDerivedTypes property.

Example 14-3. Specifying optional attribute settings with properties

```
[ExpectedException(typeof(ArgumentException), AllowDerivedTypes = true)]
[TestMethod]
public void ThrowsWhenNameMalformed()
{
    ...
```

Applying an attribute will not cause it to be constructed. All you are doing when you apply an attribute is providing instructions on how the attribute should be created and initialized if something should ask to see it. (There is a common misconception that method attributes are instantiated when the method runs. Not so.) When the compiler builds the metadata for an assembly, it includes information about which attributes have been applied to which items, including a list of constructor arguments and property values, and the CLR will dig that information out and use it only if something asks for it. For example, when you tell Visual Studio to run your unit tests, it will load your test assembly, and then for each public type, it asks the CLR for any test-related attributes. That's the point at which the attributes get constructed. If you were simply to load the assembly by, say, adding a reference to it from another project and then using some of the types it contains, the attributes would never come into existence—they would remain as nothing more than a set of building instructions frozen into your assembly's metadata. In some cases they might not even make it that far. If you're using Native AOT in conjunction with the JSON serialization mechanisms shown in Chapter 15, the relevant attributes are processed during compilation and get trimmed out of the final output.

Attribute Targets

Attributes can be applied to numerous different kinds of targets. You can put attributes on any of the features of the type system represented in the reflection API that I showed in Chapter 13. Specifically, you can apply attributes to assemblies, modules, types, methods, method parameters, constructors, fields, properties, events, and generic type parameters. In addition, you can supply attributes that target a method's return value.

For most of these, you denote the target simply by putting the attribute in front of it. But that's not an option for assemblies or modules, because there is no single feature that represents those in your source code—everything in your project goes into the assembly it produces, and modules are likewise an aggregate. So for these, we have to state the target explicitly at the start of the attribute. The specific assembly-level attribute shown in Example 14-4 will often be found in a *GlobalSuppressions.cs* file. Visual Studio sometimes makes suggestions for modifying your code, and if you want to suppress these, one option is to use assembly-level attributes.

Example 14-4. Assembly-level attributes

```
[assembly: System.Diagnostics.CodeAnalysis.SuppressMessage(
    "Style",
    "IDE0060:Remove unused parameter",
    Justification = "This is just some example code from a book",
    Scope = "member",
    Target = "~M:Idg.Examples.SomeMethod")]
```

You can put assembly-level attributes in any file. The sole restriction is that they must appear before any namespace or type definitions. The only things that should come before assembly-level attributes are whichever using directives you need, comments, and whitespace (all of which are optional).

Module-level attributes follow the same pattern, although they are much less common, not least because multimodule assemblies are pretty rare and are not supported in the latest versions of .NET—they only work on .NET Framework. Example 14-5 shows how to configure the debuggability of a particular module, should you want one module in a multimodule assembly to be easily debuggable but the rest to be JIT-compiled with full optimizations. (This is a contrived scenario so that I can show the syntax. In practice, you're unlikely ever to want to do this.) I'll talk about the `Debugg` `ableAttribute` later, in "JIT compilation" on page 656.

Example 14-5. Module-level attribute

```
using System.Diagnostics;

[module: Debuggable(DebuggableAttribute.DebuggingModes.DisableOptimizations)]
```

Another kind of target that needs qualification is a compiler-generated field. You get these with properties in which you do not supply code for the getter or setter, and also in `event` members without explicit `add` and `remove` implementations. The attributes in Example 14-6 apply to the fields that hold the property's value and the delegate for the event; without the `field:` qualifiers, attributes in those positions would apply to the property or event itself.

Example 14-6. Attribute for compiler-generated property and event fields

```
[field: NonSerialized]
public int DynamicId { get; set; }

[field: NonSerialized]
public event EventHandler? Frazzled;
```

Methods' return values can be annotated, and this also requires qualification, because return value attributes go in front of the method, the same place as attributes that apply to the method itself. (Attributes for parameters do not need qualification, because these appear inside the parentheses with the parameters.) Example 14-7 shows a method with attributes applied to both the method and the return type. (The attributes in this example are part of the interop services that enable .NET code to call external code, such as OS APIs. This example imports a function from a Win32 DLL, enabling you to use it from C#. There are several different representations for Boolean values in unmanaged code, so I've annotated the return type here with a `Mar` `shalAsAttribute` to say which particular one the CLR should expect.)

Example 14-7. Method and return value attributes

```
[LibraryImport("User32.dll")]
[return: MarshalAs(UnmanagedType.Bool)]
internal static partial bool IsWindowVisible(IntPtr hWnd);
```

C# 11.0 added a new feature for attributes that target either return values or arguments. Sometimes, attributes describe relationships between multiple parameters, or a relationship between a method's return value and a parameter. An attribute has just one target, so we refer to related arguments by name. Example 14-8 shows an example from the .NET runtime library: the string.Create method. (This method enables you to change localization and other format settings when using an interpolated string. You can write string.Create(CultureInfo.InvariantCulture, $"Value: {v}"), for example.) It uses the InterpolatedStringHandlerArgumentAttribute to tell the compiler that it wants to provide custom string interpolation handling, and that this will be managed by the DefaultInterpolatedStringHandler type. The compiler needs to know whether any of the method's other arguments are involved with the string interpolation, and this method has indicated that the provider argument needs to be passed as a constructor argument to DefaultInterpolatedStringHandler.

Example 14-8. Referring to a method argument by name in an attribute before C# 11.0

```
public static string Create(
    IFormatProvider? provider,
    [InterpolatedStringHandlerArgument("provider")]
    ref DefaultInterpolatedStringHandler handler)
```

Referring to arguments by name in a string was always slightly unsatisfactory. It's easy to mistype the name, and it is hard for refactoring tools to process these correctly—if you rename the argument, that string also needs to change. This is exactly the scenario that nameof is designed for, but you couldn't use it here because parameters were in scope only inside the method's body. C# 11.0 relaxed the scoping rules very slightly: nameof is now allowed to refer to argument names in attributes applied to the method's arguments or return value, so if you look at the source for string .Create you'll find it now looks like Example 14-9.

Example 14-9. Referring to a method argument by name in an attribute using nameof

```
public static string Create(
    IFormatProvider? provider,
    [InterpolatedStringHandlerArgument(nameof(provider))]
    ref DefaultInterpolatedStringHandler handler)
```

How are we to apply method attributes in cases where we don't write the method declaration explicitly? As you saw in Chapter 9, the lambda syntax lets us write an expression whose value is a delegate. The compiler generates a normal method to hold the code (typically in a hidden class), and we might want to pass that method to a framework that uses attributes to control its functionality, such as the ASP.NET Core web framework. Example 14-10 shows how we can specify these attributes when using a lambda.

Example 14-10. Lambda with attributes

```
app.MapGet(
    "/items/{id}",
    [Authorize] ([FromRoute] int id) => $"Item {id} requested");
```

The `MapGet` method here tells the ASP.NET Core framework how our application should behave when it receives `GET` requests on URLs matching a particular pattern. The first argument specifies the pattern, and the second is a delegate that defines the behavior. I've used the lambda syntax here, and I've applied a couple of attributes.

The first attribute is `[Authorize]`. This appears before the parameter list, so its target is the whole method. (You can also use a `return:` attribute in this position.) This causes ASP.NET Core to block unauthenticated requests that match this URL pattern. The `[FromRoute]` attribute is inside the parameter list's parentheses, so it applies to the `id` parameter, and it tells ASP.NET Core that we want that particular parameter's value to be taken from the expression of the same name in the URL pattern. So if a request came in for *https://myserver/items/42*, ASP.NET Core would first check that the request meets the application's configured requirements for authentication and authorization, and if so, it would then invoke my lambda passing 42 as the `id` argument.

 Example 9-23 in Chapter 9 showed that you can omit details in certain cases. The parentheses around the parameter list are normally optional for 1-argument lambdas. However, the parentheses *must* be present if you apply attributes to a lambda. To see why, imagine Example 14-10 without parentheses around the parameter list: it would be unclear whether the attributes were meant to apply to the method or the parameter.

Compiler-Handled Attributes

The C# compiler recognizes certain attribute types and handles them in special ways. For example, assembly names and versions are set via attributes and also some related information about your assembly. As Chapter 12 described, the build process generates a hidden source file containing these for you. If you're curious, it usually ends up in the *obj\Debug* or *obj\Release* folder of your project, and it will be named something like *YourProject.AssemblyInfo.cs*. Example 14-11 shows a typical example.

Example 14-11. A typical generated file with assembly-level attributes

```
//------------------------------------------------------------------------------
// <auto-generated>
//     This code was generated by a tool.
//     Runtime Version:4.0.30319.42000
```

```
//
//      Changes to this file may cause incorrect behavior and will be lost if
//      the code is regenerated.
// </auto-generated>
//-------------------------------------------------------------------------

using System;
using System.Reflection;

[assembly: System.Reflection.AssemblyCompanyAttribute("MyCompany")]
[assembly: System.Reflection.AssemblyConfigurationAttribute("Debug")]
[assembly: System.Reflection.AssemblyFileVersionAttribute("1.0.0.0")]
[assembly: System.Reflection.AssemblyInformationalVersionAttribute("1.0.0")]
[assembly: System.Reflection.AssemblyProductAttribute("MyApp")]
[assembly: System.Reflection.AssemblyTitleAttribute("MyApp")]
[assembly: System.Reflection.AssemblyVersionAttribute("1.0.0.0")]

// Generated by the MSBuild WriteCodeFragment class.
```

Old versions of the .NET Framework SDK did not generate this file at build time, so if you work on older projects, you will often find these attributes in a file called *AssemblyInfo.cs*. (By default Visual Studio hid this inside the project's Properties node in Solution Explorer, but it was still just an ordinary source file.) The advantage of the file generation used in modern projects is that names are less likely to drift out of sync. For example, by default the assembly Product and Title will be the same as the project filename. If you rename the project file, the generated *YourRenamedProject.AssemblyInfo.cs* will change to match (unless you added <Product> and <AssemblyTitle> properties to your project file, in which case it will use those), whereas with the old *AssemblyInfo.cs* approach you could accidentally end up with mismatched names. Similarly, if you build a NuGet package from your project, certain properties end up in both the NuGet package and the compiled assembly. When these are all generated from information in the project file, it's easier to keep things consistent.

Even though you only control these attributes indirectly, it's useful to understand them since they affect the compiler output.

Names and versions

As you saw in Chapter 12, assemblies have a compound name. The simple name, which is typically the same as the filename but without the *.exe* or *.dll* extension, is configured as part of the project settings. The name also includes a version number, and this is controlled with an attribute, as Example 14-12 shows.

Example 14-12. Version attributes

```
[assembly: AssemblyVersion("1.0.0.0")]
[assembly: AssemblyFileVersion("1.0.0.0")]
```

As you may recall from Chapter 12, the first of these sets the version part of the assembly's name. The second has nothing to do with .NET—the compiler uses this to generate a Win32-style version resource. This is the version number end users will see if they select your assembly in Windows Explorer and open the Properties window.

The culture is also part of the assembly name. This will often be set automatically if you're using the satellite resource assembly mechanisms described in Chapter 12. You can set it explicitly with the `AssemblyCulture` attribute, but for nonresource assemblies, the culture should usually not be set. (The only culture-related assembly-level attribute you will normally specify explicitly is the `NeutralResourcesLanguage Attribute`, which I showed in Chapter 12.)

Strongly named assemblies have an additional component in their name: the public key token. The easiest way to set up a strong name in Visual Studio is with the "Strong naming" section of your project's properties page (which is inside the Build section). If you're using VS Code or some other editor, you can just add two properties to your *.csproj* file: `SignAssembly` set to `True`, and `AssemblyOriginatorKeyFile` with the path to your key file. However, you can also manage strong naming from the source code, because the compiler recognizes some special attributes for this. `AssemblyKeyFileAttribute` takes the name of a file that contains a key. Alternatively, you can install a key in the computer's key store (which is part of the Windows cryptography system). If you want to do that, you can use the `AssemblyKeyNameAttribute` instead. The presence of either of these attributes causes the compiler to embed the public key in the assembly and include a hash of that key as the public key token of the strong name. If the key file includes the private key, the compiler will sign your assembly too. If it does not, it will fail to compile, unless you also enable either delay signing or public signing. You can enable delay signing by applying the `Assembly DelaySignAttribute` with a constructor argument of `true`. Alternatively, you can add either `<DelaySign>true</DelaySign>` or `<PublicSign>true</PublicSign>` to your *.csproj* file.

 Although the key-related attributes trigger special handling from the compiler, it still embeds them in the metadata as normal attributes. So, if you use the `AssemblyKeyFileAttribute`, the path to your key file will be visible in the final compiled output. This is not necessarily a problem, but you might prefer not to advertise these sorts of details, so it may be better to use the project-level configuration for strong names than the attribute-based approach.

Description and related resources

The version resource produced by the `AssemblyFileVersion` attribute is not the only information that the C# compiler can embed in Win32-style resources. There are several other attributes providing copyright information and other descriptive text. Example 14-13 shows a typical selection.

Example 14-13. Typical assembly description attributes

```
[assembly: AssemblyTitle("ExamplePlugin")]
[assembly: AssemblyDescription("An example plug-in DLL")]
[assembly: AssemblyConfiguration("Retail")]
[assembly: AssemblyCompany("Endjin Ltd.")]
[assembly: AssemblyProduct("ExamplePlugin")]
[assembly: AssemblyCopyright("Copyright © 2024 Endjin Ltd.")]
[assembly: AssemblyTrademark("")]
```

As with the file version, these are all visible in the Details tab of the Properties window that Windows Explorer can show for the file. And with all of these attributes, you can cause them to be generated by editing the project file.

Caller information attributes

There are some compiler-handled attributes designed for scenarios where your methods need information about the context from which they were invoked. This is useful for certain diagnostic logging or error handling scenarios, and it is also helpful when implementing a particular interface commonly used in UI code.

Example 14-14 illustrates how you can use these attributes in logging code. If you annotate method parameters with any of these three attributes, the compiler provides some special handling when callers omit the arguments. We can ask for the name of the member (method or property) that called the attributed method, the filename containing the code that called the method, or the line number from which the call was made. Example 14-14 asks for all three, but you can be more selective.

These attributes are allowed only for optional parameters. Optional arguments are required to specify a default value, but C# will always substitute a different value when these attributes are present, so the default you specify will not be used if you invoke the method from C# (or F# or Visual Basic, which also support these attributes). Nonetheless, you must provide a default because without one, the parameter is not optional, so we normally use empty strings, `null`, or the number `0`.

Example 14-14. Applying caller info attributes to method parameters

```
public static void Log(
    string message,
    [CallerMemberName] string callingMethod = "",
    [CallerFilePath] string callingFile = "",
    [CallerLineNumber] int callingLineNumber = 0)
{
    Console.WriteLine("Message {0}, called from {1} in file '{2}', line {3}",
        message, callingMethod, callingFile, callingLineNumber);
}
```

If you supply all arguments when invoking this method, nothing unusual happens. But if you omit any of the optional arguments, C# will generate code that provides information about the site from which the method was invoked. The default values for the three optional arguments in Example 14-14 will be the name of the method or property that called this Log method, the full path of the source code containing the code that made the call, and the line number from which Log was called.

The CallerMemberName attribute has a superficial resemblance to the nameof operator, which we saw in Chapter 8. Both cause the compiler to create a string containing the name of some feature of the code, but they work quite differently. With nameof, you always know exactly what string you'll get, because it's determined by the expression you supply. (E.g., if we were to write nameof(message) inside Log in Example 14-14, it would always evaluate to "message".) But CallerMemberName changes the way the compiler invokes the method to which they apply—calling Method has that attribute, and its value is not fixed. It will depend on where this method is called from.

> You can discover the calling method another way: the StackTrace and StackFrame classes in the System.Diagnostics namespace can report information about methods above you in the call stack. However, these have a considerably higher runtime cost—the caller information attributes calculate the values at compile time, making the runtime overhead very low. (Likewise with nameof.) Also, StackFrame can determine the filename and line number only if debug symbols are available.

Although diagnostic logging is an obvious application for this, I also mentioned a certain scenario that most .NET UI developers will be familiar with. The runtime libraries define an interface called INotifyPropertyChanged. As Example 14-15 shows, this is a very simple interface with just one member, an event called Property Changed.

Example 14-15. INotifyPropertyChanged

```
public interface INotifyPropertyChanged
{
    event PropertyChangedEventHandler? PropertyChanged;
}
```

Types that implement this interface raise the `PropertyChanged` event every time one of their properties changes. The `PropertyChangedEventArgument` provides a string containing the name of the property that just changed. These change notifications are useful in UIs, because they enable an object to be used with databinding technologies (such as those provided by .NET's WPF UI framework) that can automatically update the UI any time a property changes. Databinding can help you to achieve a clean separation between the code that deals directly with UI types and code that contains the logic that decides how the application should respond to user input.

Implementing `INotifyPropertyChanged` can be both tedious and error-prone. Because the `PropertyChanged` event indicates which property changed as a string, it is very easy to mistype the property name, or to accidentally use the wrong name if you copy and paste the implementation from one property to another. Also, if you rename a property, it's easy to forget to change the text used for the event, meaning that code that was previously correct will now provide the wrong name when raising the `PropertyChanged` event. The `nameof` operator helps avoid mistyping, and helps with renames, but can't always detect cut-and-paste errors. (It won't notice if you fail to update the name when pasting code between properties of the same class, for example.)

Caller information attributes can help make implementing this interface much less error-prone. Example 14-16 shows a base class that implements `INotifyProperty` `Changed`, supplying a helper for raising change notifications in a way that exploits one of these attributes. (It uses the null-conditional `?.` operator to ensure that it only invokes the event's delegate if it is non-null. By the way, when you use the operator this way, C# generates code that only evaluates the delegate's `Invoke` method's arguments if it is non-null. So not only does it skip the call to `Invoke` when the delegate is null, it will also avoid constructing the `PropertyChangedEventArgs` that would have been passed as an argument.) This code also detects whether the value really has changed, only raising the event when that's the case, and its return value indicates whether it changed, in case callers might find that useful.

Example 14-16. A reusable INotifyPropertyChanged implementation

```
public class NotifyPropertyChanged : INotifyPropertyChanged
{
    public event PropertyChangedEventHandler? PropertyChanged;
```

```
    protected bool SetProperty<T>(
        ref T field,
        T value,
        [CallerMemberName] string propertyName = "")
    {
        if (Equals(field, value))
        {
            return false;
        }

        field = value;

        PropertyChanged?.Invoke(this, new PropertyChangedEventArgs(propertyName));
        return true;
    }
}
```

The presence of the [CallerMemberName] attribute means that a class deriving from this type does not need to specify the property name if it calls SetProperty from inside a property setter, as Example 14-17 shows.

Example 14-17. Raising a property changed event

```
public class MyViewModel : NotifyPropertyChanged
{
    private string? _name;

    public string? Name
    {
        get => _name;
        set => SetProperty(ref _name, value);
    }
}
```

Even with the new attribute, implementing INotifyPropertyChanged is clearly more effort than an automatic property, where you just write { get; set; } and let the compiler do the work for you. But it's only a little more complex than an explicit implementation of a trivial field-backed property, and it's simpler than would be possible without [CallerMemberName], because I've been able to omit the property name when asking the base class to raise the event. More importantly, it's less error prone: I can now be confident that the right name will be used every time, even if I rename the property at some point in the future.

There's a fourth caller information attribute, CallerArgumentExpression, that is a little different: instead of telling us where the call came from, it tells us something about what the call looked like. Example 14-18 shows an excerpt from the runtime libraries' ArgumentNullException class. It declares a ThrowIfNull method that uses this attribute.

*Example 14-18. The CallerArgumentExpressionAttribute in
ArgumentNullException.ThrowIfNull*

```
public class ArgumentNullException
{
    public static void ThrowIfNull(
        [NotNull] object? argument,
        [CallerArgumentExpression(nameof(argument))] string? paramName =  null)
    {
...
```

As you can see, the `CallerArgumentExpression` attribute takes a single string argument. This must be the name of another parameter in the same method—in this case there is only one other parameter, called `argument`, so it has to refer to that. The effect is that if you call this method without providing a value for the annotated `paramName` argument, the C# compiler will pass a string containing the exact expression you used for the argument that the attribute identified. Example 14-19 shows how this `ThrowIf Null` method is typically called.

Example 14-19. Calling a method that uses CallerArgumentExpressionAttribute

```
static void Greet(string greetingRecipient)
{
    ArgumentNullException.ThrowIfNull(greetingRecipient);
    Console.WriteLine($"Hello, {greetingRecipient}");
}

Greet("world");
Greet(null!);
```

The `Greet` method needs `greetingRecipient` not to be null, so it calls `Argument NullException.ThrowIfNull`, passing in `greetingRecipient`. Because this code does not provide a second argument to `ThrowIfNull`, the compiler will provide the full text of the expression we used for the first argument. In this case, that's `"greeting Recipient"`. So the effect is that when I run this program, it throws an `Argument NullException` with this message:

```
Value cannot be null. (Parameter 'greetingRecipient')
```

One of the scenarios this attribute supports is to improve assertion messages. For example, unit test libraries typically provide mechanisms for asserting that certain conditions are true after exercising the code under test. The idea is that if your test contains code such as `Assert.IsTrue(answer == 42);` the test library could use `[CallerArgumentExpression]` to be able to report the exact expression (`answer == 42`) on failure.

You might expect the `Debug.Assert` method in the runtime libraries to use this for similar reasons, but it does not, because a single-argument overload of that method existed for years before this language feature was added. A two-argument overload using `CallerArgumentExpressionAttribute` on the second argument would be a viable candidate for code such as `Debug.Assert(status == 42);` but that also matches the single-argument method. When a method call could resolve either to a method that is an exact match, or one where the compiler has to generate code to supply missing optional arguments, it prefers the exact match. The only way to use `CallerArgumentExpressionAttribute` would be to remove the existing single-argument method, and this would not be a binary-compatible change. The .NET runtime libraries use this attribute only on exception helper methods. At the time of writing this, none of the widely used .NET testing frameworks use this on their assertion methods, nor do the popular assertion libraries, for similar backward compatibility reasons. The language feature is still relatively new, so perhaps this will change before long.

CLR-Handled Attributes

Some attributes get special treatment at runtime from the CLR. There is no official comprehensive list of such attributes, so in the next few sections, I will just describe some of the most widely used examples.

InternalsVisibleToAttribute

You can apply the `InternalsVisibleToAttribute` to an assembly to declare that any `internal` types or members it defines should be visible to one or more other assemblies. A popular use for this is to enable unit testing of internal types. As Example 14-20 shows, you pass the name of the assembly as a constructor argument.

Strong naming complicates matters. Strongly named assemblies cannot make their internals visible to assemblies that are not strongly named, and strongly named assemblies can only reference other strongly named assemblies. When a strongly named assembly makes its internals visible to another strongly named assembly, it must specify not just the simple name but also the public key of the assembly to which it is granting access. And this is not just the public key token I described in Chapter 12—it is the hexadecimal for the entire public key, which will be several hundred digits. You can discover an assembly's full public key with the .NET SDK's *sn.exe* utility, using the `-Tp` switch followed by the assembly's path.

Example 14-20. InternalsVisibleToAttribute

```
[assembly:InternalsVisibleTo("ImageManagement.Tests")]
[assembly:InternalsVisibleTo("ImageServices.Tests")]
```

This shows that you can make the types visible to multiple assemblies by applying the attribute multiple times, with a different assembly name each time.

The CLR is responsible for enforcing accessibility rules. Normally, if you try to use an internal class from another assembly, you'll get an error at runtime. (C# won't even let you compile such code, but it's possible to trick the compiler. Or you could write directly in IL. The IL assembler, *ILASM*, does what you tell it and imposes far fewer restrictions than C#. Once you get past the compile-time restrictions, then you'll hit the runtime ones.) But when this attribute is present, the CLR relaxes its rules for the assemblies you list. The compiler also understands this attribute and lets code that tries to use externally defined internal types compile as long as the external library names your assembly in an InternalsVisibleToAttribute.

Besides being useful in unit test scenarios, this attribute can also be helpful if you want to split code across multiple assemblies. If you have written a large class library, you might not want to put it into one massive DLL. If it has several areas that your customers might want to use in isolation, it could make sense to split it up so that they can deploy just the parts that they need. However, although you may be able to partition your library's public-facing API, the implementation might not be as easy to divide, particularly if your codebase performs a lot of reuse. You might have many classes that are not designed for public consumption but that you use throughout your code.

If it weren't for the InternalsVisibleToAttribute, it would be awkward to reuse shared implementation details across assemblies. Either each assembly would need to contain its own copy of the relevant classes, or you'd need to make them public types in some common assembly. The problem with that second technique is that making types public effectively invites people to use them. Your documentation might state that the types are for the internal use of your framework and should not be used, but that won't stop some people.

Fortunately, you don't have to make them public. Any types that are just implementation details can remain internal, and you can make them available to all of your assemblies with the InternalsVisibleToAttribute while keeping them inaccessible to everyone else.

JIT compilation

There are a few attributes that influence how the JIT compiler generates code. You can apply the MethodImplAttribute to a method, passing values from the Method

ImplOptions enumeration. Its NoInlining value ensures that whenever your method is called by another method, it will be a full method call. Without this, the JIT compiler will sometimes just copy a method's code directly into the calling code.

In general, you'll want to leave inlining enabled. The JIT compiler inlines only small methods, and it's particularly important for tiny methods, such as property accessors. For simple field-based properties, invoking accessors with a normal function call often requires more code than inlining, so this optimization can produce code that's smaller, as well as faster. (Even if the code is not smaller, it may still be faster, because function calls can be surprisingly expensive. Modern CPUs tend to handle long sequential streams of instructions more efficiently than code that leaps around from one location to another.) However, inlining is an optimization with observable side effects—an inlined method does not get its own stack frame. Earlier, I mentioned some diagnostic APIs you can use to inspect the stack, and inlining will change the number of reported stack frames. If you just want to ask the question "Which method is calling me?" the caller info attributes described earlier provide a more efficient way to discover this and will not be defeated by inlining, but if you have code that inspects the stack for any reason, it can sometimes be confused by inlining. So, just occasionally, it's useful to disable it.

Conversely, you can specify AggressiveInlining, which encourages the JIT compiler to inline things it might otherwise leave as normal method calls. If you have identified a particular method as being highly performance sensitive, it might be worth trying this setting to see if it makes any difference, although be aware that it could make code either slower or faster—it will depend on the circumstances. Conversely, you can disable all optimizations with the NoOptimization option (although the documentation implies that this is more for the benefit of the CLR team at Microsoft than for consumers, because it is for "debugging possible code generation problems").

Another attribute that has an impact on optimization is the DebuggableAttribute. The C# compiler automatically applies this to your assembly in Debug builds. The attribute tells the CLR to be less aggressive about certain optimizations, particularly ones that affect variable lifetime and ones that change the order in which code executes. Normally, the compiler is free to change such things as long as the final result of the code is the same, but this can cause confusion if you break into the middle of an optimized method with the debugger. This attribute ensures that variable values and the flow of execution are easy to follow in that scenario.

STAThread and MTAThread

Applications that run only on Windows and that present a UI (e.g., anything using .NET's WPF or Windows Forms frameworks) typically have the [STAThread] attribute on their Main method (although you won't always see it, because the entry point is often generated by the build system for these kinds of applications). This is an instruction to the CLR's interop services for the Component Object Model (COM), but it has broader implications: you need this attribute on Main if you want your main thread to host UI elements.

Various Windows UI features rely on COM under the covers. The clipboard uses it, for example, as do certain kinds of controls. COM has several threading models, and only one of them is compatible with UI threads. One of the main reasons for this is that UI elements have thread affinity, so COM needs to ensure that it does certain work on the right thread. Also, if a UI thread doesn't regularly check for messages and handle them, deadlock can ensue. If you don't tell COM that a particular thread is a UI thread, it will omit these checks, and you will encounter problems.

 Even if you're not writing UI code, some interop scenarios need the [STAThread] attribute, because certain COM components are incapable of working without it. However, UI work is the most common reason for seeing it.

Since COM is managed for you by the CLR, the CLR needs to know that it should tell COM that a particular thread needs to be handled as a UI thread. When you create a new thread explicitly using the techniques shown in Chapter 16, you can configure its COM threading mode, but the main thread is a special case—the CLR creates it for you when your application starts, and by the time your code runs, it's too late to configure the thread. Placing the [STAThread] attribute on the Main method tells the CLR that your main thread should be initialized for UI-compatible COM behavior.

STA is short for *single-threaded apartment*. Threads that participate in COM always belong to either an STA or a *multithreaded apartment* (MTA). There are other kinds of apartments, but threads have only temporary membership in those; when a thread starts using COM, it must pick either STA or MTA mode. So there is, unsurprisingly, also an [MTAThread] attribute.

Debugging Attributes

Some attributes have no effect on normal execution of code, but can change behavior during debugging. If you annotate a method with the DebuggerStepThroughAttribute, then by default debuggers will allow that code to run without stopping when you single-step through your code. Some code generation tools will apply this attribute so that the code they generate does not distract you while you are debugging.

If you apply the DebuggerDisplayAttribute to a class or struct, it determines how debuggers display instances of that type. For example, if you have written a Coordinate type with X and Y properties, you could annotate it with [Debugger

Display("{X}, {Y}")]. This would tell the debugger to show these property values any time it displays the value of a Coordinate.

Build-Time Attributes

Some attributes are handled as part of the build process. NuGet packages can extend the build process in various ways, and they may supply source generators that can add extra code into your project. These are often controlled by attributes. An advantage of this technique is that it works well with trimming because the attributes are processed entirely during the build, instead of using reflection at runtime.

JSON serialization without reflection

The JSON serialization mechanisms described in Chapter 15 use attributes to enable developers to control how .NET objects are represented in JSON. If you use these APIs in the most straightforward way, they will use reflection to discover these attributes at runtime. However, the .NET SDK includes a code generator that can remove any need to use reflection by processing the attributes and other type information at compile time, and generating code. Examples 15-17 and 15-18 show how to use this, so I won't repeat it here.

Regular expression source generation

The .NET runtime libraries have always offered regular expression support, but .NET 7 has introduced a new way to use these. As Example 14-21 shows, you can annotate a partial method with the GeneratedRegex attribute. This triggers a source generator built into the .NET SDK to generate C# code that evaluates the specified regular expression.

Example 14-21. Regular expression source generation

```
public partial class RegexSourceGeneration
{
    [GeneratedRegex(@"[-+]?\b\d+\b")]
    private static partial Regex IsSignedInteger();

    public static bool TextIsSignedInteger(string text)
        => IsSignedInteger().IsMatch(text);
}
```

This enables all the work of parsing the regular expression and determining how best to process it to be done at build time. This improves both startup time and throughput.

Interop

The CLR's interop services define numerous attributes. Since the attributes make sense only in the context of the mechanisms they support, and because there are so many, I will not describe them in full, but Example 14-22 illustrates the kinds of things they can do.

Example 14-22. Interop attributes

```
[LibraryImport("advapi32.dll", EntryPoint = "LookupPrivilegeValueW",
    SetLastError = true, StringMarshalling = StringMarshalling.Utf16)]
[return: MarshalAs(UnmanagedType.Bool)]
internal static partial bool LookupPrivilegeValue(
    [MarshalAs(UnmanagedType.LPWStr)] string? lpSystemName,
    [MarshalAs(UnmanagedType.LPWStr)] string lpName,
    out LUID lpLuid);
```

This uses two interop attributes that we saw earlier in Example 14-7 but in a somewhat more complex way. This calls into a function exposed by *advapi32.dll*, part of the Win32 API. The first argument to the `LibraryImport` attribute tells us that, but unlike the earlier example, this goes on to provide the interop layer with additional information. The `EntryPoint` property deals with the fact that Win32 APIs taking strings sometimes come in two forms, working with either 8-bit or 16-bit characters (some old versions of Windows only supported 8-bit text, to conserve memory) and that we want to call the *Wide* form (hence the `W` suffix). This particular API uses a common Win32 idiom: it returns a Boolean value to indicate success or failure, but it also uses the Windows `SetLastError` API to provide more information in the failure case. The attribute's `SetLastError` property tells the interop layer to retrieve that immediately after calling this API so that .NET code can inspect it if necessary. This API deals with strings, so interop needs to know which character representation is in use. It then uses `MarshalAs` on the two string arguments to tell the interop layer which of the many different string representations available in unmanaged code this particular API expects.

Prior to .NET 7, interop attributes were handled at runtime by the CLR (and that still happens if you use the older `DllImport` attribute instead of `LibraryImport`). However, that older approach relies on JIT compilation under the covers if any of the arguments or the return type need any kind of runtime processing, meaning it is unavailable if you're using Native AOT. The .NET SDK includes a code generator that looks for the `LibraryImport` attribute, and which generates code to convert between .NET and unmanaged types, enabling you to call into unmanaged APIs even when using Native AOT. (In fact, this generated code still ends up using the `DllImport` attribute, but it defines the target methods in such a way that the mappings between .NET types and unmanaged types are trivial, removing any need for the CLR to do any conversions.)

Defining and Consuming Attributes

The vast majority of attributes you will come across are not intrinsic to the runtime or compiler. They are defined by class libraries and have an effect only if you are using the relevant libraries or frameworks. You are free to do exactly the same in your own code—you can define your own attribute types. Because attributes don't do anything on their own—they don't even get instantiated unless something asks to see them—it is normally useful to define an attribute type only if you're writing some sort of framework, particularly one that is driven by reflection or compile-time code analysis.

For example, unit test frameworks often discover the test classes you write via reflection and enable you to control the test runner's behavior with attributes. Another example is how Visual Studio uses reflection to discover the properties of editable objects on design surfaces (such as UI controls), and it will look for certain attributes that enable you to customize the editing behavior. Another application of attributes is to opt out of rules applied by the static code analysis tools. (The .NET SDK has built-in tools for detecting potential problems in your code. This is an extensible system, and NuGet packages can add analyzers that expand on this, potentially detecting common mistakes specific to a particular library.) Sometimes these tools make unhelpful suggestions, and you can suppress their warnings by annotating your code with attributes.

The common theme here is that some tool or framework examines your code and decides what to do based on what it finds. This is the kind of scenario in which attributes are a good fit. For example, attributes could be useful if you write an application that end users could extend. You might support loading of external assemblies that augment your application's behavior—this is often known as a *plug-in* model. It might be useful to define an attribute that allows a plug-in to provide descriptive information about itself. It's not strictly necessary to use attributes—you would probably define at least one interface that all plug-ins are required to implement, and you could have members in that interface for retrieving the necessary information. However, one advantage of using attributes is that you would not need to create an instance of the plug-in just to retrieve the description information. That would enable you to show the plug-in's details to the user before loading it, which might be important if constructing the plug-in could have side effects that the user might not want.

Attribute Types

Example 14-23 shows how an attribute containing information about a plug-in might look.

Example 14-23. An attribute type

```
[AttributeUsage(AttributeTargets.Class)]
public class PluginInformationAttribute(string name, string author) : Attribute
{
    public string Name { get; } = name;

    public string Author { get; } = author;

    public string? Description { get; set; }
}
```

To act as an attribute, a type must derive from the `Attribute` base class. Although `Attribute` defines various static methods for discovering and retrieving attributes, it does not provide very much of interest for instances. We do not derive from it to get any particular functionality; we do so because the compiler will not let you use a type as an attribute unless it derives from `Attribute`.

Notice that my type's name ends in the word `Attribute`. This is not an absolute requirement, but it is an extremely widely used convention. As you saw earlier, it's even built into the compiler, which automatically adds the `Attribute` suffix if you leave it out when applying an attribute. So there's usually no reason not to follow this convention.

I've annotated my attribute type with an attribute. Most attribute types are annotated with the `AttributeUsageAttribute`, indicating the targets to which the attribute can usefully be applied. The C# compiler will enforce this. Since my attribute in Example 14-23 states that it may be applied only to classes, the compiler will generate an error if you attempt to apply it to anything else.

 As you've seen, sometimes when we apply an attribute, we need to state its target. For example, an attribute appearing before a method targets that method unless you qualify it with the `return:` prefix. You might think you could leave out these prefixes with attributes that can target only certain members: if an attribute can be applied only to an assembly, do you really need the `assembly:` qualifier? However, C# doesn't let you leave it off. It uses the `AttributeUsageAttribute` only to verify that an attribute has not been misapplied.

My attribute defines only one constructor, so any code that uses it will have to pass the arguments that the constructor requires, as Example 14-24 does.

Example 14-24. Applying an attribute

```
[PluginInformation("Reporting", "Endjin Ltd.")]
public class ReportingPlugin
{
    ...
}
```

Attribute classes are free to define multiple constructor overloads to support different sets of information. They can also define properties as a way to support optional pieces of information. My attribute defines a `Description` property, which is not required because the constructor does not demand a value for it, but which I can set using the syntax I described earlier in this chapter. Example 14-25 shows how that looks for my attribute.

Example 14-25. Providing an optional property value for an attribute

```
[PluginInformation("Reporting", "Endjin Ltd.",
    Description = "Automated report generation")]
public class ReportingPlugin
{
    ...
}
```

So far, nothing I've shown will cause an instance of my `PluginInformation Attribute` type to be created. These annotations are simply instructions for how the attribute should be initialized if anything asks to see it. So, if this attribute is to be useful, I need to write some code that will look for it.

Retrieving Attributes

You can discover whether a particular kind of attribute has been applied using the reflection API, which can also instantiate the attribute for you. (You could also use Roslyn, the C# compiler API, but that's beyond the scope of this book.) In Chapter 13, I showed all of the reflection types representing the various targets to which attributes can be applied—types such as `MethodInfo`, `Type`, and `PropertyInfo`. These all implement an interface called `ICustomAttributeProvider`, shown in Example 14-26.

Example 14-26. `ICustomAttributeProvider`

```
public interface ICustomAttributeProvider
{
    object[] GetCustomAttributes(bool inherit);
```

```
    object[] GetCustomAttributes(Type attributeType, bool inherit);
    bool IsDefined(Type attributeType, bool inherit);
}
```

The IsDefined method simply tells you whether or not a particular attribute type is present—it does not instantiate it. The two GetCustomAttributes overloads create attributes and return them. (This is the point at which attributes are constructed and also when any properties the annotations specify are set.) The first overload returns all attributes applied to the target, while the second lets you request only those attributes of a particular type.

All of these methods take a bool argument that lets you specify whether you want only attributes that were applied directly to the target you're inspecting or also attributes applied to the base type or types.

This interface was introduced in .NET 1.0, so it does not use generics, meaning you need to cast the objects that come back. Fortunately, the CustomAttribute Extensions static class defines several extension methods that are more convenient to use. Instead of defining them for the ICustomAttributeProvider interface, it extends the reflection classes that offer attributes. For example, if you have a variable of type Type, you could call GetCustomAttribute<PluginInformationAttribute>() on it, which would construct and return the plug-in information attribute or return null if the attribute is not present. Example 14-27 uses this to show all of the plug-in information from all the DLLs in a particular folder.

Example 14-27. Showing plug-in information

```
static void ShowPluginInformation(string pluginFolder)
{
    var dir = new DirectoryInfo(pluginFolder);
    foreach (FileInfo file in dir.GetFiles("*.dll"))
    {
        Assembly pluginAssembly = Assembly.LoadFrom(file.FullName);
        var plugins =
            from type in pluginAssembly.ExportedTypes
            let info = type.GetCustomAttribute<PluginInformationAttribute>()
            where info != null
            select new { type, info };

        foreach (var plugin in plugins)
        {
            Console.WriteLine($"Plugin type: {plugin.type.Name}");
            Console.WriteLine(
                $"Name: {plugin.info.Name}, written by {plugin.info.Author}");
            Console.WriteLine($"Description: {plugin.info.Description}");
        }
    }
}
```

There's one potential problem with this. I said that one benefit of attributes is that they can be retrieved without instantiating their target types. That's true here—I'm not constructing any of the plug-ins in Example 14-27. However, I am loading the plug-in assemblies, and a possible side effect of enumerating the plug-ins would be to run static constructors in the plug-in DLLs. So, although I'm not deliberately running any code in those DLLs, I can't guarantee that no code from those DLLs will run. If my goal is to present a list of plug-ins to the user, and to load and run only the ones explicitly selected, I've failed, because I've given plug-in code a chance to run. However, we can fix this.

Metadata-Only Load

You do not need to load an assembly fully in order to retrieve attribute information. As I discussed in Chapter 13, you can load an assembly for reflection purposes only with the `MetadataLoadContext` class. This prevents any of the code in the assembly from running but enables you to inspect the types it contains. However, this presents a challenge for attributes. The usual way to inspect an attribute's properties is to instantiate it by calling `GetCustomAttributes` or a related extension method. Since that involves constructing the attribute—which means running some code—it is not supported for assemblies loaded by `MetadataLoadContext` (not even if the attribute type in question were defined in a different assembly that had been fully loaded in the normal way). If I modified Example 14-27 to load the assembly with `Metadata LoadContext`, the call to `GetCustomAttribute<PluginInformation Attribute>` would throw an exception.

When loading for metadata only, you have to use the `GetCustomAttributesData` method. Instead of instantiating the attribute for you, this returns the information stored in the metadata—the instructions for creating the attribute. Example 14-28 shows a version of the relevant code from Example 14-27 modified to work this way. (It also includes the code required to initialize the `MetadataLoadContext`.)

Example 14-28. Retrieving attributes with the MetadataLoadContext

```
string[] runtimeAssemblies = Directory.GetFiles(
    RuntimeEnvironment.GetRuntimeDirectory(), "*.dll");
var paths = new List<string>(runtimeAssemblies);
paths.Add(file.FullName);

var resolver = new PathAssemblyResolver(paths);
var mlc = new MetadataLoadContext(resolver);

Assembly pluginAssembly = mlc.LoadFromAssemblyPath(file.FullName);
var plugins =
    from type in pluginAssembly.ExportedTypes
    let info = type.GetCustomAttributesData().SingleOrDefault(attrData =>
```

```
                    attrData.AttributeType.FullName == pluginAttributeType.FullName)
            where info != null
            let description = info.NamedArguments
                            .SingleOrDefault(a => a.MemberName == "Description")
            select new
            {
                type,
                Name = (string) info.ConstructorArguments[0].Value,
                Author = (string) info.ConstructorArguments[1].Value,
                Description =
                    description == null ? null : description.TypedValue.Value
            };

foreach (var plugin in plugins)
{
    Console.WriteLine($"Plugin type: {plugin.type.Name}");
    Console.WriteLine($"Name: {plugin.Name}, written by {plugin.Author}");
    Console.WriteLine($"Description: {plugin.Description}");
}
```

The code is rather more cumbersome because we don't get back an instance of the attribute. `GetCustomAttributesData` returns a collection of `CustomAttributeData` objects. Example 14-28 uses LINQ's `SingleOrDefault` operator to find the entry for the `PluginInformationAttribute`, and if that's present, the `info` variable in the query will end up holding a reference to the relevant `CustomAttributeData` object. The code then picks through the constructor arguments and property values using the `ConstructorArguments` and `NamedArguments` properties, enabling it to retrieve the three descriptive text values embedded in the attribute.

As this demonstrates, the `MetadataLoadContext` adds complexity, so you should use it only if you need the benefits it offers. One benefit is the fact that it won't run any of the assemblies you load. It can also load assemblies that might be rejected if they were loaded normally (e.g., because they target a specific processor architecture that doesn't match your process). But if you don't need the metadata-only option, accessing the attributes directly, as Example 14-27 does, is more convenient.

Generic Attribute Types

C# 11.0 and .NET 7.0 added support for defining generic attribute types. Showing such an attribute, and how to use it, is Example 14-29.

Example 14-29. A generic attribute type

```
[AttributeUsage(AttributeTargets.Class)]
public class PluginHelpProviderAttribute<TProvider> : Attribute
    where TProvider : IPluginHelpProvider
{
```

```
    public Type ProviderType => typeof(TProvider);
}

// Usage:
[PluginInformation("Reporting", "Endjin Ltd.")]
[PluginHelpProviderAttribute<ReportingPluginHelpProvider>]
public class ReportingPlugin
{
    ...
}
```

Since this is a fairly recent feature, it is not yet widely used. Most attribute types that need to refer to a particular type (like the ExpectedException attribute shown in Example 14-3) just take a Type object as a constructor argument. That works perfectly well, but generic attribute types have one advantage: they can define constraints for their type arguments. Example 14-29 requires that whatever type we plug in to this PluginHelpProviderAttribute<TProvider>, it must be a type that implements a specific interface, IPluginHelpProvider. If we try to use this attribute with a type that does not implement that interface, the compiler will report an error. With the old approach of passing a Type object to the attribute's constructor, you would either need to wait until the attribute is instantiated to detect the use of an inappropriate type, or write a code analyzer (which is a fairly complex task) to detect the problem at build time.

Summary

Attributes provide a way to embed custom data into an assembly's metadata. You can apply attributes to a type, any member of a type, a parameter, a return value, or even a whole assembly or one of its modules. A handful of attributes get special handling from the CLR, and a few control compiler features, but most have no intrinsic behavior, acting merely as passive information containers. Attributes do not even get instantiated unless something asks to see them. All of this makes attributes most useful in systems with reflection-driven behavior—if you already have one of the reflection API objects such as ParameterInfo or Type, you can ask it directly for attributes. You therefore most often see attributes used in frameworks that inspect your code with reflection, such as unit test frameworks, serialization frameworks, data-driven UI elements like Visual Studio's Properties panel, or plug-in frameworks. Sometimes frameworks of this kind can use the C# compiler API (Roslyn) to discover attributes at build time. This enables them to avoid relying on reflection, making them compatible with Native AOT. If you are using a framework of this kind, you will typically be able to configure its behavior by annotating your code with the attributes the framework recognizes. If you are writing this sort of framework, then it may make sense to define your own attribute types.

CHAPTER 15

Files and Streams

Most of the techniques I've shown so far in this book revolve around the information that lives in objects and variables. This kind of state is stored in a particular process's memory, but to be useful, a program must interact with a broader world. This might happen through UI frameworks, but there's one particular abstraction that can be used for many kinds of interactions with the outside world: a *stream*.

Streams are so widely used in computing that you will no doubt already be familiar with them, and a .NET stream is much the same as in most other programming systems: it is simply a sequence of bytes. That makes a stream a useful abstraction for many commonly encountered features such as a file on disk or the body of an HTTP response. A console application uses streams to represent its input and output. If you run such a program interactively, the text that the user types at the keyboard becomes the program's input stream, and anything the program writes to its output stream appears on screen. A program doesn't necessarily know what kind of input or output it has, though—you can redirect these streams with console programs. For example, the input stream might actually provide the contents of a file on disk, or it could even be the output from some other program.

 Not all I/O APIs are stream-based. For example, in addition to the input stream, the Console class provides a ReadKey method that gives information about exactly which key was pressed, which works only if the input comes from the keyboard. So, although you can write programs that do not care whether their input comes interactively or from a file, some programs are pickier.

The stream APIs present you with raw byte data. However, it is possible to work at a different level. For example, there are text-oriented APIs that can wrap underlying streams, so you can work with characters or strings instead of raw bytes. There are also various *serialization* mechanisms that enable you to convert .NET objects into a stream representation, which you can turn back into objects later, making it possible to save an object's state persistently or to send that state over the network. I'll show these higher-level APIs later, but first, let's look at the stream abstraction itself.

The Stream Class

The Stream class is defined in the System.IO namespace. It is an abstract base class, with concrete derived types such as FileStream or GZipStream representing particular kinds of streams. Example 15-1 shows three of the Stream class's members. It has several other members, but these are at the heart of the abstraction. (As you'll see later, there are also asynchronous versions of Read and Write. The latest .NET versions also provide overloads that take one of the *span* types described in Chapter 18 in place of an array. Everything I say in this section about these methods also applies to the asynchronous and span-based forms.)

Example 15-1. The members at the heart of Stream

```
public abstract int Read(byte[] buffer, int offset, int count);
public abstract void Write(byte[] buffer, int offset, int count);
public abstract long Position { get; set; }
```

Some streams are read-only. For example, when the input stream for a console application represents the keyboard or the output of some other program, there's no meaningful way for the program to write to that stream. (And for consistency, even if you use input redirection to run a console application with a file as its input, the input stream will be read-only.) Some streams are write-only, such as the output stream of a console application. If you call Read on a write-only stream or Write on a read-only one, these methods throw a NotSupportedException.

 The Stream class defines various bool properties that describe a stream's capabilities, so you don't have to wait until you get an exception to find out what sort of stream you've got. You can check the CanRead or CanWrite properties.

Both Read and Write take a byte[] array as their first argument, and these methods copy data into or out of that array, respectively. The offset and count arguments that follow indicate the array element at which to start and the number of bytes to read or write; you do not have to use the whole array. Notice that there are no arguments to specify the offset within the stream at which to read or write. This is managed by the Position property—this starts at zero, but each time you read or write, the position advances by the number of bytes processed.

Notice that the Read method returns an int. This tells you how many bytes were read from the stream—the method does not guarantee to provide the amount of data you requested. One obvious reason for this is that you could reach the end of the stream, so even though you may have asked to read 100 bytes into your array, there may have been only 30 bytes of data left between the current Position and the end of the stream. However, that's not the only reason you might get less than you asked for, and this often catches people out, so for the benefit of people skim-reading this chapter, I'll put this in a scary warning.

 If you ask for more than one byte at a time, a Stream is always free to return less data than you requested from Read for any reason. You should never presume that a call to Read returned as much data as it could, even if you have good reason to know that the amount you asked for will be available.

The reason Read is slightly tricky is that some streams are live, representing a source of information that produces data gradually as the program runs. For example, if a console application is running interactively, its input stream can provide data only as fast as the user types; a stream representing data being received over a network connection can provide data only as fast as it arrives. If you call Read and you ask for more data than is currently available, a stream might wait until it has as much as you've asked for, but it doesn't have to—it may return whatever data it has immediately. (The only situation in which it is obliged to wait before returning is if it currently has no data at all but is not yet at the end of the stream. It has to return at least one byte, because a 0 return value indicates the end of the stream.) If you want to ensure that you read a specific number of bytes, you used to have to check whether Read returned fewer bytes than you wanted, and if necessary, keep calling it until you have what you need. (On .NET Framework, you still have to do this.) Fortunately, .NET 7.0 added a new method, ReadExactly, which takes the same arguments as Read, but won't return until it either reaches the end of the stream, or is able to return as many bytes as you asked for. It also added a similar ReadAtLeast, which will never return fewer bytes than you asked for (unless it reaches the end of the stream) but can return more if the stream happens to have more available immediately.

Stream also offers a simpler way to read. The ReadByte method returns a single byte, unless you hit the end of the stream, at which point it returns a value of -1. (Its return type is int, enabling it to return any possible value for byte as well as negative values.) This avoids the problem of being handed back only some of the data you requested, because if you get anything back at all, you always get exactly one byte. However, it's not especially convenient or efficient if you want to read larger chunks of data.

The `Write` method doesn't have any of these issues. If it succeeds, it always accepts all of the data you provide. Of course, it might fail—it could throw an exception before it manages to write all of the data because of an error (e.g., running out of space on disk or losing a network connection).

Position and Seeking

Streams automatically update their current position each time you read or write. As you can see in Example 15-1, the `Position` property can be set, so you can attempt to move directly to a particular position. This is not guaranteed to work because it's not always possible to support it. For example, a `Stream` that represents data being received over a TCP network connection could produce data indefinitely—as long as the connection remains open and the other end keeps sending data, the stream will continue to honor calls to `Read`. A connection could remain open for many days and might receive terabytes of data in that time. If such a stream let you set its `Position` property, enabling your code to go back and reread data received earlier, the stream would have to find somewhere to store every single byte it received just in case the code using the stream wants to see it again. Since that might involve storing more data than you have space for on disk, this is clearly not practical, so some streams will throw `NotSupportedException` when you try to set the `Position` property. (There's a `CanSeek` property you can use to discover whether a particular stream supports changing the position, so just like with read-only and write-only streams, you don't have to wait until you get an exception to find out whether it will work.)

As well as the `Position` property, `Stream` also defines a `Seek` method, whose signature is shown in Example 15-2. This lets you specify the position you require relative to the stream's current position. (This also throws `NotSupportedException` on streams that don't support seeking.)

Example 15-2. The Seek method

```
public abstract long Seek(long offset, SeekOrigin origin);
```

If you pass `SeekOrigin.Current` as the second argument, it will set the position by adding the first argument to the current position. You can pass a negative `offset` if you want to move backward. You can also pass `SeekOrigin.End` to set the position to be some specified number of bytes from the end of the stream. Passing `Seek Origin.Begin` has the same logical effect as just setting `Position`—it sets the position relative to the start of the stream.

Flushing

As with many stream APIs on other programming systems, writing data to a `Stream` does not necessarily cause the data to reach its destination immediately. When a call to `Write` returns, all you know is that it has copied your data somewhere; but that might be a buffer in memory, not the final target. For example, if you write a single byte to a stream representing a file on a storage device, the stream object will typically defer writing that to the drive until it has enough bytes to make it worth the effort. Storage devices are block-based, meaning that writes happen in fixed-size chunks, typically several kilobytes in size, so it generally makes sense to wait until there's enough data to fill a block before writing anything out.

This buffering is usually a good thing—it improves write performance while enabling you to ignore the details of how the disk works. However, a downside is that if you write data only occasionally (e.g., when writing error messages to a logfile), you could easily end up with long delays between the program writing data to a stream and that data reaching the disk. This could be perplexing for someone trying to diagnose a problem by looking at the logfiles of a program that's currently running. And more insidiously, if your program crashes, anything in a stream's buffers that has not yet made it to the storage device will probably be lost.

The `Stream` class therefore offers a `Flush` method. This lets you tell the stream that you want it to do whatever work is required to ensure that any buffered data is written to its target, even if that means making suboptimal use of the buffer.

When using a `FileStream`, the `Flush` method does not necessarily guarantee that the data being flushed has made it to disk yet. It merely makes the stream pass the data to the OS. Before you call `Flush`, the OS might not even have seen the data, so if you were to terminate the process suddenly, the data would be lost. After `Flush` has returned, the OS has everything your code has written, so the process could be terminated without loss of data. However, the OS may perform additional buffering of its own, so if the power fails before the OS gets around to writing everything to disk, the data will still be lost. If you need to guarantee that data has been written persistently (rather than merely ensuring that you've handed it to the OS), you will also need to either use the `WriteThrough` flag, described in "FileStream Class" on page 688, or call the `Flush` overload that takes a `bool`, passing `true` to force flushing to the storage device.

A stream automatically flushes its contents when you call `Dispose`. You need to use `Flush` only when you want to keep a stream open after writing out buffered data. It is particularly important if there will be extended periods during which the stream is open but inactive. (If the stream represents a network connection, and if your application depends on prompt data delivery—this would be the case in an online chat application or game, for example—you would call Flush even if you expect only fairly brief periods of inactivity.)

Copying

Copying all of the data from one stream to another is occasionally useful. It wouldn't be hard to write a loop to do this, but you don't have to, because the Stream class's CopyTo method (or the equivalent CopyToAsync) does it for you. There's not much to say about it. The main reason I'm mentioning it is that it's not uncommon for developers to write their own version of this method because they didn't know the functionality was built into Stream.

Length

Some streams are able to report their length through the predictably named Length property. As with Position, this property's type is long—Stream uses 64-bit numbers because streams often need to be larger than 2 GB, which would be the upper limit if sizes and positions were represented with int.

Stream also defines a SetLength method that lets you define the length of a stream (where supported). You might think about using this when writing a large quantity of data to a file, to ensure that there is enough space to contain all the data you wish to write—better to get an IOException before you start than wasting time on a doomed operation and potentially causing system-wide problems by using up all of the free space. However, many filesystems support sparse files, letting you create files far larger than the available free space, so in practice you might not see any error until you start writing nonzero data. Even so, if you specify a length that is longer than the filesystem supports, SetLength will throw an ArgumentException.

Not all streams support length operations. The Stream class documentation says that the Length property is available only on streams that support CanSeek. This is because streams that support seeking are typically ones where the whole content of the stream is known and accessible up front. Seeking is unavailable on streams where the content is produced at runtime (e.g., input streams representing user input or streams representing data received over the network), and in those cases the length is also very often not known in advance. As for SetLength, the documentation states that this is supported only on streams that support both writing and seeking. (As with all members representing optional features, Length and SetLength will throw a Not SupportedException if you try to use these members on streams that do not support them.)

Disposal

Some streams represent resources external to the .NET runtime. For example, `FileStream` provides stream access to the contents of a file, so it needs to obtain a file handle from the OS. It's important to close handles when you're done with them; otherwise you might prevent other applications from being able to use the file. Consequently, the `Stream` class implements the `IDisposable` interface (described in Chapter 7) so that it can know when to do that. And, as I mentioned earlier, buffering streams such as `FileStream` flush their buffers when you call `Dispose`, before closing handles.

Not all stream types depend on `Dispose` being called: `MemoryStream` works entirely in memory, so the GC would be able to take care of it. But in general, if you caused a stream to be created, you should call `Dispose` when you no longer need it.

 There are some situations in which you will be provided with a stream, but it is not your job to dispose it. For example, ASP.NET Core can provide streams to represent data in HTTP requests and responses. It creates these for you and then disposes them after you've used them, so you should not call `Dispose` on them.

Confusingly, the `Stream` class also has a `Close` method. This is an accident of history. The first public beta release of .NET 1.0 did not define `IDisposable`, and C# did not have `using` statements—the keyword was only for `using` directives, which bring namespaces into scope. The `Stream` class needed some way of knowing when to clean up its resources, and since there was not yet a standard way to do this, it invented its own idiom. It defined a `Close` method, which was consistent with the terminology used in many stream-based APIs in other programming systems. `IDisposable` was added before the final release of .NET 1.0, and the `Stream` class added support for this, but it left the `Close` method in place; removing it would have disrupted a lot of early adopters who had been using the betas. But `Close` is redundant, and the documentation actively advises against using it. It says you should call `Dispose` instead (through a `using` statement if that is convenient). There's no harm in calling `Close`—there's no practical difference between that and `Dispose`—but `Dispose` is the more common idiom and is therefore preferred.

Asynchronous Operation

The `Stream` class offers asynchronous versions of `Read` and `Write`. Be aware that there are two forms. `Stream` first appeared in .NET 1.0, so it supported what was then the standard asynchronous mechanism, the Asynchronous Programming Model (APM, described in Chapter 16) through the `BeginRead`, `EndRead`, `BeginWrite`, and `End Write` methods. This model is now deprecated, having been superseded by the newer

Task-based Asynchronous Pattern (or TAP, also described in Chapter 16). Stream supports this through its ReadAsync and WriteAsync methods. There are two more operations that did not originally have any kind of asynchronous form that now have TAP versions: FlushAsync and CopyToAsync. (These support only TAP, because APM was already deprecated by the time Microsoft added these methods.)

 Avoid the old APM-based Begin/End forms of Read and Write. For a while they were only in .NET Framework. They were later added to .NET Standard 2.0 to make it easier to migrate existing code from .NET Framework to .NET, so they are supported only for legacy scenarios.

Some stream types implement asynchronous operations using very efficient techniques that correspond directly to the asynchronous capabilities of the underlying OS. (FileStream does this, as do the various streams .NET can provide to represent content from network connections.) You may come across libraries with custom stream types that do not do this, but even then, the asynchronous methods will be available, because the base Stream class can fall back to using multithreaded techniques instead.

One thing you need to be careful of when using asynchronous reads and writes is that a stream only has a single Position property. Reads and writes depend on the current Position and also update it when they are done, so in general you must avoid starting a new operation before one already in progress is complete. However, if you wish to perform multiple concurrent read or write operations from a particular file, File Stream has special handling for this. If you tell it that you will be using the file in asynchronous mode, operations use the value Position has at the start of the operation, and once an asynchronous read or write has started, you are allowed to change Position and start another operation without waiting for all the previous ones to complete. But this only applies to FileStream, and only when the file is opened in asynchronous mode. Alternatively, instead of using FileStream, you could use the RandomAccess class, which defines methods for performing read and write operations directly against a file handle. This class's methods all require you pass an argument specifying the position explicitly for each read and write.

.NET offers IAsyncDisposable, an asynchronous form of Dispose. The Stream class implements this, because disposal often involves flushing, which is a potentially slow operation. (This is not available on .NET Framework.)

Concrete Stream Types

The Stream class is abstract, so to use a stream, you'll need a concrete derived type. In some situations, this will be provided for you—the ASP.NET Core web framework supplies stream objects representing HTTP request and response bodies, for example, and the client-side `HttpClient` class will do something similar. But sometimes you'll need to create a stream object yourself. This section describes a few of the more commonly used types that derive from `Stream`.

The `FileStream` class represents a file on the filesystem. I will describe this in "Files and Directories" on page 687.

`MemoryStream` lets you create a stream on top of a `byte[]` array. You can either take an existing `byte[]` and wrap it in a `MemoryStream`, or you can create a `MemoryStream` and then populate it with data by calling `Write` (or `WriteAsync`). You can retrieve the populated `byte[]` once you're done by calling either `ToArray` or `GetBuffer`. (`ToArray` allocates a new array, with the size based on the number of bytes actually written. `GetBuffer` is more efficient because it returns the underlying array `MemoryStream` is using, but unless the writes happened to fill it completely, the array returned will typically be oversized, with some unused space at the end.) This class is useful when you are working with APIs that require a stream and you don't have one for some reason. For example, most of the serialization APIs described later in this chapter work with streams, but you might end up wanting to use that in conjunction with some other API that works in terms of `byte[]`. `MemoryStream` lets you bridge between those two representations.

Both Windows and Unix define an interprocess communication (IPC) mechanism enabling you to connect two processes through a stream. Windows calls these *named pipes*. Unix also has a mechanism with that name, but it is completely different; it does, however, offer a mechanism similar to Windows named pipes: *domain sockets*. Although the precise details of Windows named pipes and Unix domain sockets differ, the various classes derived from `PipeStream` provide a common abstraction for both in .NET.

`BufferedStream` derives from `Stream` but also takes a `Stream` in its constructor. It adds a layer of buffering, which is useful if you want to perform small reads or writes on a stream that is designed to work best with larger operations. (You don't need to use this with `FileStream` because that has its own built-in buffering mechanism.)

There are various stream types that transform the contents of other streams in some way. For example, `DeflateStream`, `GZipStream`, and `BrotliStream` implement three widely used compression algorithms. You can wrap these around other streams to compress the data written to the underlying stream or to decompress the data read from it. (These just provide the lowest-level compression service. If you want to work with the popular ZIP format for packages of compressed files, use the `ZipArchive` class. .NET 7.0 added a `TarFile` class for working with the *tar* archive used for similar purposes in Unix.) There's also a class called `CryptoStream`, which can encrypt or decrypt the contents of other streams using any of the wide variety of encryption mechanisms supported in .NET.

One Type, Many Behaviors

As you've now seen, the abstract base class `Stream` gets used in a wide range of scenarios. It is arguably an abstraction that has been stretched a little too thin. The presence of properties such as `CanSeek` that tell you whether the particular `Stream` you have can be used in a certain way is arguably a symptom of an underlying problem, an example of something known as a *code smell*. .NET streams did not invent this particular one-size-fits-all approach—it was popularized by Unix and the C programming language's standard library a long time ago. The problem is that when writing code that deals with a `Stream`, you might not know what sort of thing you are dealing with.

There are many different ways to use a `Stream`, but three usage styles come up a lot:

- Sequential access of a sequence of bytes
- Random access, with a presumption of efficient caching
- Access to some underlying capability of a device or system

As you know, not all `Stream` implementations support all three models—if `CanSeek` returns `false`, that rules out the middle option. But what is less obvious is that even when these properties indicate that a capability is available, not all streams support all usage models equally efficiently.

For example, I worked on a project that used a library for accessing files in a cloud-hosted storage service that was able to represent those files with `Stream` objects. This looks convenient because you can pass those to any API that works with a `Stream`. However, it was designed very much for the third style of use in the preceding list: every single call to `Read` (or `ReadAsync`) would cause the library to make an HTTP request to the storage service. We had initially hoped to use this with another library that knew how to parse Parquet files (a binary tabular data storage format widely used in high-volume data processing). However, it turned out that the library was expecting a stream that supported the second type of access: it jumped back and forth through the file, making large numbers of fairly small reads. It worked perfectly well with the `FileStream` type I'll be describing later, because that supports the first two modes of use well. (For the second style, it relies on the OS to do the caching.) But it would have been a performance disaster to plug a `Stream` from the storage service library directly into the Parquet parsing library.

It's not always obvious when you have a mismatch of this kind. In this example, the properties that report capabilities (such as `CanSeek`) gave no clue that there would be a problem. And applications that use Parquet files often use some sort of remote storage service, rather than the local filesystem, so there was no obvious reason to think that this library would presume that any Stream would offer local filesystem-like caching. It did technically work when we tried it: the storage library Stream worked hard to do everything asked of it, and the code worked correctly...eventually. But it was unusably slow. So whenever you use a Stream, it's important to make sure you have fully understood what access patterns it will be subjected to and how efficiently it supports those patterns.

In some cases you might be able to bridge the gap. The BufferedStream class can often take a Stream designed only for the third usage style mentioned previously and adapt it for the first style of usage. However, there's nothing in the runtime libraries that can add support for the second style of usage to a Stream that doesn't already innately support it. (This is typically only available either with streams that represent something already fully in memory or that wrap some local API that does the caching for you, such as the OS filesystem APIs.) In these cases you will either need to rethink your design (e.g., make a local copy of the Stream contents), change the way that the Stream is consumed, or write some sort of custom caching adapter. (In the end, we wrote an adapter that augmented the capabilities of BufferedStream with just enough random access caching to solve the performance problems.)

Text-Oriented Types

Stream is byte oriented, but it's common to work with files that contain text. If you want to process text stored in a file (or received over the network), it is cumbersome to use a byte-based API, because this forces you to deal explicitly with all of the variations that can occur. For example, there are multiple conventions for how to represent the end of a line—Windows typically uses two bytes with values of 13 and 10, as do many internet standards such as HTTP, but Unix-like systems often use just a single byte with the value 10.

There are also multiple character encodings in popular use. Some files use one byte per character, some use two, and some use a variable-length encoding. There are many different single-byte encodings too, so if you encounter a byte value of, say, 163 in a text file, you cannot know what that means unless you know which encoding is in use.

In a file using the single-byte Windows-1252 encoding, the value 163 represents a pound sign: £.[1] But if the file is encoded with ISO/IEC 8859-5 (designed for regions

---

[1] You might have thought that the pound sign was #, but if, like me, you're British, that's just not on. It would be like someone insisting on referring to @ as a dollar sign. Unicode's canonical name for # is *number sign*, and it also allows my preferred option, *hash*, as well as *octothorpe*, *crosshatch*, and, regrettably, *pound sign*.

that use Cyrillic alphabets), the exact same code represents the Cyrillic capital letter DJE: Ђ. And if the file uses the UTF-8 encoding, the value 163 would only be allowed as part of a multibyte sequence representing a single character.

Awareness of these issues is, of course, an essential part of any developer's skill set, but that doesn't mean you should have to handle every little detail any time you encounter text. So .NET defines specialized abstractions for working with text.

TextReader and TextWriter

The abstract TextReader and TextWriter classes present data as a sequence of char values. Logically speaking, these classes are similar to a stream, but each element in the sequence is a char instead of a byte. However, there are some differences in the details. For one thing, there are separate abstractions for reading and writing. Stream combines these, because it's common to want read/write access to a single entity, particularly if the stream represents a file on disk. For byte-oriented random access, this makes sense, but it's a problematic abstraction for text.

Variable-length encodings make it tricky to support random write access (i.e., the ability to change values at any point in the sequence). Consider what it would mean to take a 1 GB UTF-8 text file whose first character is a $ and replace that first character with a £. In UTF-8, the $ character takes only one byte, but £ requires two, so changing that first character would require an extra byte to be inserted at the start of the file. This would mean moving the remaining file contents—almost 1 GB of data—along by one byte.

Even read-only random access is relatively expensive. Finding the millionth character in a UTF-8 file requires you to read the first 999,999 characters, because without doing that, you have no way of knowing what mix of single-byte and multibyte characters there is. The millionth character might start at the millionth byte, but it could also start some four million bytes in, or anywhere in between. Since supporting random access with variable-length text encodings is expensive, particularly for writable data, these text-based types don't offer it. Without random access, there's no real benefit in merging readers and writers into one type. Also, separating reader and writer types removes the need to check the CanWrite property—you know that you can write because you've got a TextWriter.

TextReader offers several ways to read data. The simplest is the zero-argument overload of Read, which returns an int. This will return −1 if you've reached the end of the input and will otherwise return a character value. (You'll need to cast it to a char once you've verified that it's nonnegative.) Alternatively, there are two methods that look similar to the Stream class's Read method, as Example 15-3 shows.

Example 15-3. TextReader chunk reading methods

```
public virtual int Read(char[] buffer, int index, int count) {...}
public virtual int ReadBlock(char[] buffer, int index, int count) {...}
```

Just like `Stream.Read`, these take an array, as well as an index into that array and a count, and will attempt to read the number of values specified. The most obvious difference from `Stream` is that these use `char` instead of `byte`. But what's the difference between `Read` and `ReadBlock`? `ReadBlock` solves the same problem as `ReadExactly` does for streams: whereas `Read` may return fewer characters than you asked for, `Read Block` will not return until either as many characters as you asked for are available or it reaches the end of the content.

One of the challenges of handling text input is dealing with the various conventions for line endings, and `TextReader` can insulate you from that. Its `ReadLine` method reads an entire line of input and returns it as a `string`. This string will not include the end-of-line character or characters.

TextReader does not presume one particular end-of-line convention. It accepts either a carriage return (character value 13, which we write as \r in string literals) or a line feed (10, or \n). And if both characters appear adjacently, the character pair is treated as being a single end of line, despite being two characters. This processing happens only when you use either `ReadLine` or `ReadLine Async`. If you work directly at the character level by using `Read` or `ReadBlock`, you will see the end-of-line characters exactly as they are.

TextReader also offers `ReadToEnd`, which reads the input in its entirety and returns it as a single `string`. And finally, there's `Peek`, which does the same thing as the single-argument `Read` method, except it does not change the state of the reader. It lets you look at the next character without consuming it, so the next time you call either `Peek` or `Read`, it will return the same character again.

As for `TextWriter`, it offers two overloaded methods for writing: `Write` and `Write Line`. Each of these offers overloads for all of the built-in value types (`bool`, `int`, `float`, etc.). Functionally, the class could have gotten away with a single overload that takes an `object`, because that can just call `ToString` on its argument, but these specialized overloads make it possible to avoid boxing the argument. `TextWriter` also offers a `Flush` method for much the same reason that `Stream` does.

By default, a `TextWriter` will use the default end-of-line sequence for the OS you are running on. On Windows this is the \r\n sequence (13, then 10). On Linux or macOS you will just get a single \n at each line end. You can change this by setting the writer's NewLine property.

Both of these abstract classes implement IDisposable because some of the concrete derived text reader and writer types are wrappers around other disposable resources.

As with Stream, these classes offer asynchronous methods for reading and writing (although StreamReader doesn't implement IAsyncDisposable). Unlike with Stream, this was a fairly recent addition, so they support only the task-based pattern described in Chapter 16, which can be consumed with the await keyword described in Chapter 17.

Concrete Reader and Writer Types

As with Stream, various APIs in .NET will present you with TextReader and Text Writer objects. For example, the Console class defines In and Out properties that provide textual access to the process's input and output streams. I've not described these before, but we have been using them implicitly—the Console.WriteLine method overloads are all just wrappers that call Out.WriteLine for you. Likewise, the Console class's Read and ReadLine methods simply forward to In.Read and In.Read Line. There's also Error, another TextWriter for writing to the standard error output stream. However, there are some concrete classes that derive from TextReader or TextWriter that you might want to instantiate directly.

StreamReader and StreamWriter

Perhaps the most useful concrete text reader and writer types are StreamReader and StreamWriter, which wrap a Stream object. You can pass a Stream as a constructor argument, or you can just pass a string containing the path of a file, in which case they will automatically construct a FileStream for you and then wrap that. Example 15-4 uses this technique to write some text to a file.

Example 15-4. Writing text to a file with StreamWriter

```
using (var fw = new StreamWriter(@"c:\temp\out.txt"))
{
    fw.WriteLine($"Writing to a file at {DateTime.Now}");
}
```

There are various constructor overloads offering more fine-grained control. When passing a string in order to use a file with a StreamWriter (as opposed to some Stream you have already obtained), you can optionally pass a bool indicating whether to start from scratch or to append to an existing file if one exists. (A true value enables appending.) If you do not pass this argument, appending is not used, and writing will begin from the start. You can also specify an encoding. By default, `StreamWriter` will use UTF-8 with no byte order mark (BOM), but you can pass any type derived from the `Encoding` class, which is described in "Encoding" on page 684.

`StreamReader` is similar—you can construct it by passing either a `Stream` or a `string` containing the path of a file, and you can optionally specify an encoding. However, if you don't specify an encoding, the behavior is subtly different from `StreamWriter`. Whereas `StreamWriter` just defaults to UTF-8, `StreamReader` will attempt to detect the encoding from the stream's content. It looks at the first few bytes and will look for certain features that are typically a good sign that a particular encoding is in use. If the encoded text begins with a Unicode BOM, this makes it possible to determine with high confidence what the encoding is.

StringReader and StringWriter

The `StringReader` and `StringWriter` classes serve a similar purpose to `Memory Stream`: they are useful when you are working with an API that requires either a `TextReader` or `TextWriter`, but you want to work entirely in memory. Whereas `MemoryStream` presents a `Stream` API on top of a `byte[]` array, `StringReader` wraps a `string` as a `TextReader`, while `StringWriter` presents a `TextWriter` API on top of a `StringBuilder`.

One of the APIs .NET offers for working with XML, `XmlReader`, requires either a `Stream` or a `TextReader`. Suppose you have XML content in a `string`. If you pass a `string` when creating a new `XmlReader`, it will interpret that as a URI from which to fetch the content, rather than the content itself. The constructor for `StringReader` that takes a string just wraps that string as the content of the reader, and we can pass that to the `XmlReader.Create` overload that requires a `TextReader`, as Example 15-5 shows. (The line that does this is in bold—the code that follows just uses the `XmlReader` to read the content to show that it works as expected.)

Example 15-5. Wrapping a string in a `StringReader`

```
string xmlContent =
    "<message><text>Hello</text><recipient>world</recipient></message>";
var xmlReader = XmlReader.Create(new StringReader(xmlContent));
while (xmlReader.Read())
{
    if (xmlReader.NodeType == XmlNodeType.Text)
    {
        Console.WriteLine(xmlReader.Value);
    }
}
```

`StringWriter` is even simpler: you can just construct it with no arguments. Once you've finished writing to it, you can call either `ToString` or `GetStringBuilder` to extract all of the text that has been written.

Encoding

As I mentioned earlier, if you're using the `StreamReader` or `StreamWriter`, these need to know which character encoding the underlying stream uses to be able to convert correctly between the bytes in the stream and .NET's char or `string` types. To manage this, the `System.Text` namespace defines an abstract `Encoding` class, with various encoding-specific public concrete derived types, including `ASCIIEncoding`, `UTF7Encoding`, `UTF8Encoding`, `UTF32Encoding`, and `UnicodeEncoding`.

Most of those type names are self-explanatory, because they are named after the standard character encodings they represent, such as ASCII or UTF-8. The one that requires a little more explanation is `UnicodeEncoding`—after all, UTF-7, UTF-8, and UTF-32 are all Unicode encodings, so what's this other one for? When Windows introduced support for Unicode back in the first version of Windows NT, it adopted a slightly unfortunate convention: in documentation and various API names, the term *Unicode* was used to refer to a 2-byte little-endian[2] character encoding, which is just one of many possible encoding schemes, all of which could correctly be described as being "Unicode" of one form or another.

The `UnicodeEncoding` class is named to be consistent with this historical convention, although even then it's still a bit confusing. The encoding referred to as "Unicode" in Win32 APIs is effectively UTF-16LE, but the `UnicodeEncoding` class is also capable of supporting the big-endian UTF-16BE.

The base `Encoding` class defines static properties that return instances of all the encoding types I've mentioned, so if you need an object representing a particular encoding, you would normally just write `Encoding.ASCII` or `Encoding.UTF8`, etc., instead of constructing a new object. There are two properties of type `UnicodeEncoding`: the `Unicode` property returns one configured for UTF-16LE, and `BigEndianUnicode` returns one for UTF-16BE.

For the various Unicode encodings, these properties will return encoding objects that will tell `StreamWriter` to generate a byte order mark at the start of the output. The main purpose of the BOM is to enable software that reads encoded text to detect automatically whether the encoding is big- or little-endian. (You can also use it to

---

2 Just in case you've not come across the term, in *little-endian* representations, multibyte values start with the lower-order bytes, so the value 0x1234 in 16-bit little-endian would be 0x34, 0x12, whereas the big-endian version would be 0x12, 0x34. Little-endian looks reversed, but it's the native format for Intel's processors.

recognize UTF-8, because that encodes the BOM differently than other encodings.) If you know that you will be using an endian-specific encoding (e.g., UTF-16LE), the BOM is unnecessary, because you already know the order, but the Unicode specification defines adaptable formats in which the encoded bytes can advertise the order in use by starting with a BOM, a character with Unicode code point U+FEFF. The 16-bit version of this encoding is just called UTF-16, and you can tell whether any particular set of UTF-16-encoded bytes is big- or little-endian by seeing whether it begins with 0xFE, 0xFF or 0xFF, 0xFE.

 Although Unicode defines encoding schemes that allow the endianness to be detected, it is not possible to create an Encoding object that works that way—it will always have a specific endianness. So, although an Encoding specifies whether a BOM should be written when writing data, this does not influence the behavior when reading data—it will always presume the endianness specified when the Encoding was constructed. This means that the Encoding.UTF32 property is arguably misnamed—it always interprets data as little-endian even though the Unicode specification allows UTF-32 to use either big- or little-endian. Encoding.UTF32 is really UTF-32LE.

As mentioned earlier, if you do not specify an encoding when creating a Stream Writer, it defaults to UTF-8 with no BOM, which is different from Encoding.UTF8— that will generate a BOM. And recall that StreamReader is more interesting: if you do not specify an encoding, it will attempt to detect the encoding. So .NET is able to handle automatic detection of byte ordering as required by the Unicode specification for UTF-16 and UTF-32; it is just that the way to do it is *not* to specify any particular encoding when constructing a StreamReader. It will look for a BOM, and if it finds one present, it will use a suitable Unicode encoding; otherwise, it presumes UTF-8 encoding.

UTF-8 is a popular encoding. If your main language is English, it's a particularly convenient representation, because if you happen to use only the characters available in ASCII, each character will occupy a single byte, and the encoded text will have the exact same byte values as it would with ASCII encoding. But unlike ASCII, you're not limited to a 7-bit character set. All Unicode code points are available; you just have to use multibyte representations for anything outside of the ASCII range. However, although it's very widely used, UTF-8 is not the only popular 8-bit encoding.

Code page encodings

Windows, like DOS before it, has long supported 8-bit encodings that extend ASCII. ASCII is a 7-bit encoding, meaning that with 8-bit bytes you have 128 "spare" values to use for other characters. This is nowhere near enough to cover every character for every locale, but within a particular country, it's often enough to get by (although not always—many Far Eastern countries need more than 8 bits per character). But each country tends to want a different set of non-ASCII characters, depending on which accented characters are popular in that locale and whether a non-Roman alphabet is required. So various *code pages* exist for different locales. For example, code page 1253 uses values in the range 193–254 to define characters from the Greek alphabet (filling the remaining non-ASCII values with useful characters such as non-US currency symbols). Code page 1255 defines Hebrew characters instead, while 1256 defines Arabic characters in the upper range (and there is some common ground for these particular code pages, such as using 128 for the euro symbol, €, and 163 for the pound sign, £).

One of the most commonly encountered code pages is 1252, because that's the Windows default for English-speaking locales. This does not define a non-Roman alphabet; instead it uses the upper character range for useful symbols and for various accented versions of the Roman alphabet that enable a wide range of Western European languages to be adequately represented.

You can create an encoding for a code page by calling the `Encoding.GetEncoding` method, passing in the code page number. (The concrete type of the object you get back is often not one of those I listed earlier. This method may return nonpublic types that derive from `Encoding`.) Example 15-6 uses this to write text containing a pound sign to a file using code page 1252.

Example 15-6. Writing with the Windows 1252 code page

```
using (var sw = new StreamWriter("Text.txt", false,
                                 Encoding.GetEncoding(1252)))
{
    sw.Write("£100");
}
```

This will encode the £ symbol as a single byte with the value 163. With the default UTF-8 encoding, it would have been encoded as two bytes, with values of 194 and 163, respectively.

Using encodings directly

`TextReader` and `TextWriter` are not the only way to use encodings. Objects representing encodings (such as `Encoding.UTF8`) define various members. The `GetBytes` method converts a `string` directly to a `byte[]` array, for example, and the `GetString` method converts back again.

You can also discover how much data these conversions will produce. `GetByteCount` tells you how large an array `GetBytes` would produce for a given string, while

`GetCharCount` tells you how many characters decoding a particular array would generate. You can also find an upper limit for how much space will be required without knowing the exact text with `GetMaxByteCount`. Instead of a `string`, this takes a number, which it interprets as a string length; since .NET strings use UTF-16, this means that this API answers the question "If I have this many UTF-16 code units, what's the largest number of code units that might be required to represent the same text in the target encoding?" This can produce a significant overestimate for variable-length encodings. For example, with UTF-8, `GetMaxByteCount` multiplies the length of the input string by three[3] and adds an extra 3 bytes to deal with an edge case that can occur with surrogate characters. It produces a correct description of the worst possible case, but text containing any characters that don't require 3 bytes in UTF-8 (i.e., any text in English or any other languages that use the Latin alphabet, and also any text using Greek, Cyrillic, Hebrew, or Arabic writing systems, for example) will require significantly less space than `GetMaxByteCount` predicts.

Some encodings can provide a *preamble*, a distinctive sequence of bytes that, if found at the start of some encoded text, indicates that you are likely to be looking at something using that encoding. This can be useful if you are trying to detect which encoding is in use when you don't already know. The various Unicode encodings all return their encoding of the BOM as the preamble, which you can retrieve with the `Get Preamble` method.

The `Encoding` class defines instance properties offering information about the encoding. `EncodingName` returns a human-readable name for the encoding, but there are two more names available. The `WebName` property returns the standard name for the encoding registered with the Internet Assigned Numbers Authority (IANA), which manages standard names and numbers for things on the internet such as MIME types. Some protocols, such as HTTP, sometimes put encoding names into headers, and this is the text you should use in that situation. The other two names, `BodyName` and `HeaderName`, are somewhat more obscure and are used only for internet email—there are different conventions for how certain encodings are represented in the body and headers of email.

Files and Directories

The abstractions I've shown so far in this chapter are very general purpose in nature—you can write code that uses a `Stream` without needing to have any idea where the bytes it contains come from or are going to, and likewise, `TextReader` and

---

3 Some Unicode characters can take up to 4 bytes in UTF-8, so multiplying by three might seem like it could underestimate. However, all such characters require two code units in UTF-16. Any single char in .NET will never require more than 3 bytes in UTF-8.

TextWriter do not demand any particular origin or destination for their data. This is useful because it makes it possible to write code that can be applied in a variety of scenarios. For example, the stream-based GZipStream can compress or decompress data from a file, over a network connection, or from any other stream. However, there are occasions where you know you will be dealing with files and want access to file-specific features. This section describes the classes for working with files and the filesystem.

FileStream Class

The FileStream represents a file from the filesystem. I've used it a few times in passing already. It derives from Stream, so the preceding sections have already described most of what you need to know except for one aspect: when it comes to creating a FileStream, it offers several constructors offering a great deal of control.

We can supply various pieces of information when creating a new FileStream. Table 15-1 lists the various types you can supply to the constructor in addition to the path.[4] The most flexible FileStream constructor takes the file path and a File StreamOptions, which supports all possible settings. However, FileStream offers other constructor overloads taking various combinations of the types in that table, to simplify certain common scenarios.

Table 15-1. FileStream constructor argument types

Type	Purpose	Default
FileMode	Determines the behavior if the file already exists, or does not exist	Not applicable
FileAccess	Indicates whether we will we be reading, writing, or both	ReadWrite (Write if using File Mode.Append)
FileShare	Specifies our tolerance for other applications using the file at the same time	FileShare.Read
FileOptions	Various usage settings including async and cache write-through	FileOptions.None
FileStreamOptions	Combines all preceding settings and some less common ones	Not applicable

FileMode is normally[5] nonoptional, because FileStream needs to know whether you're expecting to create a new file, or open an existing one. Table 15-2 shows the behaviors you can choose between.

---

4 Although FileStream normally opens the file, there are constructors that accept a file handle.

5 FileMode only comes into play at the instant when a file is opened, so you don't need it with the constructors that accept a file handle.

Table 15-2. FileMode enumeration

Value	Behavior if file exists	Behavior if file does not exist
CreateNew	Throws IOException	Creates new file
Create	Replaces existing file	Creates new file
Open	Opens existing file	Throws FileNotFoundException
OpenOrCreate	Opens existing file	Creates new file
Truncate	Replaces existing file	Throws FileNotFoundException
Append	Opens existing file, setting Position to end of file	Creates new file

The FileAccess values of Read, Write, and ReadWrite are self-explanatory, but File Share is more subtle. It doesn't state how we intend to use the file; it states how other processes should be allowed to use the file while we have it open. For example, when using FileAccess.Write, we might specify FileShare.Read, indicating that we're happy for other processes to read from the file, but we want to be the only ones writing. FileShare.None demands exclusive access.

The FileShare comes into play when we try to open the file—the constructor will throw an IOException if the file is already open elsewhere in a way that conflicts with our stated requirements. (There are two kinds of conflict: our specified FileShare may be incompatible with FileAccess with which the file is already open elsewhere— perhaps we've said FileShare.Read but some other process already has the file open with FileAccess.Write. Or our specified FileAccess may be incompatible with the FileShare with which the file is already open. Perhaps we're asking for File Access.Read, but some other process has the file open with FileShare.None.) If we successfully open the file, then for as long as we keep it open, the FileAccess and FileShare we specified impose constraints on any other attempts to open the same file.

 Unix has fewer file-locking mechanisms than Windows, so these sharing semantics will often be mapped to something simpler on Linux and macOS. Also, file locks are advisory in Unix, meaning processes can simply ignore them if they want to.

While FileStream gives you control over the contents of the file, some operations you might wish to perform on files are either cumbersome or not supported at all with FileStream. For example, you can copy a file with this class, but it's not as straightforward as it could be, and FileStream does not offer any way to delete a file. So the runtime libraries include a separate class for these kinds of operations.

File Class

The static `File` class provides methods for performing various operations on files. For example, the `Delete` method removes the named file from the filesystem. The `Move` method can either move or just rename a file. There are methods for retrieving information and attributes that the filesystem stores about each file, such as `GetCreationTime`, `GetLastAccessTime`, `GetLastWriteTime`,[6] and `GetAttributes`. (The last of those returns a `FileAttributes` value, which is a flags enumeration type telling you whether the file is read only, a hidden file, a system file, and so on.) .NET 7.0 added `Get/SetUnixFileMode` methods to work with the mode flags present in Unix filesystems.

The `Exists` method lets you discover whether a file exists before you attempt to open it. You don't strictly need this, because `FileStream` will throw a `FileNotFound` exception if you attempt to open a nonexistent file, but `Exists` is useful if you don't need to do anything with the file other than determining whether it is there. If you are planning to open the file anyway, and are just trying to avoid an exception, you should be wary of this method; just because `Exists` returns `true`, that's no guarantee that you won't get a `FileNotFound` exception. It's always possible that in between your checking for a file's existence and attempting to open it, another process might delete the file. Alternatively, the file might be on a network share, and you might lose network connectivity. So you should always be prepared for exceptions with file access, even if you've attempted to avoid provoking them.

`File` offers many helper methods to simplify opening or creating files. The `Create` method simply constructs a `FileStream` for you, passing in suitable `FileMode`, `FileAccess`, and `FileShare` values. Example 15-7 shows how to use it and also shows what the equivalent code would look like without using the `Create` helper. The `Create` method provides overloads letting you specify the buffer size, `FileOptions`, and `FileSecurity`, but these still provide the other arguments for you.

Example 15-7. `File.Create` versus new `FileStream`

```
using (FileStream fs = File.Create("foo.bar"))
{
    ...
}

// Equivalent code without using File class
using (var fs = new FileStream("foo.bar", FileMode.Create,
```

---

6 These all return a `DateTime` that is relative to the computer's current time zone. Each of these methods has an equivalent that returns the time relative to time zone zero (e.g., `GetCreationTimeUtc`).

```
                    FileAccess.ReadWrite, FileShare.None))
{
    ...
}
```

The `File` class's `OpenRead` and `OpenWrite` methods provide similar decluttering for when you want to open an existing file for reading or open or create a file for writing. It also offers several text-oriented helpers, such as `File.AppendAllText`, which appends all of the text in a string to a file. This has the same effect as opening the file, wrapping it in a `StreamWriter`, writing the text, then closing the file again, but as Example 15-8 shows, it reduces all that to a single method call.

Example 15-8. Appending a single string to a file

```
File.AppendAllText(@"c:\temp\log.txt", message);
```

Be careful, though. This does not automatically add any end-of-line characters, so if you were to call `AppendAllText` multiple times, you'd end up with one long line in your output file, unless the strings you were using happened to contain end-of-line characters. If you want to work with lines, there's an `AppendAllLines` method that takes a collection of strings and appends each as a new line to the end of a file. Example 15-9 uses this to append a full line with each call.

Example 15-9. Appending a single line to a file

```
static void Log(string message)
{
    File.AppendAllLines(@"c:\temp\log.txt", new[] { message });
}
```

Since `AppendAllLines` accepts an `IEnumerable<string>`, you can use it to append any number of lines. But it's perfectly happy to append just one if that's what you want. `File` also defines `WriteAllText` and `WriteAllLines` methods, which work in a very similar way, but if there is already a file at the specified path, these will replace it instead of appending to it.

There are also some related text-oriented methods for reading the contents of files. `ReadAllText` performs the equivalent of constructing a `StreamReader` and then calling its `ReadToEnd` method—it returns the entire content of the file as a single `string`. `ReadAllBytes` fetches the whole file into a `byte[]` array. `ReadAllLines` reads the whole file as a `string[]` array, with one element for each line in the file. `ReadLines` is superficially very similar. It provides access to the whole file as an `IEnumerable<string>` with one item for each line, but the difference is that it works lazily—unlike all the other methods I've described in this paragraph, it does not read the entire file into memory up front, so `ReadLines` would be a better choice for very large files. It not only consumes less memory, but it also enables your code to get started more quickly—you can begin to process data as soon as the first line can be read from disk, whereas none of the other methods return until they have read the whole file.

Directory Class

Just as `File` is a static class offering methods for performing operations with files, `Directory` is a static class offering methods for performing operations with directories. Some of the methods are very similar to those offered by `File`—there are methods to get and set the creation time, last access time, and last write time, for example, and we also get `Move`, `Exists`, and `Delete` methods. The latter has an overload taking a `bool` that, if `true`, will delete everything in the folder, recursively deleting any nested folders and the files they contain. Use that one carefully.

Of course, there are also directory-specific methods. `GetFiles` takes a directory path and returns a `string[]` array containing the full path of each file in that directory. Similarly, `GetDirectories` returns the directories inside the specified directory instead of the files. `GetFileSystemEntries` returns both files and folders. Each of these offers an overload that lets you specify a pattern by which to filter the results, and a third overload that takes a pattern and also a flag that lets you request recursive searching of all subfolders.

There are also methods called `EnumerateFiles`, `EnumerateDirectories`, and `EnumerateFileSystemEntries`, which do exactly the same thing as the three methods in the preceding paragraph, but they return `IEnumerable<string>`. This is a lazy enumeration, so you can start processing results immediately instead of waiting for all the results as one big array.

You can create new directories too. The `CreateDirectory` method takes a path and will attempt to create as many directories as are necessary to ensure that the path exists. So, if you pass *C:\new\dir\here*, and there is no *C:\new* directory, it will create three new directories: first it will create *C:\new*, then *C:\new\dir*, and then *C:\new\dir\here*. If the folder you ask for already exists, it doesn't treat that as an error; it just returns without doing anything.

Path Class

The static `Path` class provides useful utilities for strings containing filenames. Some extract pieces from a file path, such as the containing folder name or the file extension. Some combine strings to produce new file paths. Most of these methods just perform specialized string processing and do not require the files or directories to which the paths refer to exist. However, there are a few that go beyond string manipulation. For example, `Path.GetFullPath` will take the current directory into account if you do not pass an absolute path as the argument. But only the methods that need to make use of real locations will do so.

The `Path.Combine` method deals with the fiddly issues around combining folder and filenames. If you have a folder name, *C:\temp*, and a filename, *log.txt*, passing both to `Path.Combine` returns *C:\temp\log.txt*. And it will also work if you pass *C:\temp* as the first argument, so one of the issues it deals with is working out whether it needs to supply an extra \ character. If the second path is absolute, it detects this and simply ignores the first path, so if you pass *C:\temp* and *C:\logs\log.txt*, the result will be *C:\logs\log.txt*. Although these may seem like trivial matters, it's surprisingly easy to get the file path combination wrong if you try to do it yourself by concatenating strings, so you should always avoid the temptation to do that and just use `Path.Combine`.

`Path` has platform-specific behavior. On Unix-like systems, only the / character is used as a directory separator, so the various methods in `Path` that expect paths to contain directories will treat only / as a separator on these systems. Windows uses a \ as a separator, although it is common for / to be tolerated as a substitute, and `Path` follows suit. So `Path.Combine("/x/y", "/z.txt")` will produce the same results on Windows and Linux, but `Path.Combine(@"\x\y", @"\z.txt")` will not. Also, on Windows, if a path begins with a drive letter, it is an absolute path, but Unix does not recognize drive letters. The examples in the preceding paragraph will produce strange-looking results on Linux or macOS because on those systems, all the paths will be treated as relative paths. If you remove the drive letters and replace \ with /, the results will be as you'd expect.

Serialization

The `Stream`, `TextReader`, and `TextWriter` types provide the ability to read and write data in files, networks, or anything else stream-like that provides a suitable concrete class. But these abstractions support only byte or text data. Suppose you have an object with several properties of various types, including some numeric types and perhaps also references to other objects, some of which might be collections. What if you wanted to write all the information in that object out to a file or over a network connection so that an object of the same type and with the same property values could be reconstituted at a later date, or on another computer at the other end of a connection?

You could do this with the abstractions shown in this chapter, but it would require a fair amount of work. You'd have to write code to read each property and write its value out to a `Stream` or `TextWriter`, and you'd need to convert the value to either binary or text. You'd also need to decide on your representation—would you just write values out in a fixed order, or would you come up with a scheme for writing name/value pairs so that you're not stuck with an inflexible format if you need to add more properties later on? You'd also need to come up with ways to handle collections and references to other objects, and you'd need to decide what to do in the face of circular references—if two objects each refer to one another, naive code could end up getting stuck in an infinite loop.

.NET offers several solutions to this problem, each making varying trade-offs between the complexity of the scenarios they are able to support, how well they deal with versioning, and how suitable they are for interoperating with other platforms. These techniques all fall under the broad name of *serialization* (because they involve writing an object's state into some form that stores data sequentially—serially—such as a `Stream`). Many different mechanisms have been introduced over the years in .NET, so I won't cover all of them. I'll just present the ones that best represent particular approaches to the problem.

BinaryReader, BinaryWriter, and BinaryPrimitives

No discussion of this area is complete without covering the `BinaryReader` and `BinaryWriter` classes, because they solve a fundamental problem that any attempt to serialize and deserialize objects must deal with: they can convert the CLR's intrinsic types to and from streams of bytes. `BinaryPrimitives` does the same thing, but it is able to work with `Span<byte>` and related types, which are discussed in Chapter 18.

`BinaryWriter` is a wrapper around a writable `Stream`. It provides a `Write` method that has overloads for all of the intrinsic types except for `object`. So it can take a value of any of the numeric types, or the `string`, `char`, or `bool` types, and it writes a binary representation of that value into a `Stream`. It can also write arrays of type `byte` or `char`.

`BinaryReader` is a wrapper around a readable `Stream`, and it provides various methods for reading data, each corresponding to the overloads of `Write` provided by `BinaryWriter`. For example, you have `ReadDouble`, `ReadInt32`, and `ReadString`.

To use these types, you would create a `BinaryWriter` when you want to serialize some data, and write out each value you wish to store. When you later want to deserialize that data, you'd wrap a `BinaryReader` around a stream containing the data written with the writer, and call the relevant read methods in the exact same order that you wrote the data out in the first place.

`BinaryPrimitives` works slightly differently. It is designed for code that needs to minimize the number of heap allocations, so it's not a wrapper type—it is a static class offering a wide range of methods, such as `ReadInt32LittleEndian` and `WriteUInt16BigEndian`. These take `ReadOnlySpan<byte>` and `Span<byte>` arguments, respectively, because it is designed to work directly with data wherever it may lie in memory (not necessarily wrapped in a `Stream`). However, the basic principle is the same: it converts between byte sequences and primitive .NET types. (Also, string handling is rather more complex: there's no ReadString method because anything that returns a string will create a new string object on the heap, unless there's a fixed set of possible strings that you can preallocate and hand out again and again. See Chapter 18 for more information about span types.)

These classes only solve the problem of how to represent various built-in types in binary. You are still left with the task of working out how to represent whole objects and what to do about more complex kinds of structures such as references between objects.

CLR Serialization

CLR serialization is, as the name suggests, built into the runtime itself—it is not simply a library feature. You should not use it. CLR serialization has been deprecated for a long time. Recent versions of .NET have disabled the functionality by default. (To be precise, certain types central to the operation of CLR serialization throw exceptions unless you add settings to re-enable them. This has the effect of preventing you from using CLR serialization by default, even though the underlying support mechanisms still exist in the CLR.) Microsoft has announced that in .NET 9.0 it will remove the settings that enabled you to switch it back on.

So why am I telling you about a feature that is deprecated, unavailable by default, and destined to be removed entirely? It's because it offered a useful, distinctive capability. This meant it was widely used, and it can still be tempting to use it. (This will be possible even with .NET 9.0, because the plan is to provide a NuGet package that continues to make it available.) CLR serialization can seem like a good idea, so it's important to know why not to use it.

The most interesting aspect of CLR serialization is that it deals directly with object references. If you serialize, say, a List<SomeType> where multiple entries in the list refer to the same object, CLR serialization will detect this, storing just one copy of that object, and when deserializing, it will re-create that one-object-many-references structure. This avoids duplication and also means circular references don't cause problems. (Serialization systems based on the very widely used JSON format normally don't preserve references, although the JsonSerializer described later does provide an option to do this.) Moreover, it supports cases where derived types are present—if your List<SomeType> contains a mixture of types all derived from Some Type, CLR reflection detects this. When it deserializes the list, it will create objects of the same type that were in the original list. It's also simple to use: you just apply a single attribute ([Serializable]) to a type, and the CLR automatically handles the process of writing out all of your object's fields during serialization, and reading them back in when deserializing.

This is powerful and easy to use. Why wouldn't we want it?

It's almost impossible to avoid security problems with this style of serialization. This is a consequence of the basic approach: the features I just described mean that a serialized stream describes the types of objects to create, and the values of all the fields in those objects. If you build a system that accepts serialized streams as inputs (e.g., over the network) you are enabling whoever generates those streams to create objects of any type and configuration inside your service. Security research has shown that this provides a springboard from which attackers can run whatever code they like, meaning you have effectively lost control of your system. (This is not unique to .NET by the way. Other platforms have had their own versions of this problem.) The documentation states that CLR serialization's `BinaryFormatter` "is insecure and can't be made secure," and you will see deprecation warnings when you attempt to use it. So I'm only describing CLR serialization here because it still gets used despite Microsoft's attempts to end it. (There's also one technical curiosity that exists as a result of CLR serialization. An assumption you might otherwise have made about object creation—specifically that a reference type can only be created through one of its constructors or via `MemberwiseClone`—turns out not be true, because objects can come into existence through deserialization without their constructors running.)

JSON

The JavaScript Object Notation, JSON, is a very widely used serialization format, and the .NET runtime libraries provide support for working with it in the `System.Text.Json` namespace.[7] It provides three ways of working with JSON data.

The `Utf8JsonReader` and `Utf8JsonWriter` types are stream-like abstractions that represent the contents of JSON data as a sequence of elements. These can be useful if you need to process JSON documents that are too large to load into memory as a single object. They are built on the memory-efficient mechanisms described in Chapter 18, which includes a full example showing how to process JSON with these types. This is a very high-performance option, but it is not the easiest to use.

 As the names suggest, these types read and write JSON using UTF-8 encoding. This is by far the most widely used encoding for sending and storing JSON, so all of `System.Text.Json` is optimized for it. Because of this, performance-sensitive code should typically avoid ever obtaining a JSON document as a .NET `string`, because that uses UTF-16 encoding and will require conversion to UTF-8 before you can work with these APIs.

---

7 To use this on .NET Framework, you will need to add a reference to the `System.Text.Json` NuGet package.

There's also the JsonSerializer class, which converts between entire .NET objects and JSON. It requires you to define classes with a structure corresponding to the JSON.

Finally, System.Text.Json offers types that can provide a description of a JSON document's structure. These are useful when you do not know at development time exactly what the structure of your JSON data will be, because they provide a flexible object model that can adapt to any shape of JSON data. In fact, there are two variations on this approach. We have JsonDocument, JsonElement, and related types, which provide a highly efficient read-only mechanism for inspecting a JSON document, and the more flexible but slightly less efficient JsonNode, which is writable, enabling you either to build up a description of JSON from scratch or to read in some JSON and then modify it.

JsonSerializer

JsonSerializer offers an attribute-driven serialization model in which you define one or more classes mirroring the structure of the JSON data you need to deal with, and can then convert JSON data to and from that model.

Example 15-10 shows a simple model suitable for use with JsonSerializer. As you can see, I'm not required to use any particular base class, and there are no mandatory attributes. This example uses the required keyword (new in C# 11.0) to indicate that we expect all of the properties to be set. JsonSerializer recognizes this, and will throw an exception if you try to deserialize JSON where a required property is missing.

Example 15-10. Simple JSON serialization model

```
public class SimpleData
{
    public required int Id { get; set; }
    public required IList<string> Names { get; set; }
    public required NestedData Location { get; set; }
    public required IDictionary<string, int> Map { get; set; }
}

public class NestedData
{
    public required string LocationName { get; set; }
    public required double Latitude { get; set; }
    public required double Longitude { get; set; }
}
```

Example 15-11 creates an instance of this model and then uses the JsonConvert class's Serialize method to serialize it to a string. It also passes a second, optional, argument, a `JsonSerializationOptions`. I've used it here to indent the JSON to make it easier to read. (By default, `JsonSerializer` will use a more efficient layout with no unnecessary whitespace, but that is much harder to read.)

 Example 15-11 puts the `JsonSerializationOptions` in a static field because it is inefficient to construct new options each time you deserialize. (A code analyzer built into the .NET SDK will warn you if you do that.) In applications that process JSON repeatedly, `System.Text.Json` caches information about the types being serialized to avoid repeating expensive work. It stores that inside the `JsonSerializationOptions` object, which is why you should construct the settings just once and reuse them.

Example 15-11. Serializing data with `JsonSerializer`

```
private static readonly JsonSerializerOptions SerializeIndented =
    new() { WriteIndented = true };
public static string SerializeJson()
{
    var model = new SimpleData
    {
        Id = 42,
        Names = ["Bell", "Stacey", "her", "Jane"],
        Location = new NestedData
        {
            LocationName = "London",
            Latitude = 51.503209,
            Longitude = -0.119145
        },
        Map = new Dictionary<string, int>
            {
                { "Answer", 42 },
                { "FirstPrime", 2 }
            }
    };

    return JsonSerializer.Serialize(model, SerializeIndented);
}
```

The results look like this:

```
{
  "Id": 42,
  "Names": [
    "Bell",
    "Stacey",
    "her",
    "Jane"
  ],
```

```
      "Location": {
        "LocationName": "London",
        "Latitude": 51.503209,
        "Longitude": -0.119145
      },
      "Map": {
        "Answer": 42,
        "FirstPrime": 2
      }
    }
```

As you can see, each .NET object has become a JSON object, where the name/value pairs correspond to properties in my model. Numbers and strings are represented exactly as you would expect. The `IList<string>` has become a JSON array, and the `IDictionary<string, int>` has become another JSON dictionary. I've used interfaces for these collections, but you can also use the concrete `List<T>` and `Dictionary <TKey,TValue>` types. You can use ordinary arrays to represent lists if you prefer. I tend to prefer the interfaces because it leaves you free to use whatever collection types you want. (E.g., Example 15-11 initialized the `Names` property with a string array, but it could also have used `List<string>` without changing the model type.)

Converting serialized JSON back into the model is equally straightforward, as Example 15-12 shows.

Example 15-12. Deserializing data with `JsonSerializer`

```
var deserialized = JsonSerializer.Deserialize<SimpleData>(json);
```

Although a plain and simple model such as this will often suffice, sometimes you may need to take control over some aspects of serialization, particularly if you are working with an externally defined JSON format. For example, you might need to work with a JSON API that uses naming conventions that are different from .NET's—camel Casing is popular but conflicts with the PascalCasing convention for .NET properties. One way to resolve this is to use the `JsonPropertyName` attribute to specify the name to use in the JSON, as Example 15-13 shows.

Example 15-13. Controlling the JSON with `JsonPropertyName` attributes

```
public class NestedData
{
    [JsonPropertyName("locationName")]
    public required string LocationName { get; set; }

    [JsonPropertyName("latitude")]
    public required double Latitude { get; set; }

    [JsonPropertyName("longitude")]
```

```
    public required double Longitude { get; set; }
}
```

JsonSerializer will use the names specified in JsonPropertyName when serializing and will look for those names when deserializing. This approach gives us complete control over the .NET and JSON property names, but there is a simpler solution for this particular scenario. This kind of renaming that just changes the case of the first letter is so common that you can get JsonSerializer to do it for you. Example 15-14 constructs its JsonSerializationOptions by passing an optional argument of type JsonSerializerDefaults. By passing Json SerializerDefaults.Web, we get the camelCasing style without needing to use any attributes. You can achieve the same effect by setting the JsonSerializerOptions.PropertyNamingPolicy to JsonNaming Policy.CamelCase. .NET 8.0 adds four new naming styles: KebabCaseLower (looks-like-this), KebabCaseUpper (LOOKS-LIKE-THIS), SnakeCaseLower (looks_like_this), and SnakeCaseUpper (LOOKS_LIKE_THIS).

Example 15-14. Using `JsonSerializerDefaults` to get camelCased property names

```
private static readonly JsonSerializerOptions camelCaseOptions =
    new(JsonSerializerDefaults.Web) { WriteIndented = true };
public static string AutoCamelCase(SimpleData model)
{
    return JsonSerializer.Serialize(model, camelCaseOptions);
}
```

The JsonSerializerOptions also provide a way to handle circular references. Suppose you want to serialize objects of type SelfRef, as shown in Example 15-15.

Example 15-15. A type supporting circular references

```
public class SelfRef
{
    public required string Name { get; set; }
    public SelfRef? Next { get; set; }
}
```

By default, if you attempt to serialize objects that refer to one another either directly or indirectly, you'll get a JsonException reporting a possible cycle. It says "possible" because it doesn't directly detect cycles by default—instead, JsonSerializer has a limit on the depth of any object graph that it will serialize. This is configurable through the JsonSerializerOptions.MaxDepth property, but by default the serializer will report an error if it has to go more than 64 objects deep. However, you can set the ReferenceHandler to change the behavior. Example 15-16 sets this to Reference Handler.Preserve, enabling it to serialize a pair of SelfRef instances that refer to each other.

Example 15-16. Serializing a type supporting circular references

```
private static readonly JsonSerializerOptions jsonWithRefs =
    new(JsonSerializerDefaults.Web)
    {
        WriteIndented = true,
        ReferenceHandler = ReferenceHandler.Preserve
    };
public static string SerializeWithCircularReferences()
{
    var circle = new SelfRef
    {
        Name = "Top",
        Next = new SelfRef
        {
            Name = "Bottom",
        }
    };
    circle.Next.Next = circle;
    string json = JsonSerializer.Serialize(circle, jsonWithRefs);

    return json;
}
```

To enable this, the `JsonSerializer` gives objects identifiers by adding an `$id` property:

```
{
  "$id": "1",
  "name": "Top",
  "next": {
    "$id": "2",
    "name": "Bottom",
    "next": {
      "$ref": "1"
    }
  }
}
```

This enables the serializer to avoid problems when it encounters a circular reference. Whenever it has to serialize a property, it checks to see whether that refers to some object that has already been written out (or is in the process of being written out). If it does, then instead of attempting to write out the object again (which in this example would cause an infinite loop, since it'll just encounter the circular reference again and again), the serializer emits a JSON object containing a property with the special name `$ref` referring back to the relevant `$id`. This is not a universally supported form of JSON, which is why ID generation is not enabled by default.

You can control many other aspects of serialization with `JsonSerializerOptions`—you can define custom serialization mechanisms for data types, for example. (E.g., you might want to represent something as a DateTimeOffset in your C# code but have that become a string with a particular date-time format in the JSON.) The full details can be found in the System.Text.Json documentation.

In the examples shown so far, JsonSerializer discovers our types' properties using the reflection API. This is convenient, but there are a couple of disadvantages to this. The first time a process uses reflection is relatively slow, so if your code runs in an environment where *cold start* performance (i.e., the time it takes to be able to do useful work after the process has just started) is significant, reflection can be a problem. Some cloud hosting environments don't leave code running for very long on any single machine, so you can find that even a fairly busy service experiences a surprisingly large number of cold starts. Another problem with reflection is that it makes it harder for ahead-of-time compilation to be effective, because reflection-based serialization defers work until runtime—it can make it particularly difficult for trimming to remove unnecessary code from your build output, and might not work at all with Native AOT. For these reasons, the .NET SDK includes a code generator that can generate all of the type information required for serialization at compile time, removing any need to use reflection at runtime. Example 15-17 shows how to enable this code generation.

Example 15-17. Enabling JSON serializer code generation

```
[JsonSerializable(typeof(SimpleData))]
internal partial class CodeGenSerializationContext : JsonSerializerContext
{
}
```

Although this class appears to be empty, the partial keyword enables the code generator to supply an implementation. The generator looks for classes such as this that inherit from JsonSerializerContext, and which have at least one JsonSerializable attribute. It will emit code for each attribute, including a public property with a name matching the specified type. Example 15-18 shows how to use the property generated for SimpleData.

Example 15-18. Using JSON serializer code generation

```
SimpleData? data = JsonSerializer.Deserialize(
    json, CodeGenSerializationContext.Default.SimpleData);
```

For each JsonSerializable attribute, there will be a corresponding generated property on our serialization context class. When we pass this to JsonSerializer, it will use the type information that the code generator created, avoiding use of reflection, which can enable work to commence significantly more quickly the first time this code runs, and also making it possible to use Native AOT.

JSON DOM

Whereas `JsonSerializer` requires you to define one or more types representing the structure of the JSON you want to work with, `System.Text.Json` provides a fixed set of types that enable a more dynamic approach, and which can also support significantly more efficient JSON processing. You can build a Document Object Model (DOM) in which instances of types such as `JsonElement` or `JsonNode` represent the structure of the JSON.

`System.Text.Json` provides two ways to build a DOM. If you have data already in JSON form, you can use the `JsonDocument` class to obtain a read-only model of the JSON, in which each object, value, and array is represented as a `JsonElement`, and each property in an object is represented as a `JsonProperty`. Example 15-19 uses `JsonDocument` to discover all of the properties in the object at the root of the JSON by calling `RootElement.EnumerateObject()` on the `JsonDocument`. This returns a collection of `JsonProperty` structs.

Example 15-19. Dynamic JSON inspection with `JsonDocument` and `JsonElement`

```
using (JsonDocument document = JsonDocument.Parse(json))
{
    foreach (JsonProperty property in document.RootElement.EnumerateObject())
    {
        Console.WriteLine($"Property: {property.Name} ({property.Value.ValueKind})");
    }
}
```

Running this on the serialized document produced by earlier examples produces this output:

```
Property: id (Number)
Property: names (Array)
Property: location (Object)
Property: map (Object)
```

As this shows, we are able to discover at runtime what properties exist. The `JsonProperty.Value` returns a `JsonElement` struct, and we can inspect its `ValueKind` to discover which sort of JSON value it is. If it's an array, we can enumerate its contents by calling `EnumerateArray`, and if it's a string value, we can read its value by calling `GetString`. Example 15-20 uses these methods to show all the strings in the `names` property.

Example 15-20. Dynamic JSON array enumeration with `JsonDocument` and `JsonElement`

```
JsonElement namesElement = document.RootElement.GetProperty("names");
foreach (JsonElement name in namesElement.EnumerateArray())
{
    Console.WriteLine($"Name: {name.GetString()}");
}
```

As this example also shows, if you know in advance that a particular property will be present, you don't need to use `EnumerateObject` to find it: you can call `GetProperty`. There's also a `TryGetProperty` for when the property is optional. Example 15-21 uses both: this treats the root object's `location` property as optional, but if it is present, it then requires the `locationName`, `latitude`, and `longitude` properties to be present.

Example 15-21. Reading JSON properties with `JsonElement`

```
if (root.TryGetProperty("location", out JsonElement locationElement))
{
    JsonElement nameElement = locationElement.GetProperty("locationName");
    JsonElement latitudeElement = locationElement.GetProperty("latitude");
    JsonElement longitudeElement = locationElement.GetProperty("longitude");
    string locationName = nameElement.GetString()!;
    double latitude = latitudeElement.GetDouble();
    double longitude = longitudeElement.GetDouble();
    Console.WriteLine($"Location: {locationName}: {latitude},{longitude}");
}
```

In addition to structural elements, objects and arrays, the data model in the JSON specification (*https://oreil.ly/T1Qoe*) recognizes four basic data types: strings, numbers, Booleans, and null. As you've seen, you can discover which of these any particular `JsonElement` represents with its `Kind` property. If it's one of the basic data types, you can use a suitable `Get` method. The last two examples both used `GetString`, and the second also used `GetDouble`. There are multiple methods you can use to retrieve a number: if you are expecting an integer, you can call `GetSByte`, `GetInt16`, `GetInt32`, or `GetInt64` (and unsigned versions are also available) depending on what range of values you are expecting. There's also `GetDecimal`. `JsonElement` also offers methods for reading string properties in particular formats: `GetGuid`, `GetDateTime`, `GetDate` `TimeOffset`, and `GetBytesFromBase64`.

All of the `Get` methods will throw an exception if the value is not in the required form, but it won't always be the same exception. If the JSON has a type that can't possibly contain a suitable value (e.g., you call `GetGuid` when the property's value is `false`, or you call `GetInt32` when the property is a string) it will throw `InvalidOpera` `tionException`. If the JSON type is appropriate but the value is not right (e.g., you called GetUInt32 but the number is negative, or is a floating-point value, or you called GetDateTime and the JSON value is a string, but is not a valid ISO 8601 date-time) it will throw a FormatException instead.

Each of these Get methods is also available in a TryGet form, such as TryGetUInt32. These enable you to detect when the data cannot be parsed in the expected way without triggering an exception, although there's a trap for the unwary: the TryGet forms will throw an InvalidOperationException in the same cases where the equivalent Get would—these only return false in cases where the equivalent Get method would have thrown a FormatException. If you want to avoid exceptions entirely, you should check the element's ValueKind property, and only call the TryGet method if that indicates that the JSON type is what you expect.

These types attempt to minimize the amount of memory allocated. JsonElement and JsonProperty are both structs, so you can obtain these without causing additional heap allocations. The underlying data is held in UTF-8 format by the JsonDocument, and the JsonElement and JsonProperty instances just refer back to that, avoiding the need to allocate copies of the relevant data. This can make these types significantly more efficient than deserialization in some scenarios.

Obviously, the underlying data does need to live somewhere, and depending on exactly how you loaded the JSON into a JsonDocument, it may have to allocate some memory to hold it. (E.g., you can pass it a Stream, and since not all streams are rewindable, JsonDocument would need to make a copy of the stream's contents.) Json Document uses the buffer pooling features available in the .NET runtime libraries to manage this data, meaning that if an application parses many JSON documents, it may be able to reuse memory, reducing pressure on the garbage collector (GC). But this means the JsonDocument needs to know when you've finished with the JSON so that it can return buffers to the pool. That's why we use a using statement when working with a JsonDocument.

Be aware that JsonElement.GetString is more expensive than all the other Get methods, because it has to create a new .NET string on the heap. The other Get methods all return value types, so they do not cause heap allocations.

I mentioned earlier that there are two ways of working with a JSON DOM. JsonDocument provides a read-only model that lets you inspect existing JSON. But there is also JsonNode, which is read/write. You can use this in a couple of ways that JsonDocument does not support. You can build up an object model from scratch to create a new JSON document. Alternatively, you can parse existing JSON into an object model just like with JsonDocument, but when you use JsonNode, the resulting model is modifiable. So you could use it to load some JSON and modify it, as Example 15-22 illustrates.

Example 15-22. Modifying JSON with `JsonNode`

```
JsonNode rootNode = JsonNode.Parse(json)!;
JsonNode mapNode = rootNode["map"]!;
mapNode["iceCream"] = 99;
```

This loads the JSON text in `json` into a `JsonNode` and then retrieves the `map` property. (This example expects to work with JSON in the same form as I've used in the preceding examples, with camelCased property names.) So far this doesn't do anything we couldn't do with `JsonDocument`. But the final line adds a new entry to the object in `map`. It's this ability to modify the document that makes `JsonNode` more powerful. So why do we need `JsonDocument` if `JsonNode` is more powerful? The power comes at a price: `JsonNode` is less efficient, so if you don't need the extra flexibility, you shouldn't use it.

An advantage of using either the read-only `JsonDocument` and `JsonElement` or the writable `JsonNode` is that you don't need to define any types to model the data. They also make it easier to write code whose behavior is driven by the structure of the data, because these APIs are able to describe what they find. The read-only form is typically more efficient than `JsonSerializer`, because it may enable you to cause fewer object allocations when reading data from a JSON document.

Summary

The `Stream` class is an abstraction representing data as a sequence of bytes. A stream can support reading, writing, or both, and may support seeking to arbitrary offsets as well as straightforward sequential access. `TextReader` and `TextWriter` provide strictly sequential reading and writing of character data, abstracting away the character encoding. These types may sit on top of a file, a network connection, or memory, or you could implement your own versions of these abstract classes. The `FileStream` class also provides some other filesystem access features, but for full control, we also have the `File` and `Directory` classes. When bytes and strings aren't enough, .NET offers various serialization mechanisms that can automate the mapping between an object's state in memory and a representation that can be written out to disk or sent over the network or any other stream-like target; this representation can later be turned back into an object of the same type and with equivalent state.

As you've seen, a few of the file and stream APIs offer asynchronous forms that can help improve performance, particularly in highly concurrent systems. The next chapter tackles concurrency, parallelism, and the task-based pattern that the asynchronous forms of these APIs use.

CHAPTER 16

Multithreading

Multithreading enables an application to execute several pieces of code simultaneously. There are two common reasons for doing this. One is to exploit the computer's parallel processing capabilities—multicore CPUs are now more or less ubiquitous, and to realize their full performance potential, you'll need to provide the CPU with multiple streams of work to give all of the cores something useful to do. The other usual reason for writing multithreaded code is to prevent progress from grinding to a halt when you do something slow, such as reading from disk.

Multithreading is not the only way to solve that second problem—asynchronous techniques can be preferable. C# has features for supporting asynchronous work. Asynchronous execution doesn't necessarily mean multithreading, but the two are often related in practice, and I will be describing some of the asynchronous programming models in this chapter. However, this chapter focuses on the threading foundations. I will describe the language-level support for asynchronous code in Chapter 17.

Threads

All the operating systems that .NET can run on allow each process to contain multiple threads (although if you build to Web Assembly and run code in the browser, that particular environment currently doesn't support creation of new threads). Each thread has its own stack, and the OS presents the illusion that a thread gets a whole CPU *hardware thread* to itself. (See the sidebar, "Processors, Cores, and Hardware Threads.") You can create far more OS threads than the number of hardware threads your computer provides, because the OS virtualizes the CPU, context switching from one thread to another. The computer I'm using as I write this has 16 hardware threads, which is a reasonably generous quantity but some way short of the 8,893 threads currently active across the various processes running on my machine.

Processors, Cores, and Hardware Threads

A *hardware thread* is one piece of hardware capable of executing code. Back in the early 2000s, one processor chip gave you one hardware thread, and you got multiple hardware threads only in computers that had multiple, physically separate CPUs plugged into separate sockets on the motherboard. However, two inventions have made the relationship between hardware and threads more complex: multicore CPUs and hyperthreading.

With a multicore CPU, you effectively get multiple processors on a single piece of silicon. This means that opening up your computer and counting the number of processor chips doesn't necessarily tell you how many hardware threads you've got. But if you were to inspect the CPU's silicon with a suitable microscope, you'd see two or more distinct processors next to each other on the chip.

Hyperthreading, also known as simultaneous multithreading (SMT), complicates matters further. A hyperthreaded core is a single processor that has two sets of certain parts. (It could be more than two, but doubling seems most common.) So, although there might be only a single part of the core capable of performing, say, floating-point division, there will be two sets of registers. Each set of registers includes an instruction pointer (IP) register that keeps track of where execution has reached. Registers also contain the immediate working state of the code, so by having two sets, a single core can run code from two places at once—in other words, hyperthreading enables a single core to provide two hardware threads. Since only certain parts of the CPU are doubled up, two execution contexts have to share some resources—they can't both perform floating-point division operations simultaneously, because there's only one piece of hardware in the core to do that. However, if one of the hardware threads wants to do some division while another multiplies two numbers together, they will typically be able to do so in parallel, because those operations are performed by different areas of the core. Hyperthreading enables more parts of a single CPU core to be kept busy simultaneously. It doesn't give you quite the same throughput as two full cores (because if the two hardware threads both want to do the same kind of work at once, one of them will have to wait), but it can often provide better throughput from each core than would otherwise be possible.

In a hyperthreaded system, the total number of hardware threads available is the number of cores multiplied by the number of hyperthreaded execution units per core. For example, the Intel Core i9-9900K processor has eight cores with two-way hyperthreading, giving a total of 16 hardware threads.

The CLR presents its own threading abstraction on top of OS threads. In .NET, there is always a direct relationship—each Thread object corresponds directly to some particular underlying OS thread. On .NET Framework, this relationship is not guaranteed to exist—applications that use the CLR's unmanaged hosting API to customize the relationship between the CLR and its containing process can in theory cause a CLR thread to move between different OS threads. In practice, this capability is very rarely used, so even on .NET Framework, each CLR thread will usually correspond to one OS thread.

I will get to the Thread class shortly, but before writing multithreaded code, you need to understand the ground rules for managing state[1] when using multiple threads.

Threads, Variables, and Shared State

Each CLR thread gets various thread-specific resources, such as the call stack (which holds method arguments and some local variables). Because each thread has its own stack, the local variables that end up there will be local to the thread. Each time you invoke a method, you get a new set of its local variables. Recursion relies on this, but it's also important in multithreaded code, because data that is accessible to multiple threads requires much more care, particularly if that data changes. Coordinating access to shared data is complex. I'll be describing some of the techniques for that in the section "Synchronization" on page 722, but it's better to avoid the problem entirely where possible, and the thread-local nature of the stack can be a great help.

For example, consider a web-based application. Busy sites have to handle requests from multiple users simultaneously. ASP.NET Core uses multithreading to support this, so you're likely to end up in a situation where a particular piece of code (e.g., the code for your site's home page) is being executed simultaneously on several different threads. (Websites typically don't just serve up the exact same content every time, because pages are often tailored to particular users, so if 1,000 users ask to see the home page, it will run the code that generates that page 1,000 times.) ASP.NET Core provides you with various objects that your code will need to use, but most of these are specific to a particular request. So, if your code is able to work entirely with those objects and with local variables, each thread can operate completely independently. If you need shared state (such as objects that are visible to multiple threads, perhaps through a static field or property), life will get more difficult, but local variables are usually straightforward.

Why only "usually"? Things get more complex if you use lambdas or anonymous functions, because they make it possible to declare a variable in a containing method and then use that in an inner method. This variable is now available to two or more methods, and with multithreading, it's possible that these methods could execute concurrently. (As far as the CLR is concerned, it's not really a local variable anymore—it's a field in a compiler-generated class.) Sharing local variables across multiple methods removes the guarantee of complete locality, so you need to take the same sort of care

---

1 I'm using the word *state* here broadly. I just mean information stored in variables and objects.

with such variables as you would with more obviously shared items, like static properties and fields.

Another important point to remember in multithreaded environments is the distinction between a variable and the object it refers to. (This is an issue only with reference type variables.) Although a local variable is accessible only inside its declaring method, that variable may not be the only one that refers to a particular object. Sometimes it will be—if you create the object inside the method and never store it anywhere that would make it accessible to a wider audience, then you have nothing to worry about. The StringBuilder that Example 16-1 creates is only ever used within the method that creates it.

Example 16-1. Object visibility and methods

```
public static string FormatDictionary<TKey, TValue>(
    IDictionary<TKey, TValue> input)
{
    var sb = new StringBuilder();
    foreach ((TKey key, TValue value) in input)
    {
        sb.Append($"{key}: {value}");
        sb.AppendLine();
    }

    return sb.ToString();
}
```

This code does not need to worry about whether other threads might be trying to modify the StringBuilder. There are no nested methods here, so the sb variable is truly local, and that's the only thing that contains a reference to the StringBuilder. (This relies on the fact that the StringBuilder doesn't sneakily store copies of its this reference anywhere that other threads might be able to see.)

But what about the input argument? That's also local to the method, but the object it refers to is not: the code that calls FormatDictionary gets to decide what input refers to. Looking at Example 16-1 in isolation, it's not possible to say whether the dictionary object to which it refers is currently in use by other threads. The calling code could create a single dictionary and then create two threads, and have one modify the dictionary while the other calls this FormatDictionary method. This would cause a problem: most dictionary implementations do not support being modified on one thread at the same time as being used on some other thread. And even if you were working with a collection that was designed to cope with concurrent use, you're often not allowed to modify a collection while an enumeration of its contents is in progress (e.g., a foreach loop).

You might think that any collection designed to be used from multiple threads simultaneously (a *thread-safe* collection, you might say) should allow one thread to iterate over its contents while another modifies the contents. If it disallows this, then in what sense is it thread safe? In fact, the main difference between a thread-safe and a non-thread-safe collection in this scenario is predictability: whereas a thread-safe collection might throw an exception when it detects that this has happened, a non-thread-safe collection does not guarantee to do anything in particular. It might crash, or you might start getting perplexing results from the iteration, such as a single entry appearing multiple times. It could do more or less anything because you're using it in an unsupported way. Sometimes, thread safety just means that failure happens in a well-defined and predictable manner.

As it happens, the various collections in the `System.Collection.Concurrent` namespace do in fact support changes while enumeration is in progress without throwing exceptions. However, they often have a different API from the other collection classes specifically to support concurrency, so they are not always drop-in replacements.

There's nothing Example 16-1 can do to ensure that it uses its `input` argument safely in multithreaded environments, because it is at the mercy of its callers. Concurrency hazards need to be dealt with at a higher level. In fact, the term *thread safe* is potentially misleading, because it suggests something that is not, in general, possible. Inexperienced developers often fall into the trap of thinking that they are absolved of all responsibility for thinking about threading issues in their code by just making sure that all the objects they're using are thread safe. This usually doesn't work, because while individual thread-safe objects will maintain their own integrity, that's no guarantee that your application's state as a whole will be coherent.

To illustrate this, Example 16-2 uses the `ConcurrentDictionary<TKey, TValue>` class from the `System.Collections.Concurrent` namespace. Every operation this class defines is thread safe in the sense that each will leave the object in a consistent state and will produce the expected result given the collection's state prior to the call. However, this example contrives to use it in a non-thread-safe fashion.

Example 16-2. Non-thread-safe use of a thread-safe collection

```
static string UseDictionary(ConcurrentDictionary<int, string> cd)
{
    cd[1] = "One";
    return cd[1];
}
```

This seems like it could not fail. (It also seems pointless; that's just to show how even a very simple piece of code can go wrong.) But if the dictionary instance is being used by multiple threads (which seems likely, given that we've chosen a type designed specifically for multithreaded use), it's entirely possible that in between setting a value for key 1 and trying to retrieve it, some other thread will have removed that entry. If I put this code into a program that repeatedly runs this method on several threads, but that also has several other threads busily removing the very same entry, I eventually see a KeyNotFoundException.

Concurrent systems need a top-down strategy to ensure system-wide consistency. (This is why database management systems often group sets of operations together as transactions, atomic units of work that either succeed completely or have no effect at all.) Looking at Example 16-1, this means that it is the responsibility of code that calls FormatDictionary to ensure that the dictionary can be used freely for the duration of the method.

 Although calling code should guarantee that whatever objects it passes are safe to use for the duration of a method call, you cannot in general assume that it's OK to hold on to references to your arguments for future use. Anonymous functions and delegates make it easy to do this accidentally—if a nested method refers to its containing method's arguments, and if that nested method runs after the containing method returns, it may no longer be safe to assume that you're allowed to access the objects to which the arguments refer. If you need to do this, you will need to document the assumptions you're making about when you can use objects, and inspect any code that calls the method to make sure that these assumptions are valid.

Thread-Local Storage

Sometimes it can be useful to maintain thread-local state at a broader scope than a single method. Various parts of the runtime libraries do this. For example, the System.Transactions namespace defines an API for using transactions with databases, message queues, and any other resource managers that support them. It provides an implicit model where you can start an *ambient transaction*, and any operations that support this will enlist in it without you needing to pass any explicit transaction-related arguments. (It also supports an explicit model, should you prefer that.) The Transaction class's static Current property returns the ambient transaction for the current thread, or it returns null if the thread currently has no ambient transaction in progress.

To support this sort of per-thread state, .NET offers the ThreadLocal<T> class. Example 16-3 uses this to provide a wrapper around a delegate that allows only a single call into the delegate to be in progress on any one thread at any time.

Example 16-3. Using ThreadLocal<T>

```
public class Notifier(Action callback)
{
    private readonly ThreadLocal<bool> _isCallbackInProgress = new();

    public void Notify()
    {
        if (_isCallbackInProgress.Value)
        {
            throw new InvalidOperationException(
                "Notification already in progress on this thread");
        }

        try
        {
            _isCallbackInProgress.Value = true;
            callback();
        }
        finally
        {
            _isCallbackInProgress.Value = false;
        }
    }
}
```

If the method that Notify calls back attempts to make another call to Notify, this will block that attempt at recursion by throwing an exception. However, because it uses a ThreadLocal<bool> to track whether a call is in progress, this will allow simultaneous calls as long as each call happens on a separate thread.

You get and set the value that ThreadLocal<T> holds for the current thread through the Value property. The constructor is overloaded, and you can pass a Func<T> that will be called back each time a new thread first tries to retrieve the value to create a default initial value. (The initialization is lazy—the callback won't run every time a new thread starts. A ThreadLocal<T> invokes the callback only the first time a thread attempts to use the value.) There is no fixed limit to the number of ThreadLocal<T> objects you can create.

There's one thing you need to be careful about with thread-local storage. If you create a new object for each thread, be aware that an application might create a large number of threads over its lifetime, especially if you use the thread pool (which is described in detail later). If the per-thread objects you create are expensive, this might cause problems. Furthermore, if there are any disposable per-thread resources, you will not necessarily know when a thread terminates; the thread pool regularly creates and destroys threads without telling you when it does so.

If you don't need the automatic creation each time a new thread first uses thread-local storage, you can instead just annotate a static field with the [ThreadStatic] attribute. This is handled by the CLR: it effectively means that each thread that accesses this field gets its own distinct field. This can reduce the number of objects that need to be allocated. But be careful: it's possible to define a field initializer for such fields, but that initializer will run only for the first thread to access the field. For other threads using the same [ThreadStatic], the field will initially contain the default zero-like value for the field's type.

One last note of caution: be wary of thread-local storage (and any mechanism based on it) if you plan to use the asynchronous language features described in Chapter 17, because those make it possible for a single invocation of a method to use multiple different threads as it progresses. This would make it a bad idea for that sort of method to use ambient transactions, or anything else that relies on thread-local state. Many .NET features that you might think would use thread-local storage (e.g., the ASP.NET Core framework's static HttpContext.Current property, which returns an object relating to the HTTP request that the current thread is handling) turn out to associate information with something called the *execution context* instead. An execution context is more flexible, because it can hop across threads when required. I'll be describing it later.

For the issues I've just discussed to be relevant, we'll need to have multiple threads. There are four main ways to use multithreading. In one, the code runs in a framework that creates multiple threads on your behalf, such as ASP.NET Core. Another is to use certain kinds of callback-based APIs. A few common patterns for this are described in "Tasks" on page 736 and "Other Asynchronous Patterns" on page 749. But the two most direct ways to use threads are to create new threads explicitly or to use the .NET thread pool.

The Thread Class

As I mentioned earlier, the Thread class (defined in the System.Threading namespace) represents a CLR thread. You can obtain a reference to the Thread object representing the thread that's executing your code with the Thread.CurrentThread property, but if you're looking to introduce some multithreading, you can construct a new Thread object.

A new thread needs to know what code it should run when it starts, so you must provide a delegate, and the thread will invoke the method the delegate refers to when it starts. The thread will run until that method returns normally, or allows an exception to propagate all the way to the top of the stack (or the thread is forcibly terminated through any of the OS mechanisms for killing threads or their containing processes). Example 16-4 creates three threads to download the contents of three web pages simultaneously. It uses a single `HttpClient` instance to do this, which is OK because that type is designed to be used concurrently from multiple threads.

Example 16-4. Creating threads

```
internal static class Program
{
    private static readonly HttpClient http = new();

    private static void Main()
    {
        Thread t1 = new(MyThreadEntryPoint);
        Thread t2 = new(MyThreadEntryPoint);
        Thread t3 = new(MyThreadEntryPoint);

        t1.Start("https://endjin.com/");
        t2.Start("https://oreilly.com/");
        t3.Start("https://dotnet.microsoft.com/");
    }

    private static void MyThreadEntryPoint(object? arg)
    {
        string url = (string)arg!;

        Console.WriteLine($"Downloading {url}");
        var response = http.Send(new HttpRequestMessage(HttpMethod.Get, url));
        using StreamReader r = new(response.Content.ReadAsStream());
        string page = r.ReadToEnd();
        Console.WriteLine($"Downloaded {url}, length {page.Length}");
    }
}
```

The `Thread` constructor is overloaded and accepts two delegate types. The `Thread Start` delegate requires a method that takes no arguments and returns no value, but in Example 16-4, the `MyThreadEntryPoint` method takes a single `object` argument, which matches the other delegate type, `ParameterizedThreadStart`. This provides a way to pass an argument to each thread, which is useful if you're invoking the same method on several different threads, as this example does. The thread will not run until you call `Start`, and if you're using the `ParameterizedThreadStart` delegate type, you must call the overload that takes a single `object` argument. I'm using this to make each thread download from a different URL.

There are two more overloads of the `Thread` constructor, each adding an `int` argument after the delegate argument. This `int` specifies the size of stack for the thread. Current .NET implementations require stacks to be contiguous in memory, making it necessary to preallocate address space for the stack. If a thread exhausts this space, the CLR throws a `StackOverflowException`. (You normally see those only when a bug causes infinite recursion.) Without this argument, the CLR will use the default stack size for the process. (This varies by OS; on Windows it will usually be 1 MB.) You can change it by setting the DOTNET_DefaultStackSize environment variable. Note that it interprets the value as a hexadecimal number. It's rare to need to change this but not unheard of. If you have recursive code that produces very deep stacks, you might need to run it on a thread with a larger stack. Conversely, if you're creating huge numbers of threads, you might want to reduce the stack size to conserve resources, because the default of 1 MB is usually considerably more than is really required. However, it's usually not a great idea to create such a large number of threads. So, in most cases, you will create only a moderate number of threads and just use the constructors that use the default stack size.

Notice that the Main method in Example 16-4 returns immediately after starting the three threads. Despite this, the application continues to run—it will run until all the threads finish. The CLR keeps the process alive until there are no *foreground threads* running, where a foreground thread is defined to be any thread that hasn't explicitly been designated as a background thread. If you want to prevent a particular thread from keeping the process running, set its IsBackground property to true. (This means that background threads may be terminated while they're in the middle of doing something, so you need to be careful about what kind of work you do on these threads.)

Creating threads directly is not the only option. The thread pool provides a commonly used alternative.

The Thread Pool

On most operating systems, it is relatively expensive to create and shut down threads. If you need to perform a fairly short piece of work (such as serving up a web page or some similarly brief operation), it would be a bad idea to create a thread just for that job and to shut it down when the work completes. There are two serious problems with this strategy: first, you may end up expending more resources on the startup and shutdown costs than on useful work; second, if you keep creating new threads as more work comes in, the system may bog down under load—with heavy workloads, creating ever more threads will tend to reduce throughput. This is because, in addition to basic per-thread overheads such as the memory required for the stack, the OS needs to switch regularly between runnable threads to enable them all to make progress, and this switching has its own overheads.

To avoid these problems, .NET provides a thread pool. You can supply a delegate that the runtime will invoke on a thread from the pool. If necessary, it will create a new thread, but where possible, it will reuse one it created earlier, and it might make your work wait in a queue if all the threads created so far are busy. After your method runs, the CLR will not normally terminate the thread; instead, the thread will stay in the pool waiting for other work items, which amortizes the cost of creating the thread over multiple work items. It will create new threads if necessary, but it tries to keep the thread count at a level that results in the number of runnable threads matching the hardware thread count, to minimize switching costs.

 The thread pool always creates background threads, so if it has work in progress when the last foreground thread in your process exits, that work will not complete, because all background threads will be terminated at that point. If you need to ensure that work being done on the thread pool completes, you must wait for that to happen before allowing all foreground threads to finish.

Launching thread pool work with Task

The usual way to use the thread pool is through the `Task` class. This is part of the Task Parallel Library (discussed in more detail in "Tasks" on page 736), but its basic usage is pretty straightforward, as Example 16-5 shows.

Example 16-5. Running code on the thread pool with a Task

```
Task.Run(() => MyThreadEntryPoint("https://oreilly.com/"));
```

This queues the lambda for execution on the thread pool (which, when it runs, just calls the `MyThreadEntryPoint` method from Example 16-4). If a thread is available, it will start to run straightaway, but if not, it will wait in a queue until a thread becomes available (either because some other work item in progress completes or because the thread pool decides to add a new thread to the pool).

There are other ways to use the thread pool, the most obvious of which is through the `ThreadPool` class. Its `QueueUserWorkItem` method works in a similar way to `Start`— you pass it a delegate and it will queue the method for execution. This is a lower-level API—it does not provide any direct way to handle completion of the work, nor to chain operations together, so for most cases, the `Task` class is preferable.

Thread creation heuristics

The runtime adjusts the number of threads based on the workload you present. The heuristics it uses are not documented and have changed across releases of .NET, so you should not depend on the exact behavior I'm about to describe; however, it is useful to know roughly what to expect.

If you give the thread pool only CPU-bound work, in which every method you ask it to execute spends its entire time performing computations and never blocks waiting for I/O to complete, you might end up with one thread for each of the hardware threads in your system (although if the individual work items take long enough, the thread pool might decide to allocate more threads). For example, on the eight-core two-way hyperthreaded computer I'm using as I write this, queuing up a load of CPU-intensive work items initially causes the CLR to create 16 thread pool threads, and as long as the work items complete about once a second or faster, the number of threads mostly stays at that level. (It occasionally goes over that because the runtime will try adding an extra thread from time to time to see what effect this has on throughput, and then it drops back down again.) But if the rate at which the program gets through items drops, the CLR gradually increases the thread count.

If thread pool threads get blocked (e.g., because they're waiting for data from disk or for a response over the network from a server), the CLR increases the number of pool threads more quickly. Again, it starts off with one per hardware thread, but when slow work items consume very little processor time, it will try adding threads to improve throughput.

In either case, the CLR will eventually stop adding threads. The exact default limit varies in 32-bit processes, depending on the version of .NET, although it's typically on the order of 1,000 threads. In 64-bit mode, it appears to default to 32,767. You can change this limit—the `ThreadPool` class has a `SetMaxThreads` method that lets you configure different limits for your process. You may run into other limitations that place a lower practical limit. For example, each thread has its own stack that has to occupy a contiguous range of virtual address space. If each thread gets 1 MB of the process's address space reserved for its stack, by the time you have 1,000 threads, you'll be using 1 GB of address space for stacks alone. Thirty-two-bit processes have only 4 GB of address range, so you might not have space for the number of threads you request. In any case, 1,000 threads is usually more than is helpful, so if it gets that high, this may be a symptom of some underlying problem that you should investigate. For this reason, if you call `SetMaxThreads`, it will normally be to specify a lower limit—you may find that with some workloads, constraining the number of threads improves throughput by reducing the level of contention for system resources.

`ThreadPool` also has a `SetMinThreads` method. This lets you ensure that the number of threads does not drop below a certain number. This can be useful in applications that work most efficiently with some minimum number of threads and that want to be able to operate at maximum speed instantly, without waiting for the thread pool's heuristics to adjust the thread count.

Thread Affinity and SynchronizationContext

Some objects demand that you use them only from certain threads. This is particularly common with UI code—the WPF, .NET MAUI, and Windows Forms UI frameworks require that UI objects be used from the thread on which they were created. This is called *thread affinity*, and although it is most often a UI concern, it can also crop up in interoperability scenarios—some COM objects have thread affinity.

Thread affinity can make life awkward if you want to write multithreaded code. Suppose you've carefully implemented a multithreaded algorithm that can exploit all of the hardware threads in an end user's computer, significantly improving performance when running on a multicore CPU compared to a single-threaded algorithm. Once the algorithm completes, you may want to present the results to the end user. The thread affinity of UI objects requires you to perform that final step on a particular thread, but your multithreaded code may well produce its final results on some other thread. (In fact, you will probably have avoided the UI thread entirely for the CPU-intensive work, to make sure that the UI remained responsive while the work was in progress.) If you try to update the UI from some random worker thread, the UI framework will throw an exception complaining that you've violated its thread affinity requirements. Somehow, you'll need to pass a message back to the UI thread so that it can display the results.

The runtime libraries provide the SynchronizationContext class to help in these scenarios. Its Current static property returns an instance of the Synchronization Context class that represents the context in which your code is currently running. For example, in a WPF application, if you retrieve this property while running on a UI thread, it will return an object associated with that thread. You can store the object that Current returns and use it from any thread anytime you need to perform further work on the UI thread. Example 16-6 does this so that it can perform some potentially slow work on a thread pool thread and then update the UI back on the UI thread.

Example 16-6. Using the thread pool and then SynchronizationContext

```
private void findButton_Click(object sender, RoutedEventArgs e)
{
    SynchronizationContext uiContext = SynchronizationContext.Current!;

    Task.Run(() =>
    {
        string pictures =
            Environment.GetFolderPath(Environment.SpecialFolder.MyPictures);
        var folder = new DirectoryInfo(pictures);
        FileInfo[] allFiles =
            folder.GetFiles("*.jpg", SearchOption.AllDirectories);
        FileInfo? largest =
            allFiles.OrderByDescending(f => f.Length).FirstOrDefault();

        if (largest is not null)
        {
            uiContext.Post(_ =>
            {
                long sizeMB = largest.Length / (1024 * 1024);
                outputTextBox.Text =
                    $"Largest file ({sizeMB}MB) is {largest.FullName}";
```

```
        },
        null);
    }
});
}
```

This code handles a Click event for a button. (It happens to be a WPF application, but SynchronizationContext works in exactly the same way in other client-side UI frameworks, such as .NET MAUI.) UI elements raise their events on the UI thread, so when the first line of the click handler retrieves the current Synchronization Context, it will get the context for the UI thread. The code then runs some work on a thread pool thread via the Task class. The code looks at every picture in the user's *Pictures* folder, searching for the largest file, so this could take a while. It's a bad idea to perform slow work on a UI thread—UI elements that belong to that thread cannot respond to user input while the UI thread is busy doing something else. So pushing this into the thread pool is a good idea.

The problem with using the thread pool here is that once the work completes, we're on the wrong thread to update the UI. This code updates the Text property of a text box, and we'd get an exception if we tried that from a thread pool thread. So, when the work completes, it uses the SynchronizationContext object it retrieved earlier and calls its Post method. That method accepts a delegate, and it will arrange to invoke that back on the UI thread. (Under the covers, it posts a custom message to the Windows message queue, and when the UI thread's main message processing loop picks up that message, it will invoke the delegate.)

 The Post method does not wait for the work to complete. There is a method that will wait, called Send, but you should avoid it. Making a worker thread block while it waits for the UI thread to do something can be risky, because if the UI thread is currently blocked waiting for the worker thread to do something, the application will deadlock. Post avoids this problem by enabling the worker thread to proceed concurrently with the UI thread.

Example 16-6 retrieves SynchronizationContext.Current while it's still on the UI thread, before it starts the thread pool work. This is important because this static property is context sensitive—it returns the context for the UI thread only while you're on the UI thread. (In fact, it's possible for each window to have its own UI thread in WPF, so it wouldn't be possible to have an API that returns *the* UI thread—there might be several.) If you read this property from a thread pool thread, the context object it returns will not post work to the UI thread.

The SynchronizationContext mechanism is extensible, so you can derive your own type from it if you want, and you can call its static SetSynchronizationContext method to make your context the current context for the thread. This can be useful in unit testing scenarios—it enables you to write tests to verify that objects interact with the SynchronizationContext correctly without needing to create a real UI.

ExecutionContext

The SynchronizationContext class has a cousin, ExecutionContext. This provides a similar service, allowing you to capture the current context and then use it to run a delegate sometime later in the same context, but it differs in two ways. First, it captures different things. Second, it uses a different approach for reestablishing the context. A SynchronizationContext will often run your work on some particular thread, whereas ExecutionContext will always use your thread, and it just makes sure that all of the contextual information it has captured is available on that thread. One way to think of the difference is that SynchronizationContext does the work in an existing context, whereas ExecutionContext brings the contextual information to you.

You retrieve the current context by calling the ExecutionContext.Capture method. The execution context does not capture thread-local storage, but it does include any information in the current *logical call context*. You can access this through the Call Context class, which provides LogicalSetData and LogicalGetData methods to store and retrieve name/value pairs, or through the higher-level wrapper Async Local<T>. This information is usually associated with the current thread, but if you run code in a captured execution context, it will make information from the logical context available, even if that code runs on some other thread entirely.

.NET uses the ExecutionContext class internally whenever long-running work that starts on one thread later ends up continuing on a different thread (as happens with some of the asynchronous patterns described later in this chapter). You may want to use the execution context in a similar way if you write any code that accepts a callback that it will invoke later, perhaps from some other thread. To do this, you call Capture to grab the current context, which you can later pass to the Run method to invoke a delegate. Example 16-7 shows ExecutionContext at work.

Example 16-7. Using ExecutionContext

```
public class Defer(Action callback)
{
    private readonly ExecutionContext? _context = ExecutionContext.Capture()!;

    public void Run()
    {
        if (_context is null) { callback(); return; }
        // When ExecutionContext.Run invokes the lambda we supply as the 2nd
        // argument, it passes that lambda the value we supplied as the 3rd
        // argument to Run. Here we're passing callback, so the lambda has
```

```
    // access to the Action we want to invoke. It would have been simpler
    // to write "_ => callback()", but the lambda would then need to
    // capture 'this' to be able to access callback, and that capture
    // would cause an additional allocation. Using the static keyword
    // on the lambda tells the compiler that we intend to avoid capture,
    // so it would report an error if we accidentally used any locals.
    ExecutionContext.Run(
        _context,
        static (cb) => ((Action)cb!)(),
        callback);
    }
}
```

In .NET Framework, a single captured `ExecutionContext` cannot be used on multiple threads simultaneously. Sometimes you might need to invoke multiple different methods in a particular context, and in a multithreaded environment, you might not be able to guarantee that the previous method has returned before calling the next. For this scenario, `ExecutionContext` provides a `CreateCopy` method that generates a copy of the context, enabling you to make multiple simultaneous calls through equivalent contexts. In .NET, `ExecutionContext` is immutable, meaning this restriction no longer applies, and `CreateCopy` just returns its `this` reference.

Synchronization

Sometimes you will want to write multithreaded code in which multiple threads have access to the same state. For example, in Chapter 5, I suggested that a server could use a `Dictionary<TKey, TValue>` as part of a cache to avoid duplicating work when it receives multiple similar requests. While this sort of caching can offer significant performance benefits in some scenarios, it presents a challenge in a multithreaded environment. (And if you're working on server code with demanding performance requirements, you will most likely need more than one thread to handle requests.) The Thread Safety section of the documentation for the `Dictionary<TKey, TValue>` class says this:

> A `Dictionary<TKey, TValue>` can support multiple readers concurrently, as long as the collection is not modified. Even so, enumerating through a collection is intrinsically not a thread-safe procedure. In the rare case where an enumeration contends with write accesses, the collection must be locked during the entire enumeration. To allow the collection to be accessed by multiple threads for reading and writing, you must implement your own synchronization.

This is better than we might expect—the vast majority of types in the runtime libraries simply don't support multithreaded use of instances at all. Most types support multithreaded use at the class level, but individual instances must be used one thread at a time. `Dictionary<TKey, TValue>` is more generous: it explicitly supports multiple concurrent readers, which sounds good for our caching scenario. However, when modifying a collection, not only must we ensure that we do not try to change it from multiple threads simultaneously, but also we must not have any read operations in progress while we do so.

The other generic collection classes make similar guarantees (unlike most other classes in the library). For example, `List<T>`, `Queue<T>`, `Stack<T>`, `SortedDictionary <TKey, TValue>`, `HashSet<T>`, and `SortedSet<T>` all support concurrent read-only use. (Again, if you modify any instance of these collections, you must make sure that no other threads are either modifying or reading from the same instance at the same time.) Of course, you should always check the documentation before attempting multithreaded use of any type.[2] Be aware that the generic collection interface types make no thread safety guarantees—although `List<T>` supports concurrent readers, not all implementations of `IList<T>` will. (For example, imagine an implementation that wraps something potentially slow, such as the contents of a file. It might make sense for this wrapper to cache data to make read operations faster. Reading an item from such a list could change its internal state, so reads could fail when performed simultaneously from multiple threads if the code did not take steps to protect itself.)

If you can arrange never to have to modify a data structure while it is in use from multithreaded code, the support for concurrent access offered by many of the collection classes may be all you need. But if some threads will need to modify shared state, you will need to coordinate access to that state. To enable this, .NET provides various synchronization mechanisms that you can use to ensure that your threads take it in turns to access shared objects when necessary. In this section, I'll describe the most commonly used ones.

Monitors and the lock Keyword

The first option to consider for synchronizing multithreaded use of shared state is the `Monitor` class. This is popular because it is efficient, it offers a straightforward model, and C# provides direct language support, making it very easy to use. Example 16-8 shows a class that uses the `lock` keyword (which in turn uses the `Monitor` class) anytime it either reads or modifies its internal state. This ensures that only one thread will be accessing that state at any one time.

Example 16-8. Protecting state with `lock`

```
public class SaleLog
{
```

---

2 At the time of this writing, the documentation does not offer read-only thread safety guarantees for `HashSet<T>` and `SortedSet<T>`. Nonetheless, I have been assured by Microsoft that these also support concurrent reads.

```
private readonly object _sync = new();
private decimal _total;
private readonly List<string> _saleDetails = [];

public decimal Total
{
    get { lock (_sync) { return _total; } }
}

public void AddSale(string item, decimal price)
{
    string details = $"{item} sold at {price}";
    lock (_sync)
    {
        _total += price;
        _saleDetails.Add(details);
    }
}

public string[] GetDetails(out decimal total)
{
    lock (_sync)
    {
        total = _total;
        return _saleDetails.ToArray();
    }
}
}
```

To use the lock keyword, you provide a reference to an object and a block of code. The C# compiler generates code that will cause the CLR to ensure that no more than one thread is inside a lock block for that object at any one time. Suppose you created a single instance of this SaleLog class, and on one thread you called the AddSale method, while on another thread you called GetDetails at the same time. Both threads will reach lock statements, passing in the same _sync field. Whichever thread happens to get there first will be allowed to run the block following the lock. The other thread will be made to wait—it won't be allowed to enter its lock block until the first thread leaves its lock block.

The SaleLog class only ever uses any of its fields from inside a lock block using the _sync argument. This ensures that all access to fields is serialized (in the concurrency sense—that is, threads get to access fields one at a time, rather than all piling in simultaneously). When the GetDetails method reads from both the _total and _sale Details fields, it can be confident that it's getting a coherent view—the total will be consistent with the current contents of the list of sales details, because the code that modifies these two pieces of data does so within a single lock block. This means that updates will appear to be atomic from the point of view of any other lock block using _sync.

It may look excessive to use a lock block even for the get accessor that returns the total. However, decimal is a 128-bit value, so access to data of this type is not intrinsically atomic—without that lock, it would be possible for the returned value to be made up of a mixture of two or more values that _total had at different times. (For example, the bottom 64 bits might be from an older value than the top 64 bits.) This is often described as a *torn read*. The CLR guarantees atomic reads and writes only for data types whose size is no larger than 4 bytes, and also for references, even on a platform where those are larger than 4 bytes. (It guarantees this only for naturally aligned fields, but in C#, fields will always be aligned unless you have deliberately misaligned them for interop purposes.)

A subtle but important detail of Example 16-8 is that whenever it returns information about its internal state, it returns a copy. The Total property's type is decimal, which is a value type, and values are always returned as copies. But when it comes to the list of entries, the GetDetails method calls ToArray, which will build a new array containing a copy of the list's current contents. It would be a mistake to return the reference in _saleDetails directly, because that would enable code outside of the SalesLog class to access and modify the collection without using lock. We need to ensure that all access to that collection is synchronized, and we lose the ability to do that if our class hands out references to its internal state.

 If you write code that performs some multithreaded work that eventually comes to a halt, it's OK to share references to the state after the work has stopped. But if multithreaded modifications to an object are ongoing, you need to ensure that all use of that object's state is protected.

The lock keyword accepts any object reference, so you might wonder why I've created an object specially—couldn't I have passed this instead? That would have worked, but the problem is that your this reference is not private—it's the same reference by which external code uses your object. Using a publicly visible feature of your object to synchronize access to private state is imprudent; some other code could decide that it's convenient to use a reference to your object as the argument to some completely unrelated lock blocks. In this case, it probably wouldn't cause a problem, but with more complex code, it could tie conceptually unrelated pieces of concurrent behavior together in a way that might cause performance problems or even deadlocks. Thus, it's usually better to code defensively and use something that only your code has access to as the lock argument. Of course, I could have used the _saleDetails field because that refers to an object that only my class has access to. However, even if you code defensively, you should not assume that other developers will, so in general, it's safer to avoid using an instance of a class you didn't write as the argument for a lock, because you can never be certain that it isn't using its this reference for its own locking purposes.

The fact that you can use any object reference is a bit of an oddity in any case. Most of .NET's synchronization mechanisms use an instance of some distinct type as the point of reference for synchronization. (For example, if you want reader/writer locking semantics, you use an instance of the ReaderWriterLockSlim class, not just any old object.) The Monitor class (which is what lock uses) is an exception that dates back to an old requirement for a degree of compatibility with Java (which has a similar locking primitive). This is not relevant to modern .NET development, so this feature is now just a historical peculiarity. Using a distinct object whose only job is to act as a lock argument adds minimal overhead (compared to the costs of locking in the first place) and tends to make it easier to see how synchronization is being managed.

> You cannot use a value type as an argument for lock. C# prevents this, and with good reason. The compiler performs an implicit conversion to object on the lock argument, which for reference types doesn't require the CLR to do anything at runtime. But when you convert a value type to a reference of type object, a box needs to be created. That box would be the argument to lock, and that would be a problem, because you get a new box every time you convert a value to an object reference. So, each time you ran a lock, it would get a different object, meaning there would be no synchronization in practice. This is why the compiler prevents you from trying.

How the lock keyword expands

Each lock block turns into code that does three things: first, it calls Monitor.Enter, passing the argument you provided to lock. Then it attempts to run the code in the block. Finally, it will usually call Monitor.Exit once the block finishes. But it's not entirely straightforward, thanks to exceptions. The code will still call Monitor.Exit if the code you put in the block throws an exception, but it needs to handle the possibility that Monitor.Enter itself threw, which would mean that the thread does not own the lock and should therefore not call Monitor.Exit. Example 16-9 shows what the compiler makes of the lock block in the GetDetails method in Example 16-8.

Example 16-9. How lock blocks expand

```
bool lockWasTaken = false;
object temp = _sync;
try
{
    Monitor.Enter(temp, ref lockWasTaken);
    {
        total = _total;
```

```
        return _saleDetails.ToArray();
    }
}
finally
{
    if (lockWasTaken)
    {
        Monitor.Exit(temp);
    }
}
```

`Monitor.Enter` is the API that does the work of discovering whether some other thread already has the lock, and if so, making the current thread wait. If this returns at all, it normally succeeds. (It might deadlock, in which case it will never return.) There is a small possibility of failure caused by an exception, e.g., due to running out of memory. That would be unusual, but the generated code takes it into account nonetheless—this is the purpose of the slightly roundabout-looking code for the `lock WasTaken` variable. (In practice, the compiler will make that a hidden variable without an accessible name, by the way. I've named it to show what's happening here.) The `Monitor.Enter` method guarantees that acquisition of the lock will be atomic with updating the flag indicating whether the lock was taken, ensuring that the `finally` block will attempt to call `Exit` if and only if the lock was acquired.

`Monitor.Exit` tells the CLR that we no longer need exclusive access to whatever resources we're synchronizing access to, and if any other threads are waiting inside `Monitor.Enter` for the object in question, this will enable one of them to proceed. The compiler puts this inside a `finally` block to ensure that whether you exit from the block by running to the end, returning from the middle, or throwing an exception, the lock will be released.

The fact that the `lock` block calls `Monitor.Exit` on an exception is a double-edged sword. On the one hand, it reduces the chances of deadlock by ensuring that locks are released on failure. On the other hand, if an exception occurs while you're in the middle of modifying some shared state, the system may be in an inconsistent state; releasing locks will allow other threads access to that state, possibly causing further problems. In some situations, it might have been better to leave locks locked in the case of an exception—a deadlocked process might do less damage than one that plows on with corrupt state. A more robust strategy is to write code that guarantees consistency in the face of exceptions, either by rolling back any changes it has made if an exception prevents a complete set of updates or by arranging to change state in an atomic way (e.g., by putting the new state into a whole new object and substituting that for the previous one only once the updated object is fully initialized). But that's beyond what the compiler can automate for you.

Waiting and notification

The Monitor class can do more than just ensure that threads take it in turns. It provides a way for threads to sit and wait for a notification from some other thread. If a thread has acquired the monitor for a particular object, it can call Monitor.Wait, passing in that object. This has two effects: it releases the monitor and causes the thread to block. It will block until some other thread calls Monitor.Pulse or Pulse All for the same object; a thread must have the monitor to be able to call either of these methods. (Wait, Pulse, and PulseAll all throw an exception if you call them while not holding the relevant monitor.)

If a thread calls Pulse, this enables one thread waiting in Wait to wake up. Calling PulseAll enables all of the threads waiting on that object's monitor to run. In either case, Monitor.Wait reacquires the monitor before returning, so even if you call PulseAll, the threads will wake up one at a time—a second thread cannot emerge from Wait until the first thread to do so relinquishes the monitor. In fact, no threads can return from Wait until the thread that called Pulse or PulseAll relinquishes the lock.

Example 16-10 uses Wait and Pulse to provide a wrapper around a Queue<T> that causes the thread that retrieves items from the queue to wait if the queue is empty. (This is for illustration only—if you want this sort of queue, you don't have to write your own. Use the built-in BlockingCollection<T> or the types in System.Threading.Channels.)

Example 16-10. Wait and Pulse

```
public class MessageQueue<T>
{
    private readonly object _sync = new();

    private readonly Queue<T> _queue = new();

    public void Post(T message)
    {
        lock (_sync)
        {
            bool wasEmpty = _queue.Count == 0;
            _queue.Enqueue(message);
            if (wasEmpty)
            {
                Monitor.Pulse(_sync);
            }
        }
    }

    public T Get()
```

```
    {
        lock (_sync)
        {
            while (_queue.Count == 0)
            {
                Monitor.Wait(_sync);
            }
            return _queue.Dequeue();
        }
    }
}
```

This example uses the monitor in two ways. It uses it through the lock keyword to ensure that only one thread at a time uses the Queue<T> that holds queued items. But it also uses waiting and notification to enable the thread that consumes items to block efficiently when the queue is empty, and for any thread that adds new items to the queue to wake up the blocked reader thread.

Timeouts

Whether you are waiting for a notification or just attempting to acquire the lock, it's possible to specify a timeout, indicating that if the operation doesn't succeed within the specified time, you would like to give up. For lock acquisition, you use a different method, TryEnter, but when waiting for notification, you just use a different overload. (There's no compiler support for this, so you won't be able to use the lock keyword.) In both cases, you can pass either an int representing the maximum time to wait, in milliseconds, or a TimeSpan value. Both return a bool indicating whether the operation succeeded.

You could use this to avoid deadlocking the process, but if your code does fail to acquire a lock within the timeout, this leaves you with the problem of deciding what to do about that. If your application is unable to acquire a lock it needs, then it can't just do whatever work it was going to do regardless. Termination of the process may be the only realistic option, because deadlock is usually a symptom of a bug, so if it occurs, your process may already be in a compromised state. That said, some developers take a less-than-rigorous approach to lock acquisition and may regard deadlock as being normal. In this case, it might be viable to abort whatever operation you were trying and either retry the work later or just log a failure, abandon this particular operation, and carry on with whatever else the process was doing. But that may be a risky strategy.

Other Synchronization Primitives

Although the lock keyword should be your default choice for protecting shared data in multithreaded scenarios, the .NET runtime libraries offer many specialized synchronization primitives that can be a better fit in certain cases. Table 16-1 describes the scenarios for which these are intended.

Table 16-1. Specialized synchronization types

Type	Usage
Barrier	Enables multiple threads to coordinate their work in phases.
CountdownEvent	Enables threads to wait until the CountdownEvent has been signaled some specific number of times.
ManualResetEvent, AutoResetEvent, and EventWaitHandle	Enable one thread to signal to other threads when something of interest has happened. Support cross-process notifications on Windows.
ManualResetEventSlim	Alternative to ManualResetEvent that does not support cross-process notification, but which has lower overheads when wait times are likely to be very short.
Mutex	Exclusive access similar to Monitor. Higher overhead, but with cross-process support on all operating systems.
ReaderWriterLockSlim	Higher overhead than Monitor, but can be better if locks are held for a long time and modifications are rare, because this allows concurrent readers, granting exclusive access only during writes.
SpinLock	Exclusive locking (just like lock and Monitor) that might enable lower memory usage; requires great care because subtle mistakes can make this more expensive than simpler solutions.
Semaphore	Enables a bounded level of concurrency—like a Monitor where you can configure the number of threads that are allowed to possess it simultaneously. Supports cross-process use on Windows.
SemaphoreSlim	Alternative to Semaphore that does not support cross-process notification, but which has lower overheads when wait times are likely to be very short.

Interlocked

The Interlocked class supports concurrent access to shared data, but it is not a synchronization primitive. Instead, it defines static methods that provide atomic forms of various simple operations.

For example, it provides Increment, Decrement, and Add methods, with overloads supporting int and long values. (These are all similar—incrementing or decrementing is just addition by 1 or −1.) Addition involves reading a value from some storage location, calculating a modified value, and storing that back in the same storage location, and if you use normal C# operators to do this, things can go wrong if multiple threads try to modify the same location simultaneously. If the value is initially 0, and two threads both read that value in quick succession, and if both then add 1 and store the result back, they will both end up writing back 1. Two threads attempted to increment the value, but it went up only by one. The `Interlocked` form of these operations prevents this sort of overlap.

`Interlocked` also offers various methods for swapping values. The `Exchange` method takes two arguments: a reference to a value and a value. This returns the value currently in the location referred to by the first argument and also overwrites that location with the value supplied as a second argument, and it performs these two steps as a single atomic operation. There are overloads supporting `int`, `uint`, `long`, `ulong`, `object`, `float`, `double`, `nint`, and `nuint`. There is also a generic `Exchange<T>`, where `T` can be any reference type. There is a variant called `CompareExchange`. As with `Exchange`, it takes a reference to some variable you wish to modify, and the value you want to replace it with, but it also takes a third argument: the value you think is already in the storage location. If the value in the storage location does not match the expected value, this method will not change the storage location. (It still returns whatever value was in that storage location, whether it modifies it or not.) This is often used to discover when some other thread has been using the variable at the same time as us, and to avoid concurrent modifications.

The simplest `Interlocked` operation is the `Read` method. This takes a `ref long` or `ref ulong` and reads the value atomically with respect to any other operations on the same variable that you perform through `Interlocked`. This enables you to read 64-bit values safely—in general, the CLR does not guarantee that 64-bit reads will be atomic. (In a 64-bit process, they will be unless you've taken deliberate steps to misalign data, which may sometimes be necessary to interoperate with unmanaged code. But 64-bit reads usually aren't atomic on 32-bit architectures. You need to use `Interlocked.Read` to ensure atomicity.) There are no overloads for 32-bit values, because reading and writing those is always atomic.

The operations supported by `Interlocked` correspond to the atomic operations that most CPUs can support more or less directly. (Some CPU architectures support all the operations innately, while others support only the compare and exchange, building everything else up out of that. But in any case, these operations are at most a few instructions.) This means they are reasonably efficient. They are considerably more costly than performing equivalent noninterlocked operations with ordinary code, because atomic CPU instructions need to coordinate across all CPU cores (and across all CPU chips in computers that have multiple physically separate CPUs installed) to guarantee atomicity. Nonetheless, they incur a fraction of the cost you pay when a `lock` statement ends up blocking the thread at the OS level.

These sorts of operations are sometimes described as *lock free*. This is not entirely accurate—the computer does acquire locks very briefly at a fairly low level in the hardware. Atomic read-modify-write operations effectively acquire an exclusive lock on the computer's memory for two bus cycles. However, no OS locks are acquired, the scheduler does not need to get involved, and the locks are held for an extremely short duration—often for just one machine code instruction. More significantly, the highly specialized and low-level form of locking used here does not permit holding on to one lock while waiting to acquire another—code can lock only one thing at a time. This means that this sort of operation will not deadlock. However, the simplicity that rules out deadlocks cuts both ways.

The downside of interlocked operations is that the atomicity applies only to extremely simple operations. It's very hard to build more complex logic in a way that works correctly in a multithreaded environment using just `Interlocked`. It's easier and considerably less risky to use the higher-level synchronization primitives, because those make it fairly easy to protect more complex operations rather than just individual calculations. You would typically use `Interlocked` only in extremely performance-sensitive work, and even then, you should measure carefully to verify that it's having the effect you hope—sometimes *clever* use of `Interlocked` ends up costing you more than you expect.

One of the biggest challenges with writing correct code when using low-level atomic operations is that you may encounter problems caused by the way a CPU's cache works. Work done by one thread may not become visible instantly to other threads, and in some cases, memory access may not necessarily occur in the order that your code specifies. Using higher-level synchronization primitives sidesteps these issues by enforcing certain ordering constraints, but if you decide instead to use `Interlocked` to build your own synchronization mechanisms, you will need to understand the memory model that .NET defines for when multiple threads access the same memory simultaneously, and you will typically need to use either the `MemoryBarrier` method defined by the `Interlocked` class or the various methods defined by the `Volatile` class to ensure correctness. This is beyond the scope of this book, and it's also a really good way to write code that looks like it works but turns out to go wrong under heavy load (i.e., when it probably matters most), so these sorts of techniques are rarely worth the cost. Stick with the other mechanisms I've discussed in this chapter unless you really have no alternative.

Lazy Initialization

When you need an object to be accessible from multiple threads, if it's possible for that object to be immutable (i.e., its fields never change after construction), you can often avoid the need for synchronization. It is always safe for multiple threads to read from the same location simultaneously—trouble sets in only if the data needs to change. However, there is one challenge: When and how do you initialize the shared object? One solution might be to store a reference to the object in a static field initialized from a static constructor or a field initializer—the CLR guarantees to run the static initialization for any class just once. However, this might cause the object to be created earlier than you want. If you perform too much work in static initialization, this can have an adverse effect on how long it takes your application to start running.

You might want to wait until the object is first needed before initializing it. This is called *lazy initialization*. This is not particularly hard to achieve—you can just check a field to see if it's null and initialize it if not, using lock to ensure that only one thread gets to construct the value. However, this is an area in which developers seem to have a remarkable appetite for showing how clever they are, with the potentially undesirable corollary of demonstrating that they're not as clever as they think they are.

The lock keyword works fairly efficiently, but it's possible to do better by using Interlocked. However, the subtleties of memory access reordering on multiprocessor systems make it easy to write code that runs quickly, looks clever, and doesn't always work. To avert this recurring problem, .NET provides two classes to perform lazy initialization without using lock or other potentially expensive synchronization primitives. The easiest to use is Lazy<T>.

Lazy<T>

The Lazy<T> class provides a Value property of type T, and it will not create the instance that Value returns until the first time something reads the property. By default, Lazy<T> will use the no-arguments constructor for T, but you can supply your own method for creating the instance.

Lazy<T> is able to handle race conditions for you. In fact, you can configure the level of multithreaded protection you require. Since lazy initialization can also be useful in single-threaded environments, you can disable multithreaded support entirely (by passing LazyThreadSafetyMode.None as a constructor argument). But for multithreaded environments, you can choose between the other two modes in the LazyThreadSafetyMode enumeration.

These determine what happens if multiple threads all try to read the Value property for the first time more or less simultaneously. PublicationOnly does not attempt to ensure that only one thread creates an object—it only applies any synchronization at the point at which a thread finishes creating an object. The first thread to complete construction or initialization gets to supply the object, and the ones produced by any other threads that had started initialization are all discarded. Once a value is available, all further attempts to read Value will just return that.

If you choose ExecutionAndPublication, only a single thread will be allowed to attempt construction. That may seem less wasteful, but PublicationOnly offers a potential advantage: because it avoids holding any locks during initialization, you are less likely to introduce deadlock bugs if the initialization code itself attempts to acquire any locks. PublicationOnly also handles errors differently. If the first initialization attempt throws an exception, other threads that had begun a construction attempt are given a chance to complete, whereas with ExecutionAndPublication, if the one and only attempt to initialize fails, the exception is retained and will be thrown each time any code reads Value.

LazyInitializer

The other class supporting lazy initialization is LazyInitializer. This is a static class, and you use it entirely through its static generic methods. It is marginally more complex to use than Lazy<T>, but it avoids the need to allocate an extra object in addition to the lazily allocated instance you require. Example 16-11 shows how to use it.

Example 16-11. Using LazyInitializer

```
public class Cache<T>
{
    private static Dictionary<string, T>? _d;

    public static IDictionary<string, T> Dictionary =>
        LazyInitializer.EnsureInitialized(ref _d);
}
```

If the field is null, the EnsureInitialized method constructs an instance of the argument type—Dictionary<string, T>, in this case. Otherwise, it will return the value already in the field. There are some other overloads. You can pass a callback, much as you can to Lazy<T>. You can also pass a ref bool argument, which it will inspect to discover whether initialization has already occurred (and it sets this to true when it performs initialization).

A static field initializer would have given us the same once-and-once-only initialization but might have ended up running far earlier in the process's lifetime. In a more complex class with multiple fields, static initialization might even cause unnecessary work, because it happens for the entire class, so you might end up constructing objects that don't get used. This could increase the amount of time it takes for an application to start up. LazyInitializer lets you initialize individual fields as and when they are first used, ensuring that you do only work that is needed.

Other Class Library Concurrency Support

The System.Collections.Concurrent namespace defines various collections that make more generous guarantees in the face of multithreading than the usual collections, meaning you may be able to use them without needing any other synchronization primitives. Take care, though—as always, even though individual operations may have well-defined behavior in a multithreaded world, that doesn't necessarily help you if the operation you need to perform involves multiple steps. You may still need coordination at a broader scope to guarantee consistency. But in some situations, the concurrent collections may be all you need.

Unlike the nonconcurrent collections, `ConcurrentDictionary`, `ConcurrentBag`, `ConcurrentStack`, and `ConcurrentQueue` all support modification of their contents even while enumeration (e.g., with a `foreach` loop) of those contents is in progress. The dictionary provides a live enumerator, in the sense that if values are added or removed while you're in the middle of enumerating, the enumerator might show you some of the added items and it might not show you the removed items. It makes no firm guarantees, not least because with multithreaded code, when two things happen on two different threads, it's not always entirely clear which happened first—the laws of relativity mean that it may depend on your point of view.

This means that it's possible for an enumerator to seem to return an item after that item was removed from the dictionary. The bag, stack, and queue take a different approach: their enumerators all take a snapshot and iterate over that, so a `foreach` loop will see a set of contents that is consistent with what was in the collection at some point in the past, even though it may since have changed.

As I already mentioned in Chapter 5, the concurrent collections present APIs that have similarities to their nonconcurrent counterparts but with some additional members to support atomic addition and removal of items. For example, `ConcurrentDictionary` offers a `GetOrAdd` method that returns an existing entry if one exists and adds a new entry otherwise.

Another part of the runtime libraries that can help you deal with concurrency without needing to make explicit use of synchronization primitives is Rx (the subject of Chapter 11). It offers various operators that can combine multiple asynchronous streams together into a single stream. These manage concurrency issues for you— remember that any single observable will provide observers with items one at a time.

Rx takes the necessary steps to ensure that it stays within these rules even when it combines inputs from numerous individual streams that are all producing items concurrently. As long as all the sources stick to the rules, Rx will never ask an observer to deal with more than one thing at a time.

The `System.Threading.Channels` NuGet package offers types that support producer/consumer patterns, in which one or more threads generate data, while other threads consume that data. You can choose whether channels are buffered, enabling producers to get ahead of consumers, and if so, by how much. (The `BlockingCollection<T>` in `System.Collections.Concurrent` also offers this kind of service. However, it is less flexible, and it does not support the `await` keyword described in Chapter 17.)

Finally, in multithreaded scenarios it is worth considering the immutable collection classes, which I described in Chapter 5. These support concurrent access from any number of threads, and because they are immutable, the question of how to handle concurrent write access never arises. Obviously, immutability imposes considerable constraints, but if you can find a way to work with these types (and remember, the built-in `string` type is immutable, so working with immutable data is common), they can be very useful in some concurrent scenarios.

Tasks

Earlier in this chapter, I showed how to use the `Task` class to launch work in the thread pool. This class is more than just a wrapper for the thread pool. `Task` and the related types that form the Task Parallel Library (TPL) can handle a wider range of scenarios. Tasks are particularly important because C#'s asynchronous language features (which are the topic of Chapter 17) are able to work with these directly. A great many APIs in the runtime libraries offer task-based asynchronous operation.

Although tasks are the preferred way to use the thread pool, they are not just about multithreading. The basic abstractions are more flexible than that.

The Task and Task<T> Classes

There are two classes at the heart of the TPL: `Task` and a class that derives from it, `Task<T>`. The `Task` base class represents some work that may take some time to complete. `Task<T>` extends this to represent work that produces a result (of type `T`) when it completes. (The nongeneric `Task` does not produce any result. It's the asynchronous equivalent of a `void` return type.) Notice that these are not concepts that necessarily involve threads.

Most I/O operations can take a while to complete, and in most cases, the runtime libraries provide task-based APIs for them. Example 16-12 uses an asynchronous method to fetch the content of a web page as a string. Since the `HttpClient` class cannot return the string immediately—it might take a while to download the page—it returns a task instead.

Example 16-12. Task-based web download

```
var w = new HttpClient();
Task<string> webGetTask = w.GetStringAsync("https://endjin.com/");
```

Most task-based APIs follow a naming convention in which they end in Async, and if there's a corresponding synchronous API, it will have the same name but without the Async suffix. For example, the Stream class (see Chapter 15) has a Write method, and that method is synchronous (i.e., it waits until it finishes its work before returning). It also offers WriteAsync, which, being asynchronous, returns without waiting for its work to complete. It returns a Task to represent the work; this convention is called the *Task-based Asynchronous Pattern* (TAP).

That GetStringAsync method does not wait for the download to complete, so it returns almost immediately. To perform the download, the computer has to send a message to the relevant server, and then it must wait for a response. Once the request is on its way, there's no work for the CPU to do until the response comes in, meaning that this operation does not need to involve a thread for the majority of the time that the request is in progress. So this method does not wrap some underlying synchronous version of the API in a call to Task.Run. And with classes that offer I/O APIs in both forms, such as Stream, the synchronous versions are often wrappers around a fundamentally asynchronous implementation: when you call a blocking API to perform I/O, it will typically perform an asynchronous operation under the covers and then just block the calling thread until that work completes. And even in cases where it's nonasynchronous all the way down to the OS—e.g., the FileStream can use nonasynchronous operating system file APIs to implement Read and Write—I/O in the OS kernel is typically asynchronous in nature.

So, although the Task and Task<T> classes make it very easy to produce tasks that work by running methods on thread pool threads, they are also able to represent fundamentally asynchronous operations that do not require the use of a thread for most of their duration. Although it's not part of the official terminology, I describe this kind of operation as a *threadless task*, to distinguish it from tasks that run entirely on thread pool threads.

ValueTask and ValueTask<T>

Task and Task<T> are pretty flexible, and not just because they can represent both thread-based and threadless operations. As you'll see, they offer several mechanisms for discovering when the work they represent completes, including the ability to combine multiple tasks into one. Multiple threads can all wait on the same task simultaneously. You can write caching mechanisms that repeatedly hand out the same task, even long after the task completes. This is all very convenient, but it means that these task types also have some overheads. For more constrained cases, .NET defines less flexible ValueTask and ValueTask<T> types that are more efficient in certain circumstances.

The most important difference between these types and their ordinary counterparts is that `ValueTask` and `ValueTask<T>` are value types. This is significant in performance-sensitive code because it can reduce the number of objects that code allocates, reducing the amount of time an application spends performing garbage collection work. You might be thinking that the context switching costs typically involved with concurrent work are likely to be high enough that the cost of an object allocation will be the least of your concerns when dealing with asynchronous operations. And while this is often true, there's one very important scenario where the GC overhead of `Task<T>` can be problematic: operations that sometimes run slowly but usually don't.

It is very common for I/O APIs to perform buffering to reduce the number of calls into the OS. If you write a few bytes into a `Stream`, it will typically put those into a buffer and wait until either you've written enough data to make it worth sending it to the OS or you've explicitly called `Flush`. And it's also common for reads to be buffered—if you read a single byte from a file, the OS will typically have to read an entire sector from the drive (usually at least 4 KB), and that data usually gets saved somewhere in memory so that when you ask for the second byte, no more I/O needs to happen. The practical upshot is that if you write a loop that reads data from a file in relatively small chunks (e.g., one line of text at a time), the majority of read operations will complete straightaway because the data being read has already been fetched.

In these cases where the overwhelming majority of calls into asynchronous APIs complete immediately, the GC overheads of creating task objects can become significant. This is why `ValueTask` and `ValueTask<T>` were introduced. (These are built into .NET, and .NET Standard 2.1. On .NET Framework, you can get them via the `System.Threading.Tasks.Extensions` NuGet package.) These make it possible for potentially asynchronous operations to complete immediately without needing to allocate any objects. In cases where immediate completion is not possible, these types end up being wrappers for `Task` or `Task<T>` objects, at which point the overheads return, but in cases where only a small fraction of calls need to do that, these types can offer significant performance boosts, particularly in code that uses the low-allocation techniques described in Chapter 18.

The nongeneric `ValueTask` is rarely used, because asynchronous operations that produce no result can just return the `Task.CompletedTask` static property, which provides a reusable task that is already in the completed state, avoiding any GC overhead. But tasks that need to produce a result generally can't reuse existing tasks. (There are some exceptions: the runtime libraries will often use cached precompleted tasks for `Task<bool>`, because there are only two possible outcomes. But for `Task<int>`, there's no practical way to maintain a list of precompleted tasks for every possible result.)

These value task types have some constraints. They are single use: unlike `Task` and `Task<T>`, you must not store these types in a dictionary or a `Lazy<T>` to provide a cached asynchronous value. It is an error to attempt to retrieve the `Result` of a `Value`

Task<T> before it has completed. It is also an error to retrieve the Result more than once. In general, you should use a ValueTask or ValueTask<T> with exactly one await operation (as described in Chapter 17) and then never use it again. (Alternatively, if necessary, you can escape these restrictions by calling its AsTask method to obtain a full Task, or Task<T> with all the corresponding overheads, at which point you should not do anything more with the value task.)

Because the value type tasks were introduced many years after the TPL first appeared, class libraries often use Task<T> where you might expect to see a ValueTask<T>. For example, the Stream class's ReadAsync methods are all prime candidates because buffering means these are likely to complete immediately a high proportion of the time. However, most of Stream's asynchronous methods were defined long before ValueTask<T> existed, so they mostly return Task<T>. The recently added ReadAsync overload that accepts a Memory<byte> instead of a byte[] does return a ValueTask<T>, though, and more generally, where APIs have been augmented to add support for the new memory-efficient techniques described in Chapter 18, these will usually return ValueTask<T>. And if you're in a performance-sensitive world where the GC overhead of a task is significant, you will likely want to be using those techniques in any case.

Task creation options

Instead of using Task.Run, you can get more control over certain aspects of a new thread-based task by creating it with the StartNew method of either Task.Factory or Task<T>.Factory, depending on whether your task needs to return a result. Some overloads of StartNew take an argument of the enum type TaskCreationOptions, which provides some control over how the TPL schedules the task.

The PreferFairness flag asks to run the task after any tasks that have already been scheduled. By default, the thread pool normally runs the most recently added tasks first (a last-in, first-out, or LIFO, policy) because this tends to make more efficient use of the CPU cache.

The LongRunning flag warns the TPL that the task may run for a long time. By default, the TPL's scheduler optimizes for relatively short work items—anything up to a few seconds. This flag indicates that the work might take longer than that, in which case the TPL may modify its scheduling. If there are too many long-running tasks, they might use up all the threads, and even though some of the queued work items might be for much shorter pieces of work, those will still take a long time to finish, because they'll have to wait in line behind the slow work before they can even start. But if the TPL knows which items are likely to run quickly and which are likely to be slower, it can prioritize them differently to avoid such problems.

The other `TaskCreationOptions` settings relate to parent/child task relationships and schedulers, which I'll describe later.

Task status

A task goes through a number of states in its lifetime, and you can use the `Task` class's `Status` property to discover where it has gotten to. This returns a value of the enum type `TaskStatus`. If a task completes successfully, the property will return the enumeration's `RanToCompletion` value. If the task fails, it will be `Faulted`. If you cancel a task using the technique shown in "Cancellation" on page 750, the status will then be `Canceled`.

There are several variations on a theme of "in progress," of which `Running` is the most obvious—it means that some thread is currently executing the task. A task representing I/O doesn't typically require a thread while it is in progress, so it never enters that state—it starts in the `WaitingForActivation` state and then typically transitions directly to one of the three final states (`RanToCompletion`, `Faulted`, or `Canceled`). A thread-based task can also be in this `WaitingForActivation` state but only if something is preventing it from running, which would typically happen if you set it up to run only when some other task completes (which I'll show how to do shortly). A thread-based task may also be in the `WaitingToRun` state, which means that it's in a queue waiting for a thread pool thread to become available. It's possible to establish parent/child relationships between tasks, and a parent that has already finished but that created some child tasks that are not yet complete will be in the `WaitingForChil drenToComplete` state.

Finally, there's the `Created` state. You don't see this very often, because it represents a thread-based task that you have created but have not yet asked to run. You'll never see this with a task created using the task factory's `StartNew` method, or with `Task.Run`, but you will see this if you construct a new `Task` directly.

The level of detail in the `TaskStatus` property may be too much most of the time, so the `Task` class defines various simpler `bool` properties. If you want to know only whether the task has no more work to do (and don't care whether it succeeded, failed, or was canceled), there's the `IsCompleted` property. `IsCompletedSuccessfully` tells you whether it completed without failure or cancellation. If you want to check specifically for failure or cancellation, use `IsFaulted` or `IsCanceled`.

Retrieving the result

Suppose you've got a `Task<T>`, either from an API that provides one or by creating a thread-based task that returns a value. If the task completes successfully, you are likely to want to retrieve its result, which you can get from the `Result` property. So the task created by Example 16-12 makes the web page content available in `webGet Task.Result`.

If you try to read the `Result` property before the task completes, it will block your thread until the result is available. (If you have a plain `Task`, which does not return a result, and you would like to wait for that to finish, you can just call `Wait` instead.) If the operation then fails, `Result` throws an exception (as does `Wait`), although that is not as straightforward as you might expect, as I will discuss in "Error Handling" on page 746.

 You should avoid using `Result` on an uncompleted task. In some scenarios, it risks deadlock, as does `Wait`. This is particularly common in desktop applications, because certain work needs to happen on particular threads, and if you block a thread by reading the `Result` of an incomplete task, you might prevent the task from completing. Even if you don't deadlock, blocking on `Result` can cause performance issues by hogging thread pool threads that might otherwise have been able to get on with useful work. And reading the `Result` of an uncompleted `ValueTask<T>` is not permitted.

In most cases, it is far better to use C#'s asynchronous language features to retrieve the result. These are the subject of the next chapter, but as a preview, Example 16-13 shows how you could use this to get the result of the task that fetches a web page. (You'll need to apply the `async` keyword in front of the method declaration to be able to use the `await` keyword.)

Example 16-13. Getting a task's results with `await`

```
string pageContent = await webGetTask;
```

This may not look like an exciting improvement on simply writing `webGet Task.Result`, but as I'll show in Chapter 17, this code is not quite what it seems—the C# compiler restructures this statement into a callback-driven state machine that enables you to get the result without blocking the calling thread. (If the operation hasn't finished, the thread returns to the caller, and the remainder of the method runs later when the operation completes.)

But how are the asynchronous language features able to make this work—how can code discover when a task has completed? `Result` or `Wait` let you just sit and wait for that to happen, blocking the thread, but that rather defeats the purpose of using an asynchronous API in the first place. You will normally want to be notified when the task completes, and you can do this with a *continuation*.

Continuations

Tasks provide various overloads of a method called `ContinueWith`. This creates a new thread-based task that will execute when the task on which you called `Continue With` finishes (whether it does so successfully or with failure or cancellation). Example 16-14 uses this on the task created in Example 16-12.

Example 16-14. A continuation

```
webGetTask.ContinueWith(static t =>
{
    string webContent = t.Result;
    Console.WriteLine($"Web page length: {webContent.Length}");
});
```

A continuation task is always a thread-based task (regardless of whether its antecedent task was thread-based, I/O-based, or something else). The task gets created as soon as you call `ContinueWith` but does not become runnable until its antecedent task completes. (It starts out in the `WaitingForActivation` state.)

 A continuation is a task in its own right—`ContinueWith` returns either a `Task<T>` or `Task`, depending on whether the delegate you supply returns a result. You can set up a continuation for a continuation if you want to chain together a sequence of operations.

The method you provide for the continuation (such as the lambda in Example 16-14) receives the antecedent task as its argument, and I've used this to retrieve the result. I could also have used the `webGetTask` variable, which is in scope from the containing method, as it refers to the same task. However, by using the argument, the lambda in Example 16-14 doesn't use any variables from its containing method, which enables the compiler to produce slightly more efficient code—it doesn't need to create an object to hold shared variables, and it can reuse the delegate instance it creates because it doesn't have to create a context-specific one for each call. (I put the `static` method on the lambda to tell the compiler that this was my intention. It would still generate the more efficient code even without that keyword, but this way if I accidentally tried to capture a variable, I'd get a compiler error instead of the compiler silently generating less efficient code.) This means I could also easily separate this out into an ordinary noninline method, if I felt that would make the code easier to read.

You might be thinking that there's a possible problem in Example 16-14: What if the download completes extremely quickly so that `webGetTask` has already completed before the code manages to attach the continuation? In fact, that doesn't matter—if you call `ContinueWith` on a task that has already completed, it will still run the continuation. It just schedules it immediately. You can attach as many continuations as you like. All the continuations you attach before the task completes will be scheduled for execution when it does complete. And any that you attach after the task has completed will be scheduled immediately.

By default, a continuation task will be scheduled for execution on the thread pool like any other task. However, there are some things you can do to change how it runs. Some overloads of ContinueWith take an argument of the enum type Task ContinuationOptions, which controls how (and whether) your task is scheduled. This includes all of the same options that are available with TaskCreationOptions but adds some others specific to continuations.

You can specify that the continuation should run only in certain circumstances. For example, the OnlyOnRanToCompletion flag will ensure that the continuation runs only if the antecedent task succeeds. There are similar OnlyOnFaulted and OnlyOn Canceled flags. Alternatively, you can specify NotOnRanToCompletion, which means that the continuation will run only if the task either faults or is canceled.

You can create multiple continuations for a single task. So you could set up one to handle the success case and another one to handle failures.

You can also specify ExecuteSynchronously. This indicates that the continuation should not be scheduled as a separate work item. Normally, when a task completes, any continuations for that task will be scheduled for execution and will have to wait for the normal thread pool mechanisms to pick the work items out of the queue and execute them. (This won't take long if you use the default options. Unless you specify PreferFairness, the LIFO operation the thread pool uses for tasks means that the most recently scheduled items run first.) However, if your completion does only the tiniest amount of work, the overhead of scheduling it as a completely separate item may be overkill. So ExecuteSynchronously lets you piggyback the completion task on the same thread pool work item that ran the antecedent. The TPL will run this kind of continuation immediately after the antecedent finishes before returning the thread to the pool. You should use this option only if the continuation will run quickly.

The LazyCancellation option handles a tricky situation that can occur if you make tasks cancelable (as described in "Cancellation" on page 750) and you are using continuations. If you cancel a task, any continuations will, by default, become runnable instantly. If the task being canceled was itself set up as a continuation for another task that hadn't yet finished, and if it has a continuation of its own, as in Example 16-15, this can have a mildly surprising effect.

Example 16-15. Cancellation and chained continuations

```
private static void ShowContinuations()
{
    Task op = Task.Run(DoSomething);
    var cs = new CancellationTokenSource();
    Task onDone = op.ContinueWith(
        _ => Console.WriteLine("Never runs"),
        cs.Token);
    Task andAnotherThing = onDone.ContinueWith(
        _ => Console.WriteLine("Continuation's continuation"));
    cs.Cancel();
}

static void DoSomething()
{
    Thread.Sleep(1000);
    Console.WriteLine("Initial task finishing");
}
```

This creates a task that will call DoSomething, followed by a cancelable continuation for that task (the Task in onDone), and then a final task (andAnotherThing) that is a continuation for the first continuation. This code cancels the first continuation almost immediately, which is almost certain to happen before the first task completes. The effect of this is that the final task runs before the first completes. The final and AnotherThing task becomes runnable when onDone completes, even if that completion was due to onDone being canceled. Since there was a chain here—andAnother Thing is a continuation for onDone, which is a continuation for op—it is a bit odd that and AnotherThing ends up running before op has finished. LazyCancellation changes the behavior so that the first continuation will not be deemed to have completed until its antecedent completes, meaning that the final continuation will run only after the first task has finished.

There's another mechanism for controlling how tasks execute: you can specify a scheduler.

Schedulers

All thread-based tasks are executed by a TaskScheduler. By default, you'll get the TPL-supplied scheduler that runs work items via the thread pool. However, there are other kinds of schedulers, and you can even write your own.

The most common reason for selecting a nondefault scheduler is to handle thread affinity requirements. The TaskScheduler class's static FromCurrentSynchroni zationContext method returns a scheduler based on the current synchronization context for whichever thread you call the method from. This scheduler will execute all work via that synchronization context.

So, if you call `FromCurrentSynchronizationContext` from a UI thread, the resulting scheduler can be used to run tasks that can safely update the UI. You would typically use this for a continuation—you can run some task-based asynchronous work and then hook up a continuation that updates the UI when that work is complete. Example 16-16 shows this technique in use in the codebehind file for a window in a WPF application.

Example 16-16. Scheduling a continuation on the UI thread

```
public partial class MainWindow : Window
{
    public MainWindow()
    {
        InitializeComponent();
    }

    private static readonly HttpClient w = new();
    private readonly TaskScheduler _uiScheduler =
        TaskScheduler.FromCurrentSynchronizationContext();

    private void FetchButtonClicked(object sender, RoutedEventArgs e)
    {
        Task<string> webGetTask = w.GetStringAsync("https://endjin.com/");

        webGetTask.ContinueWith(t =>
        {
            string webContent = t.Result;
            outputTextBox.Text = webContent;
        },
        _uiScheduler);
    }
}
```

This uses a field initializer to obtain the scheduler—the constructor for a UI element runs on the UI thread, so this will get a scheduler for the synchronization context for the UI thread. A click handler then downloads a web page using the `HttpClient` class's `GetStringAsync`. This runs asynchronously, so it won't block the UI thread, meaning that the application will remain responsive while the download is in progress. The method sets up a continuation for the task using an overload of `Continue With` that takes a `TaskScheduler`. This ensures that when the task that gets the content completes, the lambda passed to `ContinueWith` runs on the UI thread, so it's safe for it to access UI elements.

While this works perfectly well, the await keyword described in the next chapter provides a more straightforward solution to this particular problem.

The runtime libraries provide three built-in kinds of schedulers. There's the default one that uses the thread pool, and the one I just showed that uses a synchronization context. The third is provided by a class called ConcurrentExclusiveSchedulerPair, and as the name suggests, this provides two schedulers, which it makes available through properties. The ConcurrentScheduler property returns a scheduler that will run tasks concurrently much like the default scheduler. The ExclusiveScheduler property returns a scheduler that can be used to run tasks one at a time, and it will temporarily suspend the other scheduler while it does so. (This is reminiscent of ReaderWriterLockSlim—it allows exclusivity when required but concurrency the rest of the time.)

Error Handling

A Task object indicates when its work has failed by entering the Faulted state. There will always be at least one exception associated with failure, but the TPL allows composite tasks—tasks that contain a number of subtasks. This makes it possible for multiple failures to occur, and the root task will report them all. Task defines an Exception property, and its type is AggregateException. You may recall from Chapter 8 that as well as inheriting the InnerException property from the base Exception type, AggregateException defines an InnerExceptions property that returns a collection of exceptions. This is where you will find the complete set of exceptions that caused the task to fault. (If the task was not a composite task, there will usually be just one.)

If you attempt to get the Result property or call Wait on a faulted task, it will throw the same AggregateException as it would return from the Exception property. A faulted task remembers whether you have used at least one of these members, and if you have not yet done so, it considers the exception to be *unobserved*. The TPL uses finalization to track faulted tasks with unobserved exceptions, and if you allow such a task to become unreachable, the TaskScheduler will raise its static Unobserved TaskException event. This gives you one last chance to do something about the exception, after which it will be lost.

Custom Threadless Tasks

Many I/O-based APIs return threadless tasks. You can do the same if you want. The TaskCompletionSource<T> class provides a way to create a Task<T> that does not have an associated method to run on the thread pool and instead completes when you tell it to. There's also a nongeneric `TaskCompletionSource` for creating a nongeneric `Task`. (.NET Framework doesn't have the nongeneric one, but since `Task<T>` derives from `Task`, you can just use `TaskCompletionSource<object?>` instead.)

Suppose you're using a class that does not provide a task-based API, and you'd like to add a task-based wrapper. The runtime libraries provide an `SmtpClient` class for sending emails, and it supports an older event-based asynchronous pattern but not the task-based one. Example 16-17 uses that API in conjunction with `TaskComple tionSource<object?>` to provide a task-based wrapper.

Example 16-17. Using `TaskCompletionSource<T>`

```
public static class SmtpAsyncExtensions
{
    public static Task SendTaskAsync(this SmtpClient mailClient, string from,
        string recipients, string subject, string body)
    {
        var tcs = new TaskCompletionSource<object?>();

        void CompletionHandler(object s, AsyncCompletedEventArgs e)
        {
            // Check this is the notification for our SendAsync.
            if (!object.ReferenceEquals(e.UserState, tcs)) { return; }
            mailClient.SendCompleted -= CompletionHandler;
            if (e.Canceled)
            {
                tcs.SetCanceled();
            }
            else if (e.Error != null)
            {
                tcs.SetException(e.Error);
            }
            else
            {
                tcs.SetResult(null);
            }
        };

        mailClient.SendCompleted += CompletionHandler;
        mailClient.SendAsync(from, recipients, subject, body, tcs);

        return tcs.Task;
    }
}
```

The `SmtpClient` notifies us that the operation is complete by raising an event. The handler for this event first checks that the event corresponds to our call to `SendAsync` and not some other operation that may have already been in progress. It then detaches itself (so that it doesn't run a second time if something uses that same

`SmtpClient` for further work). Then it detects whether the operation succeeded, was canceled, or failed, and calls the `SetResult`, `SetCanceled`, or `SetException` method, respectively, on the `TaskCompletionSource<object>`. This will cause the task to transition into the relevant state and will also take care of running any continuations attached to that task. The completion source makes the threadless `Task` object it creates available through its `Task` property, which this method returns.

Parent/Child Relationships

If a thread-based task's method creates a new thread-based task, then by default, there will be no particular relationship between those tasks. However, one of the `Task CreationOptions` flags is `AttachedToParent`, and if you set this, the newly created task will be a child of the task currently executing. The significance of this is that the parent task won't report completion until all its children have completed. (Its own method also needs to complete, of course.) If any children fault, the parent task will fault, and it will include all the children's exceptions in its own `AggregateException`.

You can also specify the `AttachedToParent` flag for a continuation. Be aware that this does not make it a child of its antecedent task. It will be a child of whichever task was running when `ContinueWith` was called to create the continuation.

 Threadless tasks (e.g., most tasks representing I/O) often cannot be made children of another task. If you create one yourself with a `TaskCompletionSource<T>`, you can do it because that class has a constructor overload that accepts a `TaskCreation Options`. However, the majority of .NET APIs that return tasks do not provide a way to request that the task be a child.

Parent/child relationships are not the only way of creating a task whose outcome is based on multiple other items.

Composite Tasks

The `Task` class has static `WhenAll` and `WhenAny` methods. Each of these has overloads that accept either a collection of `Task` objects or a collection of `Task<T>` objects as the only argument. The `WhenAll` method returns either a `Task` or a `Task<T[]>` that completes only when all of the tasks provided in the argument have completed (and in the latter case, the composite task produces an array containing each of the individual tasks' results). The `WhenAny` method returns a `Task<Task>` or `Task<Task<T>>` that completes as soon as the first task completes, providing that task as the result.

As with a parent task, if any of the tasks that make up a task produced with `WhenAll` fail, the exceptions from all of the failed tasks will be available in the composite task's

AggregateException. (WhenAny does not report errors. It completes as soon as the first task completes, and you must inspect that to discover if it failed.)

You can attach a continuation to these tasks, but there's a slightly more direct route. Instead of creating a composite task with WhenAll or WhenAny and then calling ContinueWith on the result, you can just call the ContinueWhenAll or Continue WhenAny method of a task factory. Again, these take a collection of Task or Task<T>, but they also take a method to invoke as the continuation.

Other Asynchronous Patterns

Although the TPL provides the preferred mechanism for exposing asynchronous APIs, .NET had been around for almost a decade before it was added, so you will come across older approaches. The longest established form is the Asynchronous Programming Model (APM). This was introduced in .NET 1.0, so it is widely implemented, but its use is now discouraged. With this pattern, methods come in pairs: one to start the work and a second to collect the results when it is complete. Example 16-18 shows just such a pair from the Stream class in the System.IO namespace, and it also shows the corresponding synchronous method. (Code written today should use a task-based WriteAsync instead.)

Example 16-18. An APM pair and the corresponding synchronous method

```
public virtual IAsyncResult BeginWrite(byte[] buffer, int offset, int count,
    AsyncCallback callback, object state)...
public virtual void EndWrite(IAsyncResult asyncResult)...

public abstract void Write(byte[] buffer, int offset, int count)...
```

Notice that the first three arguments of the BeginWrite method are identical to those of the Write method. In the APM, the Begin*Xxx* method takes all of the inputs (i.e., any normal arguments and any ref arguments but not out arguments, should any be present). The End*Xxx* method provides any outputs, which means the return value, any ref arguments (because those can pass information either in or out), and any out arguments.

The Begin*Xxx* method also takes two additional arguments: a delegate of type AsyncCallback, which will be invoked when the operation completes, and an argument of type object that accepts any object you would like to associate with the operation (or null if you have no use for this). This method also returns an IAsync Result, which represents the asynchronous operation.

When your completion callback gets invoked, you can call the End*Xxx* method, passing in the same IAsyncResult object returned by the Begin*Xxx* method, and this will provide the return value if there is one. If the operation failed, the End*Xxx* method will throw an exception.

You can wrap APIs that use the APM with a Task. The TaskFactory objects provided by Task and Task<T> provide FromAsync methods to which you can pass a pair of delegates for the Begin*Xxx* and End*Xxx* methods, and you also pass any arguments that the Begin*Xxx* method requires. This will return a Task or Task<T> that represents the operation.

Another common older pattern is the Event-based Asynchronous Pattern (EAP). You've seen an example in this chapter—it's what the SmtpClient uses. With this pattern, a class provides a method that starts the operation and a corresponding event that it raises when the operation completes. The method and event usually have related names, such as SendAsync and SendCompleted. An important feature of this pattern is that the method captures the synchronization context and uses that to raise the event, meaning that if you use an object that supports this pattern in UI code, it effectively presents a single-threaded asynchronous model. This makes it much easier to use than the APM, because you don't need to write any extra code to get back onto the UI thread when asynchronous work completes.

There's no automated mechanism for wrapping the EAP in a task, but as I showed in Example 16-17, it's not particularly hard to do.

There's one more common pattern used in asynchronous code: the *awaitable* pattern supported by the C# asynchronous language features (the async and await keywords). As I showed in Example 16-13, you can consume a TPL task directly with these features, but the language does not recognize Task directly, and it's possible to await things other than tasks. You can use the await keyword with anything that implements a particular pattern. I will show this in Chapter 17.

Cancellation

.NET defines a standard mechanism for canceling slow operations. Cancelable operations take an argument of the type CancellationToken, and if you set this into a canceled state, the operation will stop early if possible instead of running to completion.

Note that the CancellationToken type itself does not offer any methods to initiate cancellation—the API is designed so that you can tell operations when you want them to be canceled without giving them power to cancel whatever other operations you have associated with the same CancellationToken. The act of cancellation is managed through a separate object, CancellationTokenSource. As the name suggests, you can use this to get hold of any number of CancellationToken instances. If you call the CancellationTokenSource object's Cancel method, that sets all of the associated CancellationToken instances into a canceled state.

Some of the synchronization mechanisms I described earlier can be passed a `CancellationToken`. (`Monitor` does not support cancellation, but many newer APIs do.) It's also common for task-based APIs to take a cancellation token, and the TPL itself also offers overloads of the `StartNew` and `ContinueWith` methods that take them. If the task has already started to run, there's nothing the TPL can do to cancel it, but if you cancel a task before it begins to run, the TPL will take it out of the scheduled task queue for you. If you want to be able to cancel your task after it starts running, you'll need to write code in the body of your task that inspects the `CancellationToken` and abandons the work if its `IsCancellationRequested` property is `true`.

Cancellation support is not ubiquitous, because it's not always possible. Some operations simply cannot be canceled. For example, once a message has been sent out over the network, you can't unsend it. Some operations allow work to be canceled up until some point of no return has been reached. (If a message is queued up to be sent but hasn't actually been sent, then it might not be too late to cancel, for example.) This means that even when cancellation is offered, it might not do anything. So, when you use cancellation, you need to be prepared for it not to work.

Parallelism

The runtime libraries include some classes that can work with collections of data concurrently on multiple threads. There are three ways to do this: the `Parallel` class, Parallel LINQ, and TPL Dataflow.

The Parallel Class

The `Parallel` class offers five static methods: `For`, `ForAsync`, `ForEach`, `ForEachAsync`, and `Invoke`. The last of those takes an array of delegates and executes all of them, potentially in parallel. (Whether it decides to use parallelism depends on various factors such as the number of hardware threads the computer has, how heavily loaded the system is, and how many items you want it to process.) The `For` and `ForEach` methods mimic the C# loop constructs of the same names, but they will also potentially execute iterations in parallel. `ForAsync` (new in .NET 8.0) and `ForEachAsync` also mimic these loop types, but they provide better support for asynchronous operation. Both accept a delegate that returns a task, enabling each iteration to perform asynchronous operations (equivalent to using `await` in the body of a `foreach` loop). `ForEachAsync` can work with `IAsyncEnumerable<T>` (like `await foreach`).

Example 16-19 illustrates the use of `Parallel.For` in code that performs a convolution of two sets of samples. This is a highly repetitive operation commonly used in signal processing. (In practice, a fast Fourier transform offers a more efficient way to perform this work unless the convolution kernel is small, but the complexity of that code would have obscured the main subject here, the `Parallel` class.) It produces one output sample for each input sample. Each output sample is produced by calculating the sum of a series of pairs of values from the two inputs, multiplied together. For large data sets, this can be time consuming, so it is the sort of work you might want to speed up by spreading it across multiple processors. Each individual output sample's value can be calculated independently of all the others, so it is a good candidate for parallelization.

Example 16-19. Parallel convolution

```
static float[] ParallelConvolution(float[] input, float[] kernel)
{
    float[] output = new float[input.Length];
    Parallel.For(0, input.Length, i =>
    {
        float total = 0;
        for (int k = 0; k < Math.Min(kernel.Length, i + 1); ++k)
        {
            total += input[i - k] * kernel[k];
        }
        output[i] = total;
    });

    return output;
}
```

The basic structure of this code is very similar to a pair of nested `for` loops. I've simply replaced the outer `for` loop with a call to `Parallel.For`. (I've not attempted to parallelize the inner loop—if you make each individual step trivial, `Parallel.For` will spend more of its time in housekeeping work than it does running your code.)

The first argument, `0`, sets the initial value of the loop counter, and the second sets the upper limit. The final argument is a delegate that will be invoked once for each value of the loop counter, and the calls will occur concurrently if the `Parallel` class's heuristics tell it that this is likely to produce a speedup as a result of the work running in parallel. Running this method with large data sets on a multicore machine causes all of the available hardware threads to be used to full capacity.

It may be possible to get better performance by partitioning the work in more cache-friendly ways—naive parallelization can give the impression of high performance by maxing out all your CPU cores while delivering suboptimal throughput. However, there is a trade-off between complexity and performance, and the simplicity of the `Parallel` class can often provide worthwhile wins for relatively little effort.

Parallel LINQ

Parallel LINQ is a LINQ provider that works with in-memory information, much like LINQ to Objects. The `System.Linq` namespace makes this available as an extension method called `AsParallel` defined for any `IEnumerable<T>` (by the `Parallel Enu merable` class). This returns a `ParallelQuery<T>`, which supports the usual LINQ operators.

Any LINQ query built this way provides a `ForAll` method, which takes a delegate. When you call this, it invokes the delegate for all of the items that the query produces, and it will do so in parallel on multiple threads where possible.

TPL Dataflow

TPL Dataflow is a runtime library feature that lets you construct a graph of objects that perform some kind of processing on information that flows through them. You can tell the TPL which of these nodes needs to process information sequentially and which are happy to work on multiple blocks of data simultaneously. You push data into the graph, and the TPL will then manage the process of providing each node with blocks to process, and it will attempt to optimize the level of parallelism to match the resources available on your computer.

The dataflow API is in the `System.Threading.Tasks.Dataflow` namespace. (It's built into .NET; on .NET Framework you'll need to add a reference to a NuGet package, also called `System.Threading.Tasks.Dataflow`.) It is large and complex and could have a whole chapter to itself. Sadly, this makes it beyond the scope of this book. I mention it because it's worth being aware of for certain kinds of work.

Summary

Threads provide the ability to execute multiple pieces of code simultaneously. On a computer with multiple CPU execution units (i.e., multiple hardware threads), you can exploit this potential for parallelism by using multiple software threads. You can create new software threads explicitly with the `Thread` class, or you can use either the thread pool or a parallelization mechanism, such as the `Parallel` class or Parallel LINQ, to determine automatically how many threads to use to run the work your application supplies. If multiple threads need to use and modify shared data structures, you will need to use the synchronization mechanisms offered by .NET to ensure that the threads can coordinate their work correctly.

Threads can also provide a way to execute multiple concurrent operations that do not need the CPU the whole time (e.g., waiting for a response from an external service), but it is often more efficient to perform such work with asynchronous APIs (where available). The Task Parallel Library (TPL) provides abstractions that are useful for both kinds of concurrency. It can manage multiple work items in the thread pool, with support for combining multiple operations and handling potentially complex error scenarios, and its Task abstraction can also represent inherently asynchronous operations. The next chapter describes C# language features that greatly simplify working with tasks.

CHAPTER 17

Asynchronous Language Features

C# provides language-level support for using and implementing asynchronous methods. Asynchronous APIs are often the most efficient way to use certain services. For example, most I/O is handled asynchronously inside the OS kernel, because most peripherals, such as disk controllers or network adapters, are able to do the majority of their work autonomously. They need the CPU to be involved only at the start and end of each operation.

Although many of the services offered by operating systems are intrinsically asynchronous, developers often choose to use them through synchronous APIs (i.e., ones that do not return until the work is complete). This can waste resources, because they block the thread until the I/O completes. Threads have overheads, and if you're aiming to get the best performance in a highly concurrent application (e.g., a web app serving large numbers of users), it's usually best to have a relatively small number of OS threads. Ideally, your application would have no more OS threads than you have hardware threads, but that's optimal only if you can ensure that threads only ever block when there's no outstanding work for them to do. (Chapter 16 described the difference between OS threads and hardware threads.) The more threads that get blocked inside synchronous API calls, the more threads you'll need to handle your workload, reducing efficiency. In performance-sensitive code, asynchronous APIs are useful, because instead of wasting resources by forcing a thread to sit and wait for I/O to complete, a thread can kick off the work and then do something else productive in the meantime.

The problem with asynchronous APIs is that they can be significantly more complex to use than synchronous ones, particularly if you need to coordinate multiple related operations and deal with errors. This was often why developers chose the less efficient synchronous alternatives back in the days before any mainstream programming languages provided built-in support. In 2012, C# and Visual Basic both brought language-level support out of the research labs, and since then many other popular languages have added analogous features (most notably JavaScript, which acquired a very similar-looking syntax in 2016). The asynchronous features in C# make it possible to write code that uses efficient asynchronous APIs while retaining most of the simplicity of code that uses simpler synchronous APIs.

These language features are also useful in some scenarios in which maximizing throughput is not the primary performance goal. With client-side code, it's important to avoid blocking the UI thread to maintain responsiveness, and asynchronous APIs provide one way to do that. The language support for asynchronous code can handle thread affinity issues, which greatly simplifies the job of writing highly responsive UI code.

Asynchronous Keywords: async and await

C# presents its support for asynchronous code through two keywords: async and await. Neither of these is meant to be used on its own. You put the async keyword in a method's declaration, and this tells the compiler that you intend to use asynchronous features in the method. If this keyword is not present, you are not allowed to use the await keyword.

This is arguably redundant—the compiler produces an error if you attempt to use await without async. If it knows when a method's body is trying to use asynchronous features, why do we need to tell it explicitly? There are two reasons. First, as you'll see, these features radically change the behavior of the code the compiler generates, so it's useful for anyone reading the code to see a clear indication that the method behaves asynchronously. Second, await wasn't always a keyword in C#, so developers were once free to use it as an identifier. Perhaps Microsoft could have designed the grammar for await so that it acts as a keyword only in very specific contexts, enabling you to continue to use it as an identifier in all other scenarios, but the C# team decided to take a slightly more coarse-grained approach: you cannot use await as an identifier inside an async method, but it's a valid identifier anywhere else.

The async keyword does not change the signature of the method. It determines how the method is compiled, not how it is used.

The program entry point is a special case. If you use top-level statements to avoid having to declare Main explicitly, there's no place to put the async keyword or a return type, so this is the one case where the compiler deduces whether a method is asynchronous from whether you use await.

So the `async` keyword simply declares your intention to use the `await` keyword. (While you mustn't use `await` without `async` anywhere other than in top-level statements, it's not an error to apply the `async` keyword to a method that doesn't use `await`. However, it would serve no purpose, so the compiler will generate a warning if you do this.) Example 17-1 shows a fairly typical example. This uses the `HttpClient` class to request just the headers for a particular resource (using the standard `HEAD` verb that the HTTP protocol defines for this purpose). It then displays the results in a UI control—this method is part of the codebehind for a UI that includes a `TextBox` named `headerListTextBox`.

Example 17-1. Using `async` and `await` when fetching HTTP headers

```
// Note: as you'll see later, async methods usually should not be void
private async void FetchAndShowHeaders(string url, IHttpClientFactory cf)
{
    using (HttpClient w = cf.CreateClient())
    {
        var req = new HttpRequestMessage(HttpMethod.Head, url);
        HttpResponseMessage response =
            await w.SendAsync(req, HttpCompletionOption.ResponseHeadersRead);

        headerListTextBox.Text = response.Headers.ToString();
    }
}
```

This code contains a single `await` expression, shown in bold. You use the `await` keyword in an expression that may take some time to produce a result, and it indicates that the remainder of the method should not execute until that operation is complete. This sounds a lot like what a blocking, synchronous API does, but the difference is that an `await` expression does not block the thread. This code is not quite what it seems.

The `HttpClient` class's `SendAsync` method returns a `Task<HttpResponseMessage>`, and you might be wondering why we wouldn't just use its `Result` property. As you saw in Chapter 16, if the task is not complete, this property blocks the thread until the result is available (or the task fails, in which case it will throw an exception instead). However, this is a dangerous thing to do in a UI application: if you block the UI thread by trying to read the `Result` of an incomplete task, you will prevent progress of any operations that need to run on that thread. Since a lot of the work that UI applications do needs to happen on the UI thread, blocking that thread in this way more or less guarantees that deadlock will occur sooner or later, causing the application to freeze. So don't do that!

Although the `await` expression in Example 17-1 does something that is logically similar to reading `Result`, it works very differently. If the task's result is not available immediately, the `await` keyword does not make the thread wait, despite what its name suggests. Instead, it causes the containing method to return. You can use a debugger to verify that `FetchAndShowHeaders` returns immediately. For example, if I call that method from the button click event handler shown in Example 17-2, I can put a breakpoint on the `Debug.WriteLine` call in that handler and another breakpoint on the code in Example 17-1 that will update the `headerListTextBox.Text` property.

Example 17-2. Calling the asynchronous method

```
private void fetchHeadersButton_Click(object sender, RoutedEventArgs e)
{
    FetchAndShowHeaders("https://endjin.com/", this.clientFactory);
    Debug.WriteLine("Method returned");
}
```

Running this in the debugger, I find that the code hits the breakpoint on the last statement of Example 17-2 before it hits the breakpoint on the final statement of Example 17-1. In other words, the section of Example 17-1 that follows the `await` expression runs *after* the method has returned to its caller. Evidently, the compiler is somehow arranging for the remainder of the method to be run via a callback that occurs once the asynchronous operation completes.

 Visual Studio's debugger plays some tricks when you debug asynchronous methods to enable you to step through them as though they were normal methods. This is usually helpful, but it can sometimes conceal the true nature of execution. The debugging steps I just described were contrived to defeat Visual Studio's attempts to be clever and instead to reveal what is really happening.

Notice that the code in Example 17-1 expects to run on the UI thread because it modifies the text box's `Text` property toward the end. Asynchronous APIs do not necessarily guarantee to notify you of completion on the same thread on which you started the work—in fact, most won't. Despite this, Example 17-1 works as intended, so as well as converting half of the method to a callback, the `await` keyword is handling thread affinity issues for us.

The C# compiler evidently performs some major surgery on your code each time you use the `await` keyword. In older versions of C#, if you wanted to use this asynchronous API and then update the UI, you would need to have written something like Example 17-3. This uses a technique I showed in Chapter 16: it sets up a continuation for the task returned by `SendAsync`, using a `TaskScheduler` to ensure that the continuation's body runs on the UI thread.

Example 17-3. Manual asynchronous coding

```csharp
private void OldSchoolFetchHeaders(string url, IHttpClientFactory cf)
{
    HttpClient w = cf.CreateClient();
    var req = new HttpRequestMessage(HttpMethod.Head, url);

    var uiScheduler = TaskScheduler.FromCurrentSynchronizationContext();
    w.SendAsync(req, HttpCompletionOption.ResponseHeadersRead)
        .ContinueWith(sendTask =>
        {
            try
            {
                HttpResponseMessage response = sendTask.Result;
                headerListTextBox.Text = response.Headers.ToString();
            }
            finally
            {
                w.Dispose();
            }
        },
        uiScheduler);
}
```

This is a reasonable way to use the TPL directly, and it has a similar effect to Example 17-1, although it's not an exact representation of how the C# compiler transforms the code. As I'll show later, `await` uses a pattern that is supported by, but does not require, `Task` or `Task<T>`. It also generates code that handles early completion (where the task has already finished by the time you're ready to wait for it) far more efficiently than Example 17-3. But before I show the details of what the compiler does, I want to illustrate some of the problems it solves for you, which is best done by showing the kind of code you might have written back before this language feature existed.

My current example is pretty simple, because it involves only one asynchronous operation, but aside from the two steps I've already discussed—setting up some kind of completion callback and ensuring that it runs on the correct thread—I've also had to deal with the `using` statement that was in Example 17-1. Example 17-3 can't use the `using` keyword, because we want to dispose the `HttpClient` object only after we've finished with it.[1] Calling `Dispose` shortly before the outer method returns would not work, because we need to be able to use the object when the continuation runs, and that will typically happen a fair bit later. So I need to create the object in one method

---

[1] This example is a bit contrived so that I can illustrate how `using` works in async methods. Disposing an `HttpClient` obtained from an `IHttpClientFactory` is normally optional, and in cases where you new up an `HttpClient` directly, it's better to hang on to it and reuse it, as discussed in "Optional Disposal" on page 395.

(the outer one) and then dispose of it in a different method (the nested one). And because I'm calling `Dispose` by hand, it's now my problem to deal with exceptions, so I've had to wrap all of the code I moved into the callback with a `try` block and call `Dispose` in a `finally` block. (In fact, I've not even done a comprehensive job. In the unlikely event that either the `HttpRequestMessage` constructor or the call that retrieves the task scheduler were to throw an exception, the `HttpClient` would not get disposed. I'm handling only the case where the HTTP operation itself fails.)

Example 17-3 has used a task scheduler to arrange for the continuation to run via the `SynchronizationContext` that was current when the work started. This ensures that the callback occurs on the correct thread to update the UI. The `await` keyword can take care of that for us.

Execution and Synchronization Contexts

When your program's execution reaches an `await` expression for an operation that doesn't complete immediately, the code generated for that `await` will ensure that the current execution context has been captured. (It might not have to do much—if this is not the first `await` to block in this method, and if the context hasn't changed since, it will have been captured already.) When the asynchronous operation completes, the remainder of your method will be executed through the execution context.[2]

As I described in Chapter 16, the execution context handles certain contextual information that needs to flow when one method invokes another (even when it does so indirectly). But there's another kind of context that we may be interested in, particularly when writing UI code: the synchronization context (which was also described in Chapter 16).

While all `await` expressions capture the execution context, the decision of whether to flow synchronization context as well is controlled by the type being awaited. If you `await` for a `Task`, the synchronization context will also be captured by default. Tasks are not the only thing you can `await`, and I'll describe how types can support `await` in the section "The await Pattern" on page 771.

Sometimes, you might want to avoid getting the synchronization context involved. If you want to perform asynchronous work starting from a UI thread, but you have no particular need to remain on that thread, scheduling every continuation through the synchronization context is unnecessary overhead. If the asynchronous operation is a `Task` or `Task<T>` (or the equivalent value types, `ValueTask` or `ValueTask<T>`), you can declare that you don't want this by calling the `ConfigureAwait` method passing `false`. This returns a different representation of the asynchronous operation, and if

---

2 As it happens, Example 17-3 does this too, because the TPL captures the execution context for us.

you `await` that instead of the original task, it will ignore the current `Synchronization Context` if there is one. (There's no equivalent mechanism for opting out of the execution context.) Example 17-4 shows how to use this.

Example 17-4. ConfigureAwait

```
private async void OnFetchButtonClick(object sender, RoutedEventArgs e)
{
    using (HttpClient w = this.clientFactory.CreateClient())
    using (Stream f = File.Create(fileTextBox.Text))
    {
        Task<Stream> getStreamTask = w.GetStreamAsync(urlTextBox.Text);
        Stream getStream = await getStreamTask.ConfigureAwait(false);

        Task copyTask = getStream.CopyToAsync(f);
        await copyTask.ConfigureAwait(ConfigureAwaitOptions.None);
    }
}
```

This code is a click handler for a button, so it initially runs on a UI thread. It retrieves the `Text` property from a couple of text boxes. Then it kicks off some asynchronous work—fetching the content for a URL and copying the data into a file. It does not use any UI elements after fetching those two `Text` properties, so it doesn't matter if the remainder of the method runs on some separate thread. By passing `false` to `Config ureAwait` and waiting on the value it returns, we are telling the TPL that we are happy for it to use whatever thread is convenient to notify us of completion, which in this case will most likely be a thread pool thread. This will enable the work to complete more efficiently and more quickly, because it avoids getting the UI thread involved unnecessarily after each `await`.

You might have spotted that the final call to `ConfigureAwait` in Example 17-4 doesn't pass `false`. .NET 8.0 added a new overload taking a `ConfigureAwaitOptions`. This enumeration type's `None` and `ContinueOnCapturedContext` members provide the same behavior as `false` and `true`, and it also provides access to two new capabilities. We'll look at one of these, `SuppressThrowing`, in "Error Handling" on page 776. The other, `ForceYielding`, disables an optimization. Normally, in cases where the task has already completed (described in more detail in "The await Pattern" on page 771), `await` just allows the rest of the method to proceed immediately, but `ForceYielding` causes it to act as though the task had not completed. This typically causes the remainder of the method to run on a thread pool thread when it would otherwise have run on the caller's thread. This might be useful if you know that after the `await`, you will be going on to perform CPU-intensive work, or to call some slow API that does not offer an asynchronous form, and you don't want that to tie up the caller's thread. `ConfigureAwaitOptions` is a flags-style enumeration (with `None` having the value 0) so you can ask for combinations of these behaviors.

Not all asynchronous APIs return `Task` or `Task<T>`. For example, various asynchronous APIs introduced to Windows as part of UWP (an API for building desktop and tablet applications) return an `IAsyncOperation<T>` instead of `Task<T>`. This is because UWP is not .NET-specific, and it has its own runtime-independent representation for asynchronous operations that can also be used from C++ and JavaScript. This interface is conceptually similar to TPL tasks, and it supports the await pattern, meaning you can use `await` with these APIs. However, it does not provide `Configure Await`. If you want to do something similar to Example 17-4 with one of these APIs, you can use the `AsTask` extension method that wraps an `IAsyncOperation<T>` as a `Task<T>`, and you can call `ConfigureAwait` on that task instead.

> If you are writing libraries, then in most cases you should call `Con figureAwait(false)` anywhere you use `await`. This is because continuing via the synchronization context can be expensive, and in some cases it can introduce the possibility of deadlock occurring. The only exceptions are when you are doing something that positively requires the synchronization context to be preserved, or you know for certain that your library will only ever be used in application frameworks that do not set up a synchronization context. (E.g., ASP.NET Core applications do not use synchronization contexts, so it generally doesn't matter whether or not you call `Con figureAwait(false)` in those.)

Example 17-1 contained just one `await` expression, and even that turned out to be fairly complex to reproduce with classic TPL programming. Example 17-4 contains two, and achieving equivalent behavior without the aid of the `await` keyword would require rather more code, because exceptions could occur before the first `await`, after the second, or between, and we'd need to call `Dispose` on the `HttpClient` and `Stream` in any of those cases (as well as in the case where no exception is thrown). However, things can get considerably more complex than that once flow control gets involved.

Multiple Operations and Loops

Suppose that instead of fetching headers, or just copying the HTTP response body to a file, I wanted to process the data in the body. If the body is large, retrieving it is an operation that could require multiple, slow steps. Example 17-5 fetches a web page gradually.

Example 17-5. Multiple asynchronous operations

```
private async void FetchAndShowBody(string url, IHttpClientFactory cf)
{
    using (HttpClient w = cf.CreateClient())
    {
        Stream body = await w.GetStreamAsync(url);
        using (var bodyTextReader = new StreamReader(body))
        {
            while (!bodyTextReader.EndOfStream)
            {
                string? line = await bodyTextReader.ReadLineAsync();
                bodyTextBox.AppendText(line);
                bodyTextBox.AppendText(Environment.NewLine);
                await Task.Delay(TimeSpan.FromMilliseconds(10));
            }
        }
    }
}
```

This now contains three `await` expressions. The first kicks off an HTTP GET request, and that operation will complete when we get the first part of the response, but the response might not be complete yet—there may be several megabytes of content to come. This code presumes that the content will be text, so it wraps the `Stream` object that comes back in a `StreamReader`, which presents the bytes in a stream as text.[3] It then uses that wrapper's asynchronous `ReadLineAsync` method to read text a line at a time from the response. Reading the first line may take a while because it will need to wait for the response to arrive over the network from the server, but the next few calls to this method will probably complete immediately, because each network packet we receive will typically contain multiple lines. But if the code can read faster than data arrives over the network, eventually it will have consumed all the lines that appeared in the first packet, and it will then take a while before the next line becomes available. So the calls to `ReadLineAsync` will return some tasks that are slow and some that complete immediately. The third asynchronous operation is a call to `Task.Delay`. I've added this to slow things down so that I can see the data arriving gradually in the UI. `Task.Delay` returns a `Task` that completes after the specified delay, so this provides an asynchronous equivalent to `Thread.Sleep`. (`Thread.Sleep` blocks the calling thread, but `await Task.Delay` introduces a delay without blocking the thread.)

---

3 Strictly speaking, I should inspect the HTTP response headers to discover the encoding, and configure the `StreamReader` with that. Instead, I'm letting it detect the encoding, which will work well enough for demonstration purposes.

I've put each `await` expression in a separate statement, but this is not a requirement. It's perfectly legal to write expressions of the form (`await t1`) + (`await t2`). (You can omit the parentheses if you like, because `await` has higher precedence than addition; I prefer the visual emphasis they provide here.)

I'm not going to show you the complete pre-`async` equivalent of Example 17-5, because it would be enormous, but I'll describe some of the problems. First, we've got a loop with a body that contains two `await` blocks. To produce something equivalent with `Task` and callbacks means building your own loop constructs, because the code for the loop ends up being split across three methods: the one that starts the loop running (which would be the nested method acting as the continuation callback for `GetStreamAsync`) and the two callbacks that handle the completion of `ReadLineAsync` and `Task.Delay`. You can solve this by having a local method that starts a new iteration and calling that from two places: the point at which you want to start the loop and again in the `Task.Delay` continuation to kick off the next iteration. Example 17-6 shows this technique, but it illustrates just one aspect of what we're expecting the compiler to do for us; it is not a complete alternative to Example 17-5.

Example 17-6. An incomplete manual asynchronous loop

```
private void IncompleteOldSchoolFetchAndShowBody(
    string url, IHttpClientFactory cf)
{
    HttpClient w = cf.CreateClient();
    var uiScheduler = TaskScheduler.FromCurrentSynchronizationContext();
    w.GetStreamAsync(url).ContinueWith(getStreamTask =>
    {
        Stream body = getStreamTask.Result;
        var bodyTextReader = new StreamReader(body);

        StartNextIteration();

        void StartNextIteration()
        {
            if (!bodyTextReader.EndOfStream)
            {
                bodyTextReader.ReadLineAsync().ContinueWith(readLineTask =>
                {
                    string? line = readLineTask.Result;

                    bodyTextBox.AppendText(line);
                    bodyTextBox.AppendText(Environment.NewLine);

                    Task.Delay(TimeSpan.FromMilliseconds(10))
                        .ContinueWith(
                            _ => StartNextIteration(), uiScheduler);
```

```
        },
        uiScheduler);
      }
    };
  },
  uiScheduler);
}
```

This code works after a fashion, but it doesn't even attempt to dispose any of the resources it uses. There are several places in which failure could occur, so we can't just put a single using block or try/finally pair in to clean things up. And even without that additional complication, the code is barely recognizable—it's not obvious that this is attempting to perform the same basic operations as Example 17-5. With proper error handling, it would be completely unreadable. In practice, it would probably be easier to take a different approach entirely, writing a class that implements a state machine to keep track of where the work has gotten to. That will probably make it easier to produce code that operates correctly, but it's not going to make it any easier for someone reading your code to understand that what they're looking at is really little more than a loop at heart.

No wonder so many developers used to prefer synchronous APIs. But C# lets us write asynchronous code that has almost exactly the same structure as the synchronous equivalent, giving us all of the performance and responsiveness benefits of asynchronous code without the pain. That's the main benefit of async and await in a nutshell.

Consuming and producing asynchronous sequences

Example 17-5 showed a while loop, and as you'd expect, you're free to use other kinds of loops such as for and foreach in async methods. However, foreach can introduce a subtle problem: What happens if the collection you iterate over needs to perform slow operations? This doesn't arise for collection types such as arrays or HashSet<T>, where all the collection's items are already in memory, but what about the IEnumerable<string> returned by File.ReadLines? That's an obvious candidate for asynchronous operation, but in practice, it will just block your thread each time it needs to wait for more data to arrive from storage. And that's because the pattern expected by foreach doesn't support asynchronous operation. The heart of the problem is the method foreach will call to move to the next item—it expects the enumerator (often, but not always an implementation of IEnumerator<T>) to provide a MoveNext method with a signature like the one shown in Example 17-7.

Example 17-7. The non-async-friendly IEnumerator.MoveNext

```
bool MoveNext();
```

If more items are forthcoming but are not yet available, collections have no choice but to block the thread, not returning from MoveNext until the data arrives. Fortunately, C# recognizes a variation on this pattern. The runtime libraries define a pair of types,[4] shown in Example 17-8 (first introduced in Chapter 5), that embody this newer pattern. As with the synchronous IEnumerable<T>, foreach doesn't strictly require these exact types. Anything offering members of the same signature will work.

Example 17-8. IAsyncEnumerable<T> and IAsyncEnumerator<T>

```
public interface IAsyncEnumerable<out T>
{
    IAsyncEnumerator<T> GetAsyncEnumerator(
        CancellationToken cancellationToken = default);
}

public interface IAsyncEnumerator<out T> : IAsyncDisposable
{
    T Current { get; }

    ValueTask<bool> MoveNextAsync();
}
```

Conceptually this is identical to the synchronous pattern: an asynchronous foreach will ask the collection object for an enumerator and will repeatedly ask it to advance to the next item, executing the loop body with the value returned by Current each time until the enumerator indicates that there are no more items. The main difference is that the synchronous MoveNext has been replaced by MoveNextAsync, which returns an awaitable ValueTask<T>. (The IAsyncEnumerable<T> interface also provides support for passing in a cancellation token. An asynchronous foreach won't use that itself directly, but you can use this indirectly through the WithCancellation extension method for IAsyncEnumerable<T>.)

To consume an enumerable source that implements this pattern, you must put the await keyword in front of the foreach. C# can also help you to implement this pattern: Chapter 5 showed how you can use the yield keyword in an *iterator* method to implement IEnumerable<T>, but you can also return an IAsync Enumerable<T>. Example 17-9 shows both implementation and consumption of IAsyncEnumer able<T> in action.

---

4 These are available in .NET and .NET Standard 2.1. With .NET Framework, you will need to use the Micro soft.Bcl.AsyncInterfaces NuGet package.

Example 17-9. Consuming and producing asynchronous enumerables

```
await foreach (string line in ReadLinesAsync(args[0]))
{
    Console.WriteLine(line);
}

static async IAsyncEnumerable<string> ReadLinesAsync(string path)
{
    using (var bodyTextReader = new StreamReader(path))
    {
        while (!bodyTextReader.EndOfStream)
        {
            string? line = await bodyTextReader.ReadLineAsync();
            if (line is not null) { yield return line; }
        }
    }
}
```

Since this language support makes creating and using IAsyncEnumerable<T> very similar to working with IEnumerable<T>, you might be wondering whether there are asynchronous versions of the various LINQ operators described in Chapter 10. Unlike LINQ to Objects, IAsyncEnumerable<T> implementations are not in the parts of the runtime libraries built into .NET or .NET Standard, but a suitable NuGet package is available. If you add a reference to the System.Linq.Async package, the usual using System.Linq; declaration will make all the LINQ operators available on IAsyncEnumerable<T> expressions.

While we're looking at asynchronous equivalents of widely implemented types, we should look at IAsyncDisposable.

Asynchronous disposal

As Chapter 7 described, the IDisposable interface is implemented by types that need to perform some sort of cleanup promptly, such as closing an open handle, and there is language support in the form of using statements. But what if the cleanup involves potentially slow work, such as flushing data out to disk? .NET and .NET Standard 2.1 provide the IAsyncDisposable interface for this scenario. As Example 17-10 shows, you can put the await keyword in front of a using statement to consume an asynchronously disposable resource. (You can also put await in front of a using declaration.)

Example 17-10. Consuming and implementing IAsyncDisposable

```
await using (DiagnosticWriter w = new(@"c:\temp\log.txt"))
{
    await w.LogAsync("Test");
```

```
}

class DiagnosticWriter : IAsyncDisposable
{
    private StreamWriter? _sw;

    public DiagnosticWriter(string path)
    {
        _sw = new StreamWriter(path);
    }

    public Task LogAsync(string message)
    {
        ObjectDisposedException.ThrowIf(_sw is null, nameof(DiagnosticWriter));
        return _sw.WriteLineAsync(message);
    }

    public async ValueTask DisposeAsync()
    {
        if (_sw is not null)
        {
            await LogAsync("Done");
            await _sw.DisposeAsync();
            _sw = null;
        }
    }
}
```

 Although the await keyword appears in front of the using state-ment, the potentially slow operation that it awaits happens when execution leaves the using statement's block. This is unavoidable since using statements and declarations effectively hide the call to Dispose.

Example 17-10 also shows how to implement IAsyncDisposable. Whereas the syn-chronous IDisposable defines a single Dispose method, its asynchronous counter-part defines a single DisposeAsync method that returns a ValueTask. This enables us to annotate the method with async. An await using statement will ensure that the task returned by DisposeAsync completes at the end of its block before execution continues. You may have noticed that we've used a few different return types for async methods. Iterators are a special case, just as they are in synchronous code, but what about these methods that return various task types?

Returning a Task

Any method that uses `await` could itself run slowly, so as well as being able to call asynchronous APIs, you will usually also want to present an asynchronous public face. The C# compiler enables methods marked with the `async` keyword to return an object that represents the asynchronous work in progress. Instead of returning `void`, you can return a `Task`, or you can return a `Task<T>`, where T is any type. This enables callers to discover the status of the work your method performs, it provides the opportunity to attach continuations, and if you use `Task<T>`, it offers a way to get the result. Alternatively, you can return the value type equivalents, `ValueTask` and `Value Task<T>`. Returning any of these means that if your method is called from another `async` method, it can use `await` to wait for your method to complete and, if applicable, to collect its result.

Returning a task is almost always preferable to `void` when using `async` because with a `void` return type, there's no way for callers to know when your method has really finished, or to discover when it throws an exception. (Asynchronous methods can continue to run after returning—in fact, that's the whole point—so by the time you throw an exception, the original caller will probably not be on the stack.) By returning a task object, you provide the compiler with a way to make exceptions available and, where applicable, a way to provide a result.

Returning a task is so trivially easy that there's very little reason not to. To modify the method in Example 17-5 to return a task, I only need to make a single change. I make the return type `Task` instead of `void`, as shown in Example 17-11, and the rest of the code can remain exactly the same.

Example 17-11. Returning a Task

```
private async Task FetchAndShowBody(string url, IHttpClientFactory cf)
// ...as before
```

The compiler automatically generates the code required to produce a `Task` object (or a `ValueTask`, if you use that as your return type) and set it into a completed or faulted state when the method either returns or throws an exception. A return type of `Task` is the asynchronous equivalent of `void`, since the `Task` produces no result when it completes (which is why we don't need to add a `return` statement to this method even though it now has a return type of `Task`). And if you want to return a result from your task, that's also easy. Make the return type `Task<T>` or `ValueTask<T>`, where T is your result type, and then you can use the `return` keyword as though your method were a normal, non-async method, as Example 17-12 shows.

Example 17-12. Returning a Task<T>

```
public static async Task<string?> GetServerHeaderAsync(
    string url, IHttpClientFactory cf)
{
    using (HttpClient w = cf.CreateClient())
    {
        var request = new HttpRequestMessage(HttpMethod.Head, url);
        HttpResponseMessage response = await w.SendAsync(
            request, HttpCompletionOption.ResponseHeadersRead);

        string? result = null;
        IEnumerable<string>? values;
        if (response.Headers.TryGetValues("Server", out values))
        {
            result = values.FirstOrDefault();
        }
        return result;
    }
}
```

This fetches HTTP headers asynchronously in the same way as Example 17-1, but instead of displaying the results, this picks out the value of the first `Server:` header and makes that the result of the `Task<string?>` that this method returns. (It needs to be a nullable string because the header might not be present.) As you can see, the `return` statement just returns a `string?`, even though the method's return type is `Task<string?>`. The compiler generates code that completes the task and arranges for that string to be the result. With either a `Task` or `Task<T>` return type, the generated code produces a task similar to the kind you would get using `Task CompletionSource<T>`, as described in Chapter 16.

 Just as the `await` keyword can use any asynchronous method that fits a particular pattern (described later), C# offers the same flexibility when it comes to implementing an asynchronous method. You are not limited to `Task`, `Task<T>`, `ValueTask`, and `Value Task<T>`. You can return any type that meets two conditions: it must be annotated with the `AsyncMethodBuilder` attribute, identifying a class that the compiler can use to manage the progress and completion of the task, and it must also offer a `GetAwaiter` method that returns a type implementing the `INotifyCompletion` interface.

There's very little downside to returning one of the built-in task types. Callers are not obliged to do anything with it, so your method will be just as easy to use as a `void` method but with the added advantage that a task is available to callers that want one. About the only reason for returning `void` would be if some external constraint forces your method to have a particular signature. For example, most event handlers are

---

required to have a return type of void—that's why some of my earlier examples did it. But unless you are forced to use it, void is not a recommended return type for an asynchronous method.

The program entry point (typically called Main) is a special case. The .NET runtime doesn't support asynchronous entry points, and it expects this method to return either void or int. Despite this, C# lets Main return either Task or Task<int>, in which case the C# compiler will generate a hidden method that acts as the real entry point. This calls your asynchronous Main and then blocks until the task it returns completes. This makes it possible for Main to be async (although the compiler will generate the wrapper when you use these return types even if you don't make the method async). If you use top-level statements, there will be no explicit declaration of Main, but if you use await in these statements, the compiler will choose a return type of Task, or, if you use a return statement to produce an exit code, Task<int>.

Applying async to Nested Methods

In the examples shown so far, I have applied the async keyword to ordinary methods. You can also use it on anonymous functions (either anonymous methods or lambdas) and local functions. For example, if you're writing a program that creates UI elements programmatically, you may find it convenient to attach event handlers written as lambdas, and you might want to make some of those asynchronous, as Example 17-13 does.

Example 17-13. An asynchronous lambda

```
okButton.Click += async (s, e) =>
{
    using (HttpClient w = this.clientFactory.CreateClient())
    {
        infoTextBlock.Text = await w.GetStringAsync(uriTextBox.Text);
    }
};
```

The await Pattern

The majority of the asynchronous APIs that support the await keyword will return a TPL task of some kind. However, C# does not absolutely require this. It will await anything that implements a particular pattern. Moreover, although Task supports this pattern, the way it works means that the compiler uses tasks in a slightly different way than you would when using the TPL directly—this is partly why I said earlier that the code showing task-based asynchronous equivalents to await-based code did not represent exactly what the compiler does. In this section, I'm going to show how the compiler uses tasks and other types that support `await` to better illustrate how it really works.

I'll create a custom implementation of the `await` pattern to show what the C# compiler expects. Example 17-14 shows an asynchronous method, `UseCustomAsync`, that uses this custom implementation. It assigns the result of the `await` expression into a `string`, so it clearly expects the asynchronous operation to produce a `string` as its output. It calls a method, `CustomAsync`, which returns our implementation of the pattern (which will be shown later in Example 17-15). As you can see, this is not a `Task<string>`.

Example 17-14. Calling a custom awaitable implementation

```
static async Task UseCustomAsync()
{
    string result = await CustomAsync();
    Console.WriteLine(result);
}

public static MyAwaitableType CustomAsync()
{
    return new MyAwaitableType();
}
```

The compiler expects the `await` keyword's operand to be a type that provides a method called `GetAwaiter`. This can be an ordinary instance member or an extension method. (So it is possible to make `await` work with a type that does not support it innately by defining a suitable extension method.) This method must return an object or value, known as an *awaiter*, that does three things.

First, the awaiter must provide a `bool` property called `IsCompleted`. The code that the compiler generates for the `await` uses this to discover whether the operation has already finished. In situations where no slow work needs to be done (e.g., when a call to `ReadAsync` on a `Stream` can be handled immediately with data that the stream already has in a buffer), it would be a waste to set up a callback. So `await` avoids creating an unnecessary delegate if the `IsCompleted` property returns `true`, and it will just continue straight on with the remainder of the method. (Passing `Configure AwaitOptions.ForceYielding` to `ConfigureAwait` defeats this optimization by supplying an awaiter where `IsCompleted` initially returns `false` even when the underlying task has in fact completed.)

The compiler also requires a way to get the result once the work is complete, so the awaiter must have a `GetResult` method. Its return type defines the result type of the operation—it will be the type of the `await` expression. (If there is no result, the return type is `void`. `GetResult` still needs to be present, because it is responsible for throwing exceptions if the operation fails.) Since Example 17-14 assigns the result of the await into a variable of type string, the GetResult method of the awaiter returned by the MyAwaitableType class's GetAwaiter must be string (or some type implicitly convertible to string).

Finally, the compiler needs to be able to supply a callback. If IsCompleted returns false, indicating that the operation is not yet complete, the code generated for the await expression will create a delegate that will run the rest of the method. It needs to be able to pass that to the awaiter. (This is similar to passing a delegate to a task's ContinueWith method.) For this, the compiler requires not just a method but also an interface. You are required to implement INotifyCompletion, and there's an optional interface that it's recommended you also implement where possible called ICritical NotifyCompletion. These do similar things: each defines a single method (On Completed and UnsafeOnCompleted, respectively) that takes a single Action delegate, and the awaiter must invoke this delegate once the operation completes. The distinction between these two interfaces and their corresponding methods is that the first requires the awaiter to flow the current execution context to the target method, whereas the latter does not. The .NET runtime libraries features that the C# compiler uses to help build asynchronous methods always flow the execution context for you, so the generated code typically calls UnsafeOnCompleted where available to avoid flowing it twice. (If the compiler used OnCompleted, the awaiter would flow context too.) However, on .NET Framework, you'll find that security constraints may prevent the use of UnsafeOnCompleted. (.NET Framework had a concept of *untrusted code*. Code from potentially untrustworthy origins—perhaps because it was downloaded from the internet—would be subject to various constraints. This concept was dropped in .NET, but various vestiges remain, such as this design detail of asynchronous operations.) Because UnsafeOnCompleted does not flow execution context, untrusted code must not be allowed to call it, because that would provide a way to bypass certain security mechanisms. .NET Framework implementations of UnsafeOnCompleted provided for the various task types are marked with the SecurityCriticalAttribute, which means that only fully trusted code can call it. We need OnCompleted so that partially trusted code is able to use the awaiter.

Example 17-15 shows the minimum viable implementation of the awaiter pattern. This is oversimplified, because it always completes synchronously, so its OnCompleted method doesn't do anything. If you use the await keyword on an instance of My AwaitableType, the code that the C# compiler generates will never call OnCompleted. The await pattern requires that OnCompleted is only called if IsCompleted returns false, and, in this example, IsCompleted always returns true. This is why I've made OnCompleted throw an exception. However, although this example is unrealistically simple, it will serve to illustrate what await does.

Example 17-15. An excessively simple await pattern implementation

```
public class MyAwaitableType
{
    public MinimalAwaiter GetAwaiter()
    {
        return new MinimalAwaiter();
    }

    public class MinimalAwaiter : INotifyCompletion
    {
        public bool IsCompleted => true;

        public string GetResult() => "This is a result";

        public void OnCompleted(Action continuation)
        {
            throw new NotImplementedException();
        }
    }
}
```

With this code in place, we can see what Example 17-14 will do. It will call Get Awaiter on the MyAwaitableType instance returned by the CustomAsync method. Then it will test the awaiter's IsCompleted property, and if it's true (which it will be), it will run the rest of the method immediately. The compiler doesn't know IsComple ted will always be true in this case, so it generates code to handle the false case. This will create a delegate that, when invoked, will run the rest of the method and pass that delegate to the waiter's OnCompleted method. (I've not provided UnsafeOn Completed here, so it is forced to use OnCompleted.) Example 17-16 shows code that does all of this.

Example 17-16. A very rough approximation of what await does

```
static void ManualUseCustomAsync()
{
    var awaiter = CustomAsync().GetAwaiter();
    if (awaiter.IsCompleted)
    {
        TheRest(awaiter);
    }
    else
    {
        awaiter.OnCompleted(() => TheRest(awaiter));
    }
}

private static void TheRest(MyAwaitableType.MinimalAwaiter awaiter)
{
```

```
        string result = awaiter.GetResult();
        Console.WriteLine(result);
}
```

I've split the method into two pieces, because the C# compiler avoids creating a delegate in the case where IsCompleted is true, and I wanted to do the same. However,
this is not quite what the C# compiler does—it also manages to avoid creating an
extra method for each await statement, but this means it has to create considerably
more complex code. In fact, for methods that just contain a single await, it introduces rather more overhead than Example 17-16. However, once the number of await
expressions starts to increase, the complexity pays off, because the compiler does not
need to add any further methods. Example 17-17 shows something closer to what the
compiler does.

Example 17-17. A slightly closer approximation to how await works

```
private class ManualUseCustomAsyncState
{
    private int state;
    private MyAwaitableType.MinimalAwaiter? awaiter;

    public void MoveNext()
    {
        if (state == 0)
        {
            awaiter = CustomAsync().GetAwaiter();
            if (!awaiter.IsCompleted)
            {
                state = 1;
                awaiter.OnCompleted(MoveNext);
                return;
            }
        }
        string result = awaiter!.GetResult();
        Console.WriteLine(result);
    }
}

static void ManualUseCustomAsync()
{
    var s = new ManualUseCustomAsyncState();
    s.MoveNext();
}
```

This is still simpler than the real code, but it shows the basic strategy: the compiler
generates a nested type that acts as a state machine. This has a field (state) that keeps
track of where the method has got to so far, and it also contains fields corresponding
to the method's local variables (just the awaiter variable in this example). When an

asynchronous operation does not block (i.e., its `IsCompleted` returns `true` immediately), the method can just continue to the next part, but once it encounters an operation that needs some time, it updates the `state` variable to remember where it is and then uses the relevant awaiter's `OnCompleted` method. Notice that the method it asks to be called on completion is the same one that is already running: `MoveNext`. And this continues to be the case no matter how many `await`s you need to perform—every completion callback invokes the same method; the class simply remembers how far it had already gotten, and the method picks up from there. That way, no matter how many times an `await` blocks, it never needs to create more than one delegate.

I won't show the real generated code. It is borderline unreadable, because it contains a lot of *unspeakable* identifiers. (Remember from Chapter 3 that when the C# compiler needs to generate items with identifiers that must not collide with or be directly visible to our code, it creates a name that the runtime considers legal but that is not legal in C#; this is called an *unspeakable* name.) Moreover, the compiler-generated code uses various helper classes from the `System.Runtime.CompilerServices` namespace that are intended for use only from asynchronous methods to manage things like determining which of the completion interfaces the awaiter supports and handling the related execution context flow. Also, if the method returns a task, there are additional helpers to create and update that. But when it comes to understanding the nature of the relationship between an awaitable type and the code the compiler produces for an `await` expression, Example 17-17 gives a fair impression.

Error Handling

The `await` keyword deals with exceptions much as you'd hope it would: if an asynchronous operation fails, the exception emerges from the `await` expression that was consuming that operation. The general principle that asynchronous code can be structured in the same way as ordinary synchronous code continues to apply in the face of exceptions, and the compiler does whatever work is required to make that possible.

Example 17-18 contains two asynchronous operations, one of which occurs in a loop. This is similar to Example 17-5. It does something a bit different with the content it fetches, but most importantly, it returns a task. This provides a place for an error to go if any of the operations should fail.

Example 17-18. Multiple potential points of failure

```
private static async Task<string> FindLongestLineAsync(
    string url, IHttpClientFactory cf)
{
    using (HttpClient w = cf.CreateClient())
    {
```

```
        Stream body = await w.GetStreamAsync(url);
        using (var bodyTextReader = new StreamReader(body))
        {
            string longestLine = string.Empty;
            while (!bodyTextReader.EndOfStream)
            {
                string? line = await bodyTextReader.ReadLineAsync();
                if (line is not null && line.Length > longestLine.Length)
                {
                    longestLine = line;
                }
            }
            return longestLine;
        }
    }
}
```

Exceptions are potentially challenging with asynchronous operations because by the time a failure occurs, the method call that originally started the work is likely to have returned. The FindLongestLineAsync method in this example will usually return as soon as it executes the first await expression. (It's possible that it won't—if HTTP caching is in use, or if the IHttpClientFactory returns a client configured as a fake that never makes any real requests, this operation could succeed immediately. But typically, that operation will take some time, causing the method to return.) Suppose this operation succeeds and the rest of the method starts to run, but partway through the loop that retrieves the body of the response, the computer loses network connectivity. This will cause one of the operations started by ReadLineAsync to fail.

An exception will emerge from the await for that operation. There is no exception handling in this method, so what should happen next? Normally, you'd expect the exception to start working its way up the stack, but what's above this method on the stack? It almost certainly won't be the code that originally called it—remember, the method will usually return as soon as it hits the first await, so at this stage, we're running as a result of being called back by the awaiter for the task returned by ReadLineAsync. Chances are, we'll be running on some thread from the thread pool, and the code directly above us in the stack will be part of the task awaiter. This won't know what to do with our exception.

But the exception does not propagate up the stack. When an exception goes unhandled in an async method that returns a task, the compiler-generated code catches it and puts the task returned by that method into a faulted state (which will in turn mean that anything that was waiting for that task can now continue). If the code that called FindLongestLineAsync is working directly with the TPL, it will be able to see the exception by detecting that faulted state and retrieving the task's Exception property. Alternatively, it can either call Wait or fetch the task's Result property, and in either case, the task will throw an AggregateException containing the original exception. But if the code calling `FindLongestLineAsync` uses `await` on the task we return, the exception gets rethrown from that. From the calling code's point of view, it looks just like the exception emerged as it would normally, as Example 17-19 shows.

Example 17-19. Handling exceptions from await

```
try
{
    string longest = await FindLongestLineAsync(
        "http://192.168.22.1/", this.clientFactory);
    Console.WriteLine($"Longest line: {longest}");
}
catch (HttpRequestException ex)
{
    Console.WriteLine($"Error fetching page: {ex.Message}");
}
```

This is almost deceptively simple. Remember that the compiler performs substantial restructuring of the code around each `await`, and the execution of what looks like a single method may involve multiple calls in practice. So preserving the semantics of even a simple exception handling block like this (or related constructs, such as a `using` statement) is nontrivial. If you have ever attempted to write equivalent error handling for asynchronous work without the help of the compiler, you'll appreciate how much C# is doing for you here.

> The `await` does not rethrow the `AggregateException` provided by the task's `Exception` property. It rethrows the original exception. This enables async methods to handle the error in the same way synchronous code would.

Validating Arguments

There's one potentially surprising aspect of the way C# automatically reports exceptions through the task your asynchronous method returns. It means that code such as that in Example 17-20 doesn't do what you might expect.

Example 17-20. Potentially surprising argument validation

```
public async Task<string> FindLongestLineAsync(string url)
{
    ArgumentNullException.ThrowIfNull(url);
    ...
```

Inside an `async` method, the compiler treats all exceptions in the same way: none are allowed to pass up the stack as they would with a normal method, and they will always be reported by faulting the returned task. This is true even of exceptions thrown before the first `await`. In this example, the argument validation happens before the method does anything else, so at that stage, we will still be running on the original caller's thread. You might have thought that an argument exception thrown by this part of the code would propagate directly back to the caller. In fact, the caller will see a nonexceptional return, producing a task that is in a faulted state.

If the calling method immediately calls `await` on the return task, this won't matter much—it will see the exception in any case. But some code may choose not to wait immediately, in which case it won't see the argument exception until later. For simple argument validation exceptions where the caller has clearly made a programming error, you might expect code to throw an exception immediately, but this code doesn't do that.

 If it's not possible to determine whether a particular argument is valid without performing slow work, you will not be able to throw immediately if you want a truly asynchronous method. In that case, you would need to decide whether you would rather have the method block until it can validate all arguments or have argument exceptions be reported via the returned task instead of being thrown immediately.

Most `async` methods work this way, but suppose you want to throw this kind of exception straightaway (e.g., because it's being called from code that does not immediately `await` the result, and you'd like to discover the problem as soon as possible). The usual technique is to write a normal method that validates the arguments before calling an `async` method that does the work, and to make that second method either private or local. (You would have to do something similar to perform immediate argument validation with iterators too, incidentally. Iterators were described in Chapter 5.) Example 17-21 shows such a public wrapper method and the start of the method it calls to do the real work.

Example 17-21. Validating arguments for async methods

```
public static Task<string> FindLongestLineAsync(string url)
{
    ArgumentNullException.ThrowIfNull(url);
    return FindLongestLineCore(url);

    static async Task<string> FindLongestLineCore(string url)
    {
        ...
    }
}
```

Because the public method is not marked with `async`, any exceptions it throws will propagate directly to the caller. But any failures that occur once the work is underway in the local method will be reported through the task.

I've chosen to forward the `url` argument to the local method. I didn't have to, because a local method can access its containing method's variables. However, relying on that causes the compiler to create a type to hold the locals to share them across the methods. Where possible, it will make this a value type, passing it by reference to the inner type, but in cases where the inner method's scope might outlive the outer method, it can't do that. And since the local method here is `async`, it is likely to continue to run long after the outer method's stack frame no longer exists, so this would cause the compiler to create a reference type just to hold that `url` argument. By passing the argument in, we avoid this (and I've marked the method as `static` to indicate that this is my intent—this means the compiler will produce an error if I inadvertently use anything from the outer method in the local one). The compiler will probably still have to generate code that creates an object to hold on to local variables in the inner method during asynchronous execution, but at least we've avoided creating more objects than necessary.

Singular and Multiple Exceptions

As Chapter 16 showed, the TPL defines a model for reporting multiple errors—a task's `Exception` property returns an `AggregateException`. Even if there is only a single failure, you still have to extract it from its containing `AggregateException`. However, if you use the `await` keyword, it does this for you—as you saw in Example 17-19, it retrieves the first exception in the `InnerExceptions` and rethrows that.

This is handy when the operation can produce only a single failure—it saves you from having to write additional code to handle the aggregate exception and then dig out the contents. (If you're using a task returned by an `async` method, it will never contain more than one exception.) However, it does present a problem if you're working with composite tasks that can fail in multiple ways simultaneously. For example, `Task.WhenAll` takes a collection of tasks and returns a single task that completes only when all its constituent tasks complete. If some of them complete by failing, you'll get an `AggregateException` that contains multiple errors. If you use `await` with such an operation, it will throw only the first of those exceptions back to you.

The usual TPL mechanisms—the `Wait` method or the `Result` property—provide the complete set of errors (by throwing the `AggregateException` itself instead of its first inner exception), but they both block the thread if the task is not yet complete. What if you want the efficient asynchronous operation of `await`, which uses threads only when there's something for them to do, but you still want to see all the errors? Example 17-22 shows one approach.

Example 17-22. Throwless awaiting followed by `Wait`

```
static async Task CatchAll(Task[] ts)
{
    try
    {
        var t = Task.WhenAll(ts);
        await t.ConfigureAwait(ConfigureAwaitOptions.SuppressThrowing);
        t.Wait();
    }
    catch (AggregateException all)
    {
        Console.WriteLine(all);
    }
}
```

This uses `await` to take advantage of the efficient nature of asynchronous C# methods, but it uses a new feature of .NET 8.0 to indicate that if the task faults, we don't
want an exception to be thrown. The call to `Wait` will throw an `AggregateException`
if anything failed, enabling the `catch` block to see all of the exceptions. And because
we call `Wait` only after the `await` completes, we know the task is already finished, so
the call will not block. (Alternatively, we could have not called `Wait` at all. After the
`await` we could check `t.IsFaulted` to see if it failed, and get the exception with
`t.Exception` if it did.)

Concurrent Operations and Missed Exceptions

The most straightforward way to use `await` is to do one thing after another, just as
you would with synchronous code. Although doing work strictly sequentially may
not sound like it takes full advantage of the potential of asynchronous code, it does
make much more efficient use of the available threads than the synchronous equivalent, and it also works well in client-side UI code, leaving the UI thread free to
respond to input even while work is then in progress. However, you might want to go
further.

It is possible to kick off multiple pieces of work simultaneously. You can call an asynchronous API, and instead of using `await` immediately, you can store the result in a
variable and then start another piece of work before waiting for both. Although this is
a viable technique, and might reduce the overall execution time of your operations,
there's a trap for the unwary, shown in Example 17-23.

Example 17-23. How not to run multiple concurrent operations

```
static async Task GetSeveral(IHttpClientFactory cf)
{
    using (HttpClient w = cf.CreateClient())
```

```
    {
        w.MaxResponseContentBufferSize = 2_000_000;

        Task<string> g1 = w.GetStringAsync("https://endjin.com/");
        Task<string> g2 = w.GetStringAsync("https://oreilly.com");

        // BAD!
        Console.WriteLine((await g1).Length);
        Console.WriteLine((await g2).Length);
    }
}
```

This fetches content from two URLs concurrently. Having started both pieces of work, it uses two `await` expressions to collect the results of each and to display the lengths of the resulting strings. If the operations succeed, this will work, but it doesn't handle errors well. If the first operation fails, the code will never get as far as executing the second `await`. This means that if the second operation also fails, nothing will look at the exception it throws. Eventually, the TPL will detect that the exception has gone unobserved, which will result in the `UnobservedTaskException` event being raised. (Chapter 16 discussed the TPL's unobserved exception handling.) The problem is that this will happen only very occasionally—it requires both operations to fail in quick succession—so it's something that would be very easy to miss in testing.

You could avoid this with careful exception handling—you could catch any exceptions that emerge from the first `await` before going on to execute the second, for example. Alternatively, you could use `Task.WhenAll` to wait for all the tasks as a single operation—this will produce a faulted task with an `AggregateException` if anything fails, enabling you to see all errors. Of course, as you saw in the preceding section, multiple failures of this kind are awkward to deal with when you're using `await`. But if you want to launch multiple asynchronous operations and have them all in flight simultaneously, you're going to need more complex code to coordinate the results than you would do when performing work sequentially. Even so, the `await` and `async` keywords still make life much easier.

Summary

Asynchronous operations do not block the thread from which they are invoked. This can make them more efficient than synchronous APIs, which is particularly important on heavily loaded machines. It also makes them suitable for use on the client side, because they enable you to perform long-running work without causing the UI to become unresponsive. Without language support, asynchronous operations can be complex to use correctly, particularly when handling errors across multiple related operations. C#'s `await` keyword enables you to write asynchronous code in a style that looks just like normal synchronous code. It gets a little more complex if you want a single method to manage multiple concurrent operations, but even if you write an asynchronous method that does things strictly in order, you will get the benefits of making much more efficient use of threads in a server application—it will be able to support more simultaneous users, because each individual operation uses fewer resources—and on the client side, you'll get the benefit of a more responsive UI.

Methods that use `await` must be marked with the `async` keyword and should usually return one of `Task`, `Task<T>`, `ValueTask`, or `ValueTask<T>`. (C# allows a `void` return type, but you would normally use this only when you have no choice.) The compiler will arrange for this task to complete successfully once your method returns, or to complete with a fault if your method fails at any point in its execution. Because `await` can consume any `Task` or `Task<T>`, this makes it easy to split asynchronous logic across multiple methods, because a high-level method can `await` a lower-level `async` method. Usually, the work eventually ends up being performed by some task-based API, but it doesn't have to be, because `await` only demands a certain pattern—it will accept any expression on which you can invoke a `GetWaiter` method to obtain a suitable type.

CHAPTER 18

Memory Efficiency

As Chapter 7 described, the CLR is able to perform automatic memory management thanks to its garbage collector (GC). This comes at a price: when a CPU spends time on garbage collection, that stops it from getting on with more productive work. On laptops and phones, GC work drains power from the battery. In a cloud computing environment where you may be paying for CPU time based on consumption, extra work for the CPU corresponds directly to increased costs. More subtly, on a computer with many cores, spending too much time in the GC can significantly reduce throughput, because many of the cores may end up blocked, waiting for the GC to complete before they can proceed.

In many cases, these effects will be small enough not to cause visible problems. However, when certain kinds of programs experience heavy load, GC costs can come to dominate the overall execution time. In particular, if you write code that performs relatively simple but highly repetitive processing, GC overhead can have a substantial impact on throughput.

To give you an example of the kinds of improvements that can sometimes be possible, early versions of Microsoft's ASP.NET Core web server framework frequently ran into hard limits due to GC overhead. To enable .NET applications to break through these barriers, C# introduced various features that can enable dramatic reductions in the number of allocations. Fewer allocations means fewer blocks of memory for the GC to recover, so this translates directly to lower GC overhead. When ASP.NET Core first started making extensive use of these features, performance improved across the board, but for the simplest performance benchmark, known as *plaintext* (part of the TechEmpower suite of web performance tests), this release improved the request handling rate by over 25%.

In some specialized scenarios, the differences can be even greater. I worked on a project that processed diagnostic information from a broadband provider's networking equipment (in the form of RADIUS packets). Adopting the techniques described in this chapter boosted the rate at which a single CPU core in our system could process the messages from around 300,000/s to about 7 million/s.

There is a price to pay, of course: these GC-efficient techniques can add significant complication to your code. And the payoff won't always be so large—although the first ASP.NET Core release to be able to use these features improved over the previous version on all benchmarks, only the simplest saw a 25% boost, and most improved more modestly. The practical improvement will really depend on the nature of your workload, and for some applications you might find that applying these techniques delivers no measurable improvement. So before you even consider using them, you should use performance monitoring tools to find out how much time your code spends in the GC. If it's only a few percent, then you might not be able to realize order-of-magnitude improvements. But if testing suggests that there's room for significant improvement, the next step is to ask whether the techniques in this chapter are likely to help. So let's start by exploring exactly how these techniques can help you reduce GC overhead.

(Don't) Copy That

The way to reduce GC overhead is to allocate less memory on the heap. And the most important technique for minimizing allocations is to avoid making copies of data. For example, consider the URL *http://example.com/books/1323?edition=6&format=pdf*. There are several elements of interest in here, such as the protocol (http), the hostname (example.com), or the query string. The latter has its own structure: it is a sequence of name/value pairs. The obvious way to work with a URL in .NET is to use the System.Uri type, as Example 18-1 shows.

Example 18-1. Deconstructing a URL

```
var uri = new Uri("http://example.com/books/1323?edition=6&format=pdf");
Console.WriteLine(uri.Scheme);
Console.WriteLine(uri.Host);
Console.WriteLine(uri.AbsolutePath);
Console.WriteLine(uri.Query);
```

It produces the following output:

```
http
example.com
/books/1323
?edition=6&format=pdf
```

This is convenient, but by getting the values of these four properties, we have forced the Uri to provide four string objects in addition to the original one. You could imagine a smart implementation of Uri that recognized certain standard values for Scheme, such as http, and that always returned the same string instance for these instead of allocating new ones, but for all the other parts, it's likely to have to allocate new strings on the heap.

There is another way. Instead of creating new string objects for each section, we could take advantage of the fact that all of the information we want was already in the string containing the whole URL. There's no need to copy each section into a new string, when instead we can just keep track of the position and lengths of the relevant sections within the string. Instead of creating a string for each section, we would need just two numbers. And since we can represent numbers using value types (e.g., int or, for very long strings, long), we don't need any additional objects on the heap beyond the single string with the full URL. For example, the scheme (http) is at position 0 and has length 4. Figure 18-1 shows each of the elements by their offset and position within the string.

Figure 18-1. URL substrings

This works, but already we can see the first problem with working this way: it is somewhat awkward. Instead of representing, say, the Host with a convenient string object, which is easily understood and readily inspected in the debugger, we now have a pair of numbers, and as developers, we now have to remember which string they point into. It's not rocket science, but it makes it slightly harder to understand our code, and easier to introduce bugs. But there's a payoff: instead of five strings (the original URL and the four properties), we just have one. And if you're trying to process millions of events each second, that could easily be worth the effort.

Obviously this technique would work for a more fine-grained structure too. The offset and position (25, 4) locates the text 1323 in this URL. We might want to parse that as an int. But at this point we run into the second problem with this style of working: it is not widely supported in .NET libraries. The usual way to parse text into an int is to use the int type's static Parse or TryParse methods. Unfortunately, these do not provide overloads that accept a position or offset within a string. They require a string containing only the number to be parsed. This means you end up writing code such as Example 18-2.

Example 18-2. Defeating the point of the exercise by using Substring

```
string uriString = "http://example.com/books/1323?edition=6&format=pdf";
int id = int.Parse(uriString.Substring(25, 4));
```

This works, but by using Substring to go from our (offset, length) representation back to the plain string that int.Parse wants, we've allocated a new string. The whole point of this exercise was to reduce allocations, so this doesn't seem like progress. One solution might be for Microsoft to go through the entire .NET API surface area, adding overloads that accept offset and length parameters in any situation where we might want to work with something in the middle of something else (either a substring, as in this example, or perhaps a subrange of an array). In fact, there are examples of this already: the Stream API for working with byte streams has various methods that accept a byte[] array, and also offset and length arguments to indicate exactly which part of the array you want to work with.

However, there's one more problem with this technique: it is inflexible about the type of container that the data lives in. Microsoft could add an overload to int.Parse that takes a string, an offset, and a length, but it would only be able to parse data inside a string. What if the data happens to be in a char[]? In that case, you'd have to convert it to a string first, at which point we're back to additional allocations. Alternatively, every API that wants to support this approach would need multiple overloads to support all the containers that anyone might want to use, each potentially requiring a different implementation of the same basic method.

More subtly, what if the data you have is currently in memory that's not on the CLR's heap? This is a particularly important question when it comes to the performance of servers that accept requests over the network (e.g., a web server). Sometimes, data received by a network interface won't be delivered directly into memory on .NET's heap. Also, some forms of interprocess communication involve arranging for the OS to map a particular region of memory into two different processes' address spaces. The .NET heap is local to the process and cannot use such memory.

C# has always supported use of external memory through *unsafe code*, which supports raw unmanaged pointers that work in a similar way to pointers in the C and C++ languages. However, there are a couple of problems with these. First, they would add yet another entry to the list of overloads that everything would need to support in a world where we can parse data in place. Second, code using pointers cannot pass .NET's type safety verification rules. This means it becomes possible to make certain kinds of programming errors that are normally impossible in C#. It may also mean that the code will not be allowed to run in certain scenarios, since the loss of type safety would enable unsafe code to bypass certain security constraints.

To summarize, it has always been possible to reduce allocations and copying in .NET by working with offsets and lengths and either a reference to a containing string or array or an unmanaged pointer to memory, but there was considerable room for improvement on these fronts:

- Convenience
- Wide support across .NET APIs
- Unified, safe handling of the following:
  — Strings
  — Arrays
  — Unmanaged memory

.NET offers a type that addresses all of these points: Span<T>. (See the sidebar, "Support Across Language and Runtime Versions," for more information on how the features described in this chapter relate to C# language and .NET runtime versions.)

Support Across Language and Runtime Versions

Span<T> is built into .NET and is available to any library that targets .NET Standard 2.1. You can also use it on .NET Framework via a NuGet package, System.Memory, but be aware that this package has some limitations.

First, although this NuGet package adds Span<T> and related types, it cannot modify existing libraries. To fulfill the "wide support across .NET APIs" requirement, Microsoft added numerous methods to the .NET runtime libraries. For example, new overloads of int.TryParse accept ReadOnlySpan<char> as an alternative to string. The System.Memory NuGet package can't add new static methods to int, so these new methods are not available in .NET Framework.

Second, this package provides a slightly different implementation than the one you will get when running the exact same code on .NET. These newer runtimes enable a more efficient implementation of Span<T> and related types, and provide related optimizations. This is critical to the high performance offered by the features discussed in this chapter. The latest version of the .NET Framework at the time of writing (version 4.8.1) lacks the Span<T> optimizations, and Microsoft has no plans to add them in future versions because .NET supersedes the .NET Framework. Code using these techniques works correctly on .NET Framework, but if you want to reap the full performance benefits of these techniques, you'll need to run on .NET.

Representing Sequential Elements with Span<T>

The System.Span<T> value type represents a sequence of elements of type T stored contiguously in memory. Those elements can live inside an array, a string, a managed block of memory allocated in a stack frame, or unmanaged memory. Starting with .NET 7.0 and C# 11.0, it is also possible to create a single-element span that refers to an individual field or variable without needing to use unsafe code. Let's look at how Span<T> addresses each of the requirements enumerated in the preceding section.

A Span<T> encapsulates both a pointer to the start of the data in memory and its length. To access the contents of a span, you use it much as you would an array, as Example 18-3 shows. This makes it much more convenient to use than ad hoc techniques in which you define a couple of int variables and have to remember what they refer to.

Example 18-3. Iterating over a Span<int>

```
static int SumSpan(ReadOnlySpan<int> span)
{
    int sum = 0;
    for (int i = 0; i < span.Length; ++i)
    {
        sum += span[i];
    }
    return sum;
}
```

Since a Span<T> knows its own length, its indexer checks that the index is in range, just as the built-in array type does. The performance is very similar to using a built-in array. This includes the optimizations that detect certain loop patterns—for example, the CLR will recognize Example 18-3 as a loop that iterates over the entire contents, enabling it to generate code that doesn't need to check that the index is in range each time around the loop. (On .NET Framework, Span<T> is a little slower than an array, because its CLR does not include the optimizations for Span<T>.)

You may have noticed that the method in Example 18-3 takes a ReadOnlySpan<T>. This is a close relative of Span<T>, and there is an implicit conversion enabling you to pass any Span<T> to a method that takes a ReadOnlySpan<T>. The read-only form enables a method to declare clearly that it will only read from the span, and not write to it. (This is enforced by the fact that the read-only form's indexer offers just a get accessor, and no set.)

Whenever you write a method that works with a span and that does not mean to modify the span's data, you should use ReadOnly Span<T>.

Span<T> defines an explicit conversion from arrays. Similarly, ReadOnlySpan<T> is implicitly convertible from arrays and also strings. This enables Example 18-4 to pass an array to the SumSpan method. Of course, we've gone and allocated an array on the heap there, so this particular example defeats the main point of using spans, but if you already have an array on hand, this is a useful technique.

Example 18-4. Passing an int[] as a ReadOnlySpan<int>

```
int[] numberArray = [1, 2, 3];
Console.WriteLine(SumSpan(numberArray));
```

Although Example 18-4 constructs an array, you may be surprised to discover that Example 18-5 does not, despite appearing to construct an array explicitly.

Example 18-5. Array syntax implicitly creating a ReadOnlySpan<int> directly

```
Console.WriteLine(SumSpan(new int[] { 1, 2, 3 }));
```

When you use this array initialization syntax in a place where a ReadOnlySpan<T> is required, then as long as the initializer values are all constants, the compiler can perform an optimization: it does not create a real .NET array. Instead, it embeds the initializer values directly into the compiled output as a block of binary data and generates code that obtains a ReadOnlySpan<T> that points directly to that data. This optimization relies on a couple of facts. First, spans provide no way to get hold of the underlying container. This means our code can't tell whether there really is an array behind the span, so it doesn't actually matter if no array gets created. Second, this relies on the data being read-only—since methods might run multiple times, it needs to be possible to create an identical span every time, and if we were using a writable span, it would not be possible to share the same underlying block of memory every time.

Example 18-6 shows a couple of examples in which creating a span with the same array initializer syntax really will create an array. In the first case, not all of the values are constant, so the optimization just described can't be applied. And in the second case, we assign the array into a Span<int> (even though SumSpan needs only a ReadOn lySpan<int>) so the compiler generates code that creates an array to enable the data to be modified. If the only thing we're doing with this data is passing it to SumSpan (which is allowed because Span<T> is implicitly convertible to ReadOnlySpan<T>) that's a waste, because the array will never be modified in practice.

Example 18-6. Array syntax examples that defeat the no-array optimization

```
// Creates an array because one of the initializer values is not constant.
Console.WriteLine(SumSpan(new int[] { 1, 2, DateTime.Now.Hour }));

// Creates an array because we asked for a Span<int> (not read-only).
Span<int> numberSpan = new int[] { 1, 2, 3 };
Console.WriteLine(SumSpan(numberSpan));
```

It is possible to avoid creating a real array even in these scenarios because Span<T> also works with stack-allocated arrays, as Example 18-7 shows.

Example 18-7. Passing a stack-allocated array as a ReadOnlySpan<int>

```
ReadOnlySpan<int> nonConstReadOnly = stackalloc int[] { 1, 2, DateTime.Now.Hour };
Console.WriteLine(SumSpan(nonConstReadOnly));

Span<int> constWriteable = stackalloc int[] { 1, 2, 3 };
Console.WriteLine(SumSpan(constWriteable));
```

C# disallows most uses of stackalloc outside of code marked as unsafe. This allocates memory on the current method's stack frame, so this array won't have the usual .NET object headers that an ordinary array on the GC heap would have—it's just the raw values. This means that a stackalloc expression produces a pointer type, int*, in this example. You can normally only use pointer types directly in unsafe code blocks. However, the compiler makes an exception to this rule if you assign the pointer produced by a stackalloc expression directly into a span. This is permitted because spans impose bounds checking, preventing undetected out-of-range access errors of the kind that normally make pointers unsafe. Also, Span<T> and ReadOnly Span<T> are both defined as ref struct types, and as "Stack Only" on page 796 describes, this means they cannot outlive their containing stack frame. This guarantees that the stack frame on which the stack-allocated memory lives will not vanish while there are still outstanding references to it. (.NET's type safety verification rules include special handling for ref-like types such as spans.)

As you saw in earlier chapters, C# 12.0 adds *collection expressions*, a new syntax for creating and initializing collections. These work with spans, as Example 18-8 shows. The first two collection expressions compile into code that puts the relevant data on the stack. The final one passes a collection made entirely of constant values to a method taking a ReadOnlySpan<int>, so in this case the compiler uses the same trick we saw with array initializers: it just embeds the constant values as a block of binary data in the compiled output, and creates a span pointing directly to that.

Example 18-8. Using collection expressions with spans

```
// Lives on stack (because one of the values is not constant).
Console.WriteLine(SumSpan([1, 2, DateTime.Now.Hour]));

// Lives on stack (because using Span<int> means this must be writable).
Span<int> numbersCollectionExpression = [1, 2, DateTime.Now.Hour];
Console.WriteLine(SumSpan(numbersCollectionExpression));

// Pointer to constant data embedded in DLL.
Console.WriteLine(SumSpan([1, 2, 3]));
```

If a collection expression uses the spread syntax (..) to incorporate a copy of some other collection, the size of the resulting span is not fixed at compile time—it will be determined by however large that other collection is. In these cases the compiler falls back to generating code that puts the relevant collection on the heap to avoid risking a stack overflow. If you need a span that incorporates some data from other collections and you want to avoid heap allocation, you would use stackalloc directly, and not the collection expression syntax. If you do this, you should inspect the size of that incoming data because it's generally a bad idea to put more than a few hundred bytes of data on the stack. The default stack size is not the same on all platforms, and can be changed by configuration, but it's common for the stack to be 1.5 MB in size, and if you use async and await it can be hard to predict exactly how deep call stacks will get at runtime. It is wise to choose a fairly conservative upper size limit when using stack alloc, and you should either reject data that is too large, or fall back to a heap-based code path.

Earlier I mentioned that spans can refer to strings as well as arrays. However, we can't pass a string to our SumSpan method for the simple reason that it requires a span with an element type of int, whereas a string is a sequence of char values. int and char have different sizes—they take 4 and 2 bytes each, respectively. Although an implicit conversion exists between the two (meaning you can assign a char value into an int variable, giving you the Unicode value of the char), that does not make a ReadOnlySpan<char> implicitly compatible with a ReadOnlySpan<int>.[1] Remember, the entire point of spans is that they provide a view into a block of data without needing to copy or modify that data; since int and char have different sizes, converting a char[] to an int[] array would double its size. However, if we were to write a method accepting a ReadOnlySpan<char>, we would be able to pass it a string, a

---

1 That said, it is possible to perform this kind of conversion explicitly—the MemoryMarshal class offers methods that can take a span of one type and return another span that provides a view over the same underlying memory, interpreted as containing a different element type. But it is unlikely to be useful in this case: converting a ReadOnlySpan<char> to a ReadOnlySpan<int> would produce a span with half the number of elements, where each int contained pairs of adjacent char values.

char[] array, or a `stackalloc char[]`, or could explicitly construct a ReadOnly Span<char> from an unmanaged pointer of type char* (because the in-memory representation of a particular span of characters within each of these is the same).

 Since strings are immutable in .NET, you cannot convert a `string` to a Span<char>. You can only convert it to a ReadOnlySpan<char>.

We've examined two of our requirements from the preceding section: Span<T> is easier to use than ad hoc storing of an offset and length, and it makes it possible to write a single method that can work with data in arrays, strings, the stack, or unmanaged memory. This leaves our final requirement: widespread support throughout .NET's runtime libraries. As Example 18-9 shows, it is now supported in int.Parse, enabling us to fix the problem shown in Example 18-2. The generic math feature added in .NET 7.0 defines this and a span-based TryParse in its ISpanParsable<T> interface, and since INumberBase<T> inherits from ISpanParsable<T>, span-based parsing is available for all numeric types.

Example 18-9. Parsing integers in a string using Span<char>

```
string uriString = "http://example.com/books/1323?edition=6&format=pdf";
int id = int.Parse(uriString.AsSpan(25, 4));
```

Span<T> is a relatively new type (it was introduced in 2018; .NET has been around since 2002), so although the .NET runtime libraries now support it widely, many third-party libraries do not yet support it, and perhaps never will. However, it has become increasingly well supported since being introduced, and that situation will only improve.

Utility Methods

In addition to the array-like indexer and Length properties, Span<T> offers a few useful methods. The Clear and Fill methods provide convenient ways to initialize all the elements in a span either to the default value for the element type or a specific value. Obviously, these are not available on ReadOnlySpan<T>.

You may sometimes encounter situations in which you have a span and you need to pass its contents to a method that requires an array. Obviously there's no avoiding an allocation in this case, but if you need to do it, you can use the ToArray method.

Spans (both normal and read-only) also offer a TryCopyTo method, which takes as its argument a (non-read-only) span of the same element type. This allows you to copy data between spans. This method handles scenarios where the source and target spans refer to overlapping ranges within the same container. As the Try suggests, it's possible for this method to fail: if the target span is too small, this method returns false.

Collection Expressions and Spans

I've already shown how you can use C# 12.0's new collection expression feature to initialize a span, but there's a more subtle way that these two language features interact: spans can become involved when you initialize certain other collection types with collection expressions. Some collection types define a special *create method* that C# will use if you initialize those types with a collection expression. Example 18-10 will use the ImmutableList.Create method, for example.

Example 18-10. Using a collection builder

```
using System.Collections.Immutable;

ImmutableList<int> numbers = [1, 2, 3, 4, 5];
```

Collection types can advertise a create method with the [CollectionBuilder] attribute. This method is required to accept a ReadOnlySpan<T> where T is the element type of the collection being initialized. As of .NET 8.0, only the immutable collection types define this. These types were previously quite awkward to initialize, and the simplest ways of creating them were not the highest-performing. But now, using a collection expression creates the most efficient possible initialization code.

Although not all collection types implement this, some types, such as List<T>, are known to the compiler, enabling it to generate tailored initialization code for those. But if you write your own collection type, and if its implementation details mean that you can perform initialization more efficiently if you can see all the elements up front instead of them being added one at a time, you can also implement a create method that accepts a ReadOnlySpan<T>, and declare that it is your creation method with the [CollectionBuilder] attribute.

Pattern Matching

Spans can be used with certain kinds of patterns. Chapter 2 described list patterns, a new feature in C# 11.0, and as Example 18-11 shows, you can use a span as the input to a list pattern.

Example 18-11. Using a span with a list pattern

```
static void CheckStart(ReadOnlySpan<char> chars)
{
    if (chars is ['H', .. ReadOnlySpan<char> theRest])
    {
        Console.WriteLine(theRest.Length);
    }
}
```

This pattern includes the .. syntax, denoting a slice, which matches any elements in the source not explicitly specified in the pattern. This example has a declaration pattern to capture the elements matched by the slice into a new variable called theRest. As you can see, the captured slice is also a span. Spans are particularly well suited to list patterns that capture slices, because there's no need to make a copy of the relevant subsequence. If we had used string here instead of ReadOnlySpan<char>, the compiler would need to generate code that called chars.Substring(1) to obtain a suitable value for theRest, causing a new string to be allocated. This code avoids that, and yet we can still pass this CheckStart method a string, because string is implicitly convertible to ReadOnlySpan<char>.

Since C# 11.0, it has also been possible to use a ReadOnlySpan<char> (or a Span<char>) as the input to a string constant pattern, as Example 18-12 shows. The compiler generates the code required to compare the span's contents with the string's contents.

Example 18-12. Span as input to a string constant pattern

```
static void RespondToGreeting(ReadOnlySpan<char> message)
{
    switch (message)
    {
        case "Hello":
            Console.WriteLine("Hello to you too");
            break;

        case "How do you do":
            Console.WriteLine("How do you do");
            break;
    }
}
```

Stack Only

The Span<T> and ReadOnlySpan<T> types are both declared as ref struct. This means that not only are they value types, they are value types that can live only on the stack. So you cannot have fields with span types in a class, or in any struct that is not also a `ref struct`. This also imposes some potentially more surprising restrictions. For example, it means you cannot use a span in a variable in an `async` method. These store all their variables as fields in a hidden type, enabling them to live on the heap, because asynchronous methods often need to outlive their original stack frame. In fact, these methods can even switch to a completely different stack altogether, because asynchronous methods can end up running on different threads as their execution progresses. For similar reasons, there are restrictions on using spans in anonymous functions and in iterator methods. You can use them in local methods, and you can even declare a `ref struct` variable in the outer method and use it from the nested one, but with one restriction: you must not create a delegate that refers to that local method, because this would cause the compiler to move shared variables into an object that lives on the heap. (See Chapter 9 for details.)

This restriction is necessary for .NET to be able to offer the combination of array-like performance, type safety, and the flexibility to work with multiple different containers. "Representing Sequential Elements with Memory<T>" on page 801 will show what we can do instead in scenarios where this stack-only limitation is problematic.

Using ref with Fields

Before C# 11.0, the `Span<T>` and `ReadOnlySpan<T>` types were only able to exist thanks to special support in the compiler and runtime—you couldn't write your own types that contained a `ref`-style reference. This restriction no longer exists. The basic capability that makes spans possible—the ability for a type to have a field that is effectively a `ref` to some other value—is no longer a special power available only to the span types. As Example 18-13 shows, C# 11.0 made it possible to write your own `ref`-like type.

Example 18-13. Type with a ref field

```
public readonly ref struct RefLike<T>(ref T rv)
{
    public readonly ref T Ref = ref rv;
}
```

Example 18-14 shows this type in use. The `ri` variable's `Ref` field is a `ref int` referring to the local variable `i` (because the code passes `ref i` as the constructor argument). When it modifies `ri.Ref` it is really modifying the `i` variable, so the final line displays the value 42.

Example 18-14. Using a type with a ref field

```
int i = 21;
RefLike<int> ri = new(ref i);
ri.Ref *= 2;
Console.WriteLine(i);
```

Only `ref struct` types may contain `ref` fields, for exactly the same reason that only `ref struct` types may contain other `ref struct` types such as spans: types of this kind absolutely must live on the stack, because it would otherwise be possible for a `ref` to some variable in a stack frame to end up in an object or boxed struct on the heap. That would allow the `ref` to survive after the stack frame containing the variable to which it refers no longer exists, which would mean `ref` fields were unsafe. Without this restriction, they'd be no different from pointers, and we've been able to declare pointer-typed fields since C# 1.0. But pointers are inherently unsafe. The whole point of `ref` fields is that they preserve type safety, which is why restrictions on their use exist.

Although the ability to put a `ref` in a field may seem like a relatively simple new feature, the need to ensure type safety meant that the addition of this feature had consequences. In particular, it undermines a simple assumption that used to be true before C# 11.0: if you pass some method a `ref` as an argument, it used to be safe to assume that the method was unable to retain that `ref` after it returned. But the availability of `ref` fields means that when a public method of a `ref struct` type takes an argument of some `ref` type, the caller now has to assume that the `ref struct` might store that `ref` in some `ref` field. This changes the rules about what it is safe to pass in as a `ref` or via a `ref`-like type such as `Span<T>` or the `RefLike<T>` type shown here.

For example, it's normally just fine to pass a reference to a local variable as an argument to a method (either directly as a `ref`, or via a ref-like type such as `Span<int>`). This is, in general, safe because the method won't be able to store that reference—it will not be able to use it after it returns. But if the method is a member of a `ref struct`, it *can* stash a reference passed in arguments in a field. The `ChangeTarget` method in Example 18-15 does exactly this. (As it happens, this example doesn't do anything with the stored `ref`, but we could add other members that do.)

Example 18-15. A method that captures a ref

```
public ref struct RefSmuggler<T>
{
    private ref T _ref;

    public void ChangeTarget(RefLike<T> rv)
    {
        _ref = ref rv.Ref;
```

```
    }
}
```

Because it's now possible to write code that holds on to a ref, the compiler has to apply more conservative rules. Example 18-16 tries to use the RefSmuggler<T> type to pass a reference to a local variable back out to its caller. It calls ChangeTarget to set the _ref field to refer to the local variable, but it does this on a RefSmuggler<T> passed in by ref, which means that RefSmuggler<T> will be available to whatever code calls Bad after Bad returns. This is trying to create a dangling reference—it's trying to give its caller a reference to the local variable on its own stack frame, a stack frame that will no longer exist.

Example 18-16. Attempting to enable a ref to outlive its target's stack frame

```
static void Bad(ref RefSmuggler<int> rs)
{
    int local = 123;
    RefLike<int> rli = new(ref local);
    rs.ChangeTarget(rli); // Won't compile
}
```

The compiler does not allow this, which is good, but this creates a problem. What if we had a method that takes ref-like arguments, but which didn't hold on to any reference, such as Example 18-17?

Example 18-17. A method that doesn't capture a ref but which is handled as if it did

```
public readonly ref struct NoRefCapture<T>
{
    public void UseRef(RefLike<T> rv1, RefLike<T> rv2)
    {
        rv1.Ref = rv2.Ref;
    }
}
```

This doesn't capture a ref from either of its arguments. That means that code like Example 18-18 would be safe.

Example 18-18. Code C# thinks might be attempting to enable a ref to outlive its target's stack frame

```
void LooksBad(ref NoRefCapture<int> r)
{
    int local1 = 123;
    int local2 = 456;
    RefLike<int> rli1 = new(ref local1);
```

```
    RefLike<int> rli2 = new(ref local2);
    r.UseRef(rli1, rli2); // Won't compile
}
```

Unfortunately, the C# compiler won't allow this. It applies exactly the same rules as it did in Example 18-16. We know that in this particular case there isn't really a problem because UseRef only makes immediate use of the references passed in, and it doesn't hold on to them after it returns. But the problem is that the C# compiler can't know that in general. If the NoRefCapture<T> type is defined in a library, the compiler can't know what's inside the UseRef method. (Arguably, it could inspect the IL during compilation, but that would be a bad idea because a future version of the library could change the implementation.) It can only go on the public signature of the method, and from that perspective, there's no real difference between RefSmug gler<T>.ChangeTarget and NoRefCapture<T>.UseRef. These are both members of ref struct types, so either could capture references from their inputs. That's why both examples fail to compile.

This is vexing if the method in question will never have any reason to capture its inputs. It's particularly frustrating if you wrote a library before C# 11.0 came out that includes a method of this kind, because it used to be legal: back when it simply wasn't possible to capture a ref there was no problem with this sort of method.

Fortunately, there's a solution. Our method can declare that it will never capture references from specific arguments by marking them with the scoped keyword, as Example 18-19 shows. This is part of the method's public signature, which has two effects. First, the compiler will keep us honest: if we annotated a parameter as scoped it will prevent us from attempting to capture a reference obtained through that parameter. Second, code such as Example 18-18 would not cause an error if it used this type. The compiler would know that the references passed in through these arguments won't be captured, so there will be no violation of the type safety rules.

Example 18-19. Declaring non-capture of a ref

```
public readonly ref struct NoRefCaptureWithScoped<T>
{
    public void UseRef(scoped RefLike<T> rv1, scoped RefLike<T> rv2)
    {
        rv1.Ref = rv2.Ref;
    }
}
```

Before C# 11.0 it wasn't possible for methods of this form to capture references. It's only the addition of ref fields that makes it possible. Code such as Example 18-18 never used to cause compiler errors because it used to be safe. Now it's only safe if the target method declares the argument as scoped. But what does that mean if you're using a mixture of old and new code? Your C# 11.0 or 12.0 project might use a library written in C# 10.0 that contains a method similar to Example 18-19. Since the library was written in a version of C# that didn't support ref fields, that method can't capture references, but it has parameters that, on current versions of C#, would make it possible to capture references. There was no scoped keyword in C# 10.0, so a method such as UseRef could only have a signature like the one in Example 18-17. Does that mean that such methods become unusable once you move to C# 11.0 or later?

As you'd probably expect, that's not what happens. If you're using an old library that contains code such as Example 18-17, you'll be able to call it in the way that Example 18-18 does without errors. This works because the compiler now adds attributes to the component to indicate that it was built with a version of the language in which ref fields are available. Older libraries (or any library where the project configuration specifies a version of C# older than 11.0) will not have this attribute, so if you're consuming such a library from a new project, the compiler will know that the older rules around ref handling apply. In effect, all ref-like arguments of methods of ref struct types defined in older libraries will be handled as though they were scoped.

Representing Sequential Elements with Memory<T>

The runtime libraries define the Memory<T> type and its counterpart, ReadOnlyMemory<T>, representing the same basic concept as Span<T> and ReadOnlySpan<T>. These types provide a uniform view over a contiguous sequence of elements of type T that could reside in an array, unmanaged memory, or, if the element type is char, a string. But unlike spans, these are *not* ref struct types, so they can be used anywhere. The downside is that this means they cannot offer the same high performance as spans. (It also means you cannot create a Memory<T> that refers to stackalloc memory.[2])

You can convert a Memory<T> to a Span<T>, and likewise a ReadOnlyMemory<T> to a ReadOnlySpan<T>, as long as you're in a context where spans are allowed (e.g., in an ordinary method but not an asynchronous one). The conversion to a span has a cost. It is not massive, but it is significantly higher than the cost of accessing an individual element in a span. (In particular, many of the optimizations that make spans attractive only become effective with repeated use of the same span.)

So if you are going to read or write elements in a Memory<T> in a loop, you should perform the conversion to Span<T> just once, outside of the loop, rather than doing it

---

2 Technically you could write a custom MemoryManager to do this, but the compiler and runtime would be unable to enforce safety if you did that.

each time around. If you can work entirely with spans, you should do so since they offer the best performance. (And if you are not concerned with performance, then this is not the chapter for you!)

ReadOnlySequence<T>

The types we've looked at so far in this chapter all represent contiguous blocks of memory. Unfortunately, data doesn't always neatly present itself to us in the most convenient possible form. For example, on a busy server that is handling many concurrent requests, the network messages for requests in progress often become interleaved—if a particular request is large enough to need to be split across two network packets, it's entirely possible that after receiving the first but before receiving the second of these, one or more packets for other, unrelated requests could arrive. So by the time we come to process the contents of the request, it might be split across two different chunks of memory. Since span and memory values can each represent only a contiguous range of elements, .NET provides another type, ReadOnlySequence, to represent data that is conceptually a single sequence but that has been split into multiple ranges.

 There is no corresponding Sequence<T>. Unlike spans and memory, this particular abstraction is available only in read-only form. That's because it's common to need to deal with fragmented data as a reader, where you don't control where the data lives, but if you are producing data, you are more likely to be in a position to control where it goes.

Now that we've seen the main types for working with data while minimizing the number of allocations, let's look at how these can all work together to handle high volumes of data. To coordinate this kind of processing, we need to look at one more feature: pipelines.

Processing Data Streams with Pipelines

Everything we're looking at in this chapter is designed to enable safe, efficient processing of large volumes of data. The types we've seen so far all represent information that is already in memory. We also need to think about how that data is going to get into memory in the first place. The preceding section hinted at the fact that this can be somewhat messy. The data will very often be split into chunks, and not in a way designed for the convenience of the code processing the data, because it will likely be arriving either over a network or from a disk. If we're to realize the performance benefits made possible by Span<T> and its related types, we need to pay close attention to the job of getting data into memory in the first place and the way in which this data fetching process cooperates with the code that processes the data. Even if you are only going to be writing code that consumes data—perhaps you are relying on a framework such as ASP.NET Core to get the data into memory for you—it is important to understand how this process works.

The System.IO.Pipelines NuGet package defines a set of types in a namespace of the same name that provide a high-performance system for loading data from some source that tends to split data into inconveniently sized chunks, and passing that data over to code that wants to be able to process it in situ using spans. Figure 18-2 shows the main participants in a pipeline-based process.

At the heart of this is the Pipe class. It offers two properties: Writer and Reader. The first returns a PipeWriter, which is used by the code that loads the data into memory. (This often doesn't need to be application-specific. For example, in a web application, you can let ASP.NET Core control the writer on your behalf.) The Reader property's type is, predictably, PipeReader, and this is most likely to be the part your code interacts with.

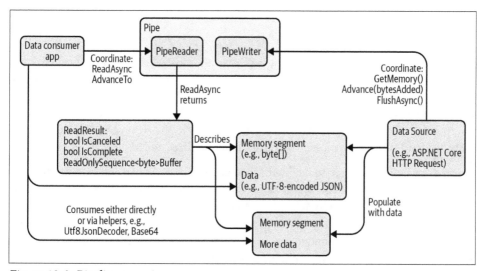

Figure 18-2. Pipeline overview

The basic process for reading data from a pipe is as follows. First, you call Pipe Reader.ReadAsync. This returns a task,[3] because if no data is available yet, you will need to wait until the data source supplies the writer with some data. Once data is available, the task will provide a ReadResult object. This supplies a ReadOnly

---

3 It is a ValueTask<ReadResult> because the purpose of this exercise is to minimize allocations. ValueTask<T> was described in Chapter 16.

Sequence<T>, which presents the available data as one or more ReadOnlySpan<T> values. The number of spans will depend on how fragmented the data is. If it's all conveniently in one place in memory, there will be just one span, but code using a reader needs to be able to cope with more. Your code should then process as much of the available data as it can. Once it has done this, it calls the reader's AdvanceTo to tell it how much of the data your code has been able to process. Then, if the Read Result.IsComplete property is false, we will repeat these steps again from the call to ReadAsync.

An important detail of this is that we are allowed to tell the PipeReader that we couldn't process everything it gave us. This would normally be because the information got sliced into pieces, and we need to see some of the next chunk before we can fully process everything in the current one. For example, a JSON message large enough to need to be split across several network packets will probably end up with splits in inconvenient places. So you might find that the first chunk looks like this:

```
{"property1":"value1","prope
```

And the second like this:

```
rty2":42}
```

In practice the chunks would be bigger, but this illustrates the basic problem: the chunks that a PipeReader returns are likely to slice across the middle of important features. With most .NET APIs, you never have to deal with this kind of mess because everything has been cleaned up and reassembled by the time you see it, but the price you pay for that is the allocation of new strings to hold the recombined results. If you want to avoid those allocations, you have to handle these challenges.

There are a couple of ways to deal with this. One is for code reading data to maintain enough state to be able to stop and later restart at any point in the sequence. So code processing this JSON might choose to remember that it is partway through an object and that it's in the middle of processing a property whose name starts with prope. But PipeReader offers an alternative. Code processing these examples could report with its call to AdvanceTo that it has consumed everything up to the first comma. If you do that, the Pipe will remember that we're not yet finished with this first block, and when the next call to ReadAsync completes, the ReadOnlySequence<T> in Read Result.Buffer will now include at least two spans: the first span will point into the same block of memory as last time, but now its offset will be set to where we got to last time—that first span will refer to the "prope text at the end of the first block. And then the second span will refer to the text in the second chunk.

The advantage of this second approach is that the code processing the data doesn't need to remember as much between calls to ReadAsync, because it knows it'll be able to go back and look at the previously unprocessed data again once the next chunk arrives, at which point it should now be able to make sense of it.

In practice, this particular example is fairly easy to cope with because there's a type in the runtime libraries called Utf8JsonReader that can handle all the awkward details around chunk boundaries for us. Let's look at an example.

Processing JSON in ASP.NET Core

Suppose you are developing a web service that needs to handle HTTP requests containing JSON. This is a pretty common scenario. Example 18-20 shows a common way to do this in ASP.NET Core. This is reasonably straightforward, but it does not use any of the low-allocation mechanisms discussed in this chapter, so this forces ASP.NET Core to allocate multiple objects for each request.

Example 18-20. Handling JSON in HTTP requests

```
[HttpPost]
[Route("/jobs/create")]
public void CreateJob([FromBody] JobDescription requestBody)
{
    switch (requestBody.JobCategory)
    {
        case "arduous":
            CreateArduousJob(requestBody.DepartmentId);
            break;

        case "tedious":
            CreateTediousJob(requestBody.DepartmentId);
            break;
    }
}

public record JobDescription(int DepartmentId, string JobCategory);
```

Before we look at how to change it, for readers not familiar with ASP.NET Core, I will quickly explain what's happening in this example. The CreateJob method is annotated with attributes telling ASP.NET Core that this will handle HTTP POST requests where the URL path is /jobs/create. The [FromBody] attribute on the method's argument indicates that we expect the body of the request to contain data in the form described by the JobDescription type. ASP.NET Core can be configured to handle various data formats, but if you go with the defaults, it will expect JSON.

This example is therefore telling ASP.NET Core that for each POST request to /jobs/create, it should construct a JobDescription object, populating its DepartmentId and JobCategory from properties of the same names in JSON in the incoming request body.

In other words, we're asking ASP.NET Core to allocate two objects—a Job Description and a string—for each request, each of which will contain copies of information that was in the body of the incoming request. (The other property, DepartmentId, is an int, and since that's a value type, it lives inside the Job Description object.) And for most applications that will be fine—a couple of allocations is not normally anything to worry about in the course of handling a single web request. However, in more realistic examples with more complex requests, we might then be looking at a much larger number of properties, and if you need to handle a very high volume of requests, the copying of data into a string for each property can start to cause enough extra work for the GC that it becomes a performance problem.

Example 18-21 shows how we can avoid these allocations using the various features described in the preceding sections of this chapter. It makes the code a good deal more complex, demonstrating why you should only apply these kinds of techniques in cases where you have established that GC overhead is high enough that the extra development effort is justified by the performance improvements.

Example 18-21. Handling JSON without allocations

```
[HttpPost]
[Route("/jobs/create")]
public async ValueTask CreateJobFrugalAsync()
{
    bool inDepartmentIdProperty = false;
    bool inJobCategoryProperty = false;
    int? departmentId = null;
    bool? isArduous = null;

    PipeReader reader = this.Request.BodyReader;
    JsonReaderState jsonState = default;
    while (true)
    {
        ReadResult result = await reader.ReadAsync().ConfigureAwait(false);
        jsonState = ProcessBuffer(
            result,
            jsonState,
            out SequencePosition position);

        if (departmentId.HasValue && isArduous.HasValue)
        {
            if (isArduous.Value)
            {
                CreateArduousJob(departmentId.Value);
            }
            else
            {
                CreateTediousJob(departmentId.Value);
            }
```

```
            return;
        }

        reader.AdvanceTo(position);

        if (result.IsCompleted)
        {
            break;
        }
    }
}

JsonReaderState ProcessBuffer(
    in ReadResult result,
    in JsonReaderState jsonState,
    out SequencePosition position)
{
    // This is a ref struct, so this has no GC overhead
    var r = new Utf8JsonReader(result.Buffer, result.IsCompleted, jsonState);

    while (r.Read())
    {
        if (inDepartmentIdProperty)
        {
            if (r.TokenType == JsonTokenType.Number)
            {
                if (r.TryGetInt32(out int v))
                {
                    departmentId = v;
                }
            }
        }
        else if (inJobCategoryProperty)
        {
            if (r.TokenType == JsonTokenType.String)
            {
                if (r.ValueSpan.SequenceEqual("arduous"u8))
                {
                    isArduous = true;
                }
                else if (r.ValueSpan.SequenceEqual("tedious"u8))
                {
                    isArduous = false;
                }
            }
        }

        inDepartmentIdProperty = false;
        inJobCategoryProperty = false;

        if (r.TokenType == JsonTokenType.PropertyName)
        {
```

```
            if (r.ValueSpan.SequenceEqual("JobCategory"u8))
            {
                inJobCategoryProperty = true;
            }
            else if (r.ValueSpan.SequenceEqual("DepartmentId"u8))
            {
                inDepartmentIdProperty = true;
            }
        }
    }

    position = r.Position;
    return r.CurrentState;
    }
}
```

Instead of defining an argument with a [FromBody] attribute, this method works directly with the this.Request.BodyReader property. (Inside an ASP.NET Core MVC controller class, this.Request returns an object representing the request being handled.) This property's type is PipeReader, the consumer side of a Pipe. ASP.NET Core creates the pipe, and it manages the data production side, feeding data from incoming requests into the associated PipeWriter.

As the property name suggests, this particular PipeReader enables us to read the contents of the HTTP request's body. By reading the data this way, we make it possible for ASP.NET Core to present the request body to us in situ: our code will be able to read the data directly from wherever it happened to end up in memory once the computer's network card received it. (In other words, no copies, and no additional GC overhead.)

The while loop in CreateJobFrugalAsync performs a process common to any code that reads data from a PipeReader: it calls ReadAsync, processes the data that returns, and calls AdvanceTo to let the PipeReader know how much of that data it was able to process. We then check the IsComplete property of the ReadResult returned by Read Async, and if that is false, then we go round one more time.

Example 18-21 uses the Utf8JsonReader type to process the data. As the name suggests, this works directly with text in UTF-8 encoding. JSON messages are commonly sent with this encoding, but .NET strings use UTF-16. So one of the jobs that the simpler Example 18-20 forced ASP.NET to do was convert any strings from UTF-8 to UTF-16. Avoiding this conversion can provide a significant performance improvement, although it does lose some flexibility. The simpler, slower approach has the benefit of being able to adapt to incoming requests in more formats: if a client chose to send its request in something other than UTF-8—perhaps UTF-16 or UCS-32, or even a non-Unicode encoding such as ISO-8859-1—our first handler could cope with any of them, because ASP.NET Core can do the string conversions for us. But since

Example 18-21 works directly with the data in the form the client transmitted, using a type that only understands UTF-8, we have traded off that flexibility in exchange for higher performance.

Utf8JsonReader is able to handle the tricky chunking issues for us—if an incoming request ends up being split across multiple buffers in memory because it was too large to fit in a single network packet, Utf8JsonReader is able to cope. In the event of an unhelpfully placed split, it will process what it can, and then the JsonReaderState value it returns through its CurrentState will report a Position indicating the first unprocessed character. We pass this to PipeReader.AdvanceTo. The next call to PipeReader.ReadAsync will return only when there is more data, but its ReadResult.Buffer will also include the previously unconsumed data.

Like the ReadOnlySpan<T> type it uses internally when reading data, Utf8JsonReader is a ref struct type, meaning that it cannot live on the heap. This means it cannot be used in an async method, because async methods store all of their local variables on the heap. That is why this example has a separate method, ProcessBuffer. The outer CreateJobFrugalAsync method has to be async because the streaming nature of the PipeReader type means that its ReadAsync method requires us to use await. But the Utf8JsonReader cannot be used in an async method, so we end up having to split our logic across two methods.

When splitting your pipeline processing into an outer async reader loop and an inner method that avoids async in order to use ref struct types, it can be convenient to make the inner method a local method, as Example 18-21 does. This enables it to access variables declared in the outer method. You might be wondering whether this causes a hidden extra allocation—to enable sharing of variables in this way, the compiler generates a type, storing shared variables in fields in that type and not as conventional stack-based variables. With lambdas and other anonymous methods, this type will indeed cause an additional allocation, because it needs to be a heap-based type so that it can outlive the parent method. However, with local methods, the compiler uses a struct to hold the shared variables, which it passes by reference to the inner method, thus avoiding any extra allocation. This is possible because the compiler can determine that all calls to the local method will return before the outer method returns.

When using Utf8JsonReader, our code has to be prepared to receive the content in whatever order it happens to arrive. We can't write code that tries to read the properties in an order that is convenient for us, because that would rely on something holding those properties and their values in memory. (If you tried to rely on going back to the underlying data to retrieve particular properties on demand, you might find that the property you wanted was in an earlier chunk that's no longer available.) This defeats the whole goal of minimizing allocations. If you want to avoid allocations, your code needs to be flexible enough to handle the properties in whatever order they appear.

So the `ProcessBuffer` code in Example 18-21 just looks at each JSON element as it comes and works out whether it's of interest. This means that when looking for particular property values, we have to notice the `PropertyName` element, and then remember that this was the last thing we saw, so that we know how to handle the `Number` or `String` element that follows, containing the value.

One strikingly odd feature of this code is the way it checks for particular strings. It needs to recognize properties of interest (`JobCategory` and `DepartmentId` in this example) but it doesn't just use normal string comparison. While it's possible to retrieve property names and string values as .NET strings, doing so defeats the main purpose of using `Utf8JsonReader`: if you obtain a `string`, the CLR has to allocate space for that string on the heap and will eventually have to garbage collect the memory. (In this example, every acceptable incoming string is known in advance. In some scenarios there will be strings in the incoming data whose values you will need to perform further processing on, and in those cases, you may just need to accept the costs of allocating an actual `string`.) So instead we end up performing binary comparisons by calling `r.ValueSpan.SequenceEqual`. Notice that we're working entirely in UTF-8 encoding, and not the UTF-16 encoding used by .NET's `string` type. (The various strings passed to `SequenceEqual` use the UTF8 string literal syntax introduced in C# 11.0—they all have a `u8` suffix. As you saw in "UTF-8 string literals" on page 85 this means that instead of producing `string` objects, the compiler embeds the UTF-8 representation of these strings directly into the compiled component, and creates `ReadOnlySpan<byte>` values pointing to the data.) That's because all of this code works directly against the request's payload in the form in which it arrived over the network, in order to avoid unnecessary copying.

Summary

APIs that break data down into the constituent components can be very convenient to use, but this convenience comes at a price. Each time we want some subelement represented either as a string or a child object, we cause another object to be allocated on the GC heap. The cumulative cost of these allocations (and the corresponding work to recover the memory once they are no longer in use) can be damaging in some very performance-sensitive applications. They can also be significant in cloud applications or high-volume data processing, where you might be paying for the amount of processing work you do—reducing CPU or memory usage can have a nontrivial effect on cost.

The Span<T> type and the related types discussed in this chapter make it possible to work with data wherever it already resides in memory. This typically requires rather more complex code, but in cases where the payoff justifies the work, these features make it possible for C# to tackle whole classes of problems for which it would previously have been too slow.

Thank you for reading this book, and congratulations for making it to the end. I hope you enjoy using C#, and I wish you every success with your future projects.

Index

Symbols

IQueryable<T> interface
    EF Core and, 523
    LINQ and, 484-486
IQueryProvider interface, 484
IReadOnlyDictionary<T> interface, 296
IReadOnlyList<T> interface, 280
is keyword in patterns in expressions, 117
is operator, 314
IsCompleted property, 772-776
IsDefined method, 664
ISet<T> interface, 301-302
ISpanFormattable<T> interface, 252
ISpanParsable<T> interface, 252
iteration statements, 46
iteration variable, 105
iterators, 282
    implementing IAsyncEnumerable<T> with,
        766
    implementing IEnumerable<T> with,
        282-286
    MoveNext triggering action, 285
IUtf8SpanFormattable<T> interface, 252
IUtf8SpanParsable<T> interface, 252

J

jagged arrays, 266-268
    flattening, 495
JavaScript Object Notation (see JSON)
JetBrains Rider, 12-15
    constructor generation, 348
    outlining, 60
    #region and #endregion directives, 60
JIT (just-in-time) compilation, 5, 191, 656
Join operator (Rx LINQ), 548-551
JSON, 696-706
    about, 696
    attributes for serialization, 659
    JsonSerializer, 697-702
        code generator, 702
    processing in ASP.NET Core, 805-810
    raw string literals, 82-84
    UTF-8 string literals, 85
JSON DOM, 703-706
JsonSerializer, 697-702
    code generator, 702
just-in-time (JIT) compilation, 5, 191, 656

K

keypress monitor example, 533

delegate-based publishing, 538
delegate-based subscription, 540
KeyValuePair<TKey, TValue>, 298

L

lambda expressions, 449-454
    default arguments, 451-454
    default lambda parameters, 451-454
    expression trees, 462-463
    ignoring arguments, 450
    inline functions via lambda syntax, 263
    LINQ where and select clauses, 480
Language Integrated Query (see LINQ)
large object heap (LOH), 373
Last operator (LINQ), 503
last-in, last-out (LIFO) list, 303
LastIndexOf method for arrays, 263
LastOrDefault operator (LINQ), 503
lazy initialization, 732-734
Lazy<T> class, 733
LazyInitializer class, 734
legal identifiers, 37
legal issues of exception messages, 420
Length property (arrays), 256
    LongLength property, 256
    rectangular arrays, 270
Length property (streams), 674
Length property example (strings), 93
let (LINQ), 480
libraries
    .dll file extension for, 13
    inheritance and library versioning, 332-338
LIFO (last-in, last-out) list, 303
#line directive, 58
linked lists, 303
LinkedList<T> class, 303
LINQ, 475-524
    deferred evaluation, 481-484
    generics and IQueryable<T>, 484-486
    introduction of, 6
    iteration via ToList or ToArray, 484
    LINQ operators, 475, 486
        (see also LINQ operators)
        LINQ providers, 475, 487
    other implementations, 522-524
        Entity Framework, 522
        LINQ to XML, 523
        Parallel LINQ (PLINQ), 523, 753
        reactive extensions, 524

About the Author

Ian Griffiths works for endjin, where he is a technical fellow. He lives in Hove, England, but can often be found on various online developer communities, where a popular sport is to see who can get him to write the longest email in reply to the shortest possible question. Ian is coauthor of *Windows Forms in a Nutshell*, *Mastering Visual Studio .NET*, and *Programming WPF*.

Colophon

The animal on the cover of *Programming C# 12* is a gray crowned crane (*Balearica regulorum*). This bird's range extends from Kenya and Uganda in the north into eastern South Africa, and they prefer to live in habitats such as open marshes and grasslands.

Adult birds stand 3 to 4 feet tall and weigh about 8 pounds. They are visually striking birds, with a gray body and pale-gray neck, white and gold wings, a white face (with a red patch above), a black cap, a bright-red throat lappet, and blue eyes. Topping all of this off (and giving them their name) is the distinctive spray of stiff gold filaments at the back of their heads.

Crowned cranes can live for up to 20 years in the wild, spending most of their waking hours stalking through the grass hunting for small animals and insects, as well as seeds and grains. They are one of only two types of crane to roost at night in trees, a feat made possible by a prehensile hind toe that allows them to grip branches. These birds produce clutches of up to four eggs; a few hours after hatching, the chicks are able to follow their parents, and the family forages for food together.

Social and talkative, crowned cranes group together in pairs or families, which at times combine into flocks of more than one hundred birds. Like other cranes, they are well-known for their elaborate mating dancing, which includes elements such as short upward flights, wing flapping, and deep bows.

Despite their wide range, these birds are currently considered endangered, threatened by habitat loss, egg poaching, and pesticide use. Many of the animals on O'Reilly covers are endangered; all of them are important to the world.

The cover illustration is by Karen Montgomery, based on a black-and-white engraving from *Cassell's Natural History* (1896). The series design is by Edie Freedman, Ellie Volckhausen, and Karen Montgomery. The cover fonts are Gilroy Semibold and Guardian Sans. The text font is Adobe Minion Pro; the heading font is Adobe Myriad Condensed; and the code font is Dalton Maag's Ubuntu Mono.